The Catholic Church and
Ireland in the Age of Rebellion
1859-1873

E. R. NORMAN

Fellow of Jesus College, Cambridge

The Catholic Church and Ireland in the Age of Rebellion

1859-1873

CORNELL UNIVERSITY PRESS

Ithaca, New York

© E. R. Norman 1965
First published 1965

First published in the United States
of America 1965

Cornell University Press

Library of Congress Catalog Card Number:
64-25406

Printed in Great Britain by
The Camelot Press Ltd., London and
Southampton

In Memory of
ASHLEY ALLEN
JOHN HOLLAND ROSE
PERCIVAL FROST

Contents

PREFACE   ix

1   The Condition of the Church in 1859   1

2   A First Phase: Rome and Education   33

3   The Church and Fenianism   86

4   Birth of the National Association, 1864-5   135

5   The University Question, 1865-6   190

6   The University Question, 1867-8   240

7   Moves Towards Disestablishment, 1866-8   282

8   Government Legislation on Church and Land, 1869-70   353

9   Episcopal Agitation: A Last Phase, 1870-3   409

BIBLIOGRAPHY   463

INDEX   477

Illustrations

Paul, Cardinal Cullen
facing page 196

Leahy, Machale, Moriarty, Woodlock
facing page 197

St Patrick's College, Maynooth
facing page 212

A Protestant View of Irish Religion
facing page 213

Preface

FOR any other part of the British Isles, an ecclesiastical view of politics comparable to that offered here might well prove to be interesting, but it would almost certainly be fairly peripheral to the main stream of political history – at least for the last hundred years. With Ireland that is not the case. There is a real sense in which the political vacuum thought often to be the characteristic of the situation in Ireland in the sixties of the last century was filled not by the Fenians – who were attempting operations outside the Constitution anyway, by armed rebellion – but by the agitation of the Catholic hierarchy. In pressing the claims of Catholic Ireland, the constitutional movement they directed (or at least, greatly helped to direct) became a substantial element in the fabric of Gladstonian Liberalism. The three Irish policies of Gladstone's First Ministry – Church, Land and Education – were all preceded by a decade of clerical agitation in Ireland. The Catholic movement tended to become incorporated into the evolving British party structure: it became one of the most significant of the sectional alliances which were forged in the 1860s, and whose coalescence, though temporary as it proved, constituted Gladstone's Liberal Party in 1868. The hopes of the Catholic bishops were indeed frustrated; they urged the Government to reforms, yet when the Government acted it was not because they had been persuaded by the bishops that the *time* had come to act, but because Fenianism had convinced them of the need to conciliate Ireland. Still, the bishops' work was not in vain. For when the Government moved, it was often along lines suggested in their demands. These were central to issues of the highest importance in general constitutional development. In any estimate of Ireland's place in nineteenth-century British history, Goldwin Smith's summary of her power of precedent must surely weight the scales. In 1862 he wrote: 'In virtue of her long unsettlement and her special claims to consideration, she is affording a clear field for the discussion of political, ecclesiastical, and social questions which the English nation, satisfied with an early and limited progress, will not suffer to be mooted directly in respect to itself.'

Between J. H. Whyte's *Independent Irish Party, 1850-9* (Oxford, 1958), and C. C. O'Brien's *Parnell and his Party, 1880-90* (Oxford, 1957), there has been no recent work on the Irish element in British history which encloses the gulf between the demise of the Independent Party and the rise of the Home Rule movement. This book is an attempt in that direction, though the type of organization described differed somewhat in nature from that examined in those other works. It tries to correct the impression left by Lord Eversley's conclusion that 'For nearly twenty years after the famine of 1846-7 there was little of interest in Irish affairs in the House of Commons.' And it attempts to show that Ireland was full of activity other than rebellion in the period; that the apparent absence of a constitutional movement has been the fruit of looking for political agitation inspired by the politicians, instead of reaching into the sanctuary whence it was in fact largely directed. Yet here there must be caution, and a right perspective. In this period the nationalists of the more militant Young Ireland tradition were quiescent although, like the Catholic Liberals, the heirs of O'Connellite nationalism, they were opposed to Fenian disruption. This study is not concerned with them except to the extent that they concerned themselves, either in sympathy or repulsion, with the agitations blown into life by the Church.

My gratitude is owing to many. But especially I must mention the many valuable suggestions as to Irish sources made by Mr T. P. O'Neill of the National Library of Ireland; the kind permission to work in his diocesan archives so freely given by His Grace the Archbishop of Dublin, Dr McQuaid, and the facilities extended there by the Chancellor, Mgr O'Regan; the hospitality of the President and Professors of St Patrick's College, Maynooth, and of the Rector of the Irish College in Rome; and the initial assistance, in planning my work in Rome, received from the late Apostolic Delegate, Archbishop O'Hara, from Father Benignus Millet of the Irish Franciscans, and from Mgr Gilbey in Cambridge. My thanks are due also to Mr Alan Bell of the National Register of Archives for help in proof-reading. Father Peadar MacSuibhne of Kildare, the editor of two recent volumes of extracts from Cardinal Cullen's letters, has been especially kind. The copies of letters from the correspondences of Cullen with Spalding in Baltimore and Gillooly in Connaught, some of which have been used in this book, were lent to me by Father MacSuibhne from private collections in Ireland.

To the Master of this College I am indebted for much encouragement, as also to Dr William Brock for many general suggestions about the writing of history. My gratitude is due further, to friends at home and in Cambridge. Lastly, to Dr Oliver MacDonagh of St Catharine's College, I express my thanks for advice, and for an interest in this work for which the expression of a bare acknowledgement hardly seems an adequate appreciation.

Selwyn College
Cambridge
26 July 1963

EDWARD NORMAN

Acknowledgements

WE wish to express our thanks to the following for their permission to include copyright material:

The Lord Ampthill, C.B.E., for two dispatches sent by Odo Russell from Rome, now held in the Public Record Office, (Crown-copyright material in the Public Record Office has been reproduced by permission of the Controller of H.M. Stationery Office); His Grace the Archbishop of Dublin for a letter of Bishop Pius Leahy to Cardinal Cullen, a memorandum by Cardinal Cullen on the rules of the National Association and a letter of Dillon to Cardinal Cullen from the Cullen Papers; The Earl of Clarendon for a letter of The Lord Ampthill to The Earl of Clarendon in 1870 from the Clarendon Papers in the Bodleian Library, Oxford; C. A. Gladstone for a letter of Dr Russell to Gladstone, a letter of Cardinal Cullen to Manning and a letter of Manning to Gladstone from the Gladstone Papers in the British Museum; The Earl Grey for a letter of Bishop Moriarty to the third Earl Grey from the Grey Papers at Durham; the Director of the National Library of Ireland for two entries from the Journal of W. F. O'Neill Daunt and for a letter of Wright to Clinton, a letter of Mayo to Warren and notes by Mayo on universities from the Mayo Papers; the Superior of the Oblates of St Charles, St Mary of the Angels for three letters of Cardinal Cullen to Manning from the Manning Papers; the President of St Patrick's College, Maynooth, for a letter of Gladstone to Russell from Dr Russell's Papers at Maynooth; Monsignor Donal Herlihy of the Pontificio Collegio Irlandese in Rome for a letter of Moriarty to Kirby, a letter of Keane to Kirby and a letter of Cardinal Cullen to Kirby from the Kirby Papers, and The Lord Strachie for a letter of Gladstone to Fortescue from the Carlingford Papers.

We are grateful to His Eminence Cardinal Agagianian the Cardinal Prefect of Propaganda for permission to translate four letters of Cardinal Cullen to Barnabo and a memorandum on Irish Endowments from the *Scritture Riferite nei Congressi, Irlanda* in the archives of the Propaganda in Rome; to the President, St Patrick's Training College, Dublin, for permission to reproduce the portrait of Cardinal Cullen; the photograph of Maynooth is by J. K. St Joseph, copyright reserved; Fr M. Harty of Maynooth, who arranged for the episcopal portraits at the College to be photographed, and Professor J. M. Plumley of Selwyn College for general assistance in the preparation of photographs.

CHAPTER ONE

Introductory: The Condition of the Church in 1859

THROUGHOUT the middle years of the nineteenth century Ireland was becoming clothed with new churches, convents and schools. 'In every part of the country', declared the Catholic bishops in a joint Pastoral of November 1859, 'we see churches rising up that rival in beauty of design and elegance of execution the proudest monuments of the zeal, the piety, and the taste of our forefathers.'[1] It was the physical change in the country which attracted the attention of Cardinal Wiseman when he visited in 1858. He could see that it was becoming stamped with Catholicity. At Dundalk he expressed surprise 'in finding that religious progress is far in advance of what is considered social improvement'.[2] The churches reflected a rising spirit of confidence returning to a land in which the old could still remember the mountainside Masses of the Penal Days, and where the young did not forget. It was a land in which the native language had only one word to denote both 'Protestant' and 'invader';[3] and which Bretherton has truly said was without a history – for all the evils of the past were re-lived as though contemporary events.[4] But there could be no mistaking the Catholic optimism of the years following the Famine; the advance of ecclesiastical institutions over the countryside belonged to a generation of clergy and laity filled, as Godkin noticed, with 'their own achievements and self-elevation'.[5] And if Wiseman saw all this in 1858, the Irish found something symbolic about his presence among them too. They turned out in their thousands to gaze upon a Prince of the Church, so that the *Dublin Review* could even remark on 'the great and almost new phenomenon which the tour elicited'.[6] O'Neill Daunt noticed it as well, in his *Journal*. 'Whatever public spirit exists in Ireland just now is rather

[1] Text in *Freeman's Journal*, 21 November 1859.
[2] *Sermons, Lectures and Speeches delivered by H.E. Cardinal Wiseman during his Tour of Ireland in August and September 1858*, Dublin, 1859, p. 124.
[3] *Freeman's Journal Church Commission*, Dublin, 1868, p. 286.
[4] C. H. Bretherton, *The Real Ireland*, London, 1925, p. 1.
[5] James Godkin, *Ireland and her Churches*, London, 1867, p. 117.
[6] *Dublin Review*, June 1859, 'Wiseman's Tour of Ireland', p. 501.

I

religious than political' he wrote a year after the cardinal had left.[1]

For all that, the buoyancy of the Catholic bishops was weighted with sadness. They watched over a people bordering from time to time on chronic disaffection. Exceptional legislation was required to keep the peace: throughout the period 1859 to 1873 Ireland was subject to the continuation of Peace Preservation Acts, and between 1866 and 1869, Habeas Corpus was suspended in the face of armed rebellion.[2] The Protestants despaired of their Catholic fellow countrymen. 'No kindness, no conciliation, no liberality, no largesses in the way of gifts can make them think or feel like British citizens.'[3] In 1870 the *Dublin Review* asked the key question of the century: whether it was possible to combine the sentiment of Irish nationality with loyalty to the Crown.[4] That is a question no longer. Yet the period following the mid-century was one in which the Catholic bishops tried a positive answer. The 'social improvement', or 'state of Ireland' question to which Wiseman had alluded, was one to which the bishops had to give their attention. The sufferings of the poor were constantly brought before them. But there was little doubt that the condition of the country had improved. Increases in trade, the rise in the rate of wages, and undertakings of public utility, combined with agricultural improvements, 'have unmistakably shown that the island has made great advances in material well-being'.[5] On the land especially the changes had been most marked. Agriculture had been transformed during the fifties as a result of emigration and price changes,[6] and the average size of farms increased, the larger ones frequently becoming devoted to pasture. Continuing agrarian agitation and discontent in Ireland seemed almost irrelevant in the face of the recovery since the Famine. But the bishops and the Catholic members of Parliament did not hesitate to show up the survival of real misery and the creation of still more by the economic changes. They were carried away in the attempt, and often denied that any material improvement had been achieved at all. 'It is a false picture', Maguire said in Parliament of the alleged progress.[7] Archbishop Leahy of Cashel lamented the passing of the small farmers.[8] The Arch-

---

[1] W. J. O'Neill Daunt, Journal, 14 August 1859.

[2] See the table of coercive measures in R. B. O'Brien, *Irish Wrongs and English Remedies*, London, 1887, p. 4.

[3] *Express* (Dublin), 19 August 1859.

[4] *Dublin Review*, April, 1870, *Is Ireland Irreconcilable?*, p. 481.

[5] *Annual Register*, 1862 (Chronicle), pp. 118 ff.

[6] R. D. Collison Black, *Economic Thought and the Irish Question, 1817-70*, Cambridge, 1960, p. 44.

[7] *Hansard*, third series, cxc, p. 1291 (10 March 1868).

[8] Kirby Papers, Leahy to Kirby, no. 101, 31 March 1863.

bishop of Dublin agreed. 'The last twenty years have pressed very heavily on Ireland', he wrote in 1867, 'and afford little ground for expecting future prosperity.' He denied bluntly that trade or agriculture were improved – at least as far as the condition of the peasants was concerned, and added that 'unfortunately our rulers either do not believe what is palpably true, or they do not wish to act, or do not know what measures to adopt in order to check the progress of ruin'.[1] Like the disciples of Toulmin Smith in England, he blamed everything on 'that system of centralization' which withdrew 'everything from this poor country to enrich the neighbouring kingdom'.[2] It is interesting that John Stuart Mill agreed that the notion of Ireland's progress was a 'fool's paradise' which the Fenian rebellions had come to prove.[3] Yet the proof is not conclusive: Fenianism may have appealed to the poor tenants, but it was conceived and led by men who certainly had not suffered by economic changes, and its roots were historic and nationalist as much as agrarian.

It was Archbishop MacHale of Tuam, in an open letter to Gladstone, of 1871, who remarked with weighty sarcasm that the steamers leaving their shores loaded with emigrants were good witness to the condition of Ireland.[4] Leahy believed that the Tenant Laws were the cause. 'If God in His mercy does not preserve to us a remnant of our people,' he warned, 'in a short time the Protestants will outnumber us.'[5] There was no danger of that, but the bishops looked on sadly as a part of the population drained away, to America and England especially. Those who came to English cities were a tangible reminder of Irish problems. The 1861 census showed that 600,000 of the twenty million people in England and Wales were Irish-born.[6] Archbishop Cullen of Dublin hinted that emigration had been 'recommended as a panacea for every evil',[7] and the Bishop of Kerry (Moriarty) felt similarly. 'The exodus of the people bids fair to solve all questions', he wrote sadly in 1864; 'They are all going.'[8]

Those Protestants and Englishmen who replied to Irish complaints of distress often had an explanation close at hand which shows that

---

[1] Manning Papers, Cullen to Manning, 8 April 1867.
[2] Spalding Letters, Cullen to Spalding, 20 August 1864.
[3] J. S. Mill, *England and Ireland*, London, 1868, p. 6.
[4] *Freeman*, 11 May 1871.
[5] Kirby Papers, Leahy to Kirby, no. 101, 31 March 1863.
[6] *The English Catholics, 1850-1950*, ed. G. A. Beck, London, 1950 ('The Irish Immigration', by Denis Gwynn), p. 279.
[7] *Freeman*, 4 June 1860, Letter of Dr Dullen to his clergy.
[8] Kirby Papers, Moriarty to Kirby, no. 93, 1 May 1864.

Ireland could be taken as an essay in 'Religion and the Rise of Capitalism'. They pointed to the prosperity of the predominantly non-Catholic province of Ulster, and referred, as did Odo Russell to Cardinal Antonelli in Rome, to the 'idle Celtic habits' of the southerners.[1] But more explicitly, this was linked with the Catholic religion. 'Catholicism, pure and simple, is not a creed to be fostered by an economical legislator as a public advantage', argued Heron, a London barrister, in his pamphlet on *The Irish Difficulty* (1868). The Protestant economic virtues were lacking, he continued, for

> Ireland is the only country in Europe where heresy has not dared to raise its head in the bosom of the Church. That aspect of Catholicism therefore is unique. It is clearly not in harmony with the received laws of economy and social progress.[2]

Examples of this interpretation of Irish problems could be multiplied. The standard Irish reply placed the blame for distress and economic ills on English misgovernment. It is curious to find so Protestant and Anglophile an Irish peer as Lord Clancarty, a member of the Trench family which was hated for its proselytizing activities in the West, agreeing that evils could not fairly be attributed to inherent defects in Irish character.[3]

The pastoral care of the Catholic Irish was entrusted to 'a regularly constituted hierarchy unbroken since the days of St Patrick',[4] and headed, at this time, by Dr Paul Cullen the Apostolic Delegate. He was born in 1803 at Ballitore (Co. Kildare), of small-farming stock. In 1813 he started attending the Quaker School in Ballitore – no unusual circumstance for the child of a Catholic family – and when thirteen he entered Carlow College. At that great seminary he studied under the famous Dr Doyle until in 1820 he travelled to Rome and became a student at the Urban College of the Propaganda. His career there was successful: he earned a reputation for some brilliance. Ordination in Rome was followed by his appointment as Rector of the Irish College, in which office he was *ex officio*, the agent of the Irish bishops. This contact with home problems, and his wide correspondence with friends in Ireland during his thirty years' residence in Rome, enabled him to keep abreast of the changing situation there. He was frequently consulted by Gregory XVI about problems both Irish and Roman. From

[1] F. O. 43, vol. 96, Dispatch no. 30, 6 April 1866.
[2] R. Heron, *The Irish Difficulty and its Solution, by a System of Local Superintendence*, London, 1868, p. 13.
[3] Clancarty, *Ireland; her present condition and what it might be*, Dublin, 1864, p. 5.
[4] Kirby Papers, O'Brien to Kirby, no. 2530, 15 March 1860.

1848 to 1849 he was Rector of the Propaganda College, remaining in Rome during the revolution and the Mazzinian Triumvirate of 1848, when Pius IX had fled to Gaeta. When Archbishop Crolly of Armagh died in 1849, the Pope named Cullen as his successor, so passing over the three names suggested by the Chapter according to custom. His consecration was at Rome in February 1850, and, following his specific mandate to unify the Church in Ireland, his first action on arrival there was to summon the first national synod since the twelfth century. It met at Thurles in August 1850 to deal with the education question, and it was therefore Cullen who presided at the condemnation of the Queen's Colleges. On the death of Dr Murray, he was translated in 1852 to the Archbishopric of Dublin, leaving the Primacy of All Ireland to Dr Dixon. Cullen was created a Cardinal at the Consistory of 22 June 1866, with the title of S. Pietro in Montorio, and became a member of the Sacred Congregations of the Propaganda, Index, Rites, and Regular Discipline. At the Vatican Council, 1869–70, his influence was great and his practical work in the interests of the 'Opportunist' party did much to secure the attainment of the definition of Infallibility. He died at his home in Eccles Street, Dublin, on 24 October 1878.[1]

It was in the fulfilment of his directions to unify the Irish Church that Cullen comes into the scope of any study of Irish history in the mid-century and after. His influence over the Church, though it did not pass uncontested, was supreme. It was with truth that the paper he dreaded most, *The Irish People*, observed in 1865 that 'one important fact is clear enough: Dr Cullen *is the hierarchy*'.[2] Clarendon was to remark in 1869 that 'the conduct of Cullen and Co.' gave 'the tone to the whole priesthood of Ireland'.[3] Yet the personal characteristics, the inner thoughts, the whole spirit of the man, have remained enigmatic. This has often been the result of the opinions of his political opponents who – in a later age when the sort of nationalism and revolutionism which the cardinal eschewed had become orthodox – came to be relied

---

[1] There is no biography of Cardinal Cullen. This outline of his life is based on: *Dictionary of National Biography*, London, 1897; W. Maziere Brady, *The Episcopal Succession in England, Scotland, and Ireland, 1400 to 1875*, Rome, 1876, vol. 1, p. 348; *Catholic Encyclopedia* (English ed.), New York, 1908, vol. IV, p. 564; Peadar Mac-Suibhne, *Paul Cullen and his Contemporaries* (extracts from letters), Kildare, 1961, vol. 1, pp. 1-59; *The Times*, 25 October 1878. For details of his family background, see 'Cardinal Cullen, Biographical Materials', by M. J. Curran, in *Reportorium Novum*, vol. 1, no. 1, Dublin, 1955, p. 213. For extracts from his public writings, see *The Pastoral Letters and Other Writings of Cardinal Cullen*, ed. P. F. Moran, Dublin, 1882.
[2] *The Irish People*, 7 January 1865.
[3] Clarendon Papers, c. 475 (4), f. 210, 25 January 1869.

upon as the sole testimony to his worth. They should not be turned aside simply on that account. But the life of Cullen is so important in the present context that the veil must be penetrated. His qualities as a priest, it need hardly be said, are not in question. His work as an ecclesiastical administrator and his 'political' opinions are.

Cullen was condemned in his own day by the Fenians, whom he, in the first place, had condemned. John O'Leary said he was 'one of the most dogmatic, domineering, and self-willed of men, with much of what he took to be, and what in a sense was, religion; but with apparently no feeling about his country other than that it was a good Catholic machine, fashioned mainly to spread the faith over the world'.[1] His memory was 'not particularly loved or liked'.[2] Cullen also had a bad press at the hands of those who took the side of Archbishop MacHale, in his many differences with the Legate. Mgr D'Alton has regretted his failure to understand Irish conditions after his long residence in Rome, and that 'he had not at any time the political acumen of Dr MacHale'.[3] Irish and English Protestants wrote him off as a haughty 'ultramontane' prelate, careless of any matter which did not tend to the aggrandizement of priestly power. 'He was a cruel man', the aged Bishop of Clogher told the visiting Archbishop of Canterbury in 1896; sent to Ireland 'to put an end to the Gallican clergy'. He could not turn in his bed, he added, without Cullen getting to hear about it.[4] When Cullen was made a cardinal in 1866, Odo Russell reported to the Foreign Office that the Irish priests in Rome did not relish the promotion, feeling that it would 'do the Pope no good in Ireland'.[5] Healy noted that when the new cardinal visited Maynooth College shortly after his elevation there was 'a latent feeling in the breasts of many of the students that he was not quite so "patriotic" as he ought to be'.[6] It was true that the supporters of parliamentary Independent Opposition indicted him for his apparent acquiescence in the defection of Sadleir and Keogh. He was often called a 'Whig' as a result – but not only by the party. Disraeli described him as 'a mere whig' in 1866,[7] and the political course followed by Cullen,

[1] John O'Leary, *Recollections of Fenians and Fenianism*, London, 1896, vol. II, p. 36.
[2] *Ibid.*, p. 51.
[3] E. D'Alton, *History of the Archdiocese of Tuam*, Dublin, 1928, vol. II, p. 47.
[4] Benson Papers (Trinity Coll. Library, Cambridge), Diary 1896, p. 274. Apart from illustrating the Irish impressions of Archbishop Benson on his tour through the country, there is no other material of Irish interest in these papers.
[5] F.O. 43, vol. 96 A. Dispatch no. 55, 29 May 1866. The Government had already decided not to interfere in the appointment – *ibid.*, Dispatch no. 17, 6 March.
[6] John Healy, *Maynooth College, its Centenary History*, Dublin, 1895, p. 459.
[7] W. F. Monypenny and G. E. Buckle, *Life of Disraeli*, revised ed., London, 1929, vol. II, p. 217.

which will be described in these pages, did in fact lead him into alliance with the Liberals. It was also Disraeli who said in the House of Commons during the debate on Maguire's Motion on the state of Ireland in 1868 –

> Great changes in Ireland have been attributed to Cardinal Cullen. I have not the honour of a personal acquaintance with Cardinal Cullen. I understand he is a distinguished member of the Liberal party. If His Eminence is of opinion that the progress of Liberal opinions under his powerful influence has operated generally in favour of the fortunes of the Holy Father, is a question which I will not ask, but which I think Cardinal Cullen in his solitude must sometimes have asked himself.[1]

The paradox lay heavily upon the Irish politics of the 1860s. Yet it is interesting that the old patriot, W. J. O'Neill Daunt, who was to do so much to bring Cullen into a Liberal alliance, could describe him as 'a most virtuous man, but narrow-minded, and not at all an Irish nationalist'.[2] There is no end to the conflict of opinion. The Dublin priest, Canon Pope, said that Cullen's 'comprehensive mind burst asunder the contracted ways of narrow-minded politicians'.[3] Two more recent Catholic authors have, from their external viewpoints, seen something of the difficulties confronting Cullen. Aubert has correctly said that 'his task was to adapt as much as possible the Irish customs to the traditional Canon law'.[4] Campana remarked that he was 'one of those men who are sufficient to make the glory of a nation and a whole epoch'.[5] It was no doubt in this sense that Bishop Moriarty wrote in 1866 that he had been 'a Borromeo for the Irish Church'.[6]

And what of the man beneath all this? The *Spectator* described Cullen as a shadowy figure 'of whom no one knows anything except that he is a Cardinal',[7] and this was true. From the loneliness of eminence he reposed his confidence in no one except those he knew well in Rome – the Pope, Cardinal Barnabo of the Propaganda, and, to a lesser extent, Mgr Kirby of the Irish College. The only exceptions to this appear to have been Patrick Moran and George Conroy – and even, to some extent, Sir John Gray, the Protestant proprietor of the Catholic *Freeman's Journal* and Liberal member of Parliament for Kilkenny from 1865 to

---

1 *Hansard*, cxc, p. 1776 (16 March 1868).
2 Daunt, Journal, 27 May 1870.
3 Thomas Pope, *The Council of the Vatican and the Events of the Time*, Dublin, 1871, p. 241.
4 R. Aubert, *Le Pontificat de Pie IX*, Paris, 1952, p. 162.
5 Emilio Campana, *Il Concilio Vaticano*, Lugano, 1926, vol. 1, p. 768.
6 Kirby Papers, Moriarty to Kirby, no. 146, 22 June 1866.
7 *Spectator*, 3 August 1872.

1875.[1] Conroy was secretary to Cullen from 1866 until his election to the see of Ardagh in 1871. He was the nephew of Dr Kieran (Primate from 1866 to 1869), and had been a student at the Armagh Diocesan College when Cullen had been Primate. After studying at the Propaganda, he returned to Ireland in 1857 to become professor of theology at All Hallows College in Dublin, which chair he relinquished on assuming the duties of Cullen's secretary in 1866.[2] Moran was Cullen's nephew. He had been vice-Rector of the Irish College in Rome until he returned home to become Cullen's assistant-secretary in 1866. He was subsequently Bishop of Ossory (1871) and finally attained to the purple as Archbishop of Sydney.[3] It is significant that both these men were admitted to Cullen's intimacy only after serving in Rome, and that the *Irish Ecclesiastical Record*, which he had established in 1864 to propagate Roman influence and practice[4], should have been entrusted to their joint editorship. Cullen kept his inmost counsel within this small household group. He communicated freely with the bishops, but rarely in his letters to them did he disclose his political motive. It was hardly surprising that the English view of him should have been shadowy. He did have a row with Newman, and for English opinion this is the only claim to greatness that he has.

Cullen was not a man of strong constitution. His frequent illnesses did not, it is true, greatly impede his work, except in 1868 when he was condemned to his bed during a critical point in the discussion of Disestablishment, but even from that place he seems to have been able to control those events which needed control. Yet he had a dislike of politics. 'The life and death of Cabinets had not the slightest influence on his conduct', the *Freeman* reported in 1859[5] – but just at a time when this was ceasing to be true. For though he wished his life to be dedicated to the administration of the Church, the circumstances of Ireland placed him in a position where it was impossible to accomplish it without political action. When he did act politically he showed a degree of opportunism. He had a bias to the Liberals, which events after 1864 particularly strengthened, and he distrusted the Conservatives who seemed to him to be the supporters of Orange ascendancy in Ireland.

[1] G. D. Burtchaell, *Genealogical Memoirs of the Members of Parliament for Kilkenny*, Dublin and London, 1888, p. 225. The *Freeman* was the mouthpiece of the hierarchy.
[2] J. J. MacNamee, *History of the Diocese of Ardagh*, Dublin, 1954, pp. 484-5; Maziere Brady, *op. cit.*, vol. 1, p. 296.
[3] Healy, *op. cit.*, pp. 541-2.
[4] 'The *Record* was, in the first place, to be a link between Ireland and Rome'. Healy, *op. cit.*, p. 541.
[5] *Freeman*, 1 September 1859.

'In political matters', Moran wrote, 'he made it a rule to support every measure from whatever political party it came that he considered conducive to the interests of Ireland.'[1] He was therefore an opportunist in no base sense, being prepared to deal only with men of sincerity. He was also experienced: the court of Rome during his years of residence was a diplomatic centre seething with political activity. It was there that he acquired a political characteristic which was new to Ireland. His view of politics became ecclesiastically-slanted; he identified political objectives with the interests of his Church. And this differed somewhat from Irish experience. There the bishops and priests, men usually of the people, had tended to ally the blessings of the Church to the aspirations of the country, and so their view of political objectives tended to be much more nationalistic in an *Irish* sense. Cullen tried to reverse the flow.

Now it is true that Cullen shared the identity held by others – especially by Moran – between the Catholic religion and the Irish nation. 'I have great confidence in the vitality of the Celtic race,' he told Spalding in 1864, 'and still more in the strength of our Catholic faith.'[2] But he was concerned with bringing discipline to a Catholicity which had only imperfectly recovered from statutory proscription. Irish nationalists could correctly castigate him for his poor knowledge of nationalist politics – but Cullen was not concerned with them. Like the nationalists, he distrusted England, but not on grounds of abstract right and the legitimacy of rule. His dislike of England expressed itself in religious terms too: the English view of Irish troubles was a *Protestant* view. The identity of Ireland's destiny with the Catholic faith was a fair one, provided he could keep Catholicism pure. Hence his obsession about proselytism. It was the contact of English Protestantism which was the greatest danger to the faith of the people. As a young man he had hoped that O'Connell would destroy the legislative Union,[3] but he had put that behind him, probably because he feared that the anarchy just beneath the surface of Irish rural life might spring the country, should a political disruption allow it, into the sort of chaos he had witnessed in the unforgettable convulsions of Rome in 1848. There could be no Gaeta for Cullen. He had acquired some positive faith in the Union, however. 'I am happy to agree with you in your admiration of the British Constitution,' he wrote to Sir Culling Eardley in 1859, 'which owes its origin to a Catholic King, and to the love of liberty which

[1] *Catholic Encyclopedia*, New York, 1908, vol. IV, p. 565.
[2] Spalding Letters, Cullen to Spalding, 12 November 1864.
[3] MacSuibhne, *op. cit.*, vol. I, p. 176.

9

animated a Cardinal Archbishop and the Catholic barons of Runny-mede.'[1] But he had given up the practice of attending the levées of the Irish court maintained by his predecessors.

He had, in fact, no political theories, only religious and ecclesiastical ones. His political opportunism led him into political positions which even the authors of the Syllabus of Errors probably imagined to be beyond the capability of the most liberal of prelates. Cullen did not realize it. 'Political and moral virtue can never be rightly dissociated from each other', he wrote in 1865,[2] for the guidance of the professional politicians with whom he was then involved in political agitation. The trouble with such a definition of politics was the necessarily arbitrary line of demarcation which would have to be drawn between issues. It was satisfactory for Cullen who, after consultation with the assembled prelates, could declare that this or that question combined political and moral virtue in the right proportions – and even then some of the bishops tended to disagree – but it was impossible for the Catholic politicians. The problem he faced in the 1860s was quite simply one of securing the changes needed in the Church, land, and education questions without disrupting society. He was to discover that whilst he could carry most of the bishops with him in his odyssey through the Statute book, on no one issue could he persuade them all. Worse: concerted action was always complicated because those who agreed with his line on one issue might disagree on another. This was less dangerous when each issue was dealt with in turn, as between 1859 and 1863 when education alone more or less occupied their attention. But after 1864 three great issues were agitated by the hierarchy concurrently. Disagreements within the camp equalled the hostilities without, and Cullen found himself wobbling precariously on top of them all. Only in one thing were the Irish bishops absolutely united. All were 'Liberal-Catholics' in the sense meant by the papacy in the nineteenth century. But not all were ultramontanes too, in the sense which Cullen gave to that term. His ultramontanism, in fact, was without personal idiosyncrasies, being in essence an attempt to bring Ireland into line with the discipline directed from Rome. His introduction of the Forty-hours Devotions and the spread of Roman dress among the clergy were signs of this. It was fortunate for Cullen that his zeal for the primacy of St Peter led Rome to turn a blind eye to the implications of the political liberalism of the Irish episcopate.

Cullen always considered the education question to be the one most

[1] Reprinted in *Nonconformist*, 21 December 1859.
[2] Cullen Papers, Notes on the National Association, 1865; f. 3.

pressing in urgency, and this was because the exposure of Catholic children to bad influence provided the easiest means for Protestants to attack their faith. When he spoke of proselytism, he usually meant just that, or sometimes, as in the Famine, the attempts of Protestant missioners to win over poor Catholics by the offer of food or tenancy.[1] Cullen saw the insidious influences at work on every side. 'Where bigotry and violent fanaticism are so rife,' he explained in his *Letter to Lord St Leonards* (1857), 'are we to be surprised that attempts should be made to divert charity from its heavenly destination, and to make it the instrument of proselytism?'[2] Open cases of direct proselytism in the tradition of the Protestant 'soupers' of the Famine era were becoming rare; proselytism under threat of eviction less so; but educational proselytism, as the *Freeman's Journal Church Commission* pointed out in 1868, had become so systematized that 'many of our most liberal men are the unconscious agents of the policy'.[3] The solution arrived at by Cullen involved far-reaching political claims on the Government in the matter of education at all levels.

With great sadness he looked out on a world in which the Catholic faith seemed to be assailed on every side. Between the assaults of the Garibaldians on the Papal States and the use of public money in Ireland to finance schools and colleges in which 'Indifferentism' was propagated, he could see no difference. Christian society appeared to be shuddering under the weight of the most alien philosophies. In the great Pastoral of August 1859, the bishops condemned 'the singular modern device of common Christianity'.[4] This was the use of scripture extracts in National Schools, which were especially selected to exclude sectarian differences. The Protestant Archbishop of Dublin, Richard Whately, who had edited them, declared his belief that the National System of Education 'was fast undermining the vast fabric of Romanism in this country'.[5] Cullen, who wrote that by this admission Whately 'threw off the mask',[6] can hardly be blamed in the circumstances for regarding the whole system of education as a nest of proselytism. Indifferentism, he could point out with some vision, would embarrass the Protestants

[1] On types of proselytism, see Fergal McGrath, *Newman's University, Idea and Reality*, Dublin, 1951, p. 24.

[2] *A Letter to Lord St Leonards on the Management of the Patriotic Fund, and application of public moneys to Proselytizing purposes*, Dublin, 1857 – in Moran, *op. cit.*, vol. 1 (xxxvi), p. 482. The paper was translated and published in Paris in 1858 (a copy of that edition is in the Cullen Papers).

[3] *Freeman's Journal Church Commission*, Dublin, 1868, Preface.

[4] *Pastoral Address of the Roman Catholic Archbishops and Bishops*, Dublin, 1859, p. 14.

[5] Quoted in *The Ireland of Today*, by 'F.T.C.D.', London, 1868, p. 14.

[6] Text of Cullen's Pastoral in *Post*, 9 August 1864.

too. He scorned the 'publications which now appear under the name of Protestant dignitaries and bishops, impugning the authority of that Sacred volume to which, in past times, they used to appeal as if it were the special foundation of Protestantism'.[1] Again it was in the schools that the danger lay: there it was possible for a Catholic child 'to be taught the opinions of a Colenso'.[2] 'The Protestant Church,' he wrote in another place, 'founded as it has been on the lust of a brutal king, propagated by fire and sword, and supported by robbery and confiscation of property, has no power to resist those dangerous encroachments of error and infidelity.'[3]

There need be no apology for the length of this introduction to Cullen: his ascendancy over the Church in these years brought a new coherence to Irish Catholicism. But it did not go unchallenged. Archbishop John MacHale of Tuam led what Dr Dixon described as 'His Holiness's Opposition in the Irish episcopal body'.[4] MacHale was a survivor from an earlier tradition of Irish Catholicism. He was born at Tirawley, Co. Mayo, in 1791, the son of an innkeeper. His earliest education, at a local school, was apparently in the Irish tongue. In 1807 he became a student at Maynooth, and after his ordination in 1814 he was appointed a lecturer in theology there. The first of his many attacks on mixed education was delivered in 1820, in his celebrated letters of 'Hierophilos'. In 1825 he was named Bishop of Maronia and coadjutor to the Bishop of Killala. It was in 1834 that he was elected Archbishop of Tuam despite opposition from the Government. In the age of O'Connell he became the most popular man in Ireland after the Liberator himself: aversion to England was his characteristic. Prior to the Vatican Council, he visited Rome only twice, and then briefly, in 1831 and 1854 – but the latter occasion saw his defeat over Independent Opposition at the hands of Cullen. MacHale's influence had begun to decline even before that of Cullen grew, however, for the Archbishop of the West reflected too greatly the prejudices and dispositions of an age which was passing away. Yet he was a legend in his lifetime: his anti-English sentiments did not lessen, and MacHale, who took a part in every political question, was always regarded as the most patriotic of the prelates. He was not to die until 1881.[5] He never in fact made the painful

---

[1] Text of Cullen's Pastoral, in *Freeman*, 27 April 1863.
[2] Text of Cullen's Pastoral, in *The Times*, 30 May 1866.
[3] *Post*, 9 August 1864.
[4] Kirby Papers, Dixon to Kirby, no. 2336, 24 March 1859.
[5] *D.N.B.*, 1897; Healy, *op. cit.*, p. 387, D'Alton, *op. cit.*, vol. 1, p. 368. There is a vast biography of MacHale, but it is especially thin on the period after 1855: Bernard O'Reilly, *John MacHale, His Life, Times, and Correspondence*, New York and Cincinnati,

readjustment to the Cullen era, and his conflicts with the Legate form a complication to the story of the Irish bishops and political action in the 1860s. Cullen and MacHale had not always disagreed, but incipient divergences over the education question blew into open conflict over the failure of the Independent Opposition party in 1854: from that point the two men were never really reconciled.[1] In February 1860, under the title 'MacHale *v.* Cullen', the *Packet* remarked that the two Archbishops 'have their squabbles, and these are chiefly caused by Dr Cullen's attempt to bring them one and all under closer subjection to Rome'. This was true in its widest sense, so was the further comment: 'Dr MacHale has thwarted him in this effort.'[2] It could be said that there was something of Gallicanism about MacHale[3] – as there had been generally about Irish Catholicism (in its organization, and rather less in its teachings) earlier in the century. MacHale continued to be remembered when Cullen had all but passed from memory. 'I once saw John MacHale,' exclaimed Kernan, in James Joyce's short story, 'Grace', 'and I'll never forget it as long as I live.'[4]

The Irish hierarchy had four archbishops: two of these have now been described. Dr Joseph Dixon, the Archbishop of Armagh and Primate of All Ireland, was also educated at Maynooth. But he was a retiring man, and though he always gave his moral support to Cullen, he took little part in the great affairs which began to stir the hierarchy anew in 1859. He died in 1866.[5] Dr Patrick Leahy, the Archbishop of Cashel, was entirely Cullen's man. Born in 1807, the son of a civil engineer, he was a student and then a professor of Maynooth, elected to the Archbishopric in 1857. His permanent memorial is the cathedral at Thurles. He was always prepared to support Cullen, and was probably the only member of the hierarchy, outside the small group of Eccles Street, who approximated to receiving his full confidence. He had never resided in Rome, but was in full sympathy with Roman discipline and was 'anxious to put in evidence the attachment of the Irish scattered over the whole earth to Papal prerogatives'.[6]

1890. For a critique of it, see Pius Devine's in the *Dublin Review*, July 1891, p. 27. Nuala Costello's *John MacHale*, Dublin, 1939, is a short sketch based almost entirely on O'Reilly.
    [1] On their early disagreements, see P. J. Corish, 'Cardinal Cullen and Archbishop MacHale', in *Irish Ecclesiastical Record*, fifth series, XCI (1959), p. 393.
    [2] *Packet* (Dublin), 8 February 1860.   [3] Emilio Campana, *op. cit.*, vol. I, p. 771.
    [4] James Joyce, *Dubliners* (1914), London, 1956 ed., p. 168.
    [5] *D.N.B.*, 1897; Brady, *op. cit.*, vol. I, p. 232; *Battersby's Catholic Directory (Ireland)*, 1867, p. 421.
    [6] Campana, *op. cit.*, vol. I, p. 771. See also; *D.N.B.*, Supplement, vol. III, London, 1901; Alfred Webb, *Compendium of Irish Biography*, Dublin, 1878, p. 287.

There were twenty-eight bishops in Ireland in 1859.[1] But of these less than a half ever formed a 'political' caucus: only they are to be found especially articulate on matters touching the action of the Government in the discussions at bishops' meetings called by Cullen in Dublin, or agitating for 'political' reforms among the people of their dioceses, or – after 1864 – attending the meetings of the National Association (or *not* attending for reasons of 'political' objection to its proceedings). This group should be listed. They were: Walsh of Ossory; Cantwell of Meath – succeeded on his death in 1866 by his coadjutor, Nulty; Keane of Cloyne; Dorrian of Connor; MacEvilly of Galway; Pius Leahy of Dromore; Derry of Clonfert; Furlong of Ferns; O'Brien of Waterford and Lismore; O'Hea of Ross; Gillooly of Elphin; Butler of Limerick – coadjutor to Ryan until 1864; and Moriarty of Kerry. The list includes 'political' bishops of all types; the last two were especially Unionist in sympathy; whereas Cantwell and Nulty sided with MacHale against Cullen over some issues.

The size of the priesthood, which had increased rapidly during the century, remained fairly static during the 1860s with a very slight upward movement. Thus in 1860 the *Catholic Directory* recorded 1,017 Parish Priests in Ireland, 984 in 1865, and 985 in 1870. There were 1,417 curates in 1860, 1,631 in 1865, and 1,734 in 1870. The numbers of the houses of the religious orders increased slightly more rapidly. The figures for 1860 are not worth quotation. The *Directory* itself admitted that returns for that year were incomplete and inaccurate.[2] But in 1865, when that position had been rectified, there were 67 houses for men, 189 for women, and 73 for priests: by 1870 this had become 89 for men, 209 for women, and 75 for priests.[3] It was a subject of frequent observation at the time that most of the secular clergy came from peasant and small-farming stock, whereas the regulars were often men of some substance before taking vows.[4] The clergy were by now customarily trained for the priesthood in the diocesan seminaries which had been founded during the century for the purpose. The Royal College of St Patrick at Maynooth was the national seminary, and it was alone in receiving State aid for its maintenance.[5] The clergy were supported entirely by the 'Voluntary System' – by the free-will offerings of the faithful. It was true that there existed a canon law obligation for the

[1] *Battersby's Catholic Directory (Ireland)*, 1860, p. 206.
[2] *Ibid.*
[3] *Ibid*, 1865, p. 241, and 1870, p. 163 – 'Ecclesiastical Summary of Ireland'.
[4] See, for example, Godkin, *op. cit.*, pp. 2 and 6.
[5] Healy's *Maynooth College* (see above), is the official history.

parishioners to support their priest, but there was no comparable provision for monks. Convents for women were erected and endowed by public subscription: monasteries and friaries were supported by voluntary offerings.[1] But the faithful had still more to provide. The *Freeman's Journal Church Commission* of 1868 considered their burden under five heads: (1) support of the bishops and parochial clergy; (2) support of the regular clergy; (3) maintenance of the churches; (4) maintenance of hospitals, and charitable institutions; and (5) maintenance of Catholic schools and colleges.[2] Additionally, sums were collected and sent annually to England for Catholic missions there,[3] and large collections were made throughout Ireland after 1859 for the upkeep both of the Catholic University in Dublin and of the Pope's temporal domains in Italy. Funds for the university also arrived from America, and expatriates often remitted money towards the building of churches in their Irish home towns. Since 1800, £5,690,995 had been spent on the erection of Catholic buildings, and the annual expenditure of the Church was estimated by the *Freeman* in 1868 as £762,030.[4] 'These figures', it remarked with truth, 'afford at once the most remarkable illustration of the persistent power of a living faith, and of the recuperative force of the Irish race.'[5] James Godkin, a Presbyterian, was astonished by the progress of Catholicism in the City of Dublin, believing the rapid ecclesiastical expansion to be without parallel in Europe.[6] It was hardly surprising that the English Dissenters should claim Irish Catholicism as an advertisement for the Voluntary System. A new Church had grown from the desiccation of penal times, and had extended a vast network of institutions over the land entirely without the assistance of endowments. This was in an age when many of the Catholic peasantry sometimes found themselves near to starvation, and material expansion, helped, at least as far as land-purchase was concerned by the Encumbered Estates Act, had nevertheless sometimes been in the face of the local opposition of Protestant landlords.[7] It was truly remarkable.

Yet in the area of administration, much of the old had continued. Ecclesiastical discipline and the parochial system had been planted anew in Ireland at the end of the eighteenth century. Cullen had been entrusted by Rome with the task of clearing up the anomalies. It was not

---

[1] *Freeman's Journal Church Commission*, Dublin, 1868, p. 375.
[2] *Ibid.*, p. 379.   [3] *Ibid.*, p. 386.   [4] *Ibid.*, p. 387.   [5] *Ibid.*
[6] Godkin, *op. cit.*, p. 94.
[7] But not always. Protestants sometimes contributed generously to funds for the erection of Catholic churches, as at Ballinasloe in 1858 – see P. K. Egan, *The Parish of Ballinasloe*, Dublin, 1960, p. 248.

easy. The great bishop of Kildare, Dr Doyle, had done much to reform ecclesiastical discipline as he found it in the thirties.[1] Godkin said he was 'the originator of that course of ecclesiastical renovation, material and spiritual, which has since his day produced such wonderful results'.[2] Indeed, the publication of Fitzpatrick's *Life* of the bishop in 1861 brought his work freshly before the hierarchy. But he had not been able to accomplish everything that Rome, in the new tides of ultramontane practice, would have Cullen perform in Ireland. And in one place very much of the relaxed discipline of the past had endured. This was in MacHale's province of Tuam. The diocese of Galway was especially bad. It had been created in 1830.

Before that time the ecclesiastical government partook in some manner of a Presbyterian or rather popular character. The vicars, as the parish priests were called, were elected by the Tribes, as also was the Warden, who, although a priest, exercised episcopal jurisdiction. The old form of ecclesiastical government had ceased for six and twenty years before Dr MacEvilly's episcopate, but the spirit of it remained. The fiscal arrangements of the diocese were in confusion. The parish priests had been more or less independent rulers. . . .[3]

MacHale himself did nothing to help MacEvilly. In fact he used his influence against him. Gillooly, another prelate in the same province, complained that in his own diocese, MacHale seemed resolved 'to interpose between me and my priests'. This sort of action, he declared, was canonically forbidden.[4] The most famous case involving MacHale and MacEvilly in disagreement over discipline in Galway concerned Father Peter Daly. That priest's interference in political matters, his attendance at public boards (he was Chairman of the Town Corporation and of the Gas Company, president of the Mechanics' Institute and of the Commercial Society, and owner and director of the Lough Corrib Steam Company),[5] and his support for mixed education,[6] made him the subject of complaint by the laity to the bishop. As an unsuccessful candidate in 1857 for the episcopal seat now occupied by MacEvilly, he did not find it easy to get on with the bishop.[7] His refusal to accept discipline resulted in his suspension early in 1862. This was supported

---

[1] See W. K. Fitzpatrick, *Life, Times, and Correspondence of Dr Doyle*, Dublin, 1861, vol. I, pp. 93 and 120.

[2] Godkin, *op. cit.*, p. 118.

[3] Brady, *op. cit.*, vol. II, pp. 234-5.

[4] Kirby Papers, Gillooly to Kirby, no. 196, 26 October 1862.

[5] *Guardian*, 15 January 1862.

[6] Kirby Papers, no. 2498, A-K (a dossier on the Daly case). See the letter of MacEvilly to Kirby, no. 2498, H., 10 June 1860.

[7] D'Alton, *op. cit.*, vol. II, p. 105.

by Cullen,[1] and confirmed by the Holy See. But when in 1865 Father Daly was again breaking through ecclesiastical discipline on every side, and was again suspended by MacEvilly, he appealed successfully to MacHale. Popular feeling went with the archbishop. A further appeal – this time to Rome by MacEvilly – secured a censure of MacHale's interference and a confirmation of the suspension.[2] The whole affair illustrates the intransigence of MacHale and of many of the lower clergy in the West. It is true that this was an extreme case, but the new order which Cullen was bringing to Ireland could find no place for even a pocket of irregularity.

The essence of Cullen's ecclesiastical policy was an attempt to knit the four provinces together to bring them into the closer direction of Roman discipline by the exercise of his legatine jurisdiction. Acton believed that 'the Irish clergy in Lamennais' time were Gallican; they were democratic; they were prepared, in matters of politics, to resist Rome'.[3] Among the characteristic qualities of 'ultramontanism' which he listed were many which Cullen was trying to enforce in Ireland – love of ecclesiastical liberty from the State, diminution of episcopal authority by the Propaganda, influence of religious orders, centralization, prevention of divisions which weakened the Church.[4] For Protestants, 'ultramontanism' implied a body of doctrines dangerous to civil allegiance which maintained the universal monarchy of the Papacy. Hence their alarm at the new order in Irish Catholicism, at 'the dangerous progress which Ultramontanism has made in Ireland within the few years which have elapsed since Cardinal Cullen's arrival from Rome'.[5] It was shortly after Cullen's arrival, in fact, that Lord John Russell alluded to the unusual circumstance of his appointment in the Parliamentary debate on 'Papal Aggression'. Not only were none of the three men named by the chapter of Armagh nominated to the vacant see, but he who was, on arrival, had dealt with matters which did not concern the internal discipline of the Church at all, at the Synod of Thurles. Russell's comment is a good summary of the suspicions so often entertained by Protestants of 'ultramontanism' as they usually understood it.

This, I think, is an instance at all events, that we have not to deal with purely spiritual concerns; that that interference, which is so well-known in all modern history of clerical bodies, with the temporal and civil concerns of the State, has

---

[1] Propaganda, *Scritture* 34, contains many papers on the Daly case from all sides in the disputes.

[2] Brady, *op. cit.*, p. 235.

[3] Acton Papers (Cambridge), Add. MS. 4969, Liberal Catholicism, p. 20.

[4] *Ibid.*, Add. MS. 5542, *Vaticana*, p. 15.

[5] *The Irish Difficulty*, by *An Observer*, London, 1868, p. 39.

been attempted, not as a system, but as a beginning – as a beginning, no doubt, to be matured into other measures, and to be exerted on some future occasion with more potent results.[1]

The period after 1859 was to provide ample occasions of proof for those who would find it in this interpretation of ultramontanism.

In a memorandum for the Irish Government on *Ultramontane Designs in 1865*, written by Johnstone Stoney of the Queen's University, three parties among the Irish priesthood were distinguished. The 'moderates' were the party of Dr Doyle and Archbishop Murray: they revered British connexion, and 'may be said to have perished amid the excesses of the Repeal agitation' in 1848. The 'old Irish' party was crude and nationalistic, and its last great member was Archbishop MacHale: it favoured Irish objectives. The third party were the 'ultramontanes', and these were now attaining to an ascendancy over the second. They looked outside Ireland for their political inspiration. Their strength was first manifest in 1859 when they secured the signatures of all the bishops to the Pastoral enunciating political demands on the Government. This was the party of Cullen.[2] Stoney's classification is a little overdrawn and clumsy, but it has caught the spirit of the changed atmosphere and direction in Irish Catholicism. His use of 'party' is too strong: the men whose sympathies he categorized did not always see themselves thus, although when the quarrel of Cullen and MacHale caused lesser ecclesiastics to take one side or another, party strife often broke the surface. Stoney followed the usage of the day in labelling the Cullen position as 'ultramontane'. But Cullen himself was not happy about the title: in 1869 he told the Powis Commissioners that he did not know 'what is meant in England by "Ultramontane" '. He was questioned about its growth in Ireland, but denied that there had been any.[3] He gave a definition which upheld the authority of the Pope but which disregarded any possibility that there might be political implications.

Ultramontanism is the teaching of those who are determined to carry out to the fullest extent the principles of their own religion, and who acknowledge in full the authority of the Pope, whom we look on as the successor of St Peter. Catholics also who are strict observers of the practices of the Church, who fast and go to confession are called Ultramontanes. Those who do not wish to act up fully to the principles and practices of Catholicity, and to submit entirely to the authority of the Pope, call those who wish to do so ultramontanes; in this sense the term is an honourable epithet for a Catholic. If I were asked, am I an

[1] *Hansard*, CXIV, p. 190, (7 February 1851).

[2] Larcom Papers, MS. 7648 (24 January 1865).

[3] *Parliamentary Papers*, 1870, XXVIII, vol. IV, Commission on Primary Education, (Ireland), Evidence, p. 1245.

Ultramontane, I would say I am in this sense – that I respect the decisions of the Head of the Church, and that I am always an obedient subject in religious matters of the Pope.[1]

Cullen was also supposed by many Protestant observers to have packed the dioceses with bishops sympathetic to Roman discipline. 'Ultramontanism may have increased its strength on the episcopal bench', noticed the *Kilkenny Moderator* in 1863, 'as the Cullenite régime progressed, but there are still several bishops who must be taken as representing the principles of the late Archbishop Murray.'[2] The archives of the Propaganda make it clear that from around 1853 and until the end of his life, Cullen's recommendation of bishops to the Roman authorities was taken by them as the determining factor. When on the demise of a bishop the chapter sent up three names in the *terna* to Rome, from among whom the vacancy was filled, he added his weight to the man of his own choice from the list. The whole business of the selection of bishops became more centralized, and the men actually appointed were often of a different quality. It was no longer customary for men to be named who had come from the diocese they were to administer; a few were chosen from religious orders; new bishops were selected from men with administrative and academic experience – there were fewer appointments from the ranks of the parish priests than had formerly been the case.[3] All this was the work of Cullen. Yet he himself denied that a change had taken place in the method of selecting bishops when questioned on it explicitly by the Powis Commissioners.[4] In this he was right: it was not the method, but its management, which had changed. And the change had been possible because the Propaganda had in Cullen someone in Ireland whose judgment they could trust to reflect their wishes. As the *Packet* put it – a good deal more crudely – 'Dr Cullen is the white-headed lad at Rome'.[5]

One of the encroachments of ultramontanism which Protestants held most severely in censure was the supposed enslavement of the Catholic laity by the hierarchy and their representatives in the localities. 'The minds of the Irish people are in the hands of the Irish priests', Moriarty told Monsell in 1868.[6] But to the extent that this was true, it had always been true, and was no work of Cullen's new order. The laity were as much to blame. In May 1870, Mgr Verot, the Bishop of Florida, told

---

[1] *Ibid.*, p. 1236.   [2] *Kilkenny Moderator*, 19 December 1863.

[3] See J. H. Whyte, 'The Appointment of Catholic Bishops in Nineteenth-Century Ireland', in *Catholic Historical Review*, April 1962.

[4] *Parliamentary Papers*, 1870, xxviii, vol. iv, Evidence, p. 1245.

[5] *Packet*, 8 February 1860.

[6] Gladstone Papers, B.M.Add.MS. 44152, f. 98 (2 March 1868).

a laughing assembly of the Vatican Council that 'it is true that the Irish believe in the Pope's infallibility; but they also believe in their priests' infallibility – and not only do they believe it, but they beat with sticks any who deny it'.[1] Yet throughout the 1860s, and before and afterwards, Protestants in England and Ireland argued that concession of the bishops' educational demands would only lead to the greater ignorance and subjugation of the Catholic laity, and some Catholics were found to agree with them. It was an argument to which the ministers of the Crown were attentive.

Thus the constitution of the Church and Cullen's endeavours with it. What of the grievances which weighed around it? First among these was the land question, the 'state of Ireland' question. But for Cullen this was a grievance to be felt, not one calling for the active agitation of the clergy – as yet. In 1859 Ireland was still too close to the insurrection of 1848 and the part taken in it by the 'Young Ireland Priests', and to the abortive alliance between the Tenant League and the Catholic Defence Association of the early fifties, for Cullen to place the legal position of the tenantry highly on any list of proposed action. MacHale could not agree, and here was another difference between the two men which the future was to see cultivated to the point of open rupture.

The existence of the Protestant Establishment was not attended with such difficulties. All the Catholic bishops were at one in believing that it should go. Yet disestablishment was to become coupled with proposals for disendowment, and over this also there were to be dissensions. But this too was laid up in the future. In 1859 the Protestant Church presented to Catholic eyes an anomaly so monstrous as almost to defy belief. The religious census of 1861 was to show that the Protestant population of Ireland numbered 693,357, compared with the Catholic figure of 4,505,265,[2] although the distribution was uneven, there being a greater concentration of Presbyterians and members of the State Church in Ulster. In 1868 Archbishop Manning told Gladstone that the existence of the Establishment 'embitters every other question'.[3] Moriarty, a moderate when it came to the question of religious endowment by the State, declared in the same year that 'religious inequality, or the Church Establishment, is the only remaining vestige of con-

---

[1] Cuthbert Butler, *The Vatican Council*, London, 1962 ed., p. 311.

[2] A. Hume, *Results of the Irish Census of 1861*, London, 1864, p. 14. It should be noticed that the figure given is for *Protestants* (i.e. members of the Establishment), and does *not* include Protestant Dissent. In Ireland, those only were called Protestants who had assented to the Thirty-nine Articles, as defined in the Test Act of 1679. See the note on this in W. F. P. Stockley, *Newman, Education and Ireland*, London, 1933, p. 92.

[3] Gladstone Papers, B.M. Add. MS. 44249, f. 33 (28 March 1868).

quest'.[1] It had contrived a situation in which 'the social repulsion between Protestants and Roman Catholics is a root of real bitterness in Ireland'.[2] That the wealth, the land, and the professions were in large part in the hands of Protestants was a commonplace of the period. It was unfortunate that the Establishment could be so easily depicted as a mere instrument of English 'oppression'. O'Neill Daunt wrote of 'the annihilation of Irish nationality wrought by the anti-Irish State Church on the minds which it influences'.[3] R. B. O'Brien pointed out that those Protestants who ridiculed the 'Italian' Church in Ireland had better look to their own. He printed a table showing that since the Reformation the Catholic archbishoprics had been held almost exclusively by Irishmen, and the Protestant by Englishmen. 'Let the reader judge which was the "Irish" and which the "foreign" hierarchy', he added.[4] For Cullen, the Establishment had about it the odour of proselytism. Not only did the Protestant clergy 'add not drops, but torrents to the waters of bitterness' in all relationships, and not only did their pulpits 'continually resound with the fiercest denunciations of Catholicity',[5] but their bishops were also the keenest supporters of the proselytism of Catholic children – in the National Schools and in the activities of their missionaries.[6] Cullen also felt that the Establishment, like the Irish Executive and the Conservative party, was deeply tainted with Orangeism. Despite all this – which amounted usually to the Parliamentary claim that the Irish Church was only a 'sentimental' grievance – the Establishment was by no means as galling as it had been. Cess had been abolished by the Temporalities Act of 1833, and tithe converted into a rent-charge in 1838 which was payable by the owners and not the occupiers of land. Many Catholics denied that the burden of tithe was removed from the tenant by the Act,[7] and in 1861 O'Neill Daunt, McCarthy Downing and a Father O'Donoghue were protesting against an increase in the tithe rent-charges made by several parsons in West Cork.[8] The diminution of actual friction caused by statutory circumscription of the privileges of the Establishment allowed the hierarchy

[1] *Ibid.*, Add. MS. 44152, f. 98, Moriarty to Monsell, 2 March 1868.
[2] Larcom Papers, MS. 7648; Memo. by Johnstone Stoney: 'Notes on Education in Ireland; Paper B' (18 July 1859).
[3] Daunt, Journal, 5 February 1862.
[4] R. B. O'Brien, *Fifty Years of Concessions to Ireland*, London, 1883, vol. II, p. 178,
[5] *Letter to Lord St Leonards*, 21 November 1857; in Moran, *op. cit.*, vol. I, (XXXVI), p. 480.
[6] Text of Cullen's Pastoral, in *Post*, 9 August 1864.
[7] See the *Freeman's Journal Church Commission*, Dublin, 1868, Fifth Report – on Tithes, p. 22.
[8] Daunt, Journal, 10 June, 6 and 8 July 1861.

to pass over it as a grievance fit for agitation until 1864. The same could not be said for the third large grievance, the education question. It was this which Cullen considered to have undoubted priority.

In February 1868 Johnstone Stoney explained to the Earl of Mayo that the great object of the bishops 'has from the beginning been, and still is, to grasp all secular education under the impious claim, first publicly announced in 1859, that Christ had sealed to ecclesiastics a monopoly of educating, when he said to His Apostles, "Go teach all nations"'.[1] It had not always been so. The Catholic prelates had co-operated with the Kildare Place Society until 1824, when their aspirations to more equitable financial assistance resulted in the Commission of 1824-27. Its deliberations soon made it plain that some sort of 'mixed' primary education was to be considered desirable for Ireland. By 'mixed' or 'united' education was meant a system whereby children of all religious denominations attended at the same schools, receiving only their religious instruction separately. In 1826 a series of episcopal resolutions declared that the hierarchy was prepared to allow such a system due to 'existing circumstances', provided that care was taken to protect the faith and morals of Catholic children.[2] The Commission reported in 1828, and its recommendations were laid before a Select Committee of the House of Commons, which prepared a system of united education for Ireland. The translation of the scheme into actuality was entrusted to Stanley, the Irish Chief Secretary. It was Stanley's *Letter to the Duke of Leinster* (October, 1831), which spoke of the united system then being created as one 'from which should be banished even the suspicion of proselytism'. So manifestly was this taken as the charter and guarantee of the new system that a copy of the *Letter* was directed to be placed in all the schools in connexion with the system.[3] Thus the National Board was established in Dublin, with Archbishop Murray as one of the Catholic Commissioners. Schools which integrated with the National System were to continue under local patronage and management; they were to be open to the inspectorate employed by the Board, and were to receive grants-in-aid. Secular instruction was to be given for four or five days a week, and separate denominational instruction on the remaining day.

Alterations in the rules of the Board, especially concerning the

---

[1] Mayo Papers, MS. 11217, Stoney to Mayo, 15 February 1868.

[2] This account of the early history of the education question is based on that in McGrath, *op. cit.*, pp. 16 ff., also James Kavanagh, *Mixed Education, The Catholic Case Stated*, Dublin, 1859; and *Parliamentary Papers*, 1870, xxviii (Powis Report), vol. 1, pp. 21-220, 'Historical Sketch of the System of National Education'.

[3] Kavanagh, *op. cit.*, p. 21n.

procedure of vesting schools, and the 'Stopford Rule' of 1847 which redefined the basis for the exclusion of children from religious instruction in a creed other than their own, inflamed the suspicions of a substantial number of the bishops. It soon became clear that a rift in the hierarchy was appearing. Dr Murray acquiesced in the changes; Dr MacHale did not. After open disagreements, a *Rescript* from Rome in 1841 left it to the bishops of each diocese to decide whether they would temporize with the Board or not.[1] In every diocese except MacHale's own, they opted for toleration. Dissatisfaction with the National System grew among the bishops, but by 1859 their policy was still one of toleration. In that year the Government contemplated extending the mixed principle into a system of intermediate schools. It was another of the episcopal educational grievances that no secondary education was provided for Catholics, and that the Protestant Endowed Schools gave an unfair advantage to the Establishment when it came to higher education. The year 1859 saw the start of a new campaign by the hierarchy against the mixed National System – but still their policy was to remain one of toleration until either they had secured changes in the System, or else they had established a sufficient number of Catholic schools independent of the Board to be able to manage without it. Cullen had refused to take the seat on the Board vacated by the death of Murray in 1852, however, and this had indicated the rising hostility. His great fear was the educational proselytism possible since the departure of the System from Stanley's original intention. It is interesting that Protestants had also opposed the System, and on the same grounds as the Catholics – that the separation of secular and religious instruction was an improper incursion into the Christian belief in the universality of all knowledge.[2] Yet as the Catholic attacks on the System developed, during the 1860s, most Protestants tended to rally round it. The Catholic bishops were often accused of having changed their position when they began to reject principles of a system they had at first supported.[3] They always replied that it was the system that had changed.

Catholic educational endeavour independent from State aid, showed the same dramatic advance which was witnessed in the building of Churches. But there could be disadvantages to turning aside completely from the National System. Thus in Tuam education was in a poor condition as there were insufficient funds to build and equip enough

[1] See P. C. Barry, 'The Holy See and the Irish National Schools', in *Irish Ecclesiastical Record*, fifth series, xcii (1959), p. 90.

[2] J. T. Ball, *The Reformed Church of Ireland*, London and Dublin, 1886, p. 244.

[3] Cullen was questioned on this in his evidence to the Powis Commissioners – *Parliamentary Papers*, 1870, xxviii, vol. iv, Evidence, p. 1259.

Catholic schools to produce an effective alternative to the National ones; it was to be seen that, in consequence, many of MacHale's flock 'became an easy prey to the proselytizers whom he used to denounce so bitterly'.[1] Elsewhere denominational schools were encouraged to supplement the National System and avoid its evils. 'It is most desirable that you should give every encouragement to the Schools that are under the care of the Christian Brothers, and of the many excellent communities of ladies with which this diocese abounds,' Cullen told the clergy of Dublin in 1864; 'schools in which, whilst secular knowledge is admirably imparted, the strongest and most salutary religious impressions are made upon the tender mind.'[2] In 1862 the *Nation* had noticed that the Christian Brothers' Schools were 'spreading every day more and more over the land'.[3] The Brothers were a lay order of Catholic teachers, established at Waterford in 1804 by Edmund Rice. From there they had radiated to every part of Ireland.[4] Cullen paid a handsome tribute to their work before the Primary Education Commissioners in 1869.[5] The Catholic education of girls was in the hands of several orders, but especially successful had been the Irish Ursuline and Presentation Orders, established at the end of the eighteenth century by Nano Nagle. 'After God', wrote William Hutch in 1875, 'the astounding success of the Presentation Order must be attributed to the fact that the Irish love education, and that they *will* have Catholic education at any cost.'[6] Of the 146 convents in Ireland in 1868, nearly all were engaged in educational work.[7] There were 112 conventual and monastic schools in connexion with the National Board in 1859, receiving grants-in-aid.[8]

When it came to university education, the bishops had not stomached the mixed principle and had provided an alternative. Trinity College in Dublin was a Protestant institution, and although a few Catholics were found among its members, it was the subject of increasing denunciation by the hierarchy. 'I shall not tell you of the heart-rending facts which have come under our knowledge respecting Catholic youths educated in

---

[1] Healy, *op. cit.*, p. 453.

[2] Text of Cullen's Pastoral, in *Post*, 9 August 1864.

[3] *Nation*, 27 December 1862.

[4] See J. D. Fitzpatrick, *Edmund Rice*, Dublin, 1945, especially p. 333; and *Edmund Ignatius Rice and the Christian Brothers*, by 'A Christian Brother', Dublin, 1926, pp. 438-97.

[5] *Parliamentary Papers*, 1870, XXVIII, vol. IV, Evidence, p. 1231.

[6] William Hutch, *Nano Nagle, her Life, her Labours, and their Fruits*, Dublin, 1875, p. 490. Also T. J. Walsh, *Nano Nagle and the Presentation Sisters*, Dublin, 1959, especially pp. 182-233.

[7] *Freeman's Journal Church Commission*, Dublin, 1868, p. 375.

[8] Kavanagh, *op. cit.*, p. 234.

the Protestant University,' Cullen wrote to the Dublin clergy in 1865 – 'of the promises of religious youth blasted, of the hopes of good mothers turned to despair, of horrible death scenes – too horrible to be described – unrelieved even by one ray of hope.'[1] The three Queen's Colleges, created at Belfast, Galway and Cork by the ministry of Sir Robert Peel in 1845 (whose son was even to suggest extending them, when Irish Secretary in 1861), with the expressed intention of providing university education for the Catholic people, had been condemned by the hierarchy at the Synod of Thurles in 1850, as injurious to faith and morals. The 'godless colleges' exuded Indifferentism in the worst manner the bishops could conceive: no provision was made in them for formal theological studies. As with the attempt to outlaw the National Schools, the question of accepting or rejecting the Queen's Colleges had occasioned differences of opinion among the bishops. Again the division was between Murray and MacHale: but this time the latter won, due to Cullen's determination to have done with the Colleges and set about creating the Catholic University which had been contemplated by the Propaganda since 1847.[2] At the Synod of Thurles the Colleges were censured in nine decrees, the fifth declaring them *penitus rejicienda et evitanda*.[3] But the condemnation was carried by only one vote. In 1859 Cullen had come to regard the Queen's Colleges as the coping stone of a system 'which slowly puts in the power of a Protestant Government all the education of a Catholic population'.[4] The story of the Catholic University which he established in their place for Catholic higher education, and Newman's unhappy Rectorship, is well known and has been admirably treated elsewhere.[5] The sort of differences which existed between Newman's view of a university, and Cullen's and MacHale's, were to reappear frequently in the negotiations between the bishops and the Government over the university question, between 1865 and 1873.

The political agitation of the bishops from 1859 to 1873 is a complicated history, with the centres of activity shifting between Dublin, Rome and Westminster. A brief account of the situation in all three places, as it was in 1859, is essential if the expansion of the Church into the vacuum in Irish political life, left after the collapse of Independent Opposition in 1854, is to be set in context.

At Westminster, the Irish Liberals were ineffective. Most were

---

[1] *Freeman*, 14 November 1865.
[2] See Fergal McGrath, *op. cit.*, pp. 63 ff.
[3] Manning Papers, Cullen to Manning, 15 March 1868 – 'Enclosure: Synod of Thurles: Queen's Colleges' (an account of the censure).
[4] Propaganda, *Scritture* 33, f. 976, Cullen to Barnabo, 2 September 1859.
[5] Fergal McGrath, *op. cit.*

unable to identify themselves with the Whig party of Lord John Russell, 'Papal Aggression', and the Ecclesiastical Titles Act. Those who did were branded in Ireland as place-hunters. There was a sense in which the Irish party were waiting for the rise of the 'advanced' English Liberals – Bright, and (though they could not have guessed this in 1859), the author of Liberal hatred of the Papal States – Gladstone himself. But until the end of 1864, when the National Association paved the way for a *rapprochement* between the Irish and the English Liberals – and that only with great internal disruption – this was by no means considered as the only likely course. In 1863 the *Dublin Review* noted that:

> To us, who recollect a time when the body of the Irish nation was in almost perfect accord with the Liberal party, fought all its battles and to some extent at all events shared in its successes, the causes which have led to the gradual and now all but complete estrangement of the Irish from the English Liberals, appear to be a matter of anxious and perhaps of profitable study.[1]

The question had never been quite as clear-cut as that: the Liberals in England were not a coherent party, and to say that in Ireland they were the descendants of O'Connell's constitutional movement and the Lichfield House compact, would be to ignore the rise in the early fifties of a third Irish party whose legacy in Irish political life after its collapse was certainly not to leave the Liberals unchanged.

The rise of the Independent Irish Party had also been the occasion of Cullen's first unhappy dabble in politics. Its policy of securing Irish concessions from the Government, not by indiscriminate co-operation with English parties, but by the creation of an independent Parliamentary group – the 'Pope's Brass Band' – continued to enjoy the support of MacHale and many of the Western and mid-Western priests long after its collapse. Many of the former 'nationalist' politicians, like G. H. Moore continued to regard it as an ideal to be strived for again. To such men Cullen's slow movement towards the Liberals during the 1860s approached political blasphemy: the more so since Cullen was attributed with a large share of the blame for bringing about the fall of the Independent Party. Cullen had consecrated the alliance between the Tenant League and the Catholic Defence Association which had given the content to Independent Opposition. That was in 1851. The excitement in Ireland over the Ecclesiastical Titles Act and the Stockport riots of 1852 had propelled the new party into serious political reality. In the general election of 1852, the Whigs were humiliated but the Independent Party enjoyed a moderate success, many elected Liberals pledging them-

[1] *Dublin Review*, April 1863, 'The Liberal Party in England and Ireland', p. 281.

selves to independence.[1] Keogh was successful at Athlone and Sadleir at Carlow. All the Independents were pledged not to accept office from a Government which did not make Irish demands Cabinet questions, but at the end of the year both Sadleir and Keogh accepted places from the Aberdeen Ministry. It was a severe blow to Irish hopes. It has been shown that their defection was by no means so decisive for the party as later Irish politicians supposed,[2] but it was followed by Cullen's withdrawal of support, carrying most of the bishops with him.[3] It is clear that he was scared both by the quality of support given to the Independent Party (his suspicion of the Young Irelanders and his fear of revolution), and by the radical interpretation frequently given to its programme in the provinces. When he withdrew the priests from politics also, in the 1854 Decrees, the fortunes of Independent Opposition were marked down. Yet even so, it would probably be mistaken to regard this as the death-blow to the party. It had suffered all along from an inherent weakness: an inability to unite on a single course of action due to the difficulty of interpreting the pledge adopted for candidates.[4] But in the eyes of many, Cullen was branded with the infamy of Sadleir's and Keogh's 'betrayal' and this was a reputation which was to dog his political actions in the next two decades. Moore and Duffy would never again have anything to do with the man who had 'betrayed and destroyed one of the greatest national movements Ireland ever possessed'.[5] O'Leary wrote in 1896 that if Cullen's name was remembered at all, it was 'generally associated with the infamous ones of Sadleir and Keogh'.[6] This all accounts for Cullen's reluctance to take part in political agitation again, and makes it all the more remarkable that he did so. It was also clear that after 1854 his sympathies were with the Liberals. 'I am sorry to see that the number of our liberal members is declining in Ireland', he wrote to Monsell, Liberal member for Limerick, in 1856; and he blamed the increasing strength of the Irish conservatives on the 'violence of the Tenant Right faction'.[7]

In turning to the position of the clergy in Ireland, it is clear that one great result of the collapse of the Independent Opposition was lasting. It is impossible to separate Cullen's drive to bring the internal affairs of the Irish Church into line with Rome from his view of the political activities of the priests. His 1854 Decrees hedging such activity were confirmed by Rome in the following year. Cullen said that the Decrees

---

[1] J. H. Whyte, *The Independent Irish Party, 1850-59*, Oxford, 1958, p. 86.
[2] *Ibid.*, pp. 110, 175.   [3] *Ibid.*, p. 113.   [4] *Ibid.*, p. 176.
[5] Charles Gavan Duffy, *My Life in Two Hemispheres*, London, 1898, vol. II, p. 268.
[6] O'Leary, *op. cit.*, vol. II, p. 51.
[7] Monsell Papers, Box 8319, 14 April 1856.

were intended 'not to destroy the influence of the clergy, but to prevent violence and imprudence'.[1] Frederick Lucas of the *Tablet* appealed to Rome against the Decrees, but was received unsympathetically, and heard from Mgr Barnabo's own lips that priests would in future be forbidden to attend political meetings in Ireland.[2] Cullen, who was in Rome at the same time – January 1855 – told him that priests would no longer be able to interfere in the selection of Parliamentary candidates unless one should be nominated who was known to be avowedly hostile to religion.[3] MacHale, also in Rome, took the chance to protest against Cullen's own interference in the internal affairs of the three Irish provinces other than Dublin. He was rebuked.[4] Cullen was delighted to hear Cardinal Antonelli remark that 'the system of so-called Independent Opposition would be likely to produce the evils occasioned in Italy by Mazzini's principles'.[5]

The Decrees of 1854 had a limited effect only; the clergy took their customarily conspicuous place in the elections of 1857 and 1859.[6] It is true that their electioneering tactics never again reached the zenith attained in 1852, but in later years its decline was not as sharp as all that. What had diminished was the even distribution of clerical participation throughout the country: but it still remained the rule rather than the exception for the clergy to assist in the selection of Parliamentary candidates, to canvass on behalf of their choice, and act as escorts on polling-days.[7] Occasionally, as at Galway and Kerry in 1872, the action of the priests was more dramatic than it had ever been before. The priests were able to supply the sort of organization for the popular side which the landlords' influence secured to the conservative interest. Cullen's Decrees could not banish that or – as Lucas warned – Irish political life would indeed fall into the hands of the revolutionists.[8] Although Bishop O'Brien of Waterford might complain that at elections the clergy 'always lose their temper, and in most intemperate language',[9] it was clear that the Decrees were always considered by Cullen to be in force, even after he had led the official return of the clergy to

---

[1] Monsell Papers, Cullen to Monsell, 10 March 1855.
[2] Edward Lucas, *Life of Frederick Lucas*, London, 1886, vol. II, p. 166.
[3] *Ibid.*, p. 185.
[4] *Ibid.*, p. 114.
[5] Monsell Papers, Box 8319, Cullen to Monsell, 10 March 1855.
[6] Whyte, *op. cit.*, pp. 123, 170.
[7] See the excellent article by J. H. Whyte – 'The Influence of the Catholic Clergy on Elections in Nineteenth-Century Ireland', in *English Historical Review*, LXXV, no. 295 (1960).
[8] Lucas, *op. cit.*, vol. II, p. 168.
[9] Kirby Papers, O'Brien to Kirby, no. 2354, 7 May 1859.

political agitation. In 1865 he warned them that their zeal for the programme of the National Association should not extend to waiving the rules of 1854.[1] Lucas's prediction had some truth in it too. 'It was unfortunate that the priests were for a time withdrawn from politics,' Bishop Dorrian wrote to Kirby in 1865, 'for people were thus driven in dispirit to combine illegally.'[2] As an explanation of the rise of Fenianism this is imperfect, but it contains a quantity of truth.

The instrument used by Cullen to co-ordinate the activities of the hierarchy, and through them the lower clergy, was the bishops' meeting. After 1859 these increased, to the dismay of MacHale, who frequently questioned their canonical regularity. But Cullen seems always to have obtained due permission from the Propaganda before summoning the bishops to Dublin. The deliberations of the meetings, which were held behind closed doors, were reported back to Rome, and usually the Resolutions passed were issued to the faithful as a joint-Pastoral. At every step in the difficult relations between the Church and the Government after 1859, the episcopate was gathered in Dublin to decide upon a united course of action. Direct approach to the Ministers was to be the favoured course. Emilio Campana wrote incorrectly that Cullen kept himself 'in the most amicable relations with the English Government'.[3] Yet he was not hostile: though he remained aloof, and when it became necessary for approaches to be made, they were almost entirely formal. After the Act of Union in 1800, the Irish Executive had survived, although the Dublin Parliament lapsed, and the co-ordination between Westminster and Dublin Castle was maintained by the Chief Irish Secretary.[4] Archbishop Murray had kept in touch with the Government by occasional attendance at the Castle, but the sign of new policy was seen when, on Cullen's appointment to Dublin, he failed to put himself in communication with the Lord-Lieutenant.[5] This was sometimes attributed to the operation of the Ecclesiastical Titles Act, and the unwillingness of Cullen to attend a court at which precedence would be conceded to Protestant bishops.[6] It is interesting that Cullen's title as cardinal after 1866 was not within the terms of the Act, and in March 1868, during the Prince of Wales' visit to Dublin, he was accorded precedence over the Protestant archbishop, who stayed away

[1] See chap. 4.
[2] Kirby Papers, Dorrian to Kirby, no. 28, 6 February 1865.
[3] Emilio Campana, *Il Concilio Vaticano*, Lugano, 1926, vol. I, p. 768.
[4] See R. B. McDowell, 'The Irish Executive in the Nineteenth Century', in *Irish Historical Studies*, IX (1954-5), p. 264.
[5] Lord John Russell noticed this – *Hansard*, CXIV, p. 189 (7 February 1851).
[6] *Parliamentary Papers*, 1867-8, VIII, *Report of the Select Committee of the House of Lords on Ecclesiastical Titles, Evidence*, p. 13.

as a result.[1] Between 1859 and 1873 the bishops were to approach all three sources of Irish Government – the Lord-Lieutenant, the Chief Secretary, and Parliament.

The relations of the Church with Rome were strictly governed. Ireland came within the administrative area of the Sacred Congregation of Propaganda because, although it had a regularly constituted hierarchy of its own, the country was in political union with England, whose hierarchy dated only from 1850, and with whose Government there existed no Concordat. Ordinarily the bishops approached the Propaganda for faculties, dispensations and decisions on controverted or unprecedented disciplinary cases. They had two ways of doing so; either by direct letter or petition to the Cardinal Prefect, or by the good offices of their agent in Rome, the Rector of the Irish College. The archives of the Propaganda are mostly filled with ecclesiastical causes, but during the period covered by this book Cullen reported with the greatest frequency – sometimes as often as once a week – on the affairs of Ireland. These letters are of the highest value. They range over the whole area of Irish problems, reporting on the state of the country, the dispositions of the Government and general political difficulties. The recipient was Cardinal Alexander Barnabo, in whom Maguire said was realized 'the fond dream of the Administrative Reformers of our own days – the right man in the right place'.[2] He and Cullen were completely in agreement. Also in this period, the Rector of the Irish College was Mgr Tobias Kirby, whose long tenure of the office lasted from 1850, when he had succeeded Cullen, until 1891 when he resigned, being by then titular Archbishop of Ephesus. The letters he received from Cullen and many of the other bishops are a valuable source of information on the inner machinations of the Irish hierarchy. It is interesting that he was so well-informed; it reduces somewhat the validity of the arguments of those who held that Cullen's years in Rome had left him out of touch with affairs in Ireland. 'I need not tell you any Irish news', Bishop MacNally wrote to Kirby in 1862, as the preface to a letter which was packed with information, 'as I know you get our newspapers, and in them almost everything appears.'[3] It is fortunate that his other correspondents were equally inconsistent.

---

[1] *Freeman*, 20 April 1868; *Mail*, 22 April 1868. It caused difficulty for the Irish Government, however – see Mayo Papers, MSS. 11161-11175 (Letter Books, 1868), Mayo to the Lord Chancellor, 23 March 1868: and questions in Parliament – *Hansard*, cxcii, p. 16 (11 May 1868) – which lasted – *ibid.*, cci, p. 1490 (27 May 1870).

[2] J. F. Maguire, *Rome, Its Ruler and Its Institutions*, second ed., London, 1859, p. 137.

[3] Kirby Papers, MacNally to Kirby, no. 15, 24 January 1862.

There were no diplomatic relations between the British Government and the Vatican, but contact was maintained by the presence in Rome of a British agent, and commercial links by the appointment of consuls.[1] In 1858 Odo Russell became agent, being, that is to say, officially transferred to Naples, according to custom, but residing in Rome. He was the nephew of Lord John Russell and had held minor diplomatic posts previously.[2] Despite his unofficial position, he was more freely admitted to the presence of Pope Pius IX than were most of the accredited representatives of the Catholic Powers. The Pope, indeed, had little deep knowledge of Irish conditions, though the activities of Odo Russell were to correct that to some extent during the 1860s. Newman was able to write, on leaving the rectorship of the Catholic University in Dublin, that though he had relied on the word of the Pope, 'I am led to think it not rash to say that I knew as much about Ireland as he did.'[3] That can be taken either way. But O'Neill Daunt recorded how Sir Bernard Burke had been told by the Pope during an audience in 1865, that he hoped he would bring his children up as Catholics. 'Why should I not?' said Sir Bernard, 'I am a Catholic myself.' The Pope had supposed he was a Protestant.[4] Odo Russell was also able to enjoy easy access to Cardinal Antonelli, the Papal Secretary of State, whose knowledge of Ireland was evidently rather better than the Holy Father's, since he made inquiry of the Propaganda for facts whenever pressed by Russell. Yet he had never left Italy, and Russell himself wrote that he was 'very slightly acquainted with the affairs of other countries'.[5] The opinions of both the Pope and the cardinal were faithfully reported to London by Russell, whose despatches, which followed the civilized Foreign Office rule of only touching on one matter in each missive, form a third valuable source of Irish affairs in Rome. When the occasion demanded it, the Government was able to exercise most effective pressure on the Vatican through his services.

The coherence of the period from 1859 to 1873 will soon become apparent. The Irish bishops were roused in the first year by Government proposals for a system of mixed intermediate education, and by English antipathy to the continued existence of the States of the Church in

[1] Sir Alec Randall, 'A British Agent at the Vatican; the Mission of Odo Russell', in *Dublin Review*, no. 479, 1959, p. 40.
[2] Noel Blakiston, *The Roman Question, 1858-70*, London, 1962. An edition of Russell's Dispatches, but leaving out almost all the Irish material. See the Introduction, pp. ix-xl, on the life of Russell.
[3] Sidney Dark, *Newman*, London, 1934, p. 67.
[4] Daunt, Journal, 7 November 1965.
[5] F.O. 43, vol. 76, Dispatch no. 7, 7 January 1860.

Italy: Wiseman's tour of Ireland in 1858 had displayed a deep consciousness both of attachment to Rome and to the national hierarchy. In 1859 also, Newman resigned as Rector of the Catholic University. The Prince of Wales delighted everyone by appearing in Rome on St Patrick's Day with a sprig of shamrock in his lapel. And in Belfast too religious sentiment was stirred, as if in preparation for retaliation to the newly-stirring south. The great Protestant Revival of 1859 was described by Cullen quite simply as 'diabolical'.[1] From the public excitement of that year, the bishops moved through a sequence of political agitation which came to an end only in 1873, the year in which, by a series of unfortunate events, they were largely responsible for the defeat of the one Ministry to which they had looked for so much: that of Gladstone.

It is certain that this can be termed 'political' agitation. It was of the standard nineteenth-century type – public meetings, associations, pressurizing the House of Commons, pledging members of Parliament, petitioning, writing and circularizing. But the characteristic noticed in the case of Cullen was also true for the other bishops. They did not desire to enter politics – that should be left to the politicians. Their concern was with matters which were, by their definition, religious. Of course the Government did not usually agree with the definition, nor did the Protestant press, which could be relied upon to howl about the political intrigues of ultramontane clerics. But the distinction maintained by the prelates must not be forgotten. The Unionist Bishop Moriarty – perhaps because he was a Unionist – expressed himself clearly on the point to Montelembert: 'It is impossible for a bishop to speak or write freely and publicly on questions . . . in which expediency and abstract right are often at right-angles.'[2] Moriarty was also to declare that 'when we descend from the heights on which God has placed us, to take part in temporal affairs, our authority does not descend with us'.[3] He could also see the dangers. 'We sometimes hear it said that the interests of religion require us to go with the people; that the alliance of religion and nationality is the great safeguard of the Church in Ireland,' he wrote in 1867. 'This depends altogether on the previous question, whether the popular mind is going right.'[4]

[1] Propaganda, *Scritture* 33, Cullen to Barnabo, f. 928, 5 July 1859.
[2] Monsell Papers, Box 8319, Moriarty to Montalembert, 16 February 1864.
[3] David Moriarty, *A Letter on Disendowment*, Dublin, 1867, p. 5.
[4] *Ibid.*, p. 24.

CHAPTER TWO

A First Phase: Rome and Education

WHEN it became apparent in 1859 that the Government was contemplating the establishment of a system of mixed intermediate education in Ireland, the Catholic bishops gave way in their determination never to enter again into 'political' questions. They could in fact do this readily. The education question was not for them 'political' – it was at the centre of the network of proselytism and indifferentism which the hierarchy had come to regard as the distinctive characteristic of the Protestant Constitution in Ireland. Around the proposal for intermediate education the bishops arranged other causes and occasions of proselytism, and the result was their Pastoral of August, which was itself supported by a meeting of Catholic Liberal Members of Parliament in Dublin at the end of the year. A sequence of agitation had opened which was to last until December 1864, when the bishops, under Archbishop Cullen, changed its quality by throwing in their lot with the Liberals in the National Association of Ireland. It is clear that in the first phase of agitation they looked for, and got, Irish Liberal support; but the Irish Liberals were not in 1859 a powerful body – they were reduced in numbers by the general election of that year, and had not yet come to that point of identity with the English Liberals in Parliament which the association with Bright, with English Protestant Dissenters, and finally with the emergent Gladstonian Party, was to characterize them after 1864. Until that time the bishops, under Cullen's lead, attempted usually to bring their own, unaided, influence to bear upon the governments. The scheme of mixed intermediate education was not put into effect – but otherwise they had no real success. Yet a new political movement *had* started. The Irish question was again in the hands of the bishops. It would not have caught fire at all, however, if Ireland had not reacted so suddenly and so decisively to the Italian question.

The design of the *Risorgimento* against the Temporal sovereignty of the Papacy is a familiar story. From the Plombières agreement in July 1858, it became almost obvious that Italian convulsion was on the cards. The Armistice of Villafranca in the same month of the following year left it to the Italians themselves – or rather to the Piedmontese and their revolutionary sympathizers in the northern states – to force a territorial settlement on the intransigent Pius IX. It was at this point, in the winter of 1859, that Irish Catholics took up the Papal cause, and were therefore hot with indignation even before Garibaldi's famous campaign in Sicily and Naples during the summer of 1860. The Papacy was defeated in armed combat on the fields of Castelfidardo, and in Ireland it was felt with the keenness of a second Battle of the Boyne.[1] A. M. Sullivan wrote of Irish feeling on the Italian question: 'On this subject there was displayed one of the most violent conflicts of English and Irish popular opinion which I have ever noted.'[2]

The matter is an extremely complicated one. Dr Beales has recently shown[3] that the picture often presented of English political crisis in 1859 is in many respects inaccurate. The Italian question did not greatly affect either the initial crisis or the general election of that year so directly or so intensely as formerly thought.[4] Nor was it the case that the minority Conservative Administration headed by Derby was so distinctively pro-Austrian and anti-Italian.[5] And it is true that Irish feeling on the question only really stirred *after* the 1859 election. But the question did have effect in the Irish elections, and it is important to realize that as early as May, when polling took place, Cardinal Wiseman in England, and the Irish bishops, backed by the public opinion on the Italian question they were just beginning to call into existence, *thought* that question to be of paramount importance. The Conservative gains in Ireland represented the *belief* of some of them that Derby was less likely than Palmerston to allow the moral weight of the British Government to be thrown on the side of Piedmont. For although all were in agreement on the importance of the question, the Irish bishops and the Catholic Members of Parliament were divided over support for Derby. The Government was defeated in the House of Commons over Parliamentary Reform on 31 March, though the dissolution was delayed until 23 April. The rump of the Irish Independent Party had been split in the debate on Reform: six voted with Derby, and five against.[6] In Ireland the clergy, still bewildered after the collapse of the Independent

---

[1] For events in Italy, see: G. F. H. Berkeley, *Italy in the Making*, Cambridge, 1932-40, vols. II and III; E. E. Y. Hales, *Pio Nono, a Study in European politics and religion in the Nineteenth century*, London, 1954; G. M. Trevelyan, *Garibaldi and the Making of Italy*, London, 1911; A. J. Whyte, *Political Life and Letters of Cavour*, Oxford, 1930; N. A. Blakiston, *The Roman Question*, London, 1962; D. Mack Smith, *Cavour and Garibaldi, 1860*, Cambridge, 1954.

[2] A. M. Sullivan, *New Ireland*, Glasgow, eighth ed., 1882, p. 210. See also, R. Dudley Edwards (ed.), *Ireland and the Italian Risorgimento*, Dublin, 1960, pp. 31-55.

[3] D. E. D. Beales, *England and Italy, 1859-60*, London, 1961.

[4] *Ibid.*, pp. 75, 163.   [5] *Ibid.*, p. 35.

[6] J. H. Whyte, *The Independent Irish Party, 1850-9*, p. 153.

programme, were sharply divided. In Meath, the bishop and clergy united to oppose Whig candidates, and in Ossory those priests who espoused the Whig were forbidden to attend a banquet in his honour.[1] Thus the 1854 decrees were put into force. As the *Dublin* pointed out in 1863, the confusion in Ireland between 'Whig' and 'Liberal' principles worked against the latter, for Catholics could still have no truck with the party of Lord John Russell and the Ecclesiastical Titles Act. The Italian question came to 'hasten and widen, if not to complete' the separation of English Liberals and Irish Liberal-Catholics.[2] So it was that at Meath where G. H. Moore was candidate, the clergy, recalling the Titles Act, told the electors that 'If ever a nation was pledged deeply and passionately against a man or a party – that nation is Ireland, and that man is Lord John Russell, and that party the Whig party.' They supported Independent action, but added significantly 'from the Tory side there was never danger to the independence of the Irish party'.[3] From Louth it was reported to Lord Naas that a cry which would catch the Catholic vote was 'Lord Derby versus Lord John Russell'.[4] From Dungarvan he heard from Maguire, who in the Parliamentary division on the Reform Bill had voted with the Government explicitly to save Rome from Italian Revolutionaries and keep out the 'dangerous incendiary', Palmerston.[5] In the election Maguire's address – as he described it to Naas – went 'the whole length for Lord Derby's foreign policy and against Russell and Palmerston'.[6]

The most dramatic intervention in the Irish elections was that of Cardinal Wiseman. He followed the tremendous success of his visit to Ireland in 1858 by supporting the Conservative interest at Waterford. The influence of his partiality rippled out to other constituencies as well. The 'alliance between the Government and Cardinal Wiseman' was much discussed during the election, the *Rambler* wryly suggesting that for the Government 'it has doubtless had its effect in adding to their unpopularity'.[7] After the election, the cardinal said that his interest had been due to the Catholics' treatment 'with more frankness and in a more

---

[1] J. J. Auchmuty, '*Acton's Election as an Irish Member of Parliament*', in *English Historical Review*, LXI (1946), p. 397.

[2] *Dublin Review*, April 1863, 'The Liberal Party in England and Ireland', pp. 283, 291, 294.

[3] Moore Papers, no. 653, 'Address of the Clergy to the Electors and People of Meath', 1859.

[4] Mayo Papers, MSS. 11036, P. Talbot to Naas, 11 April 1859.

[5] Quoted in Beales, *op. cit.*, p. 74.

[6] Mayo Papers, MSS. 11036, Maguire to Naas, 16 April 1859: 'The Whigs are furious', he added.

[7] *Rambler*, July 1859, new series, vol. 1, p. 253.

straightforward manner' by the Derby Administration than by any other.[1] But the *Rambler* also observed that many held his participation to be at the orders of a Pope in need of help against the Piedmontese.[2] Lord Campden declared that Wiseman had told him privately that he believed the Conservatives would 'do justice to the Roman Catholics'.[3] He asked the Cardinal to write to Bishop Furlong of Ferns in the Conservative interest.[4] The press carried many letters about the Waterford election, and highlighted Wiseman's letter to Blake, the sitting member, who had voted with Derby on the Reform division, in which the cardinal cited the Government's concession of Catholic army chaplains as a proof of their sincerity.[5] The disruption caused in Waterford by the election showed up in exaggerated form the sort of difficulties the political situation in Parliament had produced almost everywhere else in the predominantly Catholic constituencies. 'The priests here were divided in opinion,' the bishop (O'Brien) explained to Kirby at Rome after the polling, 'and in consequence I silenced the brawlers on both sides'.[6] Cullen told the Propaganda that 'the row which Cardinal Wiseman made during the election in Ireland has caused him much damage'.[7] It had also the unfortunate effect of making the new Government look with a jaundiced eye on the Roman Church and its election tactics. They were left prepared to believe anything. In November Odo Russell reported from Rome:

> Having gathered from conversations with French, Belgian, and Irish priests that the Pope had caused a league to be formed in Ireland under the direction of forty-two priests with a view to influence the next general election in the interests of the Conservative party, I thought it well to ask the Cardinal Secretary of State [Antonelli] whether he had any knowledge of this arrangement. His Eminence replied that he had not, and that it was quite unfounded – he understood, on the contrary, that the Irish clergy were generally more favourable to the Liberal than the Conservative Party, whilst in his private opinion he thought Lord Derby's Government more favourable to the Conservative cause all over Europe, and therefore to the unimpaired maintenance of the Pope's Temporal Power, but the Government of His Holiness always deprecated any interference in secular politics on the part of the Priesthood of foreign countries, and greatly regretted when it occurred.[8]

It is clear that Antonelli took his information from Cullen. And here the split among the Catholics was most apparent. Whilst Wiseman

---

[1] *Rambler*, July 1859, new series, p. 255.   [2] *Ibid.*, p. 254.
[3] Mayo Papers, MSS. 11036, Campden to Naas, 10 May 1859.
[4] *Ibid.*, 5 May 1859.   [5] *Guardian*, 25 May 1859.
[6] Kirby Papers, O'Brien to Kirby, no. 2354, 7 May 1859.
[7] Propaganda, *Scritture* 33, f. 888, 3 June 1859.
[8] F.O. 43, vol. 72, Dispatch no. 124, 18 November 1859.

supported the Conservatives, and MacHale the remnants of Independent Opposition, Cullen – who took no active part and did not vote, although he had voted for the two Liberal candidates for Dublin City in the 1857 election – made no secret of his sympathy with the Liberals, or his liking for the new Administration:

> The success of the Liberal Party was very cheering, [he wrote to Monsell in Limerick after the election]. The Conservatives were so identified with the Orangemen in Ireland that their continuing in power would have been most dangerous to the peace of this country. Indeed, I think it will require great energy and determination on the part of the new Liberal Government, when formed, to repair all the evils that have been done.[1]

The divisions among the clergy had materially affected the result of the elections in Ireland, however. The Conservatives got a clear majority there for the first time since 1832, winning eight seats.[2] The Conservatives gained in England too, but failing to attain a majority, they resigned on 10 June, and Palmerston took office at the head of an Administration which included both Russell and Gladstone. The Irish elections had shown a greater awareness of the Italian question than the English, but even so a more prominent issue for those standing by Derby was a personal one – keeping out the authors of the Ecclesiastical Titles Act and the wreckers of the Independent Party. In the early months of the new Government, both Cullen and MacHale expressed themselves on the Irish policy which it should pursue. In view of the conflict between the two archbishops, they made an interesting comparison. Cullen, writing to Monsell only a little over a month before the drafting of the great Pastoral, included the points which were demanded openly in it. There should be more Catholic office-holders, greater legal protection for tenants, remodelled National Education, the suppression of the Queen's Colleges, a Charter for the Catholic University, Catholic intermediate education, and provisions for Catholics in workhouses and gaols.[3] MacHale, in an open letter to Palmerston in October, testified to the superiority of Independent Opposition. But he could see hope in the nature of 'the capricious combination of parties' which had put the Liberals in power, warning Palmerston that 'the more anomalous that combination appears, and the more at variance with the rules of ordinary calculation, the stronger is the hope now felt that the measures of justice, with the promise of which we have been so long amused, cannot

---

[1] Monsell Papers, Box 8319, Cullen to Monsell, 14 June 1859.

[2] J. H. Whyte, *op. cit.*, see Appendix C, pp. 182–3, where he prints a table showing how Irish members voted in the Reform division of 1859.

[3] Monsell Papers, Box 8319, Cullen to Monsell, 14 June 1859.

be indefinitely protracted'. He demanded tenant legislation, disestablishment of the State Church, and Catholic education. Referring to divisions over the Irish elections, he wrote that 'Providing Lord Derby gave utterance to language lamenting the spread of Italian disaffection, pious Catholics forgot his jury-packing and his evictions, and fancied that an appearance of sympathy with the Holy Father should cancel all his other political and social misdeeds.'[1] God Himself, he added, and neither Derby nor Palmerston, would protect the Pope.

Although the leaders of both the great English parties were broadly in sympathy with Italian designs against the Papal States, there was good reason for supposing that an Administration under Palmerston containing Russell and Gladstone would inevitably tend to favour the *Risorgimento* more openly. Ever since the appearance of his Neapolitan letters in 1851, Gladstone had been known to favour the Italian cause, and it was his own opinion that the zeal of Palmerston and Russell 'kindled the country' on the question in 1859.[2] In 1861 he was to tell Cobden that 'the main point in which I think the existence of the present Government has been beneficial is the Italian Question'. He added: 'It is true that English opinion is now favourable to Italy, but it was not so three years ago, and we may have done something in assisting the change.'[3] By that year also, Manning had become convinced that the whole weight of the English Government was pressing to the overthrow of the Pope's dominions.[4] But in Ireland, they were persuaded of that as early as the autumn of 1859. At the end of August, Archbishop Dixon of Armagh wrote to Kirby in the confidence that wickedness was somehow always punished.

The attacks on His Holiness by Russell, Palmerston, and Gladstone have pierced the very breasts of the Irish clergy and people. The indignation of the Irish people will hurl these men from power shortly after the next meeting of Parliament, and I trust that we shall never see them in power again.[5]

In fact, as Dr Beales has shown, Russell was considering active intervention on behalf of the Italians in that month,[6] but the other two men named by Dixon remained more cautious. In Ireland, however, the idea that the whole English Administration, backed by public opinion,

---

[1] *Freeman*, 17 October 1859: letter of 15 October.

[2] John Morley, *Life of Gladstone*, London, 1905, vol. 1, p. 647.

[3] Quoted in W. E. Williams, *The Rise of Gladstone to the Leadership of the Liberal Party, 1859-68*, Cambridge, 1934, p. 58.

[4] Gladstone Papers, B.M.Add.MS. 44248, f. 152, Manning to Gladstone, 4 September 1861.

[5] Kirby Papers, Dixon to Kirby, no. 2406, 31 August 1859.

[6] Beales, *op. cit.*, p. 103.

was straining towards the Italian side, could not be held in check. Cullen
had reported to the Propaganda as early as June that 'the newspapers of
England are in favour of Sardinia'.[1] The Vatican was also convinced of
the evil intent of the British Government. In January 1860, Odo Russell,
in audience, heard the Pope declare that 'it is not in Italy that the seeds
of discontent and revolt are to be sought, but in the example of England,
the speeches of her public men, and the policy of Lord Palmerston'.
Before the Pope flew off into a rage, he had time to add that Lord John
Russell was 'our bitterest enemy'.[2] But it was more in sadness than in
anger that the Pope disclosed to him a year later his belief that 'England
is ever at work against us, favouring and assisting Revolution'; for 'your
people hate the Pope'.[3]

In this line taken by His Holiness – the familiar paradox of a constitutional country aiding the subversion of legitimate régimes – the Irish
could find their own comfort. In his famous and sensational Dispatch of
27 October 1860, Lord John Russell argued that the government of the
Pope provided so inadequately for the welfare of the people that they
looked for its overthrow as a necessary preliminary to any improvement.
Her Majesty's Government were bound to admit that the Italians themselves were the best judges of their own interests. The actions of Cavour
and Garibaldi were justified, and Italy was held *not* to be an exceptional
case, as defenders of the Temporal Power of the Papacy had always
maintained.[4] This amounted to a *carte blanche* for Revolution, and the
Irish were quite prepared for it. They had not been slow from the
beginning at showing that arguments used by the British Government
to justify Italian revolutionism were equally applicable to themselves.
In August 1859 O'Neill Daunt, referring to rumours of a French
invasion – these were legion in 1859-60 – could hold that if he should
come to Ireland, 'Napoleon's intervention would be just as legitimate as
the British interference in Italian matters advocated by Lord Palmerston'.[5] And in October of that year MacHale warned Palmerston of the
validity of such a position. 'Let those then, who are so anxious to reform
the Pontifical Government, turn their attention to the Home Department of their own, with a view to the correction of its disorders,' he
had written.[6] More bluntly still, S. B. Harper, speaking in support of the
States of the Church at a public meeting in the Hanover Rooms in

[1] Propaganda, *Scritture* 33, f. 888, 3 June 1859.
[2] F.O. 43, vol. 76, Dispatch no. 19, 31 January 1860.
[3] *Ibid.*, vol. 83A, Dispatch no. 5, 16 January 1861.
[4] Morley, *op. cit.*, vol. I, p. 649; Beales, *op. cit.*, p. 156.
[5] Daunt, Journal, 1 August 1859.
[6] *Freeman*, 17 October 1859: letter of 15 October.

London on 3 January 1860, had warned the Government 'that if the principles you are conspiring to inculcate, with regard to the Italian provinces and their rulers, had been applied to yourselves, the Irish people would have risen upon you long ago'.[1] Manning was later to tell Gladstone that the principles he had applied in the case of Italy justified every revolution that could be carried by a majority.[2]

Against such argument there could be no rejoinder in terms which the discontented in Ireland would accept. Frequently the case of Poland was pointed to. There the Catholic clergy were the leaders of insurrection against legitimate government by Russia,[3] and the Polish revolt, when it came, in 1863, received wide sympathy in England, and there was even a popular clamour for diplomatic intervention against the Cossack Czar. But this did not prevent Protestant Englishmen pointing to an apparent inconsistency in Papal policy. The Pope had at first refused a Russian request, made in 1861, to help restrain the hostility of the Polish Catholic priests – on the grounds that 'a religious movement [had] brought on persecution', and that there was no concordat with Russia.[4] Opposition to the Catholic bishops in Ireland itself also made use of the Polish case. In an article headed 'Poland and Ireland' of March, 1864, the *Irish People* (a Fenian Paper) ridiculed the inconsistency of the hierarchy, who would allow Polish priests to rebel, but not Italian peasants, or, come to that, Irish ones.[5] It is easy to understand why the bishops were so anxious to suppress Fenianism among the Catholics when it began to grow in strength early in the 1860s. They were in a dilemma. They could argue that Russell's Dispatch justified insurrection in Ireland, but if Ireland rebelled then the destruction of the Papal States must also be legitimate. The bishops stood by the traditional teaching of their Church instead: that rebellion earns damnation. Some Catholics, like Maguire, Liberal member of Parliament for Dungarvan 1852–65, and for Cork City from 1865, showed alternatively that compared with Ireland, the Papal State constituted an examplar of good government.

The *Dublin Review* summed up much of the English feeling against the Temporal Power as early as March 1859. 'All the complaints made

[1] S. B. A. Harper, *The Conspiracy against Religion and Liberties of the States of the Church, being the substance of a Speech*, London, 1860, p. 12.

[2] Gladstone Papers, B.M.Add.MS. 44248, f. 250, Manning to Gladstone, 15 January 1865.

[3] For a recent assessment, see R. F. Leslie, *Reform and Insurrection in Russian Poland, 1856-65*, London, 1963.

[4] F.O. 43, vol. 83B, Dispatch no. 105, 30 December 1861 – report by Odo Russell. In January 1862, the Vatican and the Russian Government made mutual concessions.

[5] *The Irish People*, 12 March 1864.

of the Papal Government resolve themselves, when rigidly sifted, into dislike of any Papal Government, and of ecclesiastical rule in general; not on account of any proved incapacity or inefficiency, but on account of prejudice against ecclesiastical rule, as being ecclesiastical.'[1] One particular issue was used by opponents of the Temporal Power to prove, as they supposed, the ecclesiastical tyranny which they alleged character-ized the Papal States. The Mortara Case received the widest European publicity from 1858, and on into the early sixties. Because at its core there existed an instance of proselytism, it was frequently discussed in reference to Ireland. The detail of the affair has largely been disregarded, but it is worth some examination, for non-Catholic opinion waxed hysterical over a matter deliberately inflated for the purpose of agitation into a major scandal. It played a great part in damaging the propriety of ecclesiastical government in the period immediately preceding its collapse in Italy. Maguire gave it a considerable amount of space in the second edition of his *Rome, Its Ruler and Its Institutions*, which appeared in 1859.

The story of this boy is a very simple one; and yet it has been much distorted by those who, caring nothing whatever about Edgar Mortara, his parents, his tribe, or the whole Jewish race, gladly availed themselves of his case as a vehicle for calumny, and as an opportunity for assailing and reviling the vicar of Christ.[2]

Mortara was seven years old when he was taken away from his parents at Bologna in 1858. When only eleven months old he had been baptized by a Christian servant-girl of the household whilst he was in danger of death from sickness. Now by the law of the Papal States a Jewish family was prohibited from employing Christian servants just to avoid such difficulty as that encountered over young Mortara.[3] So on the orders of Archbishop Viale-Prelà, the child was removed from his parents and given into the custody of the Church to be brought up in the Catholic religion. At the Catecumeni in Rome he was rebaptized and dedicated to the priesthood, being given the name Pius. Eventually he was to become a regular canon at the Lateran and an Apostolic Missionary.[4]

---

[1] *Dublin Review*, March 1859, 'The Government of the Papal States', p. 241.
[2] J. F. Maguire, *Rome, Its Ruler and Its Institutions*, p. 336.
[3] In 1859 Pope Pius sought to avoid a recurrence of this sort of problem by having the Roman Ghetto searched for Christian servants in Jewish households. About a dozen were found. This act, which as Maguire said, was intended for the protection of the Pope's Jewish subjects, was also made the occasion of extravagant denunciations of Papal 'tyranny'. *Op. cit.*, p. 343.
[4] For details of the case, see: J. F. Maguire, *op. cit.*, pp. 335-45; R. de Cesare, *The Last Days of Papal Rome*, trans. Helen Zimmern, London, 1909, pp. 177 ff.; *Dublin Review*, March 1859, 'The Mortara Case and the Murphy Case', pp. 19 ff.; J. Chantrel, *Annales Ecclésiastiques de 1846 à 1860*, Paris, 1861, pp. 453 ff.

Europe echoed with clamour about Mortara as soon as the case became public in 1858. Cavour spread it throughout the diplomatic world; the newspapers of Piedmont, France, England and America stormed about the cruelty of the Papal Government. After useless audiences with the Pope, the parents left the Papal States and settled at Turin where they appealed to the conscience of Europe. Napoleon III insisted upon the restitution of the child to his parents, but nothing was done. Maguire, who visited the boy in Rome and was 'struck with the unusual size of his head', declared that Mortara himself had told the Pope he would not return to his parents unless they also became Christians.[1] The whole matter played into the hands of those working for the subversion of the Temporal Power. Ridolfi de Cesare wrote, 'it was only natural that Cavour availed himself of this event to diffuse yet darker reflections upon the anomalies of the Papal Temporal Power existing in the full blaze of the nineteenth century'.[2] Public opinion in England, as usual, agreed with Cavour. On 28 April 1859, Odo Russell called on Cardinal Antonelli, accompanied by Sir Moses Montefiore, representing the Committee of Deputies of British Jews. Antonelli would only say that the child was to receive the religious education to which it was entitled.[3] Two days before, Pius IX had himself told Russell that the case was 'a closed question'.[4] On 7 November a deputation from the Evangelical Alliance, headed by Sir Culling Eardley, called on Lord John Russell in London. Russell admitted the case to be one of gross violation of parental right, but said that although they and the French Government were in agreement on the matter, they felt it was not one for the intervention of the Powers.[5] It was also Sir Culling Eardley, in his famous controversy with Archbishop Cullen in December, who wrote that 'the Mortara Case alone is enough to bring down on the Papal Government the execration of mankind', and referred to *The Times*, which had declared the affair 'conclusive for abolishing the Temporal Power of the Pope'.[6] Cullen referred him to Ireland.

The Mortara Case, in fact, was a simple one of proselytism. But it was of a non-Catholic by Catholics. In Ireland, however, the Catholics were able to cover their embarrassment by pointing to the frequent occurrence there of reverse cases, of the attempts by Protestants with official

[1] Maguire, *op. cit.*, p. 340.   [2] de Cesare, *op. cit.*, p. 179.
[3] F.O. 43, vol. 71, 28 April 1859. See a report of this meeting in the *Nonconformist*, 20 July 1859.
[4] F.O. 43, vol. 71, 26 April 1859.
[5] *Nonconformist*, 9 November 1859, 'The Mortara Case'.
[6] *Ibid.*, 21 December 1859, 'Sir Culling Eardley and Dr Cullen'.

support to proselytize Catholics. Discussion of the Mortara affair with reference to Ireland laid bare the religious jealousies on both sides, though at first the Catholics, in support of the Papal action over the Jewish child, found themselves rather on the defensive. Cullen told Eardley to remove the beam from his own eye first. Of the law of the Papal State under which Mortara had suffered, he wrote: 'this law prevailed in Rome at the very time when Charter Schools were instituted in Ireland and millions expended for the purpose of bringing up in Protestantism the children of Irish Catholics against the will of their parents, a system which still prevails to a great extent and is supported by men who speak most loudly against the Pope.'[1]

Throughout 1859 and 1860 comparisons were often made between Irish 'Mortara' cases and that in Rome – usually in the interests of Catholic defence, and as part of their propaganda to show up the active proselytism of the country. In February 1859 the case of the Murphy children of Dublin was employed in this sense. These had been removed from the Josephian Orphan House by a Protestant clergyman called Hefferman to be educated in Protestantism. Their mother could only get access to them after a court order. 'The case of Murphy is the exact parallel of that of Mortara' the *Dublin Review* exclaimed triumphantly.[2] Another *cause célèbre* was the Sherwood case of May 1860, which the *Guardian* described as 'a version of the Mortara Case'.[3] In these, Catholic opinion was tending rather to showing that Papal action was not so bad because similar things happened often in Ireland – which was at least a weak sort of defence. But in a wider sense it was possible for them to point to a vast field of proselytism, and they were encouraged by the furore over young Mortara to do so. Thus Father Lavelle – a man later to become notorious – caught the attention of Ireland during 1859-60 by his virulent campaign against proselytism and eviction carried out at Partry in West Connaught under the auspices of the Protestant Bishop of Tuam, Plunket.[4] All of Lavelle's case is not to be accepted, however, for the Catholic Bishop of the Partry area, MacEvilly of Galway, told Kirby at Rome in December 1859, and again in October 1861, that throughout the diocese 'proselytism has completely disappeared'

---

[1] *Ibid.*

[2] *Dublin Review*, March 1859, 'The Mortara Case and the Murphy Case', p. 36; also *Guardian*, 9 May 1860, 'Another Mortara case'.

[3] *Guardian*, 2 May 1860.

[4] Patrick Lavelle, *The War in Partry, or Proselytism and Eviction*, Dublin, 1861, reprinted as an Appendix in his *Irish Landlord since the Revolution*, Dublin, 1870. See O'Neill Daunt's comment on the Partry evictions, Journal, 17 December 1859, and 17 April 1860.

excepting only a case at Oughterard.[1] But he meant the open activities of Bible readers and visiting ladies. Every Catholic accepted institutional proselytism – in schools, prisons, and workhouses – as a fact. And to confirm their predisposition to imagine the worst, in the early summer of 1859 the infamous apostate Catholic, Gavazzi, toured the West preaching against Romanism.[2]

Cullen, indeed, did not hesitate to blame all the Italian troubles on the eagerness of the English Protestants to proselytize and subvert in the States of the Church. Speaking at Dublin in September 1859, he had credited British Bible agents with the Italian ruptures,[3] especially singling out Lord Shaftesbury and the Evangelical Alliance for censure, on the ground that they had indirectly financed armed rebellion against the Papacy. He also spoke of the bad example of English statesmen, and declared that 'the agents of bible societies have spread like locusts over Italy'. For the Evangelical Alliance, the charge was publicly denied by Sir Culling Eardley, but Cullen had made a point which he was to stand by. It was not without some truth, in the sense that Protestant feeling did strongly add moral weight against the Holy See. When Cavour visited London in 1856 he had found Lord Shaftesbury and the Protestant zealots the most enthusiastic of all English opinion for the Italian cause.[4] Victor Emmanuel and Garibaldi were frequently presented with Bibles in the English belief that the conversion of Italy might well follow the end of the Temporal rule of the Popes.[5] The men of the *Risorgimento*, often themselves Catholics, welcomed the support of Protestantism for their cause. In 1860 Garibaldi gave land in conquered Naples for a Protestant church.[6] Cullen withdrew nothing in the face of Sir Culling Eardley's invectives, and in a *Letter* to the Dublin clergy of January 1861, communicating to them a Papal Allocution, he stated that in Italy

Churches built and endowed for Catholic worship have been handed over to Protestants, just as St Patrick's Cathedral and Christ's Church in our city were formerly taken from our Catholic ancestors and delivered up to the followers of the so-called Reformation. . . . You will take an interest in what His Holiness states regarding the establishment of Protestant schools in Italy. It appears that

[1] Kirby Papers, MacEvilly to Kirby, no. 2479, 26 December 1859, and no. 3038, 8 October 1861.
[2] His visit to Galway caused a riot: *Guardian*, 6 April 1859.
[3] *Ibid.*, 9 November 1859. His speech was on 3 September.
[4] D. E. D. Beales, *op. cit.*, p. 24.
[5] *Ibid.*, also F.O. 43, vol. 88, which is filled with letters from English Protestant bodies supporting Garibaldi.
[6] Beales, *op. cit.*, p. 25.

the money necessary for this purpose is supplied by the biblical and revolutionary societies of England, who also provide the funds for carrying on the vile and degrading system of proselytism in Ireland.[1]

It is therefore clear that although the Italian question played some part in the Irish elections of 1859, it was only really afterwards that the acid irritation caused by English hatred of the Papal Administration burned into Irish popular opinion. Then the Irish movement for the Pope suddenly swelled into gigantic proportions. This coincided with the agreement of Napoleon III and the Pope in November to allow a congress on the Italian question to be held by the terms of the Treaty of Zürich. In Ireland, Italy became the political question of the hour, and the hierarchy stirred up a great national movement in favour of the Pope, and in the hope of influencing the British Government to work for a settlement more in his interests. In this movement the Catholics found all their complaints against their home administration reflected. It explains why the educational reform movement started by the Catholic hierarchy in August went off to such an encouraging start. 'Papal Ireland' was the label used by A. M. Sullivan to describe the peculiar atmosphere of the country in 1859 and 1860.[2]

The appearance of the revised edition of Maguire's *Rome, Its Ruler and Its Institutions* in 1859 had done much to canvass support for the Pope. It evidently had a wide sale, and was used to demonstrate how liberal the Temporal régime was. It had also the advantage of not emanating directly from the hierarchy. 'Is it possible that there can be any fairer judge of the Papal Government than a Catholic layman?' asked the *Dublin Review*.[3] In commending the work to the Catholic Young Men's Society, Cullen described it as affording 'a complete refutation of all the calumnies that have been invented against our Holy Father and his states'.[4] The bishops had started calling meetings in favour of the Pope in the various dioceses, and as the movement got under way, Cullen was delighted to notice not only that it healed the dissensions caused at Waterford and elsewhere by divisions over the general election in May, but that it promised to bring about a greater sense of Catholic unity. 'The attacks which we are exposed to', he told Bishop Gillooly in December 1859, 'ought to induce us to make every exertion to promote charity in our own ranks.'[5] In that month and in the next, massed meetings were held throughout

[1] *Freeman*, 21 January 1861.   [2] *New Ireland*, chap. XVIII.
[3] *Dublin Review*, June 1859, p. 404.
[4] Quoted in Peadar MacSuibhne, *Paul Cullen and his Contemporaries*, vol. II, p. 311 (15 November 1859).
[5] Gillooly Letters, Cullen to Gillooly, 24 December 1859.

Ireland. 'You cannot imagine anything more consoling than the deep fervent spirit of attachment to the Holy See which present circumstances are awakening among the poor country people,' Bishop Moriarty reported to Cullen from Killarney.[1] His meeting there, on 8 December, was attended by 20,000 people,[2] who were all assured by the bishop that Pius IX would 'lead the way, as he did before, in the path of liberal and enlightened reform'.[3] Sometimes the meetings expressed rather strongly the feeling against English Italian sympathy which characterized them all. Thus at Cork Dean Murphy told the people to appreciate the superiority of ecclesiastical government.

> Contrast Leo X, Paul IV and V, Pius IV and V, and Gregory XV with the monarchs of England – the Henrys, the Charleses, the Georges – (Oh! Oh!) – monsters of bigotry, lust, and imbecility, until the list was closed by her present gracious Majesty – (groans) – who has commenced a new dynasty and given an example of virtue – (No! No!). . . .[4]

At the great Mallow meeting, Bishop Keane admitted that discontent existed in the States of the Church – 'because of the imperfections of all human governments' – but asked 'Is there no discontent in Ireland?' Prolonged applause greeted that.[5] At a meeting of the Dublin clergy in the pro-Cathedral on 9 January 1860, Cullen spoke of the rights of the Holy See,[6] and at the same time 2,300 persons, headed by More O'Ferrall, M.P. for Kildare, signed a requisition addressed to Cullen calling for a Papal Meeting.[7] At that meeting the archbishop was indifferent in his condemnation of English ministers – following the position he had taken during the election. Lord Derby, he said, had called the Patrimony of St Peter a plague-spot on the map of Italy, whilst Palmerston preferred Mazzini ('that veiled prophet of modern Pantheism') to the Pope. Cavour, he declared, not without some degree of truth, appeared 'to have selected Henry VIII of England as a model'. Alderman Reynolds was hissed when he said that the Irish Catholics were loyal to the Crown, and only sporadic response was called forth when Cullen waved his hand indicating that the audience should cheer.[8] A meeting held by Archbishop MacHale at Castlebar was the occasion of similar expressions of national feeling.[9]

Although the popular enthusiasm for the Pope was great, there were those among the higher ranks of Catholic society in Ireland who would

---

[1] Cullen Papers, Moriarty to Cullen, 29 November 1859.
[2] *Ibid.*, 8 December 1859.   [3] *Freeman*, 13 December 1859.
[4] Reported in the *Guardian*, 14 December 1859.   [5] *Post*, 15 December 1859.
[6] See *The Pastoral Letters . . . of Cardinal Cullen*, ed. Moran, vol. 1 (XLIX), p. 710.
[7] *Guardian*, 11 January 1860.   [8] *Ibid.*, 18 January 1860.
[9] *Ibid.*, 25 January 1860.

have none of it. This was partly because the enthusiasm represented too nakedly a popular hostility to English policy on other matters than Italy, but more because many Catholics of position were opposed to the Temporal Power itself. Newman's journal, the *Rambler*, had come out against it early in 1859, and Cullen in reporting this to the Propaganda, anticipated some bad result in Ireland.[1] He was justified in this. It was among the aristocratic set of Catholics in the Limerick region and the south-west, many of them converts like the de Veres, who were to be dissenters from the hierarchy on the education question, who were now awkward over the Papacy. Lord Dunraven declared to Monsell in 1861 that he had found the *Rambler* view of the Temporal Power much more to his liking than the 'Manning-Faber view'.[2] Monsell, a Catholic convert since 1850, and M.P. for Limerick County since 1847, did not agree. Speaking at Limerick in December (1859) he certainly denied any hierocratic notions about the Temporal Power, but held that it was necessary to prevent the Pope becoming the subject of another sovereign. Only the States of the Church preserved his independence.[3] Stephen de Vere, former member of Parliament for Limerick County, told him bluntly in the same month that he had 'no sympathy with the Pope as a misgoverning Temporal prince', and refused to attend any gatherings at which such sympathy would be expected of him.[4] Lord Castlerosse behaved similarly. He refused to attend Moriarty's great meeting in Killarney and as a result – as the bishop explained to Cullen – completely lost his influence with the people.[5] Moriarty had found the defection of the Catholic upper classes from the Pope's cause a severe strain when he was preparing the demonstration.[6] Castlerosse, the member for Kerry, in a public letter in the press, stated that he was opposed to meetings in favour of the Pope because they could be 'a menace against both home and foreign governments'.[7] This opposition to the popular movement did not pass unnoticed in the Protestant English press, which was so anxious to play it up that it rather exaggerated it. Thus the *Nonconformist* reported that 'a regular split has taken place amongst Irish Roman Catholics'.[8] But led by Maguire and Monsell the Catholic members of Parliament mostly supported the movement, and signed an Address got up during January for presentation at

[1] Propaganda, *Scritture* 33, f. 888, 3 June 1859.
[2] Monsell Papers, Box 8319, Dunraven to Monsell, 4 September 1861.
[3] William Monsell, *A Lecture on the Roman Question*, London, 1860, p. 5.
[4] Monsell Papers, Box 8319, de Vere to Monsell, 6 December 1859.
[5] Cullen Papers, Moriarty to Cullen, 8 December 1859.
[6] *Ibid.*, 29 November 1859.   [7] *Guardian*, 7 December 1859.
[8] *Nonconformist*, 18 January 1860, 'The Italian Question'.

Westminster calling on the Government, as The O'Donoghue (member for Tipperary) declared in the House of Commons, 'to interfere in the affairs of Italy with a view to the complete restoration of the Pope's authority.'[1] Only Pope-Hennessy, the member for King's County, pointedly refused to sign, on the grounds that its authors sought favours from Palmerston. He was rebuked by Cullen.[2]

There can be no doubt that the moral weight of English Protestantism was on the Italian side, but the Government, despite calculated indiscretions like the Russell Dispatch of 1860, committed itself to neutrality after Palmerston had engineered the Cabinet into agreement.[3] When the Irish Chief Secretary, Sir Robert Peel, was in Sligo during November 1861, he defended the Government against the attacks of Cullen, on that ground. 'England is neutral in the dispute that rages between the Pontiff and the Italians', he said, but 'there is no doubt – and there ought to be none – as to the side upon which her sympathies are'.[4] Cullen, in his Pastoral at the beginning of the month, had quoted Peel's words from *Hansard* (1861) in support of the Italians, and asked what trust the Irish Catholics could put in a man who so assailed religion.[5] Peel's reply was little calculated to reassure him. But the influence of the Government – badly enough employed from his point of view – was not as bad as all that. Informally, through Odo Russell at Rome, the Government offered the Pope asylum and a palace at Malta if it should become necessary for him to flee the Italian peninsula.[6]

Compared with Catholic effort in England, as the *Dublin Review* lamented,[7] the Irish had put up a superlative show in support of the Pope. But they went even further than demonstrations and collections. They provided an army too. It has been truly said[8] that the war in Italy of 1860 was undoubtedly a struggle between two great principles: modern nationalism and the historic conception of the Church. In Ireland too these principles were engaged, but there the Church tended to identify itself with national aspirations in the limited sense the latter implied in all movements during the 1860s excepting Fenianism. And

---

[1] *Hansard*, third series, CLVI, p. 2147 (2 March 1860). See also, reference to the Address by Bishop Delany of Cork in a letter to Kirby – Kirby Papers, no. 2488, 13 January 1860.

[2] *Nonconformist*, 18 January 1860.   [3] Beales, *op. cit.*, p. 110.

[4] *Packet*, 11 November 1861.

[5] *Freeman*, 9 November 1861. See *Hansard*, CLXI, p. 1560.

[6] F.O. 43, vol. 89B, Dispatch no. 5, 7 January 1863.

[7] *Dublin Review*, February 1862, 'Papal Allocutions and Revolutionary Principles', p. 214.

[8] G.F-H. Berkeley, *The Irish Battalion in the Papal Army of 1860*, Dublin and Cork, 1929, p. 38.

over Fenianism the Irish Church was triumphant; but in Italy nationalism won. For the Irish, the opportunity of fighting for the Pope against the combined assaults of Garibaldi and the Piedmontese was 'an expression of Irish nationality in the days when the nation had no flag'.[1]

It was in January 1860 that Mgr de Mérode persuaded the Pope that a volunteer army recruited from Catholics all over Europe, might yet save the Temporal Power.[2] In April, General Lamoricière was brought from France to lead it. At an audience granted to Odo Russell at the end of January, the Pope had spoken of his desire to enlist Irish soldiers if he could do so without giving offence to the Queen.[3] There were soon reports in the English press of extensive recruitment in Ireland. A. M. Sullivan described how in March two gentlemen called at the office of his Dublin newspaper, the *Nation*, to seek his support for recruiting. He expressed some doubts about the attitude of the Government, but felt there was little they could do to impede an Irish movement since Garibaldians were being enlisted in England.[4] Sullivan was also unsure of the attitude of the bishops – who were thought to doubt whether Lamoricière's little army could ever win a battle – but he agreed to support recruiting, and toured the Irish provinces to get up enthusiasm.[5] Within a month, the first contingent left Ireland to join the service of the Pope. A committee was set up in Dublin to act as a clearing-house for recruits. It consisted of three or four men, one of whom was Canon Forde.[6] Sullivan's doubts about the bishops' attitude had proved to be unfounded. Under the Foreign Enlistment Act recruitment into service other than that of the Queen was an offence, so in Ireland it was carried on under the familiar disguise of emigration. Cullen was evidently a party to the subterfuge. Writing to Gillooly on 9 May, he referred to communication from Rome about 'employment' to be had there for the Irish, adding: 'I do not like to write much about these matters lest a false interpretation should be put on my words by our enemies, but I suppose it is quite free for anyone who wishes to emigrate, and for us to assist them if we can.'[7] Moriarty encouraged the same pretence in Kerry.[8]

Cavour complained about enlistment in Ireland, and on 16 May a proclamation was issued from Dublin Castle reiterating the penalties of the Foreign Enlistment Act,[9] and although recruiting fell off slightly

---

[1] *Ibid.*, p. vii. [2] E. E. Y. Hales, *Pio Nono*, London, 1956, p. 208.
[3] F.O. 43, vol. 76, Dispatch no. 19, 31 January 1860.
[4] A. M. Sullivan, *op. cit.*, p. 212. [5] *Ibid.* [6] *Ibid.*, p. 213.
[7] Gillooly Letters, Cullen to Gillooly, 9 May 1860.
[8] See his remarks on the difficulties involved in keeping up this disguised activity: Kirby Papers, Moriarty to Kirby, no. 2510, 15 February 1860.
[9] Berkeley, *op. cit.*, p. 22.

as a result, it continued through the summer. In the House of Commons, on the 25th, The O'Donoghue complained of the 'tyranny' of the Government in posting the Dublin Proclamation whilst at the same time countenancing the subscriptions in aid of Garibaldi. 'Her Majesty's Government', he continued, 'evidently wished success to the conspirators in Italy, and consequently were determined to crush the expression of Irish zeal'.[1] On the 10th of the month, Cardinal Antonelli had assured Russell in Rome that Irishmen enlisted in Papal service of their own free will, for 'nothing would induce the Papal Government to attempt enlistments in Ireland'.[2] This was doubtless true. The Pope, anxious to stake his defence on the legitimacy of his Temporal rule, was unlikely to allow anything which could be construed as an illegality in another State – especially one which, like England, could use any infringement of law by the Papacy as effective propaganda for the Italians. This meant that the Dublin recruiting commission was operated without sanction from Rome, and this would square with Sullivan's account and the pretences adopted about emigration. The Consul Newton reported from Rome that enlistment actually took place *after* the Irish volunteers had 'emigrated' to the Papal State.[3]

The Irish Brigade of St Patrick eventually reached just over a thousand in number. It consisted of men of all classes, though the proportion of young Catholics of position was higher than in an ordinary army.[4] This allowed the quality of 'a Crusade or Holy War', which Newton noticed, to infect the Irish.[5] But those from the lowest class certainly made their presence felt. Gregorovius observed that from their arrival in Rome, the Irish *Zouaves* would serve only under their own officers and were inclined to complain about their conditions.[6] They were 'altogether comically attired in green jackets and wide trousers, with yellow facings and epaulettes, looking like a salad garnished with eggs'.[7] The battalion was divided, and those sent to Macerata attained to new heights of dissatisfaction. Irish priests sent out from Rome to pacify them rather characteristically took their side instead.[8] In their extremity, the Macerata town authorities declared that they would prefer even a Spanish garrison to an Irish one.[9] At Ancona, where other

---

[1] *Hansard*, CLVIII, p. 1767.   [2] F.O. 43. vol. 77, Dispatch no. 65, 10 May 1860.
[3] *Ibid.*, vol. 80A, Dispatch no. 51, 26 June 1860.
[4] Berkeley, *op. cit.*, p. 21.
[5] F.O. 43, vol. 80A, Dispatch no. 51, 26 June 1860.
[6] *The Roman Journals of Gregorovius, 1852-74*, trans. G. W. Hamilton, London, 1911, p. 93.
[7] *Ibid.*, p. 113.   [8] F.O. 43, vol. 77, Dispatch no. 89, 23 June 1860.
[9] *Ibid.*

Irish recruits were sent, a British subject had to complain to the Papal Government about their riotous behaviour. He had been repeatedly assaulted by them.[1] But in the defence of Spoleto, where half the garrison was Irish, under the command of Major O'Reilly, who was in charge of all the Irish forces in the Papal army, the Irish put up an heroic effort.[2]

Despite its misgivings, the British Government offered to give the Irish recruits free passage home in October at the end of the disastrous campaign,[3] although Gladstone (then Chancellor of the Exchequer) expressed wariness about the precedent this created.[4] Odo Russell, commenting on the failure of the Papacy to re-enlist more than eighteen of the Irish into a small standing army, thought that 'the Vatican wished to keep them in Italy, fearful of the effect which the tales they would have to tell, might produce in Ireland'.[5] Those who returned to Ireland received a hero's welcome at Cork organized by Maguire.[6] The whole extraordinary episode had many results. Major O'Reilly was assured of a future, and in fact was elected as member of Parliament for Longford in 1862. He had also made himself something of an expert in Catholic educational demands, and as the Protestant *Packet* observed on his candidacy, 'the Cullenite dictatory . . . could not have found in the ultra-Papal ranks a person more offensive to the Protestant electors'.[7] Many of the Irish who fought for the Pope in 1860 were also to use their experience as officers in the American Civil War[8] – and as 'centres' of the Fenian movement in Ireland itself. The Irish Brigade had outraged English feeling,[9] and opened the eyes of the Papacy. Both the Pope and himself, Cardinal Antonelli explained to Odo Russell in July 1860, 'had not known the Irish Character to be so energetic – and he could also now appreciate the difficulties experienced by the British Government in dealing with Ireland'.[10]

The onslaughts on the Faith in which the Irish felt themselves so involved in Italy were paralleled for them in Ireland also. 'One would almost rejoice at the present calamities that have called forth so magnificent a display of Catholic feeling in Ireland', Archbishop Leahy wrote to Kirby in January 1860; 'but, in truth, it is an awful time we have

[1] *Ibid.*, vol. 75, August 1860.
[2] Berkeley, *op. cit.*, chaps. IX-XX; and J. F. Maguire, *Pius IX*, second ed., London, 1878, pp. 141-2.
[3] *Guardian*, 31 October 1860.
[4] See his letter to Palmerston, 7 October, in *Gladstone and Palmerston, being their correspondence, 1851-65*, ed. Philip Guedalla, London, 1928, p. 152.
[5] F.O. 43, vol. 78, Dispatch no. 177, 24 November 1860.
[6] A. M. Sullivan, *op. cit.*, p. 216.   [7] *Packet*, 25 February 1862.
[8] Berkeley, *op. cit.*, p. 218.   [9] Sullivan, *op. cit.*, p. 216.
[10] F.O. 43, vol. 77, Dispatch no. 100, 10 July 1860.

fallen upon.'[1] It is now time to go back to the great Catholic educational movement to which Leahy referred and which the bishops inaugurated before the Italian crisis boiled over. The Papal movement in Ireland had raised the educational demands on to a height the bishops had hardly dared to expect. The matter is a complicated one; and it is almost possible to declare with the *Rambler* of May 1859, that 'so much is doing in Ireland at the present moment in various ways in the cause of schools, seminaries, universities, and other educational establishments or associations, that we have a difficulty in entering on a subject which will prove too great for the space we can afford it'.[2]

It was in 1858 that the Irish hierarchy – particularly sensitive about the action of the State in education since the Synod of Thurles – received a shock once again. In that year the *Report* of the Royal Commission appointed to inquire into Irish endowed schools found that mere rearrangement of the existing endowments for intermediate education in Ireland would not meet the case, which they admitted, for a system of such schools for Catholics. The Commissioners therefore suggested a national system of intermediate education under local management. But the bishops were horrified to read in the *Report* that 'the provision for local management would enable the trustees to make suitable regulations for religious instruction, provided that the school, as a condition of its partaking of the grant of public money, admit of the united education of persons of all religious persuasions; and provided also, that the local managers be subject to the direct control of the proposed Board of Commissioners of Endowed Schools'.[3] To the bishops this meant the creation by the Government of a whole new network of mixed national education. As in earlier and later phases of the education question, the bishops raised questions relating to the whole field of education – primary, secondary and university – when they started a movement in the middle of 1859 which had for its object an attempt 'to anticipate and act upon the projected Government measure of intermediate education'.[4] The bishops indeed were successful in the limited field of their start. The Government did not carry out its plan in the face of their opposition. But having worked up a great movement over national education in all its branches, the bishops heightened their demands long after the projected intermediate education of 1858–59 had dropped into obscurity.

[1] Kirby Papers, Leahy to Kirby, no. 2497, 24 January 1860.
[2] *Rambler*, May 1859, new series, vol. 1, p. 123.
[3] *Parliamentary Papers*, 1857-8, XXII, (4 parts); Part I, p. 278, 'Recommendations relating to the promotion of Intermediate Education', no. 5.
[4] *Rambler*, May 1859, new series, vol. 1, p. 124.

In many respects Archbishop MacHale of Tuam anticipated the movement by the demands which issued from his Provincial Synod of Tuam at the end of August 1858. The Synod, which was attended by seven Western bishops,[1] seemed to Protestant observers as 'nothing less than a desperate attempt to wrench the control of the education of the Irish people from the National Board, and to vest it wholly and solely in the hands of the Romish hierarchy'.[2] It demonstrated the 'mortal antagonism which exists between Popery and mental enlightenment'.[3] The Address drawn up at Tuam condemned the proposals of the Royal Commission for a system of intermediate education, and indeed all national education in its existing form. Separate schools, with Catholic instruction, would alone prove satisfactory; Maynooth College maintained at public expense for the propagation of Catholic doctrine, was cited as a precedent. In an open letter to Lord Derby in November, MacHale had widened his demands further, insisting upon the suppression of the Protestant Establishment and a Tenant Act as well.[4] In November also, Archbishop Cullen told Bishop Gillooly that he saw the dangers of the National System of Education clearly, but thought that many of the bishops and priests were still favourable to it. They should not condemn it until they had agreed upon something to take its place. 'Until we have this done and agreed', he wrote, 'very little can be expected from Government.'[5] Though still cautious in October his vision included more active measures:

Some day or other I think we must come to a rupture with the Commissioners and ask for a different system. However, I agree . . . that we ought to proceed with great caution and to weigh with care the consequences of any step we are about to take. I think to do anything effectually we should have first a detailed plan of our proposed system of education drawn up and agreed on. This has not been done as yet. It seems to me that the first question that will be put to us if we ask a change is: what is the precise plan you wish us to adopt? Secondly it would be necessary for all or nearly all the bishops to be unanimous. I fear that such is not the case.[6]

Cullen's hand was forced, however. The Protestants of Ulster took up the cause of mixed intermediate education, and it became imperative that the southern Catholics should meet them with, if possible, the

---

[1] James Kavanagh, *Mixed Education – The Catholic Case Stated*, p. 197.
[2] *Mail*, 3 September 1858, 'The Tuam Synod'.   [3] *Ibid.*
[4] *Ibid.*, 26 November 1858, 'The Drum Ecclesiastic', also, *Freeman*, 26 November 1858, *Packet*, 27 November 1858, 'What the Priests Want'.
[5] Gillooly Letters, Cullen to Gillooly, 6 November 1858 (from Rome).
[6] Cullen to Pius Leahy, 30 October 1858 (from Rome): printed in MacSuibhne, *op. cit.*, vol. II, p. 269.

definite proposals of which Cullen had written. Early in 1859 he felt the way. On 30 January – when he was in Rome – he received warning from Archbishop Leahy that the question of intermediate education was assuming serious proportions.[1] And in February, Bishop Pius Leahy of Dromore let him know the extent of the engagement by both sides. In reply to Cullen's inquiry, he wrote:

> The intermediate schools to which your Grace alludes will I fear be established by the Government, and the time is rapidly passing by in which our opposition to them might be successful. The Presbyterians of Ulster, particularly in the towns, are becoming ardent in the advocacy of those schools, as they cannot educate their children for College through want of any means of giving them a classical education, and many Catholics through the same motives are preparing to join them. It would therefore be most desirable that the bishops should intimate to the people their determination to oppose a mixed system of education. . . .
>
> . . . I was informed last evening that the principal Protestants of this town [Newry], and I fear some Catholics, intend to call a public meeting to present a petition to Parliament in favour of the establishment of those schools.[2]

At the end of the month he urged that the bishops must act *before* the Government committed itself publicly to a plan of intermediate education. He felt also that Catholic members of Parliament should be sounded on the matter. If they could raise difficulties with the Ministers in London, he wrote, 'we should have time to bring the whole influence of the clergy and laity to bear upon the subject'. But he felt that other questions of national education ought not to be mixed with episcopal consideration of the intermediate schools issue, as this would extend the area in which a difference of opinion was likely to hamper their effectiveness.[3] This good advice was ignored.

Other bishops were becoming conscious of the perils of the situation. Archbishop Dixon told Kirby of the excitement over intermediate education in February. He was sure the bishops would turn out to be of one mind about it, and looked for some plan for 'bringing their unanimous voice to influence public opinion'.[4] Archbishop Leahy wrote to Cullen at the beginning of March about 'a glorious Catholic movement' in his Province in favour of Catholic intermediate education. This had been prompted, as in the north, by Protestant support for the Royal Commissioners' recommendations and the few Catholics who aided them. The majority Catholic party, he reported, saw 'that mixed intermediate schools would be so many feeders to the

[1] Cullen Papers, Pius Leahy to Cullen, 30 January 1859.
[2] *Ibid.*, 2 February 1859.
[3] *Ibid.*, 27 February 1859.
[4] Kirby Papers, Dixon to Kirby, no. 2310, 16 February 1859.

Queen's Colleges'. In Cork, Bishop Delany had put himself at the head of a great Catholic educational movement. Even so, Leahy feared divisions among the bishops over the question. He suggested one way of avoiding this in National Education generally.

I am decidedly of opinion that it would be the height of imprudence for us to denounce the National Schools as all-out Anti-Catholic. If Dr MacHale and the Connaught bishops have gone that length, they have, in my humble opinion, gone too far. If we can obtain a modification of the system, if we can obtain a larger infusion of Catholicity into the Board . . . if we can obtain a separate grant, better still. But if we ever fail in all these, still we must, I think, *tolerate* the National System, and use it as best we can, for *want of better*, for *fear of worse*.[1]

Tension was released somewhat by a statement in Parliament on 18 March by Derby. The Bishop of Down and Connor, in presenting petitions to the Lords in favour of mixed intermediate education asked when the Government intended to introduce its measure. In reply, Derby assured the Bishop that the matter was in hand, but due to the difficulties of any settlement, he could not promise a Bill that session.[2] Lord Naas, who had been Chief Irish Secretary in 1852 and again in 1858, told Monsell privately that the Government had abandoned the idea of a Bill altogether. But it was evident that in the elections – now seen to be inevitable – the Whigs would probably be returned to form an administration. In reporting Naas's news, Dixon added: 'the tug of war will be with the Whigs'.[3] In February he had said that if they were in office they would 'make a desperate effort to establish mixed middle-schools as auxiliaries to the Queen's Colleges'.[4] So the respite occasioned by Derby's statement was only felt to be temporary. 'I trust the mind of the whole country is beginning to perceive the dangers of mixed education', Bishop Leahy wrote to Cullen at the end of March.[5]

The outline of the bishops' course of action had been prepared. At this time three other elements came into the scene. One was a great meeting in Cork on intermediate education, another the movement to get a Charter for the Catholic University, and the last the publication of a book on the National System by James Kavanagh. The three fused in the public mind – and in the minds of the bishops – making it certain that when the Church finally drew up its demands to put before the Government, they would cover the whole field of education.

[1] Cullen Papers, Leahy to Cullen, 2 March 1859.
[2] *Hansard*, CLIII, p. 308.
[3] Kirby Papers, Dixon to Kirby, no. 2336, 24 March 1859.
[4] *Ibid.*, no. 2310, 16 February 1859.
[5] Cullen Papers, Pius Leahy to Cullen, 29 March 1859.

James Kavanagh, who had been headmaster of the Marlborough Street Model School in Dublin, was appointed superintendent of National Schools in 1845 and became Head Inspector in 1847, which post he held until he resigned from the Board in 1858. He was a Roman Catholic. As he related to the Powis Commissioners in 1868, 'there was only about a year between the time I withdrew from connexion with the Board and my appointment to the Catholic University', where he became professor of mathematics; 'in that interval, I published a work reviewing the principles, the working, and the results of the National System'.[1] This was *The Catholic Case Stated*, which was published anonymously on 17 March 1859. There was some controversy at the time over the reason for Kavanagh's resignation from the Board, and this is not worth examining, except to notice that Archdeacon Stopford in his reply to *The Catholic Case* pointed out that he left on 'merely personal' grounds, and 'apparently without any misgiving that the system had become a proselytizing snare'.[2] Kavanagh himself wrote that his book was to 'enable the Catholic clergy and people, the Government, Parliament, and the public generally, to approach the settlement of the question, with a full knowledge of its bearings'.[3] He explained the need for this at length in several places in the book, and especially tried to show the width of vision implied:

> Through deference to the Mitre, few Catholic laymen have written upon the subject of education – even upon its working and results – Catholic Members of Parliament, and the men who take a leading part in public life, regard it as forbidden ground, and beyond the pale of public discussion; so that, owing to these and other causes, there is more general ignorance upon the subject, or at all events, less reliable or available information, either in Books, or in the Journals and Periodical Literature, than on almost any other public question. The relations of Catholics to the State, in the matter of education, are not confined to the National Schools, they extend to the important classes of destitute and offending youth, in Workhouses, Prisons, and Reformatories, to Regimental and Military Schools, to the Queen's Colleges, and Trinity College, upon all of which it is most desirable that full and clear information should be put before the Hierarchy in order that their working, in relation to Catholics, should be known and understood.[4]

His desire was to be realized. The bishops' Pastoral of August covered the wider ground he had indicated. The bulk of the book was a detailed, examination of the National System showing the large extent to which

[1] *Parliamentary Papers*, 1870, xxviii, vol. iii, *Evidence*, p. 395 (12 June 1868).
[2] E. A. Stopford, *A Letter to the Rt. Hon. Alexander MacDonnell, Resident Commissioner of National Education, in Reply to the Catholic Case Stated, etc.*, Dublin, 1859, p. 7.
[3] Kavanagh, *op. cit.*, p. 14.   [4] *Ibid.*, p. 380.

it was bent in the interest of proselytism. In particular he attacked the Stopford Rule and the departure from the original intentions of Lord Stanley. The six Catholic Commissioners on the Board were no safeguard for faith and morals; he ridiculed their lack of activity and their readiness to side with the proselytizers.[1] The whole tone and operation of the Board was anti-Catholic.[2] He had many recommendations to offer. There should be an Irish Council on Catholic education,[3] and he was able to show, at the end of the book, 'how the present National Schools can, readily, with little derangement, and not much additional expense, be fitted for the application of the British or Denominational System'.[4] Such a cause he thought the bishops ought to adopt, and to demonstrate the seriousness of their intention, they could withdraw Catholic children and teachers from schools under Protestant patrons, and from all Model Schools.[5]

Most of Kavanagh's case was accepted by the hierarchy. But his last recommendation they could not accept. It has already been seen that Leahy counselled the toleration of the System until Catholic schools were ready as an alternative. The bishops everywhere adopted that course of action. Only MacHale did not. Kavanagh dedicated his book to the hierarchy, and wrote that he had produced it 'in obedience to a call of the Church'.[6] Now that was not strictly true. There seems little doubt that he told Cullen of its preparation in the autumn of 1858, but the Archbishop wrote of Kavanagh at that time, 'it is doubtful whether he can do any good as he writes merely because he was set aside by the Board, or rather degraded'.[7] The success of the book when it appeared in March of the following year induced Cullen to draw in a little. Bishop Leahy informed him that at Newry 'Mr Kavanagh's book has caused an excitement which must be attended with beneficial results'.[8] Cullen himself wrote warmly in appreciation to its author in July.[9] The *Nation* agreed that it was a landmark in the movement for Catholic education.[10] In fact, *The Catholic Case Stated* was riddled with errors, and was misleading – Kavanagh had selected evidence on the criterion of laying before the prelates what he knew they wanted to read. He was a statistician who presented only the statistics for his side of an argument.

[1] Kavanagh, pp. 149, 230, 258.   [2] *Ibid.*, p. 290.   [3] *Ibid.*, p. 381.
[4] *Ibid.*, p. 393. The practical soundness of this suggestion is undoubted: it was to be recommended by the Powis Commissioners in 1870.
[5] *Ibid.*, p. 400. Model Schools were those in which teachers in training resided.
[6] *Ibid.*, p. iii.
[7] Gillooly Letters, Cullen to Gillooly, 6 November 1858.
[8] Cullen Papers, Leahy to Cullen, 29 March 1859.
[9] See his letter, printed in MacSuibhne, *op. cit.*, vol. II, p. 290.
[10] *Nation*, 13 August 1859.

Many of his errors of fact and of emphasis were corrected by Archdeacon Stopford's *Letter* in reply, although Stopford himself had a case to argue and he likewise was not as objective as he pretended. 'The priests have failed to control the parents' liberty, and it is demanded through Mr Kavanagh that the State should do it for them,' he wrote.[1] Yet the bishops accepted the book, and it was employed as the source for all their invectives against the National Board. Even Myles O'Reilly – who became no mean expert in educational matters – referred to Kavanagh as giving the authentic Catholic case.[2] Cullen relied on Kavanagh's book for information, but its author was by no means to become his right hand man as has been suggested.[3] It is true that the archbishop valued his ability with statistics, and recommended him to Manning on that account, but he always referred to him distantly as one whose services were valued but upon whom he chanced only occasionally. It was not without some truth, however, that the *Packet* observed sourly that 'no man can henceforth be considered a good Catholic who does not worship Mr James Kavanagh'.[4]

The university question was the second new element in the spring of 1859. The Catholic University in Dublin was in transition: Newman, who ceased officially to be its Rector in August,[5] had for some time been on the way out, and Cullen had become persuaded of the need for a Royal Charter of incorporation as the only sure way of enabling a fair competition with the Queen's Colleges.[6] In March 1859 an approach was made to the Derby Administration with this in view. It seemed, as the *Freeman's Journal* wrote, as though the Government which had conceded Catholic army chaplains in 1858 might well allow a Charter now.[7] A deputation was got up to see Disraeli, the Leader of the House. It contained Protestants as well as Catholics, the speakers being Maguire, Deasy and Bowyer. Twenty-three of the thirty-one Irish bishops had written letters authorizing the deputation to make use of their names. In his, the Bishop of Kerry (Moriarty) stated that a chartered Catholic University was a necessary complement to the Catholic intermediate education for which they were also hoping.[8] Disraeli promised the

[1] Stopford, *op. cit.*, p. 15.
[2] Myles O'Reilly, *Two Articles on Education, Reprinted from the Dublin Review*, London, 1863; I, p. 26.
[3] See MacSuibhne, *op. cit.*, vol. II, pp. 274-5, who discusses and rejects this view too.
[4] *Packet*, 13 August 1859, 'The Romish Synod'.
[5] McGrath, *Newman's University*, p. 478.
[6] See Cullen's letters of 1858 – Monsell Papers, Box 8319, Cullen to Monsell, 7 May 1858 (two letters).
[7] *Freeman*, 23 March 1859.
[8] *Rambler*, May 1859, new series, I, p. 126; also, McGrath, *op. cit.*, p. 484.

deputation he would raise the question of a Charter in the Cabinet, and he 'distinctly held that the question ought not to be dealt with as one involving any rivalry between the Queen's Colleges and the Catholic University, but on its own merits'.[1] In fact the Government fell on the Reform question before that of a Charter could be considered. In view of the difficulties over the matter encountered in the negotiations between the hierarchy and the Government on the Charter question from 1865 to 1868, it is unlikely that one could have been granted in 1859 anyway. There were difficulties on the episcopal side too: as early as May 1858, Cullen had realized that MacHale would not consent to a Charter.[2] He continued his opposition. At the end of March 1859 he wrote telling Maguire that the application to the Government for a Charter 'had never been submitted to nor authorized by any meeting of the Irish episcopacy'.[3] Maguire himself was not to appear too pleasing to the bishops over this question. He insisted on seeking to raise the Charter directly in the Commons during July. This earned the disapproval of Archbishop Leahy who warned that the Protestant temper of the House would produce a debate injurious to the university itself: much better to approach the Government by deputation as they did in March. 'You have no right to proceed in this matter without consulting the Catholic Bishops', he told him.[4] Maguire did not continue his course of action when he was instructed by Cullen (at Leahy's request) to give it up.[5] Leahy also distrusted Maguire for seeming to 'force upon the public the belief that he has the confidence of the Catholic bishops. I would not place much confidence in him', he added, 'I would not allow him to make the public believe I did.'[6]

The third element was the Cork meeting on intermediate education. This was held on 2 March 1859 in the Catholic cathedral, and was attended by the Bishops of Cork, Cloyne, Kerry and Ross, by members of Parliament, deputy-lieutenants, magistrates, 300 priests and 8,000 Catholic laymen. The most important resolution passed was that 'no form of intermediate education is suited to a Catholic people, unless it be granted to them in separate schools, and on terms always strictly in accordance with the teaching and discipline of the Catholic Church'.[7] Bishop Delany of Cork declared his doubt that there was a single

[1] *Rambler*, p. 126.
[2] Monsell Papers, Cullen to Monsell, 7 May 1858.
[3] Kirby Papers, Dixon to Kirby, no. 2336, 24 March 1859.
[4] Cullen Papers, Leahy to Maguire, 2 July 1859.
[5] *Ibid.*, Leahy to Cullen, 11 July 1859.
[6] *Ibid.*, Leahy to Maguire, 2 July 1859 – note by Leahy on the copy he sent to Cullen.
[7] *Rambler*, May 1859, new series, vol. 1, p. 124.

Catholic who supported mixed education; and Maguire told the meeting that the Government were 'waiting for your unanimous verdict before they attempt to legislate'.[1] But the bishop's confidence was hardly well-founded. Lord Fermoy had held a separate meeting in favour of mixed education in February at which Catholic laymen were present.[2] The Protestant Bishop of Cork assured the Government that the unanimity of the Catholics was the result of coercion. He described how a pack of friars 'marshalled and drilled a loathsome mob of scum and refuse of society – ruffians of the lowest class – blackguard boys and prostitutes' to disrupt the rival educational meeting; 'the priests literally shaking their fists at a Roman Catholic gentleman who ventured to rebuke their violence'.[3] The great Cork meeting of 2 March triggered off smaller ones through the country. Cullen was certain it had done great good in helping to persuade the Government of the need to correct the National System too. 'I suppose it will be too arduous a task to overthrow it', he wrote, though 'Dr MacHale probably will consent to nothing else.'[4]

It is therefore clear that by the summer of 1859 these three elements had produced a blueprint for a coherent and comprehensive programme of demands on Catholic education. The correction of the National System, Catholic intermediate schools, and a Charter for the university, remained the three and indissolubly united parts of the bishops' educational policy. It now needed only a meeting of the hierarchy to organize and pilot a distinct movement.

The Decrees of the Tuam Synod of August 1858 occasioned a circular sent by the Propaganda to the Irish sees in February 1859. It concerned National Education, and the proposed intermediate system, requesting returns from each Province on the state of education. Cullen said that the Propaganda inquiry was to prevent effect being given to MacHale's total condemnation of the National Schools at the 1858 Synod,[5] and it must therefore be seen as a triumph for Leahy's view that the existing system should be tolerated until a replacement was ready.[6] The circular also recommended a national meeting of the bishops to consider educational matters.[7] This was called for 2 August by Cullen as

---

[1] *Ibid.* For Kavanagh's testimony to the importance of the meeting in the Catholic educational movement, see *The Catholic Case Stated*, p. ix.

[2] Larcom Papers, MS. 7648: Notes on Education in Ireland, *Paper B*, by G. Johnstone Stoney; 10 July 1859.

[3] *Ibid.*, Enclosure, B. 1, Copy of a Letter from William, Bishop of Cork, 11 February 1859.

[4] Cullen to Pius Leahy, 14 April 1859; printed in MacSuibhne, *op. cit.*, vol. II, p. 287.

[5] *Ibid.*, vol. II, p. 283; 9 February 1859.

[6] The replies from the archbishops are in Propaganda, *Scritture 33*.

[7] *Rambler*, May 1859, new series, I, p. 126 gives the text of the circular.

Legate. In July, Archbishop Leahy wrote to him in some disquiet.

We have need to look forward to this next meeting with no small anxiety, [he wrote]. There has been no meeting of equal importance since the Synod of Thurles. What is most to be apprehended is a division among the bishops – a thing that in present circumstances could be disastrous to us. The great question before us is that of the National Education System.[1]

The scare occasioned by the *Report* in favour of mixed intermediate education was passing, and the whole field of education would clearly be under review at the meeting. Leahy repeated to Cullen his belief that the system must be tolerated whilst they urged the concession of a separate grant on the Government. They should work to spread the Christian Brothers and other teaching orders – in preparation for the contingency of being obliged to throw up the entire National System if it came to that at some future point. And *no* recommendations should be made to the Holy See for the present: it was essential that the bishops be left alone 'to do the best we can with the Government'.[2] Bishop Gillooly also feared that the meeting would provide 'the usual manifestation of weakness and disunion'.[3] In writing round to settle arrangements with the bishops, Cullen outlined a most comprehensive agenda. It was: (1) The present state of the National System of Education; (2) The proposed system of intermediate education; (3) The Catholic University, and any other questions upon Education, 'or the protection of our Religion'.[4]

The Government received its information on the rising Catholic educational movement from George Johnstone Stoney, who, on 18 July, sent Cardwell, the Irish Chief Secretary, papers on National Education.[5] In his Paper B, he wrote to Cardwell, he had endeavoured 'to state some of the chief grounds of the importance of united as contrasted with separate education, so far as they relate to the Catholic part of the population of Ireland'.[6] Paper B started by differentiating between Catholicism as a religion and as a 'politically-interfering system' It was the latter which was relevant in the education question. Separate education was demanded as part of a whole policy for the aggrandizement of the priesthood and the depression of the laity. Therefore no

---

[1] Cullen Papers, Leahy to Cullen, 11 July 1859.   [2] *Ibid.*
[3] Kirby Papers, Gillooly to Kirby, no. 2391, 28 July 1859.
[4] Monsell Papers, Box 8319, Cullen to Moriarty, 5 July 1859.
[5] Larcom Papers, MS. 7648. They were prepared initially to provide Cardwell with information to answer Pope-Hennessy's motion in the Commons on 22 July 1859. It was Stoney's Paper B which McGrath discussed in his *Newman's University* (p. 483). He was unable to identify its author, and appears to have used a wrongly dated copy.
[6] Larcom Papers, MS. 7648, Stoney to Cardwell, 18 July 1859.

Charter should be granted to the Catholic University, for Irish Catholicism was 'the great bar of all progress'. It was vain to wait for the laity to speak out against the priests. They would not come out against the 'social thraldom under which they groan'. The Catholic gentry formed a moderate party, and it was in a bid to obliterate them by Catholic education that the condemnation of the Queen's Colleges, and the present educational demands, were undertaken by the hierarchy. But if the united system of education was maintained for the future, 'it will have cultivated a respect for England and a feeling of united interests pervading all denominations through the country, and it will be progressively weakening the *political*, while it leaves untouched the *religious* sway of the priests over our Roman Catholic fellow-countrymen'.[1] With this sort of information to hand the bishops were to have a formidable task indeed if they were to persuade the Government.

The Catholic bishops assembled at St Kevin's Chapel in Dublin on 2 August 1859. Cullen evidently had some hope that the Government might listen to them: in July he had reported to the Propaganda that 'the present Government will not do justice to the Catholics, but at least it is not so hostile as the fallen Government'.[2] The meeting lasted four days, and, as Bishop Keane wrote to Kirby, 'no one ever remembered such a meeting, so general was the agreement and so cordial the union that bound the whole body together'.[3] The National System, intermediate education, the Queen's Colleges and the Catholic University came under review, the Archbishop of Cashel acting as secretary. The resolutions of the prelates were issued in the form of a joint Pastoral, and it is clear from Cullen's report to the Propaganda that they were to be taken as a triumph for Archbishop Leahy's view of National Education over Archbishop MacHale's. The resolutions, he informed Cardinal Barnabo

are not perhaps very clear, but in point of fact they reveal the perils and disadvantages of the National Schools, although at the same time they admit that many of these schools may admit many Catholics without risk, and that it would not be prudent to publish any condemnation until the Catholics themselves shall be in a position to finance their own schools, or be able to obtain from the Government subsidies for separate schools.[4]

Leahy was instructed by the bishops to write to the Propaganda giving a full account of the reasons why it was necessary to oppose the existing

[1] *Ibid.*, Paper B.
[2] Propaganda, *Scritture* 33, f. 928, Cullen to Barnabo, 5 July 1859.
[3] Kirby Papers, Keane to Kirby, no. 2402, 18 August 1859.
[4] Propaganda, *Scritture* 33, f. 948, Cullen to Barnabo, 10 August 1859.

arrangement of National Education. When he did so he also transmitted a Latin text of the resolutions.[1] MacHale was instructed to draw up a memorandum for the Viceroy showing the case for separate schools and outlining the feelings of the bishops on the university question too. It is interesting that in reporting on this to the Propaganda, MacHale urged the Cardinal-Prefect to reconsider the decrees of his 1858 Synod of Tuam on the National System. It will be remembered that the tenth Chapter of those decrees totally rejected the System, but that the Propaganda had failed to allow this in the circular letter of February. MacHale now felt himself able to point out that 'there is nothing in that Chapter which is not found judged in far weightier words, and in the same sense, by the meeting of all the bishops'.[2] It is obvious that behind the unanimity of the assembly, Cullen and MacHale were still widely at variance.

The memorial to the Viceroy (Lord Carlisle) which he drew up and presented on behalf of the bishops, was dated 5 August. It ruminated over the dangers of the National System to Catholic faith and morals; protesting against the 'systematic refusal' to recognize the bishops' legitimate authority to direct and superintend the education of their flocks. The bishops, it declared, had no wish to interfere with the 'proper management of the public funds over which the civil Government should exercise control'. But mixed education was incompatible with Catholicity, and it requested the concession of separate schools, pledging the bishops to use every constitutional means of obtaining them.[3]

An Address of fidelity was also sent to the Holy See by the meeting, and this referred to the need for protection 'from the evil influences of a dangerous system of education'. It was not until the end of the year that the Pope replied – but when he did he fully approved their censure of the mixed schools.[4]

The resolutions of the meeting were published very shortly afterwards, as part of a *Pastoral Address of the Roman Catholic Archbishops and Bishops to the Catholic Clergy and People of Ireland.* The Pastoral caused the greatest excitement not only in Ireland but in the English press also, and will therefore bear close examination – especially as it came to be the blueprint for a decade of agitation. 'The education of the Catholic Youth of Ireland holds a foremost place among the questions affecting the present and future well-being of our country,' it began; 'it is

---

[1] Propaganda, *Scritture* 33, f. 941.

[2] *Ibid.*, 33, f. 953, MacHale to Barnabo, 13 August 1859.

[3] *Parliamentary Papers*, 1860, LIII, 659: Copy of Memorial of the R.C. Prelates relative to National Education in Ireland.

[4] Both these letters are conveniently printed together in the *Post*, 3 January 1860.

intimately connected with the interests of our holy faith itself.'[1] The bishops must watch over it and 'pronounce with authority how far the teachings of secular knowledge may or may not be in conformity with the unerring, never-changing standard of Catholic faith'. In a phrase which was picked up by the Protestant press and which remained the watchword of the bishops throughout the long educational struggle which lay ahead, they quoted the words of Christ from the Gospel: 'Go, teach all nations.'[2] The Pastoral next reviewed the events leading to the episcopal meeting: the Letter of the Propaganda – the summons by the Apostolic Delegate – the assembly.[3] Religion, it continued, was a necessary supplement to the laws of the land, and if it were absent 'highly but badly educated people might overturn – as they have overturned – the altar and the throne'.[4] This looked ahead to Cullen's later argument that there was an identity between the Fenian leaders and those educated in mixed schools.

The actual resolutions passed by the bishops on 5 August were printed in the middle of the Pastoral. They made the demands already recited, and these were summarized in the First Resolution:

> That schools for Catholic youth should be such as to insure for them the benefit of a safe secular education, and adequate religious instruction in the faith and practices of the Catholic Church. They should be, therefore, so subordinated to bishops in their respective dioceses as that no books may be used in them for secular instruction to which the Ordinary shall object; and that the teachers, both as to appointment and removal, and the selection of all books for religious instruction, and the arrangements for it, be under the control of the same Ordinary.
>
> That the principles enunciated can be adequately embodied and acted upon in this country only on a system of education exclusively for Catholics.[5]

The remaining eight resolutions rehearsed specific objections to aspects of mixed education in the existing system. The text of the Pastoral then resumed, calling upon the peoples' help 'by meetings, petitions, and all other constitutional means' in securing alteration to the National System and a flat rejection of any proposal for mixed intermediate education.[6] Difficulty might be avoided if the Government should allow grants for the schools, seminaries and colleges which the bishops had already established. The Queen's Colleges were again condemned, on the authority of the Holy See. A letter would be sent to the Chief

---

[1] *Pastoral Adress of the Roman Catholic Archbishops and Bishops*, Dublin, 1859, p. 3 (also in Moran, vol. i, p. 682).
[2] *Ibid.*, p. 4. [3] *Ibid.*, p. 5. [4] *Ibid.*, p. 6. [5] *Ibid.*, pp. 7-8.
[6] *Ibid.*, p. 10.

Secretary requesting the concession of the points made in the resolutions; 'nor do we anticipate any long delay to our wishes' the bishops added.[1] Then, as Kavanagh had recommended, they turned to the risks of proselytism in a wider field. More funds for the Catholic University would place it in a stronger position to demand a Charter.[2] The operations of the Poor Law Board were censured, as were 'attempts to "Protestantize" Catholic children in the Workhouses', and the continued absence of Catholic navy chaplains.[3] In concerning themselves with the condition of the tenants the bishops were careful to state that it was a matter of charity – 'we by no means step out of our own province'. The law allowed eviction without compensation, and so was at fault. Too many landlords 'enforce their rights under the operation of a one-sided law', and had even evicted tenants who had voted against the candidate they had themselves sponsored. 'The Natural and Divine Law, humanity and justice, the peace and good order of society – all demand the application of a speedy remedy to this too-long tolerated evil.'[4] The Pastoral closed by enjoining support for the Temporal Power of the Pope through its present perils, and agitation for the questions raised by the bishops even, if necessary, making it the condition of support to Parliamentary candidates.[5]

There was an immediate press reaction to the Pastoral. The *Nation* rejoiced at the end of the 'painful division in the Catholic ranks, alike amongst prelates and politicians which had characterized the preceding thirty years'.[6] The *Freeman* was to be disappointed in its optimistic belief that every Protestant would approve the great principle of denominational education,[7] and that the Pastoral would 'influence the legislation of the next session' of Parliament.[8] It gave its unreserved support to the episcopal programme. The object in view, it reported, was 'to render any system devised not only accessible but *acceptable* to all whom it is intended to benefit'. Ireland alone, the *Freeman* continued, did not have the denominational system: the experiment of mixed education had been tried and it had failed.[9] The Irish Protestant press came out solidly against the Pastoral. The *Packet* remarked sarcastically that its author 'will merit canonization at the least', and regretted the 'frantic efforts being made by the ultramontane press to blow into importance the recent assembly of the Cullen prelates'. The Catholic laity had better look out, for the bishops were to meet again shortly on the Catholic

[1] *Pastoral Address of the Roman Catholic Archbishops and Bishops*, Dublin, 1859, p. 11.
[2] *Ibid.*, p. 12. [3] *Ibid.*, pp. 14-15. [4] *Ibid.*, pp. 16-17. [5] *Ibid.*, p. 20.
[6] *Nation*, 13 August 1859. [7] *Freeman*, 19 August 1859.
[8] *Ibid.*, 20 August 1859. [9] *Ibid.*

University, and there could be little doubt that they would then be forced to educate their sons in 'the gloomy medievalism' of the Catholic University.[1] Four days later the same paper pointed to the familiar Protestant belief that the clergy as well as the laity were having their former moderation crushed by Cullen's 'ultramontanism'. 'All ecclesiastics beneath the Legate are now under pressure' it observed of the effect of the Pastoral.[2] The *Daily News* remarked on the growing prosperity of Ireland: 'but the master-spirit of evil – religious discord – has not disappeared', and the renewed educational conflict was an occasion of it.[3] 'The Old Struggle – Priest v. People' was the title of an article on the Pastoral in the Dublin *Evening Mail* which took the same view as the *Packet*, and even held that 'active Protestant interference can do good' in the educational field.[4] The *Packet* went further again, declaring that the manner of summoning the Episcopal meeting exhibited 'in the clearest way that the social and political interests of the R.C. laity are under the absolute control of a foreign authority'.[5]

The English press stormed against the Irish bishops, and the *Freeman* thought it prudent to remind them that the denominational grants which they denounced as 'Italian', 'ultramontane', and 'monkish' were in fact made in England.[6] The *Nation* declared that the press in England had shown itself utterly ignorant of Irish realities, and used their outburst over the Pastoral as proof that only Independent Opposition could benefit the Irish people.[7] A reaction of 'Political Protestantism' was hinted at by the *Nonconformist*.[8] And one Irish Catholic paper, the *Cork Examiner* accused the bishops of inconsistency for turning round now upon a system from which they had benefited so greatly in the past.[9] This was an argument frequently to be employed against them in the subsequent decade. Cullen wrote of English press reaction that, 'instead of refuting the arguments of the Pastoral, they insulted the bishops'. This confirmed his belief that education could never safely be entrusted to men of such bigotry and ignorance.[10] As a result of the excitement

---

[1] *Packet*, 13 August 1859, 'The Romish Synod'.   [2] *Ibid.*, 16 August 1859.
[3] *Daily News*, 18 August 1859.   [4] *Evening Mail*, 19 August 1859.
[5] *Packet*, 20 August 1859.
[6] *Freeman*, 25 August 1859. For general comment on the adverse English press, see *Dublin Review*, February 1860, 'Irish National Education' by Aubrey de Vere, pp. 351 ff.
[7] *Nation*, 26 August 1859, 'The Irish Bishops and the British press'.
[8] *Nonconformist*, August 1859.
[9] Printed in the *Packet*, 25 August 1859, as 'A Solitary Gallican Protest'.
[10] *Freeman*, 10 October 1859, Cullen's 'Letter on some recent instances of Bigotry and Intolerance'. He expressed the same opinion in his letter to Propaganda on 2 September. If the System were not dangerous, he wrote, it 'would not enjoy so much the favour of the unbelievers and heretics' – *Scritture* 33, f. 976.

James O'Ferrall, a Catholic Commissioner, resigned from the National Board of Education, although other anticipated resignations were not forthcoming.[1]

Accordingly with the promise made in the Pastoral, the bishops communicated the resolutions to the Chief Secretary, Cardwell, who sent a formal reply to Cullen acknowledging the importance of the question and indicating that the Government would send an answer in due course.[2] Meanwhile in Dublin the bishops were preparing for a second meeting, to deal with the Catholic University, and several of the Catholic Liberal members of Parliament were canvassing support for a meeting to discuss Parliamentary action on the Pastoral. Cardwell received two public letters from James Kavanagh during the interlude. Both went exhaustively into the evils of the Irish National System.[3] As the prelates' and the politicians' meetings came on, the mounting public excitement in Ireland over the Italian question was providing a public opinion calculated to believe the worst of the British Government.

The bishops were due to assemble again during October to discuss the university – although, as Keane told Kirby, 'other matters will not be overlooked'.[4] This presumably meant that any reply received from the Government would come under review. But no reply had come when they met on 19 October. This meeting lasted three days and the university was the only topic discussed.[5] Newman's resignation from the office of Rector was approved, and the administration of the university was vested in the four archbishops and two bishops from each province. A general collection was ordered in all the parishes throughout Ireland to assist maintenance expenses. MacHale opposed everything. As Cullen explained to the Propaganda, he contested the authority of the meeting, saying that as it was not a Synod it had no power to act.[6] This was an argument he was to use in the defence of his dissensions at many episcopal gatherings during the 1860s. The pattern laid out in 1859 of periodical bishops' meetings was maintained during the sixties. Cullen could only point out – as he did to MacHale in October 1859 – that the meeting had been convoked on an instruction from the Sacred Congregation. MacHale favoured the total condemnation of Newman's policies, complaining of the appointment of Englishmen to Chairs, and

[1] *Guardian*, 24 August 1859.   [2] *Liverpool Mercury*, 25 August 1859.

[3] Printed in *Freeman*, 24 September, and 30 September 1859 'The Education Crisis'.

[4] Kirby Papers, Keane to Kirby, no. 2420, 23 September 1859.

[5] Propaganda, *Scritture 33*, Cullen to Barnabo, 11 November 1859. In August, a committee of twelve prelates had been appointed to draw up a report on the state of the Catholic University for the October meeting.

[6] *Ibid.*

objecting to the plan for parochial collections. Cullen justified his over-ruling of these to the Propaganda thus:

> If things ended in this way the bishops would be placed before the public as a divided body incapable of reaching a decision, and with the danger of reviving the scandals of the past when after every episcopal meeting some of the bishops published their dissent from what the others had done. Thank God that this time we were able to free ourselves from such a situation. Some of the bishops, disgusted by Mgr MacHale's opposition, urged me to break with him, but others including myself believed it better to overcome everything by patience, and to prefer any sacrifice to the public knowledge of our disagreement.[1]

Happily, he was able to persuade MacHale to sign the Address in favour of the university, but the cracks had become dangerously obvious. The illusions of the August meeting were seen to have cleared, and Cullen himself admitted the present occasion was 'in truth not very consoling'. He saw that with their demands on National Education before the Government, any sign of division among the bishops would prove fatal for their chances. It was this consideration, he said, which made him avoid a rupture with MacHale.[2] The Pastoral Address on the university was issued to the press and was in circulation shortly after the close of the meeting, on 21 October.[3] It reiterated the demand for a Charter, and put the case for a separate Catholic institution quite simply – 'Protestant Universities are not suited for a Catholic people'. In a *Letter* to his clergy on *Some recent instances of Bigotry and Intolerance* early in October, Cullen had shown up the continuing dangers to Catholic faith and morals in proselytizing institutions. 'Ex operibus eorum cognoscentis eos' he had quoted.[4] Together with the Pastoral on the Catholic University and the August Pastoral and resolutions, this made the Catholic case complete in its presentation.

The bishops waited for the reply of the Government, Cullen believing it to be delayed by the preoccupation of the Ministers with foreign affairs.[5] On the day of the episcopal meeting over the university, Kavanagh had addressed another open letter to Cardwell, warning him of courses of action – or 'means of coercion' as he called them – available to the bishops if their demands were rejected. These amounted to more or less a complete withdrawal from all association with the National

---

[1] *Ibid.* [2] *Ibid.*

[3] *Freeman* – Text of the Pastoral – 21 November 1859; Moran, vol. i, p. 701.

[4] *Freeman*, 10 October 1859; Moran, vol. i, p. 652.

[5] Propaganda, *Scritture* 33, Cullen to Barnabo, 11 November 1859. But to Monsell, he suggested that Cardwell's delay might be an expedient to prevent their moving before the meeting of Parliament – Monsell Papers, Box 8319, Cullen to Monsell, 20 November 1859.

System.[1] None of the bishops but MacHale would have allowed that, and Cardwell was evidently unimpressed. When his letter finally came, on 28 November 1859, it was a glowing testament on the benefits of the Irish National System. Mixed education was upheld:

> Her Majesty's Government observe with regret that some of the demands preferred in the Memorial [of the bishops] are wholly incompatible with the maintenance of these principles. If those demands were conceded, the national system would be overthrown; and a system of sectarian education substituted for it, calculated to revive social divisions in Ireland, and to stimulate feelings which it is the object of every just and liberal government to allay.[2]

Cullen sent on the reply to the bishops.[3] All that Cardwell had suggested was that perhaps a reconsideration of the rules of the National Board might meet some of the prelates' objections. Only Bishop Moriarty of Kerry seems to have found any satisfaction in that. Replying to Cullen on 8 December, he revealed his scepticism of the virtue of separate schools. They would allow the Protestants to establish institutions of even worse proselytizing tendencies. And at present they were not really badly off. 'We can never be exposed to the dangers of a mixed system in a country where there is nothing to mix – where all are Catholic.' They had the advantage of all the State grants too.[4] There was much truth in what he said – Cardwell in his letter had quoted the Commissioners' Report to show that of the 5,335 schools under the Board, 3,683 were controlled by Catholic patrons, and that 80 in every 100 teachers were Catholic. So true was this, that in 1870 the Powis Commission recommended that most of the National System was virtually denominational and should be legally recognized as such. Moriarty was always to be out of step with the other bishops over Education, and his views at this time were no comfort to Cullen.

Unexpected consolation came from another direction. The Catholic Liberal members at last met and pledged their support to the episcopal demands. In August, The O'Donoghue and Maguire had issued a circular suggesting such a meeting, but it had been delayed.[5] There was

---

[1] *Freeman*, 19 October 1859.

[2] *Parliamentary Papers*, 1860. LIII, 659 (p. 2), Cardwell to Cullen, 28 November 1859.

[3] Monsell Papers, Box 8319, Cullen to Monsell, 7 December 1859.

[4] Cullen Papers, Moriarty to Cullen, 8 December 1859. The 1859 Report of the Commissioners of National Education in Ireland (*Parliamentary Papers*, 1860, XXVI, p. xxix), gave a Return on the extent of mixed education in National Schools, for the quarter ending 31 December 1859. It showed that only $3\frac{1}{2}$ per cent of the Catholic pupils received their secular instruction in schools conducted exclusively by Protestants, whereas $16\frac{7}{10}$ per cent of Protestant pupils were comparably under Catholic teachers.

[5] *Packet*, 26 August; *Evening Post*, 26 August; *Guardian*, 31 August 1859.

F

much speculation on the design behind their meeting, especially as Cullen had kept himself aloof so long from political matters. It was necessary for the *Freeman*, on his behalf, to announce that the Liberal members' promotion of the Pastoral was *not* the sign that Archbishop Cullen was forming a new Parliamentary party. The politicians acted on their own initiative, without prompting from the hierarchy.[1] This was certainly true; Cullen did not countenance the formation of a Parliamentary party until the end of 1864. But at the same time, the phrasing of the Pastoral left Catholic members of Parliament with little choice. Cullen reported the matter simply to the Propaganda: 'Several members of Parliament have also declared that they will support the demands of the Archbishops which appear to them reasonable and moderate.'[2] Bishop Keane claimed that the Government tried to prevent the Catholic Liberals from holding a meeting,[3] but there is little evidence to support him. Association of the Pastoral demands with the Liberals was not altogether an unmixed blessing for the Church anyway. In September, the *Tablet* printed a letter attacking the bishops for connecting themselves with 'Whiggery'.[4] Cullen himself told Monsell early in December that he thought 'the meeting of M.P.s will do no good but I have no influence with those who are promoting it'.[5]

The Liberal Members met privately at the Northumberland Hotel in Dublin on 15 December. Eleven were present,[6] Corbally taking the chair. Colonel White, a Protestant, dissented from the meeting's resolution to support the Temporal Power of the Pope.[7] Seven resolutions were passed upholding the points made in the Pastoral – which, the Members declared in their first resolution, 'contains a fair exposition of the present wants of Ireland', so that they could avail themselves of their position and influence, as members of Parliament, 'to press upon the Government the just demands put forward in that important document'.[8] But the *Nation*, arguing for Independent Opposition, remarked that the Liberals had done nothing about the episcopal demands in the past, and that if they could 'palter with such demands as those which

---

[1] *Freeman*, 1 September 1859. The *Cork Examiner* (4 September), held the same.
[2] Propaganda, *Scritture* 33, f. 976, Cullen to Barnabo, 2 September 1859.
[3] Kirby Papers, Keane to Kirby, no. 2420, 23 September 1859.
[4] *Tablet*, 24 September 1859, letter from Pierse Creagh of Dublin.
[5] Monsell Papers, Box 8319, Cullen to Monsell, 7 December 1859.
[6] *Evening Mail*, 16 December 1859, 'The Pope's Eleven'. They were: J. F. Maguire, The O'Donoghue, J. Pope-Hennessy, E. MacEvoy, J. A. Blake, Col. White, J. Lanngai, Dr Brady, P. O'Brien, R. M. Bellew, and M. Corbally. Bowyer, Dunne, McMahon and Redmond, who were not present, allowed their names to be used.
[7] Resolution 7.
[8] *Evening Mail*, 16 December 1859, Resolution 1.

they have thus evaded and nevertheless be acceptable on the hustings to bishops and people, then the Pastoral has been issued in vain'.[1]

The education movement, like the contemporaneous one in favour of the Papal State, had caught on in the Irish dioceses, however. Popular meetings in support of the Pastoral were held in December and the first two months of 1860 at Kilkenny, Thurles, Cloyne, Ross and Meath.[2] From Galway, Bishop MacEvilly reported the receipt of petitions to Parliament from every parish in the diocese.[3] And so successful was the organization of petitions in the diocese of Elphin by Bishop Gillooly that Cullen copied his method in Dublin.[4] Early in March Cullen prepared a massive reply to Cardwell (no doubt encouraged by the enthusiasm shown for the educational demands by the country), which occupied nine columns when printed in the newspapers.[5] Archbishop Dixon thought it strong enough to elicit at least some concessions from the Government.[6] Cullen himself told Moriarty that though it asked for the separate system, it did not preclude them from accepting any other concessions which might be offered. He feared that if disagreement should now appear among the bishops Rome would condemn the entire National System. It would also give the Government reason to 'urge on their most dangerous plan of taking education altogether into their own hands'.[7] Moriarty signed; but the Bishops of Clonfert and Cork did not – nor did MacHale. He refused Cullen's request to sign on the ground that the Government had firmly announced their intention of standing by the National System and that a second approach could get no further.[8] When pressed by Cullen he complained of the evils 'of sending round letters to bishops soliciting their signatures for various objects without the opportunity of mutual consultation'.[9] It was clear that he was hedging for more weighty reasons than those he offered. The next three years were to see his differences with Cullen sharpen still more until in 1864 they all but exploded over the Lavelle Case.

The second letter to Cardwell was followed up by a *Letter* of Cullen to his clergy read throughout the Diocese of Dublin on 3 June 1860, on the evils of emigration and mixed schools. Of the latter he observed sadly

---

[1] *Nation*, 17 December 1859.   [2] *Ibid.*, 4 February 1860.
[3] Kirby Papers, MacEvilly to Kirby, no. 2479, 26 December 1859.
[4] Gillooly Letters, Cullen to Gillooly, 8 February 1860.
[5] *Guardian*, 18 April 1860. For the text of the letter of 18 March to Cardwell, see Moran, vol. II, p. 74.
[6] Kirby Papers, Dixon to Kirby, no. 2542, 14 March 1860.
[7] Monsell Papers, Box 8319, Cullen to Moriarty, 23 March 1860.
[8] MacHale to Cullen, 13 March 1860 – published in Bernard O'Reilly, *John Mac-Hale*, vol. II, p. 523.
[9] *Ibid.*, vol. II, p. 524.

that 'the continual and dangerous warfare carried on most actively for years against the faith of poor Catholic children has obliged me to address you repeatedly'. The Irish echoes of the Mortara Case rang from his warning about 'the scandalous practice of kidnapping or buying Catholic children for the purpose of educating them in a religion different from that of their parents'.[1] In Parliament, the Earl of Clancarty had moved on 30 April for copies of the correspondence between Cardwell and the bishops, declaring that the House would be surprised to learn that the hierarchy had repudiated the National System.[2] In the Commons on 17 July, Butt moved unsuccessfully for an Address to the Queen on National Education. He sought an inquiry to discover what changes could be made in the rules of the Board which would allow the Irish people to avail themselves of National Education without violating their consciences. 'The question involved,' he said, 'was whether Ireland was to be treated in the same manner as this country.'[3] Cardwell replied with a eulogy of the National System.[4] Also in July, nineteen Catholic members of Parliament – including Acton – sent a joint letter to Cardwell in support of Catholic education for Ireland.[5] The Parliamentary vote for Irish education came on 16 August, MacHale attempting to influence Irish members to vote only for a separate system by an open letter to Palmerston in which he reviewed, once again, all the educational grievances.[6] But it was too late. In his speech on the 16th, Cardwell announced some changes in the arrangement of the National Board. Another paid Commissioner was to be added, and other 'minor points' were declared to be in the Government's consideration. The actual vote of money was up by £21,000 on that of the previous year.[7]

Cullen had supposed that modification of the Board's rules might be proposed by Cardwell, and had been anxious to get his second letter dispatched well in time to allow any changes to reflect its requirements.[8] But Cardwell's proposal for a second paid Commissioner, and his hints about scriptural instruction in Model Schools, an 'Irish tone' in schoolbooks, and greater liberty of action by the patrons of vested schools, were simply marked down as 'trivial alterations' by the *Freeman*.[9] In a further letter in the press to Palmerston, MacHale said distinctly that

---

[1] *Freeman*, 4 June 1860.   [2] *Hansard*, CLVIII, p. 313.
[3] *Ibid.*, CLIX, p. 2037.
[4] *Ibid.*, p. 2059. For an account of the debate, see the *Annual Register*, 1860 (History), pp. 200 ff.
[5] *Parliamentary Papers*, 1861, XLVIII, 683.   [6] *Freeman*, 17 August 1860.
[7] *Irish Times*, 17 August 1860.
[8] Monsell Papers, Box 8319, Cullen to Moriarty, 23 March 1860.
[9] *Freeman*, 18 August 1860.

nothing could be expected from an Administration which supported the Italians. 'The varied schemes that have been successively adopted and enforced by the British Government for the destruction of the Catholic religion in Ireland,' he wrote, 'are viewed by the people in the same light as their recent hostile policy for the destruction of the Pope's power.'[1] The *Irish Times*, attacking Cardwell for his 'subserviency to ultramontanism', argued that the Catholic laity were about to be betrayed by the Ministers into the hands of the priests, who, 'in order to create an appearance of sympathy on the part of the laity with themselves, mixed up the question of National Education with Tenant-Right, sympathy with the Pope, and half a dozen other questions'.[2] Cullen admitted to Moriarty that many of the Catholic gentry opposed the episcopal demands, and that he feared above all else that education might fall into the hands of 'the Irish Cavour party'. The Catholic Commissioners were useless safeguards.[3] The question of the Commissioners was discussed at a meeting of fourteen bishops in the middle of October. Moriarty held that good Catholics should not be excluded from office, but the Archbishop of Cashel and the other prelates were opposed. Not more than three of the bishops were satisfied with Cardwell's proposed modifications, but all were prepared to give them a trial.[4]

It was in December that Cardwell announced what he termed the 'reconstruction' of the Board. There were to be ten Catholic and ten Protestant members.[5] MacHale made it clear at once – in yet another press letter to Palmerston – that 'the bishops are not directly or indirectly parties to this new scheme'. The new appointments were intended only to increase ministerial patronage, he held, and the only course now open to the hierarchy was 'open, earnest, vigorous, and persevering resistance'.[6] In his Lenten Pastoral of February 1861, the Bishop of Clonfert compared the delighted acceptance by the Government of the exclusion of the Catholic Church from education in Ireland, with that in Italy.[7] The bishops waited to see what would happen next.

At this point it will be useful to interrupt the course of the education movement to examine the work of Cullen in reference to the Poor Law. This he also saw as a field of proselytism, and in February 1861, when a Select Committee was appointed to examine its operation in Ireland, Cullen saw his chance to unmask all. The Irish Poor Law had been

---

[1] *Freeman*, 29 August 1860.   [2] *Irish Times*, 17 August 1860.
[3] Monsell Papers, Box 8319, Cullen to Moriarty, 7 October 1860.
[4] *Ibid.*, Cullen to Monsell, 28 October 1860.   [5] *Mail*, 26 December 1860.
[6] *Freeman*, 21 January 1861.   [7] *Ibid.*, 19 February 1861.

passed in 1838: it provided a county rate and workhouse ('indoor') relief[1] on the English model, but its unsuitability for Irish conditions had been revealed in the famine of 1846–8, when it had temporarily broken down, and outdoor relief had to be undertaken. Cullen had been concerned about cases of proselytism in the workhouses for some years, and had already put together a sizeable number of notes on the question when the Select Committee was appointed.[2] The *Dublin Review* had shown in 1859 that workhouse proselytism was of the same quality as that which occurred in prisons and workhouse-schools. Of the last, it remarked that 'hundreds, nay thousands, of the children of Catholic parents are thus brought up in Protestantism'. Only an effective means of registering the denominations of inmates could overcome it.[3] Catholic suspicion – especially after the Mortara Case – was aroused by notices in the press like that of April 1860, announcing that two paupers ('represented to be amongst the most intelligent in the workhouse') had applied to the Mullingar Board of Guardians to have their religion changed from Catholic to Protestant.[4] The dismissal of Father Fox from the chaplaincy of the South Dublin Union in August of the same year, had underlined for Cullen especially the absence of any real control by the bishops even over the Catholic pastorate in the workhouses.[5]

When Cardwell moved the appointment of the Poor Relief Select Committee on 22 February 1861, he said he did not really 'believe that any important changes were likely to result'.[6] But Cullen did not heed that. He set about gathering facts and influencing Irish opinion, for he was to be called to give evidence. In an undated note of about this time, which he headed 'Why a Catholic Bishop interferes in the Poor Law Question',[7] his first point was that Catholic rites could not under present arrangements be properly performed, and that regular Catholic chapels should be provided in the workhouses. Another note listed 'leading points upon which Catholic testimony' before the Select Committee 'should be prepared and methodized'. Twenty-one of these concerned 'defects in the law', and six, 'defects and abuses in its administration'.[8] He also prepared a petition from the bishops to the House of Commons, praying for Catholic representation on the Poor Law Board and in the

---

[1] On the operation of the law in Ireland, see Adolphe Perraud, *Ireland in 1862*, Dublin, 1863, pp. 309 ff.

[2] These are now in a large folder in the Cullen Papers.

[3] *Dublin Review*, June 1859, 'Prison and Workhouse Grievances', p. 427 (a review of C. A. Russell's *The Catholic in the Workhouse*, London, 1859).

[4] *Guardian*, 4 April 1860.

[5] For details of the case, see *Parliamentary Papers*, 1860, LVIII, 941.

[6] *Hansard*, CLXI, p. 862.   [7] Cullen Papers.   [8] *Ibid.*

inspectorate, and for a separate place of Catholic worship in each poor-house.[1]

Cullen was hopeful that good might come of the Committee's inquiry, and told Monsell that he hoped he would keep an eye on it. 'The system may even be improved', he added.[2] On 19 March he wrote to all bishops inviting them to meet in April, and fixing the Poor Laws as the fifth point of the agenda. He asked them also to submit evidence on the evil working of the laws.[3] The Committee called witnesses during May and June;[4] Cullen was heard on 27 of May. He used his appearance to give vent to a manifesto of the Catholic case against proselytism in the workhouses. He pointed to the 'considerable number of workhouses in Ireland in which the master, the matron, the clerk, the schoolmaster and schoolmistress, are all Protestants or Presbyterians, and where no official in the workhouse is a Roman Catholic'.[5] He presented a letter from Gillooly, showing that at Sligo the Guardians consistently refused to appoint Catholic officers, and additionally Cullen was able to cite many comparable instances from the Dublin region.[6] He had much to say also on the procedure of appointing chaplains. Under 1 & 2 Vict. cap. 56, section 48, the right of appointment belonged solely to the Poor Law Commissioners, and the tenure then obtained only at their pleasure. As none of the Commissioners were Catholics the method was open to grave abuse, and it was, Cullen declared, 'quite in opposition to the discipline of the Roman Catholic Church'.[7] 'It is schismatic', he repeated later in his evidence, 'for a board of lay Commissioners to give authority to a clergyman to act as chaplain without the sanction of the bishop of the diocese.' It was worse: it was 'an invasion of the rights of the Roman Catholic Church'.[8] Finally, he dwelled on evils of the workhouses which concerned persons of all religions. All were agreed, he said, in considering 'a workhouse the most dangerous place that any poor man or poor boy can go to, on account of the profligate language and improper stories which they hear, and the bad example set before their eyes'.[9]

Of the twenty witnesses who appeared before the Committee, sixteen were connected in some way with the Poor Law administration. This

[1] Cullen Papers. The signatures of three archbishops are on p. 2. MacHale had not signed.

[2] Monsell Papers, Box 8319, Cullen to Monsell, 2 March 1861.

[3] Gillooly Letters, Cullen to Gillooly, 11 March 1861.

[4] On its work, see Perraud, *op. cit.*, pp. 356 ff.

[5] *Parliamentary Papers*, 1861. x, 1, Report from the Select Committee (Commons) on Poor Relief (Ireland), Evidence, p. 183. There is a copy of the Evidence with Cullen's own annotations in the Cullen Papers.

[6] *Ibid.*, p. 191.   [7] *Ibid.*, p. 181.   [8] *Ibid.*, p. 192.   [9] *Ibid.*, p. 185.

left only four who could be called independent witnesses.[1] It was therefore hardly surprising that, as Cardwell had predicted, the Committee's Report did not contemplate any drastic changes. It was suggested that Catholics be placed on the Board, but the mode of appointing chaplains was to remain unaltered, and although a separate room might be provided in workhouses for Catholic services no specific arrangement was to be made for it. But there was one recommendation which satisfied Catholic demands – the method of registering the denomination of children was to be altered so that every foundling was not automatically registered as a Protestant.[2] It was too late in the Parliamentary session for the Report, which was made in June, to be the subject of legislation at once. Cullen was displeased. 'I suppose the poor will be doomed to remain for years to come in their present deplorable state', he wrote to Monsell.[3]

When it became apparent that legislation was to be introduced early in the new year, the bishops met in Dublin (23 January 1862) with a large body of influential laymen to consider the Poor Laws. The meeting passed resolutions on the lines suggested by Cullen in his evidence to the Select Committee, and a petition to Parliament was organized.[4] Meanwhile in Parliament, on 14 February, Sir Robert Peel, now the Chief Secretary, introduced a Bill to give effect to the Committee's recommendations. Cullen considered most of the provisions of the Bill to be irrelevant to the evils of which he had spoken so strongly, but he called for Catholic members of Parliament to oppose especially clause XI, which suppressed the privilege enjoyed by religious, educational, and charitable buildings of exemption from the payment of poor-rates. He told Monsell to use all his influence against it: 'It is monstrous to tax our churches in Ireland, and leave the churches in England free.'[5]

Perraud wrote that the Bill was like most Irish measures: 'it corrects or abolishes certain abuses of detail; leaving untouched, indeed approving of, those of which Ireland most complains.'[6] From this point it was left to the localities to win concessions for themselves. The concession by the Ballinasloe Board of Guardians of the right of the Sisters of Mercy to visit the workhouse, was only made in 1863 after a long and celebrated

---

[1] Perraud, *op. cit.*, p. 357.
[2] *Parliamentary Papers*, 1861, x, 1, and Perraud, p. 359.
[3] Monsell Papers, Box 8319, Cullen to Monsell, 8 July 1859.
[4] Perraud, *op. cit.*, p. 361.
[5] Monsell Papers, Box 8319, Cullen to Monsell, 7 March 1862.
[6] Perraud, *op. cit.*, p. 360.

conflict[1] and against the opposition of Lord Clancarty. It represents, in an exaggerated form, the easing of the system which was accomplished elsewhere.

There was one other subject of Government legislation which touched Catholic interests. It was in February 1861, the same month as the appointment of the Poor Law Committee, that Monckton-Milnes introduced his Marriage Law Amendment Bill, which, had it passed, would have legalized marriage with a deceased wife's sister. Milnes himself declared that he was not concerned with ecclesiastical questions,[2] but Cullen could hardly agree, and Archbishop Leahy instructed Monsell to familiarize himself completely with Catholic doctrine on the point in order to be in a position to present a coherent case against the Bill.[3] The bishops also felt their interests closely involved in Cairns's marriage registration proposals. 'Parliament cannot legislate on Catholic doctrines and practices without making great blunders', Cullen wrote of them. He especially distrusted Cairns – as an Orangeman and a high Conservative.[4] His Committee of 1861 was followed in 1862 by a Bill applicable only to Ireland. It provided for registration, though Cairns said it was moved principally in the interests of Protestant Dissenters.[5] Cullen found many of its provisions objectionable, especially as the existing registrars of marriage – all Protestants – were to remain unchanged.[6] His effort to get the Bill's operation limited to Protestant marriages failed,[7] but it was fortunately withdrawn after a second reading.[8] Monsell secured the passage of a safe Registration Act for Ireland in 1863,[9] and by April of the following year, Cullen was able to assure him that it was working smoothly and satisfactorily.[10]

The worst area of proselytism and danger to Catholic interests was still National Education, however. After the reconstruction of the Board

[1] For details of the case, see P. K. Egan, *The Parish of Ballinasloe*, Dublin, 1960, pp. 254–61.

[2] *Hansard*, CLXI, p. 845.

[3] Monsell Papers, Box 8319, Leahy to Monsell, Whitsunday, 1861. On the fate of the Bill, see *Annual Register*, 1861 (History), p. 155.

[4] Monsell Papers, Box 8319, Cullen to Monsell, 18 May 1861. Sir Hugh Cairns was M.P. for Belfast, 1852-56; he became Attorney-General, and then Lord Justice of Appeal, in 1866.

[5] *Hansard*, CLXV, p. 490 (19 February 1862).

[6] Monsell Papers, Box 8319, Cullen to Monsell, 7 March 1862.

[7] *Ibid.*, 4 March 1862.

[8] *Hansard*, CLXVII, p. 1314 (2 July 1862).

[9] Introduced 26 February 1863, *ibid.*, CLXIX, p. 856; royal assent, 28 July 1863 (26 & 27. Vict. cap. 90).

[10] Monsell Papers, Box 8319, Cullen to Monsell, 22 April 1864. See also his Pastoral on Marriage Registration in Moran, vol. II, p. 228, 22 December 1863.

by Cardwell, the bishops waited for their next meeting before deciding on a move. This had been fixed for 23 April 1861. The intransigence of the Ministers was demonstrated again before it came on. Butt moved for a Committee on Irish National Education on 19 April, but withdrew in the face of Cardwell's insistence on the success of the Irish system.[1] At the bishops' meeting, national and university education, marriage legislation, military and workhouse chaplains and their mode of appointment, and the Poor Laws, were all under discussion.[2] Keane told Kirby that the divisions over the education question were less evident at the meeting, and that 'union of thought and action may with greater certainty be expected in future'.[3] But it was MacHale's absence which probably accounted for the accord. He remained at Tuam. The assembled prelates appointed Dr Woodlock, the President of All Hallows College, to the rectorship of the Catholic University, vacant since the resignation of Newman. The Pastoral Address which they issued at the end of the meeting condemned as unsatisfactory the changes to the National Board of Education and once again called on the Government to concede the denominational system.[4] There matters rested through the summer – a summer in which Ireland was visited by Queen Victoria.

In November the press made much of a paper quarrel between Cullen and Peel, the Chief Secretary. The latter, on a tour of Ireland, had spoken of a plan for a new Queen's College in Dublin. Cullen blazed out against him in a Pastoral on 9 November,[5] and there was some truth in the *Packet*'s belief that it was Peel's sympathy with the Italians which was the real cause of the outburst,[6] especially since Cullen gave some space to quotation from his speeches in favour of the *Risorgimento*. The unlucky Peel had also written to prominent Catholic laymen, inviting them to contribute towards the foundation of scholarships and exhibitions at the Queen's Colleges, and this also was lashed by Cullen. His opinion, expressed to Gillooly, that 'Sir Robert Peel appears to be a dangerous man', did not make for peaceful intercourse between the bishops and the Government.[7] For the calm of Ireland, the Protestant *Mail* recommended that no more be heard of the Dublin College

[1] *Hansard*, CLXII, p. 854. See *Annual Register*, 1861 (History), pp. 161 ff., on Butt's subsequent motion, and Cardwell's similar treatment of it.

[2] Cullen's report of the meeting is in Propaganda, *Scritture* 34, Cullen to Barnabo, 12 June 1861.

[3] Kirby Papers, Keane to Kirby, no. 2955, 1 May 1861.

[4] Moran, vol. I, p. 828, Pastoral Address of the Archbishops and Bishops of Ireland assembled in Dublin, 23 April 1861.

[5] Text in *Freeman*, 9 November 1861.   [6] *Packet*, 9 November 1861.

[7] Gillooly Letters, Cullen to Gillooly, 12 November 1861.

scheme.[1] Its advice was followed. That of Whalley, the Protestant doyen of Parliament, that Peel should press on and 'be to Ireland in spiritual matters what Garibaldi has been to Italy', was not.[2] The clash of Cullen and Peel was in fact the last thunderclap of a storm. While the *Packet* asked if Peel had really 'plucked the string from Dr Cullen',[3] the truth was that after the *impasse* reached at the beginning of the year, the bishops were turning themselves increasingly to matters relating to the still unchartered Catholic University, and the MacManus funeral[4] and its aftermath had shown them that potentially a greater danger even than mixed education was arriving among their flocks – Fenianism.

The new Rector of the Catholic University, Bartholomew Woodlock, was considering plans for a charter in December 1861 – by extending the charter of the Maynooth Board so that it should become applicable to the College in St Stephen's Green – for 'university-schools', under the control of the bishops, and the provision of Catholic intermediate education.[5] In these, he had the support of both Monsell and Bishop Moriarty. Peel's injection of new spirit into the Queen's Colleges had had the effect of forcing the bishops to realize that a war on the university front could find them very badly placed. Over primary education they had a majority of Catholic patrons in National Schools, and could anyway fall back on the Christian Brothers and other teaching orders. But on university education it was impossible for them to have effective alternatives. The Catholic University could not give legally-valid degrees, it was short of funds, opposed by MacHale, and neglected by students. In October, MacEvilly had reported that the Galway Queen's College was filled with Catholics,[6] and it was to prevent such a state of affairs that the bishops gave a renewed impetus to the Catholic Charter plan. Moriarty declared in his Pastoral on Education in March 1862, that it was safer to send children to Trinity College, Oxford or Cambridge, than to the 'godless and graceless institutions', the Queen's Colleges, 'which represent the indifferentism and infidelity of modern society'.[7] What the bishop called at the same time, in a letter to Kirby, 'the worn-out topic of education',[8] was still agitated by the bishops in their Pastorals, but the Catholic University predominated. The Corporations of Kilkenny and Limerick memorialized the Government on the need

1 *Mail*, 14 November 1861; 'Sir Robert Peel and Dr Cullen'.
2 In a speech in London: *Chronicle*, 28 November 1861.
3 *Packet*, 2 December 1861.   4 See chap. 3.
5 Monsell Papers, Box 8319, Woodlock to Moriarty, 12 December 1861.
6 Kirby Papers, MacEvilly to Kirby, no. 3038, 8 October 1861.
7 *Freeman*, 11 March 1862.
8 Kirby Papers, Moriarty to Kirby, no. 44, 20 March 1862.

for a Charter, and, what is most remarkable in the circumstances, Protestant support helped the Charter agitation along.[1] At a meeting of the Dublin Corporation in April 1862, Alderman D'Arcy moved a resolution urging a Charter on the Government. It was warmly seconded by Dr John Gray, who cited the Charter of the Laval Catholic University in Canada as a precedent.[2] Gray, to be knighted in 1863, was a Protestant educated at Trinity College, Dublin, the proprietor of the *Freeman's Journal*, and was to become one of Cullen's closest allies and one of those foremost in Catholic agitation after 1864. Other corporations soon followed after Dublin, and, as the *Freeman* reported, a great movement of public opinion offered its support to the Charter plan.[3]

The Catholic Bishop of Cloyne had suggested in his Lenten Pastoral that co-operation between Catholics and Protestants on educational matters was to be desired.[4] It began to look as though his words had not been in vain. On 8 May, the Protestant patriot, William Smith O'Brien, wrote publicly to Bishop Butler of Limerick to express his satisfaction at the growth of the Charter movement.[5] It was therefore rather surprising that at this moment the bishops should be called together by Cullen to discuss and resolve upon a whole spectrum of Irish grievances. To some extent this is explained by the fact that Cullen was instructed by Cardinal Barnabo, on the orders of the Pope, to assemble the bishops on the education question.[6] But, as usual, Rome was merely reacting to information imparted to it by Cullen himself, even if somewhat tardily. Perhaps he saw in the popularity of the Charter movement a favourable opportunity to renew the pressure on National Education which he had to some extent released after the *impasse* of the previous year. When the bishops met, from 6 to 9 May, they approved resolutions on Education, the Charitable Bequests Amendment Bill, the Poor Laws, Registration of marriages, secret societies, the Protestant Establishment, and on 'the prevailing distress'. Petitions on these topics were drawn up for circulation along with the resolutions themselves.[7] The petition on education recited all the familiar grievances against the National Schools and asked for the denominational system. No mention was made of the Catholic University.[8] The balance was redressed somewhat by The O'Conor Don, member for Roscommon, whose observations in the Commons on

---

[1] *Freeman*, 18 March 1862.   [2] *Ibid.*, 14 April 1862.
[3] *Ibid., Guardian*, 16 April; *Post*, 1 May 1862.   [4] *Freeman*, 7 March 1862.
[5] *Post*, 8 May 1862.
[6] Gillooly Letters, Cullen to the bishops (a circular), 5 April 1862.
[7] Larcom Papers, MS. 7651. Resolutions adopted by the Archbishops and Bishops of Ireland, at a meeting held in Dublin.
[8] *Ibid.*

Irish Education on 22 May were directed principally to the evils of the Queen's Colleges.[1] Monsell insisted that in Ireland, Catholics were debarred from obtaining degrees by their conscientious objections to attendance at them.[2]

The chances for an early grant of a Charter were squashed on 5 July 1862. On that day a deputation from the Catholic University called on Palmerston in London to ask for a Charter. Monsell had prepared their visit by writing to Gladstone suggesting a meeting with him in order to outline courses of action which would satisfy the Catholics but 'involve no compromise of principle on the part of Parliament'.[3] But his advice does not seem to have got through to Palmerston, who when he saw the deputation at Cambridge House, rejected their request without hesitation: 'Her Majesty's Ministers have made up their minds as to the nature of the education suitable for Ireland: they are firmly convinced that the best system of education for that country is a mixed system.'[4] The keen disappointment this statement caused in Ireland must have prompted the demonstrations of the faithful which accompanied the ceremonial laying of the foundation stone of new buildings for the Catholic University in Dublin on the 20th.[5] The Irish Government considered suspending the procession by enforcing the Party Processions Act, but decided against it after consultations with London.[6] A Grand Orange Soirée at the Dublin Rotundo was the scene of protests against the Catholic Ceremony – the 'Popish College' was denounced and Lord Palmerston's name greeted with hissing.[7] But the *Freeman* warned that by the popular enthusiasm for the ceremony, the Catholics 'made their election – took their side – declared their determination'.[8]

Yet it was clear that their determination alone was not enough. The great movement which the hierarchy had started in 1859, for Catholic Education, was running down. It had been upheld for a time by the strong anti-English feeling inspired by the Italian question, and by the *ad hoc* demonstrations got up to support the bishops over their demands. But when the Government failed to satisfy them on both National Education and the Catholic University Charter, there was nothing they could do to keep up the movement. A sustained and permanent agitation was the only answer. The years 1863 and 1864 were generally ones

[1] *Hansard*, CLXVI, p. 2031.

[2] For a summary of the debate, see *Annual Register*, 1862 (History), pp. 39 ff.

[3] Gladstone Papers, B.M.Add.M.S. 44152, f. 96, Monsell to Gladstone, 2 July 1862.

[4] *Freeman*, 7 July 1862.

[5] James MacCaffrey, *History of the Catholic Church in the Nineteenth Century*, Dublin, Waterford and St Louis (Mo.), 1909, vol. II, p. 245; *Freeman*, 20 July 1862.

[6] Larcom Papers, MS. 7672.

[7] *Irish Times*, 15 July 1862.   [8] *Freeman*, 21 July 1862.

of political inactivity by the bishops. They saw also the growth of Fenianism. But they should be considered as the gestation period for the National Association of Ireland as well. The bishops, indeed, did not cease to pronounce upon the education question in their Pastorals, but without a simultaneous movement of public opinion behind them, their warnings only had the effect of keeping their demands on record.

Several occurrences which kept the question alive did have lasting influence. One was the publication in the *Dublin Review* of two articles on education by Myles O'Reilly, the former leader of the Papal brigade and now member of Parliament for Longford. These were in November 1862, and April 1863. Following the first – on the National System – O'Reilly wrote hopefully to Kirby that in Ireland 'we are ready to fight in all ways'.[1] This article had shown that the circumstances of the Reformation in Ireland, where Protestantism never became the Church of the people, meant that education had come to be looked upon 'as a right and duty of the State'.[2] This had not been the fate of education in England. When he argued 'the striking injustice of making the tax-payers of the country pay for the support of schools to rival and oppress those which they voluntarily support',[3] he was close to the arguments pioneered for religious purposes in England by Dissenters in their campaign against the payment of Church Rate. His general theme was that the State, as in England, should assist all education financially but enforce no system of its own. That would mean the denominational principle for Ireland.[4] The second article, on university education, examined practice abroad, especially in Belgium where he went in the autumn of 1862 to discover facts for himself.[5] His conclusion was that a Charter should be granted to the Catholic University which would allow the full authority of the Papacy and the hierarchy to be perpetuated.[6] Both articles were welcomed by the bishops and by the Rector of the Catholic University – who testified to their excellence in a letter to Kirby.[7] The second was to be quoted frequently in subsequent years as an authority on the university question, and it was in fact comparable in public estimate with Kavanagh's work on the National System.[8]

[1] Kirby Papers, O'Reilly to Kirby, no. 220, 21 November 1862.

[2] Myles O'Reilly, *Two Articles on Education*, London, 1863, i, 'The Connection of the State with Education', p. 17.

[3] *Ibid.*, p. 30.   [4] *Ibid.*, p. 35.   [5] *Ibid.*, ii, 'University Education', p. 62.
[6] *Ibid.*, p. 90.

[7] Kirby Papers, Woodlock to Kirby, no. 157, Sacred Heart, 1863.

[8] Kavanagh himself paid tribute to O'Reilly's work on education – in his *Letter* to the bishops: *Freeman*, 2 December 1864.

Cullen also made a permanent pronouncement on the education question in June 1863. After his election at Tralee, Thomas O'Hagan, the Irish Attorney-General, made a speech containing favourable references to the National System. It was published as a pamphlet. Cullen replied at once, declaring the real question to be 'whether the National System is free from the dangers of proselytism'.[1] He held most strongly that it was not, and that almost the entire object of the mixed system was to get Catholic children 'under the control of Protestant or Presbyterian patrons or teachers'.[2] Cardwell's reconstitution of the Board was attacked,[3] and the central office in Marlborough Street, 'from the Resident Commissioner to the Head Porter, through every one of its departments, exhibits Protestant ascendancy'.[4] The whole organization was nothing but the vehicle of proselytism, and especially galling was the appointment of apostate Catholics with the intention of presenting bad examples to Catholic youth. This had happened at the Royal Hibernian School, the Convicts' Prison, the Poor Law Office, numerous workhouses, and in every Model School.[5] Even since the reconstruction of the Board, Model Schools had been intruded upon the Catholic peoples of Enniscorthy, Sligo, Londonderry, Omagh and Parsonstown, in defiance of the local declarations of the bishops.[6] Cullen's pamphlet was dismissed by the Protestant press. 'A mere glance across this broad page of bigotry and intolerance was sufficient to show that it was only the old story done up in a variation of abusive expletives', was the *Mail*'s summary.[7] Peel's visit to the West Connaught Protestant Mission in the same month, and his speech at a meeting held to raise money for the mission, also drew invectives against proselytism from the archbishop in his June Pastoral. Bibles, he wrote, were not 'the best food for the starving peasantry'.[8] Yet at least one of the grievances of which he had complained was removed during this year. Catholic prison chaplains, paid by the State, were provided by an Act introduced by the Government.[9]

Although the bishops continued to stand by the policy of tolerating the mixed schools until the National System was altered or until they

[1] *Letter of the Most Revd. Dr Cullen to the Rt. Hon. Thomas O'Hagan, M.P., and the Commissioners of National Education, on National Education, in reference to his speech at the late Tralee Election*, Dublin, 1863, p. 3. (Text also in Freeman, 18 June 1863, and Moran, vol. II, p. 180.)

[2] *Ibid.*, p. 3.   [3] *Ibid.*, p. 8.   [4] *Ibid.*, p. 11.   [5] *Ibid.*, p. 17.

[6] *Ibid.*, p. 20.

[7] *Mail*, 19 June 1863, 'Dr Cullen and the Attorney-General'.

[8] 'Pastoral on the Temporalities of the Church, State of the Country, and Education', in *Freeman*, 30 June 1863.

[9] *Annual Register*, 1863 (History), pp. 69 ff.

had provided institutions of their own, Catholic teachers and children were removed from Model Schools. As Kavanagh had shown in his book, these schools provided the worst occasions of proselytism due to their residential character.[1] At Galway Bishop MacEvilly, who regarded the Model Schools as 'Queen's Colleges in miniature',[2] had opened Catholic secondary schools as an alternative to them at the beginning of 1863. In a Pastoral at the time, he declared that the Government was not to be trusted over education.[3] The experiment was successful. At a bishops' meeting in Dublin in September the clergy were called upon to withdraw all Catholics from the Model Schools and provide suitable alternatives. On education generally, the bishops recited all their familiar arguments of 1859. 'Nothing has occurred in the interim which has elapsed', the *Freeman* remarked, 'to reconcile them to either the system or its administration'.[4] A flurry of Protestant anger was caused by the decision of the Board in November 1863 to allow the training of teachers at any school in the National System of certain standing, and not exclusively in the Model Schools, as this advantage fell chiefly to the Catholic convent schools connected with the Board. There was such a howl in the Protestant press, Butler wrote in his Pastoral, 'as if the whole empire were going to pieces'.[5] An Ulster deputation waited on the Lord-Lieutenant to protest.[6] Kavanagh, although claiming that his sole object was 'to overthrow both Board and System alike', wrote publicly to the Lord-Lieutenant to protest against the protestors.[7] In Parliament, on 14 June 1864, Sir Hugh Cairns moved that the new rules 'as regards their operation on the aid afforded to Convent and Monastic Schools' were 'at variance with the principles of National Education'.[8] His motion was lost, but as the *Freeman* pointed out, the old leaven of ascendancy was still fomenting in a Protestant Legislature.[9]

The year had provided another example of the same thing. On Sunday, 3 April, Garibaldi arrived in London, and the British nation 'went out of its ordinary course of folly into an extravagant and hideous act of lunacy'.[10] To the Irish Catholics, the popular enthusiasm which

[1] Kavanagh, *op. cit.*, pp. 291 ff.

[2] Kirby Papers, MacEvilly to Kirby, no. 75, 6 March 1863.

[3] *Freeman*, 9 January 1863; Pastoral of 3 January.   [4] *Ibid.*, 16 September 1863.

[5] *Ibid.*, 26 February 1864.

[6] Parliamentary Papers, 1864, XLVI, 371; *Northern Whig*, 18 March 1864 (report of an Ulster protest meeting).

[7] *Freeman*, 5 March 1864; letter of Kavanagh to Lord Carlisle. See also his previous letter to Carlisle – *ibid.*, 9 February 1864.

[8] *Hansard*, CLXXV, p. 1761.   [9] *Freeman*, 17 June 1864.

[10] *Dublin Review*, July 1864, 'Garibaldi in England', p. 138.

the visit provoked in England confirmed again the growing feeling that if anything would be gained, some more effective means of applying pressure would have to be devised. For some, however, the revolution preached by the Fenians seemed more to the point. Cullen scorned the public reception of Garibaldi by so many members of the Government: 'having paid such honours to the representative of violence, perfidy, and revolution, and having sown in the wind, they may reap the storm'.[1] It is interesting that the one tangible English result of the visit was the formation of the Reform League, and it was to become grievously involved in Fenianism.[2] There is a sense in which the inauguration of the National Association in December was its one tangible Irish result. The first burst of the episcopal movement had run down, and the bishops were to try co-operation with the Liberals instead. To the education grievance, they added the Church and the Land. But before turning to that, it will be well to follow through the reactions of the Catholic Church to the shadow which hung over Ireland for a decade or more. Fenianism brought the troubles to Cullen which the *Risorgimento* had thrust upon Pius IX.

[1] Monsell Papers, Box 8319, Cullen to Monsell, 28 April 1864.
[2] F. E. Gillespie, *Labour and Politics in England, 1850-1867*, Duke Univ. Press, 1927, p. 293.

CHAPTER THREE

The Church and Fenianism

IRISH and English writers alike have emphasized the Fenianism of the 1860s, the first because it seemed proof of the determination of the Irish for national consciousness, the second because it provided yet another instance of the impossibility of governing a people so imbued with the instinct of sedition. This emphasis has allowed much else of value in that period to escape notice; but it is curious that the effect produced on the Catholic Church by the advent of Fenianism has not been examined. Perhaps this has been due to the conflict of evidence and the inexactness of some of it. Let it be said at once that the matter must to a certain extent remain obscure. Often the sort of evidence that would be most telling is quantitative evidence – and there is a definite absence of that, so that it is beyond the limits set by the available material ever to know the attitudes adopted at different times by the clergy in anything but a necessarily inconclusive way. But the task is not impossible, for the magnitude of the issue caused much to be written.

It was often difficult for contemporaries to understand what Fenianism really was, hence one problem for the retrospect of the historian. Information was difficult to come by (and even more difficult to evaluate once obtained) simply because the Society was secret. Many agrarian outrages during the decade were doubtless perpetrated by Ribbonmen, and attributed erroneously to the Fenians, for Ribbonism, though lessened in influence, was still extant in these years. Cullen always depicted Fenianism as a Mazzinian organization affiliated with a general movement of European revolutionism;[1] but this can only mean philosophical affiliation rather than actual, for although Stephens and O'Mahony had associated with continental revolutionaries during their brief exiles in Paris, and probably learned a little of secret organization there,[2] Irish-American Fenianism was unique in character, and even

---

[1] Propaganda, *Scritture* 35, Cullen to Barnabo, Epiphany 1865: 'If the Fenians will acquire influence among us religion will suffer, and the Mazzinian doctrines will achieve more than that which the Anglican heresy will ever be able to achieve. Let us hope, however, that this bad grass will not take deep root. . . .' And *ibid.*, Cullen to Barnabo, 29 September 1865: 'Although they enjoyed the favour of Father Lavelle and some of his friends, it is certain they belonged to the school of Mazzini or of Garibaldi.'

[2] A. M. Sullivan, *New Ireland*, p. 198.

when Fenians were found outside Britain or America – in Italy for example – they were not affiliated brother organizations but simply Irish expatriates, harmless with their dramatic and futile plotting.[1]

There need be no doubt as to who actually were Fenians, however, for they were clearly defined by the nature of their organization and their oath,[2] and this made them quite distinct from other revolutionaries like the St Patrick's Brotherhood and the Ribbonmen. The Irish organization was modelled by Stephens on that created by O'Mahony in America. Enrolment was in Circles or groups, officers being styled A's, B's, and C's according to seniority.[3] Stephens was styled the Central Organizer of the Irish Republic (C.O.I.R.). He appointed missionaries who created distinct 'Circles' in localities where not more than fifty persons had taken the Fenian oath, the missioner himself then becoming 'B' or 'Centre' of the Circle so brought into being.[4] The Circles were to receive military training, organize new Circles, and upset journals or public meetings of a 'distracting' character. The whole Society was centralized in Dublin, and after the summer of 1863 its own paper *The Irish People*, edited by O'Leary, Kickham, and Luby, was sent out weekly. The oath was equally distinctive, and, unlike Ribbonism, which had almost as many oaths as there were lodges in Ireland, was the same everywhere. In reply to an inquiry from the Propaganda about Fenianism which he received in August 1865, Archbishop Leahy of Cashel sent back a brief account which included the full text of the oath:

Feniani duplicem habent formam juramenti, unam solemniorem, aliam minus solemnem eandem fere atque priorem nisi quod brevior sit. Forma solemnis est haec – 'I . . N . N . . do in the presence of God Almighty, solemnly swear allegiance to the Irish Republic now virtually established, that I will yield implicit obedience to the commands of my superior officers. Fearlessly now do I take this oath in the spirit of a true Irish soldier of liberty:

SO HELP ME GOD.[5]

[1] F.O. 43. vol. 102, Joseph Severn to Lord Stanley, 29 January 1868, is exceptional and probably inaccurate. Severn had been assured by Mgr Berardi that 'the Fenians and the Italian revolutionists have combined together' and were acting with great 'secrecy and cunning' – so secret, in fact, that he could find out nothing about them.

[2] For a brief account of the origins of Fenianism see R. B. O'Brien's *Fifty Years of Concessions to Ireland*, vol. II, pp. 201 ff.; and A. M. Sullivan, *op. cit.*, pp. 200–4, and pp. 232–47.

[3] In Ireland the Society was properly known as the 'Irish Revolutionary Brotherhood', or 'I.R.B.'

[4] A. M. Sullivan, *op. cit.*, p. 236. Also: 'Fenianism appears to have been organized, as a ship is built, in water-tight compartments' – *Dublin Review*, April 1868, 'The Case of Ireland before Parliament', p. 499.

[5] Propaganda: *Scritture* 35, Leahy to Barnabo, 10 August 1865. The following is amusing: 'Very evidently many of the rank and file were not quite clear as to what the

Yet the reason for the success of Fenian infiltration is obscured by a conflict of evidence. In a sense Conor Cruise O'Brien has caught the spirit of the appeal it made to the young: it was its 'Parnellism' – by which he means the quintessence of revolt against Church, society, and family. The fate of Donnel in O'Faoláin's *Nest of Simple Folk* rings true. A young man found all his dislike of the tyranny of the priests suddenly drawn out by listening to the speeches of James Stephens. So also apparently did many, in the reality of the 1860s.[1] Cullen saw Fenianism as a reaction to Orangeism.[2] A writer in the *Dublin Review,* doubtless thus earning MacHale's gratitude – for it must have been his opinion too – regarded Fenianism as the natural outcome of Cullen's suppression of Independent Opposition in 1855,[3] and the increasing disillusionment of the Irish people with Parliamentary action.[4] Many were agreed that the Land Question was the root of the matter,[5] and still others (and these will be examined later) that it was a movement against the Catholic Church, or one organized by the Catholic Church against the Protestant Constitution. Goldwin Smith, writing as an historian, as he pointed out, attributed Fenianism to national aspirations quite independent, he claimed, of economic or religious issues.[6] There was similar disagreement at the time as to the word "virtually" meant; for much merriment arose during some of the trials when the approvers declared they were sworn to obey "the Irish Republic now *virtuously* established".' A. M. Sullivan, *op. cit.,* p. 236n.

[1] C. C. O'Brien, *Maria Cross, Imaginative Patterns in a Group of Modern Catholic Writers,* London, 1963 ed., p. 88.

[2] As early as 1859 he wrote to Barnabo 'there is reason to fear that some secret societies will be formed to offer protection from the oppression and insults of the Orangemen' – Propaganda, *Scritture* 33, no. 928, Cullen to Barnabo, 5 July 1859. He had said the same of Ribbonism: 'It was established in opposition to Orangeism, and the great probability is that it will never cease to exist as long as Orangeism shall be encouraged by the gentry. . . .' – Monsell Papers, Box 8319, Cullen to Monsell, 30 August 1852.

[3] *Dublin Review,* April 1867, p. 395: 'those who dug the grave of Independent Opposition in Ireland dug the foundations of Fenianism at the same time.'

[4] Such disillusionment, no doubt real enough, was a debating commonplace in the 1860s. An example is furnished by The O'Donoghue who during the second reading of Dillwyn's Motion on the Church in 1865 said that the fruitless repetition of the question in Parliament only strengthened the impression in Ireland that 'there was no use in appealing to the House of Commons' – 28 March 1865, *Hansard,* third series, CLXXVIII, p. 394. And Cullen wrote to Gladstone in 1869 that only the Fenians would be gratified by the adoption of the Church Bill as amended by the Lords, 'as it will give them an opportunity of proclaiming that Ireland can expect nothing good from British legislation'. Gladstone Papers, B.M.Add.MS. 44421, f. 150, Cullen to Gladstone, 14 July 1869.

[5] See John Stuart Mill's *England and Ireland,* for this view of the case, one most influential at the time.

[6] Goldwin Smith, *The Irish Question: Three Letters to the Editor of the Daily News,* London, 1868, p. 5 (Letter 1).

stations of the men who joined. It was generally believed that they were persons of no account,[1] though Manning warned his countrymen that 'no greater deception could we practise on ourselves than to imagine that Fenianism is the folly of a few apprentices and shop-boys', for it was sustained by 'the traditional and just discontent of almost a whole people'.[2] Unlike Ribbonism, the Fenian Society was not exclusively Catholic in membership: Thomas Clarke Luby for example was a Protestant, whose uncle was a Senior Fellow of Trinty College. Dr Leahy was clear on the point in his Memorandum for the Propaganda. 'Feniani, quamvis ut plerique Catholici, nolunt Societatem esse exclusive Catholicam, omnino rejiciunt characterem Catholicum, quem dicunt esse noxium libertati Hibernae, volentes ut quam plurimi Protestantes mixti Catholicis Societati aggregentur, Protestantes tamen procul abeunt. . .'.[3] Though impossible to prove, it is most likely that many of the earliest Fenian recruits were Irishmen from the Papal Brigade of 1860, returning home disillusioned with the service of the Pope, but willing to recapture their crusading zeal in the service of the 'virtually established' Irish Republic. Justin McCarthy described how, in November 1860, twenty-eight Tipperary men who had belonged to the Brigade gave a public reception in Kickham's home town, Mullinahone. The Fenian himself read an Address signed by the twenty-eight, which denounced the tyranny of England and contained Fenian sentiments. The men were asked by Kickham to 'scatter the seed'.[4] In fact the overwhelming majority of the Fenians were Catholics;[5] it was a commonplace of the times that it was only they who were really disaffected.

It is difficult to see how Catholics could belong both to the Fenian Society and the Church (which offered excommunication for the former membership) unless they made a mental distinction between the Church and the clergy – the sort of distinction, in fact, which reformers of the United Church of England and Ireland always insisted on

[1] The Earl of Mayo said in the Commons that 'In Ireland itself the disaffection is exclusive to the lowest class alone: unlike 1798 and 1848 when men of position and intellect were leaders'. Debate on Maguire's motion for a Committee on the State of Ireland, 10 March 1868, *Hansard*, cxc, p. 1354. But many of the Fenian leaders were the veterans of '48.

[2] During the Lords' debate on the second reading of the Church Bill the Duke of Marlborough quoted these words (spoken by Manning at a public meeting in May 1866) as 'words of incitement – of almost revolutionary incitement'. 26 June 1868, *Hansard*, cxciii, p. 35.

[3] Propaganda, *Scritture* 35, Leahy to Barnabo, 10 August 1865.

[4] J. H. McCarthy, *Ireland Since the Union*, London, 1887, p. 183.

[5] See Newdegate's speech in the Commons: 12 March 1868, *Hansard*, cxc, p. 1633.

throughout the century. It would perhaps be unkind to say that such a nice point was beyond the intelligence of the rank-and-file Fenians, but it would be unwise, for such a conception was entirely foreign to the spirit of Catholicity, and the Irish devotion to their priesthood was of world renown.[1] The possibility that some of the parish priests were not quite so much opposed to the Fenian sympathy of many of their charges as Cullen liked to imagine, will be considered in due course. In many places where the local clergy took a firm stand there must have been friction, as at Skibbereen in Co. Cork, where the Roman Catholic Fenians burned their parish priest, a Father Collins, in effigy, because they suspected him of betraying an attorney's clerk named Keane who had been administering the Fenian oath in the parish.[2] The Bishop of Ross (O'Hea) threatened to excommunicate all involved unless suitable reparation were made.[3] *The Irish People* observed that 'the effigy burning in Skibbereen proves how strongly the people feel on this subject', and used it as conclusive of the evil effects of priests meddling in politics.[4] The unhappy Father Collins tried to justify himself by swearing in front of magistrates that he had only condemned secret societies and not spoken of Keane. But when he was applauded by the Protestant press he was taken as guilty by the Fenians. A great national fund was organized to help the defence of the attorney's clerk.[5] It could even be suggested that the Government encouraged the discord of priests and people by delay of its proceedings against the Fenians, so allowing as long a time as possible for the local conflicts among the Catholics to work the maximum damage.[6] Cullen himself believed this.[7]

The primary object of Fenianism was the establishment of an Irish Republic and as surely as the Catholic Church impeded the way, so it also was not infrequently condemned along with the Government, especially early in the decade. *The Irish People*[8] ridiculed the hierarchy and charged the priests with duping the masses. Most of its articles

[1] 'No clergy is more justly popular than the Irish Catholic clergy. It has fought for the faith, for liberty, and for the poor.' Jules de Lasteyrie: *French Thoughts on Irish Evils*, London, 1868, trans. (from '*L'Irelande et les causes de son misère*', in *Revue des Deux Mondes*), p. 26.

[2] *Guardian*, 28 December 1864.   [3] *Guardian*, 4 January 1865.

[4] *The Irish People*, 21 January 1865.   [5] *Ibid.*, 11 March 1865.

[6] W. J. O'Neill Daunt, Journal, 5 December 1865 – although the Castle had Pierce Nagle, a spy in the Fenian office for eighteen months prosecution was delayed 'Just because that movement sowed discord between the people and the priests wherever it took root, and so far was agreeable to the British power, that hates Catholicity . . .'.

[7] Spalding Letters, Cullen to Spalding, 17 September 1864.

[8] '"The Irish People", their organ, is as bad as a Mazzinian Paper . . .' Kirby Papers, Cullen to Kirby, no. 246, 9 December 1864.

which were offensive to the Church were the work of Charles Kickham;[1] but it was an American writer who criticized the Irish hierarchy for appearing to be 'actuated by the long ago exploded doctrine of the Divine Right of Kings and passive obedience; whilst the Polish hierarchy thinks the people have some rights, and acts upon the Catholic doctrine, that all political powers come from God *to* the people, and through the people to the Government established by them'.[2] Yet Kickham soon took up the Catholic inconsistency over Poland and argued it in his favour.[3] His articles on 'Priests and Politics', in which the clergy were indicted for holding the people aloof from political wisdom,[4] though they were by no means so violent as Cullen pretended, were especially loathed by him.

In fine, the movement could be described in these years, as it was by Dr Leahy, as 'directe et formaliter adversus Religionem Catholicam'.[5] Cullen was equally satisfied with this opinion[6] and always rejoiced to see the Fenians emphasize the demarcation between the Society and the Church, for this[7] enabled their condemnation to proceed with more exactitude and clarity. Informed opinion in Parliament held that the Society sought to undermine Protestant and Catholic Churches indiscriminately,[8] and it was Manning's belief that this attitude had crossed the ocean: 'The American Irish are practically without religion, except a burning hatred of England for its religious persecution in Ireland.'[9] In America, in fact, the Fenians had been condemned by all the bishops

---

[1] O'Leary, *Recollections of Fenians and Fenianism*, vol. II, p. 12.

[2] *The Irish People*, 9 April 1864.

[3] O'Leary, *op. cit.*, vol. II, p. 13; *The Irish People*, 12 March 1864.

[4] For example, *The Irish People*, 4 June 1864.

[5] Propaganda, *Scritture* 35, Leahy to Barnabo, 10 August 1865.

[6] *Ibid.*, Cullen to Barnabo, 12 January 1866: 'Although the Fenian movement is a plot principally directed against the Catholic Church, the Protestants pretend to believe that it is the Catholics who conspire against them, and using these pretexts they have started to dismiss the poor Catholics from every sort of employment, and to replace them with Protestants.'

[7] 'The Fenians are coming out in their true colours. In Tipperary they abused and insulted the priests – so much the better as some of the priests there were rather bitten with Young Irelandism.' Kirby Papers, Cullen to Moran, no. 43, 2 March 1865.

[8] For example, Earl Granville's speech on the second reading in the Lords of the Habeas Corpus Suspension (Ireland) Act Continuance Bill, 27 May 1867: 'Fenianism was equally opposed to the Protestant and Catholic Churches' – *Hansard*, CLXXXVII, p. 1122. Others discounted religion as an element: 'Present disturbances in Ireland were not caused by religious grievances. The Fenian movement had no connexion with religion, and the Fenians themselves were dead to all religious considerations'. Sir Frederick Haygate on Gray's motion for a committee on the Temporalities and Privileges of the Established Church, 7 May 1867, *ibid.*, CLXXXII, p. 117.

[9] Gladstone Papers, B.M.Add.MS. 44249, f. 8, Manning to Gladstone, 22 September 1867.

in Irish areas, using the censures of the episcopate in Ireland as their precedent. *The Irish People* was not slow in pointing out that this was tautological, for Cullen claimed to base his censures on those of the bishops in America.[1] It is true that fewer of the American clergy were obedient to the strictures, and the laity even less so. The revolutionary preaching of Father Moriarty of Philadelphia echoed as far as Ireland, from whence he was aided by Lavelle's donations.[2] The fate of Father Venuta, who tried in vain to prevent his flock attending a Fenian meeting at Hudson City, and earned their execration for his pains,[3] became well known in England and Ireland too. It served as a grim warning to the Irish Government.[4] Cullen went so far as to suspect that the Fenians were 'encouraged by those who wish to keep up the Protestant Church',[5] and if this suggests an absence of Fenian propaganda against that Church, it is Whiteside, the champion of the Establishment, and the member of Parliament for Dublin University, who supplies an explanation, by his realization that the promoters of Fenianism 'have too much good sense to think that a revolution could be accomplished by agitation with respect to Church grievances'.[6] It is clearly seen that just beneath the surface, assertion could be met with counter-assertion, but it is quite evident that the general tenor of Fenian doctrine was in conflict with Catholicism; 'its members openly proclaimed their enmity to the Romish hierarchy and priesthood . . . as enemies of the nation to be swept away and destroyed.'[7]

It was hardly surprising that the Church hit back. It had, in fact, a positive obligation to do so,[8] since secret societies were forbidden by Rome, principally in the Encyclical of Leo XII *Quo graviora* issued on

[1] *The Irish People*, 19 March 1864.

[2] Spalding Letters, Cullen to Spalding, 12 November 1864; *The Irish People*, 18 June 1864.

[3] *Daily News*, 6 January 1865, from the *New York World*, 17 December 1864.

[4] Larcom Papers, MS. 7648, 'Memorandum on Ultramontane designs in 1865', by Johnstone Stoney, Note C.

[5] Kirby Papers, Cullen to Kirby, no. 246, 9 December 1867.

[6] Speech in the Commons on Gray's Motion on the Church, 10 April 1866, *Hansard*, CLXXXII, p. 1047.

[7] *Annual Register*, 1865 (History), p. 174.

[8] 'The Catholic Church condemns oath-bound secret societies. . . . Firstly, regarding the sanctity of an oath, it denies that anyone who chooses can, for any purpose he pleases, formally administer or impose that solemn obligation. Secondly, having regard to the safety of society, of public order, of morals and religion – it prohibits the erection of any such barrier between the objects and operations of a society, and authoritative examination or judgment. Over this critical and important issue the Fenian movement on its very threshold was plunged into a bitter war with the ecclesiastical authorities of the Catholic Church.' A. M. Sullivan, *op. cit.*, p. 237.

13 March 1826,[1] and supplemented with numerous other Papal censures.[2] Even so there was no lack of difficulty in interpreting them. In April 1864, Cullen sought Kirby's advice concerning a long letter written by Father Lavelle in the Tuam *Patriot* on secret societies, in which 'he endeavours to show that the Fenians do not come under the Bull of Leo XII' and pointed to the gravity of the case should Lavelle press his point: 'If the *et* in Leo XII Bull can be taken conjunctively, it would appear there is no censure against societies who endeavour to subvert the Church but respect the throne. Does not that appear absurd? Get us some decision on this point.' But he was able to console himself in the face of the Fenians, as they 'appear to incur the censure, for by fomenting revolutions, they injure and assail both Church and State'.[3] In fact, there was a greater divergence of opinion in Ireland on how the censures should be defined than Cullen suggested. Writing to the same person at about the same time, Bishop Moriarty was explicit, and his letter deserves quite full quotation:

> ... In your last you spoke of the danger of secret societies. The difference of opinion amongst ecclesiastics here as to the meaning of the Papal bulls on the subject is causing much mischief. Dr Cullen and others declare that Fenians and members of the Society of St Patrick incur censures *ipso facto* – and others and some bishops say no, because these societies though against the State are not against the Church, and that the bulls require that the Society should be not only secret but opposed to Church and State. Since the beginning of the Phoenix Society I have made the joining of any secret society bound by oath a reserved call, and I have commanded the priests not to give Absolution until the society should be renounced *in foro externo*. ... I have found this plan very effective. My dear friend, some of us by our abuse of government drive the people into disaffection and the spirit of rebellion. We can not blame them if they are more logical than canonical in their conclusions. I have brought upon myself much obloquy by taking another path. Time will tell. ...[4]

With due consistency the Order of Freemasons was included among the Papal censures of secret societies,[5] though this cannot have stemmed from a particularly wide personal knowledge possessed of that Order by

---

[1] For a summary of Papal censures of secret societies, see E. Cahill, *Freemasonry and the Anti-Christian Movement*, Dublin, 1929, p. 119-29.

[2] Quoted in the text of the Syllabus Errorum (1864) as: Encyclical, *Qui pluribus*, 9 November 1846; Allocution, *Quibus quantisque*, 20 April 1849; Encyclical, *Noscitis et nobiscum*, 8 December 1849; Allocution, *Singulari quadam*, 9 December 1854; Encyclical, *Quanto conficiamur*, 10 August 1863. (See Anne Freemantle, ed., *The Papal Encyclicals*, Mentor ed., New York, 1956, p. 145.)

[3] Kirby Papers, Cullen to Kirby, no. 86. 15 April 1864.

[4] *Ibid.*, Moriarty to Kirby, no. 93, 1 May 1864.

[5] Letter against Freemasonry from the Propaganda to the Archbishop of Dublin, 7 July 1863 – text in *Irish Ecclesiastical Record*, new series, III, p. 322.

the Pope, who, in 1861, lamenting the Prince of Wales's decision to join it, added in conversation to Odo Russell that 'he believed from the perusal of a little book which he had bought at Montevideo years ago, that the principles of Freemasonry were anti-Christian'.[1] Cullen, however, was conscious of the dangers, which, characteristically, he exaggerated. Predicting that in a short time all the offices in Ireland would be filled by Protestants 'and generally by Freemasons', he concluded that the principal authorities in the army and indeed in every department of State belonged to that Society, 'so we are in bad hands'. His moral was that this set a poor example to the Fenians.[2] Cullen plainly misunderstood the development of things in England when he went on to assert that like the Fenians, all the workmen of England were now bound in 'secret societies' aimed at strikes – 'Why should they not, when the highest classes are all sworn Freemasons?' During the Lords' Debate on the second reading of the Church Bill, the Earl of Derby noted Cullen's recent threat to excommunicate all Roman Catholics *ipso facto* if they attended the Dublin Masonic Ball in honour of the Prince of Wales: 'I can only say that if His Excellency imagines that the Freemasons of England stand in the same footing with the Carbonari and other secret societies . . . I can only say that it is a signal proof of the ignorance of infallibility.'[3]

Thus came the Pastorals issued by members of the hierarchy against the Fenian and other secret societies. Following the MacManus affair in 1861, Cullen had warned of the evils of secret societies in his Pastoral at the end of November, on the Feast of the Immaculate Conception. Those joining them, he had written, were excommunicated *ipso facto*.[4] A bishops' meeting in May 1862, considered the matter fully and their resolutions 'warn Catholics against all such combinations, whether bound by oath or otherwise' – this phrase was evidently aimed at the Brotherhood of St Patrick – and yet assured the faithful that their bishops 'cannot be blind to the many injustices they suffer'.[5] At a bishops' meeting in August 1863, one of the resolutions passed concerned the St Patrick's Brotherhood:

Several bishops having represented to the meeting that a society exists called the Brotherhood of St Patrick, having for its object the support and defence by arms of what is called in the oath of membership the Irish Republic, or

[1] F.O. 43, vol. 83A, Dispatch no. 5, 16 January 1861.
[2] Kirby Papers, Cullen to Kirby, no. 128, 5 April 1867.
[3] 17 June 1869, *Hansard*, CXCVI, p. 32.
[4] *Post*, 3 December 1861; see also Moran, *op. cit.*, vol. I, p. 863 (LVIII).
[5] Text in *Freeman's Journal*, 27 May 1862. See Larcom Papers, MS. 7651; and Moran, vol. II, p. 134 (IV).

proposing to itself other such illegal ends, and that societies of the same character, though sometimes not bound by oath, exist in some dioceses, it was resolved to condemn all such associations.[1]

It is clear that the bishops were confusing the Brotherhood directly with the Fenians. Cullen himself used the terms interchangeably in a letter to Spalding of 1864.[2] One result was that *The Irish People* was able to claim that the Church had not condemned Fenianism at all, but only the St Patrick's Brothers.[3] Pastorals continued to hammer the revolutionaries into the 1870s, and these crystallized the declared episcopal opposition for all time.[4] So it was that Dr Leahy was able to inform the Propaganda that 'Episcopi Hibernici . . . monuerunt adversus hanc Societatem periculosam et perniciosam'.[5] The pulpit as well as the Pastoral thundered anathema. Among the Mayo Papers is a 'Sermon on Fenianism' preached in St John's Catholic Cathedral, Limerick, on Sunday 16 December 1866, by the Very Reverend the Administrator of the Cathedral, Dr M. Fitzgerald:

> We are all commanded by the Divine Law to be subject to the higher power. . . . The Church has ever been guided by this doctrine in all her laws against secret societies. In fact her laws on this very subject are a mere development of the principles of St Paul, and a practical application of them to the various wants of every age. In Italy she condemns the Carbonari, in France the Socialist, and here at home, alike and equally—the Fenians.[6]

There follows a passage which Naas underlined:

> Neither priest, nor bishop, nor Cardinal, nor even the Pope, could give Sacraments to a person who persists in a sinful course. If, for example, a Fenian became suddenly ill in this Parish, and if I were to attend him . . . it would be my duty to advise him, to exhort him, to point out to him the danger to which his eternal Salvation was exposed; but if all failed I should let him die without the Sacraments.[7]

Even in the days of Ribbonism's worst excesses, Cullen had goaded the clergy against them.[8] Now he veritably pressurized them. The British Government were assured by 'a priest of high standing' in Rome that

---

[1] *Freeman*, 16 September 1863.
[2] Spalding Letters, Cullen to Spalding, 20 August 1864.
[3] *The Irish People*, 12 March 1864.
[4] See Moran, *The Pastoral Letters . . . of Cardinal Cullen*, vol. II. These closely follow the same formula, and those of other bishops emulated them.
[5] Propaganda, *Scritture* 35, Leahy to Barnabo, 10 August 1865.
[6] Printed as a handbill by the *Munster News*, 'to meet the demands of the public', and found in the Mayo Papers, MS. 11188, and *The Times*, 22 December 1866.
[7] *Ibid.*
[8] Monsell Papers, Box 8319, Cullen to Monsell, 30 August 1852: 'The clergy (Catholic) have done everything in their power to banish secret societies.'

the 'Papal Government have strictly forbidden the Irish clergy to take any part whatever in this conspiracy and have ordered them to warn against it in the Confessional',[1] an assurance which the Holy Father himself confirmed to Gladstone during an audience in 1866.[2] Many expressed themselves satisfied with the effect on the lower clergy of the episcopal strictures;[3] and the *Dublin Review* cautiously declared that 'the English Government has the zealous and active aid of the Irish Catholic clergy in opposing the action of the Revolution in Ireland'.[4] Expressing his gratification that 'all the priests and bishops' had acted well, keeping 'the people from going mad' during the March insurrection of 1867, Cullen rejoiced to find that Lord Naas admitted in the Commons that twenty-nine National Schoolmasters had joined the rebels: 'This ought to convince our rulers that education without religious control is well calculated to promote revolution.'[5] Cullen, in fact, was sure of the case. In his papers there exists a memorandum headed 'The Fenian movement: its connection with the *Mixed* System of Education'. Not only did this hold that 'no single instance has yet turned up of any of the parties accused in Ireland of Fenianism having received their education in the Schools of the Christian Brothers, the Catholic Colleges, or the Catholic University', but also that in Fenianism it was possible to 'witness the *real* effects of a system that restricts or removes all those higher influences which alone can secure the well-being of individuals, of society, or of states'. There followed a list of known Fenians showing their places of education. These were Trinity College, the Queen's Colleges, or the National Schools.[6] To Spalding he wrote in 1865 that O'Leary had lost his faith in a Queen's College.[7]

[1] F.O. 43, vol. 91A, Dispatch no. 13, 1 February 1864.

[2] 'He spoke warmly against Fenianism, and declared the decided hostility to it of his clergy in Ireland: which hostility, in any point that might come before him, he always approved and seconded.' Memorandum written by Gladstone of a conversation with His Holiness Pope Pius IX on 22 October 1866: Gladstone Papers, B.M.Add.MS. 44755, f. 101 (Add.MS. 44234, f. 218 is the Italian text).

[3] *Guardian*, 28 February 1866: 'The Priests are denouncing Fenianism on every side and warning their flocks against it.'

[4] *Dublin Review*, July 1867, 'Irish Questions', p. 204. But this support was set at a premium by contestants in the Concurrent Endowment affray. The reviewer continued: 'but we are not certain that the efficacy of their action would be increased if they were to confront their people in the new character of pensioners of the State . . .'. From a different viewpoint, and assuming the disaffection of the clergy, the author of *The Government Proceedings Against Fenianism*, London 1865 (a short pamphlet), favoured endowment, since by diminishing the priests' influence among their flocks 'they would be thought to be in league with the governing powers. Their only consistent course would be to recommend fidelity to the Sovereign.' (p. 13.)

[5] Kirby Papers, Cullen to Kirby, no. 86, 12 March 1867.　　[6] Cullen Papers.

[7] Spalding Letters, Cullen to Spalding, 2 December 1865.

Cullen never forgot this ultimate proof of the soundness of his views on education. Giving evidence to the Powis Commissioners on 24 February 1869, he was again able to contrast the Christian Brothers' Schools, which could claim only one Fenian pupil, with those of the National System: 'He did not say the training schools were hot-beds of Fenianism, but many of those superficially educated young men were connected with Fenianism.'[1] It seemed that everything had played into his hands.

In February 1866, Cullen reflected on his campaign against the Fenians in a letter to Barth. Woodlock: '. . . It was the opposition given to the MacManus funeral in Dublin, and the continued denunciations of the Fenians, that prevented the successful spread of that mischievous organization through every part of the country. Nothing but the influence of the clergy saved us from the greatest evils. . . .'[2] He had touched on a curious event, 'the ridiculous affair of MacManus' bones'.[3] Terence Bellew MacManus had been convicted for his leading part in the '48, sent to Van Diemen's Land, escaped to San Francisco in 1851, and died there in 1861. Several Irishmen then resident in America – in the hope of raising sympathy and funds for Fenianism, as it later transpired[4] – arranged for his exhumation, shipment, and re-burial in Dublin. 'The Irish race in America seemed to make of the funeral a demonstration of devotion to the old land. The Irish at home were seized with like feelings. . . .'[5] The body arrived at Queenstown on 30 October 1861 amidst great excitement, and was reinterred at Glasnevin on Sunday 10 November, when the funeral oration was preached by Lavelle. The regular chaplain to the cemetery did not appear – he was obeying the prohibition placed on the whole affair by Cullen,[6] who himself regarded Lavelle's address as a great scandal.[7] Cullen suspected that only the Fenians would profit from the popular enthusiasm, and refused to allow a lying-in-state or other public ceremonial in his churches,[8] a course which was expressly approved by Cardinal Antonelli,[9] who at the same time linked Fenianism with continental revolu-

---

[1] *Parliamentary Papers*, 1870, XXVIII, vol. IV, p. 1226.

[2] Monsell Papers, Box 8319, Cullen to Woodlock, 25 February 1866.

[3] *Guardian*, 4 November 1863.

[4] The moving spirit of the demonstration was O'Mahony, Head Centre of the American Fenians. See *The Irish People*, 13 February 1864.

[5] A. M. Sullivan, *New Ireland*, p. 245.

[6] John O'Leary, *Recollections of Fenians and Fenianism*, London, 1894, vol. I, p. 169.

[7] Gillooly Letters, Cullen to Gillooly, 12 November 1861.

[8] Sullivan, *op. cit.*, p. 246.

[9] Cullen Papers, Kirby to Cullen, 6 December 1861; and the same to the same, 14 December 1861.

tionism, and opined that the Irish clergy would follow Cullen's lead. Cullen explained his anxiety to Monsell:

In Dublin some foolish people following up MacManus manifestation are establishing clubs thro' the city. The persons engaged in this work call themselves Brothers of St Patrick ... I wish the leaders could be caught and prosecuted. All the clergy are active in opposing the movement, so I hope it will not spread.[1]

As on other occasions, Cullen's prohibition did not receive total respect. On Sunday 3 November, a requiem office for the repose of MacManus's soul was chanted at Maynooth by the students. 'Rarely have they assembled on such solemn occasion with such hearty good will . . . and while they prayed that his soul might rest in peace, they wished every success to the cause which he represented.'[2] But the clergy generally opposed the demonstration as Cullen had demanded, and five years later, the Fenian leaders admitted that it was an expedient intended to encourage their movement.[3] Thus the veracity of Cullen's instinctive depicture of the entire proceedings as calculated to injure religion.

Cullen's hostility to the Fenians proved to involve personal risk. In 1864 he might boast that a good many Fenians were leaving the Society since his denunciation of them,[4] but in the course of time exasperated Fenians, doubtless more in the hope of publicity at a time when their cause was flagging than from any real intention, were threatening his life. He reported to Propaganda in February 1866 that he was receiving letters 'in which they state that I will have to pay dearly for having declared that the Fenians will be excommunicated by the Church'.[5] After the issue of his December Pastoral in the same year, in which he reiterated the censures, rumours were once more abroad concerning his imminent assassination,[6] but like other whispers of the same happening they proved to be without content, and it is doubtful if they were taken seriously.

It has already been seen that in some places there was opposition

---

[1] Monsell Papers, Box 8319, Cullen to Monsell, 8 January 1862.

[2] *Morning News*, 6 November 1861. Quoted in *Fenianism and Romanism*, by John Thomas Waller, Second Letter to the Editor of the Clare Freeman, 27 February 1866. It should be noticed that this is a Protestant source, and it is unlikely that Maynooth students had any real sympathy with Fenianism as such.

[3] See A. M. Sullivan, *op. cit.*, p. 246.

[4] Kirby Papers, Cullen to Kirby, no. 86, 15 April 1864.

[5] Propaganda, *Scritture* 35, Cullen to Barnabo, 18 February 1866. He prefixed the information with his stock explanation: 'It appears as if in religious matters they are Mazzinians, and they have learned from that chief partizan the use of the dagger.' But he was resolute; 'I and the Dublin clergy will not cease to exhort the people to be on their guard against the designs of secret societies.'

[6] *Guardian*, 19 December 1866.

to the priests in reward for their loyalty to injunctions of the hierarchy in prohibition of Fenianism. 'Disaffection against the authority of the Church', wrote a *Dublin Review* contributor in 1865, 'is also, we suspect, more general, and it is certainly more openly testified than at any previous period we can recall.'[1] O'Neill Daunt noticed a curious state of affairs in Cork City:

> When the priests condemned Fenianism in the Confessional and refused the Sacraments to persons connected with it, many of the Fenian youths of Cork gave up going to Confession to priests who had been educated at Maynooth, but some of them confessed to priests brought up in foreign seminaries. . . . Maynooth priests, being educated at the expense of the State, are suspected of being more or less in the English interest.[2]

But in most localities where priest and people were irrevocably polarized by the advent of Fenianism, there was not even friction, due to the absence of a point of contact, since the Fenians were 'entirely independent of any priestly or religious influence';[3] or, as Goldwin Smith put it, 'their denunciations have been given to the wind. They have no control over the matter whatever.'[4] Bishop Keane clearly enunciated the dangers to Kirby in 1866:

> The great question of the day is that of 'Fenianism'. It is destined to exercise an extraordinary influence on the future relations between priests and people. . . . For some years past, several complaints were made by the people against what they called the inactivity and neglect of the priests. In plain words, it was said, over and over again, that 'the priests don't care about us any longer. They and the upper class Catholics who expect places are well enough off, and they no longer feel for the suffering of farmers and working people.' This language and sentiment have prepared many to adopt . . . conspiracy against a government that refused redress.

His final warning was significant: 'If once the masses throw off the respect they have always had for their priests, then will come the real Irish difficulty for England and for all concerned.'[5]

Although Cullen felt he could rely on the clergy to oppose Fenian designs, there was no accounting for Father Lavelle – nor, where that priest was concerned, for Dr MacHale. Lavelle's vice-presidency of the

---

[1] *Dublin Review*, April 1865, 'Wanted, A Policy for Ireland', p. 436.
[2] Daunt, Journal, 12 September 1865.
[3] *Annual Register*, 1865 (History), p. 174. 'But where is the force in Ireland to resist the Fenians? The Archbishop and the hierarchy said that the multitude contained in that conspiracy had broken away from the authority of the Church, and the heads of the Church no longer able to control them.' Whiteside on Gray's motion in the Commons on the Irish Church, 10 April 1866, *Hansard*, CLXXXII, p. 1049.
[4] Goldwin Smith, *op. cit.*, Letter 1, p. 6.
[5] Kirby Papers, Keane to Kirby, no. 24, 6 February 1866.

St Patrick's Brotherhood, his overt identity with the Fenian cause, his consequent friction with the hierarchy, resulted in a further deterioration of the relations between Cullen and MacHale, already damaged by the political disagreements of 1854 and their lack of accord on the education question. The 'Lavelle Case', as the numerous incidents involving that priest came to be called, was without doubt the greatest clerical scandal of the decade, equalled, perhaps only in that following by the case of O'Keeffe. Little purpose can be served by going through much of a distressing story:[1] but the effect of Lavelle on the bishops, and especially on Cullen, was of a magnitude it is almost impossible to exaggerate.

At Maynooth, Patrick Lavelle was held to be one of the most outstanding students of his time. It was after his ordination, when he was sent as a professor to the Irish College in Paris, that the first signs of his stormy character became clear. After quarrelling with the President, he returned to Ireland, taking first a curacy in Mayo and then the pastoral charge of Partry in 1858.[2] It was there that what Mgr D'Alton called his 'stirring career' began.[3] Lavelle's name gained its national currency as a result of his legal battle with Lord Plunket and others over the Partry proselytizing evictions of 1859 and 1860.[4] His is a clear instance of the appeal of Fenianism to those already agitating the Land question. It is true that he never had any formal connexion with the Fenian Society as such, but the St Patrick's Brotherhood of which he was the prime moving spirit, was condemned by the hierarchy as a secret society, and because of its popular identity with Fenianism. Lavelle assured Cullen in vain that the St Patrick's Brotherhood was not a secret society.[5] His activities apparently belied his professions. In 1862 he was preaching sedition in Dublin, and at the same time began writing to the 'Mazzinian' press; but even this was not his earliest association with Fenianism, for he had taken a conspicuous part in the MacManus demonstration of 1861. Cullen appealed to MacHale to suspend Lavelle, without result; for as *The Irish People* boasted in 1864, the Western archbishop had publicly blessed the Fenians by acknowledging their alms.[6] In February 1864 Lavelle went to Rome to present his case against Cullen at the

---

[1] Propaganda, *Scritture* 34 and 35 are bulky with material on Lavelle – Cullen's reports; Lavelle's depositions and petitions. The press closely reported the unhappy priest's every word.
[2] D'Alton, *History of the Archdiocese of Tuam*, vol. II, p. 69.
[3] *Ibid.*, vol. II, p. 358.
[4] See his *War in Partry*.
[5] Cullen Papers, Lavelle to Cullen, May (no date, but 1863).
[6] *The Irish People*, 26 November 1864.

Propaganda. He had submitted on some points to his own archbishop in November 1863 – MacHale himself being constantly goaded into action by Cullen and Rome.[1] Yet still nothing happened, and Cullen was unprepared to find satisfaction in Lavelle's vague assurances, especially as his support for Fenian activities was maintained without interruption. For Cullen, MacHale was now equally to be blamed for rending the seamless robe of the Church's opposition to revolution. The subsequent petitioning and cross-petitioning at Propaganda is of no concern here: but the case of Lavelle as it appeared to Cullen in the critical year of 1864 was certainly not unconnected with his determination to throw in his lot with the National Association at its foundation in December.

It seems quite evident that Cullen was determined to brand MacHale with Lavelle's infamy. When in May 1863 MacHale declared himself a subscriber to the *Irishman*, Cullen wrote to Kirby that that journal was 'a newspaper very wicked for the past' and MacHale's defence of the journal would be 'in the hope of amendment, but he ought to have waited to see some signs of penitence. The *Irishman* is the organ of St Patrick's Brotherhood.'[2] In February 1864 he pounced again. O'Mahony, Head Centre of the American Fenians, sent a monetary contribution from his Society to MacHale, who duly acknowledged the gift in the public press and sent it to charities in some depressed localities of the diocese. Dr Duggan, the Catholic Bishop of Chicago, had already condemned Fenianism. Cullen hinted darkly of civil penalties ahead. 'If the Fenians carry out their project of invading Ireland, Dr MacHale will get into trouble for his communications with them.'[3] In March the Legate was informing Kirby of a sinister association between Lavelle and MacHale, indeed, their relationship was alleged to be that of an identity of opinions,[4] and worse, that MacHale had used the expression 'benevolent Fenian Brotherhood' in the Dublin press.[5] By April, he was aspiring to force MacHale's hand; 'If he is forced to punish Lavelle for his concessions to the said society, the people will see they cannot support them.'[6] Earlier that month, MacHale had sent three autographed portraits of himself to be sold at a Chicago Fenian Fair,

---

[1] Cullen sent Gillooly, one of the bishops in MacHale's Province, the copy of a letter from Rome ordering the archbishop to deal with Lavelle, in December 1863 (Gillooly Letters).

[2] Kirby Papers, Cullen to Kirby, no. 152, 22 May 1863.

[3] *Ibid.*, Cullen to Kirby, no. 39, 19 February 1864.

[4] *Ibid.*, Cullen to Kirby, no. 57, 15 March 1864.

[5] *Ibid.*

[6] Propaganda, *Scritture* 34, Cullen to Barnabo, 8 April 1864.

organized to raise funds for the Society, and his action[1] was well publicized in the Chicago Fenian newspapers. Cullen again hinted of censures: 'Dr Duggan prohibited the fair – and yet the lion raises his voice in favour of it, even though by doing so he may compromise himself with the powers that be.'[2] And in July: 'Many are beginning to say what is true, that it is a great scandal that the Archbishop does not carry out the Pope's instructions.'[3] In June, Bishop MacEvilly of Galway had taken up the Cullen line with a complaint that the Connaught *Patriot* (a 'malicious Garibaldian rag, which is sometimes heretical, sometimes schismatical, and at all times personally offensive to the Head of the Church'), was 'the avowed organ of Dr M. [*sic*]'. He stated further, that when first started the Tuam clergy were expected to get it, and that when about a year previously the *Patriot* had begun to fail and a useless appeal made to the clergy to support it, the archbishop had sent with his subscription of £3 a letter 'declaring it to be the true organ of Catholicity in this part of the country'.[4] The Propaganda at last responded to Cullen's entreaties for a suspension of Lavelle, and in commenting upon this to Kirby his suspicions knew no bounds:

I hope Dr MacHale will after the last letter take some steps against Lavelle. It is too bad to oblige the Holy See to occupy itself so often with that unhappy priest. One word from Dr MacHale two years ago ordering Lavelle to stay in his parish, and not to act as vice-president of the St Patrick's Brotherhood, would have saved himself and that priest from great evils. I wrote several times to Dr MacHale calling his attention to the conduct of his subject – but all was in vain. His Grace appears to be infatuated about that worthless man. Perhaps also there is another motive, probably Lavelle has letters in his hands which he would publish were he suspended, and their publication might not be agreeable to Dr MacHale. . . .[5]

The letter from Propaganda instructed Cullen to call a meeting of the Irish Episcopate to agree on some decision about Lavelle. The meeting was held in Dublin in October.[6] MacHale attempted to obstruct the deliberations, but Cullen insisted that the matter was clearly in the hands of the Pope, and that interference was now impossible. He read out the letter of Propaganda, and the bishops were of one accord that

[1] For the importance attached to this by Irish Fenians, see *The Irish People*, 1, 19, 28 March, and 14 May 1864.

[2] Kirby Papers, Cullen to Kirby, no. 86, 15 April 1864.

[3] *Ibid.*, Cullen to Kirby, no. 140, 19 July 1864.

[4] *Ibid.*, MacEvilly to Kirby, no. 115, 14 June 1864.

[5] *Ibid.*, Cullen to Kirby, no. 159, 21 August 1864.

[6] Kirby Papers, Cullen to Kirby, no. 208, (?) October 1864. (A report of the meeting which was, of course, held in secret, probably at Marlborough Street.)

they should proceed to state their opinions as instructed in it. 'Dr MacHale spoke over and over, and did all he could to impede progress', Cullen reported. 'We were at the question for about 4½ hours. I made every Bishop speak.' Their Lordships 'lectured' MacHale for his defence of Lavelle, and censure was agreed upon. MacHale was evidently unmoved; 'I think he will still sink or swim by that hero', Cullen noted.[1]

Despite the censure of Lavelle's conduct by the bishops, the priests of the Tuam diocese rallied to support him. The diocesan clergy presented an address to their patriotic archbishop in December, expressing regret that the Pope had misunderstood MacHale's political opinions, and compelled him to visit with censures 'for undue interference in politics, a clergyman who has certainly done good service in extirpating heresy and proselytism'.[2] They added that all Lavelle had written on politics could not be justified, but might well be tolerated. The Address did not mention that priest's connexion with the St Patrick's Brotherhood. Cullen wrote: 'Dr Gillooly says that no priest in his diocese will sign the address. I suppose that all the priests of Tuam and Clonfert will.'[3] Lavelle's silence was not secured. Just previous to the Fenian risings of March 1867 his voice was heard praising them again. He was also the author of a long letter against Manning upholding revolutionary doctrines, which was published in a pocket edition.[4] Cullen was perhaps not surprised to find himself next; this time Lavelle's barbs issued from a series of letters in New York newspapers.[5] 'These personal attacks do not harm me very much,' he reported to Cardinal Barnabo, 'but it is really very naughty to publish bad revolutionary doctrines, and to incite resistance in some poor artisans and farmers who are in consequence exposed to certain destruction.'[6] This was mild coming from Cullen.[7]

In October 1867 he was able to associate Lavelle and MacHale again. The former was entertained at a dinner in the Dublin Rotundo, and Cullen accused MacHale: 'Probably this is a move to encourage the Fenians in this City', he wrote; 'It looks very ugly in Dr MacHale to allow such a thing.'[8]

Now it is unfortunate that reliance on O'Reilly is imperative if

[1] Kirby Papers, Cullen to Kirby, no. 208, (?) October 1864.
[2] Quoted in Cullen's letter to Kirby, *ibid.*, no. 246, 9 December 1864.
[3] *Ibid.*
[4] Manning Papers, Cullen to Manning, 8 and 13 February 1867.
[5] Propaganda, *Scritture* 35, Cullen to Barnabo, 5 March 1867.   [6] *Ibid.*
[7] Indeed its mildness may have other explanation. See p. 118.
[8] Kirby Papers, Cullen to Kirby, no. 368, 10 October 1867.

MacHale's reply to these assertions is to be found,[1] as his work is particularly thin at this point, but in one place the veil is lifted. In April 1862 an American priest had written to MacHale to discover whether the Fenian Society should be encouraged or not.[2] O'Reilly has printed the archbishop's reply.[3] He said first that he was 'not able to furnish the information looked for, having no knowledge of its constitution or its rules', but 'from a recent controversy in Ireland regarding kindred subjects' he had no hesitation in saying that such associations should be 'cautiously inquired into'. Then, significantly, he added that the St Patrick Brotherhood in Ireland disowned secret oaths or symbols, and that inquiry should be directed as to whether these existed among American Fenians. One passage seems flatly untrue – and MacHale must have known this even as early as the date of this letter:

> In this diocese we are strangers to the Fenian Brotherhood as well as to the Brotherhood of St Patrick and the Young Men's Societies.[4] And the reason is, because we deem the sacred bond of Catholicity[5] . . . to be the most effectual of all associations for rigorous and legitimate action in promoting both the spiritual interests of the Church and the civil welfare of the people. . . .[6]

He concluded by warning the people against being 'seduced by wicked and artful leaders into dangerous political courses under the mask of patriotism', and countered this by alluding indirectly to the opposite extreme of the Sadleir-Keogh 'betrayal'.[7] O'Reilly admits that his subject refused to denounce the men who had led the Fenian insurrections, on the ground that those taken were to be tried before William Keogh, and packed juries:[8] 'Dr MacHale recoiled from such inhumanity.' It is with truth that he observes 'This was another fruitful theme

[1] Bernard O'Reilly, *John MacHale*. Others have complained of the poverty of this massive work, but due to the loss of the MacHale Papers, which O'Reilly had in his possession when writing, it is almost all there is to go on. For the period here considered, O'Reilly searched the papers for evidence that MacHale hated secret societies and sought to further his favourite hope of genuine independent opposition. 'Had the constitutional principles and policy advocated through life by the Archbishop of Tuam been adopted by a unanimous clergy and a united people . . . the Ireland of the nineteenth century would have known of secret societies and unlawful associations nothing but the name.' *Op. cit.*, vol. 2, p. 526.

[2] O'Reilly, *op. cit.*, vol. 2, p. 532.   [3] *Ibid.*, p. 533, 28 April 1862.

[4] Dean O'Brien's movement – it was non-political. See M. J. Egan's *Life of Dean O'Brien*, Dublin, 1949.

[5] It will be recalled that in 1864 MacHale defined the objects of 'Catholicity' as being enunciated in the *Connaught Patriot*. See Kirby Papers, no. 115, 1864.

[6] O'Reilly, *op. cit.*, vol. 2, p. 533 (from MacHale MSS.)   [7] *Ibid.*

[8] And because 'The Fenian conspiracy was born, grew and flourished in the very dioceses where the bishops had espoused the fatal course adopted by the Delegate Apostolic, and where, in consequence, the priests were forbidden "to meddle in

of declamation against the Archbishop of the West, and of misrepresentation at the Vatican. . . .'[1]

It is only possible to conclude from all this that Cullen saw a real danger in Lavelle – all the more so because of the clear personal and ideological link he perceived between that priest and the Archbishop of Tuam. Indeed, at a time when the bulk of the clergy were supporting his proscription of Fenianism, that link must have been the major bias in his mind at the inception of the National Association of Ireland. His correspondence certainly shows him developing it with marked emphasis. The episcopal participation – not to say domination – in the Association, founded just after his triumph over Lavelle, and avowedly intended to remove the bite from the appeal of Fenianism, together with MacHale's subsequent relations with the Association,[2] supply much indirect evidence supporting that conclusion.

Now it is clear that there was not wanting a suspicion in the minds of some Protestants that the Catholic clergy were in some compromising way involved with Fenianism. They had felt the same about Ribbonism. Patrick Murphy's description of a pilgrimage to Croagh Patrick includes a scene where 'Phoenix-Men' initiated some of the young pilgrims 'into the mysteries of Ribbonism' – an initiation which included secret signs and an oath, and at which 'secret plans and purposes were intimated'. The occasion, he felt, was quite suitable, for the dogmas the novices professed to believe were that faith need not be kept with heretics, and that forfeited civil and ecclesiastical property was to be restored to its 'original owners'.[3] A pamphleteer of 1858 had been more explicit still: 'There is nothing in Ribbonism that is not Romanism; the gun of the Ribbonmen is one with the canon law of Rome.'[4] Even as late as

politics", and bishops and clergy had lost touch of the people.' O'Reilly, *op. cit.*, vol. 2, p. 545. Presumably he refers to Co. Cork especially, but Connaught had no lack of Fenian supporters.

[1] *Ibid.*, continuing in grand style, '. . . But no current of abuse and slander was ever powerful enough to make him utter a word, write a line, or perform a single act contrary to what he deemed truth and justice towards the lowliest or highest of the misguided men, led astray by too ardent a love of country and the despair begotten of ceaseless oppression.'

[2] See chap. 4.

[3] *Patrick Murphy on Popery in Ireland, or Confessionals, Abductions, Nunneries, Fenians, and Orangemen. A Narrative of Facts*, London, 1865, p. 20. This work is historically inaccurate no doubt, and there is in the above a confusion between Fenianism and Ribbonism, but it is of importance in postulating the extra-Parliamentary viewpoint of G. H. Whalley, the M.P. for Peterborough, who was the anonymous author of *Patrick Murphy*. This sort of view, though old-fashioned in the House, still had a very wide acceptance outside it.

[4] William Johnston, *Ribbonism and its Remedy: A Letter to the Earl of Derby*, Dublin, 1858, p. 3.

1871 Dr Nulty of Meath complained that a prominent landowner, George Augustus Rochfort Boyd, had said his Pastoral, while apparently condemning Ribbonism, 'did not strike him that the bent of it was against the Ribbon Society'.[1] It is clear that Protestants were often quite willing to doubt the depth of Catholic loyalty to the Crown in a general sense,[2] and to some Fenianism provided an occasion of proof. It is interesting that Johnston had traced the connexion of the Church and Ribbonism through the Confessional,[3] as it was by the use of the Confessional that Rome assured the British Government of Catholic loyalty,[4] and in the Confessional that Patrick Murphy saw the seeds of rebellion. 'But whoever thought in Ireland of intruding upon the secrecy of the Confessional?' he asked, 'Why, it is understood in every court there, that a priest is not to be interrogated against his will; and while every other subject of Her Majesty may be incarcerated for contempt of court, priests of Rome may pass with impunity.'[5] His solution was extreme: 'When it is distinctly understood that for the life of the first Protestant gentleman sacrificed by the hands of an assassin a priest will be hung, agrarian crime in Ireland will be a thing of the past, for then no absolution for murder will be granted in the Confessional.'[6] There were certainly moments when open signs of disloyalty could be trying to the hierarchy – as at a Dublin meeting of January 1860 in favour of the Temporal Power, when Alderman Reynolds was hissed when he declared that Irish Catholics were loyal to the English Crown.[7] Indeed, it was the Italian question which posed the difficulty of what was called 'double allegiance' in its most critical form, as the British Government's policy was so manifestly injurious to that of the Pope. A Catholic could accept this quite frankly: 'he holds emphatically what has been invidiously called the doctrine of a double allegiance; of obedience due to the Pope and the Catholic Episcopate on all matters within their sphere'.[8] Suspicion, of course, arose out of the definition of that sphere, and to whom belonged the right of defining it; and even in disregard of this nicety it could be asserted, as it was by Newdegate, that Ultramontane opinions supported 'a devotion to the ambition of the Holy See which would be totally incompatible with their allegiance to a

---

[1] Letter of the Most Revd. Dr Nulty, Bishop of Meath, to Lord Hartington, Chairman of the Westmeath (Outrage) Committee, 26 April 1871, p. 3. (Can be found in the Gladstone Papers, B.M.Add.MS. 44616, f. 139.)

[2] See chap. 7, p. 292.   [3] Johnston, *op. cit.*, p. 4.

[4] See F.O. 43, vol. 91A, Dispatch no. 13, 1 February 1864; quoted above.

[5] Patrick Murphy, *op. cit.*, pp. 66-7.   [6] *Ibid.*, p. 112.

[7] *Guardian*, 18 January 1860. See chap. 2.

[8] *Dublin Review*, April 1867, 'Catholic and Party Politics', p. 384.

Protestant Government';[1] or more broadly still, that 'the Ecclesiastical Organization of the Church of Rome may without doubt be asserted to be the most powerful of all other secret societies, and where it runs counter to temporal interests it is by far the most mischievous'.[2]

Some of the arguments used in Parliament by the Protestant rump tended to depict Fenianism as a plot inspired by the hierarchy. This is plainly untrue, but should be examined briefly if only by way of elimination, and for the interesting light it throws on the worst that could be thought of Catholic practice. Whalley, M.P. for Peterborough, said bluntly that Fenianism 'was entirely the result of the teaching of the doctrines and discipline of the Roman Catholic Hierarchy'.[3] Newdegate, M.P. for North Warwickshire, acknowledged the loyalty of some Irish Catholics, but pointed to the influence of a 'sect' in their Church which was dominant at Rome.[4]

It is this sect which stirred up the Polish Rebellion. It is this sect which has sworn perpetual hostility to every government that is not Catholic; and I more than suspect that this sect is at the bottom of the Fenian movement, not only in Ireland, but in New York. There are those, and I speak from information,[5] who are connected with that sect, and a particular order of the Church of Rome,[6] who have stimulated and are still stimulating this disposition to rebellion in Ireland, as they stimulated the rebellion in Poland. . . .

His coping stone was the statement that the Irish hierarchy 'are said to have lent themselves to the Fenian rebellion'.[7] In May 1869, Stapleton said he knew 'nothing more humiliating in ecclesiastical history than the connexion between the Fenians and the Roman Catholic clergy'.[8] But perhaps the most extreme assertion of all was that which had been made by Whalley in moving for a Committee on Fenianism in the middle of the Commons' second reading of the Transubstantiation Declaration Bill in May 1866:

[1] Debate on Maguire's Motion, 13 March 1868, *Hansard*, cxc, p. 1641.
[2] Mayo Papers, MS. 11217, G. Johnsone Stoney to Mayo, 15 February 1868.
[3] Second reading in the Commons of the Habeas Corpus Suspension (Ireland) Act Continuance Bill, 23 May 1867. *Hansard*, clxxxvii, p. 983.
[4] Debate on Maguire's Motion, 13 March 1868; *Hansard*, cxc, p. 1633.
[5] Which he did not intimate.   [6] His favourite Jesuits.
[7] *Hansard*, cxc, p. 1639.
[8] Debate on the Commons' second reading of the Church Bill; 31 May 1869; *Hansard*, cxcvi, p. 1017. 'In the beginning,' he continued, 'the R.C. bishops had gone so far as to refuse the Sacraments of their Church to the members of the Fenian Brotherhood on the authority of a Papal Bull, which, *ipso facto*, excommunicated all members of secret societies.' But this had not prevented the offering by priests of prayers for the three men executed at Manchester 'who had died without renouncing Fenianism'.

Evidence would be given before such a Committee to show that the move-ment was neither more nor less than a deliberate organisation, in accordance with all the antecedents of the Roman Catholic Church – to gain the objects of the Roman Catholic Hierarchy by force, if necessary, by means of a bargain with the Government, in pursuance of which this, and similar little bills, were to be given as the price of keeping the Fenians in check. . . .[1]

A further Protestant linking of the Church with Fenianism must not be overlooked, although it is almost as highly-coloured, much of its evidence based on the activities of Father Lavelle, whose importance Protestants did not exaggerate, for it has been seen that Cullen was prompted to action by that priest, but whom Protestants tended to mistake as typical of the clergy generally. These were the two letters of John Thomas Waller of Castletown, Co. Limerick, to the editor of the *Clare Freeman*.[2] 'Fenianism is thoroughly and essentially a Roman Catholic movement', he wrote, 'it originated in the teaching of the Roman Catholic priests, it was nourished and fostered by their influ-ence.'[3] When he said additionally, that 'it is in accordance with the principles of their Church' he was on less safe ground. Much of his evidence in the first *Letter* concerned speeches made at the Dublin meeting of August 1864 to raise the O'Connell Monument,[4] and were given to show what was incontestably true – that many of the clergy were steeped in disaffection to the Government. Brother John Con-cannon, O.S.F., of Mount Bellew Monastery, Co. Galway, who wrote to Michael Scanlan, a Fenian Centre, is represented as feeling urged 'to bring under the notice of the Fenian Brotherhood' the terrible distress of the country. 'Is the galling yoke of British misrule to continue always?' he asked the Fenian; 'Oh, may the God of Mercy forbid such Deordina-tion!' and he prayed for 'the independence of the bleeding country. . . .'[5] His second *Letter* is sub-titled 'Are the Roman Catholic Priests loyal?', and, like the first, it provided evidence of disaffection – this time drawn from speeches of ecclesiastics at meetings of the National Association of Ireland – and further quotation from Lavelle.

Among the arguments used in the Concurrent Endowment debate[6] about Voluntaryism there was one which contained much truth: that

---

[1] 8 May 1866, *Hansard*, CLXXXIII, p. 638. The second part of Whalley's point is not, in fact, without some degree of truth: see chap. 7, p. 320n.

[2] *Fenianism and Romanism*. The two letters were written in February 1866, and later published as a pamphlet.

[3] Waller, *op. cit.*, First Letter, p. 1. There is some truth here: see F.O. 43, vol. 96A, Dispatch no. 30, 6 April 1866; and Kirby Papers, Moriarty to Kirby, no. 93, 1 May 1864 – both noticed elsewhere in this chapter.

[4] See chap. 4, p. 136.   [5] June, 1864. Quoted in the First Letter, p. 3.
[6] See chap. 7.

the Irish secular clergy were a peasant clergy, reflecting the social and political beliefs of the class from whom they were drawn, and, being dependent on that class for voluntary contributions, were naturally reluctant to gainsay those beliefs should their superiors recommend such a course. 'This clergy . . . still carry, though ceasing to be oppressed, the spirit of social and political opposition to a point beyond what the circumstances require . . . united to the poor by so many bonds, subsisting on the charity of the wretched, they must partake of the passions that lead to crime, however stringent may be the curb they place on crime. . . .'[1] To the extent that the clergy may not have been unfavourable to Fenianism, here is the entire reason.

In reply it could be said that the clergy were not a revolutionary class. The Pope said that the Irish bishops 'were true to the existing order of things' though desiring a few changes, in education for example.[2] The Protestant Vicar-nominate of Boyle charitably declared that the loyalty of the Irish priesthood 'with the exception of a few factious priests here and there (usually soon silenced by their own bishops)' admitted of no question. Priests as a general rule never favour revolutions; 'They love the *status quo*.'[3] Lord Stanley, no less, said that the Irish clergy were not at all given to 'revolutionary views', and were men of 'exemplary personal conduct'.[4] But in the face of this, the fact remains that in this actual decade the Catholic priesthood had preached rebellion in Poland, even in Italy their loyalty to the Papal State was not always to be counted on,[5] and this is not to advert to the part played by the 'Young Ireland Priests' in the '48.[6]

[1] Jules de Lasteyrie: *French Thoughts on Irish Evils*, London, 1868 (trans. of 'L'Irelande et les causes de son misère', in *Revue des Deux Mondes*), p. 27. James Godkin said that the priests had rebellion in their blood – *Ireland and her Churches*, London, 1867, p. 2.

[2] W. E. Gladstone, 'Memorandum of a Conversation with H.H. Pope Pius IX on the 22 October, 1866, Gladstone Papers, B.M.Add.MS. 44755, f. 101.

[3] Orlando T. Dobbin, *A Plea for Tolerance toward our Fellow-subjects in Ireland who profess the Roman Catholic Religion*, London, 1866, pp. 7-8. The interesting point about exceptions was seconded by Goldwin Smith (*op. cit.*). After saying that the clergy have 'always instinctively felt that the revolutionary spirit threatens creeds as well as thrones' (Letter I, p. 5), he agrees that 'of course there are exceptions, especially among the poorer priests' (Letter 1, p. 6).

[4] Speech during the Commons' Observations on the State of Ireland, 30 April 1869, *Hansard*, CXCV, p. 2001.

[5] Odo Russell, on the testimony of a party of English tourists who had just arrived in Rome from Umbria and the Marches, wrote in his dispatch that 'Even the peasants, led by their parish priests, on whose fidelity the Vatican had placed almost implicit reliance, voted against the temporal rule of the Popes', F.O. 43, vol. 78, Dispatch no. 170, 11 November 1860.

[6] Not all of these had favoured actual rebellion. Pockets of them survived: 'The

Waller's second *Letter* had ended by asking whether the confidence being reposed in the priests was warranted 'by the simple fact that the priests think the time has not arrived when they can *successfully* rebel against England, though they pant for the day when the time shall come'.[1] This was written on 27 February 1866. Among the Mayo Papers is a letter from Thomas R. Wright to Lord Charles Clinton, written in October of the same year, which says the same thing. It is such a lucid exposition of the view suggested by Waller – that the clergy, though sympathetic to Fenian designs, were biding their time – that one passage is given here in full:

> . . . I know, my Lord, that much reliance is placed on the priests and the police, and men in power imagine that the country is safe while they are opposed to the conspiracy. I have reason to know that the priests are not opposed to it. Some of them, not from love to England, but from fear of failure, speak against it, because they think that it will fail, and that the punishment will be terrific, and that in the scuffle their cause will suffer and their people be annihilated: they are making political capital out of it at this moment, and they say if the Land Question were settled, and the Established Church abolished, Fenianism would be at an end – but they know in their hearts that nothing will satisfy the Fenians but the destruction of the landlords of this country, the separation of Ireland from England, and the total uprooting of Protestantism. Others of the priests, and they are the most numerous, are heart and hand with the movement, and if a rising once take place, they will be in the foremost ranks, and bid it God's speed.[2]

The last point did not prove true in the rising of 1867, and in the trials which followed it (as indeed in all the Fenian trials) no evidence of priestly participation was introduced. Wright also submitted that his local resident magistrate at Clonakilty (Co. Cork)[3] was 'a creature of the priests' who had constantly reported to the Government that there was no appearance of Fenianism in the district, though this was a conscious falsehood 'made to serve an end'.[4]

The talk in Parliament and elsewhere of episcopal plots was absurd, and Protestant opinion must be treated with the greatest caution in this regard. But were some of their milder allegations true? What of internal Catholic evidence that some of the clergy were not quite so opposed to Fenianism as it seemed? First let it be said that this is sparse in Ireland:

worst party we have now to deal with are the said Young Irelanders – they are numerous in Wexford – there are some in Meath – elsewhere they are not very powerful.' Kirby Papers, Cullen to Kirby, no. 3, 2 January 1867.

[1] Waller, *op. cit.*, p. 4.

[2] Mayo Papers, MSS. 11142–11145, Wright to Clinton, 26 October 1866. The letter was apparently passed on by Clinton to Naas.

[3] Named as Mr Fitzgerald.   [4] *Ibid.*

doubtless the hierarchy would seek to discount the evidence of anything contrary to the official line – and certainly would not wish to preserve anything really discreditable among their own papers.[1] Doubtless also at a local level most evidence would be Confessional, and uncommitted to paper; whilst everywhere it was true that 'a Roman Catholic priest will seldom commit himself to documentary evidence; indeed, priests will write nothing which can possibly affect themselves or the Church'.[2] It is therefore surprising to learn straight off that Moriarty confirms Thomas Wright's suspicion about the priests and the hope of rebellion:

> The clergy will preach against rebellion on account of the evils it will bring on the people, but I am sure that their almost unanimous opinion is that if there was a fair chance of success it would be lawful, nay *dulce et decorum*.[3]

In the same place he explains the grave disaffection of the priests. It is caused by religious inequality. The clergy, he says, form an 'intermediate class' between the gentry and the people, but unlike the former, are not attached to British connexion – far from it; 'You are met with clerical opposition everywhere.'[4] Manning in the same year gave tidings equally alarming. Ireland's growing Republicanism – which was American, not Red Republicanism – was spreading; 'This is invading even the clergy: and if it establishes itself in the pastors you will have lost the people.'[5]

Far from this supposed reserve of the clergy in the face of certain defeat, however, was Father Lavelle. Openly – and it has to be admitted, fearlessly – he was alone in preaching the Right to Rebel on the grounds of Catholic doctrine.[6] In February 1862, he gave a lecture at the Rotundo in Dublin entitled 'The Catholic Doctrine of the Right of Revolution',

[1] It is significant that most of the evidence concerning the Fenians in this sense is to be found outside Ireland – in Rome particularly.

[2] Murphy, *op. cit.*, p. 216.

[3] Gladstone Papers, B.M.Add.MS. 44152, f. 98, Moriarty to Monsell, 2 March 1868. Earl Russell quoted Moriarty during the Lords' debate on his motion for a Royal Commission on the Church, 24 June 1867: 'We all know that through the lower orders of the people the opinion is unquestioned that if rebellion could be successful it would be lawful.' *Hansard*, CLXXXVIII, p. 359.

[4] Gladstone Papers, B.M.Add.MS. 44152, f. 98.

[5] Gladstone Papers, B.M.Add.MS. 44249, f. 19. Manning to Gladstone, 11 February 1868.

[6] The right to rebel is a complex and diffuse doctrinal point. Traditionally it existed only in the face of tyranny, though only a minority following the sixteenth century Spanish Jesuit Suarez would have allowed the legitimacy of tyrannicide. Preachers of the right to rebel in the nineteenth century took their stand, not on the postulate that faith need not be kept with heretics, but that bad government terminated the divine permission to rule. In the face of European revolution, and because the Papal State formed an awkward example, the Papacy would never concede the right, and temporized in the case of Poland rather than face embarrassment.

the drift of which was that Ireland was so misgoverned that she had a right to revolt against the Queen, and in doing so she would have the sanction of the Church.[1] Though against the teaching of the Church of England, he argued, it was perfectly consistent with that of his own. In a letter to the *Tablet*[2] he amplified his opinion that Fenianism was in accordance with the Catholic Faith:

1. According to all Catholic Divines (Bossuet alone, perhaps, excepted), oppressive rulers may be deposed by their subjects.
2. No subjects in the world are more refinedly oppressed than the Irish people of the present day.
3. Therefore, we have the general and indisputable right to set aside our tyrannical rulers.
4. However, at this moment it would be madness or wickedness to make the attempt, because resistance would be useless.
5. Still, we have not alone the right, but we are bound by the duty, of making all preparations in our power against the day when our oppressor will herself be battling for her existence,[3] and when our efforts will be morally certain of success. Is this treason? I am then a traitor. Is this disloyal? So am I.

Early in 1868 he was at it again, this time occasioning a question in the Commons, asked by Bentinck of the Irish Attorney-General, Warren. Lavelle had spoken at Dublin in a room 'placarded with the suggestive names of MacManus, Meagher, Wolfe Tone', declaring that he would not preach a revolt against English authority just yet, though 'he laid it down on the word of a priest that resistance to authority simply so taken, was never condemned by the Catholic Church'. Tremendous cheering greeted this. So far from condemning, he went on, the Church actually bestowed her divinest blessing on people standing up against unjust authority ('Deafening cheers'). 'The dim prospect was near the dawn.' He would never furl his flag and one day 'and shortly, too' it would fly over 'a free and emancipated people'.[4] Others, whilst not going so far, were obviously in the same class. At the O'Connell Monument meeting of August 1864, in Dublin, Father Quaide was quoted in *The Times* as saying that although he had a horror of bloodshed, 'if the time came, if the circumstances arose, and if those means existed which

---

[1] *Guardian*, 12 February 1862.   [2] *Tablet*, 8 August 1863.

[3] It was a popular Fenian argument, following the traditional Irish revolutionary belief that 'England's difficulty is Ireland's opportunity', that England would be best defeated when at war with either France or America. See, for example, the *Irishman*, 24 August 1867.

[4] 16 March 1868. Mr Warren replied that his speech, which had taken place two or three months previously, though it violated the law, was not to entail its author in a prosecution since, 'regarding the circumstances', this was inexpedient: *Hansard*, cxc, p. 1674.

would make it justifiable to resist to the death the oppression of the country, he held it would be perfectly legitimate to do so'.[1] This sort of thing had very little meaning – it was born of emotion, and whilst indicating disaffection, is not to be taken at its face value.

In these matters Cullen has little to say. Occasionally a case cropped up for his attention: an Augustinian friar and an American priest in 1865,[2] Father Anderson and a Christian Brother in 1869;[3] but these can be allowed as Orlando Dobbin's 'few factious priests here and there'. Nevertheless, the Irish Government was concerned about the priests' attitude to Fenianism. A secret memorandum of February 1868 revealed that a Father Mullen, 'said to be a priest of the neighbourhood of Mullingar',[4] attended a Fenian Council held in Dublin. Writing to the Under-Secretary, Sir Thomas Larcom, the Earl of Mayo observed 'we know trouble of him before . . . he is said to be a centre of activity and influence in his district', and ordered a watch to be kept on his movements. 'Other priests', he affirmed, 'are said to have attended this meeting, and I fear from what I hear, the movement is spreading among that body.'[5] Another official source – the British agent – provides evidence from the most Catholic centre, Rome itself.

The Papal Government was familiar enough with Fenianism because of the presence of Fenian recruits in the Irish Brigade, and because of the representations of both the British Government and the Irish hierarchy. The activity of Fenian exiles for the cause in Italy was not really to be taken seriously however, as it had about it a certain cloak-and-dagger effect,[6] and, of course, the absence of any hope of a follow-

[1] Quoted from *The Times* in Waller, *op. cit.*, First Letter, p. 1.

[2] 'I have discovered that an Augustinian friar who lives here in Dublin, and a priest from America also residing here, were associated in the infamous journal, 'The Irish People' which continually contained articles against religion and against the Catholic clergy.' Propaganda, *Scritture* 35, Cullen to Barnabo, 29 September 1865.

[3] The other case was at the Dunganon Christian Brothers' establishment, where the Superior General removed a Brother Grace who had 'kept company with the Fenians, and it seems he is imbibing their ideas'. Father Anderson, who had a writ pending against the R.C. Bishop of Waterford, had been associated with Lavelle in a Fenian festival at Cork for liberated Fenian prisoners. Propaganda, *Scritture* 36, Cullen to Barnabo, 23 March 1869. (This Bro. Grace is not to be confused with the Bro. John Augustin Grace who gave evidence before the Powis Commissioners: see Report, *Parliamentary Papers*, 1870, XXVIII, vol. III, p. 375.)

[4] Mayo Papers, MS. 11188, Secret Memo. for the Irish Government, 18 February 1868.

[5] *Ibid.*, MSS. 11161-11175 (Mayo's Letter-Books); Mayo to Larcom, 18 February 1868.

[6] As, for example, in 1868 when the Anglo-Roman Carabiniere Wright overheard three Irish Fenians plotting in the Coliseum to stage demonstrations in Rome, Florence, Zürich, and Genoa: F.O. 43, vol. 102, Joseph Severn to Lord Stanley, 19 February 1868.

ing. But as the British agent, Odo Russell, pressed the danger of Fenianism in Ireland, the inquiries made by the Propaganda of the situation produced alarming evidence. The first occasion on which Rome mentioned the issue to Odo Russell was reassuring. In a Papal audience of January 1866 he was told that the principles of Fenianism were clearly condemned in the latest Encyclical against Freemasons and secret societies in general, and the Pope expressed his hope 'that the evil would be soon suppressed altogether'.[1] Yet a telegram from Clarendon at the Foreign Office seeking (in vain, as it happened) an authentication of the rumour that James Stephens was in Rome[2] caused Russell to look again at the question. On 6 April, he thanked Cardinal Antonelli for the course pursued by the Pope in regard to the Fenians, and took the opportunity of expressing regret that the Roman Catholic clergy in Ireland 'had not during the last twenty years opposed the secret societies and revolutionary organisation of part of their flocks, which had at last culminated in Fenianism'[3] – the complete dissolution of all the ties by which society is held together 'including the Roman Church and her priests', who had unhappily been 'active apostles of disaffection', teaching the people that all the misfortunes which their own 'idle Celtic habits' had brought upon them, were attributable to the Government. The people had come to believe that they would enjoy every earthly blessing if they could shake off the yoke of England. 'The people now thought they could do it, but not intending to do things by halves, they meant also to get rid of those who had preached disaffection to them, and in the end the Roman Catholic clergy now shared the dangers which threatened the very government they had so long opposed.'[4] Cardinal Antonelli could not admit the accuracy of this view, which he considered extreme. It was true that the Irish clergy had many just causes of complaint, of which 'they had spoken with that freedom which the British Government allots to all her subjects'. But the charge that the clergy had not opposed secret societies was manifestly disproved by the late Encyclical – and the Cardinal emphasized that obedience was one of the first principles the clergy had to observe. 'The Pope's condemnation of Fenianism', he assured, 'was therefore nothing new and was in accordance with the true principles of the Church.' It gave him satisfaction to think that the co-operation of the clergy might prove an assistance to the British Government in maintaining peace and order in Ireland.[5]

[1] F.O. 43, vol. 96A, Dispatch no. 7, 23 January 1866.
[2] *Ibid.*, telegram, 16 February 1866.   [3] *Ibid.*, Dispatch no. 30, 6 April 1866.
[4] *Ibid.*
[5] F.O. 43, vol. 96A, Dispatch no. 30, 6 April 1866. Clarendon wrote from the

On the morning of 4 May, Russell called again on the Cardinal Secretary of State, and intimated the more serious charge that he had received 'reliable information according to which the priests in many places in Ireland had joined the Fenian movement and were known to receive the Confessions of Fenians and to sympathise generally with them'.[1] Antonelli was annoyed and expressed his difficulty in crediting such a thing as disobedience in the face of Papal censure. 'Priests, however, were human Beings', he added, 'and consequently liable to fail occasionally . . . and to give way sometimes to political passions.' Something that looks rather like a double bluff followed. Antonelli asked Russell for names and localities, and these were refused, since the Cardinal 'could easily obtain the further details he might stand in need of through the sources of information at his disposal'. The Irish College, or the Irish priests in Rome 'who appeared to me to be wonderfully aware of Fenian proceedings in Ireland' were suggested by Russell as a likely source of confirmation of his account – which was, he would repeat, not in the least exaggerated. Furthermore, the Pope's authority was just as much at stake as was that of Her Majesty. But at this point their discussion was interrupted by the arrival of the Austrian ambassador, and Russell left to hurried assurances by the Cardinal that his 'earnest and immediate attention' would be directed to the matter.[2] He did so, and when the two men met again on 15 May, Antonelli admitted that he had been in the wrong, for after repeating their former conversation to the Pope, His Holiness had confirmed the account given by Russell with 'private letters which had just reached him from Ireland'.[3] But the evil was fortunately limited 'to one or two cases only of disobedience', which the Pope had already caused to be visited with reminders of their duties. Antonelli, returning Russell's bluff, and doubtless also safeguarding against the possibilities of civil penalties being meted out in Ireland, said that he 'could not at that moment recollect the names of those priests', but that they had swiftly been reprimanded. There the matter in Rome rested for a year and a half.

In January 1868, forty Fenians were discovered amongst Irish Catholics who had come to enlist in the Papal army, and imparting this news to Russell on the 7th, Cardinal Antonelli added 'that he had

Foreign Office approving the language which Russell had used at this interview. *Ibid.*, F.O. to Russell, 19 April 1866.

[1] F.O. vol. 96A. Dispatch no. 38, 4 May 1866.

[2] *Ibid.*, Russell's reluctance to name actual instances of Fenian priests was because at this stage he did not know any: the concluding part of the Dispatch requests Clarendon to supply him with 'a list of the priests who have joined the Fenian movement'.

[3] F.O. 43, vol. 96A, Dispatch no. 45, 15 May 1866.

ordered the Propaganda to reprimand an Irish Bishop' – whose name was not given – 'for having encouraged Fenian demonstrations in his Diocese'.[1]

In the same month, the official *Correspondance de Rome* reprinted as 'Les fénians et l'Angleterre' an article translated from *L'Osservatore Romano*, giving the Papal opinion that 'Le fénianisme est manifestement destiné par la Providence à punir l'Angleterre de ses fautes et de ses erreurs contre la justice, contre le droit, contre les gouvernements et contre les peuples'. This inference is clearly British support for European Liberalism, especially that of Italy.[2]

Also at this time the Propaganda was known to be planning a Scottish hierarchy, and Russell warned Antonelli of the risk of another 'Papal Aggression' outburst in Britain should this be carried into effect. It would upset the sincere desire among all classes to conciliate the Irish Catholic clergy, who could 'do so much to encourage or repress' Fenianism.[3] In March, during an audience, Russell was allowed to learn of the Pope's disappointment that Lord Clarendon did not approve of Cardinal Cullen, who, the Pope said, had assisted Her Majesty's Government in the suppression of Fenianism, and would continue to do so, since he had himself condemned 'the Garibaldians of England'.[4] Signs of Fenian sympathy by the clergy had not abated, however. The Under-Secretary of State, Mgr Berardi, was not surprised, to learn that many Fenians might be priests;[5] and the carabiniere Wright assured the Consul, Joseph Severn, that several Irish priests he could point out were Fenians.[6] But at this point Odo Russell left the question for two years, and of the effect on Rome of the important Irish movement following the Manchester executions, he relates nothing. Before it is attempted to bring greater coherence in the matter of the Fenians and the clergy, it will be well to look at that Irish movement, and at one

[1] *Ibid.*, vol. 101, Dispatch no. 4, 7 January 1868. These demonstrations were probably for the Manchester 'Martyrs'. The bishop was almost certainly MacHale.

[2] *Correspondance de Rome*, 11 January 1868.

[3] F.O. 43, vol. 101, Dispatch no. 14, 21 January 1868. The Scottish Hierarchy was dropped – but as much because of the difficulty of finding a prelate suitable to head it (after Errington had refused) as because of a fear of disrupting the chances for concession in Ireland.

[4] F.O. 43, vol. 101, Dispatch no. 32, 26 March 1868.

[5] 'So much the worse, for they shall have the severer punishment', he said; F.O. 43, vol. 102, Severn to Stanley, 22 January 1868.

[6] F.O. 43, vol. 102, Severn to Stanley, 19 February 1868. He seems to have meant Irish priests resident in Rome, and these could not be excused for being removed from the centre of Fenianism, and so mistaking its real intentions, for it has been seen that there were enough active Fenians in Rome itself to allow of no misunderstanding.

other episode which preceded it, and which assists comprehension of the difficulty of Cullen's position.

Just after the Fenian rising of 1867 in Kerry, the bishop of the diocese condemned the movement in a sermon at Mass in the Cathedral of Killarney on 17 February. He praised the people for not joining the Fenians whom he identified generally with European revolutionism.[1] It was reported in the press[2] that several young men were seen to leave the building while Moriarty was speaking – but this was denied by Lord Naas in Parliament, who quoted a letter from the bishop correcting misinterpretations.[3] The sermon had been the most severe censure of the Fenians yet to fall from episcopal lips. It had concluded with an affirmation that hell was not hot enough nor eternity long enough for their punishment. The phrase had immediate and wide publicity,[4] prompting anger among many in Ireland, and much respect in Parliament.[5] Dismay was to be expected: Kerry was a Fenian stronghold. So were the continued signs of popular disapproval, and 'unusual opposition' was offered to the collection of the annual dues in the diocese.[6] Additionally, the sermon started a rift in the Catholic population, which, quite as much as the Home Rule issue, caused the clerical and lay determination to prefer Mr Blennerhassett and to disobey Dr Moriarty in the famous Kerry election of 1872. When in November 1869 the lay and clerical Catholics of the diocese presented £700 to defray the expenses to be incurred by the bishop's attendance at the Vatican Council, a certain partisan spirit was involved in the subscription, and it was indeed with truth that it could be said that 'the present is not without a gratifying political significance. The Bishop had been a constant advocate of loyal and constitutional principles, and he has given determined opposition to the Revolutionary schemes of the 'National' Party. . . .'[7] And in replying to the deputation which had made the presentation, the bishop, conscious of the significance of the occasion, made direct allusion to those principles and again condemned sedition.

[1] *The Times*, 20 February 1867.   [2] *Guardian*, 20 February 1867.
[3] *Hansard*, CLXXXV, p. 1090 (27 February 1867).
[4] And was not forgotten: 'Didn't old Bishop Moriarty condemn the Fenians, and say that they were in league with French Freemasons and the Italian Carbonari; and that they were about to bring atheism to the country, and that hell wasn't hot enough nor eternity long enough to punish them?' Brendan Behan, *Borstal Boy*, 1961 ed., p. 254.
[5] In his Motion in the Lords for a Royal Commission on the Church, Earl Russell quoted the bishop, 'a prelate who, as we know, was commended by the present Chief Secretary for Ireland for his patriotic sentiments, who used all the influence of his power to oppose and defeat the schemes of the Fenians, and who, on every occasion, has professed his loyalty to the Crown . . .' 24 June 1867, *Hansard*, CLXXXVIII, p. 359.
[6] *Guardian*, 12 February 1868.   [7] *Ibid.*, 24 November 1869.

Moriarty followed up the sermon with his *Letter on Disendowment*[1] which was being printed when the Fenian risings of March occurred.[2] Its effect was supplementary:

We are not believers in the chances of rebellion. We never believed for a moment that Fenianism would succeed in revolutionizing the country. We denounced it as an American swindle. Yet Fenianism, with all its fraud and falsehood, with all its braggart cowardice, and with that hatred of religion which marked its every utterance, found sympathy and raised strange hopes in the Irish poor. And unfortunately the Irish poor means the Irish people.[3]

Yet the sermon excited anger in a surprising place. Cullen's first censure was mild:[4] 'He is very much blamed for so foolish an exaggeration' he wrote to Kirby[5] a few days after the event. Increased publicity of the sermon induced greater anger: 'Dr Moriarty's saying that eternity was not long enough and hell not hot enough for the Fenians has given great offence – I wish he could be called to an account for it. . . . Dr Moriarty was first a Young Irelander[6] now he has gone into the opposite extreme. . . .'.[7] Now this is curious, for the plain meaning of the cardinal's words is that the bishop's censure is to be desired because he has gone to the opposite extreme from Young Irelandism (a title which Cullen uses in an inexact sense), and this can only be an implied censure of unconditional loyalty, and that on a question concerning which the Catholic Church had already taken an unconditional stand, namely secret societies. *A propos* the Fenians, the cardinal in the first quarter of 1867 seems conciliatory indeed. In the same letter to Kirby he went on to endorse the sound judgment of no lesser ecclesiastic than Father Lavelle. 'In the *Connaught Ranger* of last week there is a fierce letter against him [Moriarty] signed Patrick Lavelle. The worst of the letter is that it tells a good deal of truth.'[8] It is clear that Cullen had other

---

[1] David Moriarty, *A Letter on the Disendowment of the Established Church*.

[2] *Ibid.*, p. 20 n.

[3] *Ibid.*, p. 19. Henry William Wilberforce wrote to him on 1 April 1867, congratulating him on his *Letter* – 'how exactly it was timed, just after your glorious showing up of the Fenian folly'. Monsell Papers, Box 8319.

[4] It is curious that Waller cites Moriarty for seditious opposition to the Government, (*Fenianism and Romanism*, Second Letter, p. 27), but this was written before the events being narrated here. This should still excite caution in crediting Waller's other evidences.

[5] Kirby Papers, Cullen to Kirby, no. 59, 22 February 1867.

[6] This change in Moriarty's opinions is exaggerated, and his increased bias to British connexion was not as recent as Cullen implies. At the first stirrings of the Phoenix Conspiracy in 1858, Moriarty called on A. M. Sullivan, editor of the *Nation*, to enlist the aid of that paper in warning the people from joining the society. See A. M. Sullivan, *op. cit.*, pp. 201-2.

[7] Kirby Papers, Cullen to Kirby, no. 100, 18 March 1867.

[8] *Ibid.*, Cullen to Kirby, no. 100, 18 March 1867.

reasons to be distrustful of Moriarty, who was out of step with the hierarchy on the questions of National Education and Concurrent Endowment. It must be remembered also that the Fenian risings of 4 and 5 March 1867, in Cork, Tipperary, Dublin, Louth, Limerick, Clare and Waterford, had already taken place when Cullen was denouncing Moriarty to Kirby. Thus the explanation given by Dr Corish[1] – that Cullen's annoyance stemmed from his belief that Moriarty had disturbed any chance that might otherwise have obtained of bringing calm and normality in the aftermath of what was apparently an unsuccessful (Kerry) rising – has considerable merit. The most satisfactory explanation of Cullen's ire seems to be his fear that any high condemnation of Fenianism at that critical moment, would enhance the increasing disaffection of the Catholic people from their pastors. In the Commons, Maguire made the point that recently the Roman Catholic clergy 'had stood between the people in Ireland and the counsels of violent men, thus compromising to a certain extent, their influence with their flocks'.[2] And in December, during the 'Martyrs' excitement Manning told Gladstone that 'very praise of the Catholic bishops for their firm attitude at this time, lessens the sympathy of our people, and that because it renders us suspect of the English policy of contempt and coercion'.[3] Fear of increasing this tendency was probably Cullen's motivation in this private condemnation of the Bishop of Kerry. If he felt that a critical moment had been reached, he cannot have considered it of long duration, for his Pastoral of 12 March,[4] issued before his letters to Kirby, roundly condemned Fenianism and enjoined the obligation of allegiance. The matter is obscure. Probably his letters to Kirby, intended, as were most of his letters in that series, for dissemination at Propaganda, reflected his policy differences from Moriarty, and were intended rather as personal ammunition. In the autumn of the same year he encountered a national issue of the same quality, but in a greatly enlarged form.

On the morning of the 23 November 1867, William Philip Allen, Michael Larkin, and Michael O'Brien were executed at Salford Jail.

[1] In *Reportorium Novum*, III, no. I, 1961-2, 'Cardinal Cullen and the National Association of Ireland', p. 47.

[2] In the debate on Gray's motion for a Committee on the Irish Establishment, 7 May 1867. *Hansard*, CLXXXVII, p. 176. He had warned Gladstone in 1865 about the 'dangerous feeling which exists in the country, and of which Priests and *Bishops* are now the victims, through unpopularity and loss of influence'. Gladstone Papers, B.M.Add.M.S 4405, f. 271, J. F. Maguire to Gladstone, 25 March 1865.

[3] Gladstone Papers, B.M.Add.MS. 44249, f. 14, Manning to Gladstone, 20 December 1867.

[4] Text in *Freeman*, 15 March 1867.

The story has become a familiar one, although the increased sympathy between many of the Catholic clergy in Ireland and the Fenians, a result of the effect produced by the executions, has not been explored. 'Colonel' Thomas J. Kelly, who had planned James Stephens' escape from Richmond, assumed leadership of the Fenian Party on Stephens' withdrawal to America. On 11 September 1867, he and 'Captain' Deasy were arrested for vagrancy in Manchester, but were not recognized, and it was only after a remand that 'Williams' and 'White' proved to be of more significance. Their escape was planned by Manchester Fenians[1] and at half-past three on Wednesday 18 September, as the prisoners were driven off on a further remand to the county jail at Salford, the escape was attempted under a railway arch at Bellevue, by the armed assault of some thirty men. Kelly and Deasy were carried off to safety by their rescuers, but five Fenians were captured, and a policeman in the prisoners' wagon, Sergeant Brett, was shot and killed. The five were arraigned for the murder of Brett, found guilty, and sentenced; Thomas Maguire being subsequently pardoned, and Edward Condon reprieved. Much doubt as to the propriety of the trial was ventilated at the time – much more in Ireland than in England – but there can be little real fault, for by the strict procedure of the law the conspirators of the outrage were guilty, even though, as they claimed at the trial, Brett was killed accidently when they were trying to shoot off the lock of the hatch on the prison wagon. It is true, however, that the panic which swept England during the trial produced a public opinion little calculated to bear with much sympathy for the Fenians in the dock. In Ireland all was dismay. The news of the executions of Allen, Larkin, and O'Brien was accompanied by the information that the bodies of the three men had been buried in quicklime in unconsecrated ground within the jail. 'Here was a stroke which went home; a barbed and poisoned arrow that pierced the heart of Ireland. This branding of their inanimate bodies with infamy, this denial of Christian burial in consecrated earth, wounded the most sensitive feelings of Irishmen.'[2] This was the normal process of law in the case of murderers, but Irishmen saw the trial as a political one, and the murder as patriotism. 'This is a foul judicial murder. . . . The murder of those three men will widen the breach between this country and England.'[3] As the news spread, sympathy for the Manchester 'Martyrs' deepened. 'I never knew Ireland to be more deeply moved by mingled feelings of grief and anger.'[4] Priests every-

[1] For an account of the rescue and its effects, see R. B. O'Brien, *Fifty Years of Concessions to Ireland*, vol. II, pp. 225-8.

[2] A. M. Sullivan, *op. cit.*, p. 291.   [3] Daunt, Journal, 26 November 1867.

[4] A. M. Sullivan, *op. cit.*, p. 292.

where prayed for the three dead men on the Sunday following the executions. Mock-funeral demonstrations were got up; Cork's on 1 December leading the way. In Killarney, The O'Donoghue headed the procession,[1] although the bishop, Moriarty, had addressed his clergy in a circular letter condemning masses for the dead Fenians.[2] In Parliament Lord Claud Hamilton accused The O'Donoghue of 'the countenance he had given to Fenianism' in a clear allusion to his part in the procession; and pointed to the condemnation by his own bishop – a proof that The O'Donoghue did not represent the feelings of the Catholic body.[3] That in Dublin on 8 December was led by John Martin and A. M. Sullivan. The celebrated *Declaration* of the Limerick Clergy, examined elsewhere,[4] was drawn up, as Lowe emphasized in the Commons, after the priests had celebrated a Mass in honour of the 'Martyrs'.[5]

The prayers at Mass for the three men, and even requiems held in their honour in many places, at once caused some embarrassment to Cullen and to most of the hierarchy. It was quite evident that many of the lower clergy were in full sympathy with the wave of public feeling so conducive, by implication, to the Fenian cause.[6] Cullen saw just retribution in the happenings. 'The English have given large sums to Garibaldi to assail the Pope'; he wrote, 'now as they have done to others so it is done to themselves.'[7] He let the clergy know that it was right to pray for the three men, and even to say private Masses for them, but that no public manifestation should be made to approve their conduct. 'In Tuam', he wrote sadly to Kirby, 'Dr MacHale assisted at a High Mass for them.'[8] At Cove in Co. Galway, in Lavelle's parish, when such a Mass was celebrated 'the peasantry gathered from many miles around'.[9] Affairs in the Church were getting out of hand and initiative was passing to the local clergy. Cullen, seeing breakers ahead, wrote again to Kirby:

The poor men who suffered at Manchester are made heroes and martyrs of because they belonged to that class . . . undoubtedly under the ban of the Church.

[1] The O'Donoghue was no Fenian, and had refused overtures made to him by Stephens in 1865: see Sir Charles Gavan Duffy, *My Life in Two Hemispheres*, vol. II, p. 256.
[2] *The Times*, 3 and 6 January 1868.
[3] *Hansard*, CXC, p. 1620. It would perhaps be truer to say that it was Moriarty who did not represent those feelings. See the condemnation of him in turn by the *Nation*, 7 January 1868.
[4] See chap. 8.   [5] *Hansard*, CXC, p. 1486.
[6] Though Kelly, writing to the *Irishman* on 22 October had said: 'I take occasion publicly to deny that I have declared any general movement in connection with the trials in Manchester', *Irishman*, 26 October 1867.
[7] Spalding Letters, Cullen to Spalding, December 1867.
[8] Kirby Papers, Cullen to Kirby, no. 11, 7 January 1868.
[9] *Guardian*, 1 January 1868.

They are not honoured or prayed for because they were good men or died penitent, but because they were Fenians. The great processions were got up not for prayers, but to make a display in favour of Fenianism. . . . The only object of getting up High Masses, and offices, was to promote Fenianism.[1]

But in Rome itself matters were no better, and Cardinal Antonelli had to explain to Odo Russell that about forty Fenians in the Papal Army had endeavoured – unsuccessfully, due to timely action by the Pontifical authorities – to arrange 'a Mass in favour of Allen and Larking' at Sant Andrea della Fratte.[2] At least with the Dublin clergy Cullen had some success. In the procession of 8 December there were no priests, and one informed English observer went so far as to credit the Irish clergy generally with using their influence to persuade their flocks not to join the processions.[3] Yet there were still Masses and offices in eighteen Dublin City churches[4] – a fact which the *Nation* lauded with relish. To Cullen it must have seemed like the MacManus affair all over again. If in 1861 that episode had injected the Fenians with new life and an increased membership, at least the clergy had frowned; in December 1867 the position was changed, and a disaffected clergy were near to sinking themselves heart and hand with a disaffected and increasingly Fenian-sympathized population.

Action by Cullen was, happily for him perhaps, forestalled. On the 6 December 1867 Derby had asked Mayo to require the Law Officers to consider the question 'whether a meeting convened for the purpose of expressing sympathy with men condemned to death for murder in aid of Fenians, may not be looked on as a seditious meeting, and expose the leading authors to a prosecution'.[5] On 12 December, four days after the Dublin procession, a Viceregal Proclamation was issued declaring the funeral processions illegal. Martin and Sullivan were prosecuted for their part at Dublin, but acquitted when the jury disagreed.[6] The Proclamation must have been immensely satisfying to Cullen, though he kept his silence. The Bishop of Kerry was appreciative in a note to Mayo:

In common with many others I feel grateful to the Government for having stopped these disgraceful and demoralizing processions. The people were being betrayed into a public approval of Fenianism. . . .[7]

[1] Kirby Papers, Cullen to Kirby, no. 43, 7 February 1868.
[2] F.O. 43, vol. 101, Dispatch no. 4, 7 January 1868.
[3] *Annual Register*, 1867 (Chronicle, December).
[4] Kirby Papers, Cullen to Kirby, no. 11, 7 January 1868.
[5] Mayo Papers, MS. 11202, Derby to Mayo, 6 December 1867.
[6] Sullivan was subsequently convicted and imprisoned on a seditious publications indictment.
[7] Mayo Papers, MS. 11156, Moriarty to Mayo, 14 December 1867.

The people, he continued, were submitting to the ban. They did so elsewhere, and slowly passion cooled. Cullen's worst fear of a large-scale and open clerical support for the Fenian cause was not to come to pass before his eyes, but it is no exaggeration to consider the outburst over the Manchester 'Martyrs' as a near thing. Though the hierarchy held to the denunciations expressed in their Pastorals, the attitude of the lower clergy to Fenianism had changed along with that of the mass of the Catholic population. In March, Maguire enunciated the new order of things for the benefit of the Commons: 'As a mere conspiracy, Fenianism is not very formidable; but as a principle pervading the Irish Nation, and actively influencing the minds of many who have never thought of becoming avowed Fenians, I look upon it as more serious than I can easily find words to express.'[1] And in May, Mr Serjeant Barry said that Fenian sentiment was spreading widely 'and had extended into a higher grade recently than it had reached before'.[2] 'For the first time during years,' wrote A. M. Sullivan, 'the distinction between Fenian and non-Fenian Nationalists seemed to disappear' as a result of the 'Martyrs' demonstrations, 'and the national or popular element came unitedly and in full force to the front.'[3] Aubrey de Vere wrote of the funerals – 'thousands attended them who had previously opposed Fenianism'.[4] The *Freeman* observed that it now had 'thousands of passive sympathisers among the peasantry'.[5] No matter how slight the shift of ground, this curious episode had given a distinct encouragement to the lower clergy, who had once again reposed in the unreserved admiration of their people, and seemed once more to be united with popular political aspirations. In April 1869, the *Dublin Review* hit exactly on the revised attitude of the clergy:

Fenianism has borrowed from Italy, from France, from America, certain characteristics of secret organization; and it has been able withal to present itself before the world on various striking occasions, as if it had, to a degree which Continental revolutionary movements have never professed to possess, the sympathy of strong sections of the Catholic clergy. This sympathy has certainly only been a kind of posthumous sympathy, limited to such objects as the saying of Masses for the souls of executed Fenians, or the collections of funds for the relief of the families of incarcerated Fenians. Still, it marks a difference at which we can now only glance, but which it would be idle to ignore, between the Fenian Society and the Italian Carbonarism. . . . It became possible to found the

[1] Introducing his motion for a Committee on the State of Ireland, 10 March 1868. *Hansard*, cxc, p. 1301; (he used Mr Keane, a Protestant, for his authority).

[2] Speech in the Commons' debate on the second reading of the Church Bill; *ibid.*, cxcii, p. 773.

[3] A. M. Sullivan, *op. cit.*, p. 292.

[4] Grey Papers, de Vere to Grey, 24 December 1867.

[5] *Freeman*, 24 January 1868.

Society in consequence of the disorganised and demoralized state of Irish Catholic politics; and these same conditions have rendered it difficult for the ecclesiastical authorities of the country to deal with it frankly and effectively.[1]

It is now possible to distinguish two phases in the relationship of the clergy with Fenianism: though only really one – consistent though not completely united opposition – between the hierarchy and the Society. The first, from 1858 to 1864 or 1865, saw the whole Catholic Church in roughly unanimous hostility to Fenianism, and this was the period of which A. M. Sullivan wrote, 'the quarrel eventuated in the Fenians denouncing the priests as deadly foes of Irish nationality, and the priests denouncing the Fenians as enemies of the Church; men who would overthrow the altar and destroy society'.[2] The second phase only really became apparent with the wave of public sympathy just related, but it is evident that its period of gestation can be dated much earlier, perhaps from 1865,[3] though the change was slow of realization. No doubt the withdrawal of frontal attacks by Fenians on the Church had something to do with this – they must have realized the impossibility of an anti-Church assault in the face of Irish sentiment. Attack was also more difficult – for in 1865 *The Irish People* had been suppressed by the Government. The suspension of Habeas Corpus again in Ireland in 1866 drove Fenianism into a misleading quiescence for a time, and this also helps to explain the slowness with which change was apparent, for with an absence of Fenian incident, there lacked also a yardstick with which to measure the clergy's reactions. But the growing disaffection in Ireland, so eloquently evidenced, must in some places have conveyed itself from the flock to the pastor. Here the effect of Voluntaryism and the closeness of the clergy to the people can speak for itself. Fenianism also became increasingly Irish, and proportionately less American, since despite the influx of Irish-American volunteers at the end of the American Civil War, by March 1867 the Irish were acting independently of American aid,[4] and in February 1868 it was decided at a Dublin Council meeting that Irish Fenians should stand aloof from the American organization,[5] where there were quarrels over leadership. This also

---

[1] *Dublin Review*, April 1869, 'Mr Gladstone's Irish Policy', pp. 454-5.

[2] A. M. Sullivan, *op. cit.*, p. 238. It is interesting that Sullivan agrees that this period was ending after 1864.

[3] Evidence quoted from Odo Russell's dispatches makes it clear that from the very beginning of 1866, Rome was concerned with the question of the clergy and Fenianism – due to his prompting.

[4] A. M. Sullivan, *op. cit.*, p. 274; though there were still many American military staff concealed in the country, affairs were no longer directed in co-operation between both countries.

[5] Mayo Papers, MSS. 11161-11175 (Letter-books), Mayo to Larcom, 18 February 1868.

must have helped those clergy so disposed to see the Society as a home movement close to the interests of their people. A growing awareness that waiting on governmental action was futile must have been an early stimulus. The courses recommended in the great 1859 Pastoral were all unfulfilled. In March 1866 the episcopal negotiations with the Government on university education ended after the rejection of all the bishops' demands; and the prevailing clerical depression was summed up quite simply by Cullen himself: 'The Government will do nothing good.'[1] The National Association of Ireland, founded explicitly to counter Fenianism, concentrated more on the Church than the Land questions, failed to attract much of a Parliamentary following, and so for many local clergy must have contributed to that loss of priestly faith in the Constitution to which Moriarty gave evidence.[2] Peripheral matters may have played a part. Some priests may have reacted favourably to the Fenians against the employment of Judge Keogh in the Fenian trials, in view of his (never forgiven) part in the 'betrayals' of 1854.[3] The raid by police constables on the crypt of the Catholic Cathedral at Armagh in 1866 found the Fenians and the churchmen equally outraged. The matter was raised in Parliament, but nothing could gloss over what the *Freeman* called 'the desecration of the sanctuary'.[4] The differences of MacHale and Cullen over issues related to Fenianism must also have allowed parish priests to take their pick between them, and this would have landed those opting for MacHale on the frontiers of Fenianism. It is impossible to determine the extent of Lavelle's following, but it has been seen that the diocesan priesthood of Tuam were certainly not opposed to him.[5]

This second phase surfaced with the outburst of popular sympathy evinced in Ireland by the Manchester executions, and it seems only to have declined with the decline of Fenianism itself.

Before looking at that, let it be noticed that the sympathy was sustained during the following two years in the support shown by the clergy to the general movement favouring the Fenian convicts. Cullen himself had given example here, by his intercession to the Lord-Lieutenant in May 1867 for the reprieve of Burke. Thomas Burke had been sentenced

---

[1] Kirby Papers, Cullen to Kirby, no. 19, 2 February 1866.

[2] Gladstone Papers, B.M.Add.MS. 44152, f. 98, Moriarty to Monsell, 2 March 1868.

[3] *Irishman*, 5 November 1867 – 'Judge Keogh Again': 'Judge Keogh is the very last Judge on the bench before whom any prisoner accused of Fenianism would wish to be tried. The feeling may be a very wrong one, but it unquestionably exists. . . .'

[4] *Freeman*, 17 March 1866. See also *Hansard*, CLXXXII, p. 847 (23 March 1866), and a collection of letters in the Larcom papers (MS. 7591) dealing with the Government's difficulties over the curious affair.

[5] Evidenced by their Address to MacHale of 1864.

to death for his part in the Fenian risings, and several deputations had been unable to shake either the Lord-Lieutenant or Lord Derby in their determination to see the matter through. So Cullen himself went to the Castle. His chances of success were reasonable, for at the recent Lord Mayor's Dinner the Viceroy (Abercorn) had been so delighted by the conciliatory tone of Cullen's address on charity that he had asked him to attend at the Castle as Catholic prelates had formerly done. Cullen had declined.[1] His visit over the case of Burke was not his only appearance at court,[2] but it was a rare enough occurrence to show the importance in which he held the affair. The Government found itself awkwardly placed. On one side it was assured that 'leniency in the cases of the convicts Burke and others would be mistaken . . . for weakness, and hence would tend to encourage the spirit of disloyalty which would otherwise receive a severe blow'.[3] On the other were warnings like that of Mazzini – 'Burke will be the Robert Emmet of 1867'.[4] In the end Burke got his reprieve.[5] Cullen's intervention played an undoubted part. Dr Corish raises the interesting question of why Cullen acted on that occasion but not in favour of the Manchester men,[6] and concludes that 'the circumstances were very different', as the former matter was primarily an Irish, but the latter was an English question. The circumstances were different indeed, but it is more probable that the difference lay not in the location but in the changed balance of opinion about Fenianism within the Irish Church itself. It is far more likely that Cullen did not wish to appear to lend his support to the Fenian murderers at a time when he saw the initiative in the Church's policy towards their Society passing into the enthusiastic hands of the lower clergy.

Popular sympathy for the Fenian convicts ran high in these last two years of the decade, and in many places, as at Cork on St Patrick's Day 1869,[7] contributions were levied at Mass for the benefit of the released prisoners and the families of those still in penal servitude. Manning was condemned by Newdegate in the Commons for his conduct over these collections. When approached by some Fenians, the archbishop admitted that he was identified with them in their general objects, but differed as to the means. Newdegate was triumphant: 'He left the

---

[1] Kirby Papers, Cullen to Kirby, no. 100, 18 March 1867.
[2] As Moran believed – *Catholic Encyclopedia*, English ed., New York, 1908, vol. IV, p. 565.
[3] Mayo Papers, MSS. 11146-11160, F. Petrie to Naas, 25 May 1867.
[4] Quoted in Nicholas Mansergh, *Ireland in the Age of Reform and Revolution*, London, 1940, p. 57.
[5] *The Times*, 17 and 29 May 1867.   [6] Patrick Corish, *op. cit.*, p. 49.
[7] *Guardian*, 24 March 1869.

question open, and said he would consider it: is not this aiding treason?'[1] The question of the convicts had an importance too in keeping back some Irish support for Gladstone – who was told by Maguire that the continued imprisonments were the one barrier to complete trust in him by the Irish: 'The most loyal Catholics – Bishops, Priests, Magistrates, men of wealth and station – earnestly desire their freedom.'[2]

The Amnesty Association had in fact been started as a result of the agitation of two clerical members of the National Association, Dr Spratt and Canon Pope. In May 1867, they had got up a requisition for a public meeting in Dublin which, when held, called on the Queen to extend her mercy to the Fenian convicts.[3] From that point the movement spread and increased in influence. There were some differences among its adherents as to the quality of the convicted for whom mercy was to be desired. Monsell thought that those who had committed acts of personal violence ought still to be detained, but felt also that the amnesty should be so large as to make such men the exception and not the rule.[4] Yet the position of the bishops in relation to the movement was not an easy one for Cullen to decide upon. At a great aggregate meeting for the release of the Fenians, held in Dublin on 26 January 1869 and attended by MacSwiney and Butt, letters of support were read from the Archbishop of Tuam, and from the bishops of Ross, Dromore and Elphin.[5] These three bishops had all been among Cullen's most loyal allies. Now they were found in alliance with Father Lavelle – from whom a letter was also read at the meeting. But Cullen assured Chichester Fortescue, the Chief Secretary, that no collections in aid of the Fenian prisoners made in Dublin would have his permission,[6] and Moriarty denied that a collection had been made in Killarney, adding his sorrow at finding that the same could not be said for Limerick.[7] Cullen, in fact, sent a letter to his clergy requesting them to inform their flocks that he would have no part in the Amnesty movement, pledging his support to the Government, and declaring that he would withhold permission for collections.[8] Collections were authorized in the diocese of Cloyne by Bishop Keane, however.[9] And the movement

---

[1] Commons' Committee on the Irish Church Bill, 15 April 1869; *Hansard*, cxcv, p. 867.
[2] Gladstone Papers, B.M.Add.MS. 44422, f. 40, Maguire to Gladstone, 17 September 1869.
[3] *The Times*, 10 May 1867.
[4] Carlingford Papers, CP. 3/74, Monsell to Granville, 7 January 1869.
[5] *The Times*, 27 January 1869.
[6] Carlingford Papers, CP. 3/80, Cullen to Fortescue, 14 March 1869.
[7] *Ibid.*, CP. 3/86, Moriarty to Monsell, March 1869.
[8] *The Times*, 15 March 1869.   [9] *Ibid.*, 18 March 1869.

prospered through two bodies – the original committee for the release of Fenian convicts, and the Amnesty Association.[1]

Cullen's dislike of the movement was shared by Clarendon, the Foreign Secretary, and by Spencer, the Lord-Lieutenant. The former pointed to the inconsistency of the position occupied by the clergy who supported it: 'the men whom they extol as heroes and martyrs, and whose liberation they excite the populace to demand, are Fenians.'[2] He heard from Odo Russell that the bishops, then in Rome for the Vatican Council, favoured the release of the Fenians as the only way to stop the 'wild and seditious meetings'. They admitted that the convicts were 'wild beasts', but felt that they could always be deported after release.[3] Moriarty advised that there were many supporters of Gladstone's Administration who might well defect to the Opposition over the proposed land legislation should the Government release agrarian criminals.[4] Clarendon used the bishop's opinion as proof that even his brother prelates must really believe that the Fenians 'would no more scruple in cutting the Holy Father's throat than they would the Lord-Lieutenant's if they got the chance'.[5] But the movement for their release was powerful. It received wide publicity in England during the struggle over the disqualification of O'Donovan Rossa, who was elected as member of Parliament for Tipperary at the end of 1869.[6] Some Irish members, led by MacCarthy Downing, took up the cause of all the prisoners, and in petitioning the Prime Minister, he did not hesitate to point out the backing he had been given by bishops and priests.[7] Spencer advised against release, not because he felt his throat jeopardized, but because the growing agrarian crime in Ireland was hardly a suitable indication that things had quietened down, and the proclamation of a Republic in France had stimulated a degree of popular sympathy among the Irish which showed that the Fenian programme was not yet dead.[8] But there was sympathy for the fate of the prisoners even among the Protestants in Ireland, especially since the convicts were treated in the same way and in the same gaols as common

[1] *The Times*, 24 June 1869.

[2] Clarendon Papers, c. 475 (4), f. 270, Clarendon to Odo Russell, 28 January 1870.

[3] *Ibid.*, c. 487, f. 120, Russell to Clarendon, 24 January 1870.

[4] *Ibid.*, enclosure: Moriarty to Russell, 25 January 1870, c. 487, f. 124.

[5] *Ibid.*, c. 475 (4), f. 280, Clarendon to Russell, 7 February 1870.

[6] Earl Kimberley, *A Journal of Events during the Gladstone Ministry, 1868-74*, ed. Ethel Drus, *Camden Miscellany*, vol. XXI, 1958, p. 10.

[7] Carlingford Papers, CP. 1/136, MacCarthy Downing to Gladstone, 26 October 1870.

[8] *Ibid.*, CP. 2/15, Spencer to Gladstone, 13 September 1870.

felons.[1] Consciences were stirred by the findings of an inquiry into their conditions, and in 1871 many of the prisoners were granted a conditional pardon.

Early in 1870 came the Papal condemnation of Fenianism by name: it is the last chapter in the story of the Church and the Fenians. So again the centre of activity moves to Rome, where the Irish bishops were still gathered for the Vatican Council. Now it is important to notice that the initiative came from the British Government and not from either Cullen or the Propaganda, and that the occasion was provided once more by the excesses of Lavelle. It is clear that as early as 1868, Monsell was thinking along the line that a decree from the Pope might end revolution in Ireland. 'Have you got the rules of the Fenian Association?' he wrote confidentially to Mayo. 'If you can send their rules to me, I have strong reason to believe that we shall be able to get a stronger denunciation of Fenianism, made by the highest authority in the world, that has ever yet been made.'[2] Nothing came of this. But when the proceedings in Parliament to abolish the Irish Establishment were met in Ireland itself only by a renewal of agrarian crime, informal probes of the Papacy began, to see what could be done about helping the bishops to outlaw the Fenians. The case was difficult, for the criminals were held by the Government to be abetted by large numbers of parish priests. At first only an injunction from Rome to Cullen in favour of order and condemning crime was sought. 'We could not *ask* for anything of the kind,' Clarendon told Odo Russell, 'but if you could lead the cardinal to *suggest* it, you would do the Government a service.' Gladstone particularly desired it.[3] When Russell questioned Antonelli on the activities of the clergy on 4 May 1869, the cardinal replied that the state of Ireland 'filled him with horror and distress', adding that 'the Irish character was incomprehensible'. Yet he was certain that Cullen would see that the sympathies of the lower clergy did not run away with them.[4] This was slender comfort to Clarendon, whose impatience grew. 'The fact is', he wrote with irritation, 'that the priests have with such continuous pertinacity educated their flocks in disloyalty to the Crown, and defiance of England, that they find themselves powerless now if they attempt to preach or warn in a different sense.' Cullen, who was 'thoroughly disaffected', he distrusted most of all.[5]

Clarendon followed this up in mid-December by citing the case of

[1] James Macaulay, *Ireland in 1872*, London, 1873, p. 309.
[2] Mayo Papers, MSS. 11161-11175, Monsell to Mayo, 29 January 1868.
[3] Clarendon Papers, c. 475 (4), f. 231, Clarendon to Russell, 19 April 1869.
[4] *Ibid.*, c. 487, f. 43, Russell to Clarendon, 5 May 1869.
[5] *Ibid.*, c. 475 (4), f. 237, Clarendon to Russell, 17 May 1869.

Father Ryan, the parish priest of New Inn, Cahir, who had remained uncensured by the hierarchy even though he had actually encouraged the tenants to assassinate their landlords. Odo Russell was instructed to contact Bishop Moriarty in Rome ('as he is the only one of them on whom reliance can be placed'), through the good offices of Acton. He should suggest to the bishop that orders might be given to the clergy to preach against sedition. Manning was useless, he felt, for this purpose, as he would fall immediately under the influence of the distrusted Cullen.[1] Russell followed out these instructions, establishing contact with Butler of Limerick and MacEvilly of Galway as well as with Moriarty, finding them 'well-disposed and ready to talk, but it takes time to gain their confidence'.[2] At the same time he brought up the charges Clarendon had made in an interview with Antonelli, giving as his reason that 'neither Cardinal Cullen nor Dr MacHale appear to notice the sermons and writings of Fathers Lavelle and Ryan in Ireland, and none of the Irish bishops appear to reprove them'.[3] Antonelli explained that the Pope had repeatedly condemned Fenianism, and in the recent *Bull of Censures*[4] anathematized the class of secret societies to which Fenianism belonged. Russell countered by saying that no one in Ireland would read the Bull and that unless the Pope struck at the root of the evil, Lavelle would continue writing in favour of Fenianism and Ryan would go on preaching in favour of agrarian outrages, 'and the bishops would be open to suspicion'. He requested what he called an '*ex-cathedra*' utterance, determined to be up to the minute. Antonelli finally seemed well-disposed, and promised to draw the Pope's attention to the necessity of immediate action.[5]

Russell repeated all that the cardinal had said to the Irish bishops he had contacted, and the fruit of this was a meeting of all the Irish prelates at which it was decided, as Moriarty reported, 'to appeal to the Pope for greater powers than they have hitherto enjoyed to condemn Fenianism in his name'.[6] The Government in England put on pressure. A dossier of priestly incitement to Fenianism and outrage compiled by Spencer was sent to Rome as ammunition for Russell's next assault. With it went Clarendon's instructions:

> We ask no favour of Rome, but in the interest of the Church and the credit of religion Rome ought to interfere and prevent the R.C. clergy from running

[1] Clarendon Papers, c. 475 (4), f. 257, Clarendon to Russell, 13 December 1869.
[2] *Ibid.*, c. 487, f. 108, Russell to Clarendon, 1 January 1870.
[3] F.O. 43, vol. 106, Dispatch no. 2, 2 January 1870.
[4] *Latae Sententiae*, Article 4, condemned secret societies.
[5] F.O. 43, vol. 106, Dispatch no. 2, 2 January 1870.
[6] Clarendon Papers, c. 487, f. 112, Russell to Clarendon, 7 January 1870.

political riot as they do in Ireland. The subject requires to be treated with tact and caution, but upon that I shall offer no advice as you know better than anybody how and when and with whom to handle it.[1]

Russell gained an audience with the Pope. This took place on the morning of 13 January. The Pope said it was a misfortune that the bishops were all in Rome when their presence was most needed at home to combat Fenianism – 'the enemy of Church and State'.[2] Russell explained the position exactly as he saw it, how 'among the lower clergy were many who sympathized with the Fenians, denounced their bishops, criticized their theology, condemned their pastorals, encouraged disobedience, crime, sedition, and undermined the spiritual authority of the Pope in Ireland'. If His Holiness would consult the bishops, he would find that they needed his immediate assistance in pacifying Ireland, and to 're-establish their authority over the lower clergy'. He declared also that 'a single word from His Holiness to the Irish clergy in support of episcopal authority, and stringent instructions to the bishops to suspend offending priests' would give the example of respect for authority so much required in Ireland. The clergy could always count on the support of the civil authority whenever they were willing to accept it. At last the Pope said he would again consult the Irish bishops about such measures as Russell had indicated.[3] But the Pope had in fact authorized a Decree condemning Fenianism *by name* on the previous day, although it had not yet been issued.

Cum dubitatum fuerit a nonnullis, an societas Fenianorum comprehensa censeatur inter Societates damnatas in Pontificiis Constitutionibus, Santissimus Dominus Noster Pius Divina Providentia Papa IX. exquisito prius suffragio Eminentissimorum Patrum Cardinalium contra haereticam pravitatem in universa christiana Republica Inquisitorum generalium, ne fidelium, praesertim simplicium, corda cum evidenti animae discrimine pervertantur, inhaerens decretis alias a S. Congregatione Universalis Inquisitionis in similibus editis, praesertim decreto fer. IV. die 5 Iulii 1865 decrevit ac declaravit, Societatem Americanam seu Hibernicam Fenianorum appellatam comprehendi inter societates vetitas ac damnatas in constitutionibus summorum Pontificum et praesertim in nuperrima Ejusdem Santitatis Suae edita quarto Idus Octobris 1869: Incip. *Apostolicae Sedis* qua sub num. 4.[4]

By the 21st of the month, Russell had still not learned of the Decree,[5] and accordingly carried on his diplomatic agitation. But on the 23rd,

[1] Clarendon Papers, c. 475 (4), f. 270, Clarendon to Russell, 8 January 1870.
[2] F.O. 43, vol. 106, Dispatch no. 13, 13 January 1870.
[3] *Ibid.*
[4] Dated 12 January 1870. For the full text, see *Irish Ecclesiastical Record*, new series, VI, p. 240.
[5] Clarendon Papers, c. 487, f. 118, Russell to Clarendon, 21 January 1870.

Manning and Moriarty called to let him know of it. Manning said he hoped the Government saw the importance of the Decree as it would undoubtedly expose the bishops to great 'hostility and persecution' in Ireland. Both prelates expressed a hope that the Government would refrain from exposing their prior knowledge until the publication of the Decree in Ireland, in order to avoid any further weakening of the bishops' authority. Russell reported all this, adding that 'neither of the two prelates seemed to know that I had spoken to the Pope . . . and attributed the measure in question to Cardinal Cullen's influence'.[1]

Poor Cullen had told Kirby in 1868 that he thought Odo Russell a bad theologian, and would 'not like to follow his guidance in regard to the Fenians'.[2] Now he had been instructed by the Pope to call a meeting of the bishops in Rome[3] to agree to a condemnation of the Fenians along lines suggested by Russell to Antonelli and the Pope himself. Moriarty felt that the Decree, which should bring peace to Ireland, ought to be followed by the release of the Fenian prisoners.[4]

The Decree was published in Ireland by the Vicars-General (in the absence of the bishops) at the end of February. In many places there was an uproar. Cullen and Manning had not even won the golden opinions for which they had hoped from the English press. Thomas Mozley, *The Times* correspondent in Rome, depicted their action as 'a piece of toadyism to the British Government'.[5] Mgr MacClosky, the Archbishop of New York, was known to be in despair at the effect the Decree would produce in America, and it could always be pointed out, as it was by Mozley, that the condemnation applied only to America and Ireland, whereas it was well known that almost every Irishman in London was a Fenian.[6] Odo Russell reported that:

> The American bishops are angry at the Decree because they prefer the Fenian to the Britisher – but the Irish bishops generally, with the exception of MacHale, are well-disposed and ready to write vigorous pastorals as you will see, and the more so as their Vicars-General will have to bear the brunt of the condemnation in Ireland, while they are safe in Rome – for all expect and dread the vengeance of the Fenians.[7]

Antonelli tried to persuade him that Infallibility would be the destruction

[1] F.O. 43, vol. 106, Dispatch no. 23, 23 January 1870.
[2] Kirby Papers, Cullen to Kirby, no. 43, 7 February 1868.
[3] Clarendon Papers, c. 487, f. 120, Russell to Clarendon, 24 January 1870 (reports Moriarty's account of the episcopal meeting).
[4] *Ibid.*, c. 487, f. 124 (enclosure), 26 January 1870.
[5] *The Times*, 17 February 1870; Gladstone Papers, B.M.Add.MS. 44249, f. 146, Manning to Gladstone, 20 March 1870.
[6] *The Times*, 17 February 1870.
[7] Clarendon Papers, c. 487, f. 142, Russell to Clarendon, 20 February 1870.

of Fenianism. Russell could only reply that if the Pope succeeded in extirpating revolution from Ireland, he might even think it was true.[1] He was instructed to keep Antonelli up to the mark over carrying out the Decree, otherwise, said the distrustful Clarendon, the Irish bishops would 'slip through his fingers'. He did not care about the American bishops: 'I don't believe that the Pope and Council together will make them denounce the Fenians, i.e. their flocks.'[2] But Cullen was faithful to the Papacy once again. His Lenten Pastoral in March 1870 duly condemned the Fenians, as well as Freemasonry and the French plays about to be performed at the Theatre Royal in Dublin.[3] When it was read at the Pro-Cathedral in Dublin, some of the congregation left the building in protest.[4] All those parts of it touching Fenianism were deliberately omitted in a chapel near Dublin when the priest read the Pastoral to his parishioners[5] – who were, as a result, delighted to find themselves treated to a long harangue about French immodesty. The *Irishman* printed letters, allegedly from Catholic priests, criticizing the Pope's action.[6]

The 1870 Decree was largely without effect, however, for Fenianism itself, as a serious political influence in Ireland, was already a spent force. Cullen set himself to win back the initiative partly lost to the lower clergy during the excitement over the Manchester 'Martyrs'. He still argued that the influence of the Fenians was responsible for opposition to Gladstone's Land Bill – and this was doubtless true in a broad sense. He wrote of the 'external influence' roused by the presence in Ireland of American adventurers, preparing the minds of the 'poor simple people' for resistance to authority. He blamed outrages on the unbridled licence of the press.[7] To Gladstone he hinted that a new suspension of Habeas Corpus might get rid of the adventurers, and that action might be taken to curtail the 'Fenian' press.[8] In part his hints were acted upon. The Peace Preservation (Ireland) Act,[9] passed against the background of increasing violence in Westmeath and Mayo, was welcomed by the bishops, who especially praised the provision for suppressing seditious newspapers.[10] Clarendon admitted that the section of the Act dealing with the press was the

---

[1] *Ibid.*   [2] F.O. 361/1, Clarendon to Odo Russell, 1 March 1870.
[3] *The Times*, 17 March 1870.   [4] *Ibid.*
[5] *Guardian*, 18 May 1870.   [6] *The Times*, 28 February 1870.
[7] Gladstone Papers, B.M.Add.MS. 44425, f. 243, Cullen to Gladstone, 12 March 1870.
[8] *Ibid.*
[9] 33 & 34 Vict. cap. 9. See *Hansard*, CC, pp. 81, 641, 788.
[10] Clarendon Papers, c. 487, f. 166, Russell to Clarendon, 10 April 1870.

result of Cullen's letter to Gladstone.[1] Cullen also feared that Fenianism had carved a niche which 'the infamous International Society' might fill.[2] This was not without a grain of truth. Marx himself had taken a part in exposing the prison treatment of O'Donovan Rossa and other Fenians in British gaols. Henri Rochefort and Gustave Flourens, both subsequently involved with the Paris Commune, had also campaigned for the Fenian prisoners, in the French press.[3] In 1871, Rossa expressed sympathy with the Commune and the International Workingmen's Association in a letter to the *Irishman*.[4] But Devoy held that the Fenians had no affiliations with movements outside Ireland, except for the Brotherhood and Clan na Gael in America.[5] Cullen was also alarmed by reports in the press of a union between the Home Rulers and the *International*.[6] These were unfounded.

Cullen would have to turn elsewhere for his troubles. Fenianism receded as Gladstone started 'doing something for Ireland'. With the closing of the decade there came a change in the location of the dangers to the unity of the Church. O'Keeffe was to become the new Lavelle of the seventies; but the controversy centred round his name was about ultramontanism, not Fenianism. The Home Rulers arrived in time to see the receding heels of the Fenians. There was no letting up for Cullen. But if the nature of his problems changed somewhat then, so did the method he sanctioned in 1864 to deal with the old ones. The education movement of 1859, weakened by the lack of sustained agitation, was to be allied with two other great questions. It was the bishops' reply to the challenge of the Fenians, so it is now necessary to turn to the National Association of Ireland.

---

[1] F.O. 361/1, Clarendon to Russell, 28 March 1870.

[2] Propaganda, *Scritture* 36, Cullen to Barnabo, 26 September 1871.

[3] *Devoy's Post Bag, 1871-1928*, ed. W. O'Brien and D. Ryan, Dublin, 1948, vol. 1, p. 19.

[4] *Irishman*, 24 June 1871.

[5] John Devoy, *Recollections of an Irish Rebel*, London, 1929, p. 118.

[6] Manning Papers, Cullen to Manning, 13 October 1871 (especially refers to an article in *Saunders*, 13 October).

CHAPTER FOUR

Birth of the National Association
1864-5

'A FEW days ago', wrote Cullen to the Propaganda at the beginning of 1865, 'I profited from a great meeting which was held here in Dublin to elucidate the greatest dangers to the Church and to Ireland. All the people who gathered, there were about five thousand persons present, greatly applauded my words; so much so, that one may hope that in Dublin evil influence will not make much progress.'[1] The evil of which he wrote was, of course, Fenianism; and the meeting was that which inaugurated an important constitutional movement, subsequently almost entirely forgotten.[2] The National Association of Ireland was one of the more happy results of Fenian organization, for it was established to provide an alternative, safe, and constitutional means of securing the redress of Irish grievances. Cullen and the bishops were less concerned with taking active steps against Fenianism (beyond condemnations in their Pastorals) whilst that movement seemed restricted to a lay minority. But in the course of 1864 the affair of Lavelle suggested that the Fenians could find potential material for their infection among the lower clergy.[3] The fear this consideration engendered, especially in Cullen, and the frustration following the failure of the Government to concede any of the points in the 1859 Pastoral, lead nearly all of them to plunge into the quagmire of Irish politics. It was a brave move urged on by pressing necessity, especially as it meant facing over again the sort of bitterness and disillusionment that had accompanied the dissolution of the Independent Opposition Party in 1855 – Cullen's only previous experience of political organization. But the choice lay between the risk of another charge of betrayal, or the threat which Fenianism held out to

[1] Propaganda, *Scritture* 35, Cullen to Barnabo, 6 January 1865.
[2] Its only other treatment has been in a recent essay by Dr P. J. Corish of Maynooth College, 'Cardinal Cullen and the National Association of Ireland', in *Reportorium Novum* (Dublin Diocesan journal), III, no. 1, 1962.
[3] '. . . opposition to the influence of the clergy was an overt element; and it is said that one of the principal motives which induced the Hierarchy to take so prominent a part in founding the National Association . . . was the alarming spread of Fenianism and other secret seditious Societies.' *Dublin Review*, April 1865, 'Wanted, a policy for Ireland', p. 436.

him in the possible decline of religion and triumph of 'Mazzinianism'.[1] The hierarchy resolved to take the risk. For a decade the National Association worked to inform public opinion of Irish grievances, but its primary objective when founded was to bring about a united and coherent action by the prelates and Irish Catholic politicians, in co-operation with the Liberals. Within a year of its foundation it had been split by the old dissensions of the 1850s, Cullen was ceasing to be so intimate with its counsels, and some of its members had seceded. The crucial period of the Association's history is, therefore, its first year; and as it is in this period also that Cullen's opinions were found most closely identified with it, a detailed analysis of the origins and early stages of the Association will be worth while.[2]

It was not only the affair of Father Lavelle and the dangers of Fenianism which inspired Cullen and the bishops to support the establishment of a new constitutional agitation. In the period immediately preparatory to its formation, the threat of Orangeism was seen equally to be approaching a point of precipitation. Cullen was ever conscious of it. 'The Orangemen would be very glad to get an opportunity of trampling on the people and again establishing their ascendancy', he was to write in 1866; 'I fear them far more than the Fenians.'[3] The middle of 1864 provided him with ample evidence that his fears were not entirely unfounded, in the occurrence of a series of curious but significant events, sparked off by the great O'Connell demonstration in August.

This was got up to lay the foundation stone of a national memorial to O'Connell at the lower end of Sackville Street in Dublin. The clergy were prominent on the committee which planned and staged the procession on Monday, 8 August, in which Church dignitaries participated. It is important to note, in view of subsequent events, that many Protestants took part in the proceedings.[4] Cullen, Dixon, Leahy (of Cashel), M'Nally, Gillooly, Butler, Keane, O'Hea, Dorrian and Leahy (of Dromore) represented the hierarchy in the procession, of which the *Freeman* reporter said 'We have seen many demonstrations, but none, within our memory, at all approached in grandeur the sublime spectacle of yesterday.'[5] The demonstration terminated with a grand banquet at which many of those who later helped in the organization of the

---

[1] Propaganda, *Scritture* 35, Cullen to Barnabo, 6 January 1865.

[2] It is unfortunate that the Minutes books of the National Association are lost; but newspaper reports are full, and the published papers of the Association, as well as references in correspondence, allow its history to be written with some precision.

[3] Kirby Papers, Cullen to Kirby, no. 339, 7 December 1866.

[4] *Freeman's Journal*, 9 August 1864.

[5] *Ibid.*

National Association were present, and it is reasonably likely that, even if a new constitutional movement was not mooted in concrete terms during these proceedings, or at the meetings of the committee which arranged them, at least some of the laymen who took part were persuaded that agitation in the spirit of O'Connell was now again a possibility, and some of the bishops could see that political gatherings were not, *ipso facto*, injurious to the integrity of the Church. It is in this sense that Cullen's own fears were unfulfilled, for he had written to Kirby that he would go to the procession if no row threatened, but not the banquet since 'there will probably be a row there'.[1] Others of the bishops who processed but did not dine were probably similarly disposed, and at the banquet it was left to O'Hea to explain that large numbers of the bishops would have attended 'if their duties had not called them elsewhere'.[2] The Archbishop of Cashel's speech included a justification of the attendance of those clergy who were there – they had rendered service in the struggle for Catholic Emancipation – but it is curious that even he, who so heartily threw himself into the National Association once formed, and became its most regular episcopal member, should have considered such an apology necessary. Other speeches came from men who were later members of the Association; from MacSwiney (who presided), Gray, Dillon, Maguire and Kavanagh.[3] It is significant that the title chosen for the new association when it was formed was suggestive of O'Connell's organization of 1836. He had shrunk from the use of 'National Association' at that time, preferring to leave such a title to a point in the future at which it would seem more suitable.

Reviewing the closing year of 1864, *The Times* in a leading article noticed that the O'Connell demonstration 'would have been speedily forgotten if it had not provoked an untoward reaction at Belfast' – thus summarizing the Orange Riots which it declared also 'fairly illustrates the inherent difficulty of governing Ireland'.[4] This northern reaction must be considered together with Fenianism as tearing open for the hierarchy and for those laymen who founded the Association the dangers of the situation in Ireland, and as conditioning their minds for a new movement. The O'Connell demonstration was not of itself an offensive act, although the streets of Dublin were filled with persons wearing green sashes and rosettes, but the Belfast Protestant mob could not let the triumphant rejoicings of their opponents pass off without a counter-demonstration. It was of a nature highly offensive to Catholic susceptibilities. O'Connell was burned in effigy by the Belfast mob, and the ashes

---

[1] Kirby Papers, Cullen to Kirby, no. 145, 28 July 1864.   [2] *Freeman*, 9 August 1864.
[3] *Ibid.* and *The Times*, 10 August 1864.   [4] *The Times*, 31 December 1864.

placed in a real coffin from the lid of which Roman candles were let off.[1] The Catholics retaliated by raiding the Pound District – an Orange stronghold – and hurling stones at the windows of Protestant chapels. On 10 August regular affrays started between mobs on both sides, and then disturbances were renewed with an increased intensity between the 15th and the 18th of that month.[2] The Roman Catholic bishop (Dorrian) issued an address to his flock urging them to peace, but both sides seemed beyond remonstrance. By the 29th Belfast was quiet; but in the fighting seven persons had died, and 150 were seriously injured; and for some little while small bitter outbreaks occurred in other towns. In Dundalk the Catholics burned King William in effigy and there was an anti-Orange riot in Cork City,[3] although the *Freeman* claimed that in the predominantly Catholic towns 'such exhibitions of sectarian hate as have recently disgraced Belfast are never witnessed',[4] and O'Neill Daunt expressed the same opinion in his *Journal*,[5] adding, however, that 'it is fortunate for the interests of morality that all Protestants are not Orangemen'. The Government set up a Commission to inquire into the Belfast riots, but the real lesson to be had from these events was read by the men who formed the National Association – it was that the public must be presented with a programme to alleviate the appalling divisions in Irish society which the rioting had symptomized.

The founders of the National Association must also have received an example and some encouragement from the establishment of Martin's National League at the end of January, 1864. It had long germinated in Martin's mind, and in 1861 Dillon had been joined with Moore and The O'Donoghue in contemplating the chances for such a body.[6] It is interesting that Dillon did not join the League in 1864, although it was a constitutional society founded explicitly, like the National Association at the end of the year, to counteract Fenian designs. Dillon was probably put off by its sole programme of Repeal: he had moved a long way from 1848.[7] It was left to The O'Donoghue to join Martin in running the League.[8] MacHale gave his support.[9]

---

[1] *Annual Register* 1864 (Chronicle for August): 'The Riots in Belfast'.
[2] *Ibid.*
[3] *Ibid.*
[4] *Freeman*, 7 September 1864.
[5] Daunt, Journal, 20 August 1864.
[6] P. A. Sillard, *Life and Letters of John Martin*, second ed., Dublin, 1901, p. 164.
[7] John Blake Dillon, a Younger Irelander and one of the founders of the *Nation* newspaper, had fled the country after his part in the '48 rebellion. He was now a Liberal.
[8] *Ibid.*, p. 166.
[9] *Guardian*, 17 August 1864.

How the idea of the National Association may have had its first expression is therefore rather obscure, but by the autumn it was well enough known that a new movement was about to be inaugurated. A. M. Sullivan writes of private negotiation or 'interchange of views' going on in this period between the English Liberation Society and prominent English Liberals on the one side, and between Irish ecclesiastical and lay politicians on the other 'with a view to restoring cordial relations, or effecting a new alliance, between Irish and English Liberalism'.[1] This is substantially true, and O'Neill Daunt's efforts for creating a working alliance with the Liberation Society were one of its later fruits. But the ecclesiastical element in these communications is less certain – probably Dr Leahy of Cashel was concerned.[2] Cullen can have had no part in them. Early arrangements for the projected Association were undoubtedly made by MacSwiney, Kavanagh, Dillon, Gray and Devitt, but they must have been working within terms of reference agreed upon by informal consultations with available clergy, for it was Dillon, on the same platform with Cullen, who leaked the first definite announcement of the new Association. Even before this, however, MacSwiney had started circulating a requisition for an aggregate meeting to consider Irish problems and some ways of settling them. But the National Association was in origin essentially a society organized by the laity, acting in the certain knowledge that the hierarchy would endorse their proceedings and render active support. Thus *The Times* was guilty of misplaced emphasis when it reported 'that a new Catholic association is about to be organized under the guidance of the Bishops. It is said that the only laymen admitted to their intimate councils on this subject are the present Lord Mayor, Mr MacSwiney, Alderman Dillon, and Mr Devitt, a member of the town Council.'[3]

At the first monthly meeting, on 20 January 1865, MacSwiney announced that the new Association 'had its birth in the Mansion House'.[4] On 4 November preceding, Dillon had written to let Daunt know that a new agitation for Tenant Right, Disendowment of the State Church, and Free Education 'is contemplated by all the Bishops and a large number of laymen'.[5] On 23 November Cullen presided at a

---

[1] A. M. Sullivan, *New Ireland*, p. 301.

[2] This would accord with his later agreement of opinion, about such an alliance, with Daunt; but the point will only be settled decisively when the archives of the diocese of Cashel, at Thurles, are opened for inspection.

[3] *The Times*, 9 December 1864. MacSwiney, the Lord Mayor, was a Dublin draper.

[4] *The Irish People*, 25 February 1865.

[5] Daunt, Journal, 5 November 1864.

meeting of the friends and patrons of St Brigid's Orphanage held in St Kevin's Chapel, Marlborough Street, and at which Dillon and MacSwiney spoke. Dillon denounced the Church Establishment and the evils of proselytism with very little reserve, and announced that an effort was shortly to be made 'to bring the force of the people of Ireland to bear on this question'.[1] The *Nation*, reporting the meeting, said that 'Alderman Dillon, evidently by previous arrangement, virtually launched the new association'.[2] The report said also:

A new Association has been in process of formation for some time past in Dublin; having chiefly for its object the abolition of the Established Church. All the movements have been kept private, except from some few members of the clergy and laity here; for you will be glad to learn that, so far from being opposed to legitimate political action, it is mainly to his Grace the Archbishop and his clergy that this endeavour to reconstruct an Irish Parliamentary Party for the obtaining of Irish Measures, is owing. Alderman Dillon and the Lord Mayor are the only Laymen (beside Mr Devitt) who, so far as my knowledge extends, have been admitted to any share in the confidential deliberations up to the present; but the sanction of three Archbishops, has, I believe, been obtained for the work in hand. . . .[3]

Writing on 1 December to the archbishops and bishops on the Education question through the columns of the *Freeman*, Kavanagh declared that education would form an important part of the programme of the forthcoming Association.[4] Thus through the speculation and hints in the press the National Association was announced, and public expectation mounted as the requisition for the aggregate meeting proceeded on its rounds. Many of the City Corporation signed it *en masse*;[5] so did a large number of Catholic magistrates[6], but some of the Tenant-League priests refused to do so.[7] Gillooly, the Bishop of Elphin, addressed a circular to his clergy urging them to sign with the assurance that 'the project of such an organization has been for some time under consideration'.[8] Twenty-four prelates signed the requisition, several hundred parish priests and curates, and many of the Liberal M.P.s. It stated that a meeting was requested 'for the purpose of forming an association for the following objects – a reform of the law of landlord and tenant, securing to the tenant full compensation for valuable improvements; the abolition of the Irish Church Establishment; and the perfect freedom of Education in all its branches'.[9]

[1] *The Irish People*, 26 November 1864.
[2] *Nation*, reprinted in *The Irish People*, 26 November 1864.   [3] *Ibid*.
[4] *Freeman*, 2 December 1864.   [5] *The Times*, 9 December 1864.
[6] *The Irish People*, 24 December 1864.   [7] *Ibid*.
[8] *The Times*, 9 December 1864.   [9] *Freeman*, 30 December 1864.

MacHale refused to sign the requisition when it was sent to him by Dillon, and published his reasons in an open letter in the public newspapers.[1] His letter was dated 6 December. In it he acknowledged the importance of the subjects of the proposed deliberations, but added the rider that 'though there is no question regarding the importance of the objects, it is not so with the agency proposed to carry them into serious and practical effect'. He pointed a parallel between the present zeal to found an association and that which had issued in the great Association of 1851; 'and from its fate, and the consequences that followed, one may draw a lesson in estimating what would be probably the result of the projected association'. There followed reflections on the treachery of Sadleir and Keogh. 'Are we then justified in expecting from the Association now contemplated more favourable results?' Presumably not; and he declined his signature after a fairly pointed reference to Cullen: 'I cannot enter into alliance with any who manifest no regret for the violation of former solemn engagements.'[2]

The Aggregate Meeting was arranged for Thursday 29 December, and as the time drew near so there also grew a degree of consternation: for the Protestant Vigilance Committee had threatened to set the Liffey on fire if it was held. On 28 December the Grand Orange Lodge of Ireland held a special meeting at which they condemned the proposed Popish one,[3] reminding MacSwiney that by his oath of office as Lord Mayor he was interdicted from attempting to procure the subversion of the Church Establishment – which was one of the known objects of the Aggregate Meeting. The twofold nature of the danger which necessitated the formation of the National Association was underlined at this eleventh hour by a Fenian threat too. In its leader of 24 December *The Irish People* stigmatized the proposed association as a trick by would-be place-hunters: 'There will be men on the Rotundo platform on Thursday who will haunt the back stairs at the Castle in the evening.'[4] And, more violently, a Fenian broadsheet circulated in Dublin, demanding

---

[1] *The Irish People*, 24 December 1864. (It is significant that MacHale should include this Fenian paper among those he requested to publish his letter, but it is quite clear from the Editor's note that he did.) Also in B. O'Reilly, *John MacHale*, vol. II, p. 536. On 18 December, MacHale had written to Dr Denvir, Bishop of Down and Connor: 'It is not to the objects of the Association that any objection is made. But I rather fear that, instead of sincerely and earnestly labouring for the attainment of these laudable objects, some will make use of them to forward their own selfish purposes. This fear is founded on recent experience . . . nor is there any peculiar reason to hope that a similar deception will not be again practised.' *Ibid.*, p. 541.

[2] See a brief allusion to this in D'Alton, *History of the Archdiocese of Tuam*, vol. II, pp. 77-8.

[3] A. M. Sullivan, *op. cit.*, p. 305.

[4] *The Irish People*, 24 December 1864 – 'Doctor Cullen's Agitation'.

that no toleration should be given to 'a revival of the slavish organisation' and inciting all 'Nationalists' to keep their powder dry.[1]

Accordingly, precautions to preserve the peace and order of the meeting were taken by Devitt. A hundred men with white rods were appointed to exclude undesirables from the Rotundo. They were recruited chiefly from the city coal-porters 'and other unwashed but muscular citizens'.[2] The platform was especially elevated so that it could not be easily scaled, but the new tiers so added were decently hidden beneath green baize. The meeting was called for twelve o'clock, yet long before that hour the Round Room of the Rotundo was densely packed, and so were the approaches to it. Seven prelates attended: Cullen, Leahy of Cashel, Gillooly, Kilduff, Keane, O'Hea and Nulty. MacHale did not, nor did Dixon of Armagh, but the latter had signed the requisition. MacSwiney took the chair and Dillon and Devitt were appointed secretaries to the meeting.[3]

MacSwiney expressed his delight at finding that his last public act as Lord Mayor identified him with a constitutional movement 'having for its object the complete emancipation of his creed and country from those oppressive and offensive laws which still disgraced the statute book, and weighed like a mill-stone round the necks of the people'. He stated again the objects for which their association was to be formed, although these were by now well known: first, a measure of landlord and tenant law reform, securing to the tenant full compensation for valuable improvements; secondly, the disendowment of the Irish Church Establishment, so placing all the religious denominations on a footing of complete equality, whilst at the same time protecting the vested interests of individuals; and thirdly, perfect freedom of education, securing to the parent entire control of the education of his child, and allowing the State the supervision of the public funds granted for that purpose. These proposals were received with cheers. He then concluded his few remarks by appealing to the people 'not to heed the counsels of those who would seek to turn them aside from the sure and safe paths of constitutional agitation'.

The secretaries read letters from those unable to be present, among them an important one written from Rochdale by Bright; and addressed to MacSwiney who had invited him to attend:

I am glad to see that an effort is to be made to force on some political advance in your country. The objects you aim at are good, and I hope you may succeed.

[1] A. M. Sullivan, *op. cit.*, p. 305.   [2] *The Times*, 31 December 1864.
[3] This account of the meeting is based on the very full one given in the *Freeman's Journal*, 30 December 1864.

On the question of landlord and tenant, I think you should go further, and seek to do more. What you want in Ireland is to break down the laws of primogeniture and entail, so that in course of time and by a gradual and just process, the Irish people may become the possessors of the soil of Ireland. A legal security for tenants' improvements will be of great value, but the true remedy for your great grievance is to base the laws which affect the land upon sound principles of political economy. With regard to the State Church, that is an institution so evil and so odious under the circumstances of your country that it makes one almost hopeless of Irish freedom from it, that Irishmen have borne it so long. The whole Liberal Party in Great Britain will, doubtless, join with you in demanding the removal of a wrong which has no equal in the character of a national insult in any other civilized and Christian country in the world. If the popular party in Ireland would adopt as its policy free land and free Church, and would unite with the popular party in England and Scotland for the advance of liberal measures, and especially for the promotion of an honest amendment of the representation, I am confident that great and beneficial changes might be made within a few years. We have on our side numbers and opinion, but we want a more distinct policy and a better organization, and these, I hope, to some extent, your meeting may supply.[1]

Bright's letter is important not only in the sense in which it was offered – as a gesture of support – but because it foreshadows many of Bright's own later actions, especially with reference to his schemes for Irish peasant proprietorship. He secured a clause in the 1870 Land Act which reflected the line he takes here on that subject. It is interesting also that the National Association did not really ever go further on the Land question, as he suggested it should, though they did give some support to Parliamentary reform.

After the reading of Bright's letter, Cullen rose to propose the resolution on the Church, and was greeted with prolonged applause. Cullen's speech on this occasion is undoubtedly the most coherent and emphatic enunciation of his political opinions ever made in public. It will repay a close study.[2]

He started with a frank declaration of his position: 'I do not hesitate to undertake the advocacy of the measures referred to in the requisition on which this meeting has been called, and to declare my concurrence in them.' They were measures, he said, for the welfare of the native land of which all were so rightly proud; and were so self-evidently just that they left 'no room for any discussion or for serious dissension'. They were unconnected with party politics; and, in fine, he could not see how any

[1] *Freeman*, 30 December 1864. Also printed in A. M. Sullivan, *op. cit.*, pp. 305-6. The letter was read out by Whiteside in his speech on Gray's motion on the Church, (10 April 1866). *Hansard*, third series, CLXXXII, p. 1048.

[2] *Freeman*, 30 December 1864. Also printed in Moran, *The Pastoral Letters . . . of Cardinal Cullen*, vol. II, p. 283, (xvi), 'Discourse delivered at a meeting of the citizens of Dublin'.

men of whatever party, could fail to accede to them. It is perhaps significant, in view of the later order of priorities set upon the three points of the Association, that Cullen turned first to deal with education:

> It is in order that Ireland may be able to resume her former mission among the nations of the earth that I am anxious to assist in freeing education from the trammels which prevented its growth for the past; were I not ready to take part in so patriotic and religious a work, I would be unworthy of the name of a Christian bishop. . . .

As long as the people were left in ignorance, he added, little could be expected from them; but there was something worse than ignorance, and that was 'infidel, or unchristian education'; this was so dire that it 'prepares children for a career of wickedness in this world, and blasts their prospects in the world to come'. (This was greeted with loud cheers.) He was aware that Catholics had been accused of opposing enlightenment, but the facts were contrary to such a supposition, for Catholics had built schools and universities everywhere, and had nowhere contrived to 'confine the mind and to enslave the intellect' – a phrase recalling Lord John Russell's Durham Letter. He spoke at some length on the evils of the National System of Education, urging that the time was now at hand for proper change. They should not cease their efforts until they should have a university comparable in its rights and privileges with the Protestant universities; Catholic Model and Training Schools; Catholic inspectors and the use of Catholic books and practices in National Schools; and, echoing the words of the 1859 Pastoral, 'the recognition of the rights of bishops who were sent by Christ to teach all nations'. Government control of public schools should be limited to the right of providing that the funds be properly expended; there should be no further State intervention. Whilst advocating 'the *right* of Catholic education for a Catholic people', he would not, of course, refuse the same right to the Protestants, 'but protest against any ascendancy on their part'. Prussia and Austria had given their Catholic subjects the rights he was now demanding – even in England the Catholics enjoyed the benefits of the denominational system. He closed his remarks on education by hoping that the National Association would 'bring the education question to a happy issue'.

Cullen turned next 'merely to glance' at the Land question: 'It is one surrounded with inextricable difficulties,' he said, 'but its settlement is of vital importance to the country.' The facts could speak for themselves. In the last twenty years Ireland had lost three million of her inhabitants by emigration, and this continued apace. Agriculturally, the country was still backward, and the wretched quality of the land was often the reflection of insecure tenures. With high rent, no leases, and low prices for cereals, the present poverty was likely to increase. Trade had deserted many of the country towns which as a result were falling into decay; and the manufacture of 'nearly everything necessary for domestic purposes' had almost entirely vanished, and the consequence was an enormous drain of capital away from Ireland – an evil aggravated by the remission of rents to absentee landlords. It was not for him, on that occasion, to say how this state of things came about, but it must be admitted that 'present evils are in great part to be traced back to past misrule and to the misdeeds of bygone generations'.

Their present duty, he asserted, was to use every *constitutional* means to change this state of affairs. The temptations of Orangeism and Fenianism were to be resisted:

. . . for it is foolish, it is wicked, to speak of having recourse to violence and bloodshed, or to expect anything good from illegal combinations and secret societies. Those who invoke the aid of foreign armies, those who talk of civil war, resistance to established authorities and revolutionary movements, are the worst enemies of Ireland and its ancient faith. . . . It is our duty . . . to walk in the footsteps of the great Liberator, Daniel O'Connell. (Hear, hear.) By peaceful means and by force of reason, without violating any law, he broke the chains which bound Ireland. . . .

The columns of *The Irish People* and the Orange press should be ignored, and constitutional action pursued. They should call upon the Legislature to enact that tenants should receive compensation for all valuable improvements. Referring to Bright's letter, he said that something 'more effectual' might be done after this first step; 'and free-trade, as established in regard to almost everything else, may be extended to land'. Meanwhile, they might consider whether they could not apply to Ireland laws comparable to those which at one time protected the tenants in England from extermination.[1] Cullen made other positive suggestions, on land, some of which were drastic indeed:

It might be desirable also to examine whether it would not be well to deprive all tenants-at-will, or tenants without a proper lease, of the electoral franchise, which to them is the occasion oftentimes of loss or persecution; to deprive, at the same time, the landlords of the power of distress in regard to the same tenants, and to subject the landlords to the payment of all taxes on farms let without leases. Such enactments would encourage the owners of the fee to give a fair tenure to the occupiers of the land, and would undoubtedly tend to improve the condition of the tiller of the soil. However, in every change the rights of property ought to be recognized.

1 Presumably this referred to measures in restraint of enclosure in sixteenth- and seventeenth-century England. This he thought to find comparable with Irish 'clearances'.

Whether these measures were possible or not, he added, it was clear that something must be done; for there was nothing in the nature of the Irish people which prevented their prosperity, so the way to its attainment must lie in legislative change.[1] He brought his observations on land to an end by reiterating the great difficulty of the question, and claiming that his own ideas were but thrown out for discussion.

And so he passed to a consideration of the Church question. The Establishment, he postulated, must be considered not as a religious, but a civil institution – and having said that, he lapsed into a long account of its history. In the present century, he claimed, it was the Protestant dignitaries who had demonstrated their intolerance and bigotry by their assaults on Catholic education; who had opposed Emancipation; who were the great promoters of the Ecclesiastical Titles Act. The evils of the Establishment were not intangible either, for 'the principles acted on by the establishment are still embodied in Protestant oaths'; and these oaths were the cause of the unhappy factions and parties into which Ireland was divided. Yet despite the protection of law, the Establishment was revealed as a complete failure in the 1861 census, which census showed at the same time that 'the old Catholic faith is still the religion of the land, deeply rooted in the affections of the people'. He illustrated this point with statistical evidence culled from the census report; and went on to add quotations from Sidney Smith, Lord Chancellor Campbell, Dr Johnson, and Lord Brougham, to show just how monstrous the Establishment was. He observed further that his remarks on that Church were offered free from 'theological or canonical considerations', but was careful to add also that it was 'condemned by the wickedness of its origin, which stemmed from the lust, the avarice, and the despotism of Henry VIII and his daughter'. It was intruded on Ireland by force and maintained as a perpetual obstruction to civil liberty; finally,

. . . it has been always the fruitful source of dissensions in the Country, never more so than at present, when Protestant ministers have established a sort of traffic in the souls of poor children, hoping, by educating them in error, to prop up the tottering Establishment and increase its members, and when, with the aid of gold from England, they are carrying on a most insulting system of pecuniary proselytism, a system founded on bigotry and intolerance, and distinguished by its hypocrisy and total absence of Christian Charity.

Cullen then proposed his resolution:

That the entire ecclesiastical revenues of Ireland, amounting to upwards of £580,000 annually, are appropriated to the maintenance of a Church which,

[1] This assumption of Cullen's that legislation could change virtually anything shows just how liberal and English his outlook was.

146

(according to the latest census), counts among its members only 691,872 persons – being less than one-seventh of the entire population of this island. That this singular institution was originally established, and has always been maintained, by force, in opposition to reason and justice, and in defiance of the will of the great majority of the Irish people. That we, therefore, resent it as a badge of national servitude, offensive and degrading, alike to all Irishmen, Protestant as well as Catholic.

Cullen resumed his seat amid long-continued cheering; and his motion, being seconded by Mr Ignatius Kennedy, was put and carried unanimously. Dillon had divided the anti-Church resolution into two parts, and W. J. O'Neill Daunt had now to move the second half.[1] Before he stood up, Maguire expressed his belief, in a whisper, that Cullen had left him nothing to say, to which Daunt replied (also *sotto voce*), 'He has not touched one of my points'.[2] Daunt had become a Catholic in 1831, under the influence of Father Matthew, the Apostle of Temperance. He had actively supported O'Connell and the Repeal Association, and had actually become O'Connell's secretary, but was by this time in virtual retirement at Kilcascan in Co. Cork.

Whereas Cullen's resolution was declaratory, Daunt's proposed the positive demand of Disendowment – 'as a condition without which social peace and stability, general respect for the laws, and unity of sentiment and of action for national objects, can never prevail in Ireland' – and though vested interests were to be protected, the churches on a new footing of equality were to subsist entirely on voluntary contributions.

At the outset Daunt held that what they were in fact demanding was the secularization of the ecclesiastical State revenues of Ireland, and their application to public purposes of general utility to the nation: thus putting up a claim which was to be the subject of a considerable amount of contention during subsequent phases of the Church question, both in Ireland and at Westminster. He went on to recall that in December 1857 in the Lords, Derby had deprecated the proposed intervention of the State to help the propagation of Christianity in India. But here was a terrible paradox: for Derby 'would not force a Christian State Church upon the heathens of India, but he would force a Protestant State Church upon the Catholics of Ireland'. Happily, however, the members of the Liberation Society in England were now ready to help the Irish in their struggle for freedom from religious establishments. These men were the exponents of voluntaryism, and the Irish Catholics, who had more than 300 years' trial of that principle, could proclaim its success.

[1] Daunt, Journal, 28 December 1864. [2] *Ibid.*, 29 December 1869.

The Church property of Ireland was originally given by Catholics, and the very existence of another Church holding that property 'was inevitably productive of animosity and strife'. He went further: the Establishment was only maintained to foster discord in Ireland; it was an incomparable example of the Anglo-Irish policy of *'divide et impera'*. Daunt's motion was seconded by Digby, and like all the others on that day, it was carried unanimously.

It fell now to the Archbishop of Cashel, Patrick Leahy, to propose the resolution on Land, and like Cullen's it was declaratory, merely stating the injustices. The general theoretical assumptions of Leahy's speech reflected natural law notions about the nature of property, held in a curious balance with respect for existing rights of property. 'What has anyone a better right to consider his own', he asked, 'than the labour or capital a tenant employs in improving his land?' If law will not allow such a tenant compensation 'no law of man's making can divest the act of its inherent injustice'. Yet his observations were tempered with moderation. The existing statutes were only opposed to justice 'in some respects', and *à propos* landlords and tenants 'there are good and bad upon both sides'. He was also anxious to forestall any criticism that might be prompted by the sight of Catholic bishops stirring discord by taking part in a movement favouring the tenants; to this he could only reply that they were Ministers of Justice as well as of Peace. (This caused cheering.) He was encouraged to continue:

> If we now enter into the arena of politics, it is but to ask for justice for a long-suffering people. We come forward respectfully, but firmly, to call upon the government . . . to ameliorate . . . the condition of a people whose welfare has been sadly neglected. Therefore are we here today. And let no one say we have not a right to be here. We have a perfect right. We are bishops, but so are we Irishmen . . . we claim the right to speak and to act within the laws . . . to meet and petition for the redress of what we feel to be grievances.

These words may well be taken as a general apologia by the prelates for their part both in the Aggregate Meeting, and in the new Association. Leahy followed up by stressing that it was emigration – the drain of the people from the land – that 'has brought us bishops to the determination not any longer to remain quiescent'. Now was the time to speak out. Now they had come forth from the sanctuary 'to break a silence which, perhaps, we have too long kept', and what they were going to demand was that the Government should fulfil its most sacred duty in the compact between rulers and people (*'salus populi lex suprema'*), and preserve them from desiccation. The fruit of its failure would certainly be the forfeiture of the confidence of the Irish nation.

This weighty declaration was seconded by Maguire, who applauded the return of the prelates to what he described as the battle which necessity imposed upon the nation to fight. Further: he was confident that within two years the Government would make the agrarian demands of the Irish people the subject of legislation. The Land question, he affirmed, must have pre-eminence. They could wait for the settlement of the Church and education questions, 'but the settlement of the Land question we cannot do without, and we cannot afford to wait too long'.

Dr Keane, the Bishop of Cloyne, added the positive resolution on Land, which called for a measure of tenant compensation. The Land he described as 'the question of questions', more fundamental than the insults of the Establishment or the dangers of mixed education. His remark was quoted and applauded in Sir John Gray's *Freeman* Leader.[1] Keane faced squarely the fact that the last comparable great meeting had inaugurated a movement which terminated in pledge-breaking and betrayal, and he acknowledged the difficulty in which this now placed them, accounting also as it did for the lack of 'the thrilling enthusiasm of bygone days' which had marked the announcement of their new Association. But if even only twenty good men were returned to Parliament there could be success; they could impress the ministers with the gravity of Irish questions 'by their silent looks and determined countenances', and accept no compromise from any party until a final settlement should be secured. It was a critical moment. 'The fate of the country trembles in the balance.'

After Synan[2] had seconded Keane's resolution, Dr Gillooly, the Bishop of Elphin, spoke on education. It had a twofold object – 'the knowledge and fulfilment of our natural or social duties, and the knowledge and services of God, and in this twofold sense education is called secular and religious'. But it was to the parent alone that the right of educating his child in the secular sense belonged, and to the priest in the religious, and 'in no sense whatever does education belong by right to the State'. Over the consciences of men, the State has no control (loud cheers). And in England a just and free constitution, inherited from Catholic times, allowed education to be left to pastor and parent, and so it should be in Ireland. It did, however, belong to the State to protect their educational rights and to assist in providing the means of education. A large part of Gillooly's speech was a consideration at length of the action of the Government over education in Ireland,

---

1 *Freeman*, 30 December 1864. Gray wrongly attributed the expression 'question of questions' to Leahy.

2 The Limerick J.P. and Parliamentarian; a Liberal.

pausing to demand the English system for his own country, and finally to put his resolution, which was seconded by Myles O'Reilly. It deplored State interference in education, and embodied the points he had just enumerated in his speech.

A resolution of gratitude to those working in the interests of Ireland was then proposed by Professor Sullivan of the Catholic University and John Lawlor, Mayor of Waterford, and the meeting reached, at last, that point for which all had waited for what was by then some hours.

Richard Devitt, a Dublin City Councillor, rose to propose the resolution for the foundation of the new Association. In view of the great importance that the exact text of this resolution and the rules contained therein later assumed in the history of the Association, though at the cost of some tedium, it will be given in full:[1]

That an association be now formed for the purposes indicated in the foregoing resolutions, that its title and fundamental rules shall be as follows:

1. The association shall be called the National Association of Ireland. Its objects shall be – 1st. To secure by law to occupiers of land in Ireland compensation for all valuable improvements effected by them. 2nd. The disendowment of the Irish Protestant Church, and the application of its revenues to purposes of national utility, saving all vested rights. 3rd. Freedom and equality of education for the several denominations and classes in Ireland.

2. The Association will seek to realize its objects by convincing, as far as possible, all men of their fairness and utility, by fostering a rational and intelligent patriotism, by uniting the people for mutual aid and protection, and by placing in representative positions, both imperial and local, men from whose principles and character they may anticipate a disinterested and effective support.

3. The Association will not support any political party which shall not in good faith co-operate with it in establishing by law the tenants' right to compensation, or in procuring the disendowment of the Established Church. Neither will it recommend, or assist in the election of, any candidate who will not pledge himself to act on the same principle.

4. No member of the Association shall be bound by, or answerable for, any opinion expressed, or language uttered by any other member at any of the meetings thereof.[2]

5. The affairs of the Association shall be managed by a Committee, who shall appoint such officers as they may deem necessary, shall fix the times and places for holding public meetings, and shall appoint a chairman to preside at each meeting.

6. The Committee shall also have power to make bye-laws for the regulation of their own proceedings and of the general business of the Association, provided

[1] Quoted in full in the *Freeman* report, 30 December 1864.
[2] The fourth rule may well reflect Cullen's personal insistence: if he were to join a political agitation, he would not regard it as unreasonable that safeguards should exist to avoid embarrassment to him in the event of its meetings being swayed by persons of more extreme opinions.

that such bye-laws shall accord with the general scope and objects of the Association, and that no such bye-laws shall contravene any of these fundamental rules; and provided that such bye-laws shall be passed at a meeting of not less than ten members.

7. At the public meetings of the Association it shall be the duty of the Chairman to prevent violent or illegal discussion; and if any member shall, in defiance of the decision of the Chairman, persist in such discussion, the Chairman shall thereupon have power to declare the meeting adjourned, and shall bring the conduct of the member so offending under the notice of the Committee at its next meeting.

8. The Committee, at a meeting to be especially convened for that purpose, shall have power to expunge from the list of members and associates, the name of any person so offending; and the person whose name shall be so expunged shall thereupon cease to be a member of, or an associate, as the case may be.

9. The accounts of the Association shall be audited and published at such intervals as the Committee may deem expedient – such intervals not to exceed six months.

10. Every person approving of the objects of the Association, and accepting its rules, whose admission shall be moved and seconded at a public meeting thereof, may be admitted and remain a member, on handing in to the Secretary an annual sum of one pound, and may be admitted and remain an associate on paying an annual subscription of one shilling.

11. These fundamental rules shall not be abrogated, added to, or in any respect altered, unless by the vote of the Committee passed at two successive meetings (called by special notice for the purpose) and confirmed by the Association at a public meeting thereof.[1]

Devitt also moved, as an addition to the resolution, that the following persons, having each subscribed a pound, should be the original members of the Association: Dr Cullen, Alderman MacSwiney, Dr Gillooly, Dr Dorrian, Dean O'Connell, Alderman Dillon, Alderman Plunkett, Mgr Woodlock, Dr Quinn, Canon Forde, Canon MacCabe, J. Connolly, Dr Spratt, L. Carolan, P. M. Fay, J. J. Kennedy, Canon Farrell, Canon Roche, Canon MacMahon, Professor Kavanagh, M. Matthews, Major O'Reilly, M.P., Canon Lee, J. Manley, R. Williams, D. Dolan, and M. Cassidy. Devitt's original resolution was then seconded by Canon Redmond of Arklow, and after a vote of thanks to the Chair, the meeting dispersed, the prelates receiving loud and prolonged ovations as they walked to the street. So ended the great Aggregate Meeting. It had lasted six hours'[2]

Public reaction was immediate and varied. Gray's *Freeman's Journal* gave the National Association a heartening send-off, rejoicing that the threatened Orange disruption of the meeting had not occurred. It expressed delight that Cullen had proclaimed himself a follower of the policy of O'Connell, and assured its readers that there was no doubt that

---

[1] *Freeman*, 30 December 1864.   [2] *The Times*, 31 December 1864.

the Catholic prelates who had inaugurated the new Association would take every necessary step to unite all parties in a concerted attempt to secure reforms.[1] *The Times* remarked on the absence of lay respectability and influence from the meeting, finding it strange 'that the clerical and episcopal pressure that must have been brought to bear upon the mercantile community was so generally resisted'.[2]

Commenting retrospectively, in 1869, however, whilst disapproving some of the tactics it saw the importance of the Association's existence. 'We fully admit the right of the Irish Roman Catholics, with their bishops at their head, to agitate in favour of any legislation which they deem beneficial to their temporal and spiritual interests', *The Times* then conceded. It went even further, owning that the 'formation of an Irish Association for the enlightenment of English opinion' was 'a healthy sign'.[3] *The Irish People* lamented this renewed interference of priests in politics, and Kickham writing their leader, was especially annoyed that Cullen had 'devoted part of his prosy speech to a denunciation of *The Irish People*'.[4] It took the view both now, and on subsequent occasions, that the National Association was a smoke-screen put up by Cullen to prevent the people from getting the only effective amelioration – national independence.[5] A writer to the *Irish Times*, who signed himself 'An Irish Catholic' – but probably was not – expressed disgust at a meeting so evidently packed and organized for a favourable result; it was a 'most glaring outrage on common decency', and those who sought to articulate their dissent from the speakers were assaulted by special constables.[6] A further correspondent, in the *Dublin Evening Mail*, pointed out that by the Act of 33 Geo. III, cap. 29 (Ireland) the Aggregate Meeting, and the new Association were plainly illegal.[7] Returning to review the new agitation in a more critical vein, on 2 January, *The*

---

[1] *Freeman*, 30 December 1864 (leader).

[2] *The Times*, 31 December 1864.

[3] *Ibid.*, 19 January 1869.

[4] *The Irish People*, 31 December 1864. Cullen's denunciation was in that part of his speech where he warned the people against illegal political action. (See *Freeman* report.)

[5] *Ibid.*, 21 January 1865: 'Public Delinquents.'

[6] *Irish Times*, 30 December 1864.

[7] *Dublin Evening Mail*, 31 December 1864. The Act of the Irish Parliament referred to states: 'All assemblies elected, or appointed to represent, or assuming a right to represent, the people of this realm, or any number or description of the people, under pretence of petitioning for, or in any other manner procuring an alteration of, matters established by law in Church and State, save and except the members of Parliament, and save and except the Houses of Convocation, duly summoned by the King's writ, are unlawful assemblies.' The Act was, of course, an anachronism, but it exemplified in its way the continuance on the Statute book of those penal laws about which Catholics protested.

Times noticed that Bright's hope that the Association would co-operate with the English Liberal Party was unlikely of fulfilment, for 'Irish Liberals of every shade and class kept away from the meeting'. This was not entirely true, nor was the further claim that the few lay members were 'unknown to fame'.[1] This could hardly be said of MacSwiney, Dillon and Maguire. The *Nonconformist*, speaking for English Liberal Dissenters, upheld Bright's claim, and welcomed the new Association for which they had been waiting, since 'all efforts here have been paralyzed by Irish inaction'. Therefore, 'there can be no doubt . . . as to the readiness of the vast majority of Liberals in England to lend Ireland a helping hand'. So far as the new society gave itself to the work of Disendowment, so far would it receive Liberal support.[2]

Bishop Dorrian writing to Kirby at Rome, was cautious: 'The new Association is sound at heart, but the country will be a long time in coming to believe *that*, after having been so often betrayed.' But he was sanguine enough to feel it might 'work its way and do good in time'.[3] Bishops MacEvilly and Gillooly wrote to Kirby with more hope, endorsing the objects of the Association.[4] Both these last mentioned prelates came from MacHale's Province, and it is interesting that Dorrian's caution reflected the reasons which kept MacHale out of the National Association – the risks of a repetition of the 'betrayals' of the Independent Party of the fifties.

MacHale was prevailed upon again to join, this time by Daunt, who wrote to him on 6 January. His object was explicitly to assure His Grace that there would be no repetition of 1850s, and he had reason to know that all the prelates in the new Association were completely in earnest, and were thus the guarantors that it would be conducted straightforwardly.[5] This was no comfort to MacHale, who had always regarded Cullen as an accomplice in Sadleir's and Keogh's pledge-breaking. He replied to Daunt on the 13th:

It is unnecessary to enumerate the obvious causes of the deep distrust in the recent movement. They are found in the studied forbearance from any reference to the treachery already practised on the Irish people. One of the deepest, however, is the restriction of our country's misery to subordinate grievances, without daring even to allude to the prolific parent of wrong [the Union] from which all the rest derive their noxious vitality[6].

1 *The Times*, 2 January 1865.   2 *Nonconformist*, 4 January 1865.
3 Kirby Papers, Dorrian to Kirby, no. 28, 6 February 1865.
4 *Ibid.*, MacEvilly to Kirby, no. 53, 10 March 1865; and Gillooly to Kirby, no. 80, 12 April 1865.
5 B. O'Reilly, *op. cit.*, vol. II, p. 539; and N. Costello, *John MacHale*, Dublin, 1939, p. 129.
6 B. O'Reilly, *op. cit.*, vol. II, p. 541.

There could be no reply to this, for if there was one thing the Association could never consider within its terms of reference, it was the abolition of the Union. Yet Daunt did reply; to insist that even if the dangers suggested did exist, the archbishop's adhesion to the Association would neutralize them. And again he wrote – on the 18th, with the same arguments, and emphasizing that he also hated the Union, but was not thereby prohibited from seeing good in the Association. 'Conceive the effect upon the public mind', he wrote, 'if the Archbishop of Tuam appeared in the ranks of the Movement as a leader, carrying a resolution against place-hunting'.[1] But it was useless: MacHale would not be persuaded.

Still, one more attempt was made, but this time more indirectly. Dillon approached G. H. Moore in the hope that he would prevail upon MacHale in an attempt to bring about a general reconciliation with Cullen.[2] Moore visited MacHale after discussing the possibilities with Dillon, and apparently found him amenable.[3] He was left with the impression that it would not be MacHale's fault if such an understanding was not produced, though the archbishop evidently believed that mediation was unnecessary and that the suitable method of effecting it was by direct communication between himself and Cullen. This must evidently have left the initiative with Cullen, and may well explain why, if Cullen took it up, MacHale took part in the settlement of the dispute about the Association's rules in June 1865.[4] On 15 February, Dillon acquainted Cullen with Moore's conversation with MacHale, and, writing to Moore before doing so, he said that he would be surprised if he did not find Cullen 'well-disposed to make every reasonable advance and concession to his Grace of Tuam . . . in *principle* I do not believe there is a shred of difference between the two prelates. The objects of the Association were equally approved by both . . .'.[5] He added also, for MacHale's benefit, that the Rules of the Association, and the absence of all place-hunters from its membership, afforded the guarantee of an honest and independent policy. It is interesting to find Moore acting in this way, for he was as opposed to the National Association as MacHale, and for the same reasons. He also had little regard for

[1] B. O'Reilly, *op. cit.*, vol. II, p. 543.

[2] The event is alluded to, *en passant*, in Terence de Vere White's *The Road of Excess*, Dublin, 1946, p. 234.

[3] Moore Papers, no. 728, Moore to Dillon, 13 February 1865, in which Moore felt also 'that a sincere and cordial understanding between him and the Archbishop of Dublin would be of incalculable advantage to the Irish Church'.

[4] But this must remain speculation. There is no documentary evidence to show that any such conciliatory communications took place between Cullen and MacHale.

[5] Moore Papers, no. 729, Dillon to Moore, 15 February 1865.

Cullen, although he was anxious to let Dillon know that between the two archbishops he took no sides, and entertained 'no feeling towards either of these distinguished prelates'.[1]

The first committee of the National Association on 31 December was held in the rooms at 7 Lower Ormand Quay which had been taken for the purpose. The Association at last received actual expression and planned organization.[2] The first monthly meeting was arranged for 20 February 1865. But before that, on 31 January, Cullen issued a Pastoral addressed to the secular and regular clergy of his diocese, and enclosing a copy of his address at the Aggregate Meeting with each copy of the Pastoral. He went again over the matters there discussed, with rather different elaborations of detail and illustration, but with essentially the same emphasis.[3] A section on education included a diversion on the evils of Trinity College, where so many Catholics had lost their faith, and where even those who did not actually lose it were still found to retire from the College 'without a grain of Catholic spirit'. The Pastoral again condemned the Queen's Colleges and the mixed system of National Education – the latter is especially picked on by Cullen, for the recent Syllabus of Errors, he pointed out, had three express censures of that type of education.[4] For its programme on these matters, as well as on the tenant and Church question, he unreservedly urged the clergy to give their whole support to the Association. But he warned them also to be directed by the Decrees of 1854, 'for the guidance of clergymen in reference to temporal matters', and which were approved by the Holy See. And for their certain guidance he also sent a copy of these Decrees with each Pastoral. With this proviso, the clergy are urged to action.

As so many respectable laymen have undertaken to conduct the business of the Association, and so many priests and bishops have already given in their adhesion to it, it would afford me great pleasure to see . . . your influence in obtaining associates and members. . . . In promoting this undertaking, of course none of us can be expected to neglect any of our duties, or to do anything inconsistent with the ecclesiastical state.[5]

The first meeting of the Association, held in one of the smaller rooms of the Rotundo on 20 February, was attended by less than 200 persons, a large proportion of whom were priests.[6] MacSwiney in the Chair

[1] *Ibid.*, no. 728, Moore to Dillon, 13 February 1865.
[2] Daunt, Journal, 31 December 1864.
[3] *Freeman*, 31 January 1865.
[4] He refers the clergy to the Syllabus, which was to be printed in the *Irish Ecclesiastical Record* for February 1865.
[5] *Freeman*, 31 January 1865.
[6] *The Times*, 22 February 1865; *The Irish People*, 25 February 1865.

spoke optimistically on their prospects, though he referred to his receipt of several anonymous letters threatening his life if he should endure in the present agitation. Devitt gave the roll of members as now numbering 305, with 748 associates. He read a letter from the Archbishop of Cashel intimating that forty or fifty clergymen in his diocese, whom he had chanced upon at the funeral of a priest, had joined. Dillon also spoke encouragingly, and so did Kavanagh and Woodlock.[1] It was left to Archdeacon O'Brien to go further than the declared objects of the Association, when he hinted that it constituted a Union which might be useful for many things besides those immediately in view; but it would 'carry him half-way and he would find the means of going the other half himself'. O'Brien's joining the Association[2] was considered an immense accession of strength, in some ways offsetting the failure of MacHale, for he also was an outspoken and popular 'nationalist' priest. But he was also a risk – and to some, perhaps to Cullen, an embarrassment. On 6 March a meeting of the twenty National Association clergy of his archdeaconry in Limerick, at which O'Brien presided, drew up a 'Declaration of Right and Resolve', which pledged them to work for national independence; and as *The Times* observed, 'it would appear from this that national independence is one of the objects of the Association, although it is not in the programme'.[3] The Declaration even went so far as to hint at revolutionary action if tenant claims should not be conceded,[4] and many of the speeches at the meeting had a decidedly popular character. The Rev. Mr Lynam denounced the gentry with contempt as '*shoneens*',[5] for their failure to support the National Association. Fr Synan hailed the Archdeacon as the new O'Connell – 'in fact, O'Connell was a schoolboy to him'.[6] The committee of the Association must have wished to be saved from its friends.

MacSwiney had spoken of the threats he had received. In the Dublin Corporation he was to be offered more, though rather more passively. When on 1 January he resigned the office of Lord Mayor to Barrington (a Quaker), and Sir John Gray moved a vote of thanks, it was opposed

---

[1] It was probably at this meeting that the *Address of the Committee of the National Association of Ireland to the People of Ireland* was drafted. It asked for support and outlined the objects of the Association. It was circulated as a broadsheet, a proof copy of which is in the Cullen Papers.

[2] See M. J. Egan, *Life of Dean O'Brien*, p. 109.

[3] *The Times*, 9 March 1865.

[4] *Ibid.*, see also comment by the *Express* (Dublin), 20 October 1865, on the anti-English slant of some of the speeches.

[5] The word has the same flavour as our 'nouveaux-riches' when used in a pejorative sense.

[6] *The Times*, 9 March 1865; and *The Irish People*, 11 March 1865.

by Bonsell and Norwood on the grounds of MacSwiney's lack of political impartiality, which had been seen so manifestly in his part over the O'Connell demonstration and the Aggregate Meeting.[1] After an angry exchange, Gray's motion was carried by 31 to 10 votes.[2]

The three points of the National Association were perhaps to be one of its weaknesses. The advocacy of three series of measures simultaneously involved too much diffusion of interest. The Association should have concentrated on one point only, and used it as a focus of the discontent expressed also in others. This was recommended by the *Nonconformist*,[3] which selected the Church question as the safest priority, since it was most likely to secure English Liberal support. The Liberals in the Association should have learned their lesson from the Anti-Corn Law League, much of whose effectiveness had resulted from its partiality of interest, and its bending and relating of all questions to the single one of its selection. The parallel was not lost at the time, for the *Freeman* in its editorial on the Aggregate Meeting aspired to think that the men of the new Association would 'base it on the experience of the half-dozen men who carried the repeal of the Corn Laws'.[4] Bright should have pressed the point on the Association. But in fact the National Association never did urge its three points equally at the same time – it tended to concentrate on them singly. Unhappily, the members could not always agree as to which of the points should be accorded priority, and this was to be productive of internal dissension and even of secessions from the Association. Yet there were greater causes of weakness, which will be considered later, and it must not be forgotten that Martin's National League, which had only one point (Repeal of the Union) failed, and many years before the National Association.[5] There was a real sense in which many Irishmen had lost faith in constitutional agitation. The history of the deliberations and activities of the Association therefore shows a changing emphasis in the priorities of the questions under its notice.

[1] The point was made also by Lefroy on 17 May 1865 during the Commons' second reading of the Roman Catholic Oath Bill. He held MacSwiney's oath of office to have been broken by his part in the Aggregate Meeting – *Hansard*, CLXXIX, p. 433.

[2] *The Times*, 4 January 1865. See also A. M. Sullivan, *op. cit.*, p. 312.

[3] *Nonconformist*, 4 January 1865 – 'On this side of the Channel there will be doubt as to the practical wisdom of giving to one Association a three-fold object.'

[4] *Freeman*, 30 December 1864. And at a meeting of the Association on 19 June 1865, MacSwiney said that they were inoculating public opinion as did 'Cobden and the Anti-Corn Law League'. *Freeman*, 20 June 1865.

[5] It was wound up early in 1867. See P. A. Sillard, *op. cit.*, p. 182: 'The main cause of its failure was the apathy of the people to support constitutional means of achieving their freedom while they were carried away by the idea of successful insurrection.'

During the Commons' discussion of the Church Bill in 1869, Newdegate referred to the first stirrings of the Association. 'How did Cullen begin the Movement?' he asked; 'he commenced by attacking the oath which was taken by Roman Catholic members, and which bound them not to assail the Established Church. It was thus he fulfilled the commission which he received from Rome, and the fresh instructions which the Encyclical of 1864 conveyed.'[1] Sir John Gray was entrusted by the Association with the advocacy of the oath question in the Dublin Corporation,[2] and a grand political discussion resulted at its special meeting called for the purpose on 18 February. It must almost have appeared to be the National Association sitting as a corporation in the Mansion House. Gray moved for the adoption of a petition to Parliament praying for the abolition of 'obnoxious oaths'[3] and the substitution of a uniform oath which should be simply one of allegiance to the Crown. The censure vote on MacSwiney on 1 January had brought the whole question of 'obnoxious oaths' before the Association and the Corporation. Early in the meeting the Conservatives walked out, and this left a Liberal rump led by members of the National Association, two of whose most prominent members, MacSwiney and Dillon, then spoke in favour of Gray's motion, which was passed amid cheering. Deputations to the Lord-Lieutenant and Chief Irish Secretary were then agreed upon.[4] Before that to Lord Wodehouse effected its commission, the Corporation of Limerick joined that of Dublin in demanding a petition on offensive oaths,[5] and were followed in this by the municipal bodies of Cork, Waterford, Clonmel, Kilkenny, Drogheda, Wexford, Carlow, Nenagh, Thurles, Templemore, Enniscorthy, Kingstown and Dalkey.[6] The combined deputation presented their case to Wodehouse on 20 March.[7] It was an impressive success for the National Association.

The Land question was the next to receive the Association's close attention. At the usual weekly meeting of the committee, on 28 February, a letter was read from Dr O'Connor, Bishop of Saldes (but resident in Dublin: it was a title *in partibus infidelium*).[8] He believed,

---

[1] *Hansard*, cxcv, p. 852 (15 April 1869).

[2] *The Irish People*, 1 July 1865. Kickham, the writer of the article, also asked speculatively, 'would it be too much to suppose that the Association entrusted Sir John Gray with a question with which Sir John Gray had previously entrusted the Association?'

[3] *The Times*, 20 February 1865.

[4] *Ibid.*

[5] *Ibid.*, 6 March 1865.

[6] The Sligo Corporation took the view of the Dublin Conservative opposition, that it was not constituted to discuss any but purely municipal matters – *The Times*, 22 March 1865.

[7] *The Times*, 22 March 1865.   [8] *Freeman*, 1 March 1865.

especially after a conversation with an unnamed gentleman 'of considerable influence in the country', that the Land question should form the first in priority of the three pledges to be proposed to candidates for election to Parliament:

... that nothing else would satisfy the people, and that if the land question were placed first, and made in a special manner a condition for a return to parliament, it would attach the whole country to the Association ...[1]

Dillon, he wrote, would doubtless have no objection, and he recommended the committee to decide and publish its decision throughout the country. Dillon evidently determined to bide his time, for he made no observation on the letter, and instead moved for the addition of Mr Philip Callan of Cookstown to the committee. After which the meeting adjourned.

In March the office of the Association dispatched a circular with copies of a petition on religious endowments in Ireland, and in support of Dillwyn's forthcoming motion in the Commons on the Irish Church.[2] But it was the Land question which occupied their time. On 11 April the committee sent out a list of *'Suggestions for the Amendment of the Landed Property (Ireland) Improvement Act'* of 1860,[3] with an accompanying explanatory letter signed by Dillon, as its Chairman.[4] This announced that as the Act had been referred to a Special Committee of the House of Commons, with a view to inquiring into the causes which had prevented its effective operation, it was desirable that Irish public opinion should sanction some specific proposals. This committee had been appointed in March on the motion of Maguire, now a leading member of the Association, and it was to report that the Cardwell Act was a dead letter. Another member, the Bishop of Cloyne (Keane) gave evidence.[5] Dillon now proposed that no claim for compensation should be made by any tenant unless he had been evicted by his landlord, and that the onus of proof of improvement must rest upon the tenant who, in order to sustain his claim, must prove not only that the value of the land had increased, but that any increase was due to his improvements. Against any claim for improvements, the landlord may set arrears of rent and damage caused to his land by mismanagement or bad cultivation. Proposed legislation would therefore only effect where eviction was of an *improving and solvent tenant*. And

---

[1] *Ibid.*
[2] Dillwyn's motion was introduced on 28 March 1865. See *Hansard*, CLXXVIII, p. 383. The Association's circular was dated 20 March, and signed by Dillon and Devitt as hon. secretaries. There is a copy in the Cullen Papers.
[3] 23 & 24 Vict. cap. 153.
[4] Cullen Papers.
[5] *Parliamentary Papers*, 1865 (402) XI, *Report of the Select Committee.*

by giving a lease for thirty-one years the landlord could protect himself against any claim for improvements previously made; in such cases the tenant could make no claim for improvements made during the lease unless he had duly notified the landlord of his intention to make them, and by specifying their estimated cost; and the landlord should then have the option of making the improvements himself, and charging an increased rent of 5 per cent on the cost as estimated by the tenant. Improvements made by written agreements between landlord and tenant would not be affected by the proposed legislation. These suggestions were certainly within the terms of the National Association's land policy, and Dillon emphasized this by adding that their object was 'not to transfer property from one class to another, but rather to stimulate improvement, and to furnish motives for the creation of property' from waste lands. These suggestions, he wrote, were thrown out solely to elicit an expression of opinion.[1]

These were moderate propositions, but they expressed the increasing movement of the committee towards according the Land question a greater importance; though others would have preferred something more radical and immediate. It is perhaps significant that whilst Dillon's committee were preparing their *Suggestions*, Maguire was writing to let Gladstone know that the Land question 'is regarded in Ireland by the leaders and followers of that [popular] party as *the* question of the day, *transcending all others in importance and urgency*'.[2] This feeling of urgency erupted with a first-class internal row in the Association, which, after active and auspicious beginnings ran into a dispute involving disagreement about its rules; and that in a way which questioned its very *raison d'être* and resulted in permanent division.

Meath was the spearhead for a movement to secure changes in the National Association, and its coadjutor bishop, Nulty, acting in concert with gentlemen not actually members, but who took part in the subsequent reform discussions of 28 April, was responsible for it. This is clearly seen in a letter to Cullen written by the secretary, Nicholas Whyte.[3] The clergy of Meath had been conspicuous in the tenant agitation of the 1850s, and although Nulty had attended the Aggregate Meeting he was evidently dissatisfied with the direction and methods of the Association. On 26 April he presided at a county meeting held in Navan which resolved to inaugurate a New Tenant Right Society.[4] This

[1] Cullen Papers.
[2] Gladstone Papers, B.M.Add.MS. 44405, f. 271, Maguire to Gladstone, 25 March 1865.
[3] Cullen Papers, Whyte to Cullen, 25 April 1865.
[4] *Freeman*, 4 December 1865.

did not come into existence until November, and it is reasonable to suppose that the bishop temporized in the hope of succeeding in his effort to mould the National Association to his liking. His Lenten Pastoral of March 1865 condemned Irish members of Parliament for – as Cullen related it to Kirby – 'having prostituted their influence to the Whig government'. Cullen was already wary: 'the priests are very much inclined to go astray in their denunciations', he wrote.[1] It is clear that Nulty and the Meath clergy were after a return to the Independent Opposition policy of the fifties, and so looked for the withdrawal of the Association from its professed alliance with the Liberals. They hoped to reconstruct the rules in such a way as to make them result more logically in Independent Opposition. But it was the primacy of the Land question which was their motive, for they felt it was unlikely to attain to a settlement satisfactory to Irishmen if its consideration waited on an English political party. It looked as though the question of Independent Opposition would break up the Association, and so vindicate MacHale.[2]

A special private meeting of prominent members of the Association and of those seeking changes, was called for 28 April. 'The object of the meeting will be to consider some proposals for modifying the Rules of the Association so as to render them more universally acceptable.'[3] Cullen was asked to attend.[4] But it is evident from Dillon's remarks to the members at the public meeting on 19 June that the Committee were already unfavourable to any changes, having considered the matter at some time previous to 28 April.[5] Dillon told them that 'most persons who have taken an interest in the proceedings of the Association are aware that some dissatisfaction was expressed from time to time with the Rules of the Association, on the ground that the principle of Independent Opposition was not to be found in them. . . . The majority of the Committee were of a different opinion.'[6]

The meeting on 28 April was attended by Cullen, O'Hea, Gillooly, Dorrian, Nulty, some Dublin priests, and representatives of the Meath clergy. Keane was in the Chair.[7] A lengthy discussion ended with a decision to alter Rule 3, dividing it into two new rules which were in substance those printed in a circular of 5 May, but the reason for their

[1] Kirby Papers, Cullen to Kirby, no. 52, 16 March 1865.
[2] And also the *Dublin Review*, which now supported it with vigour: see January 1866, 'The New Parliament', and April 1866, 'Signs of an Irish policy'.
[3] Cullen Papers, Whyte to Cullen, 25 April 1865.
[4] *Ibid.*
[5] *Freeman*, 20 June 1865.
[6] *Ibid.*
[7] Since this was a private meeting there was no press report, but Dorrian refers to it in his letter to Kirby. Kirby Papers, Dorrian to Kirby, no. 93, 2 May 1865.

being printed at all at that stage was caused by the ambiguity of the last sentence of the new Rule. 3. This required that before the Association could allow its Parliamentary representatives to support an administration, 'a measure of effectually securing compensation to the occupiers of the soil for all improvements by which annual letting value is increased' must become a Cabinet measure. The new rules were to be put before the whole Association as its constitution required, but unhappily someone at the meeting handed them to the press, and the result was that the *Irish Times* was able to declare that by the new rules the Association seemed to be no longer pledged to Disestablishment. This indeed was not an unfair construction of the last line of Rule 3.[1] Nor is it unfair to assume that it was a member of the Independent Opposition party who gave the information to the press, thereby hoping to secure them from further discussion and the risk of further redrafting.[2] If so, he was mistaken. The Association was forced to send round a printed circular giving the revised text of the new Rules 3 and 4, announcing the press leak as the reason.[3] The rules were to be submitted to a General Meeting in the following form:

III. This Association pledges itself to the policy of complete Parliamentary Independence, and will support no candidate for Parliament, who will not pledge himself to vote for all the objects of the Association, and further, to vote (on all questions involving confidence in the Ministry) in opposition to any government that will not adopt and make a Cabinet question a satisfactory measure of Tenant Compensation; that question being deemed by the Association as of pressing urgency.

IV. The acceptance of place or the solicitation of favours from Government is incompatible with an independent attitude towards the Ministry, and, therefore, it shall be a recommendation from this Association to all Irish constituencies to bind their representatives to accept no place and to solicit no favour from any Government which, by the foregoing rule, they shall be bound to oppose; and to bind their representatives, further, to take council with the party in the House of Commons who hold the principles of the Association, and to *act in accordance with the decision* of the majority.[4]

It will be seen at once that the new rules went to some lengths to conciliate supporters of Independent Opposition, and those also who held to the primacy of the Land question, although the retractions

[1] As Dillon admitted at the General Meeting of 19 June. *Freeman*, 20 June 1865.

[2] This assumption is made also by Corish in *Reportorium Novum*, III, no. 1, 1961–2, p. 32.

[3] Cullen Papers. The circular is dated 6 May 1865, and signed by Nicholas Whyte.

[4] *Ibid.* The words in italics were crossed out by Whyte in Cullen's copy, who inserted in their place 'adopt and act upon the policy approved by . . .'. The new Rules 3 and 4 should be compared with the original Rule 3, and the extent of the conciliation will be appreciated.

required by the *Irish Times* gaffe must have nullified the effects for the latter. But it has been suggested already that those who pressed the Land question into more radical tenant demands were also those who favoured independent opposition. Some of the opposition who had been at the meeting of the 28 April regarded the slight alteration to Rule 3 in the circular of 6 May as a breach of faith, and alleged it as the reason why they could not join the Association.[1] These were evidently the gentlemen in Nulty's party.[2]

It was at this point that Cullen drafted a memorandum on the rules changes which is of the greatest importance, for it shows his own decided opinions as to what had by then become a crucial struggle inside the Association. The paper is long, and composed with the utmost care: probably there never was more than the one copy written out by Cullen himself, and this is filled with erasures and amendments.[3] It reveals also the considerable part he took in the deliberations over the whole question.

His reason for writing, he began, was that his opinion had been asked. In the first place, he regretted that changes in the original rules had been thought necessary at all:

> On the one hand, the interchange of views which took place at the Conference on the 28th of April, between some members of the General Committee and the Gentlemen from the Country who desired explicit explanations of the Committee's views, satisfied me that there was no real difference of opinion on the subjects discussed; on the other I felt all along that any alterations even of the language in which the fundamental principles of an Association such as ours had been expressed, was calculated to expose us to the charge of instability and fickleness of purpose, while affording a seeming triumph to our enemies, to render many even of the adherents to our principles timid and apprehensive, lest perchance even the very principles and conditions upon which they had joined the Association were actually, or at any future period might be, altered.[4]

He went on to consider the reconstructed form of the rules. The revision he approved in general terms, for as the rules now stood they approached more nearly to the full sense of the Aggregate Meeting at which the original ones were drawn up 'confessedly in a hurry, in the last moments of a very protracted conference'. Particularly, he agreed that the Association's Parliamentary policy should be one of complete

---

[1] Dillon disclosed this on 19 June. See *Freeman*, 20 June 1865.
[2] Referred to in the letter of Whyte to Cullen, 25 April 1865. Cullen Papers.
[3] Cullen Papers. The memorandum is undated, but it evidently belongs to this point in the sequence of events, since Cullen states at the beginning that he has had the 'amended form of the Resolution of the 28th of April before me for some days'. This amended form would refer to the circular of 6 May.
[4] Cullen Papers.

independence from both the great English parties – at least in the present early stage of things when they hoped to influence the election of members to Parliament. Both great parties were now similarly undeserving of the Association's confidence and co-operation; one of them was traditionally and actually connected with that (Conservative Protestant) party in Ireland which was hostile to Catholicism, the other (Whig) having anti-Catholic and anti-Irish tendencies, and whose leading men had severed the tie which had previously secured the support of the Irish Catholic group in Parliament for the Liberal Party. 'The Irish representatives should therefore be perfectly indifferent to the party claims of either.' As a third party, though few in number, they would be united for Irish interests.[1] He continued:

> I am nevertheless pleased that in your amended modification, you continue to use the words parliamentary Independence, instead of *Independent Opposition*.[2] The latter phase is, I think, open to misconstruction . . . as meaning a blind and indiscriminate opposition to every measure, irrespective of its merits, emanating from a government like the present.

It is true, he added, that this interpretation had been denied by its leading exponents, both clerical and lay, but it was equally the case that the phrase had been circulated as 'the watch-word of an extreme, impracticable, and unsound line of Parliamentary action'. Similarly, he welcomed the proposed test of the sincerity of those expounding Parliamentary independence as thus defined: that of an obligatory vote against a Government hostile to the objectives of the Association, and expressly limited to questions purely of confidence in the Ministry of the day. For this limitation recognized the 'incontestable right', not to say bounden duty, of members of Parliament to exercise their trust as their own consciences indicated. As votes of pure confidence were a seldom occurrence in Parliamentary experience, the test imposed by the new rule was therefore 'reduced to an abstract question'; but even so, a test that was inadequate was preferable to one based on an unsound principle. However, the knowledge that independent support could be secured from such an Irish group to a censure motion, might well lead to the more frequent proposal of such votes.[3]

[1] Here Cullen shows himself true to his claim that the new rules were a more coherent representation of the opinions expressed at the Aggregate Meeting, for this small 'third party' was then held by Bishop Keane to be the *sine qua non* for Irish objectives: see *Freeman*, 30 December 1864.

[2] He had erased 'for the terms first proposed'; but it is clear from this, that in the first draft of the new Rule 3 at the meeting of 28 April, the Independent Opposition party had carried their demand.

[3] Cullen acknowledged that this point was made by one of the prelates at the meeting of 28 April.

Cullen turned next to consider the modified statement of the objects of the Association. These now consisted of all the original points, and not, as it had seemed from the press construction of Rule 3, only one of them. But he feared that there was room even yet for some misinterpretation; 'for as the resolution now stands, it would appear to place the Association itself, as such, in an attitude of indifference to the merits of a candidate for Parliamentary honours who might perchance adopt what a particular constituency might consider the most important two-thirds of the Association's programme'. The Association should still support men who would refuse to expel a Government from power which had the serious intention of giving 'at least a large instalment of justice to Ireland' – he meant one prepared to deal in the Church and education questions.[1] He therefore hoped that before the final adoption of the revised rules at a general meeting 'a distinct and formal declaration' might be given on this point. Also – and this was an important modification of all his preceding remarks – it should be understood that the line of action traced out in the resolution 'applies to the Association as such, and not to its members in their individual capacity'.

Respecting the new Rule 4, he was entirely in agreement that nothing could be more reprehensible than the conduct of a man who entered Parliament pledged to a course of action which he did not then pursue; who bartered that confidence reposed in him by the people for place and gain. Yet a distinction existed, recognized by the Conference of 28 April, between the 'corrupt solicitation of favour', and the right of Irish Catholics to an 'active and proportionate share in the administration of their country'. Some Catholics must hold appointments, since by filling certain offices they are in a position to protect Catholic interests. The phrasing of the new rule should express this distinction. Constituencies should choose men of high personal character: for these only can be relied upon to keep their trust, and to men of any other disposition, mere verbal pledges entered into at the hustings are worthless.

He came now to one last point, and it concerned the new ruling of enforcing representatives into unanimity by majority decisions. Unanimity was certainly desirable, and it was never more wanted. But if it was forced in detail, then it would overrule the consciences of the representatives, and that was not to be desired. 'The Authority to legislate vested indeed by the act of the people in their representatives, comes from GOD', and was therefore a matter of conscience to be determined

---

[1] It must be realized that Cullen would not wish to see the existing Government fall, since the hierarchy were at the time negotiating with it on the university question (see chap. 5).

upon in each instance by personal responsibility and not by the decisions of majorities. On this point also, he would like to see some other form of expression in the new rules. All legitimate means must, of course, be employed to serve 'unanimity of action amongst Irish popular representatives', but not the enslavement of conscience.[1]

It was left now to a general meeting of the Association to determine on the new rules, according to the Constitution.[2] Time was becoming crucial, for the general election approached in July, and the long dispute was making the signs of internal vacillation and division apparent to the public.[3] A general meeting was called for 5 June, but on that day placards went up in Dublin announcing its postponement until the 19th of the month. The delay was doubtless the reflection of discussion of Cullen's points behind the scenes, and the speeches of Dillon and MacSwiney at the meeting when it was finally convened bore all the marks of being the result of a desperate effort to present the case of the committee in such a favourable light as still – at the late hour – to hold the Association together.

The Pillar Room of the Rotundo was the scene of the meeting on the 19th. It was well attended, with large numbers of priests prominent, but Dr Conaty of Kilmore was the only bishop present. The secretary, Whyte, said that letters had been received from Leahy of Cashel, Gillooly, O'Hea and Dorrian. Cullen did not attend, and his opinions were not directly referred to by any of the speakers. MacSwiney in the Chair spoke first: a long discussion of the positive achievement of the Association, evidently intended to dazzle the opposition into submission. Their work had supplemented the efforts of their friends in Parliament,[4] and as each question arose the Association had got up petitions in Ireland, and the committee had forwarded facts and figures to friendly members for use in debates. These had been most important for Maguire's motion on land,[5] and Dillwyn's on the Establishment.[6] They were supplying The O'Donoghue with information to help his forthcoming motion on Education[7] as they had helped Monsell similarly with the oaths question.[8] And it was the Association which had initiated the

---

[1] Cullen Papers.
[2] Rule 11: 'These fundamental Rules shall not be abrogated, added to, or in any respect altered, unless by vote of the Committee passed at two successive meetings (called by special notice for the purpose) and confirmed by the Association at a public meeting thereof.'
[3] As *The Times* pointed out, 7 June 1865.
[4] The account of this meeting is based on the *Freeman* report, 20 June 1865.
[5] *Hansard*, CLXXVIII, p. 570 (31 March 1865).
[6] *Ibid.*, p. 383 (28 March 1865).
[7] *Ibid.*, CLXXX, p. 541 (20 June 1865).   [8] *Ibid.*, CLXXVIII, p. 24 (21 March 1865).

movement against those oaths, and he went on to refer to the way it had been taken up by their members in the Dublin Corporation. He urged them to 'rally round the National Association of Ireland, the only Association which in their day was calculated to unite the prelates, the priests, and the people of Ireland'. He besought them to lay aside their differences, and settle for the principle that – in plain reference to the vital question at issue – a parliamentarian's character and honesty were more reliable than mere pledges.[1]

It was then left to Dillon to move the addition of fifty names to the membership of the committee, an extraordinary enlargement which showed the need to widen the basis of the Association, and so, at the same time, to lessen some of the opposition, which had all come from the localities. Most of the additions were clergy, but O'Neill Daunt and J. A. Dease, Synan of Limerick and MacCarthy Downing were in the list. So was Archdeacon O'Brien of Limerick. The new clergy were probably almost entirely supporters of the committee's stand in the rules dispute, although MacCarthy Downing and Dease may have been added in a brave bid for their support. If this was the motive, Downing's speech later in the meeting showed that it was misguided. Dillon proposed the Election Address, drawn up by the committee, which was at the same time a manifesto of their position on the new rules. The Association was to organize a committee in each constituency, entrusted with examining the character and record of the existing representative, who, if he had been faithful to his trust, was not to be rejected. In no case was there to be any dispensing with a 'clear, explicit, and written' avowal of adherence to the principles of the Association. Significantly, reform of the law of Landlord and Tenant was to be put as a question of 'paramount urgency and importance'. The crucial phrase opposed a point made by Cullen in his memorandum, and it must be supposed that its appearance in the Election Address represents some considerable adjustment in the committee: 'In all cases where it is possible, you will do well to have an understanding with your representatives that they will oppose every government which will not incorporate that measure with its policy, or at least afford it a sincere and efficient support.'[2]

Dillon then passed on, as he put it, to 'offer to the Meeting a few words of explanation of some transactions which have recently taken place in the Committee.' He reviewed the growth of dissatisfaction with the rules by those professing the principle of Independent Opposition,

---

[1] This was an enunciation of the distinction for which Cullen had contended in his memorandum.

[2] Text in the *Freeman*, 20 June 1865.

and the committee's feeling that it was mostly unwarranted, since any man going into Parliament pledged to the Association's rules as they originally were, would 'inevitably hold himself independent' of existing parties. A majority of the committee had favoured conciliation, however, and the result was the meeting of 28 April. He alluded *en passant* to the affair of the *Irish Times*, the subsequent slight alteration in the phrasing of Rule 3, the circular to the members giving the revised text, and the offence taken by some as a result. The rules to be submitted to the meeting were those as altered and printed in the circular.

MacCarthy Downing rose to confess that he was still unclear about Dillon's meaning, and proceeded to put the case of the more moderate of the opposition. Were the rules agreed at the meeting on 28 April to be abandoned or not? The resolutions of that meeting had been adopted with only one dissentient. If the present meeting allowed the issue to go unresolved, he believed it would be 'the funeral day of the National Association'. He represented simply that party which sought to bind members returned to Parliament against taking places, he said, while he was ready to adopt any resolutions that would retain the principles of those of 28 April – for if they were laid aside, he would feel obligated to retire from the Association. This declaration was applauded. Downing was prepared, however, to see further amendments, but not, apparently, those circularized by the committee on 6 May. He therefore proposed the following motion as a compromise:

That the resolutions agreed to at the Conference on the 28th of April last, be affirmed, subject to such amendments as a committee hereafter to be appointed may deem necessary, preserving the principles therein enunciated.[1]

This was passed unanimously.

Before the special committee could be convened, however, some of the bishops met at Maynooth on the 21st, and discussed the rules informally.[2] They agreed to meet again the following day at Coffrey's Hotel in Dublin, when MacHale, Derry, Keane, Dorrian and Nulty, Dillon and Cullen, assembled at 10 o'clock. It is surprising to find MacHale in these discussions; perhaps it reflects the conciliation which Dillon and Moore tried to bring about between him and Cullen, or perhaps, even, he hoped to find room for his own peculiar manœuvres in a reformed Association with more radical rules. But whatever the reason, he still did not join, although so amicable was the impression he made at Coffrey's Hotel that Dorrian was left optimistic[3] and so was Dillon. MacHale said that he would at once join, 'if the Association consisted only of those then

[1] Text in the *Freeman*, 20 June 1865.
[2] Kirby Papers, Dorrian to Kirby, no. 141, 27 June 1865.   [3] *Ibid.*

present, but he would watch if it would follow the policy now agreed upon, and then act accordingly'.[1] Cullen also seems to have managed to get on with MacHale. The bishops drew up a revised version of the rules agreed upon originally on 28 April.

The meeting of the Special Committee allowed for in MacCarthy Downing's motion met also on the 22nd, after the bishops had conferred.[2] It consisted of the same men, with the additions of Gillooly and Kilduff; and again Cullen and Dillon attended. The rules agreed upon by the prelates at Coffrey's were passed unanimously and issued to the press:

The Association pledges itself to the policy of complete Parliamentary Independence, and the electorate shall in all cases be urged to bind their representatives, not only to vote for all the objects of the Association, but also to oppose any government which shall not incorporate with its policy, or otherwise efficiently support, a satisfactory measure of tenant compensation – that measure being deemed one of pressing exigency and paramount importance.

That as it is impossible to give an honest and efficient advocacy in parliament to measures, and at the same time to incur personal obligations to a minister who is opposed to those measures, the electors should bind their representatives to accept no place or *honour*[3] for themselves, and incur no personal obligation to any minister who shall not support a satisfactory measure of tenant compensation.

That there should be an understanding between the electors and their representatives, that the latter should take counsel together, so as to secure general uniformity of policy and a combined action for the ends of the Association.[4]

This agreement was made amid refreshing cordiality, and was intended as a moderate compromise solution. There the rules question remained. It was no mere technical squabble, for the fabric of Irish political aspirations was involved in it, as well as the very life of the National Association, which was near to falling asunder on the same issue which had caused the collapse of Independent Opposition in the preceding decade. But the hopes of winning MacHale were at once found to be worthless. He had promised Dorrian that he might pledge himself to the Association in writing should it go the right way after their rules changes, and the 'proper time' arrive.[5] Yet on the 27th, the day on which Dillon reported the successful compromise on the rules to the committee of the Association,[6] there was a public dinner for Gavan Duffy, who was

---

[1] *Ibid.*   [2] *Freeman*, 24 June 1865.

[3] This clause was insisted upon by Cullen. 'Dr Cullen made the part about place-seeking by suggesting the word "honour" should be added.' Kirby Papers, Dorrian to Kirby, no. 141, 27 June 1865.

[4] Text in the *Freeman*, 24 June 1865.

[5] Kirby Papers, Dorrian to Kirby, no. 141, 27 June 1865.

[6] *Freeman*, 28 June 1865.

visiting Ireland from Australia, at which a letter from MacHale was read. It was dated 24 June, and stressed that nothing short of complete Independent Opposition would satisfy him. G. H. Moore – significantly taking sides – blasted out at Cullen and his Association, in a speech which bitterly recalled the betrayals of the fifties.[1]

The clergy of Meath and their bishop were also unappeased, yet waited to see how the Association would come out in the elections. But apparently dissatisfied, and annoyed that the Land question was being dealt with no more radically by an Association with revised rules, they withdrew from it in November 1865. They should have realized that the revision of the rules was, as Dillon said, a matter of words with 'reference to phrases and forms of speech exclusively, and that on principles there is no difference whatever'.[2] The spirit of the Association had not altered in their favour at all. The bishop and priests of Meath met at Navan on 6 November and formed an association of their own, the "Meath Tenant Right Society".[3] On the 26th they published an Address which announced the union of the clergy and laity 'to stay the course of eviction'. It also attacked the proposed meeting of the Liberal M.P.s to be held in Dublin under the auspices of the National Association. And, as though in summary of their whole division from that Association, it affirmed with emphasis that 'the *one* – the *great* – the *sole question for Ireland is the Land question*. Other agitations – such as that against the Established Church – are got up for party purposes'. They pledged themselves to the prelate who was most outspoken in condemning place hunters, 'the oldest and best friend of Ireland – the great Archbishop of Tuam'.[4]

A few others fell off as a result of the rules question. Myles O'Reilly resigned from the Association, explaining in a letter to its secretary in January of the next year, that when the rules had been changed he had written to Cullen and Dillon indicating his withdrawal for that reason.[5] Dease resigned also. The Association had come through its crisis without dissolution, but its careful, almost equivocal, balance was little calculated to retain within it those whose susceptibilities had provoked the crisis.

Following immediately upon the rules question, which was at once the symptom and occasion of dissensions, the elections in July 1865

---

[1] Duffy, *My Life in Two Hemispheres*, vol. II, p. 268.
[2] *Freeman*, 20 June 1865.
[3] *Ibid.*, 4 December 1865.
[4] Text in the *Freeman*, 4 December 1865.
[5] This letter, and that from J. A. Dease, were read at the public meeting of the Association on 23 January 1866 – see the *Freeman* report, 25 January 1866.

were equally crucial to the Association. Unfortunately the result was hardly satisfactory, even though MacSwiney made out a case for their success; 'nearly all the new members have declared for some part of our programme', he told the Association, and those few who had subscribed to their entire programme would make up for the smallness of their number by the extent of their influence.[1] This was in the tradition of Keane's claim that twenty good men would be sufficient. Dillon was returned as one of the members of Tipperary, Gray for Kilkenny and Synan for Limerick; and these were the only really outstanding successes the Association had. The Louth election in April had been a fair indication of the way the general election could go, for there the priests set aside the nominees of the Association and adopted a Liberal Protestant candidate, Tristram Kennedy, who was elected,[2] causing paradoxical satisfaction to *The Irish People*.[3] The Louth clergy, under the direction of Dean Kieran, were moving for the reconciliation of the Irish Catholics with the Liberal Party – a movement to which Chichester Fortescue was a party.[4] This was not of course outside the terms of the Association, even as it was left by the changed rules, but the Louth clergy simply acted independently of it. Curiously, the Association received help from an unexpected quarter. In a Pastoral Letter, Nulty urged the voters to support those who would endorse the Association's programme, though he was careful to add 'especially the Tenant compensation question', and that only those should be selected who had pledged themselves not to take places.[5] In the circumstances this can only be construed as an ambiguous support. It is interesting that one of the few candidates who did declare for the whole programme was Isaac Butt, at Youghal.[6] He was defeated.[7]

The lack of success in the 1865 elections may well reflect the weakened state of the National Association after its internal troubles, especially as these troubles were directly concerned with electioneering questions and the proper mode of representation, but there was another reason

1 *Ibid.*, 26 July 1865. Also reported in *The Irish People*, 29 July 1865. At the meeting of 18 October, Archbishop Leahy of Cashel also expressed satisfaction with the election results. Speaking chiefly on the continuing dangers of Fenianism, he stressed the urgency of convincing the Irish people of the effectiveness of Parliamentary action – *The Times*, 20 October 1865. Sentiments like these, which could be multiplied in example, underline the crucial nature of the rules dispute.

2 *The Times*, 8 April 1865; and 17 April 1865.

3 'Doctor Cullen was completely ignored at Louth'. *The Irish People*, 29 April 1865.

4 Carlingford Papers, CP. 3/38, Fortescue to Kieran, 19 April 1865.

5 There is a copy of the Pastoral in the Cullen Papers.

6 O'Leary, *Recollections of Fenians and Fenianism*, vol. II, p. 165.

7 De Vere White, *op. cit.*, p. 192.

also. The candidates who adopted the programme were dubbed Whigs. In September, even Dorrian was disheartened by what he imagined to be the partial support given by the Association to the Whigs.[1] When MacSwiney told the Association that the few men returned to Parliament in their interest would co-operate with the Liberal Party in England[2] it must have seemed to those disappointed by the compromise solution of the rules question that this was a true description.[3] Perhaps more people than usual agreed with *The Irish People* when it reported in April that the election results would show that the Association had not been able 'to get up even the empty show of a parliamentary movement'.[4] The disruption of the rules question, and the election results coming afterwards, appearing to summarize the consequences, mark the close of a phase of the Association's history. It was by no means at an end; its work continued to be important and even decisive. It took up the Church question and assisted the bishops in their determination to stand by the voluntary principle, although its part in Land questions was less influential, since its voice on those matters spoke with the ambiguity which combining divisions both inside its membership and outside imposed upon it. It took little part in the movement seeking modification of the 1870 Land Bill. Education it hardly touched, for in this the bishops, under Cullen's lead, preferred to act independently, and by the time that Gladstone came to deal with the university question – in 1873 – it was already weakened by the secession of some of the leading members to the Home Rule movement. It finally dissolved at the end of that year. These activities will be considered later when those topics of the period after 1866 are examined. But the second half of 1865 marked a decided change in the Association, and it was something of a decline. It will be seen that Cullen's own support flagged. So did that of local organization, which had never really evolved effectively anyway. The Association had failed within a year of its inauguration to hold even the clergy together – in this the final ending of the hope of gaining MacHale's support, and the secession of the Meath clergy were crucial – let alone the laity, many of whom had hardly started active co-operation, awaiting early developments to see how the Association would turn out. They had had their answer. It will be well, therefore, to pause at this moment in

[1] Kirby Papers, Dorrian to Kirby, no. 216, 28 September 1865.
[2] *Freeman*, 26 July 1865; and *The Irish People*, 29 July 1865.
[3] 'We said from the first that the "National Association" was intended to support the Whigs. No one can now doubt that we were right. Its policy of "independent opposition" was a fraud'; *The Irish People*, 29 July 1865, commenting on the election results.
[4] *The Irish People*, 29 April 1865.

the Association's history, and take stock of the significance of its existence and operation. To do so will certainly lay bare the political work-
ings of Ireland for the period. If an impression has been formed that
the Association was merely the corpse of Irish Parliamentary aspiration
thrown down on the dissecting table and opened up merely to be
found empty – an impression its opponents tried to convey – then
it requires severe modification. The internal strife must not be
allowed to hide the fact that the Association, despite quiverings of
unease at the time of the rules question, did endorse active co-operation
with the Liberals, and it took the initiative and most prominent
part in reuniting the Irish Catholic body with that party, and in
this it prepared the way for the Irish measures of Gladstone's first
Ministry.

After the Aggregate Meeting of 1864, Sir John Gray had written in the
Freeman that 'there are already indications of a desire to unite with the
advancing Liberal Party in England, and this, perhaps, is the most
hopeful thing we see connected with the new body'.[1] The laymen behind
the Association at its origin were all Irish Liberals – Dillon, Maguire,
Gray, O'Reilly and MacSwiney. (Some of the 'nationalist' politicians
like Moore and Martin would have no truck with them, both because of
this political allegiance, and because, like MacHale, they could not
bring themselves to co-operate with Cullen.)[2] When they became the
Association's representatives in Parliament it was obvious that they
would have worked in the interests of the party to which they were
already committed, even had there been no other body holding their
allegiance.[3] But such another body now existed: it was even supported by
Bright, and by the Liberation Society. Further, some immediate means
were needed to bring the Association's case to Parliament with the 1865
elections at hand, and with no machinery except the voice of the clergy
set up by the Association for managing local contests in their interests,[4]
it was no surprise when Liberal candidates pledged themselves and so
secured its support.

It has been seen that Bright tendered allegiance to the Association at
its inception. Indeed, it was his participation in Irish questions which,
Trevelyan observed, writing of 1865, caused him 'to dominate the heart

[1] *Freeman* (leader), 30 December 1864.
[2] For the case of Moore, see Duffy, *op. cit.*, vol. II, p. 268; and on Dillon's place in
the Association, see p. 243.
[3] James Aytoun, *The Irish Difficulty*, London, 1866, p. 14: 'All the Parliamentary
influence both of the priests and Catholic laymen is exercised in favour of the Liberal
Party.'
[4] *Freeman*, 20 June 1865.

and mind of Liberals'.[1] He and Dillon on the one hand,[2] and O'Neill Daunt and the Liberation Society on the other, brought about the *rapprochement* of the English Liberals and those Irish Catholics sympathetic to the National Association, even sometimes of those not actually members; though of the latter class, some, like Monsell and The O'Donoghue were already working in the English Liberal interest anyway, and chose to remain independent of the Association when it was established. Bright corresponded with the secretaries of the Association, giving frequent assurances of continued support.[3] At the Annual Meeting of January 1867 a resolution was passed expressing thanks to him for his promise of sympathy and support.[4] Eulogy of Bright, in fact, became almost a characteristic of Dillon and his group in the Association, and he took care in preparing a grand banquet for his hero in Dublin,[5] for 30 October 1866. Unhappily Dillon died on 15 September; but the banquet was still held, occasioning much bitterness among Irish Conservatives.[6] Bright spoke of Irish evils and their remedies, making a plea for united action.[7] Cullen, who was not at the banquet, but who received Bright when he called upon him on 31 October,[8] was pleased that he would put down the Protestant Church. 'I hope he will stop there' he wrote to Kirby.[9]

The issues involved in the rules question were concerned with the whole idea of working in with the Liberals. The Independent Opposition critics were unsuccessful in changing the basis of the Association's Parliamentary activities, but for a time Cullen, and even Dillon, were cautious of too emphatic a declaration in favour of co-operation with an existing political party. This was seen in Cullen's memorandum on the rules, and in Dillon's speech to the general meeting on 19 June 1865. When it became apparent that real healing of the wounds was not to

[1] G. M. Trevelyan, *Life of John Bright*, London, 1913, p. 247. The case was probably not as straightforward as Trevelyan suggested, but the Irish question certainly received a greater place in Bright's mind as a result of the National Association's publicity.

[2] Justin McCarthy, *Ireland since the Union*, p. 164. See also, on Dillon's connexion with Bright over the union of their two parties, *The Times*, 18 September 1866 (recording Dillon's death).

[3] See, for example, his letter read at the meeting in March, 1866. *The Times*, 9 March 1866.

[4] *The Times*, 11 January 1867.

[5] G. M. Trevelyan, *op. cit.*, p. 349.

[6] A. M. Sullivan, *op. cit.*, p. 308.

[7] McCarthy, *op. cit.*, p. 166.

[8] *Guardian*, 7 November 1866; *The Times*, 2 November 1866. Eighteen bishops replied to the invitation to the banquet, but none attended.

[9] Kirby Papers, Cullen to Kirby, no. 296, 30 October 1866.

come to pass, and the Meath clergy were ready to go their own way, Dillon's confidence returned, and he and the committee began to organize a meeting of the Irish Liberal members of Parliament. Cullen never did resume his former position, at least as far as the Association was concerned, since for reasons which will be suggested shortly, he was by the second half of 1865 ceasing to identify himself so completely with it.[1]

The meeting of Irish members organized by Dillon and the Association committee was on 5 December in the Dublin City Hall. Some twenty members of Parliament attended,[2] their sitting lasting until a late hour. It was held behind closed doors. Colonel Greville took the Chair and Dillon acted as secretary.[3] The number present was slightly less than the thirty that Dillon had told Cullen he hoped would come: 'any reasonable measures put forward by such a body will be certain to receive a favourable hearing at the hands of the Government.'[4] He looked for the support of these men, and then the Association would provide them with the justification, in the form of petitions, to carry it through. Dillon had also consulted Daunt, who was not at the Conference, but who urged him to pledge the assembled members to deal with the Church question according to the Voluntary principle.[5] 'Place it on any other ground', he noted, 'and you lose the English Voluntaries and Dissenters; you change them from friends into enemies.'[6] He need not have feared. The assembled members agreed in their resolutions to pursue a common policy on the questions which constituted the Association's three points, Land, Church, and Education, and co-operation with the English Liberal Party was allowed for.[7] The Irish members were apparently to support Parliamentary reform[8] in return. Sir John Gray, in

---

[1] Cullen was present, it is true, at a meeting of the Association in October when Dillon attempted to resolve difficulties over the proposed meeting of Irish M.P.s – see the *Freeman*, 19 October 1865; and *The Times*, 20 October 1865. But by November Dillon was urging Cullen to resume active support of the Association – see Cullen Papers, Dillon to Cullen, 24 November 1865.

[2] They were F. Greville (Longford Co.), G. Bryan (Kilkenny Co.), J. Bagwell (Clonmel), M. Corballis (Meath Co.), W. Moore (Tipperary Co.), E. Synan (Limerick Co.), R. Armstrong (Sligo), R. Devereux (Wexford), M. O'Reilly (Longford Co.), G. Barry (Cork Co.), P. Urquhart (Westmeath Co.), J. Dillon (Tipperary Co.), J. Maguire (Cork), J. Blake (Waterford), Sir J. Power (Wexford), Sir P. O'Brien (King's Co.), Sir J. Gray (Kilkenny), The O'Donoghue (Tralee), O. Stock (Carlow), and J. O'Reardan (Athlone). This was less than half the Irish Liberal members.

[3] *The Times*, 7 December 1865.

[4] Cullen Papers, Dillon to Cullen, 24 November 1865.

[5] Daunt, Journal, 30 November 1865.

[6] *Ibid.*, 5 December 1865.

[7] Text of the resolutions in the *Freeman*, 8 December 1865.

[8] *Guardian*, 10 January 1866.

a speech to his constituents at Kilkenny, declared that he and the others at the Dublin meeting were 'most anxious to go into the same lobby with Mr Bright and his friends'.[1] As the meeting was held privately, there are unfortunately no press reports of its discussions, so how the balance of the members worked itself out is now impossible to determine.

The great importance of the meeting must be judged, however, not by any results touching the actions in the House of those who attended so much as by the position of the Association which it demonstrated. Dillon had brought it right back to full co-operation with the Liberal Party, the careful compromise of the rules question notwithstanding. The *Dublin Review*, commenting upon the political alliance with the Liberals confirmed at the Dublin meeting, made the somewhat valid point that though Dillon had put the National Association's case on the question of Independent Opposition, his explanations would certainly 'not read well in context with the recent resolutions'.[2] It is true that when compared with the revised rules they appear to belong to a different order of things.

From this point, the Association always continued to ally its action with the Liberals, or at least until the university question in the early seventies revealed the inherent incompatibilities between Liberalism and Irish Catholicism. The alliance was largely dictated by the issues, and especially by the growth of the Church question to 1869. The Catholic members of the Association in Parliament, though a small body, were certainly active. Soon after the 1865 election even the *Express*, on 20 October, claimed that its members' action in the House 'has resulted in the Government evincing a desire to meet the agitators by concessions'. During the debate of Gray's motion on the Church in April 1866, Whiteside spoke of its author's connexion with the Association, and the influence thereby exercised by the Irish hierarchy in politics. It seemed natural that Catholic politicians should ally themselves in this way, for a large and articulate section of the 'advanced' Liberals in England consisted of 'Political Dissenters', whose language and opinion on the question of religious establishment and endowment were identical with those of the great majority of the Catholic party in Ireland. A surprising degree of political sophistication is shown by the National Association in all this. The Liberals, it must be remembered, were frequently denounced on the grounds of Whiggery.[3] They were

[1] *Guardian*, 10 January 1866.

[2] *Dublin Review*, January 1866, p. 183.

[3] A. M. Sullivan, *op. cit.*, p. 307. Of the Association: 'public feeling in Ireland was strongly in favour of the objects it had proposed; but the objection to fusing with the English Whig-Liberal party for *any* object seemed all but insuperable.'

therefore the party of Lord John Russell and the Ecclesiastical Titles Act. The 'advanced' Liberals were certainly opposed to Papal claims in Italy, and had paid homage to Garibaldi in 1864 when he was in England. When the Association was started, Cullen and the bishops must have closed their eyes to most of the tenets of Liberalism, and allowed the laymen to proceed with their party alliance, almost solely because union with an existing party seemed the only realistic method of securing redress, accepting the facts of Irish politics, threatened by Fenianism and Orangeism, as they were. They could hardly have seen in 1864 what the English did not know until 1867, that Gladstone would rise to the leadership of the Liberal Party in the way he did – pledged to reform Irish grievances. The National Association played a large part in producing the information, and its small band in the House the climate of opinion, on which Gladstone drew, although in any assessment, his actual conversion to the urgency of Irish questions must be attributed to the violence of the Fenians. Nevertheless, the Association's shot in the dark, by favouring the Liberals, came near in one respect – the solution of the Church question – to hitting the target.

In addition to the cultivation of the Liberal alliance, the Association also secured the good offices of the Liberation Society, thanks to the efforts of O'Neill Daunt. This body, founded in London in 1853 as the 'Society for the Liberation of the Church from State Patronage and Control', was evolved from the Religious Freedom Society and the Anti-State Church Association.[1] Its success and growth was largely the work of Edward Miall,[2] and J. Carvell Williams who was its secretary from 1853 until 1877, and with whom Daunt treated.[3] The unlikely co-operation of the Irish Catholic hierarchy with the most 'advanced' of English and Scottish Dissenters, notorious for their opposition to Catholicism, was hardly something that could have been predicted; but just as the alliance between the Association and the Liberals was reciprocal, so also was the working agreement that came about with the Liberation Society. By the terms of the first, the Association was to support parliamentary reform in return for Liberal support on the Church and land questions, and at a meeting in April 1866 MacSwiney

---

[1] For an outline of its early history and activities, see B. L. Manning, *The Protestant Dissenting Deputies*, Cambridge, 1952, especially pp. 50–2.

[2] Liberal M.P. for Rochdale 1852–7, and for Bradford 1869–74. He also founded the *Nonconformist* in 1841. He was a Congregationalist, and had risen to prominence for his rôle in the agitation against English Church Rate.

[3] A Welsh Congregationalist; secretary of the Anti-State-Church Association from 1847 until it became the Liberation Society in 1853, when he became secretary to that body. Carvell Williams was closely associated with the Dissenting Deputies, on whose committee he sat, and which worked in co-operation with the Liberation Society.

renewed the pledge, stating that the destiny of the Association hinged on the course they adopted on the question of Reform.[1] The terms agreed upon with the Liberation Society were also straightforward: all would work for the disendowment of the Irish State Church and the general recognition of the Voluntary System, in return for which the Irish Catholics should support the cause of disendowment when it was demanded for England after a successful issue in Ireland.

O'Neill Daunt first encountered the potential of the Liberation Society, when, after an early anti-State-Church Meeting of August 1856, which he had sponsored at Clonakilty (Co. Cork), the Society opened correspondence with him on the Irish Church question – a correspondence which was to last until his death in 1894. C. J. Foster was deputed by the Society to visit him in Ireland, and views were exchanged on the best methods of proceeding in the agitation.[2] Writing in his Journal in 1869, Daunt summarized the great results that were to follow this Conference. After the Clonakilty meeting, he wrote:[3]

Thenceforth I kept up a correspondence with the Liberation Society on the one hand, and with some leading Catholic prelates on the other, in the hope of getting both parties to work in the same harness. It was no easy task to get Irish ecclesiastics to place confidence in the Liberation people whose anti-Catholic bigotry in theological matters was notorious. And if their attacks on Maynooth had continued, the junction of forces so necessary to our success would have been impossible. So I induced the Liberation Committee to suspend all action against Maynooth, which concern was certain to be wound up whenever the final day of the State Church should arrive. This secured harmonious action. In December 1864 poor Dillon, MacSwiney, and the Catholic prelates founded the National Association; and the question, whether to adopt Voluntaryism, or a division of the endowment between the Churches, then hung in the balance among some of the founders.[4] Dillon was strenuously pressed to avoid the Voluntaries, and to pin our fortunes to such people as Russell, Grey and the slippery Whig party in general.[5] I told him that such a course would destroy our chance of being emancipated from the State Church.

In this Daunt was right, for the only possible basis for an alliance with the Liberation Society was Voluntaryism. They had nothing else in common. The dropping of the Maynooth question by the Society is

[1] Meeting of 18 April 1866. Dillon made the same point in a letter to the Association. *Freeman*, 19 April 1866.

[2] W. J. O'Neill Daunt, *A Life Spent for Ireland*, ed. by his daughter, London, 1896, p. 130.

[3] Daunt, Journal, 26 July 1869.

[4] An account of the Association's position on the question of religious endowments and on the problem of what to do with the revenues of a disendowed Irish Church, is given in chap. 7.

[5] By Monsell. Daunt, Journal, 5 December 1865. This occurred just before Dillon's meeting with the Irish Liberal members in Dublin.

interesting. As early as 1859 Daunt had seen it as a difficulty, but felt it 'could easily be accommodated on a conference between accredited leaders from both countries'.[1] In September 1862 the Liberationists still held it to be indissolubly bound up with the Church question: so much so, that until Irish Catholics could be induced to give up the Maynooth endowment, the question of the Establishment could never be approached coherently.[2] Daunt could see this too, though he did not see the need, which the Society did at that time, to dispose of the grant first; for him it would lapse together with the State Church endowment. Daunt's letter urging the Society to abandon opposition to Maynooth was read at a committee meeting in London on 31 October 1862. It stated plainly that this would be a gesture tending to obtain the support of Irish Catholics for its Church objectives.[3] The Society's affirmative reply was sent to Daunt on 14 November.[4] Its recipient was in a strong position to treat with the Society in this way, as his support was evidently most highly regarded by them – in June of the same year, they had invited him to join their Executive Council, an honour which he declined with regret on grounds of health and the impossibility of his travelling to London for meetings.[5]

In 1863 Daunt and Leahy (of Cashel) were unable to induce the Society to support their attempts to get up petitions against the Church in Ireland. Carvell Williams gave as his reason the insurmountable prejudices of the existing Government and the futility of petitioning it.[6] But when the National Association was founded, the Liberation Society's committee at once sought information regarding its programme, resolving that the secretary should communicate with Daunt for this object, and resolving further to publish Daunt's speech at the Aggregate Meeting.[7] Daunt's reply was received and minuted by the committee early in February,[8] and was apparently found satisfactory, for in March the Society gave its active support, through its sympathizers in

---

[1] *Nonconformist*, 14 December 1859. Daunt's letter is reprinted from the *Freeman's Journal*.

[2] *Nonconformist*, 24 September 1862 (containing comment taken from the Society's journal, the *Liberator*).

[3] Liberation Society's Minute Books, vol. III, p. 76.

[4] *Ibid.*, vol. III, p. 78.

[5] Daunt, Journal, 18 June 1862. Daunt declined a similar invitation in May 1865 – significantly, perhaps, in the early months of the National Association's life. *Journal*, 29 May 1865.

[6] *Ibid.*, 25 November 1863. See also the reasons given at the annual meeting of the Liberation Society on 5 May 1864 – *Nonconformist*, 11 May 1864.

[7] Liberation Society's Minute Books; Council of 6 January, vol. III, p. 234.

[8] 7 February 1865; *ibid.*, p. 242.

Parliament, and through its press, to the oaths question which was the first plunge into action made by the Association.[1]

From this point Daunt's correspondence with Carvell Williams became prolific,[2] but the Society evidently felt it best to leave it to Daunt to bring about a corroborated working agreement between the two bodies. This he did, both by pressing the need for such an agreement whenever he had the opportunity to do so, and by approaching individual prelates in this interest. He had, in fact already started doing so, and at the Aggregate Meeting he had spoken of 'a powerful and growing confederation in England of men who have formed themselves into a society for the liberation of religion', and which 'stretched forth to them the right hand of fellowship'.[3] And writing to persuade MacHale to join the Association, on 13 January 1865, he had assured that archbishop that he had that week received 'the strongest assurances of active support' for the Association's effort to disendow the Church, 'from the Central Committee of the English Liberation Society', and added 'their alliance is an element of strength of the utmost importance'.[4] He seems to have concentrated most of his attention on the Archbishop of Cashel, and it was through him, probably, that the working agreement received its connexion with the episcopal members of the Association's committee.[5] Writing at the time of the death of Leahy in 1875, Daunt paid tribute to his efforts in that behalf: 'it is more than doubtful whether I could have effected a working union between the English voluntaries and the Irish hierarchy unless he had helped me'.[6] The Liberation Society helped to prepare agitation in favour of Gray's motions of 1866 and 1867, advising in its early stages,[7] and in most other parliamentary business in which they had a common interest. In September 1867 Carvell Williams came to Ireland, visiting Daunt and several of the bishops.[8] When, after the rules question, the Association's support for the Liberals became

[1] Liberation Society's Minute Books; Council of 6 January, vol. III, p. 255. They agreed to support Monsell's motion in the House. They also worked for Dillwyn's motion, which was sponsored directly by the Society, and which the National Association aided by petitions.

[2] As the acknowledgements of letters received in his *Journal* indicate.

[3] *Freeman*, 30 December 1864.

[4] B. O'Reilly, *John MacHale*, vol. II, p. 542.

[5] See remarks on the Thurles archives in an earlier note. It is interesting that on Dillon's death in 1866, Daunt suggested to Leahy that Edward Miall should adopt his seat in Tipperary. But this was not followed up due to Leahy's insistence that Miall could have no hope of being elected there – Daunt, Journal, 22 September and 2 October 1866.

[6] Daunt, Journal, 29 January 1875.

[7] *Ibid.*, 25 December 1865; Liberation Society's Minute Books, vol. III, p. 351.

[8] See chap. 7.

more apparent, and when the Church question assumed priority, the working agreement between the two societies was much more easily effected, and Carvell Williams' visit reflected this. Knowledge of their co-operation became widespread, and caused some comment in Parliament during Church debates in the latter part of the decade.[1] Like the Association's co-operation with the Liberals, their 'working union' with the Liberation Society eventually lapsed over Catholic educational claims in the early 1870s.[2]

The National Association worked through other societies as well, especially the Dublin Corporation, where an identity of membership between its Liberal leaders and the Association was apparent in the prominence in both of Dillon, Gray, MacSwiney, Devitt and Plunkett. Other Irish municipal bodies became linked with the Association's programme, usually by acting with the Dublin Corporation to pass resolutions and organize petitions in favour of proposed action. This happened during the oath question of 1865, and again over land and Church proposals.[3] But this was all fairly indirect. Occasionally other organizations sent pledges of sympathy to the Association, but these were merely declaratory, and were not followed up by any active measures.[4] MacSwiney supported the English Reform League in 1867, by arranging meetings to appoint Irish deputations to attend the League's demonstrations in Manchester, Birmingham and London;[5] but this also had only indirect connexion with the Association. Cullen was of opinion that the Reform League misrepresented Irish grievances, and MacSwiney may well have organized the deputations in obedience to Cullen's wish that someone should set them right.[6] MacSwiney's combination of allegiance to the Association and to other movements was not, of course, unique. O'Neill Daunt was both a committee member of the Association and a presiding officer of Martin's National League.[7] In July 1868 Cullen supported MacSwiney's Central Franchise Association with an open letter and a subscription of five pounds. Its object was

---

[1] See chap. 7.

[2] Liberation Society's Minute Books, vol. IV, p. 486.

[3] For example, *The Times*, 9 and 16 April 1866.

[4] Such was the case with the Lancashire Catholic Electoral Registration Association, which promised electoral support to the objects of the National Association in a letter to Cullen of the 19 January 1865 – Cullen Papers.

[5] *The Times*, 17 January 1867, reports such a meeting in Dublin on the 15th.

[6] See Cullen's letter to the National Association, read at the Annual Meeting of 8 January 1867 – *The Times*, 10 January 1867.

[7] Sillard, *op. cit.*, pp. 169–70. Martin disliked 'the evil of two or more organizations instead of one', but felt that he and Dillon were unlikely to fall out, and thought that the National Association would help forward the object of the League (pp. 172–3).

to register the names of those citizens enfranchised by the new Reform Bill on the role of voters of the city of Dublin. In his letter of 10 July, Cullen expressed the hope that the new voters would help the return of men pledged to redress Irish grievances.[1]

It must now be asked why the National Association was a relative failure; why it failed in the sense that it was unable to hold the clergy and laity together in a coherent programme of agitation. 'It must be admitted that there is something anomalous in the position of this Association,' wrote *The Times* early in 1867; 'it is so attenuated and retiring, apparently so destitute of Parliamentary and popular support, and so ill supplied with funds, though enjoying in a larger measure than any other political society in this country the blessings of the Church'; and continued 'in fact, it may be said to have been ushered into the world by the hierarchy, who have ever since watched over its cradle and prayed for its prosperity. Why, then, does it not prosper?'[2] This was a little overdrawn: the work of the Association in the second half of the decade and until it petered out in 1873, was still valuable. Even if it had become a somewhat sectional agitation, a group of bishops were still active in it, lead by Leahy (of Cashel) and including Gillooly especially – and sometimes Cullen – and nominally the entire hierarchy with the exceptions of MacHale and Nulty. The last named did give at least the negative assurance in 1868 that he was not opposed to the Association on the Church question, whilst still upholding the primacy of land.[3]

The secession of the Meath clergy, and of some lay members of the committee, over the rules question, was the Association's most serious loss. Moriarty of Kerry was never connected with it, although he signed the requisition in 1864. He never greatly dissented from it, as did MacHale and Nulty, but the stand of the Association on the voluntary principle of endowments, in explicit condemnation of his own published views to the contrary, meant that he would never join.[4] O'Neill Daunt never ceased in his exertions for the Association, and the part he took in its deliberations on the Church question, in the spirit of the working agreement with the Liberation Society, was of the greatest importance.[5] The death of Dillon[6] on 15 September 1866 was a severe blow. He was the Association's most active lay member.[7] But Sir John Gray remained

---

[1] *The Times*, 14 July 1868.
[2] *Ibid.*, 11 January 1867. The article went on to notice the smallness of the attendance at its meetings.
[3] The Meath *Declaration*: see *The Times*, 7 September 1868.
[4] See the proceedings of the meeting of 27 June 1867, in the *Freeman*, 29 June 1867.
[5] Discussed in chap. 7.   [6] D'Alton, *op. cit.*, vol. II, p. 78.   [7] *Ibid.*

consistent, persisting in representing its programme in the House, and propagating its virtues in his newspaper, the *Freeman*. Yet still the Association was not achieving the success looked for. The great weakness that has already been discussed was the diversification of the Association's programme into *three* points, rather than one, and this was fundamental and ineradicable. For even if, as tended to happen, different sections pressed one point to the exclusion of others in importance, this did not overcome, but only added to the weakness since it could, and did, bring the Association near to collapse when members disagreed on the criterion of importance to be adopted.

There were many institutional weaknesses. It was rather too much a Dublin movement, even after the addition of the fifty new committee men in 1865. These came mostly from the provinces, but it was by then too late to persuade the more ardently 'nationalist' elements stronger in the provinces that the decisions of the Association sitting in Dublin on the rules question would ever create an effective political line. Too late also was the resolution of May 1868 which added to the Executive Council the names of men representative of the different districts of the country, a resolution which MacSwiney said had for its object the widening of the basis of the Association.[1] Organization in the provinces was still left to the local clergy; but one reason for the sponsorship of the Association by the hierarchy in 1864 had been the suspicion in the light of the Lavelle case especially, that some of the local clergy were disaffected from constitutional action. And it has been seen that by early 1868, after the affair of the Manchester executions, opinion among the lower clergy flowed quite decidedly towards a more tolerant attitude to the Fenians, and towards a more final despair with constitutional agitation which Gladstone's Bills did little, really, to dispel.[2] Indeed, Disestablishment in 1869 removed much of the sting of Orangeism, and so at the same time one of the justifications for the National Association's existence. The local clergy were therefore not to be counted on. Very little local organization was the result. The Association had also some financial difficulties. The income from subscription was not enough to meet the expenses incurred by the printing and circulation of petitions – even though this was, except for the cost of the hire of the rooms at Ormond Quay, and later at 68 Middle Abbey Street, about the only large charge there must have been on the Association's funds.[3] Dillon

---

[1] *Freeman*, 27 May 1868. Committee meeting of 26 May.   [2] See chap. 8.

[3] In the first Parliamentary session of 1866 the Association had managed to organize the incredible number of 514 petitions on the tenant question, and 357 on the Church question. This was announced by Kavanagh at the meeting of 18 April 1866, *Freeman*, 19 April 1866.

estimated that £500 or £600 would be needed to get up petitions in 1865, and found that there seemed to be not a penny of that amount then available.[1] In 1867 a petition against tithe adjustments had to be dropped for the reason that the Association had run out of funds.[2]

Clearly the impression is that the members never fully entrusted their objectives to the Association. It was not really so damaging that success at Parliamentary elections did not go too frequently to men pledged wholly to the Association's programme, although such lack of success had a detrimental effect on those in England who looked to this as a criterion of worth; for the Association had other ways of stirring public opinion, even if the most common of these was the getting up of petitions, which needed someone in the House to present them and argue their points. But the small band in the Commons never acted with the same consistency and uniformity as the representatives of the Liberation Society there, and that despite the fact that the revised rules of 1865 expressly required some such uniformity of action. Its absence was the price paid – as the Independent Opposition party had said it would be – for the Liberal alliance. That alliance came to mean that when a Liberal leader emerged with his own programme for Ireland the Association would find itself in a dilemma. Thus there is a sense in which the rise of Gladstone to the leadership of the Liberal Party frustrated the Association. His three-fold policy of conciliation for Ireland followed the three points of the Association in name, but was vastly different in the extent to which it was prepared to go. This left the Association and its representatives in Parliament with the desperate choice between urging innumerable amendments to his proposed legislation, or implementing the revised Rule 3 and so opposing his Government. The history of their attitudes between 1868 and 1873 is the story of how they opted for the first alternative on the Church Bill, were then divided about the Land Bill, and finally, and probably with some relief, for the strain was considerable, slumped into opposition on the University Bill. Rule 3 was implemented when the Irish voted in 1873 to turn out the first Gladstone Government. But their inability to retain consistency in these oscillations knocked the life out of the National Association.

The episcopal members of the Association were also guilty of failing to entrust their case completely to the Association. Between 1865 and

[1] Cullen Papers, Dillon to Cullen, 24 November 1865.

[2] Daunt, Journal, 20 June 1867. It would be useful to know more about the Association's financial position, but in the absence of its books this is difficult. By Rule 9, accounts were to be published at least every six months, but this does not seem to have been kept.

1868 they negotiated directly with the Government on the university question without any particular reference to the Association, and this was started even before the rules question had divided it and so, perhaps, rendered such action excusable. At all times there took place too much crucial discussion on the lines of the Association's programme, but without reference to it, for it to have remained the clearing-house for Irish agitation. At the Aggregate Meeting, Cullen had warned the clergy always to keep within the canonical decrees governing their legitimate participation in politics. By that very definition the bishops themselves determined their position in relation to the Association's objectives, not on the platform of its meetings, but at the occasional meetings of the hierarchy in Dublin. Yet the National Association became both a mover of public opinion and its reflection. Kavanagh said it had 'prepared the public mind for legislation, dispelling prejudice, refuting fallacies, and spreading . . . information'. This was, in itself, no small thing.

The *Dublin Review*, as usual, made wise comment when it remarked in 1865 that the National Association would have stood more chance of success had it been founded at the time of the issue of the bishops' Pastoral in 1859.[1] 'It is probable, indeed, that the power of political association over the country at large is seriously diminished since O'Connell's time, and even since the time of the Catholic Defence Association and the Tenant League; and that more may and can be effectively done by local action.'[2] This was just what the National Association was unable to do.

One final source of weakness must be suggested: the vacillating position of Cullen himself towards the Association. He seems to have blown alternately hot and cold towards it, sometimes endorsing its proceedings with warmth, and at others he is found being urged not to give it up altogether. It is curious that there is scant reference to the Association in his correspondence, though his failure to keep the Propaganda informed of the detail of its activities may well represent the reserve he imagined Rome would have towards any sort of agitation which could be shown to be allied with political Liberalism. O'Neill Daunt noted his amusement to find himself at the 1864 Aggregate Meeting supporting a programme of Disestablishment, when the union of Church and State had just been upheld in the Syllabus of Errors,[3] especially as he had spoken 'in the immediate presence and with

---

[1] *Dublin Review*, April 1865, 'Wanted, a policy for Ireland', p. 439.   [2] *Ibid.*

[3] *Syllabus Errorum* (1864), condemned Proposition 55: 'The Church ought to be separated from the State, and the State from the Church'. From the Allocution *Acerbissimum*; 27 September 1852. (English text in Anne Freemantle, *The Papal Encyclicals*, New York, 1956, p. 149.)

full approbation of the Pope's Irish legate'. He absolved himself with the thought that he was 'in no way bound by the Pope's political notions'.[1] But could Cullen say the same? A year later, the *Dublin Review*, referring to the Syllabus, pointed to the impossibility of any legitimate alliance with the Liberal Party 'for its principles are the utter negation of our principles'.[2] And in 1869, again with reference to Disestablishment, *The Times*, writing of the Archbishop of Cashel's speech in its favour at the National Association, assured its readers that 'the Syllabus of Pio Nono places under a stern anathema the proposition' of religious equality.[3] It is certainly true that in supporting the National Association, Cullen was courting another condemned proposition – that of Indifferentism.[4]

Yet Cullen approved the alliance with the Liberals by implication, in his speech at the Aggregate Meeting, when he endorsed the entire proceedings. He was prepared also to work with a man like Dillon, whose political background included exile for a part taken in that rebellion of 1848 which Cullen considered the most monstrous of outrages. He was friendly towards Bright, and though not present at the Dublin banquet held in his honour in 1866, he sent a letter, read at the dinner, which praised Bright without reservation,[5] and he even received him at his house in Eccles Street – a rare privilege. In a letter to the Association's Annual Meeting in 1867 he hinted at the benefits to be received from the English Liberals, although expressing the (vain) hope that they would be as concerned about the education question as they were showing themselves to be with Disestablishment.[6] This was in the face of the views Cullen had expressed in his memorandum on the rules question in 1865, which, though moderate and conciliatory, had still looked to a Parliamentary policy of the Association which 'should be one of complete independence of both the great English Parties'.[7] Probably, like Dillon, he took up positions during that struggle over the rules from which, when the conciliation had been seen to have failed anyway, he afterwards withdrew.

Despite the complete identity between his own opinions and those of the Association which he made at the Aggregate Meeting, it was only a year later, after the rules dispute, that Cullen made a partial withdrawal

---

[1] Daunt, Journal, 29 December 1864.
[2] *Dublin Review*, January 1866, 'The New Parliament', p. 187.
[3] *The Times*, 19 January 1869.
[4] *Syllabus Errorum*, Proposition 15: 'Every man is free to embrace and profess that religion, which guided by the light of reason, he shall consider true.' From the Allocution *Maxima quidem*; 9 June 1862. (English text in Anne Freemantle, *op. cit.*, p. 145.)
[5] *The Times*, 2 November 1866.
[6] *Ibid.*, 10 January 1867.
[7] Cullen Papers.

from its meetings and counsels. His elevation to the Sacred College early in 1866 may have weighed with him when making this decision. He would have felt (no doubt correctly) that his position in reference to political agitation was changed by his cardinalate: he could not risk compromising the policy of Rome by actions the Association might take with his direct concurrence. In November 1865 at the time when he was completing his arrangements for the meeting of Liberal members, Dillon wrote pleading with Cullen not to give up his part in the Association:

> It is because I clearly see this great opportunity, and am apprehensive that it may pass away from us, that I am tempted to urge your Grace not to give up the good work in the inauguration of which you assisted a year ago. . . . If the friends of the Association will now fail to exert themselves in its behalf, not only will all the good work of which it is capable remain undone, but our enemies will point to its failure as evidence that the country is indifferent regarding the objects for which it was established. To prevent these disastrous results, I take the liberty of urging your Lordship to continue your patriotic efforts on behalf of the Association.[1]

It was apparently of little avail. Cullen continued to remain identified with the Association – indeed, it was always popularly supposed to be 'Cullen's Association'[2] – but he tended to keep at a distance. He supported its objects by vague letters of support which were read at meetings,[3] always maintaining his subscriptions, but very rarely attending in person. In this he contrasts with the Archbishop of Cashel, who was punctilious in appearing. Cullen was almost certainly instrumental in getting the Association's meetings going again after their discontinuance during the winter of 1867-8. A letter from him was read by MacSwiney at the first resumed meeting of the committee on 20 March. It congratulated the Association on its past work, and even went so far as to make some positive suggestion about improvements in the Land Acts.[4] This was something of a vote of confidence, for almost certainly one of the reasons that had caused Cullen's withdrawal from an active part in the Association was a fear that its land programme would become more radical than he could personally countenance, under pressure from those disappointed over the rules changes, but who had given up their membership. It is also probable that, notwithstanding this letter, and his

---

[1] Cullen Papers, Dillon to Cullen, 24 November 1865.

[2] See, for example, this view put forward by the Protestant Bishop of Tuam during the Lords' debate on the Church Bill in 1869 – *Hansard*, cxcvii, p. 105 (17 June 1869).

[3] For example, the Annual Meeting on 8 January 1867 (*The Times*, 10 January 1867); at a special meeting of the committee on 20 March 1868 (*ibid.*, 23 March 1868); and at a meeting on 13 January 1869 (*ibid.*, 15 January 1869).

[4] *Freeman*, 21 March 1868, and *The Times*, 23 March 1868. For Cullen's actual suggestions about leases in his letter, see chap. 8.

speech at the Aggregate Meeting, Cullen was more cautious on land questions than he liked to admit in public. The National Association he envisaged as an agitation primarily on the Church question – even on education he must have been reluctant to allow it a free hand, for he dealt directly with the Government on that question. In this sense there was some substance in the charge made by *The Irish People* in 1865 that Cullen had supported the Association 'as a bait to catch the masses of the people', and so prevent their agitating more serious matters.[1] It has been said that the three points were given different orders of priority by different groups in the Association: Cullen plunged decisively for the Church question.

Cullen's especial concern for the resumption of the meetings in March 1868 probably represents his fears about the increased tolerance and even sympathy for the Fenians after the Manchester executions. His activity indicated the renewed threat of Fenianism within the Church itself. The Martyrs' masses were responsible. Even so, having got the thing going again – and that without direct participation – he continued to remain at a distance. Yet, as will be seen, Cullen's partial withdrawal from the Association was not a part of his general withdrawal from politics. It was only an indication that he was influencing matters in another way, mostly by contact with Manning and the bishops on one hand, and with members of Parliament (and here he did not restrict himself to representatives of the Association) on the other.

After the rules question, Cullen probably saw danger in too close a union with the Association, for with the secession of the Meath clergy, plus the failure of many bishops to concern themselves actively, he perceived that the Association was just as likely to cause a rupture among the hierarchy as to heal its latent divisions. He did not care about the failure to win over MacHale – he had always been prepared to act independently and in opposition to MacHale's views, for he alone had the ears of Rome – but his hope that the new movement would attract him was genuine enough. When he all but compromised himself over the rules question, it was probably in the belief that MacHale might come over if moves at least towards Independent Opposition were allowed, especially as Dillon and Moore had worked for goodwill between the archbishops. Cullen was also anxious not to be drawn into deep waters by actions of the Association; he did not wish to burn his fingers again as he had done over the Catholic Defence Association.

[1] *The Irish People*, 14 January 1865: 'We do not believe that Dr Cullen expects to get Tenant Right. He tells us himself that it is a question surrounded by "inextricable difficulties".' The Association was 'got up somewhat on the principle of the celebrated razors that were made, not to shave, but to sell'.

To say, with Dr Corish,[1] that in the development of the National Association Cullen's 'political opinions emerge rather clearly' is to appreciate the importance of his attitude towards it, although perhaps to undervalue some of the subtlety of his position. But it is also to suppose either that he endorsed its proceedings fully, which he did not, at least after 1865, or that he could have stopped any of its proceedings which he found distasteful, which he could not. Did Cullen see that the National Association was failing, and so keep out? This is to overstate even his caution. Cullen, who was always unlucky with politics, simply found to be true what his instinct had told him all along, that although it was possible for a Catholic prelate to embrace Liberal opinions, parties established to realize them turned out, in the process, to be far from Catholic.

[1] P. J. Corish, 'Cardinal Cullen and the National Association of Ireland', in *Reportorium Novum*, III, no. 1, 1961–2, p. 14.

CHAPTER FIVE

The University Question
1865-6

THE Irish bishops, like Catholic bishops everywhere, placed the highest priority on the attainment of an education for their people which perfectly safeguarded faith and morals. The circumstances of Ireland cast university education as the most hopelessly removed from that object.[1] Bishop MacEvilly of Galway wrote in 1866 that he knew of 'no other question which is so peculiarly *our question*, as nothing else so directly affects the souls of men and the salvation of generations yet unborn'.[2] During 1865 the bishops became involved in a series of communications and negotiations with the Government, which ended in 1866 with the grant of a Supplemental Charter to the Queen's University. The sequence of events is complicated, but it is necessary to consider them closely, for the matters under review were important. The question of Irish university education was central to the whole debate on higher education in nineteenth-century Britain. Much of the discussion over Ireland which occurred before 1871 had reference to the concept of a university which the English Test Act[3] of that year embodies, especially as Fawcett's extenuated moves to open Trinity College, Dublin, had aired the difficulty of erasing religious tests. In May 1870, in the course of the debate on the Test Bill, Gathorne Hardy summarized a decade of Irish experience when he asked if the Government were 'going to say that the denominational system is good for Ireland but not for England?'[4] And in June of the same year, Gladstone observed to Manning that 'already the shadow of Irish education is cast darkly over the English Bill'.[5] Manning, who had always supported denominational education

---

[1] 'If education is to have any influence at all, it must have an influence for good or evil upon the faith and morals of the young man, during that "most impressionable period of life", in which, ordinarily speaking, he passed through a University Course.' John MacDevitt, *University Education in Ireland and 'Ultramontanism'*, Dublin, 1866, p. 26.

[2] Kirby Papers, MacEvilly to Kirby, no. 3, 5 January 1866.

[3] 34 & 35 Vict. cap. 26.

[4] *Hansard*, third series CCI, p. 1238 (23 May 1870; second reading).

[5] In reply to Manning's inquiry as to whether the Government intended doing anything for the Catholic University in Dublin. Gladstone to Manning, 22 June 1870;

for Ireland, regretted the passing of the English Test Act in his Lenten Pastoral for 1872. The Act 'de-christianized', he held, and education ought never to be separated from religion.[1] Once again Ireland was to provide precedents for English reform – and for the manner of effecting reform. This was seen at the time. Remarking on a speech by Wodehouse, the Lord-Lieutenant of Ireland, on the Government's proposals for Irish universities, *The Times* noticed in October 1865 that 'when this new University is established, Ireland, in its education as in so many other things, will be, theoretically at least, far ahead of England and Scotland'.[2] The Irish debate was also usually admixed with questions of National Education – and the rules of the Irish Board for its system of secular instruction had to give close attention to the rights of conscience. When England received the beginnings of a comparable system in the 1870 Forster Act, the mechanism worked out to safeguard minority religious opinion in Ireland was found to be applicable there too. It was a short step from the Stopford Rule to the Cowper–Temple Clause. The history of the university question in these years had internal significance too. The opinions of the bishops were brought out more clearly than at any other time by the exigency of negotiation with the Government, and they were not always united.[3]

In his Westcott Lecture for 1962, *Westcott and the University*, Professor Chadwick pointed to the changed 'emphasis and atmosphere' in university education which occurred in England during the nineteenth century. He quoted Newman to show that in the early Victorian ideal the object of a university was to educate undergraduates, and if intellectual advance issued out of the university, it was only a byproduct. The religious office of the university was training up citizens who pursued goodness and possessed the key to knowledge; they could become equally parsons or politicians on the result. But after 1871 especially, this had all changed – 'the emphasis in all university education was moving away from the appropriation of received truth, to a responsible judgment about conflicting opinions'.[4] This was largely

printed in D. C. Lathbury, *Correspondence on Church and Religion by W. E. Gladstone*, London, 1910, vol. II, p. 140.

[1] *Freeman*, 15 Feburary 1872.   [2] *The Times*, 16 October 1865.

[3] Moody does not regard the period about to be examined here as 'a crucial stage' in the history of the Irish university question. He lists four such stages: 1793-5, 1845-50, 1873-82 and 1901-8. T. W. Moody, 'The Irish University Question of the Nineteenth Century,' in *History*, XLIII, 1958, p. 93. The present chapter is an attempt to adjust the list. Walsh regarded the university question as falling into four periods too, of which that started in 1866 was 'the period of hopeful reform'. W. J. Walsh, *The Irish University Question, The Catholic Caste*, Dublin 1897, p. 36.

[4] W. O. Chadwick, *Westcott and the University*, Cambridge, 1963, p. 10.

reflected in the results of the altered statutory provisions relating to religious belief at Oxford and Cambridge colleges. The difference of emphasis and atmosphere between 1832 and 1872, 'or even more narrowly between 1852 and 1868, was so marked as to be revolutionary'.[1] Now much of the experience of university reform acquired by the English politicians who effected the statutory changes for England came from their dealings with Irish higher education. The sequence of events in the Irish side of the reform movement – for it can be called such – gives weighty content to Professor Chadwick's chronology. The united secular education of the Queen's University, so carefully upheld by the Legislature even when contemplating widening its constitutional basis, and the suggestions to open Trinity College fellowships to every shade of religious dissent, were the Irish precedents for England. The failure of the attempt to charter and endow a denominational (Catholic) university or college in Ireland – not for want of trying – is not unassociated with the English problem either. Professor Chadwick mentions Pusey's proposal to the Wesleyan Conference of 1868 for concurrent endowment of denominational colleges at English universities, by appropriations from the foundations of existing Anglican colleges.[2] That plan, and any like it were destined to failure for the very reason that the principle upon which it rested had been emphatically rejected in the case of the Dublin Catholic University. When Gladstone introduced his resolutions on the Irish Church in May 1868, it was his way of putting a stop to the chance of concurrent endowment, not only of universities in Ireland, but of churches too. He did it because of his Liberal persuasion that united secular education was more desirable than the old system of State endowment and religious inequality. Having made his point in Ireland, it was not to be withheld from England.

In their memorial to Sir George Grey in January 1866, the Irish bishops said that 6,360 Roman Catholics were receiving higher education in Ireland, but on unfair terms. They had no way of obtaining legally-recognized degrees.[3] This was a crucial matter for them, for there was a recurrent risk that Catholic youth would resort to Trinity College or to the Queen's University – both of which were under episcopal condemnation.[4] It has been seen before that their favoured solution was the

---

[1] W. O. Chadwick, *Westcott and the University*, Cambridge, 1963, p. 1.   [2] *Ibid.*, p. 12.

[3] *Parliamentary Papers*, 1866, LV, 243, 'Copies of Memorials addressed to the Secretary of State for the Home Department by the Roman Catholic Prelates in Ireland, on the subject of University and National Education in Ireland, and of Correspondence relating thereto', Enclosure 1, p. 6.

[4] Thus Auchmuty correctly says that the Irish university question could not be settled 'as long as Roman Catholic students did not feel themselves adequately catered for'. J. J. Auchmuty, *Irish Education, A Historical Survey*, Dublin, 1937, p. 139.

incorporation of the Catholic University in Dublin. The negotiations of 1865-6, and of 1868, had this end in view on both sides – the episcopal and the Governmental. But the attempts to reach a common agreement upon terms ended in failure, and as McGrath has said, the real cause of the ultimate failure of the Catholic University was its lack of a charter.[1] For Cullen, the protection of Catholic youth from the proselytism and indifferentism of mixed universities was supremely urgent. Writing in 1902, Archbishop Walsh claimed a duty 'that all Irish Catholics owe to the memory of that great prelate, of whom it can be said . . . that to him . . . the credit is due that there is a University question, alive and clamouring for settlement on the line of absolute equality for Catholics'.[2] So importantly did Cullen and the bishops regard educational matters, that from the very beginning of the National Association they were prepared to sap much of its authority by dealing directly with the Government, and without reference to it, whenever the opportunity was presented. They probably also saw that its working co-operation with the Liberal Party whilst useful on the Church question was unlikely to bear fruit on educational matters. The bishops' demands threw most clearly into relief an English and Protestant distrust of ultramontane designs on Irish education and confirmed the belief of the 'advanced' Liberals with whom the National Association was in accord, that united secular education should not only be preserved at all costs in Ireland, but should be extended to England as well. It is interesting that Gladstone could write in June 1865 that 'the ultramontane spirit is more rampant among the Roman Catholics of England than in Ireland',[3] and then in December of the same year, after attending an interview with the four Irish archbishops, so reverse that belief as to admit that he 'never thought of the expediency and necessity of defending the R.C. laity against their own Prelates!'[4] The unfortunate problem for the bishops was that some lay Catholics were sympathetic to this view, and the negotiations with the Government were to be immensely complicated by intervention of some of these men, usually with the lead of Monsell. Also prominent was W. K. Sullivan, Professor of Chemistry at the Catholic University, and a disciple of Newman's. He worked to uphold the laity, all of whom, 'while anxious for Catholic Education, distrust, if they do not absolutely disbelieve, in the capacity

[1] McGrath, *Newman's University*, p. 497.

[2] W. J. Walsh, *Trinity College and the University of Dublin*, Dublin, 1902, p. 2.

[3] Gladstone Papers, B.M.Add.MS. 44758, f. 83, Memorandum on The O'Donoghue's motion, 8 June 1865.

[4] Carlingford Papers, CP. 1/3, Gladstone to Fortescue, 25 December 1865.

of the Irish priests to conduct a good system of lay education'.[1]

It was The O'Donoghue's motion in June 1865 that again threw open the whole question of education in Ireland, for although it was directed at university reform, and led into the negotiations of the bishops with the Government, the resulting area of debate took in the National System of Education as well. There had been a noticeable relaxing of strife over Irish university education[2] as the bishops' hopes of achieving anything of the Government, in the backwash from their 1859 demands, grew less. The O'Donoghue's motion, by convincing the Government of the need to take some action on Irish universities,[3] drew in the bishops too. But it is important to notice, first, that The O'Donoghue acted on his own initiative, he was not backed by any Irish party like the National Association, nor was the Catholic University consulted by him; and secondly, that the bishops only took up the fight again after they had been informally approached and encouraged to do so by the Government.

In the couple of months preceding his motion there had been a little discussion of Irish education: The O'Donoghue did not act in a vacuum, for although he was not a party to any of these stirrings he cannot have been ignorant of them entirely. In April, Chichester Fortescue, M.P. for Louth, and Chief Secretary in 1865-6, had disclosed, in a letter to Dean Kieran at Dundalk, his preparedness to consent to a 'radical change' in the National System – a system which he upheld, but to the details of which he did not feel wedded.[4] Manning, who was to play no small part in subsequent developments, attempted in May to persuade Gladstone to action on the Catholic University and on Irish education generally. He felt that the Catholic University should be chartered and its degrees thereby recognized in law, and expressed the hope that Gladstone would take up the matter and secure the desired end.[5] Gladstone agreed to see Woodlock, the Rector of the Catholic University, but believed that the safest course was to qualify Irish educational establishments to send their pupils for examination and degree to the Queen's University[6] – a view which looked forward to the Supplemental Charter Scheme of the following year. On 1 June

[1] Monsell Papers, Box 8319, Sullivan to Monsell, 1 June 1866.
[2] W. K. Sullivan, *University Education in Ireland, A Letter to Sir John Acton*, Dublin, 1866, p. 4.
[3] John MacDevitt, *op. cit.*, p. 2.
[4] Carlingford Papers, CP. 3/38, Fortescue to Kieran, 19 April 1865.
[5] Gladstone Papers, B.M.Add.MS. 44248, f. 270. Manning to Gladstone, 6 May 1865.
[6] *Ibid.*, Add.MS. 44248, f. 274, Gladstone to Manning, 9 May 1865.

Judge Keogh delivered a lecture in Dublin on 'Milton's Prose', in the course of which he lauded Milton's justification of God's ways 'by asserting the right of all men to exercise unrestrained their intellectual faculties . . . to determine *for themselves* what is truth and what is false-hood'[1] – a phrase which was at once picked up and made the occasion of yet another execration of the unhappy judge. Cullen joined in this; the opinion Keogh had expressed was a frontal attack on the claim of the Church to 'teach all nations' and to determine faith and morals.[2] Keogh had in a phrase denied the educational claims that Cullen had made in his Pastoral of January 1865 announcing the National Association. In that place Cullen had emphasized the crucial nature of education, since it was that 'on which the future welfare of our religion chiefly depends'.[3] But although he made full demand in the Pastoral for Catholic education at all levels, to receive the same State financial aid that the existing mixed system obtained, he did nothing about it until moved by the Government later in the year.

In May, The O'Donoghue gave notice of his motion praying for a Charter of Incorporation for the Catholic University. From the beginning the Government were prepared to conciliate. Grey asked Lord Wodehouse, the Lord-Lieutenant of Ireland, if there was any other plan which, whilst satisfying Catholic demands, did not go quite so far as incorporation.[4] Wodehouse replied that he had heard nothing of the question until lately, but referred to a suggestion of allowing the Queen's University to confer degrees upon affiliated colleges, of which the Catholic University could be one, though expressing some doubt as to whether the Catholics would ever accept connexion, even in this way, with the condemned Queen's Colleges.[5] Gladstone's attitude to The O'Donoghue's notice, doubtless formulated with care after his receipt of Manning's appeal, appears in notes he made on 8 June in anticipation of the coming debate. He saw no difficulty in resisting the motion, provided it could be done on tenable grounds, but their present position with regard to higher education in Ireland seemed to him to be

[1] *The Times*, 2 June 1865.
[2] *Ibid.*, see also John MacDevitt, *op. cit.*, p. 14.
[3] *Freeman*, 31 January 1865.
[4] Cabinet Paper of 25 November 1865; Grey to Wodehouse, 23 May 1865. This paper was printed for Cabinet use, and reviewed some of the official correspondence on the Irish university question throughout the year. There is a copy in the Gladstone Papers – B.M.Add.MS. 44604, f. 52 – with Gladstone's own annotations. Hereinafter referred to as 'Cabinet Paper, 25 November 1865'.
[5] *Ibid.*, Wodehouse to Grey, 24 May 1865. He cited O'Reilly's objections to such affiliation in his *Dublin Review* articles (wrongly given by him as *Dublin University Magazine*), of 1863-4.

'totally untenable'. Catholic medical students in Dublin who believed that their education ought to be directed by their own Church were unable to obtain degrees, and legal students could not proceed to the bar with the same facility or rapidity, as Protestants if they did not possess a degree. In this sort of way, he felt, '*civil disabilities* are still in 1865 attached to *religious opinions*; and this in the matter of education, which the State professes, and desires, and spends much money, to encourage'. If the Roman Catholics would accept the affiliation of their existing College to London University, it would be well. But if they would not, then he did not see how the Government could resist the concession of a Charter to them.[1]

Gladstone's expression of the idea that the Dublin Catholic University could be affiliated to London was not indeed to be entertained, for effort became concentrated on the abortive attempt to reconstruct the Queen's University into an Irish London University. But the idea was not irrational. Wiseman had allowed English Catholics to attend the Universities of Oxford and Cambridge, where they could not of course take degrees because of the existence of the religious test until 1871, but Manning enforced prohibition on this in 1864-5, on the ground that these universities were 'mixed' and so occasioned dangers to the Catholic undergraduates' faith and morals.[2] He obtained advice from Cullen on the evils of Catholic attendance at such universities.[3] Newman's attempt to found an Oratory at Oxford, intended as the nucleus of a Catholic college, was also squashed, although it is interesting that it had the support of Monsell[4] – much to Cullen's disgust.[5] After the prohibition on Oxford and Cambridge, the only one Catholics were allowed to attend was the secular London University, a curious paradox. Although Propaganda in 1867 interdicted attendance at 'non-Catholic' universities, which should have applied to London, it became clear in experience that it was only the former definition against 'Protestant universities' which was taken to apply.[6] Manning was prepared to put up with that much, for it quietened those who favoured the Oxford

---

[1] Gladstone Papers, B.M.Add.MS. 44754, f. 83, 8 June 1865.

[2] See E. S. Purcell, *Life of Cardinal Manning*, London, 1895, vol. II, pp. 288-303; and V. A. McClelland, *Cardinal Manning, His Public Life and Influence, 1865-1892*, London, 1962, p. 92.

[3] Shane Leslie, *H. E. Manning, His Life and Labours*, London, 1921, p. 184.

[4] Kirby Papers, Cullen to Kirby, no. 20, 31 January 1865; and Monsell Papers, Box 8319, Simson to Monsell, 18 December 1864.

[5] For the details of this proposal and its fate, see Meriol Trevor, *Newman, Light in Winter*, London, 1962, pp. 346-59, and 582-636; and V. A. McClelland, *op. cit.*, p. 93.

[6] H. O. Evennett, 'Catholics and the Universities', in *The English Catholics, 1850-1950*, ed. G. A. Beck, p. 316; and Leslie, *op. cit.*, p. 187.

Paul, Cardinal Cullen
from the portrait at St. Patrick's College, Dublin

Leahy   Machale

Moriarty   Woodlock

The portrait of Woodlock is at St. Mel's College, Longford;
the other three at St. Patrick's College, Maynooth

college plan, and anyway, except for the Catholic University in Dublin, which was intended for the whole British Isles but never in fact fulfilled that object, there was no alternative until the Kensington College came into existence in 1874. The same could not be said for Cullen; he already had his own (if unchartered) university and had declared most strongly against both the Queen's Colleges and Trinity. London he would have regarded as identified in error with these. Comparison between Irish university plans, as they developed in the next couple of years, and the English Oxford college scheme, did not, however, go unexamined.[1]

As the time came on towards The O'Donoghue's motion, Grey's suspicion that it had some justice waxed strong. Like Gladstone, he saw the grounds for the complaint that degrees could only be had in Ireland by passing through colleges forbidden by the hierarchy. 'However much we may desire to promote mixed education', he wrote to Wodehouse, 'we cannot compel all Roman Catholics to agree with us.' He still regarded chartering the Catholic University as inadmissible, but suggested instead the *system* of London with its affiliated colleges; 'it works here with satisfaction to the Roman Catholics'.[2] Wodehouse was convinced of the inevitability of some change 'sooner or later', and confirmed Grey's suggestion. But there would be objections to interfering with the Queen's Colleges: Berwick, President of the Galway College, had already represented the seriousness of these, and maintained that if students of the Catholic University could obtain degrees there from some central examining body, the bishops would tighten their declarations against the Queen's Colleges into a positive ban. On the other hand, the President of the Cork College, Kane, was not unfavourable; and Henry of Belfast felt that his College would be little affected by such a change as it was almost exclusively Presbyterian anyway. Wodehouse also made the point which became the basis for subsequent discussion:

> The easiest way of admitting the students from the R.C. Universities to degrees would be to extend the powers of the Queen's University so as to enable the Senate to grant degrees to students from any Colleges who passed the prescribed examination. The composition of the Senate would, however, require to be altered, and its re-arrangement would be a very delicate matter. Still, if the Roman Catholics accepted the scheme, the difficulties would not be insuperable.[3]

[1] *Dublin Review*, July 1868, 'Catholic University Education in Ireland', p. 235.
[2] Cabinet Paper, 25 November 1865. Grey to Wodehouse, 15 June 1865.
[3] *Ibid.*, Wodehouse to Grey, 16 June 1865. This proposal must have been discussed in the Cabinet almost immediately, for Grey had sought Wodehouse's opinions with the Cabinet deliberations especially in mind.

He went also to some pains to show that such a concession would not undermine the mixed National System. The cases were quite distinct. The National Schools had no privileges comparable to the giving of degrees, and a child educated in a denominational school was in the same position as one educated nationally. It was only higher education that required modification, 'especially when in England Roman Catholics are, through the action of the London University, placed upon a perfect equality'.[1] The Cabinet concurred in Wodehouse's view when his letter was read to them by Grey.[2]

On 20 June, The O'Donoghue moved, at last, in the Commons 'That an Address be presented to Her Majesty, representing to Her Majesty that conscientious objections to the present system of University Education in Ireland prevent a large number of Her Majesty's subjects from enjoying the advantages of a University Education, and praying that such steps may be taken as will remedy this grievance.'[3] Catholics, he affirmed in his speech, could not go to the existing university institutions without falling under the disfavour of the Church. In Belfast, where the total number of students was 405, only 22 were Catholics; in Cork there were 263 of whom 123 were Catholics; in Galway there were 169 and 78 of these were Catholics; and in Trinity College only 45 of the 1,000 students were Catholics. Thus the total number of students in the legally recognized Irish universities was 1,837, of whom the number of Catholics was only 268.[4] What, then was the remedy? It was a simple one he said. Let a Charter of Incorporation be granted to the Catholic University which already existed in Dublin, but which had no existence in law. The Catholics who had founded it had contributed £130,000 for its support, and they did not ask for a grant of public money, but only for a charter. The Catholics of Canada and Australia had chartered universities, so why could not those of Ireland make use of the precedents?[5] The Catholic University was of good standard, and he was 'authorized to say, on the part of the heads of the Catholic University, that they courted the fullest publicity, and earnestly desired that all their arrangements should be submitted to the most searching scrutiny'.[6] This last claim by The O'Donoghue was denied by Professor Sullivan of the university.[7]

Sir George Grey replied for the Government. He regretted the opposition of the Roman Catholic hierarchy to mixed education, and

---

[1] Cabinet Paper, 25 November 1865. Grey to Wodehouse, 15 June 1865.
[2] *Ibid.*, Grey to Peel, 19 June 1865; Grey to Wodehouse, 21 June 1865.
[3] *Hansard*, CLXXX, p. 541.   [4] *Ibid.*, p. 543.   [5] *Ibid.*, p. 545.
[6] *Ibid.*, p. 546.   [7] W. K. Sullivan, *op. cit.*, p. 4.

considered Catholics mistaken in forgoing the advantages it offered, but they could still not shut their eyes to the facts. There were Protestants as well as Catholics who entertained 'feelings of aversion and distrust' towards the Queen's Colleges.[1] He made the distinction emphasized by Wodehouse between mixed primary education and universities with the right of giving degrees; 'to that extent I think there is reasonable ground of complaint, and it is one the justice of which the Government admit'.[2] But they could not consent to chartering the existing Catholic institution, on the principle that it was bad to multiply the number of bodies conferring degrees.[3] They proposed instead 'an enlargement of the powers of the Queen's University in Ireland, by amending its Charter, so as to remove the restriction which now prevents it from granting degrees to any students except those who have passed through the course of instruction in one or other of the Queen's Colleges, and thus adopting a system analogous to that found to work satisfactorily in the University of London'.[4] This also followed Wodehouse. He anticipated an 'earnest rivalry' between the different institutions which, he believed, would promote a high educational standard.[5]

It was left to Whiteside to repeat the allegation of Berwick, and of Peel,[6] that if such an alteration were made in the Queen's University, Cullen and the bishops would implement their threat to withhold the sacraments from any who did not send their sons to the college which would be under their direct supervision.[7] But Monsell welcomed the proposal,[8] sweeping aside the opposition of Cairns and Newdegate, and also of Pope-Hennessy (M.P. for King's Co.) who still demanded an independent Catholic Charter.[9] Having secured promised action by the Government, The O'Donoghue withdrew his motion.

Grey was satisfied; all reasonable men, and all the Roman Catholic members of the House with the exception only of Pope-Hennessy, were fully satisfied. Dunne wrote to let him know the concurrence of Woodlock and Sullivan, believing the Government's proposal would materially improve the educational condition of Ireland.[10] Wodehouse was delighted that it was his plan which had been adopted.[11] Sullivan approved also

[1] *Hansard*, CLXXX, p. 551.   [2] *Ibid.*, p. 552.   [3] *Ibid.*, p. 554.
[4] *Ibid.*, p. 555.   [5] *Ibid.*, p. 556.
[6] Cabinet Paper, 25 November 1865; Peel to Grey, 18 June 1865.
[7] *Hansard*, CLXXX, p. 560.   [8] *Ibid.*, p. 567.
[9] *Ibid.*, see also, W. K. Sullivan, *op. cit.*, p. 4.; and *Annual Register*, 1865 (History). Pope-Hennessy raised the matter again a few days later, by asking if the Government had had secret negotiations with the hierarchy on their proposal. This drew an emphatic denial from Grey.
[10] Cabinet Paper, 25 November 1865. Grey to Wodehouse, 21 June 1865.
[11] *Ibid.*, Wodehouse to Grey, 22 June 1865.

of the idea that competition between the Colleges would benefit education, believing that as a result a high uniform standard would be attained.[1] Grey had now two points to consider; these, as he wrote to Wodehouse, were whether under the new Charter, the Queen's University should be empowered to grant degrees to all who passed its examinations, as at London, or whether degrees ought to be given only to those from affiliated colleges; secondly – and this was much more difficult – how the Senate should be so constructed as to command the confidence of all parties. This last must be done, 'while retaining in the hands of the Crown the absolute nomination of its members'.[2] This point he knew to be essential to the success of the scheme. It was to be that which disturbed the Irish bishops.

Cullen was sceptical at first; especially as the general election was due in July:

> The Government seem disposed to incorporate the [Catholic] University as a College, giving it the right to possess property, etc., and then to establish a National University which will not teach but merely confer degrees. Belgium and France have something of this kind. The Government has not communicated anything officially, so we do not know what they will do. Probably the whole business may be an electioneering trick.[3]

Dr Dorrian was more sanguine. He saw a prospect of obtaining an arrangement for the Catholic University which would not lower its status, leave education in the hands of the bishops, and would incorporate the existing institution, giving it 'proper and safe' representation on the Senate. 'But we had better say little', he wrote to Kirby, 'till all danger of adverse influence is over.'[4] Not only the professors of the Catholic University, but the Catholic party generally, were reported by *The Times* as regarding the Government statement as a most important concession, and generally as satisfactory.[5] Yet some Ulster Liberals regarded it as a triumph for the enemies of united education[6] – the very thing Grey had tried to show it was not – but they bided their time, probably awaiting the arrangement of detail.

Meanwhile the details were already being considered. Again the basic proposals came from Wodehouse, in answer to Grey's two points. He favoured the London University system (the 'open system') of granting degrees to any who qualified, because if it should be restricted only to those from affiliated colleges, grave difficulties would arise as to

[1] W. K. Sullivan, *op. cit.*, p. 5.
[2] Cabinet Paper, 25 November 1865. Wodehouse to Grey, 22 June 1865.
[3] Kirby Papers, Cullen to Kirby, no. 140, 27 June 1865.
[4] *Ibid.*, Dorrian to Kirby, no. 141, 27 June 1865.
[5] *The Times*, 23 June 1865.   [6] *Ibid.*

which colleges should be so affiliated. This would be dangerous too: for the body determining affiliation would be the Senate, which, since it was to be composed of men already at odds about religion, could not be relied on, and in fact the fewer the number of questions referred to it the better. Above all, in arranging their plan, the Government should not attempt to consider 'the best form of university', but what was most just for Ireland, otherwise they would become involved in 'discussions of the most difficult character'. Also, if there were no affiliated colleges, the bishops would not be able to censure those who did not choose to enter their own, and so their ultramontane design of a monopoly over education would be frustrated. But although the 'open system' was the most satisfactory it remained to be seen whether the hierarchy could be induced to accept it, and he was not hopeful. On the other hand, should the Catholic University be affiliated, it would sink to the level of a college ('You cannot affiliate an University to an University'), and this, he felt, was why many Roman Catholics, whilst they would accept the present scheme as a first step, would really like the Belgian system. There four separate universities came under one body for examination and the conferring of degrees. They would thus prefer no interference with their College, even to the extent of affiliation. It was because of this that he hoped they would be more agreeable to the 'open system'. Grey's second point, the reconstitution of the Senate, was, he agreed, more difficult. O'Hagan had spoken with him on it, and believed that the hierarchy would insist that certain of their numbers should be *ex officio* members of the Senate. Wodehouse could not approve that, not only because the *ex officio* principle was bad, but because it would admit an even worse one – that ecclesiastics, as such, have a right to control education. They must conciliate, and let 'ultramontane' bishops have a 'potential voice' in the Senate if it were demanded, but they should not sit there as an indefeasible right. The numbers of Catholics and non-Catholics in the Senate should balance equally, as was the case at that time with the National Board of Education and the Bequests' Board. There were then only four Catholics on the Senate, which consisted of twenty-four, so eight more would have to be added if this suggestion were adopted. In the letter in which he put these views for the Government's consideration, he said also that Monsell and O'Reilly in London could be consulted by Grey over the details, and that O'Hagan was going over to help.[1]

On 7 July, Monsell met Wodehouse in Dublin: he pressed strongly for a Charter incorporating the Roman Catholic University as a College,

[1] Cabinet Paper, 25 November 1865. Wodehouse to Grey, 28 June 1865.

and although he was undetermined on the exact terms of such a charter, he indicated that those granted to King's and to University College, London, would be appropriate. He mentioned Lampeter College in the same sense. Wodehouse felt that he would probably be satisfied with the 'open system' though he would have preferred complete affiliation ('close system'). He also suggested to Monsell that they might employ the form of the revised Charter of London – which had started 'close' but had moved to the 'open system', so allowing the admission under certain conditions of students from non-affiliated colleges. This would enable the Government to mention the Queen's Colleges and the Catholic University 'College' in the new Charter. Monsell, apparently agreeable, outlined a Senate of half ecclesiastics, half laymen, and with power of filling vacancies by election. His own suggestions were Corrigan and Kane, Cullen, Russell (of Maynooth), Moriarty, Canon Forde (of Dublin), O'Reilly, Woodlock, O'Conor Don, Aubrey de Vere, O'Hagan and Sullivan. This met with Wodehouse's approval, and in forwarding the list to Grey, he added also the name of Monsell himself. He was now clear that their plans turned on the question of the grant of a Charter to the Catholic University as a college. If this was not conceded, the plan would fail.[1]

The Cabinet had met on the 6th and discussed the Irish University plan, but had postponed any decision.[2] Delays were inevitable; even if there were no opinions still to be sounded, the close proximity of the general election impeded progress. Grey, meanwhile, could see no objection to incorporating the Catholic University as a college, but waited for the opinion of the Irish Law Officers on the legality of such a proceeding before bringing it before the Cabinet. This was sent to him from Dublin on 22 July. In an accompanying note, Wodehouse announced O'Hagan's identity with Monsell's views.[3] This was an important factor, for Grey had great confidence in O'Hagan's judgment.[4] The Law Officers, James Lawson and Edward Sullivan, believed that the powers of the Crown to grant a charter to an exclusively Roman Catholic college or university in Ireland were so doubtful that they could only safely be exercised with the sanction of Parliament. The Crown could, however, create any new College or university, provided it was not intended for the exclusive use of Roman Catholics, and in such an institution they could hold office and take degrees. But should the

---

[1] Cabinet Paper, 25 November 1865. Wodehouse to Grey, 7 July 1865.
[2] *Ibid.*, Grey to Wodehouse, 7 July 1865.
[3] *Ibid.*, Wodehouse to Grey, 22 July 1865.
[4] *Ibid.*, Grey to Wodehouse, 7 July 1865.

charter be silent on the matter of religion it would create a college open to all denominations, and although its exclusively Catholic governing body might mean that in fact only Catholics would attend it, that would not invalidate the charter.[1] To this opinion, the Irish Attorney-General added, for clarity, that there was no legal objection to the governing body being composed entirely of Catholics.[2]

This was decisive. There was no longer any question of chartering the Roman Catholic institution as a university, and the Government plan could mature. At the Cabinet on 24 July no objection was raised to Grey's suggestion of chartering it as a college, and a draft of such a proposed charter was ordered.[3]

At this point, Bruce (Vice-President of the Committee of Privy Council for Education), who was afterwards to make informal representations to the hierarchy on the plan, left for Ireland on private matters, but was referred by Grey to both Wodehouse and Monsell.[4] The latter was already becoming worried about the bishops. He had heard from Woodlock at the beginning of July that they would 'not give up the College founded by the people', although he, and apparently Woodlock, regarded such a stand as misconceived.[5] More O'Ferrall (M.P. for Kildare) distrusted them both, and said so to Cullen. He also advised the utmost caution:

I believe there never was a period since the agitation of the veto, of so much danger to Catholic interests. The Government are ready to purchase, and we have people willing to treat, but as long as the Bishops are no party to a treaty there is no danger. When the Government state their plan, the Bishops will give their opinion, without being influenced by any acts, opinions, or engagements entered into by any individuals, lay or clerical. I believe I am right in stating that this will be the course adopted by the Bishops.[6]

Monsell was emphatic about the error of the bishops' insistence on desiring to see the governing body of their proposed college exclusively ecclesiastical. He had outlined the plan for a senate to Wodehouse at their meeting on the 7th, and he explained in a letter to Grey on 27 July that it was constructed on the principle of Maynooth. He could not see why the bishops objected to that too. He undertook to sound the

---

[1] *Ibid.* The Law Officers' opinion is dated 20 July. Its provisions are based on the Relief Act (10 Geo. IV, cap. 7), which had not removed previous legal declarations that no exclusively Roman Catholic college or university could be founded in Ireland.

[2] *Ibid.*, Wodehouse to Grey, 23 July 1865.

[3] *Ibid.*, Grey to Wodehouse, 25 July 1865.

[4] *Ibid.*, and Grey to Monsell, 27 July 1865.

[5] Cullen Papers, More O'Ferrall to Cullen, 5 July 1865.

[6] *Ibid.*

bishops and attempt to elucidate their concrete proposals.[1] Meanwhile he was preparing a gathering at his house, Tervoe, Co. Limerick, to discuss the university question.

In the first week of August O'Hagan, Aubrey de Vere, Moriarty, and Butler (Bishop of Limerick) gathered at Tervoe as Monsell's guests. They were joined by Bruce, who had come from meeting Corrigan, Sullivan, and Dunne, and by Woodlock. There was to have been a meeting of the hierarchy in Dublin on the university question in the middle of the week, but it was postponed until 22 August.[2] Woodlock and Butler left to go up to Dublin, but came back bringing the news of the postponement – but no other; they had been unable to ascertain the course the bishops would take.[3]

The discussions at Monsell's left Bruce with the impression that the bishops' support must be won by concessions. Above all they feared, he imagined, giving the appearance of sanctioning the principle upon which the condemned Queen's Colleges had been established. It was suggested to him that they would favour a change in the title of a reconstituted Queen's University – 'Royal Irish University' would be acceptable to them. Monsell and O'Hagan favoured the opening of the burses, then limited to the Queen's Colleges, to general competition and Bruce endorsed this strongly. There was also some sign in the discussion that the advocates of affiliation were weakening.[4] Bruce also noted jealousy among the lay Catholics of the growth of episcopal power in Ireland – but this was to be expected, for those he met at Tervoe were principally the anglophile liberal Catholics and 'Limerick convert' set.[5] He anticipated opposition by the bishops to Monsell's suggested alteration in the Catholic College Charter allowing for the governing body to be half lay and half ecclesiastic. Throughout these discussions he was most careful not to commit the Government on any point.[6]

Reflecting on the Tervoe meeting, Woodlock felt only disappointment, but he could still see some good points in the Government plans. 'You may remember', he wrote to Monsell on 11 August, 'that when the proposal was made last June in London, I was well pleased with it: since then I have been most anxious, and worked very hard, to obtain the Bishops' concurrence in carrying it out; at the same time I said that its value would depend on the way it was carried out.'[7] He did not now

---

[1] Cabinet Paper, 25 November 1865. Monsell to Grey, 24 July 1865.
[2] *Ibid.*, Bruce to Grey, 7 August 1865.
[3] *Ibid.*, Bruce to Grey, 9 August 1865.   [4] *Ibid.*
[5] See chap. 7 on the opinion held by this group on the Church question.
[6] Cabinet Paper, 25 November 1865. Bruce to Grey, 9 August 1865.
[7] Monsell Papers, Box 8319, Woodlock to Monsell, 11 August 1865.

believe that it was being carried out satisfactorily. He had understood Grey to mean that their Catholic College was to be placed on as good a footing as the Queen's Colleges, although he realized it did not imply a monetary grant. Grey had spoken in the House of a race between the colleges, but the competition would hardly be fair if their own college started as 'but one of the numerous schools and Colleges throughout Ireland to which the new University is to be open'. And the Queen's Colleges were to continue with all their endowments and buildings. He would like to see the Government acting with the Catholics in 'a more liberal spirit'; so half-hearted were their concessions, that he now felt almost indifferent to the result of the approaching deliberations of the bishops. He would follow any instructions they might give him, but as he felt at that point in the evolution of the plan, he would be inclined to turn down a seat on the Senate if one were offered him. He would allow his students to get 'all the advantages they can in the scramble' but he was really of opinion that Catholics should temporize: if the plan worked when in effect, then they could join it. He asked Monsell to make these feelings known to Bruce, who, he urged, must confer directly with the bishops, preferably at their forthcoming meeting in Dublin, and place the Government proposals before them in more detail.[1]

MacHale also felt the need for more information regarding the details, and wrote to Grey requesting them.[2] He was told in reply that the principle on which the Government would act had been given in his speech (on The O'Donoghue's motion), and that details of the arrangements could not be disclosed until they had been submitted to, and approved by the Cabinet.[3] MacHale was, as could only be expected from his past record on university matters, evidently antagonistic. Once again, Cullen despaired. 'Dr MacHale has not done anything for the Catholic University in the last thirteen years. He condemns everything, but gives nothing, and will take no part', he wrote to Kirby on the 14th.[4] Nor was he hopeful of the coming meeting of the bishops. He was ignorant of the Government's intentions, and saw little chance of the bishops agreeing about anything; but unless something *were* obtained from the Government, the Queen's Colleges 'will go ahead'. Still the position seemed impossible: 'The division among the Bishops and Dr MacHale's

---

[1] *Ibid.* Monsell's final views, as expressed at the time of the bishops' meeting, are given in his 'Memorandum on the University Question', in the Cabinet Paper of 25 November (Item 36).

[2] *Parliamentary Papers*, 1866, LV, 243, 'Copies of Memorials', p. 3; MacHale to Grey, 9 August 1865.

[3] *Ibid.*, p. 3; Grey to MacHale, 12 August 1865.

[4] Kirby Papers, Cullen to Kirby, no. 180, 14 August 1865.

opposition' could not only place their meeting in jeopardy, it also encouraged the people to withhold subscriptions from the Catholic University, and some priests, trading on MacHale's example, encouraged them.[1] Yet despite this Bruce, who was remaining in Dublin for the bishops' meeting, was able to find some hope in his reading of Cardinal Barnabo's letter instructing Cullen to call it, which was shown to him by Moriarty. It seemed to him to be so worded as to imply that Cullen was favourable to at least serious consideration of the Government plans. Meanwhile, Monsell and other laymen were moving away from the 'open' scheme to affiliation again, in order to secure official recognition of their Catholic College.[2] Bruce counselled concession as the only safe means of saving the day.

The twenty-seven bishops met in Dublin on 22 August, and on the second and last day Bruce submitted proposals through Dr Butler for their consideration.[3] He refused to offer them officially, or give any assurance that if they were accepted by the bishops, the Government would adopt them.[4] His heads of proposal were:

1. That the Charter granted to the Queen's University be withdrawn, and a new Charter be granted to a Body to be called 'The Royal Irish University'.

2. That the Senate of such University consist of an equal number of Roman Catholics and Protestants.

3. That the number of Members of the Senate be 32, in the first instance; to be named by Her Majesty's Government, after consultation with the heads of the different bodies to be represented.

4. That of these 32 members, 6 be specially named as Government nominees. 6 more shall be selected at first and ever after from the religious bodies in the following proportions, *viz.* 3 Roman Catholic prelates, 2 prelates of the Established Church, and 1 member from the Synod of Ulster; 8 shall consist of those whose places are to be supplied hereafter by election by the whole body of graduates; and 12 whose places shall be supplied, as vacancies occur, by election, the Protestant by the Protestant, the Catholic by the Roman Catholic members of the Senate.

5. That the Colleges expressly affiliated by the Charter be, in the first instance, the Queen's Colleges and the Roman Catholic College; that the Senate have the

[1] Kirby Papers, Cullen to Kirby, no. 180, 14 August 1865. Four dioceses had given nothing to the Catholic University that year, and eight or ten had given very little.

[2] Cabinet Paper, 25 November 1865. Bruce to Grey, 17 August 1865.

[3] *Ibid.*, Bruce to Grey, 1 September 1865. There was some feeling that Bruce would actually attend the meeting, but he did not – partly, perhaps, as the *Nation* suggested subsequently (16 December 1865), because of the Archbishop of Tuam's fears for the independence of hierarchy.

[4] Cabinet Paper, 25 November 1865. 'Memorandum of Basis for the foundation and Government of proposed Irish University, suggested by Mr Bruce to the Right Revd. Dr Butler, August 23, 1865, it being clearly understood that while Mr Bruce is prepared to recommend to her Majesty's Government the adoption of such basis, he is unable to guarantee, and expressly declines to guarantee, such adoption.'

power of affiliating on demand such other Colleges as they may deem proper, with further power if experience should prove that it is unadvisable or impracticable to maintain the distinction between Colleges admitted and excluded; to admit all persons, wherever educated, who are able to pass the required examination.

6. That there be one uniform matriculating examination for all who present themselves.

7. That either by the application of existing or the creation of new endowments, honours and scholarships be provided so as to place the rewards of merit equally within the reach of all members of the University.

8. That the University may hold (over and above premises for its immediate purposes) any other lands, buildings, etc., not exceeding an annual value of £10,000 at time of taking, etc.

Roman Catholic College. It is understood that a Charter for this College will be granted in terms to be approved by Her Majesty's Government. The following scheme is suggested as likely to be approved – That the 4 R.C. Archbishops be the Visitors; that the property of the College be vested in them, or such other trustees as may be thought proper by the present governors; that the Governing Body be the Rector and Professors. The Rector to be appointed by the visitors, who shall also have power to reject, for special errors in faith, morals, or conduct, after due inquiry, any Professor appointed by the governing Body, and to dismiss upon the like grounds any existing Professor. Power of holding land to the value of £10,000 a year.[1]

It will be seen that these proposals were reflections of the conciliation which Bruce had urged on the Government. By Point 5 the 'close' principle of affiliation was upheld, and although provision is made for the Royal to go the same way as the London University, and evolve to the 'open' system, yet the power of determining this is vested in that body to which Wodehouse had said it ought never to belong – in the Senate. Point 7 is Monsell's and O'Hagan's recommendation about burses. The proposed Charter of the Roman Catholic College placed it firmly under the control of the hierarchy.

Bruce heard – no doubt from Dr Butler – that the great majority of the bishops expressed themselves in favour of the proposals.[2] But Cullen evidently considered it an inadequate statement of the Government plan, though he outlined as much as he knew in a letter to Kirby, in which he asked him to find out the opinion of Rome on it.[3] Many Catholics, he said, (doubtless meaning those especially who had met at Tervoe), would favour the bishops' agreement to the idea that

[1] *Ibid.*   [2] *Ibid.*, Bruce to Grey, 26 August 1865.
[3] Kirby Papers, Cullen to Kirby, no. 191, 27 August 1865. The letter is in Italian. The *Nation*, reviewing the August meeting of the bishops, reported (16 December 1865): 'The Holy Father replied that it was for the Irish prelates in council assembled to consider what the English Government really meant to offer, and then, after full deliberation, to lay the matter before the Holy See for its decision.'

bishops should become members of the Senate, since they would obtain some influence on education questions as a result. 'On the other hand,' he felt, 'it would seem strange that the hawks and the doves, the light and the darkness, be placed together to form a united body, and to direct the higher teaching of the country.' Under the proposal for joint examination, however, many things could be tolerated which they would have had to oppose had teaching been involved; and although the Senate would be mixed, the schools and colleges would not. But the bishops were unable to decide anything without a 'detailed exposition' of the plan. All they had done was to appoint the four archbishops to treat with the Government through Grey, and the meeting had been adjourned until more information had become available through their efforts. Cullen asked Kirby to secure a note from the Propaganda instructing him to hold such a meeting – for without it MacHale would introduce discussions about his authority to act in the way suggested.[1] MacHale was certainly at his most intractable, but O'Reilly has correctly suggested that he suspected the Government of not treating with them earnestly.[2]

Bruce had foreseen that the meeting might appoint deputies to discuss the proposals, but he imagined they would treat either with himself or with Wodehouse.[3] Their decision to meet Grey seemed to him, and to Monsell and O'Hagan, absurd. Wodehouse thought similarly, but could see some general good in the idea of 'occasional direct contact between the Roman Catholic prelates and the Government'.[4] Meanwhile the press carried much exaggeration and misconception upon what was actually happening between the Government and the hierarchy.[5] The *Nation*, repeating allegations printed in the *Tablet*, thought that the bishops were about to accept an endowment of £25,000 a year as a condition of sinking the Catholic University to the level of a Queen's College.[6]

---

[1] Kirby Papers, Cullen to Kirby, no. 191, 27 August 1865.

[2] Of these negotiations, O'Reilly wrote: 'In all these negotiations the Archbishop of Tuam adhered inflexibly to his own principles and rules of conduct; and here again his sagacity proved that he knew the Ministers well, and that nothing was to be expected from them but such concessions as a compact unity in the episcopal body, and a compact and independent party in the House of Commons, would compel them to yield to the Catholics of Ireland.' B. O'Reilly, *John MacHale*, vol. II, p. 523. MacHale was himself certainly doing little to secure episcopal unity, but doubtless this was because the episcopate, at least as represented in the National Association, had shown themselves by August 1865 most reluctant to bring about the second condition – Independent Opposition.

[3] Cabinet Paper, 25 November 1865. Bruce to Grey, 17 August 1865.

[4] *Ibid.*, Bruce to Grey, 26 August 1865.

[5] *Nation*, 16 December 1865: 'The guilty fears of the Whig–Orange press led them to spread the most extravagant rumours.'

[6] *Ibid.*, 23 September 1865.

Cullen wrote to Grey requesting the interview on 27 August,[1] stressing that Catholics still reserved their right to equality in education, but that they would not refuse concessions which might diminish 'the evils and injustice of which they have had so long to complain', though such acceptance was not to be taken for acquiescence in mixed education. He also raised their grievances over National Education, referring to the episcopal letter to Cardwell of March 1860. In reply, Grey temporized, using his absence from London as an excuse.[2] When he had learned that the bishops intended to deal directly with Grey, Bruce had suspected that they would raise Catholic grievances generally, in addition to the university question.[3] Cullen's letter proved him right, as Grey himself observed.[4] He could not see any good resulting from an interview at that time, since without reference to other members of the Government he had nothing additional to say. Also, he wanted Bruce to attend, with members of the Cabinet, and could not see the possibility of organizing such a gathering before November. Even so, they would have to be especially careful to avoid their actions appearing to be dependent on the approval of the bishops.[5]

Here matters rested until the interview took place in December. Some clarity was brought to the discussion in the intervening period, however, by the speech which Wodehouse delivered at the annual meeting of the Queen's University on 15 October. He upheld the mixed principle, recognized the need for changes dictated by the requirements of Catholic conscience, and outlined again the Government plan.[6] He said nothing new, but this was the first time it had received public announcement. *The Times* thought it was 'something very like a surrender' of the principle of mixed education; it had the vision to perceive what indeed would have been true, that the new university would be a precedent.[7] The Protestant press generally regarded the plan as a triumph of ultramontanism and a betrayal of the Irish laity.[8] On 17 October, there was another episcopal meeting in Dublin, which, due to the interest engendered by Wodehouse's speech, was widely noticed in the press. But it was a private meeting and no statement or declaration was issued by it. Cullen was evidently pleased with the Government's position and with the temper of the meeting. On the

---

[1] *Parliamentary Papers*, 1866, LV, 243.

[2] Cabinet Paper, 25 November 1865. Grey to Cullen, 28 August 1865.

[3] *Ibid.*, Bruce to Grey, 26 August 1865.

[4] *Ibid.*, Grey to Bruce, 29 August 1865.   [5] *Ibid.*

[6] *Freeman*, 17 October 1865.   [7] *The Times*, 16 October 1865.

[8] Thus, for example, the Dublin *Mail*, 18 October 1865.

following day he wrote to Spalding expressing his belief that the Government might even abolish the mixed system of education.[1] The four archbishops and seventeen bishops attended, probably to exchange considered opinions about the reactions to the now publicized negotiations.[2] The *Express* took the view that conciliation was forced on to the Government by the activity of the small group of National Association members in the House after the 1865 election – but this was unnecessarily machiavellian, for the Government plans were maturing before the election anyway.[3] But Dr Gillooly, speaking to the National Association on 18 October, noted an 'honest desire to conciliate' Ireland, by 'just and impartial legislation'.[4]

Protestant opposition to the Government proposals mounted, but it was not representative of all Protestant opinion. It has been seen that at least two of the heads of the Queen's Colleges were not opposed to the plan, at least as it stood, in somewhat vague terms, and at the inauguration of the Presbyterian Magee College at Londonderry on 10 September, Gibson, a leading member, spoke encouragingly of it.[5] On the other hand, the non-subscribing Presbyterians of Ireland represented against it to the Lord-Lieutenant.[6] Public opinion was disturbed in October by a curious sequence of events in Belfast which seemed to confirm Protestant fears of ultramontane education, and which certainly hardened their opposition. The Catholic bishop, Dorrian, had joined issue with the 'Catholic Institute' of that city in April over its rules. The Institute was a literary society with a reading-room, and the bishop demanded four conditions for its continued operation. They amounted to episcopal control and supervision of its management and membership, and of the newspapers which were to be allowed in its reading-room. The incidents attending this demand came to a head in October, and ended, after the bishop had threatened to withhold the sacraments from those who would not submit to his requirements, in the voluntary closure of the Institute in November by its members. The whole affair received the widest publicity, and seemed to be an attack by the episcopacy on the educational rights of the laity.[7]

[1] Spalding Letters, Cullen to Spalding, 18 October 1865.
[2] This was the opinion of *The Times* (20 October 1865), the *Freeman* (18 October 1865) and *Saunders* (18 October 1865).
[3] *Express*, 20 October 1865.
[4] *The Times*, 20 October 1865.
[5] Cabinet Paper, 26 November 1865. Wodehouse to Grey, 23 October 1865. Enclosed is a copy of Gibson's speech.
[6] *Ibid.* (enclosures).
[7] *Mail* (Dublin), 27 October 1865; *The Times*, 3 and 20 November 1865. For a justification of the bishops' actions, see MacDevitt, *op. cit.*, pp. 15-18. The case was

In November, Wodehouse received a memorial got up by Professor Nesbitt and signed by thirty-seven Queen's professors, objecting to the proposed alterations.[1] On 6 December a public meeting was held in Belfast of the graduates of the Queen's University; their *Statement*, which they published, condemned the proposed changes to their university, though acknowledging that they were as yet vaguely known.[2] It was also suggested that the meeting was convened irregularly, since the great majority of the Catholic graduates knew nothing about it. As a result they sent a counter-memorial to Earl Russell putting the Catholic case.[3] It was probably awareness of this sort of feeling which induced Cullen, in his Pastoral of 9 November appealing for collections for the Catholic University, to attack Protestant education with some bitterness, especially warning of the evils of Trinity College.[4]

Towards the end of October, Grey had decided that the best way of bringing the matter before the Cabinet again would be by submitting to them the draft of an amended Charter for the Queen's University, and he asked Wodehouse to produce one, leaving out reference to Point 7 of Bruce's memorandum (scholarships) as it should have separate consideration.[5] Wodehouse agreed, using Bruce's memorandum as a basis,[6] and employing the Irish Attorney-General (Lawson) for the actual drafting.[7] It was sent to Grey on 20 November.[8] It followed Bruce's memorandum closely, except that Point 4 was revised so that it was not necessary, in the Senate, for Protestants alone to elect Protestant Senators, and Catholics the Catholics. For as Wodehouse felt, 'the wall of separation between the two creeds is surely high enough already without the Government building it higher?'[9] In the revised arrangement, each new member of the Senate was to be elected by all existing members irrespective of their religion. This would also provide for the unlikely exigency of a Jew seeking election.[10] Bruce himself approved of the change.[11] Wodehouse did doubt the wisdom of one

also referred to, as evidence of Catholic educational despotism, by Lord Claud Hamilton during the debate in May 1867 on Gray's motion. *Hansard*, CLXXXVII, p. 175.

[1] Cabinet Paper, 25 November 1865. Wodehouse to Grey, 16 November 1865. (The memorial is an enclosure.) Also in *Parliamentary Papers*, 1866, LV, 'Copies of Memorials', p. 19.

[2] *Statement Adopted by the Graduates of the Queen's University in Ireland.* Belfast, 1865. Also in *Parliamentary Papers*, 1866, LV, 'Copies of Memorials', p. 26.

[3] W. K. Sullivan, *op. cit.*, p. 6.   [4] *Freeman*, 14 November 1865.

[5] Cabinet Paper, 25 November 1865. Grey to Wodehouse, 30 October 1865.

[6] *Ibid.*, Wodehouse to Grey, 1 November 1865.

[7] *Ibid.*, Wodehouse to Grey, 6 November 1865.

[8] *Ibid.*, Wodehouse to Grey, 20 November 1865.

[9] *Ibid.*   [10] *Ibid.*, Wodehouse to Grey, 21 November 1865.

[11] *Ibid.*, Bruce to Grey, 23 November 1865.

provision in the proposed charter, that of binding the Crown to appoint a certain number of Catholic and Protestant bishops, as it seemed to recognize the right of ecclesiastics to control lay education.[1] But on this point Bruce was immovable. Unhappily, he maintained, Ireland was 'a priest-ridden country', and although subservience could only be removed by education, those who were subject would not consent to an education unsanctioned by their bishops. Admit the bishops to the Senate, therefore, and they would be powerless for mischief; but if they were excluded they would soon undermine the comprehensive system of education now proposed.[2]

In December, after the meeting with the four archbishops, Fortescue wrote to all who had been present on the Government side, seeking opinion on the question of *ex officio* bishops on the Senate. Gladstone could see the difficulty which this might cause, but found no abstract objection. He did fear the Government moving too far in advance of English public opinion.[3]

Now that a firmer basis existed for negotiation the four archbishops went to London to meet Grey. The interview took place in the first week of December. Representing the Government, Grey had with him Cardwell, Gladstone and Bruce. Sir John Gray apparently acted as *amicus curiae*.[4] The archbishops were unanimous in their views, and as MacHale was present, this is a fair indication that they confined themselves to matters on which all four *could* agree. They did not discuss the Catholic University as a result.[5] First they raised, as Grey and Bruce had feared, the general grievances of Catholics with the National System of Education, and once again repeated their demand for the denominational principle. Secondly, regarding the Queen's Colleges, they suggested that two of them, Cork and Galway, should become Catholic colleges, and the third, Belfast, Presbyterian. Trinity was to be placed on an equal footing with the others, and to remain exclusive to the Established Church. Such an arrangement would be no more than a recognition of the facts, as things had tended to settle themselves naturally very much in this sort of way. Thirdly, on the Model Schools,

---

[1] Cabinet Paper, 25 November 1856. Wodehouse to Grey, 20 November 1865.

[2] *Ibid.*, Bruce to Grey, 23 November 1865.

[3] 'For if we set that against us, all our good intentions will come to little', he said in reply to Fortescue: Carlingford Papers, CP. 1/3, Gladstone to Fortescue, 25 December 1865.

[4] *Nation*, 16 December 1865.

[5] The three other archbishops would probably have preferred to keep MacHale out of the negotiations as he had already expressed himself against them on principle, but it was necessary, in order to maintain the appearance of episcopal unity, for him to be present.

St. Patrick's College, Maynooth, Co. Kildare, June 1963

A Protestant view of Irish Religion : 'Monks in Ireland burning the Bible'
Cartoon from *The Bulwark or Reformation Journal*, 1852

the Government party were already convinced that the existing state of affairs was unsatisfactory to all concerned, and though they were prepared to consider doing something, they did not go so far as the four archbishops, who stigmatized them as miniature 'infidel Colleges'. Fourthly, they insisted that the revenues of Trinity College were so used as to exclude four-fifths of the population from their benefits; and they suggested that the State appropriate a large part and expend it on a less exclusive educational system. These appear to be all the propositions discussed at the interview,[1] and although they were treated fully, and in a frank and conciliatory spirit, the archbishops' introduction of general educational grievances had prevented negotiation on the intended purpose of the meeting – the Government University Scheme.[2]

Writing to inform the Propaganda of the recent developments, Cullen was still cautious:

> The Government, however, has not made any official statement, because I imagine it did not want us to examine its proposals, and the Ministers did not want to give definite promises so as not to commit themselves in Parliament. In conclusion, up to now, this whole matter has been dealt with privately, and without having put down anything in writing with the Ministers.[3]

According to the terms of their agreement at the meeting of 22 and 23 August, the bishops had now to meet again in Dublin to consider the results of the interview with Grey. It was duly called for Thursday, 19 December, to be held, as usual, in the Presbytery in Marlboro' Street.[4] The meeting lasted two days. MacHale did not attend, nor did he write to explain his absence. Cullen was glad[5] – it enabled the bishops to proceed without his trenchant opposition to almost everything. Cullen outlined the subject of their deliberations to the Propaganda:

> The meeting devoted its entire attention to the question of Primary and Higher Education, and it was decided to send a memorandum to the Government explaining our position, and requesting the concessions to which we have a right with regard to University and Secondary Education. We have shewn that nothing has yet been done for the Catholics, while within the Protestant University of Dublin, endowments of great value, and other income, have been

[1] *Nation*, 16 December 1865. There appears, unfortunately, to be no reference to these discussions in the Cullen Papers.

[2] *Ibid.* This report seems to be accurate, though it came from a source evidently sympathetic to MacHale. Its editorial comment expresses the MacHale view that nothing would really be conceded by the Government. The *Guardian* (13 December 1865) hinted that the interview with Grey was about a charter for the Catholic University, but this was merely a supposition that the meeting would discuss the point for which it was called – which it did not.

[3] Propaganda, *Scritture* 35, Cullen to Barnabo, 24 December 1865.

[4] Monsell Papers, Box 8319, Cullen to Moriarty, 8 December 1865.

[5] Kirby Papers, Cullen to Kirby, no. 297, 22 December 1865.

conceded to the members of the Established Church, who are very few compared with the Catholics, and furthermore, the Queen's Colleges have also been richly endowed; which Colleges have been condemned, and are used only by the Presbyterians, and by those who do not take much notice of religion.[1]

They had therefore decided, at the meeting, to demand a charter and endowment for the Catholic University,[2] and they framed a draft charter which would 'leave all power in the hands of the Bishops'.[3] This was evidently their reply to the suggested line such a charter should follow which Bruce had made as the last point in his *Memorandum*. At least the bishops said nothing to condemn, (nor to approve), the proposed Royal University at the meeting,[4] and their draft charter was at any rate an attempt to state the terms on which they could join it. Their draft placed the four archbishops as perpetual Governors of a Roman Catholic incorporated college. Other life Governors were named in the instrument; they were to be Bishops Derry, Kilduff, O'Brien, Walshe, Gillooly, Furlong, Flannery and Pius Leahy. The four archbishops were to be the Visitors, with supreme authority in the college 'in all things'. A vacancy among the life Governors was to be filled by the nomination of the *ex officio* Governors, and they were to appoint the rector and vice-rector. They were also to appoint professors and members of the faculties, and to remove them. This charter the bishops were to describe in their memorandum to Grey, as 'borrowed in its main details from that of King's College, London'.[5]

At least the assembled prelates considered the proposed Royal University seriously, and determined to consider it with even greater earnestness should it prove not to sanction mixed education or the Queen's Colleges, and to allow a suitable Charter to their existing institution. But as Cullen pointed out, the great difficulty was whether bishops should sit on the proposed Senate. At the meeting, while some said they might, others were opposed to the suggestion.[6] Yet all were determined not to accept any place on the Senate if the Holy See had not first declared that acceptance was permissible.[7] The meeting considered their other educational demands, and embodied them in a second memorandum to Grey. 'The question now is,' Cullen wrote, 'shall we get anything from the Government? I fear not – if not, it is probable that our [Catholic] University will fall, as many bishops and

---

[1] Propaganda, *Scritture* 35, Cullen to Barnabo, 24 December 1865. [2] *Ibid.*
[3] Kirby Papers, Cullen to Kirby, no. 297, 22 December 1865. [4] *Ibid.*
[5] The text of the draft drawn up at this meeting was printed in the Memorandum to Grey: *Parliamentary Papers*, 1866. LV, 'Copies of Memorials', Enclosure I, p. 9.
[6] Kirby Papers, Cullen to Kirby, no. 297, 22 December 1865.
[7] Propaganda, *Scritture* 35, Cullen to Barnabo, 24 December 1865.

priests won't make collections, and Dr MacHale prohibits them in his diocese.'[1] The existence of this probability in Cullen's mind is almost certainly the explanation of his willingness to conciliate with the Government, and of his compromise in the following year. The Pope himself was pleased that the archbishops had met Grey, and looked for a satisfactory settlement.[2] So Cullen was left with a free hand.

The two Memorials to the Government drawn up at the bishops' meeting were tidied up in the verbal form of their drafting, and then sent to Rome. Cardinal Barnabo replied by telegraph that the Propaganda had no objection to them.[3] Copies were then sent out to the bishops together with a petition to the Queen for a Charter.[4] The way for the presentation of the Memorials, and a preparation of public opinion, was provided by an open letter to Fortescue which Kavanagh sent to the *Freeman* on 5 January 1866.[5] In it, he lingered on the evil of speaking out on a question about which negotiations between the bishops and the Government were pending, but it was a necessary evil, for the cause of Catholic education was being assailed on every side. He again put the case for denominational education at all levels, and execrated the Queen's Colleges. In a second letter, which appeared on 13 January, he criticized in detail the principles and history of Irish education as given in the *Statement* of the Queen's Graduates.[6] Kavanagh's appeals to the public were not superfluous. Opposition from within the Queen's University to the proposed new Charter was growing, and so was Protestant opposition generally.[7] There was a widespread feeling that the position of the Government over the whole matter was somewhat incongruous. At a Dublin Protestant meeting called to condemn the alterations to the Queen's University, one man 'expressed his astonishment that the project to establish and endow a sectarian University should be proposed or favourably regarded by a

[1] Kirby Papers, Cullen to Kirby, no. 297, 22 December 1865. MacEvilly was more hopeful that the meeting would produce a good result and lead to the settlement of the education question, *ibid.*, MacEvilly to Kirby, no. 3, 5 January 1866.

[2] He expressed himself thus when Odo Russell was received in audience on the 23 January 1866. F.O. 43, vol. 96A, Dispatch no. 7.

[3] Monsell Papers, Box 8319, Cullen to Moriarty, 10 January 1866.

[4] This petition is printed in *Parliamentary Papers*, 1866, LV, 'Copies of Memorials'.

[5] *Freeman*, 6 January 1866, 'Freedom of Education', a letter of James Kavanagh to Chichester Fortescue, Chief Secretary for Ireland.

[6] *Ibid.*, 13 January 1866, a second letter of Kavanagh's to Fortescue.

[7] The Ulster National Education Association was drawing up a memorial to the Lord-Lieutenant against the proposed alteration of the Queen's University. Their memorial, dated 18 January 1866, is in *Parliamentary Papers*, 1866, LV, 'Copies of Memorials', p. 38. For an account of their deputation, and Wodehouse's reply, see the *Mail*, 24 January 1866.

Liberal Government, which had always professed to desire the abolition of sectarian restrictions on the Universities'.[1]

The Presbyterian body felt that their interests were being sacrificed to a conclave of bishops by a Government determined, as the Dublin *Mail* said, to support a 'lay Maynooth'. It noticed also that Sir John Gray was shortly to move against the Irish Established Church in the Commons, and asked whether 'there may not be another "arrangement" between the Government and the Roman bishops in this case also?'[2] Meanwhile the *Dublin Review* watched the education negotiations with scepticism, doubting that any good could come from the co-operation of Irish Catholics and English Liberals.[3]

On 14 January, Cullen sent the two Memorials to Grey, one on universities and one on the National System of Education, and with them the petition to the Queen for the incorporation of the Catholic University.[4] All of these papers had been signed by twenty-nine prelates. Praying for their consideration, Cullen pointed out that 'they contain very little more than the statements which the four Archbishops had the honour of making to you in the interview'.[5] But the important point was that Cullen was still insisting on a general airing of Catholic educational grievances, and in this he and the bishops must bear a responsibility for the difficulties which were to arise in the way of a settlement. For as with the three points of the National Association, *all* their educational grievances were too widely diffused for effective concurrent consideration, even though in moving them on the principle of denominational education they could claim that only recognition of that principle would give satisfaction.

The first Memorial, on the university question, started by taking the line of The O'Donoghue's motion. 'The effects of this penal legislation still remain; and Catholics, deprived of the endowments of former times, are left without any institution supported by the State, in which they can, with safety to faith and morals, cultivate the higher studies and take out academical degrees.' Despite the admission of Catholics to non-foundation scholarships and to some subordinate professorships at Trinity College, they were still left without redress, for that College was imbued with 'an anti-Catholic spirit'. Nor were the Queen's Colleges

[1] Meeting at the Religious Institution Rooms, December 1865. Speech of John Ramsay Esqr., *Mail*, 22 December 1865.

[2] *Mail*, 15 February 1866.   [3] *Dublin Review*, January 1866, p. 184.

[4] On the extent of the bishops' demands, see Thomas Andrews, *Stadium Generale, A Chapter of Contemporary History*, London, 1867, pp. 42-3.

[5] *Parliamentary Papers*, 1866, LV, 'Copies of Memorials', p. 5. Cullen to Grey, 14 January 1866.

fulfilling the objects of their establishment, for in them the mixed system produced all the evils of indifferentism. It went on to enumerate the present benefits of the Catholic University – but all of these were frustrated by the illegality of its degrees. Yet the proposal of the Government was in the right direction:

> In the changes referred to, as we understand them, we recognize a token of the willingness of Her Majesty's Government to grant an instalment of justice in educational matters to which our flocks are entitled, but, if unaccompanied by an endowment of our Catholic University, and a reconstruction of the Queen's Colleges, we cannot regard them as satisfactory to the Catholics of Ireland . . . without an endowment, the proposal of the Government would confer but little, if any, substantial benefit upon our Catholic University; for degrees can be obtained through the London University, and property can be acquired and transmitted without a Charter by availing of certain legal expedients. Without rearranging the Queen's Colleges on the principles of the denominational system . . . much of the evil and injustice of which Catholics complain will remain unredressed.[1]

But taking the proposal as evidence of goodwill, the bishops would co-operate because they were hopeful that the Government would allow concessions. Seven were listed.[2] They were a Charter for the Catholic University as a college within the new Royal University, a draft charter being suggested;[3] an endowment for the Catholic College to secure equality with other institutions – this was just, for Catholics contributed to the public funds which supported these others; burses and scholarships for the college; the 'Catholic University College' to be empowered to affiliate colleges and schools to itself; examinations were not to be hostile in any way to Catholicism (Points 5 and 6); and that the Queen's Colleges be 'rearranged' on the denominational principle.[4]

The second Memorial covered the entire field of National Education. It demanded the simple recognition of denominationalism, by the removal of all restrictions on religious teaching in National Schools, and the reshaping of the rules of the National Board accordingly. If this were done, many Catholic schools run by regular orders could be taken into connexion with the Board and so share in the grants of public money. Proselytism could be avoided by a return to the safeguards of Lord Stanley's *Letter to the Duke of Leinster*, (1831). Model Schools should be abolished; some might become denominational training schools. In short, the Catholics should enjoy the complete denominational

---

[1] *Ibid.*, Enclosure i, p. 8.
[2] *Ibid.*, p. 9. Also given in Macaulay, *Ireland in 1872*, p. 390.
[3] *Parliamentary Papers*, 1866, LV, 'Copies of Memorials', Enclosure i, p. 9.
[4] *Ibid.*

system – 'seeing it is so good for England, why not apply it to Ireland too?'[1]

Grey replied on 30 January. He ignored the second Memorial, and on the first stated emphatically that the Government did not consider the Queen's Colleges failures, and could not therefore alter the principles on which they were conducted. But they were hopeful that the new Queen's University Charter with a revised Senate would prove satisfactory – certainly it would fulfil the objects the Government intended. They were prepared to grant a Charter to the Catholic University, but not in the form proposed by the bishops. The archbishops might be constituted Visitors, but its governing body should contain 'a considerable proportion' of laymen. The Government were quite willing to suggest a form of Charter which they would deem suitable. They could never allow power in it to enable the Catholic institution to affiliate schools and colleges to itself, for that right belonged only to a university.[2]

Grey's reply was something of a blow to Cullen. 'I do not know what we shall do next about the education question,' he wrote to Kirby, 'the Government will do nothing good. They put us to a great deal of trouble, but after all we get nothing.'[3] He and Woodlock called on Fortescue to find out what part of their hopes could be salvaged. Woodlock did the talking, Cullen apparently still preferring not to commit himself. He demanded the exclusive right of graduation in the new university for the Catholic College and the Queen's Colleges, with the power, posited in the memorial, of affiliation of colleges and schools to the Catholic College. Fortescue reported the demand to Moriarty – one of the two prelates at the Tervoe meeting in 1865 and known to be unsympathetic to the Cullen policy on education. Woodlock's position implied that no Catholic could obtain the degrees of the new university except through the Dublin Catholic College. 'This would be utterly inadmissible,' he wrote to Moriarty, 'and could blow up our whole scheme from the very foundation.' It was essential that the Government prepare their proposed Charter for the Catholic University at once.[4] Cullen's reply to Grey, of 11 February, stated the dissatisfaction of the prelates, but they would not make any declaration until they had seen the two

[1] *Parliamentary Papers*, LV, 'Copies of Memorials', Enclosure 2, p. 11. Both memorials are also printed in Moran, *Pastoral Letters . . . of Cardinal Cullen*, vol. II, p. 443 (XXVII), and p. 450 (XXVIII).

[2] *Parliamentary Papers*, 1866, LV, 'Copies of Memorials', p. 15. Grey to Cullen, 30 January 1866.

[3] Kirby Papers, Cullen to Kirby, no. 19, 2 February 1866.

[4] Monsell Papers, Box 8319, Fortescue to Moriarty, 5 February 1866.

proposed Charters – of the Royal University and of the Catholic College.[1]

The urgency of Fortescue's request for the Charters had apparently fallen on receptive ears, however, for also on the 11th, after his dispatch of the letter to Grey, Cullen was shown a draft of the university Charter, which was not yet complete, by Monsell. The Senate was to consist of thirty-four. Two Catholic bishops were to be elected by the body of bishops. The three Queen's Colleges, the Catholic University, and the Magee College (this was still open to doubt)[2] were to be affiliated to the university.[3] In the next week, he received the rest of the provisions from Monsell. The Crown was to fill up the first vacancy on the Senate, the second by the Senate itself, and the third by the graduates of the Queen's University. The Charter for the Catholic College secured its power to hold property, but insisted on lay representation at the governing body. Cullen could see no good in either. Of the first, the method of filling vacancies he felt sure would 'exclude all Catholic influence', and provide an immense Protestant majority on the Senate for the next fifty years 'and would always make it a point to select a Catholic who retains that name for the purpose of injuring his Church more effectually'. He suggested Kane and Keogh as likely bad candidates. Monsell he distrusted, as he now did Professor Sullivan, for adopting the Government view.[4]

It seemed as if the game was up. While the Charters were in preparation, Cullen had sent Woodlock to London to be at the centre of activity. Now he despaired of any use Woodlock might serve by remaining there.[5] Yet he remained just in case further developments should require him. He saw Gladstone, but apparently without learning anything new.[6] He did make contact with Manning, forwarding copies of the bishops' memorials to him, but only learning from him the belief that the Government were bent on secularizing education in Ireland.[7] Manning, who was to take such an equivocal part in later phases of the Irish university question, was not yet ready to join hands with the Irish bishops – he was too involved still with smoothing the waters which had been disturbed by his succession to the see of Westminster.

[1] *Parliamentary Papers*, 1866, LV, 'Copies of Memorials', p. 17. Cullen to Grey, 11 February 1866.
[2] The Bishop of Londonderry (Kelly) told Cullen that Magee College, after four months of existence, had six Presbyterian professors and two lay professors. It had only twenty-three pupils, and Cullen felt disgusted that so small an institution should be mentioned in a Royal Charter. Woodlock Papers, Cullen to Woodlock, 28 February 1866.
[3] Woodlock Papers, Cullen to Woodlock, 11 February 1866.
[4] *Ibid.*, Cullen to Woodlock, 18 February 1866.   [5] *Ibid.*   [6] *Ibid.*
[7] *Ibid.*

Meanwhile, Cullen's objections to the Government proposals as outlined in the Charter for a Catholic College had crystallized under two heads[1]. First he objected to the mode of appointing the professors, and secondly to the exclusion of the bishops from all control over the Catholic College. Of the first, he called the method outlined in the Charter, the method of *Concursus*, the method that had driven all outsiders from office at Maynooth. The Charter vested the appointment of professors in the Rector and professorial body, subject to a veto by the bishops. Cullen felt this would eventually lead to a collision between the bishops and the college officers. Of the second the exclusion of the bishops from entire government of the college would also mean the final ending of all their interest in it, and so they would cease to provide funds for its maintenance. Unless the Government gave an endowment, their proposed Charter would dry up other sources of income. Cullen objected further to the suggested incorporation of 'the Rector and Professors' to the exclusion of the archbishops and bishops.[2] He could see little hope, and suggested no ways out, when he wrote to the Propaganda.

> The Government has rejected all our requests . . . they are trying to make us give up what we have, without giving us any compensation. I imagine that the discussion of the National System of Education will end in the same way. . . .[3]

He was also conscious that the other prelates shared his despair. The Archbishops of Cashel and Tuam wrote to him against the proposed Charter, both expressing distrust of the Government's intentions.[4]

It was at this point, as though in realization of Cullen's worst fears, that James Lowry Whittle published his pamphlet, *Freedom of Education: What it Means*. Whittle was a Trinity College Catholic, and the object of his essay was the exposure of ultramontane designs on Irish Education. The 'mysterious utterances' of the Government last June were now seen by him to imply that the Catholic College in Dublin was to receive recognition from the State: 'The few observations I have to make', he wrote, 'are directed against this broad proposition.'[5] He appealed in the interests of the 'educated Catholics' who felt no zeal for ultramontanism, for the bishops' demands were directed principally against their independence.[6] It was quite true that the laity had been told by their pastors that it was better to leave their sons without any university

---

[1] Monsell Papers, Box 8319, D. B. Dunne to Monsell, 17 February 1866.
[2] *Ibid.*
[3] Propaganda, *Scritture* 35, Cullen to Barnabo, 18 February 1866.
[4] Woodlock Papers, Cullen to Woodlock, 18 February 1866.
[5] J. L. Whittle, *Freedom of Education: What it Means*, Dublin, 1866, p. 5.
[6] *Ibid.*, p. 8.

education rather than send them to a non-Catholic institution; yet the figures showed that the laity did not believe it, and sent their sons to such universities, but the arguments of The O'Donoghue used in his motion assumed that they did.[1] The episcopal demands on the university question were the demands of a mere faction of Irish Catholics: prompted by the fear revealed in the encyclical *Quantâ curâ* that non-ultramontane Catholics would increase in strength.[2] This faction aimed at the subversion of liberal education, hence the surprise that many had experienced at finding the Government dealing with it. Whittle was anxious to dispel any suggestion that publication of his opinions would cause scandal to his Church; he had 'always thought it a greater scandal to allow it to pass uncontradicted that ultramontanism is Catholicism'.[3] The pamphlet evidently sold well, as it ran into a second edition within a month. Protestant opinion rejoiced to find in a Catholic author a clear confirmation of their predisposition to vilify ultramontanism.[4] Cullen thought Whittle's pamphlet was 'as ignorant as it is presumptuous'.[5]

Despite the circulation of the proposed Charter, the Government was still prepared to shift ground a little. Sullivan saw Fortescue on 18 February, and was informed that the wishes of the bishops would be met, at least to the extent that the body to be incorporated would be the (existing) Board of Bishops of the Catholic University and the college authorities. Fortescue also explained that the Government were considering the bishops' demands on National Education, but that there was some delay because of the illness of MacDonnell, the resident Commissioner of Education, and their resulting inability to have the opinion of the National Board.[6] On the 20th, Sullivan and Dunne called to let Cullen know Fortescue's mind. They had the impression that Fortescue would be glad to have the university question settled one way or the other as soon as possible.[7] This was no doubt because he had advised the Government of the supremely pressing danger of Fenianism and sought to clear the decks to deal with it. The day before his meeting

---

[1] *Ibid.*, p. 13.   [2] *Ibid.*, p. 55.   [3] *Ibid.*, p. 68.

[4] *Mail*, 20 March 1866, 'A Gallican Movement in Ireland' – leader on Whittle's pamphlet. For a counterblast to Whittle, see MacDevitt, *op. cit.*, especially pp. 6-18. Pamphlets were also written against the university proposals by Professor Cairns and Sir Dominic Corrigan. For a moderate criticism of these, see W. K. Sullivan, *op. cit.*, especially pp. 33-47; and *Dublin Review*, July 1866, 'Irish Writers on University Education'.

[5] Woodlock Papers, Cullen to Woodlock, 22 February 1866. It was also 'a strong proof of the necessity of a Catholic College'. *Ibid.*, Cullen to Woodlock, 28 February 1866.

[6] Monsell Papers, Box 8319, D. B. Dunne to Monsell, 19 February 1866.

[7] *Ibid.*

with Sullivan, the Government had given the three readings at one sitting to the Habeas Corpus Suspension (Ireland) Bill.[1]

Cullen was still cautious. He now felt that perhaps the difficulties of getting a solution safe for Catholics were so great that they ought to put off the chartering of the Catholic University to a better time. Suddenly he switched to the 'open' plan, and instructed Woodlock in London on 22 February to probe the chances of suppressing all mention of the Queen's Colleges and the Catholic University College in the proposed Charter. 'Let the new University be a mere examining body', he suggested to him. 'If that were done the Bishops would accept.'[2] If not, it would be better to exclude the bishops from the Senate, and have on it two reliable priests instead. Cullen wrote on these lines to the other archbishops at the same time, and let Woodlock know that he would not himself accept a place on the Senate, MacHale would not, and nor, he imagined, would Dixon or Leahy when they replied.[3] Cullen now began to move strongly towards the 'open' plan: that plan which in June 1865 it had seemed the bishops would never accept, and the plan most favoured by Wodehouse. Out of this movement there grew the Catholic acceptance of Supplemental Charter. It was caused by Cullen's realization of the hopelessness of attaining his demands in the terms of reference of the proposed Charters. Also, the bishops, with the (to him) dishonourable exceptions of Moriarty and Butler, both of whom had been at the Tervoe meeting with Monsell in 1865, would, like the archbishops, have nothing to do with the new Senate.[4] He saw the difficulty of recommending anything without getting into new difficulties: 'we have asked to have the Queen's Colleges remodelled; the new Charter will confirm them'. Not one of the conditions in their Memorial to Grey had been conceded.[5] He was also afraid that 'patriots of the *Nation* School' were awaiting their chance to assail the bishops, and that it would arise if they should accept a small measure of justice as a great boon.[6] The Fenians would also join in to condemn the bishops if it could be shown that they had done anything to sanction the Queen's Colleges, either directly or indirectly.[7] Therefore it seemed better to Cullen that they should keep the name of their Catholic College

[1] *Hansard*, CLXXXI, p. 667. On Fortescue's part in its preparation, see Grey's reference to his advice on p. 678.

[2] Woodlock Papers, Cullen to Woodlock, 22 February 1866.

[3] *Ibid*. He also asked Woodlock to acquaint Gladstone with his revised attitude. *Ibid.*, Cullen to Woodlock (I), 23 February 1866.

[4] *Ibid.*, Cullen to Woodlock (II), 23 February 1866.

[5] *Ibid.*, and Monsell Papers, Box 8319, Cullen to Woodlock, 25 February 1866.

[6] Monsell Papers, Box 8319, Cullen to Woodlock, 25 February 1866.

[7] *Ibid.*

out of the Charter, leaving it to the Senate to receive the college, together with the Queen's Colleges, into connexion with it by its own action.[1] But his attitude was not hardened too much; he was still receptive to any further moves.

Sir Robert Peel had given notice that he would ask the Chancellor of the Exchequer (Gladstone) about the proposed alteration in the Queen's University. It was fixed for 23 February. Cullen instructed Woodlock in London to write afterwards recounting reactions, for, writing to him on the morning of the appointed day, he supposed that 'our future course will depend on what occurs tonight'.[2] Cullen wrote also to Sir John Gray, urging him to action on the university, and asked Woodlock to get Dillon to study it – and even Bright.[3] Monsell, Sullivan and Dunne called to see him on the 23rd as well, and pressed him to 'accept things just as they are'. Cullen replied that as the Government was doing nothing for them, they could hardly expect the bishops to do anything, and that anyway, he could not declare his support for the Government Charter without the concurrence of the other bishops. Monsell threatened to tell Fortescue that all was up then, and left in annoyance.[4] Peel duly asked his question,[5] although it was rephrased to suggest that no alteration would in fact be made, but Gladstone replied that the intentions of the Government were unchanged, that he could not place a copy of the proposed Charter on the table of the House since correspondence was still in progress, and the Government had not yet determined upon all the points that it should embrace. The matter would be brought to the House when the Government asked it to vote sums for the proposed scholarships.[6] Lowe secured an understanding that no alterations to the university would be recommended to the Crown without first receiving the sanction of the House.[7] With the question therefore still in a formative and uncertain state on both sides – with Cullen as well as with the Government – it looked as if it would be even longer before a settlement could be arrived at.

Cullen evidently desired the opinion of the Government on his tentative endorsement of the 'open' plan, and Myles O'Reilly was dispatched to Fortescue, at that time still in Dublin, on 27 February.

---

[1] *Ibid.*   [2] Woodlock Papers, Cullen to Woodlock (III), 23 February 1866.
[3] *Ibid.*
[4] *Ibid.*, and Kirby Papers, Cullen to Kirby, no. 39A, 23 February 1866, which also describes the interview with Monsell. Cullen felt that Monsell's anger was provoked by his desire to be able to announce to his constituents 'that the education question was settled to the satisfaction of the bishops'. Woodlock Papers, Cullen to Woodlock, 28 February 1866.
[5] *Hansard*, CLXXXI, p. 964.   [6] *Ibid.*, pp. 966–7.   [7] *Ibid.*, p. 968.

Fortescue received the idea favourably, thinking that the Government would consent to omit all mention of colleges in the Charter, and so place all schools on a common level. Cullen saw the disadvantages, but as he said on hearing Fortescue's opinion, at least no principle was sacrificed.[1] Fortescue also felt that a Charter satisfactory to the bishops could be drafted for the existing Catholic University.[2] He asked O'Reilly to submit suggestions to him in writing 'with a view', as O'Reilly put it, 'to conciliate the different proposals on the subject of a Charter of incorporation for the R.C. College founded by the bishops in Dublin; and to reconcile the just claims of the Bishops with the right of the civil government to secure adequate guarantees for the literary character of the institution proposed to be chartered'.[3] The importance of his suggestion is that it shows the extent to which Cullen was still holding out for a Charter like that submitted to Grey with the Memorial of 14 January. O'Reilly admitted Fortescue's objection that the power of the Visitors in that Charter was too vaguely defined in being stated to be 'supreme – and in all other things'; and that as it stood the bishops' Charter could allow the Governors to appoint any number of wholly unqualified persons to a faculty. But these objections, he felt, did not concern the essential principles at stake. He clarified his position by suggesting a modified plan, by which the college would be governed by the Chancellor and Governors, a Rectorial Council, and the Visitors. He also saw the advantages to both sides of a State endowment; it would secure greater educational equality between the denominations, and it would allow the State some control of the affairs of the college by representation in its government:

> How many of the difficulties attending the Charter we have been discussing would be solved if the State contributed, and had consequently some rights. . . . If the State supported no Colleges it would be all fair. It now wholly supports one class and refuses to the other.[4]

Cullen doubted Fortescue's readiness to concede points, and although he advised Woodlock in London to see Fortescue, who was about to return there, he was of the opinion that nothing should be believed 'except what you get in black and white', for it was clear to him that the Ministers 'are only seeing how they can get on'.[5] He was also convinced that before leaving for London, Fortescue had been advised by Monsell and Sullivan not to yield to the bishops[6] – which was probably true.

---

[1] Woodlock Papers, Cullen to Woodlock, 28 February 1866. [2] *Ibid.*
[3] Monsell Papers, Box 8319, O'Reilly to Fortescue (undated). [4] *Ibid.*
[5] Woodlock Papers, Cullen to Woodlock, 28 February 1866.
[6] *Ibid.*, Cullen to Woodlock, 1 March 1866.

Now it is clear that whilst favouring the 'open' plan for the Irish University, about his own Catholic institution Cullen was hardening, and would only consider a charter which was shorn of compromise. In the end, he thought, it would be necessary to get up a deputation to the Government requesting 'a real University with the power of giving degrees, and an endowment'. This would have just as much chance as their present trifling demands. He was at least happy in the consolation that when the people should learn that the Catholic claims had been rejected by the Government, they would stand by their bishops.[1] He therefore prepared to face the failure of the protracted moves, writing to Propaganda,

Our negotiations with the Government on the Education question have not yet ended, but I do believe that they will have no result. Up to now, the Government was trying to make us approve of the Queen's Colleges, at least indirectly, at the same time promising us, by way of compensation, only trifles. I have written to the Secretary of State for Ireland that it would be useless for them to put forward these proposals, and that we are quite determined to maintain at any cost the condemnation of the Queen's Colleges. . . . The present Government is full of Liberals by name, who are declared enemies of Catholic Education and wish to introduce, at any cost, infidelity in the Schools of Ireland.[2]

Woodlock was recalled to Dublin.[3] The publication of the papers and the correspondence between the prelates and the Government placed an outline of events in the hands of the public early in March.[4] The gap in their letters, representing the period of the interview with Grey in London, was noticed unfavourably by the press – it looked like the sort of secret cabal which ultramontanes thrived on. And in outline, without the whole and complicated series of probings which had occurred and which has just been described, the published papers made it appear that the Government had retreated a little from their first position, though as the *Mail* remarked, they still offered more than the public could agree to give.[5] Most men were in some confusion as to what exactly had been settled and what had not. Aubrey de Vere asked Monsell if the whole thing was to fall through after all.[6] The *Dublin Review* was surprised that

[1] *Ibid.*
[2] Propaganda, *Scritture* 35, Cullen to Barnabo, 6 March 1866. On the other hand, the *Daily News* took the more common view that the Government proposals 'are not only inconsistent with the principles of the Liberal Party, but disastrous to the cause of liberal education throughout the country' (15 February 1866).
[3] Woodlock Papers, Cullen to Woodlock, 1 March 1866.
[4] This was the publication of the 'Copies of Memorials', *Parliamentary Papers*, 1866, LV, 243.
[5] *Mail* (Dublin), 7 March 1866.
[6] Monsell Papers, Box 8319, de Vere to Monsell, 9 March 1866.

the bishops had apparently waived their claim to a special Charter for the Catholic University, *as a university*, and speculated on their future courses.[1] Sullivan suggested to Monsell that if the Government could be induced to draw up the points of a Charter for the Catholic University *as a college*, and make concrete proposals, the present bitterness and disappointment about the university question would be mitigated. He also deprecated – apparently forgetful of the way the bishops had described the draft charter in the memorial of 14 January – the determination of the Government 'to treat us to a second edition of the London University'.[2] This only showed how far out of touch he was with the drift of Cullen's thought.

Yet although the hopes of a settlement were virtually written off, some action was still pending. In a letter to Wodehouse on 20 March, Grey had asked him to direct a draft Charter for the Queen's University to be drawn up. Legislation would be required, for the Law Officers had advised that the powers of the Chancellor, Senate and Convocation were at that time too limited to allow them to grant degrees under a Supplemental Charter without it.[3] Thus Grey moved in that direction which Cullen had indicated he also could go. In the Supplemental Charter the 'open' plan was put into practice, and in the way Wodehouse had originally desired in June 1865 – by starting the new Queen's University on the 'open' plan instead of proceeding to it from the 'close' system as at London. The Government always intended that the Supplemental Charter should be the first step,[4] the step that could be taken by the Crown, without legislation, and that legislation to enlarge the Charter and develop it should follow. Circumstances prohibited further development, and it remains to be seen how the bishops received the Supplemental Charter.

But before the Royal Patent issuing the Charter was sealed on 25 June, the bishops turned from the quagmire into which the university question seemed to have settled, and looked instead to the points of their second Memorial to Grey – on the National System. Speaking at the National Association on 18 April, MacSwiney said that they had little to hope for on the education question from Earl Russell, but that there were some members of the Government – he mentioned Gladstone – who might

---

[1] *Dublin Review*, April 1816, 'Signs of an Irish Policy', p. 492.

[2] Monsell Papers, Box 8319, Sullivan to Monsell, 13 April 1866.

[3] *Parliamentary Papers*, 1866, LV, 285, Grey to Wodehouse, 26 March 1866. For the opinion of the Law Officers, see Cabinet Paper, 25 November 1865 (enclosure no. 15).

[4] This was stated by Grey in the Commons on 17 April in reply to a question by Aytoun. He said that they intended legislation to give effect to the intention outlined in the letter to Wodehouse of 26 March. *Hansard*, CLXXXII, p. 1506.

help them.[1] He was mistaken. On the same occasion Kavanagh announced that the university negotiations had 'hopelessly broken down, as they dare not accept the terms offered'. And he offered little hope on National Education either, merely suggesting that all Catholic Schools should be withdrawn from connexion with the Board, as the bishops had done over the Kildare Place Schools in 1826.[2] Cullen did not go so far, but, as he told the Propaganda, 'with regard to the National Schools, I do not think anything will be achieved, but we shall be obliged to take counteracting measures, to minimize the damage caused by the Government's Model Schools.'[3] And in this he was wise, for the Government were prepared to concede a substantial part of the Catholic case against the utility of these schools anyway.

It was O'Reilly who took the education demands to Parliament, apparently in accordance with the wishes of Cullen.[4] O'Reilly had originally planned to bring on his motion at the beginning of March, but had postponed it when Gladstone represented that the correspondence still going on between the Government and the bishops had not reached an issue.[5] At that time Cullen had been urging Gray, Dillon and Maguire to support O'Reilly.[6] On the same day that O'Reilly moved in the House, 15 May, Gillooly said at the committee of the National Association that they had been led to believe that the Government would propose educational measures satisfactory to them, and that although nothing fulfilling that condition had yet appeared, it was not too late.[7] O'Reilly moved for a Select Committee 'to inquire what changes may, with advantage, be made in the System of National Education in Ireland, in order to allow greater freedom and fullness of religious teaching in schools attended by pupils of one religious denomination only, and to guard effectively against proselytism, and protect the faith of the minority in mixed Schools'.[8] He mentioned the postponement of his motion,

---

[1] *Freeman*, 19 April 1866.   [2] *Ibid.*

[3] Propaganda, *Scritture* 35, Cullen to Barnabo, 9 May 1866.

[4] This would seem to be implied by an undated letter of O'Reilly's to an unnamed bishop, in the Cullen Papers. It urges the recipient to persuade Cullen to get Monsell to vote with the independent Catholics instead of with the Government, but requests that direct allusion must not be made to his own wish to use Cullen's influence in this way, as it would give a handle to the opposition in Parliament. The person who originally put the Cullen Papers in order of years assigned this one to 1865, but although the internal evidence is far from conclusive, it seems to agree more with the present state of the education question. O'Reilly suggests a compromise: abolition of Model Schools, the establishment of Denominational Training Schools, and the rescinding of the Stopford Rule.

[5] Cullen Papers, O'Reilly to Cullen (also undated).

[6] Woodlock Papers, Cullen to Woodlock, 28 February 1866.

[7] *Freeman*, 16 May 1866.   [8] *Hansard*, CLXXXIII, p. 1002.

but saw also, on reflection, that the reply of the Government to the bishops' Memorial gave little hope that they were 'disposed to meet the wishes of the Roman Catholics'.[1] He reiterated all the demands of that Memorial. He and The O'Conor Don, who seconded the motion, were not opposed to National Education; they simply asked that it should be so administered as to become acceptable to the majority of the Irish people. The motion was well received, and as the rules for the prevention of proselytism were already under the consideration of the Commissioners of Education, and as Fortescue gave an assurance that the present position of Model and Training Schools should receive the attention of the Government, it was withdrawn. The *Freeman* was satisfied. It saw in the short debate a degree of progress on the issue of 'free education'.[2] As when The O'Donoghue moved the university question in 1865, so now the motion of an Irish member propelled the Government into action. The Charter question seemed quietly to be slipping from the public mind and from the attention of the bishops. In his Pastoral for St Kevin on 22 May, Cullen underlined the changed direction, by opening a searing attack upon proselytizing educational institutions.[3]

Then, suddenly, the Government were defeated on 18 June on Dunkellin's motion on Parliamentary Reform[4] and after reference to the reluctant Queen at Balmoral, Russell and the Cabinet announced their retirement to the House on the 26th. There was no election, and Derby took office on 9 July, with Disraeli as Chancellor and Lord Naas (who became the Earl of Mayo in 1867) as Irish Secretary. It was thought in Ireland that Naas would not accept the modifications in the National System which the dying Government had indicated.[5] But the Russell Administration was working on its Irish policy even during its last month despite the Parliamentary crisis.

Nobody expected the Government to fall, and when it was initially defeated on 18 June, 'the sensation was almost beyond precedent'.[6] On 19 June Fortescue wrote to the Commissioners of National Education announcing the decision of the Government not to extend the present system of Model Schools. Their reason was not the Catholic objection to the attacks on faith and morals alleged to occur in those schools, although the hostility of the Catholic community was given as a factor which had weighed with them, but the inadequacy of the existing system, which only turned out 400 teachers annually, although 900 were

---

[1] *Hansard*, CLXXXIII, p. 998.   [2] *Freeman*, 18 May 1866.
[3] *Ibid.*, 30 May 1866. See also Moran, *Pastoral Letters . . . of Cardinal Cullen*, vol. III, p. 1 (1), 'Pastoral Letter for the Feast of St Kevin,' 22 May 1866.
[4] *Hansard*, CLXXXIV, p. 639.   [5] *Freeman*, 24 May 1866.
[6] John Morley, *Life of Gladstone*, vol. I, p. 840.

needed. They proposed the establishment of Model Schools under local management.[1] Detailed proposals were presented to the Board at a special meeting in Dublin on 26 June. The concessions were quite large. Chaplains of the different denominations were to be provided at each Model School, and provision was made for the establishment of denominational boarding-houses attached to each. This last was explicitly stated in Fortescue's letter to be a way of overcoming the threat to faith and morals which the Catholic bishops claimed was inherent in the present schools.[2] The Board approved the principle of the changes at a further special meeting on 30 June,[3] and without binding themselves to adopt any particular details, they sent back their approval to Fortescue,[4] 'keeping always in view the fundamental principles of United Secular Education'. The new Government did not follow up Fortescue's suggestion. Instead a new rule issued by the Board in the middle of July, but planned by Fortescue at the end of the old Government,[5] was allowed to pass into effect. By it 'no pupil who is registered by its parents or guardians as a Roman Catholic is to be permitted to remain in attendance during the time of religious instruction in case the teacher giving such instruction is not a Roman Catholic. . . . And further, no pupil is to be permitted to remain in attendance during the time of any religious instruction to which its parents or guardians object.' This did not satisfy Kavanagh, the Catholic self-appointed spokesman on the National System, who ridiculed the pretension of the new rule to be a return to the original intention of Lord Stanley. It *excluded* no child from religious instruction *unless the parents or guardians objected*; whereas Stanley's rule of 1833 *assumed* the objection of the parent to his child receiving any other than his *professed* religious instruction.[6] It is interesting that this sort of experimenting to safeguard denominational interests in the Irish system of mixed education, provided the actual experience for the adoption of the Cowper–Temple clause in Foster's English Education Act of 1870.

The new Government was hardly expected to deal with the National System, for one of the last acts of Russell's had been the Supplemental Charter, and Irish interest swung back, once again, to the university

[1] *Parliamentary Papers*, 1866, LV, 213, Correspondence between Her Majesty's Government and the Commissioners of National Education.

[2] A copy of the minutes of this meeting of the Board, and of that of the 30th, are in the Mayo Papers, MS. 11217.

[3] *Ibid.*   [4] *Parliamentary Papers*, 1866, LV, 213 Reply of the Board, 2 July 1866.

[5] *Hansard*, CLXXXIV, p. 721.

[6] *Freeman*, 28 July 1866, 'The New Rule of the National Board; a letter of James Kavanagh to the Catholic Archbishops and Bishops'. Kavanagh did not doubt the good intentions of the Government, but felt it had been ill-advised by the Board.

question. On 25 June the seal had been affixed to the patent granting a Supplemental Charter to the Queen's University. The important phrase was: 'And we do further will and ordain that all persons, although not educated in any of the Colleges [the Queen's Colleges] mentioned or referred to in Our Said Charter shall be admitted as candidates for matriculation in the said University, and after such matriculation, as candidates for any of the said degrees or distinctions.'[1] On 27 June, six members were added by name to the Senate, by the usual procedure of Royal Letter. On 5 July, Fortescue, replying to a question by Lowe, made the first announcement to Parliament that the Charter had been granted by the Crown. He repeated the advice of the Law Officers that such a Charter, if followed by legislation to effect those parts of their plan not in the Royal competence, would fulfil the Government's intentions for Irish university education. All the Charter did was to enable the existing Queen's University to confer degrees on all who passed its examinations, without regard to their places of education. Now a Bill was required 'to place the new class of graduates upon an equal footing, as to all rights and privileges, as members of convocation and corporate bodies, with existing graduates of the University'. This bill, which was almost complete, would also provide for an increase in the Senate.[2]

In February, Gladstone had said that Parliament would be informed before any such Charter should go before the Crown.[3] This had not happened, and on 9 July Peel referred to the Supplemental Charter and to Gladstone's breach of good faith.[4] He raised the matter again on the 16th – and between the two dates, on the 11th, the Senate of the University had voted to postpone consideration of the Charter.[5] In reply to Peel, Grey hoped that the Senate would decide to accede to it, 'in the interests of religious peace in Ireland'.[6] Fortescue denied the accusation that Gladstone was guilty of a breach of faith,[7] and Lawson emphasized that the Supplemental Charter was only an enabling meas-

---

[1] *Parliamentary Papers*, 1866, LV, 217, 'Copy of Patent granting Supplemental Charter to the Queen's University in Ireland'.

[2] *Hansard*, CLXXXIV, p. 720.   [3] *Ibid.*, CLXXXI, p. 968.

[4] *Ibid.*, CLXXXIV, p. 755.

[5] Peel had attempted to induce the Senate to reject the Supplemental Charter outright, but he could only secure a postponement of what was admittedly almost certain rejection. Sullivan asked Monsell to let Parliament know that only half the Senate was present on this occasion, as late notice of the meeting meant that it came as a surprise. He feared that Peel would use the vote of the Senate in his own favour during the debate – which is what he did. Monsell Papers, Box 8319, Sullivan to Monsell, 15 July 1866.

[6] *Hansard*, CLXXXIV, p. 863.   [7] *Ibid.*, p. 872.

ure – it was up to the Senate to decide whether they would act under it or not; 'it is optional'.[1]

The fate of the Supplemental Charter is well known in the history of Irish education,[2] but the attitude of the Catholic Church to it has only been imperfectly appreciated. It must not be supposed – as Walsh thought – that the Charter was a new move by the Russell Government to which the Church then brought its critical scrutiny.[3] It has been seen in this chapter that it was the outcome of a long series of negotiations and manoeuvrings to which the bishops were a party, and that it was never intended to stand on its own, for circumstances attendant on the change of Government prevented the full development of the Russell Administration's plan, which provided for legislation to supplement the Supplemental Charter. In the following year, Fortescue was to say that the Supplemental Charter 'was avowedly and notoriously incomplete, it never having been intended that it should stand without the accompaniment of an Act of Parliament'. The Bill of the old Administration was ready and would have been introduced, had not the Government suddenly fallen: 'in fact,' he said, 'the separation of the Charter from the Bill had only been caused by the accident of Parliamentary warfare.'[4] Thus as matters stood when the Russell Government resigned, an 'open' university was provided for, although it never actually came into existence because of the opposition of some members of the Senate to the Charter. But even had it stood, it could never in the long run have proved satisfactory to Catholics without the intended supplementary legislation to create privileges for external members and alterations in the composition of the Senate. The Charter for the Catholic College was also left undone, as negotiations with the bishops had not been resumed after March 1866. But they had never been formally broken off, and had the change of Government not occurred when it did, it is not impossible to suppose, in view of the readiness of the bishops to deal with Mayo in 1868,[5] that a suitable arrangement might have been reached in the

[1] *Ibid.*, p. 875.

[2] See W. Haslett, *Queen's University of Ireland: the Supplemental Charter Considered*, Dublin, 1867; W. J. Walsh, *The Irish University Question, the Catholic Case*, Dublin, 1897, especially pp. 36-7; McGrath, *Newman's University*, p. 491.

[3] Walsh, *op. cit.*, p. 36. Walsh saw the Supplemental Charter as deliberate Government policy; as an end in itself rather than half a measure which circumstances prevented being completed. Thus he saw the passage of that Charter as 'the commencement of the period of hopeful reform'. He complained (p. 37) that it 'left untouched the great and irritating grievance' that public endowments were still to be in the hands of non-Catholics – but it has been seen that legislation to provide scholarships was also prevented by the change of Government.

[4] *Hansard*, CLXXXVII, p. 1435 (31 May 1867).

[5] See chap. 6.

second half of 1866.[1] It was a misfortune that the 'open' plan should have been launched in so imperfect and partial condition. Cullen, who was prepared to accept the 'open' principle, was not able to behold a good example of its expression in the Supplemental Charter.

Sullivan, who had impressed upon Fortescue the urgency of issuing the Charter and laying a Bill before Parliament as soon as possible, accepted the Charter as a first step. He had seen Fortescue on 30 or 31 May, and been assured that a Bill to alter the composition of the Senate was on the way. He had already felt, however, that it would not pass that year, but was certain eventually. Sullivan pressed him to pass it at once as it would help to ward off Irish distrust. He also saw that the Charter would occasion the final collapse of the Catholic University, but felt that the bishops would be glad of an excuse no longer to have to meet its expenses. They would see 'that the principle of a Catholic University can be better maintained by connecting the diocesan and other schools with the new Queen's University'. But this was not altogether a good thing, he believed, since the Catholic University still had lay professors. They were being removed gradually, and if Catholic education were thrown back into the provincial seminaries, the priests would get a complete hold on it.[2] Sullivan and Monsell worked to prevent the Irish members from voting against the Government during the crisis over Dunkellin's motion, although their work could have been made easier, as Sullivan said, if Fortescue would make some effort to mix with the Irish members as Bruce had done.[3] Cullen was in London at the beginning of June – on his way to Rome to receive the red hat – and Sullivan hoped that the Government would be a little gracious to him on his return.[4] He also hoped that legislation was still possible, even after the fall of the Government, for some Catholics might be put off from accepting the Supplemental Charter unless something could be done about the university examinerships.[5] At that time, under an arrangement engineered by Peel when Irish Secretary in 1862, examiners were professors of Queen's Colleges whose stipends for that purpose were met by the suppression of a few chairs and a diversion of £600 from the annual Parliamentary grant. In order to carry this into effect, the Charters of the Queen's Colleges had been revoked, and new ones granted, in August 1863. By 1865 it was customary for the professors in each subject

---

[1] The *Dublin Review* expected the continuance of the negotiations with the bishops. July 1866, p. 88.

[2] Monsell Papers, Box 8319, Sullivan to Monsell, 1 June 1866.

[3] *Ibid.*, Sullivan to Monsell, 3 June 1866.   [4] *Ibid.*

[5] *Ibid.*, Sullivan to Monsell, 15 July 1866.

to conduct university examinations. It can therefore be seen that Sullivan had a point: 'So long as the examiners would be selected exclusively from Queen's College professors, no students would be likely to be sent up for examination with the sanction of the bishops.' But he wrote round urging Catholics to look favourably on the Supplemental Charter, telling them 'not to reject it, because it is still incomplete'.[1]

With Cullen in Rome, it fell to his nephew Moran to explain to Kirby the turn of events, and also to confirm Sullivan's thoughts about the Catholic University – but for the opposite reasons:

> The Education Question is now *in statu quo*. Mgr Woodlock sent a copy of the new Charter to His Eminence [Cullen]. The best sign of its being some use to us is, I think, the fact that Peel and the Orange faction are in terrible hubbub about it. The Catholic University, however, has great difficulties to contend against, and not the least is the intrinsic evil of having had a complete staff of laymen appointed its professors in the commencement,[2] who now of course look upon it in the light of a monopoly.[3]

The *Dublin Review* admitted that there could be a valid division of opinion among Catholics on the Supplemental Charter. The present scheme was a compromise, since the Irish bishops had abandoned their 'higher ideal' of a chartered Catholic University for what they considered more attainable – but Catholics were entitled not to agree with the wisdom of this step down.[4] By 1868 the *Dublin* was anxious to show that this compromise was in no way comparable to the scheme for a Catholic college at Oxford, by which Catholic youth would have lived in the midst of Protestants at a distinctively Protestant university. The Supplemental Charter did not mean that Irish Catholics had any local connexion with a mixed university; their only connexion was that of examination.[5] The *Dublin* was correct in supposing that the Irish bishops were prepared to work through the Supplemental Charter – Woodlock had said he would not prevent his students from seeking degrees under any such arrangement. But Catholic opinion waited upon Cullen's return and the attitude the Queen's Senate would take to the Charter. The former occurred on 12 August,[6] but the new Cardinal

---

[1] *Ibid.*   [2] See McGrath, *op. cit.*, especially pp. 196–7.
[3] Kirby Papers, Moran to Kirby, no. 168, 19 July 1866.
[4] *Dublin Review*, July 1866, p. 98.   [5] *Ibid.*, July 1868, p. 235.
[6] Dublin was illuminated for Cullen's return as Ireland's first cardinal. There was some fear that public peace might be disturbed. See the curious letter by 'A father of females' to Lord Naas, asking that some action be taken by the Government to prevent the celebrations: 'The alarm, my Lord, and terror of delicate females in the apprehension of a night attack is at present dreadful and ought to be calmed by some assurance.'

decided to bide his time and see how things worked out; the latter, due to the postponement at the meeting in July, not until October.

Derby was evidently not *au fait* with the whole question of Irish university education, and as the crucial meeting of the Senate came on, he had to ask Naas what it was all about.[1] The Government, in fact, had become noticeably cool in its attitude to the Irish Catholics, and *The Times*, remarking on this, noticed that the spirit of Protestant ascendancy 'seems to be excited to a higher pitch than it has been for a long time'.[2] The discussion of the Supplemental Charter both in the Senate and the Convocation were the occasions for its manifestation. The Senate met at Dublin Castle on 6 October to decide, as they supposed, the fate of the Supplemental Charter. Lord Chancellor Blackburne moved its rejection, and was seconded by Earl Rosse. This motion was lost by two votes, and the Senate accepted the Charter and rejected a further motion by Peel for the postponement of its consideration.[3] On 19 October, Convocation met on the same question, and after an excited debate, declared the acceptance of the Charter 'inexpedient'.[4] But this had no effect on the Senate, which during November drafted a series of regulations which were then published to put the Supplemental Charter into effect.

It was thought that the future of the Charter was assured. In Rome Gladstone, taking time off after the fall of the Russell Government, explained the state of the Irish University question and the steps taken by that Government to the Pope.[5] Monsell wanted Sullivan to send copies of the regulations drafted by the Senate on matriculation to each of the bishops. Sullivan approved, though he regarded immediate action

(Mayo Papers, MSS. 11142-11145, letter of 6 August 1866.) Cullen himself was impressed by his kindly reception, and especially recalled that the Protestants joined the Catholics in signs of good feeling, 'a thing very rare in Ireland' he wrote. Spalding Letters, Cullen to Spalding, 10 November, 1866.

[1] Mayo Papers, MSS. 11142-11145. Derby to Naas, 4 October 1866. This is strange: it was he who founded the Irish National System of Education in 1831, but was apparently out of touch on the university question.

[2] *The Times*, 31 October 1866.

[3] *Freeman*, 8 October 1866. The voting was 11 to 9 in favour of the Charter. See also reference to the vote by Naas in reply to a question from Fortescue in May 1867; *Hansard*, CLXXXVII, pp. 1441 ff.

[4] *Hansard, ibid.*

[5] At an audience on the 22 October 1866: Gladstone Papers, B.M.Add.MS. 44755, f. 101, 'Memorandum of a Conversation with His Holiness Pope Pius IX'. (Also printed in D.C. Lathbury, *op. cit.*, vol. II, p. 395.) Gregorovius said that Gladstone advised the Pope 'to make a virtue of necessity', but he meant about the Roman, and not the Irish university question. *The Roman Journals of Ferdinand Gregorovius*, pp. 262-3 (4 November 1866).

as premature as they should wait 'until the question of the Colleges shall have been settled'. He could see the benefit, 'and I think the advisability of taking immediate advantage of the new privileges'. An assistant secretary should be appointed, he thought, and one on whom Catholics could rely, to facilitate the working of the Senate's regulations, and to help college authorities interpret them.[1] A committee of the Senate was sitting in Dublin during November to receive applications from colleges which wished to be recognized by the Queen's University as fit institutions to submit candidates for its matriculation and degrees.[2] Sullivan had made application on behalf of the Catholic University, hence his desire to wait until 'the question of the Colleges shall have been settled' before approaching the bishops. Carlow College had also applied. Both had been accepted at a meeting at which only three of the five members of the committee attended – Brady, Chief Justice Monahan and Sir Dominic Corrigan. Chief Baron Piggot, arriving late at the meeting had begged them to reconsider, and to send a questionnaire to every college seeking recognition under the Supplemental Charter 'with a view of determining accurately the real condition of each'.[3] They had agreed to hold another meeting on 27 November, but at that, only Brady, Corrigan and Piggot attended, since Lord Talbot, who sided with Piggot was ill and the Chief Justice was attending to legal matters. The result was that the Chief Baron was outvoted and the original resolution to accept both the Catholic University and Carlow was passed and presented to the Senate in the Report of the committee.[4] Sullivan agreed with Piggot, and was persuaded to make a bid for Monsell's adhesion to Piggot's next move, which was to ask the Senate to refer the Report back to the committee, and to add more members to the committee at the same time. Sullivan wanted an immediate settlement: the first examinations under the new Charter were to be in January, and he wanted the recognition of colleges to be made well before that time. But he had supported Piggot for interesting reasons. He did not want the recognition of Carlow – for if that happened then Clongowes College would almost certainly make a successful application. And that would mean that Catholic education would fall entirely into the hands of ecclesiastics, and as both those colleges were seminaries staffed wholly by priests, they would 'monopolize lay education'. No one had ever thought of Carlow

---

[1] Monsell Papers, Box 8319, Sullivan to Monsell, 28 November 1866.

[2] Thomas Andrews, *Studium Generale, A Chapter of Contemporary History*, London, 1867, p. 61.

[3] Monsell Papers, Box 8319, Sullivan to Monsell, 28 November 1866. The manoeuvres of the committee are explained fully in this letter.

[4] *Ibid.*

as a university before; 'it remained for Sir Dominic Corrigan and Mr Brady to discover the high and hitherto unknown merits of those institutions'. If the Senate accepted the Report, he would withdraw the application from the Catholic University, 'and leave to Dr Woodlock or someone else the task of asking for recognition, if the University or the Bishops should think fit to share the honours of recognition with every grammar school in the country'.[1] Sullivan, in fact, was pressing the point which Grey had made in 1865, that the multiplication of universities was undesirable. It is a question that is with us still. Kavanagh, whom Sullivan called the 'Secretary of Education to the Cardinal',[2] was strongly in favour of Carlow's claim, and in representing its qualifications for recognition to Fortescue early in the new year, he warmly endorsed the operation of the Charter: 'I trust, however, before many months to see all narrow restrictions swept away, and the full benefits of the Supplemental Charter granted to the Irish Catholics.'[3]

The restrictions to which Kavanagh alluded were more serious than he evidently imagined, and before anything could be done about the recognition of colleges, an injunction issued by the Master of the Rolls on 3 December restrained the Senate's execution of its new regulations, pending legal action brought against the Supplemental Charter by three Queen's graduates. The Senate duly cancelled the matriculation examination planned for 7 January.[4] *The Times* speculated that the delay in giving effect to the Supplemental Charter would prove to be pleasing to the Catholic bishops, for they had 'accepted the arrangement reluctantly, as a compromise, but they seem now to expect that they will get a Charter of their own'.[5] They were not wrong in this: as Naas was to say in May of the following year, the Government would consider what action to take when the courts had finally finished with the Supplemental Charter.[6] It transpired, in 1868, that that action was the offer of a Catholic University Charter.

Meanwhile, on 20 December, at the annual meeting of the Catholic University, Woodlock spoke on the Supplemental Charter. It can be assumed that his opinions were those of Cullen too, not only because of their close identity during the discussion in February, but because Cullen presided at this meeting. Whilst making severe reservations about the Charter, Woodlock was also at pains to show that the new attempt in

---

[1] Monsell Papers, Box 8319, Sullivan to Monsell, 28 November 1866. The manoeuvres of the committee are explained fully in this letter.
[2] *Ibid.*, Sullivan to Monsell, 1 June 1866.
[3] Carlingford Papers, CP. 3/55, Kavanagh to Fortescue, 4 January 1867.
[4] *The Times*, 11 December 1866.   [5] *Ibid.*
[6] *Hansard*, CLXXXVII, p. 1445 (31 May 1867).

the courts to exclude them even from that was hardly what they deserved. The regulations published by the Senate on the conditions for obtaining degrees did not, he said, contain anything objectionable to Catholics, and many of his students intended to present themselves for the matriculation examination when it was eventually held. The recent events had stopped them from doing so immediately. The bishops had not been consulted when the Supplemental Charter was issued, and 'no arrangement can meet with the full approval of Catholics which does not place Catholic education on a perfect equality with every other system of education.' The Catholic University gave numerous benefits, and these would be risked 'if not most assuredly lost' under the arrangements proposed by the Supplemental Charter. But despite all that, he felt he should express the sense of injury inflicted on Catholics and on the Catholic University, by the present attempts to deny them even 'the small advantages' which the Supplemental Charter was to have conferred.[1] It is clear that the bishops were still waiting to see what would happen to the Charter – but it is equally evident that whilst using its provisions for their benefit, they in no sense felt that it was a just solution of their grievance. But then it was never intended as such by the Government, at least in the incomplete form which was then on trial.

Now a new Charter which the Queen's University had accepted in 1864 made provision for the first time in its constitution for the establishment of Convocation.[2] The injunction issued by the Rolls Court, which had arrested the Senate's further realization of its regulations under the Supplemental Charter, resulted from an action by three members of Convocation who claimed that under the 1864 Charter the power of accepting or rejecting the Supplemental Charter was not vested exclusively in the Senate but jointly in Senate and Convocation. Their petition against the Corporation of the Queen's University, some members of the Senate, and their secretary, was heard before the Rolls Court in Dublin during April 1867.[3] The petition prayed for a declaration that the provisions of the Supplemental Charter of 1866 were inconsistent with the provisions of the 1864 Charter, and that the resolution of the Senate in October purporting to accept the Supplemental Charter was void. It asked also for an injunction to restrain the

---

[1] *The Times*, 22 December 1866.

[2] See reference to the implications of this by Naas in May 1867, in *Hansard*, CLXXXVII, pp. 4, 1441 ff. Previous Charters had been granted to the Queen's University in 1850 (under the provisions of 8 & 9 Vict. cap. 66) and in 1852. These had been surrendered upon the grant of the new Charter of 1864.

[3] *McCormac and Others* v. *the Queen's University*.

respondents from surrendering the 1864 Charter, and from matriculating or conferring degrees on any persons other than those qualified under that Charter. The Master of the Rolls delivered his judgment on 16 April. He said he had nothing to do with the policy which had directed the grant of the Supplemental Charter – it was not within his terms of reference – 'but the change was obviously a very fundamental one'.[1] Yet the parties who had instituted the present suit were not the proper ones to do so; they had no *locus standi*, and on that ground he dismissed the case. But he also stated that in his opinion the court had jurisdiction to decide the question as to whether the 1864 Charter could be constructed favourably to the petitioners, and it was his opinion that it had *not* vested the power of accepting or rejecting the Supplemental Charter exclusively in the Senate, but he could not give a legal declaration on the matter until it was raised in a proper and technical petition to the court.[2]

It was, as a result, quite clear that the Supplemental Charter would almost certainly prove to be without effect. The Master had advised that a proper manner of procedure for a new hearing would have to show that the injuries sustained under the new Charter by the petitioners were neither pecuniary nor personal, and that the injury must be of a public nature inflicted upon all members of the Convocation, and not merely on three of them. The proper course was an information in the name of the Attorney-General at the relation of the injured parties.[3] The *Cork Examiner* expressed its disgust at that: 'it is only the narrowest spirit of sectarian intolerance which would say that a Presbyterian doctor was injured because a Catholic got a diploma.'[4] A new suit was started, however, and the Government were pressed by Fortescue, first on 6 May,[5] and again on the 31st: on the latter occasion he asked them 'to interpose and anticipate the possible results of litigation, either by sanctioning and completing by further legislation the plans of the late Government, or by providing something wiser and better'.[6] Naas replied that the Government would wait until the fate of the Charter had been settled in law before acting on its own.[7] But it was to prove impossible for them to wait until 1 February 1868, on which day the Rolls Court granted a

[1] *Express* (Dublin), 17 April 1867.   [2] *Ibid.*, and *Hansard*, CLXXXVII, p. 4.
[3] *Express*, 17 April 1867.   [4] *Cork Examiner*, 18 April 1867.
[5] *Hansard*, CLXXXVII, p. 3. Question by Fortescue on the intentions of the Government, 'whether they intend to bring in a Bill to remove doubts as to the validity of the acceptance by the Senate of the Supplemental Charter of last year'.
[6] *Ibid.*, p. 1438. It is significant that he considered throwing open Dublin University to all denominations, whilst maintaining the separate identity of Trinity College, as a course of action 'wiser and better'. This was the core of Gladstone's plan in 1873.
[7] *Ibid.*, p. 1445.

perpetual injunction against the enforcement of the Charter in an almost empty court.[1] The cause of the Charter had been given up as lost long before that, and the bishops had begun to turn their attention to the growing volume of discussion on the Church question. But they did not cease to press their university claims and when Mayo came up with a plan for a Catholic university they again entered into negotiations with the Government.

[1] *The Times*, 3 February 1868. See also Walsh, *op. cit.*, p. 37, for a brief note on the end of the Charter.

CHAPTER SIX

The University Question
1867-8

WHEN the Master of the Rolls gave his first judgment on the Supplemental Charter in April 1867, it became obvious that the long series of negotiations started by the Russell Administration in 1865 had ended finally in failure. The Government through Naas had declared that it would wait for the completion of legal procedure against the Charter before producing a plan of its own,[1] but the delay in the Rolls Court meant that the last rites were not performed for the Charter until February, 1868. The Government did not, indeed, produce its plan for a chartered Catholic University until after that date, but from the middle of 1867 it was probing Catholic opinion on the university question, just as Grey and Bruce had done in 1865. The bishops were themselves quick to get off to a new start after the first Rolls Court decision, and so was Fawcett, who turned for the first time to the solution of the question which he was to press with almost the regularity of Spooner's former motions against Maynooth – a solution to be secured by the abolition of religious tests at Trinity College, Dublin.

The bishops began by considering a plan by Dr Andrews of the Belfast Queen's College,[2] when nine of them met in the middle of April at the Catholic University Board under Cullen's chairmanship. Andrews had suggested that Maynooth should be constituted a university, and become, in fact, the 'Irish Catholic Oxford'. It was originally intended for laymen as well as ecclesiastics, and under his proposed arrangement, medical students would continue to get their professional training elsewhere but they could take the degrees of the University of Maynooth. The Board did not accept this plan, however, but one which had occurred to Woodlock when he had read Andrews's pamphlet.[3] By this, the existing Catholic University could acquire legal recognition, not by making Maynooth a university, but by creating a 'St Patrick's University' of which the present Maynooth Board would be the Senate. It would have under it two colleges – Maynooth and the Catholic Univer-

[1] *Hansard*, third series, CLXXXVII, p. 1445 (31 May 1867).
[2] Thomas Andrews, *Studium Generale*, especially pp. 79 ff.
[3] Monsell Papers, Box 8319, Woodlock to Moriarty, 16 April 1867.

sity College in Dublin. The Dublin College would comprise the Arts, Science, Law and Medicine faculties; Maynooth the Theological and Moral Sciences.[1] Cullen could see many advantages in this: the most likely way of giving a grant to the university would come from placing a sum of money annually at the disposal of the Maynooth Board for the maintenance of a second college.[2] Woodlock felt it was advantageous to have no question of creating a new body, but only of extending the powers of an old one, and that body, the Maynooth Board, received £26,000 a year of public money. Further, it already met once a year at Maynooth, and once at Dublin; it was a mixed body, composed of bishops and laymen, and, 'in fine, it enjoys the confidence of the Bishops, of the Governments and of the Public'.[3] Above all, the position of the Church at the head of Catholic education would be secured by the plan, yet at the same time, he was persuaded, 'the Queen's Colleges Party and the friends of mixed education would not . . . oppose this scheme, as they have opposed and will oppose any interference with the Queen's University'.[4] The plan could be moved by the Maynooth Board itself when the bishops should direct them to do so. But first the Catholic University Board, after approving the plan, instructed Woodlock to write to the bishops for their views, and ask their advice on the best way of urging the scheme on the Government.[5]

Some sort of action was imperative. After the deflation of the high hopes the Supplemental Charter had inspired – at least as regards the legality of degrees – the Catholic University was especially weakened. 'The professors are dropping away, the students are becoming fewer, and the funds are diminishing', Sullivan wrote to Monsell. In fact, 'it can hardly be said to exist', and he reflected bitterly that the loss of each lay professor caused rejoicing in the camps of the hierarchy, for they had clerical replacements at hand.[6] He was rather over-drawing the picture, but it was true that the Catholic University had lost prestige by the public's realization that the bishops were prepared to trade it in to the Government in return for a university which would legalize its degrees.

On 18 June, Fawcett, the Radical member for Brighton, attempted his settlement of the Irish University question. His motion in the Commons was for the abolition of all religious tests at Trinity College, Dublin, and

[1] *Ibid.*, Woodlock to Moriarty, 18 April 1867.
[2] *Ibid.*, Woodlock to Moriarty, 16 April, 1867.
[3] *Ibid.*, Woodlock to Moriarty, 18 April 1867.
[4] *Ibid.*, Woodlock to Moriarty, 16 April, 1867.
[5] *Ibid.*, Woodlock to Moriarty, 18 April 1867.
[6] *Ibid.*, Sullivan to Monsell, 3 May 1867.

for the opening of fellowships and foundation scholarships to persons who did not profess the religion of the Establishment. It is interesting that his motion was defeated, after an equality of votes, only by the customary adverse vote of the Speaker.[1] It is difficult to predict what might have happened had Fawcett succeeded on this occasion. The importance of his move is not only that it was the first of his many attempts on the same plan, but that its terms of reference were to become English; his attempt to abolish religious tests in Ireland was in 1871 to be turned to account in application to Oxford and Cambridge.

The proposal of the Catholic University Board to bring a 'St Patrick's University' into being was quietly dropped, not, probably, because of lack of support among the bishops – for Cullen favoured it – but because it seemed as if the Government was itself about to make proposals.[2] Cullen advised Barnabo at the Propaganda at the end of July that a meeting of the bishops would be needed in September or October to consider the state of the Church question, and that of the universities:

> It also appears as if the Government is willing to establish a Catholic University, or to endow the one we have already. It is therefore desirable that the Archbishops should be in agreement on these matters. If your Eminence deems it desirable, you could give me the necessary instructions, and the authority to convene the Archbishops, and I could therefore hold the proposed meeting with some hope of a successful outcome. If the Archbishops do not agree among themselves, there is danger that they might divide, and so nothing good will result.[3]

The reason for Cullen's belief in the imminency of Government action was provided by the intervention of Manning. From May 1867 until March of the following year he was in regular communication with Disraeli and 'represented himself as fully acquainted with the views of Cardinal Cullen and the other leaders of Roman Catholic opinion'.[4] In 1865 Manning had written to Cullen that they had 'such an identity of principles that we need only a fuller and more personal knowledge of each other to renew the union which once partially existed'.[5] The reign of Wiseman had mitigated against such a union, for although of

---

[1] *Hansard*, CLXXXVIII p. 55. See also the remarks by W. J. Walsh in *The Irish University Question*, p. 38.

[2] The Derby Government did not decide to take up a definite scheme as quickly as Fergal McGrath suggests, however. See his *Newman's University*, p. 491.

[3] Propaganda, *Scritture* 35, Cullen to Barnabo, 30 July 1867.

[4] Monypenny and Buckle, *Life of Benjamin Disraeli*, vol. II, p. 345.

[5] Shane Leslie, 'Irish Pages from the Postbags of Manning, Cullen and Gladstone', in *Dublin Review*, October 1919, p. 163. He prints a letter of Manning to Cullen, 8 December 1865. In his *Life* of Manning (London, 1921, p. 194), Leslie gives the date of this letter as 19 January 1866.

Irish extraction, and despite the success of his tour of Ireland in 1858 (when he was honoured more for his office than for himself – he was the first cardinal to visit Ireland since the Reformation), he was distrusted in many clerical circles there.[1] Bishop O'Brien of Waterford said in 1860 that 'Wiseman would like to have the Irish Church at his feet', and see their 'ancient and independent hierarchy absorbed by England'. The antidote to Wiseman's designs which he suggested, helps to explain the absence of union between the two hierarchies to which Manning referred: 'we should always keep ourselves separated from the English in those public demonstrations; for otherwise they would extinguish us as a distinct national hierarchy.'[2] Manning was anxious to heal the division between them. Fenianism, the distress of the Irish countryside, the renewed assaults on the Irish Establishment, all gave him a chance to identify himself with Cullen and the Irish bishops – and so did the university question. In February 1866 he started inviting the Irish Catholic Members of Parliament to his Tuesday evening receptions, in order to 'keep up relations with them and with Archbishop Cullen'.[3] At the same time Mgr Talbot urged him from Rome to bring the English, Scotch and Irish bishops into line, and declared that Wiseman's inability to produce combined action (which would have 'no little political influence') had been due to the unwillingness of the Irish bishops, for they had been afraid of the cardinal.[4] Manning was able to assure Talbot that in the previous month Cullen had written expressing his readiness 'to form a union with the English bishops'.[5] He had apparently agreed to join action with Manning to oppose the Government should it 'meddle in Italy'.[6] The English bishops agreed to common action with the Irish at their meeting in April 1866, and Manning was sure that 'if we could devise some occasion for a joint act, they are all ready to unite in it'.[7]

Manning relied on his personal influence with ministers, especially with Gladstone.[8] They were of course old friends, and the silence between them occasioned by Manning's entry of the Roman Church after the Gorham case, in 1851, had ended in 1861.[9] Throughout the sixties they corresponded on the Roman question, although taking

---

[1] V. A. McClelland, *Cardinal Manning, His Public Life and Influence, 1865-92*, London, 1962, p. 162.

[2] Kirby Papers, O'Brien to Kirby, no. 2530, 15 March 1860. It is odd that O'Brien was bishop of that diocese in which Wiseman had spent a few boyhood years, having attended at school in Waterford.

[3] Purcell, *Life of Cardinal Manning*, vol. II, p. 392.

[4] *Ibid.*   [5] *Ibid.*, p. 393.   [6] *Ibid.*, p. 395.

[7] Leslie, *Dublin Review*, October 1919, p. 165.   [8] Purcell, *op. cit.*, p. 383.

[9] John Morley, *Life of Gladstone*, vol. I, p. 387, n. 2.

opposite views of the Temporal Power. In 1868 Manning was able to tell Gladstone that his 'communications with Ireland are direct and truth-worthy'.[1] He was trusted in Rome as a spokesman on Irish affairs – in 1868 Antonelli told Odo Russell that the opinions publicly expressed by Cullen and Manning on Irish questions were those of the Papal Government.[2] And he was accepted by Parliament as representing the opinions of the Irish bishops.[3] But the renewed accord between Gladstone and Manning in the 1860s, which was to endure until they fell apart again, over the Vatican Decrees controversy in 1874[4] was of little use for immediate action on the Irish University question in 1867, since Gladstone was in opposition to the Conservative Administration. Manning was therefore to make overtures to Disraeli, and when he succeeded Derby as Prime Minister in February 1868 he added as his excuse that 'It is my privilege to stand neutral between political parties'.[5] He accordingly arranged for Woodlock to meet Disraeli, and in his letter to Disraeli of 21 May, giving the time of the interview, Manning wrote:

> I am able to say, of my own knowledge, that any favourable proposal from Government on the subject of the Catholic University would not only encounter no opposition, but would be assisted. I believe I may say that this includes the grant of a Charter. What I write is not from second-hand. I can add that the 'Chief' I conferred with is in the front, and he fully recognizes the need of removing the Catholic education of Ireland from the turbulent region of politics.[6]

On 17 August 1867 Cullen wrote replying to Manning's inquiry about his feeling on the university proposals which the Government were beginning to consider, and which he had written about to him. Cullen said he was 'altogether in favour of a Catholic University with an independent charter for itself, and altogether under Catholic control'. This was also the desire of all the bishops with the possible exception of Moriarty. He was aware that some of the Catholic M.P.s were opposed to the plan, and favoured instead the system of London University – but when this had been attempted, in the Supplemental Charter, it 'had pleased no party', and so never passed into effect.[7] Manning therefore

[1] Gladstone Papers, B.M.Add.MS. 44249, f. 19, Manning to Gladstone, 11 February 1868.

[2] F.O. 43, vol. 101, Dispatch no. 57, 22 December 1868.

[3] See, for example, the Duke of Marlborough's assumption that this was the case – *Hansard*, CXCIII, p. 33 (26 June 1868).

[4] J. L. Hammond, *Gladstone and the Irish Nation*, London, 1938, p. 137.

[5] In a letter of Manning's to Disraeli of 26 February 1868; quoted in Monypenny and Buckle, *op. cit.*, vol. II, p. 346.

[6] *Ibid.*, p. 345.

[7] Manning Papers, Cullen to Manning, 17 August 1867. Also quoted by Leslie, *Dublin Review*, October 1919, p. 181.

urged Disraeli to disregard hostile expressions from Irish Members. 'I am now able to state', he wrote again on 20 August, 'that they do not represent the sense and desire of Cardinal Cullen or the Irish Bishops.'[1] The part taken by Manning explains Cullen's belief that the Government were about to do something on the university question. Manning remained self-appointedly at the centre of that question, in 1868 and again in 1873, and succeeded in embarrassing Disraeli, Gladstone and Cullen in turn. He gave assurances when he should not have done so because they had no foundation in the opinions of others, and he led men to suppose that he had the entire confidence of others when he had not.

Cullen must have told Sir John Gray of Manning's intervention, for the *Freeman's Journal* contained a leader on 12 August which described the university question as 'well-nigh settled'. A Charter was to be granted to a Catholic university, and with it a reasonable endowment. For the present the Queen's University and Trinity College would continue undisturbed. The Government were said to have arrived at a settlement on those lines, although it was not to be communicated to Parliament until February.[2] That was the month in which the Master of the Rolls was to deliver his last words on the Supplemental Charter.

Also in August, the Government appointed a Royal Commission to inquire into Irish Primary Education, to sit under the chairmanship of Lord Powis. The *Freeman* thought this hopeful too (although it meant some delay while the Commission gathered its evidence) for 'the friends of free education believe the evidence in favour of the denominational system will be so overwhelming that Parliament cannot resist its adoption'.[3] The Commission on the Church was also getting down to business at this time, and just as its opponents claimed it was a Tory delaying tactic to put off immediate consideration of the Establishment, so they saw that a comparable Commission on Education could reflect a similar expedient. The Government knew well that consideration of the university question in 1866 had been complicated when the bishops insisted on airing the entire question of education at all levels at the same time. The issue of the Powis Commission meant that a case could be made out by the Government for temporizing on the National System should the bishops again bring it up in the course of the university proposals they were to be asked to consider in March 1868.

In February 1867 Cullen had told Manning that he thought Naas and Derby appeared 'disposed to maintain the mixed system' of National

---

[1] Monypenny and Buckle, *op. cit.*, vol. II, p. 345.
[2] *Freeman's Journal*, 12 August 1867.   [3] *Ibid.*

Education.[1] But he was prepared to welcome the Commission, as it would enable the Catholics to state their claims and the evidence on which they were based. He doubted if the Commission itself would result in the end of the National System because it was too favourably regarded by Protestants.[2] And he was to remark bitterly that when the Commissioners were finally appointed it would be found to illustrate the maxim 'no Irish need apply'.[3] But by the end of February, Cullen had become more hopeful. 'Here we are in a fair way of getting rid of mixed education,' he wrote to Spalding in Baltimore, 'a royal Commission now will probably get the separate or denominational system introduced into Ireland.'[4] His only fear was that a Catholic Commissioner might be named who would sympathize with the National System. On 18 August, he wrote to Kirby:

> I fear Dr Moriarty will be put forward by the high Catholics as the representative of the Catholic body – he would perhaps defend mixed education and propose that Catholics should take a portion of the income of the Protestant Church. It would be most important for us to have a general declaration of the Bishops as to their own views as a body.[5]

His fear was realized: Moriarty was offered a place on the Commission. Cullen could never allow that – in the previous year he had intimated Moriarty's unsoundness on education to the Propaganda; he was an 'outspoken partisan of all the controversies on education'.[6] Moriarty on the Commission would, he was sure, give rise to the impression that the Irish bishops were more divided over the education question than they were in fact. On 7 September a bishops' meeting was called for 1 October, to consider the education and Church questions. Cullen acted quickly. 'The moment is very critical', he wrote to Kirby.[7] To Moriarty himself he wrote advising delay in answering the invitation to the Commission. He should wait to see what the bishops felt at the forthcoming meeting, for if the offer were accepted without consulting them, they would probably be inclined not to co-operate. 'If they sanction your acceptance of the office,' Cullen added, 'of course they will assist you.'[8] He then made his preparations to insure

[1] Manning Papers, Cullen to Manning, 7 February 1867, also quoted by Leslie, *Dublin Review*, October 1919, p. 165.

[2] Propaganda, *Scritture* 36, Cullen to Barnabo, 18 January 1868.

[3] Monsell Papers, Box 8319, Cullen to Monsell (undated, but certainly January 1868).

[4] Spalding Letters, Cullen to Spalding, 29 February 1868.

[5] Kirby Papers, Cullen to Kirby, no. 294, 18 August 1867.

[6] Propaganda, *Scritture* 35, Cullen to Barnabo, 17 May 1866.

[7] Kirby Papers, Cullen to Kirby, no. 323, 7 September 1867.

[8] Monsell Papers, Box 8319, Cullen to Moriarty, 19 September 1867.

that there was no risk of that happening. Dr Russell, the President of Maynooth, and Lord Dunraven had also been asked to join the Commission, and Cullen was aware that a rejection of Moriarty by the bishops would prompt their refusals too, for he regarded all three as 'weak and yielding men' who were no fit spokesmen of the Catholic cause.[1] Moriarty himself would be supported by a faction of lay Catholics, and no greater harm could be done.[2] The *Freeman* agreed with Cullen's diagnosis of the situation: 'one bad or doubtful selection would taint the whole inquiry.'[3]

The meeting of the bishops took place on the 1, 2 and 3 October, and all were present except two who were unwell – O'Brien and Feeny. MacHale stayed for only the first two days, but was, as Cullen said, 'much more agreeable than ever I saw him before'.[4] After a discussion of the Church question they turned to the matter of Moriarty and the Commission. All were united in telling him not to accept. He did not help himself by saying that if the Commission produced a report condemning the bishops' educational demands, he would sign it.[5] The bishops took the view which Cullen expressed: 'he would probably have gone great lengths with the Government, and this was the reason why he was selected.'[6] As a result of the meeting, Moriarty did not accept; nor subsequently, did Russell and Dunraven.

Sir Robert Kane did. He was a Catholic, but an opponent of the bishops' demands; and Cullen consoled himself with the consideration that 'he will not be able to do much harm as he is a layman. A bishop would have ruined us if he went astray.'[7] The bishops at the meeting renewed their educational demands, and pledged themselves to support the Catholic University.[8] And, most importantly, Dr Leahy, the Archbishop of Cashel, and Dr Derry of Clonfert, were deputed by the body of bishops 'to treat with the Government about a Charter for the Catholic University, *and other educational matters*'. Derry was proposed by Cullen himself, because 'he is very determined against the mixed system'.[9] The meeting was held, as Cullen said, just in time; 'otherwise

---

[1] Kirby Papers, Cullen to Kirby, no. 368, 10 October 1867.
[2] *Ibid.*, Cullen to Kirby, no. 398, 31 October 1867.
[3] *Freeman*, 12 August 1867.
[4] Kirby Papers, Cullen to Kirby, no. 368, 10 October 1867.
[5] *Ibid.*   [6] *Ibid.*
[7] *Ibid.*, Cullen to Kirby, no. 398, 31 October 1867.
[8] It was probably this pledge of support which caused MacHale to leave before the end of the meeting – at least Cullen thought so (*ibid.*, Cullen to Kirby, no. 368, 10 October 1867). The resolutions adopted by the bishops at the meeting are in P. F. Moran, *The Pastoral Letters . . . of Cardinal Cullen*, Dublin, 1882, vol. III, p. 71 (VII).
[9] Kirby Papers, Cullen to Kirby, no. 368, 10 October 1867.

we would have been divided into several parties, losing all our influence'.[1] Manning wrote promising the support of the English bishops for the Irish educational demands.[2]

At the distribution of prizes at the Catholic University on 23 October, Cullen followed the spirit of the agreement to support the institution made by the prelates at their meeting. He expressed confidence that the university would prosper, although warning that progress would be slow. But the people of Ireland would support them. 'Talent is never wanting in Irishmen,' he said, 'but industry and perseverance are often wanting.'[3] At this point the perseverance of Maguire again led him to raise the question of a Charter for the Catholic University in Parliament. On 22 November 1867 he asked the Chief Secretary what course the Government intended to adopt on the matter. Mayo, in replying, said that Irish university education was at that time receiving the attention of the Government, and would shortly come before the House.[4] It was by now well known that the Government plans were maturing on the line of considerable conciliation to the Catholics. In October, the *Dublin* had considered it 'perfectly in accordance with the policy of the present Government to give a Charter to the Catholic University', and pointed to the precedent they had created in 1852 by chartering the Catholic University of Canada; 'if we are not misinformed, they have already intimated their disposition to do the same in the case of Ireland'.[5] But the Government had to tread with the utmost caution, for they had not only to conciliate the Irish Catholics, but to keep their own minority party in the Commons united. Truckling to the Cullen party could be dangerous. The Irish Attorney-General, Warren, intimated to Mayo the anxiety occasioned in his constituency (University of Dublin) by his reply for the Government to Maguire's question. He was especially anxious that the Government should pledge itself never to admit Catholics to the governing body of Trinity College, or any university which could control Trinity. Such a measure, wrote Warren, would '*kill* the allegiance of your best friends in Ireland'. He had no 'political objection' to the plan of chartering a Roman Catholic university affiliated with Maynooth, and having a governing body such as the Maynooth Commissioners might desire.[6] This, of course, was the plan considered so favourably by the Catholic University Board in April of that year.

[1] Kirby Papers, Cullen to Kirby, no. 398, 31 October 1867.
[2] *Ibid.*
[3] *Post,* 24 October 1867.
[4] *Hansard,* cxc, p. 142.
[5] *Dublin Review,* October 1867, 'An Irish Session', p. 522.
[6] Mayo Papers, MS. 11217, Warren to Mayo, 1 December 1867.

Mayo replied to dismiss Warren's anxieties, referring the 'gossips in College' to the Government's opposition to Fawcett's motion of June. That had shown that they would not tamper with Trinity College.[1] At the same time he emphasized the dangerous position Trinity was in while the university question remained unresolved – it ran the risk of losing everything. He then outlined two possible courses. First was the creation of a Roman Catholic university 'which would stand somewhat in relation to the Roman Catholics that Trinity College, Dublin, does to the members of the Established Church'[2] —a phrase which received wide currency in 1868. The second course was 'a much more comprehensive and useful plan':

> The outline of this scheme would be to leave to Trinity College, the Queen's Colleges, and the new Roman Catholic College all their distinctive principles of government and teaching, their property and endowments, but to create a degree-giving Body to which all Irish students in Arts and perhaps in Medicine would have to submit their claims before obtaining a degree – leave the [Parliamentary] Representation of T.C.D. as it is, and give a member to a constituency created out of all the rest of the other Colleges. The advantage of this scheme over every other must be at once apparent. It would avoid the great evil recognized by all . . . the multiplication of Universities in one Kingdom, which tends to the lowering of the standard of Education for the purpose of attracting students – it would place all on an equality and so give the race to the strong (we know who the strong would be) – it would combine all the advantages of United Education without its admitted evils, and, above all, if accepted by the three parties it would settle the question for ever.[3]

Trinity College, he submitted, would retain all her present advantages, whilst her wealth would give her ascendancy over all other colleges in Ireland.[4] He saw that difficulties would arise in filling up the details of the plan, but he was sure it was the right solution. The letter is interesting, for it shows the extent to which the Government now felt themselves committed. It is also interesting that in February 1868 they preferred the first of Mayo's two proposals. The plan for a chartered Catholic university then outlined was therefore evidently intended to be followed up by wider university arrangements. Like the plan of the

[1] *Ibid.*, Mayo to Warren, 3 December 1867. It will be remembered that Fawcett's motion was only lost by the adverse vote of the Speaker, but the Conservatives, in a minority in the House anyway, had all voted against it. So had the Irish Catholic members.

[2] *Ibid.*

[3] *Ibid.*

[4] The *Dublin Review* had made the same point: 'So far as Trinity College is concerned, a separate Charter for the Catholic University seems to be the one available means of preserving its endowments for the exclusive use of Irish Protestants.' October 1867, p. 522.

Russell Administration before it, consideration of the Mayo plan was to be cut in half by parliamentary accident. But that plan, unlike the Supplemental Charter, had not actually passed into effect when the Conservatives fell over Gladstone's resolutions.

As the year closed, Cullen held a meeting of the clergy of the Dublin diocese to consider Catholic education. It had the important effect of drawing public interest to the question on the eve, as it were, of the start of discussions on the university. Notice in the press tended to harden the opinions on both sides. The meeting was held at the pro-Cathedral on 18 December. Cullen emphasized the importance of their agreeing to a concerted effort. It was the misfortune of Catholics, he said, that education was 'very commonly employed as an engine for assailing the true religion'.[1] They were assembled to insist on free education, totally independent of State control; indeed

Experience teaches us that Government, and especially Governments composed of men of various religions, when they usurp the charge of schools, always spread irreligious opinions. . . .[2] Such have been the unhappy results of State Education in France and Belgium and other countries. Irreligion has spread, and at the same time a spirit of socialism and revolution.[3]

He quoted Burke, and then, paradoxically, listed some *rights* to which the Irish Catholics were entitled. These were a Catholic university, with both charter *and* endowment; Catholic intermediate education; and Catholic seminary education. He turned next to quote the *Letter of Propaganda* which declared that no Catholic could attend 'non-Catholic universities' without exposure to sin.[4] A resolution, proposed by Dean O'Connell, and seconded by Dr Curtis (a Jesuit) was carried unanimously. It posited 'That Education, to be a source of blessings, must be animated and controlled by religion; separated from religion, it is productive of innumerable evils to individuals and society'.[5] A second resolution upheld the right of Catholic parents to determine the education of their children.

The *Freeman* eulogized the proceedings, and supposed, correctly, that

[1] *Freeman*, 19 December 1867.

[2] It is interesting that this compares with Gladstone's argument against some religious Establishments, that a State cannot be said to have a conscience when it is clear that it is divided in its religious convictions. See chap. 7.

[3] *Freeman*, 19 December 1867.

[4] Letter of 1867. This was applicable to England especially, and came in support of Manning's campaign against the Oxford Catholic college plan. See H. O. Evennett, 'Catholics and the Universities', in *The English Catholics, 1850-1950*, ed. G. A. Beck, p. 316.

[5] *Freeman*, 19 December 1867. Cullen's speech is also printed in Moran, vol. III, p. 123 (x).

before the Government acted they would have to communicate with the Catholics to ascertain their views on university education. It also observed that the question could be resolved under two heads – a charter for the Catholic University 'of the same character and confessing the same privileges as the Charter conceded to the London University and to the Queen's University', and a 'liberal endowment' – 'by such wise concessions the question of University education would be settled'. Trinity College and the Queen's Colleges could pursue their own course as at that time.[1] The *Irish Times* prepared to open a new Protestant campaign against sacerdotalism in education: the object of the Dublin diocesan meeting was 'to seize upon the control of secular education'. It seemed to its leader-writer that the clergy, realizing they could not rely upon the support of their own laity over education, were hoping to force them into submission by the help of the State. 'Ultramontanism,' he observed, 'like the Celtic race, finds its last refuge in the most western parts of Europe.'[2] The *Dublin Review* made the useful point that Cullen's meeting had shown clearly the two senses in which 'Education' was being considered. According to the 'secularists' it meant 'the development of intellect', but the definition in Dean O'Connell's resolution showed that it must be something 'animated and controlled by religion'.[3] Unhappily for Catholic aspirations, the claim of the *Freeman* that 'all who are not philosophic Liberals with strong tendencies of Positivism'[4] recognized the need to combine religious and secular instruction, was not to prove true in reference even to the Conservatives. And when Gladstone came to deal with Irish universities at the end of 1872, the Catholics found themselves in the hands of a man who was limited in the concessions he could make by having among his supporters just those 'philosophic' Liberals whom the *Freeman* most dreaded.

It is important to notice that the proceedings of this meeting combined the university question with consideration of the other branches of education. It looked as if the pattern of 1866 would be repeated. The only new element in the situation was the intervention of Manning. He concentrated his energies to secure a Charter from Disraeli, but he also turned to other Irish questions, and in his *Letter to Earl Grey* of 12

[1] *Freeman*, 20 December 1867. It can be seen that, as in the case of the bishops' claims of 1866, the powers proposed for the Catholic Charter were very wide. But the plan outlined by Gray in the *Freeman* was not so dissimilar from that in Mayo's letter to Warren as to rule out any possibility of a successful adjustment.

[2] *Irish Times*, 20 December 1867.

[3] *Dublin Review*, April 1868, p. 523. (This number also contains a review of the published proceedings of the Dublin meeting.)

[4] *Freeman*, 20 December 1867.

March 1868, he suggested courses which could ameliorate the condition of the Irish by reforming the land laws and abolishing the Established Church.[1] During the second half of December, and in the first of January, 'Manning was lending his assistance in maturing the Ministerial plan' for a Catholic Charter.[2] He saw Disraeli on at least two occasions, and communicated his impressions to Cullen, although he was still far from expecting much from the Government.[3] On 1 February 1868, the Rolls Court in Dublin granted a perpetual injunction against the operation of the Supplemental Charter, and so the way was opened for the Government to move their plan.

Mayo considered the possibilities in a memorandum now to be found among his papers.[4] At the beginning he saw the unpleasantness of the situation in which he was placed:

> Any plan proposed by the Government for the erection of an University at which Irish Catholics could be educated would, if acceptable to the Irish R.C. bishops, be at least boldly and thankfully received by the R.C. laity, and would be violently opposed by the Protestant Party. Again, anything falling short of an acceptance of the proposal of the Irish bishops would be magnified by them into a grievance – perhaps an insult – and in this line they would be supported by the R.C. laity for party purposes, or to obtain cheap popularity.[5]

He was certain that neither Maynooth nor the Queen's Colleges were suitable foundations for any Government plan, and proposed instead a Royal Commission which would consider applications for a charter from 'any institution in the *United Kingdom*', which was to impart 'a liberal education' in any two of the four faculties of Theology, Law, Medicine, and Arts (or Philosophy). The Commissioners should look into the means possessed by applicants to fulfil their claims; 'the means being money, buildings, books, museums, laboratories, a corps of distinguished professors, and the probability of resort of students'. The consequence of the wide application of the Commission would be, he imagined, that an English Catholic university would be founded before long, 'for the Irish gentry would attend it, and return to Ireland better

---

[1] H. E. Manning, *Ireland, A Letter to Earl Grey*, printed as a pamphlet, in London, March 1868, also in his *Miscellanies*, London, 1877, vol. I, p. 213. (See chap. 7 for an evaluation of this work.)

[2] Monypenny and Buckle, *op. cit.*, vol. II, p. 346.

[3] Leslie, *Dublin Review*, October 1919, p. 182, Manning to Cullen, 14 January and 24 January 1868.

[4] Mayo Papers, MS. 11217, 'Notes on University Education – Ireland'. It is undated, but attached to a memorandum by Stoney, to which it obviously refers and which is dated 15 February 1868.

[5] *Ibid.*

subjects'.[1] The Crown would be advised to incorporate any institution favourably regarded by the Commission. Each college would be allowed absolute liberty of management, but examinations were only to be made in the presence of three Assistant Commissioners (or if the Commission had expired, of three men named by the Crown for the purpose). Any university so established would require assistance, and Parliament should empower municipal corporations to erect or grant the use of existing buildings to these universities, in addition to any grants and the endowments of Chairs – 'subject to terms of agreement between the Corporation and the University'. Any existing legislation, which should be found impeding the ability of a university to hold property, must be repealed. He would propose to Parliament 'votes to subsidize such institutions on the same plan as Primary Schools are assisted in England', and votes for prizes. He was in agreement with his predecessors of 1865-6, Grey and Wodehouse, that free-trade in university education was beneficial, and that 'two or three contests between rival universities would do much more to secure good policy than any attempt to dragoon men into indifferentism or infidelity by mixed education'. Under the plan, the supporters of mixed education, freethinkers, and Catholics, could all be satisfied with an education according to their beliefs. If the Irish bishops wanted a university under their exclusive control, and could get money, professors and students, they could have it under the plan. Mayo was conscious that the multiplication of universities would be dangerous should a chartered body fail – but he was sure that the Commissioners who were to report on examinations would be able to detect and check failure before university education *per se* was brought into contempt. 'The University of Durham', he wrote, 'has never distinguished itself, but I am not aware that the low estimate in which its degrees are held has done any harm.' He was strongly opposed to endowment of poor scholars, for the significant reason that the supply of educated men for the public service was ample, and endowment of poor scholars would only increase applicants; and he quoted the Bishop of Ghent's[2] *bon mot* that a university degree was 'a cheque on the Government . . . if they honour it they make an employee a bureaucrat; if not a revolutionist'.[3]

Mayo had asked the opinions of Johnstone Stoney at the Queen's University, and the long memorandum he submitted in reply represents

1 This was a pious hope. When Manning and Capel established their Kensington College in 1874 the Irish did *not* resort to it – but then it also was unchartered, and so unable to grant legally recognized degrees.

2 The Prince de Broglie.

3 Mayo Papers, MS. 11217, as above.

a fair statement of the Protestant case. It was not one favourable to that direction in which Mayo was tending. Stoney wrote: 'I must confess that continued thought leaves me only more averse from a measure so retrograde in its intellectual aspect, so disastrous politically, so emasculating to our moral nature as the imposing upon Ireland of a Catholic University would inevitably be, or become.'[1] His reasons followed, at some length. They are a sophisticated version of the old Protestant fear that Catholic education enslaved the mind, and that the Catholic laity must in any situation be saved from that, by the rejection of the demands of their bishops. The ecclesiastical organization of the Church of Rome was, he wrote, 'the most powerful of secret societies, and where it runs counter to temporal interests, it is by far the most mischievous'. He outlined the familiar contrast between the relative freedom of the Irish Catholicism of O'Connell's time and the modern excess of ultramontanism. The bishops' educational claims 'first publicly announced in 1859' were now in danger of succeeding; and since education is 'the cardinal point in which lay and ecclesiastical interests clash' any concessions to them would place Irish education at their feet. In every country in Europe, it was the educational claims of their Catholic hierarchies which had given rise to struggles between Church and State, and everywhere the laity had been articulate enough to join the opposition to exclusive control by the bishops. But in Ireland, unhappily, lay thought 'is in the main not Roman Catholic'. Government countenance of a 'priest-ridden university' would simply have the vile effect of extinguishing even that small quantity of free lay thought which continued still: 'No constitution for a Catholic university can be devised, which, in the peculiar circumstances of Ireland would not in the long run become priest-ridden.'[2]

Working, therefore, for some suitable manœuvre, Stoney proceeded upon an examination of the nature of university education. He discussed three different meanings attaching to it. First were the Universities of Oxford and Cambridge as they were from the time of Laud until the reforms of the 1850s; in this sense a university was a body under the control of its own colleges, which examined candidates trained in *them*, and not by *itself*. The London University, however, has given an 'entirely new and strange meaning' to the word 'university'; it is here a body putting its whole faith in examination. Thirdly, there was 'the original meaning of the word' – universities such as Oxford and Cambridge were before the Laudian Statutes, 'and to which they are rapidly

---

[1] Mayo Papers, G. Johnstone Stoney to Mayo, 15 February 1868.
[2] *Ibid.*

returning since the recent legislation which restored the independence of the university'.[1] In this definition a university is a corporation by which its students are both taught and graduated – and it is to this that Irish university education should tend, 'and thus convert a crisis of great difficulty into a mine of fortune'.

Stoney suggested a plan which would give an Irish realization of that concept of university – a plan which was to be followed in its essential outline by Gladstone's proposals of 1873, and which was to be consecrated in Archbishop Walsh's *Trinity College and the University of Dublin* (1902).[2] Trinity College was to be disentangled from the University of Dublin. It was to be a constituent college of that university, as it was technically at that time anyway, and the University of Dublin was to be widened to become the 'University of Ireland'. It was unfortunate that in the beginning Trinity College had been invested with too much power over the university: by his plan, Stoney would have reconstituted it according to the phrase in Queen Elizabeth's Charter – *'Mater Universitatis'*, the nucleus of an university. This was, he claimed, merely 'an intention to which effect has not yet been given.' Laud's subjugation of universities to Colleges, having produced a backwash in Ireland, had prevented its fulfilment. If the plan were carried, existing Fellows of Trinity should be appointed to Chairs in the University of Ireland, so would the professorial staff of the Catholic University in Dublin. The Galway Queen's College would be absorbed by the Dublin Catholic College. The Cork College would become a great school, comparable to the Royal Belfast Institution. The Belfast College would become a college of the new university. The Government should propose the endowment of a Catholic College or Hall at the outset. The immediate religious difficulties could be at least partially resolved on this wise:

> The Theological Faculty of the University should be many-sided as it is in Bonn, Tübingen, and Breslau. The instruction in this Faculty would also be exceptional in not being delivered in the University buildings: that of the Established Church being given in Trinity College; that of the Roman Catholics at Maynooth; that of the Presbyterians in the Theological College of Belfast.[3]

[1] The Acts of 1854 and 1856.

[2] In discussion of Fawcett's motions to abolish tests at Trinity College the hierarchy condemned the idea on the ground that by it Trinity was merely converted into another 'godless college' – and that in the centre of Dublin where it could do maximum harm. In his *Trinity College and the University of Dublin*, Archbishop Walsh argued that Trinity was quite separable from the university: its founders envisaged more than one college in the university. He hoped to see 'a Catholic College, on a footing equal in all respects with that of Trinity College, in the University of Dublin' (p. viii).

[3] Mayo Papers, MS. 11217, Stoney to Mayo, 15 February 1868.

If it could be skilfully presented, such a plan might be found acceptable at both Trinity College and the Catholic University – the former ought to be swayed by the forewarning that it was the only chance of keeping their College government closed to Dissenters, for if no settlement came soon to the university question, public opinion would compel it to be thrown open.[1] And in opposition to Mayo's predisposition to allow the multiplication of institutions, Stoney pointed out that 'the feeling of Parliament is undoubtedly in favour of one University'.

His proposal, which he finally summarized as 'Denominational Colleges, and a University so many-sided as to be thereby undenominational', would be a practical compromise which the bishops might well be induced to accept. The withdrawal of the Queen's Colleges at Cork and Galway could be represented as great concessions to them, and if a sufficient number of Catholic staff were appointed in the university, Catholic students would be able to receive instruction exclusively from members of their own Church. 'It may further be hinted' to the bishops, he added correctly and with some foresight, 'that after the next Parliament meets there is reason to apprehend that all negotiations will become vastly more difficult.'[2] But Stoney's plan, so prophetic of later developments in the Irish university question, was set aside by Mayo, who in the end presented only his own to the Cabinet for discussion.

Mayo did not announce his plan to Parliament until 10 March. In the meantime he did not communicate with the Irish bishops – but he had no need to do so, for Cullen was able to suggest the conditions which they would agree to through Manning. Cullen also sent Woodlock to London as he had done in 1866, to be on the spot during the formative weeks of the Government plan. Dr Leahy and Dr Derry, the two prelates deputed by the bishops to treat with the Government at their meeting in October 1867, were not to prove as amenable as Cullen had imagined, however.

Manning saw Disraeli on 19 February 1868, and was faced with definite propositions. He was asked if the Irish bishops would accept a Charter for the Catholic University if it were made without the offer of an endowment and with the admission of laymen into its government. Manning wrote urging Cullen to accept. An endowment, he pointed out, would probably come 'by the force of events' anyway, in time, and should the laity be admitted to government, 'is it not possible to reserve the supreme control of the bishops over all its sytem?'[3] Cullen's reply is

---

[1] This was the point made by the *Dublin Review* (October 1867, p. 522).
[2] Mayo Papers, MS. 11217, Stoney to Mayo, 15 February 1868.
[3] Leslie, *Dublin Review*, October 1919, p. 182, Manning to Cullen, 20 February 1868.

lost; but its content is expressed in Manning's letter to Disraeli of 22 February. He believed that Irish bishops would stick out for an endowment, but that the admission of laymen into the government of everything but the theological, moral and religious matters, would be accepted by them. Manning felt that this was 'ample basis for a conference', with 'great probability of satisfaction to both sides'. He urged Disraeli to communicate the plan directly to Cullen when the Cabinet thought fit, and to the two deputed bishops – who would willingly come over to London if desired.[1]

Manning also urged Cullen to send over Leahy and Derry, begging him to keep it secret, however, to avoid perils from adverse public comment.[2] But the two bishops were holding back. They had refused Cullen's suggestion that they should meet the Irish Parliamentary representatives when he had put it to them in January.[3] Now both refused to accept a Charter without an endowment. Leahy wanted the bishops to assemble and make a declaration to that effect, but Cullen, in urging him to go to London to learn from the Prime Minister directly what the Government intended to do, said that there was no point in convening the bishops until the Government's intentions could be known officially. Derry, who was unwell, did not wish to travel to London, and was annoyed with Disraeli for not replying to the letter which he and Leahy had written on 23 October 1867, requesting some information of the Government's intentions and suggesting negotiations.[4] Cullen told Woodlock to remain in London to see what turn events might take.[5] Manning saw the intransigence of Leahy and Derry as a real threat to success, and once again pressed acceptance of a Charter without endowment upon Cullen. He made the suggestion which Stoney had put to Mayo: that the Irish bishops should be made aware of the fact that they would not get a Charter out of the Liberals.[6]

Cullen's own opinions on the plan of a Charter without endowment do not show directly, but he was becoming impatient of Leahy and Derry, whom he called 'touchy'. 'If they go on in this way', he wrote to Woodlock, 'they will do nothing – but mischief.' Derry he thought worse than Leahy in this; both would be blamed if good was prevented by their

---

[1] Disraeli evidently sent this letter to Mayo, in whose papers it is to be found. MSS. 11161-11175, Manning to Disraeli, 22 February 1868.

[2] Leslie, *Dublin Review*, October 1919, p. 182, Manning to Cullen, 21 February 1868.

[3] Woodlock Papers, Cullen to Woodlock, 29 January 1868.

[4] *Ibid.*, Cullen to Woodlock, 28 February 1868.

[5] *Ibid.*

[6] Leslie, *Dublin Review*, October 1919, p. 183, Manning to Cullen, 29 February 1868.

'high horse' attitude.[1] He was suspicious of the motives of the Government, but his approval of at least the principle of their plan was shown when he said to Woodlock that although the bishops had stipulated that a Charter without endowment would be unsatisfactory, 'there is not a word to indicate that it would not be accepted'.[2] Woodlock was thinking of getting the development in the university question presented in Rome, evidently with Cullen's approval, for he enjoined Woodlock not to let Leahy or Derry know of the idea.[3] It did not come to anything, probably because the new state of the question passed away with such rapidity – it did not last beyond June – that there was never anything to represent at Rome anyway. In a way Cullen was playing a double game. The two prelates deputed by the body of bishops to treat with the Government were ignored by him. He dealt instead with Woodlock, whom he had sent to London for the purpose, and with Manning. He had reason for doing so in view of the intransigence of the two prelates, but that did not make his procedure proper.

The Cabinet discussed Irish policy on 2 March. It was a long sitting, and they decided to decline any immediate legislative action on land questions.[4] They were also able to avoid discussing the Church since the Commission was at the time sitting on it. There was thus a real sense in which their existence was pinned to a satisfactory settlement of education. They could not touch primary education until the Powis Commission reported, so they resolved that Mayo should announce the intention of the Government to grant a charter to *a Roman Catholic university*, and that a suggestion should be thrown out about dealing with financial support for buildings.[5] The choice of the university question as the one on which to make their stand was not a wise one. For as Moriarty wrote to Monsell on the very day that the Cabinet met, the first need of the Government was to cure disaffection, and the education

[1] Woodlock Papers, Cullen to Woodlock, 1 March 1868.

[2] *Ibid.*, refers to the letter of the bishops to Grey of 14 January 1866 (*Parliamentary Papers*, 1866, LV, 243), of which Cullen had just sent a copy to Manning.

[3] Woodlock Papers, Cullen to Woodlock, 1 March 1868.

[4] This is Mayo's account. According to Disraeli's (given to the Queen, and therefore to be preferred for accuracy) the Cabinet resolved to bring in a Land Bill, and to appoint 'another Devon Commission'. *The Letters of Queen Victoria*, second series, *1862-78*, ed. G. E. Buckle, London, 1926, vol. I, p. 510; Disraeli to the Queen, 4 March 1868. It is clear from Parliamentary debate that the Government intended land legislation (see chap. 8). For an account of this Cabinet, see also H. J. Hanham, *Elections and Party Management, Politics in the time of Disraeli and Gladstone*, London, 1959, p. 210.

[5] Mayo Papers, MSS. 11161-11175 (1868 Letter-books); Mayo to Abercorn, 2 March 1868. In it Mayo also wrote of his proposed speech in Parliament on the Charter – 'I shall have a pretty stiff job to announce all this' was his closing remark.

question 'can never be a cause of popular disaffection, because it touches only a class which is not disaffected, and because those who want education most feel the want least'.[1] Moriarty advised action on the Church as the solution. Gladstone was to show the soundness of this when he attempted to put an end to the Mayo university plan by proposing his famous Resolutions on the Church in its place. It is interesting that Monsell gave Moriarty's letter to Gladstone.[2]

Writing to inform the Queen of the Cabinet's decision, Disraeli made it clear that the Charter would only be allowed 'provided the governing Body contained such a decided lay representation as would prevent its being a sacerdotal institution'. Lord Derby had agreed to the Mayo plan not as the best, but as the only practicable solution of the question, and Disraeli informed the Queen:

> It is doubtful whether the R.C. prelates will accept our offer. If they do not, upon them will rest the responsibility of rejecting fair and liberal terms. If they do, I think our Protestant friends will acquiesce for fear of sanctioning worse.[3]

Disraeli also referred in this letter to the communication he had received from Leahy and Derry suggesting negotiations with the Government before the measure reached Parliament. He had declined this offer, but expressed his wish, after his proposition had been made public, to 'listen considerately to any criticism and suggestions made by the Prelates'.[4] The House would receive the plan badly if the first confidence had not been reposed in them.

Cullen was now convinced that it was better to accept a Charter without endowment than to wait any longer,[5] but he still instructed Woodlock in London to agitate for both.[6] Leahy and Derry at last

[1] Gladstone Papers, B.M.Add.MS. 44142, f. 98, Moriarty to Monsell, 2 March 1868. His argument that those most in need of education were the least likely to realize it, has interesting affinities with Dr Chalmers's justification of religious endowment – that those most in need of religion were the least likely to realize the fact. See Thomas Chalmers, *Lectures on Religious Establishments*, London, 1838, Lectures II and III. Chalmers applied this idea to the voluntary principle – to show the inadequacy of a 'free-trade' in religion, and again Moriarty's affinity is apparent. He was the only Catholic bishop who argued against that principle in the Church discussions of 1867-9, and with reasons closely resembling those of Chalmers. (See Moriarty's *Letter on Disendowment*, Dublin, 1867.) Both men drew on a common source: S. T. Coleridge.

[2] Among whose papers it has survived.

[3] *The Letters of Queen Victoria, 1862-78*, vol. I, p. 510; Disraeli to the Queen, 4 March 1868.

[4] *Ibid.* It will be recalled that his tardiness in replying to the two bishops was occasioning them some annoyance.

[5] Woodlock Papers, Cullen to Woodlock, 3 March 1868.

[6] Woodlock in London appeared 'to have acted as a sort of *aide-de-camp* to carry messages between them [the bishops] and the Irish Office'. *Express* (Dublin), 23 May 1868.

agreed to go to London if Disraeli would give them an interview.[1] In anticipation of the coming debate in the House, Cullen also sent Manning statistical evidence of Catholic children receiving religious instruction from Protestants.[2] Woodlock was further instructed to 'act on' the Catholic members of Parliament, and Cullen gave his final assessment of the position before the debate:

> I think we ought to accept the Charter without endowment. I think the great bulk of the bishops are of the same opinion. However, Dr MacHale will be for not accepting, and also I suppose Dr Leahy and Dr Derry, who will have some influence on account of the commission they got. A greater difficulty will arise if the ministry propose to grant the Charter to a mixed body of bishops and laymen. Then I daresay the bishops might reject it.[3]

Woodlock put this position to Manning, who felt as a result that the bishops would not be able to accept the Government plan.[4] The debate came on 10 March.

The Government had chosen Maguire's motion for a Committee on the State of Ireland as the occasion for the announcement of their Irish policy. This was made on the 10th. Maguire ranged over every cause of Irish discontent. Touching education, he condemned Trinity College as a 'monstrous anomaly', and contrasted it with the support given by the Catholic people to their own university in Dublin. Parliament he indicted for having done its best 'to blot out the intellect of the Catholic people of Ireland', by its educational measures.[5] But a burst of laughter had greeted his solemn assertion 'that the Catholic people of Ireland are the most tolerant and liberal people in the world'.[6]

Mayo covered the points which Maguire had raised, meeting argument with argument.[7] He could not agree that the primary education of Ireland was a grievance. It was entrusted almost entirely to teachers nominated by the patrons of the schools, and as four out of every six of these were Catholics, no one could say there was 'an unnational element in the system of education'.[8] In 1866 the number of schools enrolled under the National Board was 6,600, of which 4,000 were under

[1] Woodlock Papers, Cullen to Woodlock, 4 March 1868 (two letters).
[2] *Ibid.*, Cullen to Woodlock, 6 March 1868. He sent a copy of the Parliamentary *Return* ordered by O'Reilly on the 13 July 1864.
[3] *Ibid.*, Cullen to Woodlock, 8 March 1868.
[4] *Ibid.*, Cullen to Woodlock, 10 March 1868.
[5] *Hansard*, cxc, p. 1308. The debate is also discussed in R. B. O'Brien, *Fifty Years of Concessions to Ireland*, vol. II, pp. 236-9.
[6] *Hansard*, cxc, p. 1306.
[7] See Mayo Papers, MS. 11216, 'Notes of a Speech on Maguire's Motion' (apparently wrongly dated for 19 May 1868), in which Mayo sketched the points he made. The University proposal is mentioned in Morley's *Life of Gladstone*, vol. I, p. 876.
[8] *Hansard*, cxc, p. 1358.

the direct patronage of the Roman Catholic clergy.[1] Trinity College, Dublin, he said, may indeed have retained its Protestant character, but it had been 'conspicuous among all Universities for liberality'. Prizes and scholarships, and at that very time, several professorships, were held there by Catholics. He did not believe there was any considerable body of opinion in Ireland hostile to Trinity, which 'ever since 1793 has led the way in all the questions of University Reform'.[2] Moreover, the Queen's University had done its work 'admirably'; but he could see the justification of those who could not allow their sons to go there because of objection on religious grounds.[3] The attempt of the late Government, in the Supplemental Charter, to remedy that objection, had failed due to resistance. The present situation was not ideal: if they could start again, doubtless it would be best to have *one* university for the whole country, but that was impossible now. For at that time three systems of education were operating in Ireland – denominational (the Catholic 'University'), semi-denominational (Trinity), and secular (Queen's).[4] He then turned to outline his plan for 'a third University' which could be founded 'without injuring the existing institutions', and, in words echoing the solution he had passed over in his note to Warren of December 1867,[5] a university 'which would, as far as possible, stand in the same relation to the Roman Catholic population as Trinity College does to the Protestant'.[6] It should be as free as possible from Government control. They therefore proposed advising Her Majesty to grant a Charter to a Roman Catholic university, which, he stressed, would *not* be like the existing Catholic institution. It was to have a Charter, a Chancellor, a Vice-Chancellor, and a government of four prelates, the President of Maynooth, and six laymen, all Catholics. The elective principle would be completely recognized, and the teaching officers, together with the general body of graduates, would have 'a potent voice' in the selection of the governing body.[7] The Government, he affirmed, had not yet been in consultation with any of the interested parties, for the good reason that a large part of the Supplemental Charter's failure had been because it came upon the House, and upon the Queen's University, by surprise. But they were open to any suggestions which might be made, although in any modifications, they could never allow the lay element and the elective principle to be lost.[8] The State would provide initial endowment – not for colleges but for scholarships – but detail of this was still undecided.[9]

---

[1] *Ibid.*, p. 1367.   [2] *Ibid.*, p. 1381.   [3] *Ibid.*, p. 1382.   [4] *Ibid.*, p. 1383.
[5] Mayo Papers, MS. 11217, Mayo to Warren, 3 December 1867.
[6] *Hansard*, cxc, p. 1384.   [7] *Ibid.*, p. 1385.   [8] *Ibid.*, p. 1386.   [9] *Ibid.*, p. 1387.

In the Commons on 12 March, Fawcett asked the Chief Secretary not to advise the Crown to grant a Charter until Parliament had expressed itself upon the plans either by granting or refusing the public money which was to be required in it. Mayo replied that the Government desired only to act in concert with Parliament, but that 'an erroneous impression' had appeared relative to his late speech. It seemed 'generally supposed' that the university the Government proposed to found in Dublin did not resemble any institution in the kingdom. What he had in fact said was quite the reverse. 'It was that the Charter proposed *did* resemble to a certain extent, the Charters given to similar institutions in the United Kingdom; but that the institution they proposed bore no resemblance whatever to the R.C. University now existing in Dublin.'[1]

The long debate which followed Mayo's declaration of the plan was to be three times adjourned, until finally, on 16 March, Maguire withdrew his motion 'being quite satisfied with the results'.[2] On the 12th, Horsman had attacked the university plan amid a welter of contrary arguments revealing the evils of ultramontane designs on Irish lay education. In short, the Government were about to 'overthrow the system of education which was England's best gift to Ireland'.[3] Lowe saw the move in a similar light: any grant of a sectarian university would be retrogressive:

> It is utterly contrary to my idea of doing business, that this House should be asked to agree to a scheme, the whole essence of which depends upon the consent of the R.C. hierarchy . . . we should not be making a concession to the R.C. population but to the R.C. hierarchy, an Ultramontane hierarchy – a hierarchy that has an electioneering influence; and it is that influence which you are seeking to buy by sacrificing the R.C. laity.[4]

On the 13th, Fortescue observed that the plan carried the denominational principle further than 'any responsible minister had ever attempted to carry it'. He hinted at the type of reform suggested by Stoney to Mayo. He wanted, he said, to make the University of Dublin a 'truly national University – Queen Elizabeth and her advisors could

---

[1] *Hansard*, CXC, p. 1456.   [2] *Ibid.*, p. 1791.   [3] *Ibid.*, p. 1462.

[4] *Ibid.*, p. 1500. Mayo was not as sensitive of the position of the Roman Catholic laity. 'They are the most contemptible party in the Empire', he wrote on learning from the Irish Lord Chancellor that Lowe's point was supported by the appearance of opposition by some Irish lay Catholics to the Government plan. 'They support the priests' candidates at elections, or become members themselves – they vote against conservative principles on every occasion – and they come whining to us to protect them against a problem which they never lose an opportunity of supporting in their attacks on our Church and our Land.' Mayo Papers, MSS. 11161-11175 (Letter-books, 1868), Mayo to Lord Chancellor Blackburne, 16 March 1868.

never have forseen that by the middle of the nineteenth century the majority of the Irish people could still be Catholics'.[1] Fortescue did not elaborate, but it is important that from this point the Gladstonian Liberals considered an Irish university settlement almost exclusively along these lines. Newdegate truly said that the proposed university would introduce an anomaly into the educational system of Ireland; and then, citing evidence culled from Whittle's pamphlet, he showered venom upon the ultramontanism of the hierarchy.[2] They could not allow so important a matter to be settled without an inquiry. The lay element proposed by the Government for the Catholic University had, he pointed out, been condemned by the present Pope in his Syllabus of Errors of 1864.[3] The debate was resumed on 16 March, and Monsell condemned the plan[4] as not producing religious equality in education. Only an endowment could secure that. Anyway, he thought the multiplication of universities an evil, citing American experience as evidence, and favoured instead Fortescue's hinted nationalization of Dublin University, with separate colleges affiliated to it.[5] Gregory (member for Co. Galway) upheld the Irish bishops on the ground that evidence was lacking to show that the Irish laity desired to be protected against their doctrinal teaching.[6] Viscount Castlerosse felt the university plan need not detain their serious attention, as there was 'not the remotest chance' of carrying it, and referred to the opinion of Leahy and Derry that the weight of reason favoured the endowment of the existing Catholic University, not the creation by the State of a new one.[7]

Gladstone was impressed by the inadequacy of the Government's

[1] *Hansard*, cxc, p. 1599.   [2] *Ibid.*, pp. 1635-41.   [3] *Ibid.*, p. 1641.

[4] Much to the surprise of his friend de Vere, who wrote to Moriarty, 'I fear Monsell will not like Lord Mayo's proposition about the Catholic University: but I think it an excellent one. It would give both a Charter and an endowment to *a* Catholic University, just such as Dr Newman wished for.' Monsell Papers, Box 8319, de Vere to Moriarty, 15 March 1868.

[5] *Hansard*, cxc, p. 1692. Monsell also told Mayo that his plan was only proposed in order to save Trinity College, and added ('significantly' – as Mayo commented): 'I want to get hold of Trinity College, Dublin, but if this is not carried we must get in there before long.' Mayo Papers, MSS. 11161-11175 (Letter-books, 1868), Mayo to Blackburne, 16 March 1868.

[6] *Hansard*, cxc, p. 1710.

[7] *Ibid.*, p. 1733. Leahy and Derry had produced a 'Statement on the University Question' which they had circulated to the Catholic members of Parliament. Gladstone also referred to it in his speech, *ibid.*, p. 1753. The terms set by the prelates for acceptance of a Charter were given on page 9 of the *Statement*: 'Equally certain is it that the bishops will not forgo the right of authoritative supervision with respect to any possible plan of University Education, in its bearing on the faith and morals of their flocks. That is a right inherent in the office of the bishop. . . . It includes the right of intervening in the selection of teachers, of watching over them, and, if necessary, of removing them.'

vision, and said they had failed to see 'that we have reached a crisis in the affairs and in the State of Ireland'.[1] Regarding higher education ('for I do not think that, at this moment, there is any question distinctly raised with regard to the primary and popular education of Ireland'[2]), the present plan was anachronistic. The proposed foundation of universities and colleges in 1868, to be supported by annual grants from the Consolidated Fund, was not a scheme conforming to the spirit of the age. The Maynooth grant was no precedent, since it was a legacy from the old Irish Parliament.[3] But the university question *was* related to that of the Church, for if the Irish Establishment were to be ended, the position of Dublin University – 'the National University' – would require consideration.[4] Thus Gladstone gave notice of the trend ahead. It was also at the close of this speech that he made his famous statement on the Irish Church, that 'that Church, as a State Church, must cease to exist'.[5]

Disraeli, in closing the debate on the 16th, declared the absence of any intention by the Government of *endowing* the proposed Catholic University. They were simply urging the House to adopt a measure which necessity required; he had not heard in the debate a single objection to the scheme which would bear 'the slightest discussion'.[6] He deplored the way ultramontanism had been bandied about the House.[7]

Cullen received the declaration of the plan by Mayo with his usual caution, writing to congratulate Maguire on his speech, and evidently agreeing with Manning that a sufficient basis existed for negotiation.[8] Mayo had stated his readiness to consider modifications of the plan in his speech. But Manning was mistaken in supposing – as he did in his letter to Cullen – that Mayo's speech proposed both Charter and endowment. He told Cullen that 'this is our moment', and that he had written

[1] *Hansard*, CXC, p. 1741.

[2] *Ibid.*, p. 1750 – a position which Gladstone continued to maintain, doing nothing, when in office, to give effect to the proposals of the Powis Commission's Report. He did think of legislation on the basis of the report, but decided that action in the face of a renewed anti-Catholic feeling would be unwise.

[3] *Ibid.*, p. 1752.

[4] *Ibid.*, p. 1755.

[5] *Ibid.*, p. 1764.

[6] *Ibid.*, p. 1775. In a letter at this time Mayo wrote: 'I only proposed a vote for a few hundreds a year (I believe it would have been under a thousand), for a Catholic University'; quoted in W. W. Hunter, *A Life of the Earl of Mayo*, London, 1875, vol. 1, p. 92.

[7] *Hansard*, CXC, p. 1776.

[8] Woodlock Papers, Cullen to Woodlock, 12 March 1868.

begging Gladstone not to obstruct the Government's settlement.[1] His letter crossed with one from Cullen asking Manning to secure more details, since he feared that the university plan, as outlined in Mayo's speech, might draw premature adverse declarations from some of the bishops, and this would compromise their chances of a settlement, and perhaps even occasion dissensions among them. It was important to know whether the Chancellor and Vice-Chancellor were to be bishops, for if they were laymen, it would reduce the ratio to eight lay to four episcopal members of the university government:

> It would be also important to know how the laymen are to be chosen. We have some laymen in Ireland who are as hostile to the rights of the Church as our open enemies. Probably the choice of Government would fall upon men of that class, in which case the education of the country would not at all be safe.[2]

Manning's appeal to Gladstone 'not to diminish the possibility' of the Government's plan being realized was based on his belief that giving over Irish education to the Catholic Church was the only way of 'keeping Ireland from American anarchy'. At least the plan, which would need modification before being accepted in Ireland, was capable of treatment.[3] But Gladstone did not need to be impressed by the dangers of Fenianism to the whole fabric of Irish society – it was his acute realization of that threat which convinced him of the futility of the Government's present half-measure. He replied that it was a hopeless scheme; he could never support 'a plan for endowing a "denominational" University *for the first time* out of the Consolidated Fund, when Parliament has for thirty years been endeavouring to get rid of all such grants'. The battle of the moment would not be upon the education, but upon the Church question.[4]

Gladstone's opinion reflects the turn he was to give to treatment of the Irish question. The crucial aspect of the plan was the concession of denominationalism and the possibility of endowment. It was on the evening of the day he wrote to Manning that Mayo declared in the House that endowment was not intended for the proposed university, but this did not cause Gladstone to withdraw his objections. His Liberalism could not embrace – even in the peculiar circumstances of Ireland – any arrangement which suggested endorsement of the

---

[1] Leslie, *Dublin Review*, October 1919, p. 183, Manning to Cullen, 11 March 1868. It was on the day after this letter was written that Mayo made his speech in the House clarifying the point about endowment raised by Fawcett's question.

[2] Manning Papers, Cullen to Manning, 11 March 1868.

[3] Gladstone Papers, B.M.Add.MS. 44249, f. 26. Manning to Gladstone, 11 March 1868.

[4] *Ibid.*, B.M.Add.MS. 44249, f. 28, Gladstone to Manning, 12 March 1868.

principle of concurrent endowment by the State. The battle over this principle was fought out on the Church question, but it can be seen clearly that Gladstone and the Liberals allied it in their minds with educational grants too. The trend, as Gladstone wrote to Manning, was in the direction of united education: the Liberals were the friends of that movement in Ireland, just as they were to be in England. Cullen was correct in assuming that he would get nothing from the Liberals over education. Hence the readiness with which he would see the bishops open negotiations with the Government on the basis of Mayo's plan.

Dr Russell, the President of Maynooth, was another who accurately diagnosed the situation. He urged Gladstone not to allow a summary rejection of the Mayo Plan by the Liberals, for when they came to deal with the great question of Ireland themselves, as they must do shortly, they would have deprived themselves of the confidence of the Catholics if they had just brought about the end of a university plan which was regarded by Catholics as at least a step in the right direction. The condition of Ireland must be admitted as exceptional. 'You cannot deal with the Irish now exactly in the way which best approves itself to your theoretical notions', he told Gladstone. The Irish must be conciliated according to their own notions, and one of these was denominational education. They would be alienated from the Liberal Party should the Government plan be vetoed by Liberal opposition. Russell recalled a conversation in which Gladstone had admitted that although he considered the Irish Catholics wrong about education, he could see also that they had a right to what they desired. He asked Gladstone to act on that admission in the present case, or the 'cordial union' between the Irish and the Liberal Party would be lost.[1] But he had written while the debate continued in Parliament, and when, two days later, Gladstone spoke, Russell was satisfied that he appreciated the rights of Catholics to higher education and he sympathized with the view, there expressed, that the Government plan was not the right one.[2] Gladstone also wrote to reassure him. He had never desired a Charter for a Catholic university, he wrote, 'but I have felt so strongly the Roman Catholic grievance in respect to higher education' that he would have allowed a simple charter to pass. But the present 'reckless policy' of the Government was to grant an endowment at the same time, and that 'at once placed the question on a new footing' which made it impossible for him and his colleagues to countenance it.[3] It is interesting to find Gladstone holding

[1] Gladstone Papers, B.M.Add.MS.44414, f. 155, Russell to Gladstone, 14 March 1868.
[2] *Ibid.*, B.M.Add.MS. 44414, f. 208, Russell to Gladstone, 25 March 1868.
[3] C. W. Russell's Papers, Gladstone to Russell, 23 March 1868.

to the question of endowment well after Mayo and Disraeli, the latter in his speech on the 16th, had declared that it was not involved.

Woodlock was able to send Cullen a circular on the university plan, which had apparently been drawn up for the information of interested parties.[1] The Chancellor and the six laymen were to be elected by convocation – a method which Cullen felt would only occasion dissension, 'and in the end would put us in the hands of demagogues'. The Senate, he thought, should fill up vacancies, as this would give the governing body some unity. The circular also made it clear that there was to be no endowment for the present, 'except for the expenses of the University'. Cullen interpreted that as including the salaries of professors.[2]

For some time, he had been urging Leahy and Derry to join Woodlock in London. On 14 March, Mayo at last replied to their letter of 23 October 1867, in which they had announced their commission to negotiate with the Government. His failure to reply until this time had, it will be remembered, been a major cause of the touchiness of the two prelates. Now he sent them a confidential memorandum on the university plan, which was, in effect, a proposed constitution, and invited them to communicate with him in any way they might choose.[3] On the same day this letter was sent, Manning had an interview with Disraeli, and was impressed with his sincerity in desiring to carry the measure, and with his frankness in agreeing that it required the sanction of the Irish bishops. Manning therefore urged Cullen to get the bishops to 'examine and pronounce upon the plan'. In the meantime he would try to get the provisions of the governing body modified. He again affirmed that they could expect nothing so favourable from the Liberals.[4] Cullen replied most positively:

> Though the Charter is not what we would wish, yet I think it ought to be accepted with some modifications. The Chancellor's election ought not to be left to Convocation. As for the election of the six laymen, I suppose it might be left to the graduates, though it would be safer in the hands of the Senate. I think it would be better not to hold a meeting of our bishops until something final is arranged. Dr MacHale would appeal to Rome against us and stop all negotiations. If things were finally agreed on by Dr Leahy and Dr Derry with

[1] Woodlock probably got it from Manning, but it is clear from the debate in Parliament that its existence was unknown to the members. There seems to be no surviving copy, but its content is obvious from Cullen's letter.

[2] Woodlock Papers, Cullen to Woodlock, 13 March 1868.

[3] *Parliamentary Papers*, 1867-8, LIII, 779; Correspondence relative to proposed Charter to a Roman Catholic University (Ireland), p. 2; Mayo to Leahy, 14 March 1868.

[4] Leslie in *Dublin Review*, October 1919, p. 183, Manning to Cullen, 14 March 1868.

the Ministers, the bishops would all agree to them, and the Holy See would not object. But if the things be brought to an appeal before Rome the delay would be too great. Dr MacHale, I am sure, would prevent anything from being done at a meeting if held at present.[1]

Cullen also consulted many of the Dublin clergy, all of whom appeared to favour accepting the proposed Charter if some slight adjustment could be made in the governing body. He pressed Woodlock to tell this to Cogan (M.P. for Kildare), Maguire and Sir John Gray.[2] He wrote himself to Gray, to Murphy (M.P. for Cork) and Sir George Bowyer. The Catholic members were to do all in their power to get a settlement of the university question this time. 'It will be well to make the best terms we can,' he wrote, 'but our Liberal friends appear determined to defeat all our hopes.'[3] It was the stand Gladstone made against the Charter which brought out suspicion in Cullen – a suspicion which was not to make Gladstone's subsequent attempts 'to do something for Ireland' any easier. In this sense Dr Russell was wise to caution Gladstone against the position he adopted over the Charter. His chances of success on Church and land might have been prejudiced by the impression his present action produced in Cullen, who wrote at this point:

I never liked Gladstone since he wrote his letters against Naples. He first misrepresented things and then when he was refuted he refused to retract. This shows that he is not a lover of justice. What trust can we place in him in Irish affairs? I suppose his opposition will prevent the Government from going on with the Charter.[4]

Mayo's letter to Leahy and Derry had enclosed a draft of a proposed constitution for the Catholic University. This was substantially the same as that which was appended to a draft 'Royal Letter' by the Irish Attorney-General (Warren) on 23 March, for use as the basis of discussion at the interview arranged for the following day between the two deputed prelates and the Government representatives. That is to say it was the detailed statement of the Mayo plan before any suggestion of modification had got to work on it.[5] The preamble of the 'Royal Letter' followed that of the draft Charter submitted to Grey by the bishops in 1866.[6] It adverted to the existence of the Catholic

[1] Manning Papers, Cullen to Manning, 15 March 1868. The first two sentences of the letter are quoted in V. A. McClelland, *Cardinal Manning*, p. 168.
[2] Woodlock Papers, Cullen to Woodlock, 15 March 1868.
[3] *Ibid.*, Cullen to Woodlock, 16 March 1868.
[4] *Ibid.*, Cullen to Woodlock, 17 March 1868.
[5] Mayo Papers, MS. 11217, 'Draft of a Royal Letter for Charter; Roman Catholic University, Ireland. Settled by the Attorney-General', 23 March 1868.
[6] 14 January 1866. See chap. 5.

institution in Dublin, and 'in order to render complete and satisfactory the courses of education to be followed' there, it was constituted one of the colleges 'affiliated to the University intended by US to be incorporated'. In this and any other affiliated colleges which might appear, the students would be enabled to receive the degrees already taken in other universities in Britain. The new university was to be called 'The Roman Catholic University of Ireland,' and its incorporated government was to consist of a Chancellor, Vice-Chancellor, and Senators, all professing Catholics, and all of whom were to be named in the 'Royal Letter'. Of the Senators, four were to be Catholic bishops; the President of Maynooth was to be an *ex officio* Senator; six laymen; and the Rectors of the Colleges of the Catholic University of Ireland. Five Senators were to be elected, one by each faculty in the existing college or in other colleges to be affiliated. A vacancy in the Chancellorship was to be filled by election by the Convocation, and his deputy, by nomination by himself. Vacancies among the four bishops were to be filled by the body of bishops who would select from their own number; and among the six laymen by election by Convocation.

The other arrangements of the new Charter followed exactly those of the Queen's University's 1864 Charter – so exactly that the draft in the Mayo Papers is actually on pages torn from a copy of the Queen's Charter with the necessary adjustments written in. Now it is important to notice that the provisions of the Queen's Charter which resulted from the use of a State grant from the Consolidated Fund – fees fixed with the approbation of the Treasury Commissioners, the requirement of the Lord-Lieutenant's warrant for meetings of the university, and the provision for an annual progress report to be submitted to him – were *not* erased from the copy which formed the basis of the new Charter. They were only marked as queries. It is thus quite evident that the Government had still not entirely dismissed the possibility of endowment for the Catholic University.[1] The 1864 Queen's Charter had been that in which Convocation was allowed for, and hence the part given to Convocation in the Catholic University. But the row over the Supplemental Charter's ratification caused the drafting of the powers of Convocation to be more closely circumscribed in the

---

[1] The *Dublin Review* for April 1868, reporting the clergy meeting called in Dublin by Cullen, contained, in Newdegate's reading, 'a distinct claim to endowment for the R.C. University after it was chartered' – Newdegate in the Commons' Committee on the resolutions, 7 May 1868 – *Hansard*, CXCI, p. 1906. Woodlock also continued to hope that an endowment would be granted, even if only by the force of events: 'an endowment would be sure to come very soon; as soon as the Protestant Church is disendowed'; Kirby Papers, Woodlock to Kirby, no. 75, 15 April 1868.

present instrument. To the Senate was given the power to determine what colleges should be affiliated to the Catholic University, and the appointments of rectors, vice-rectors, professors and tutors, in all such affiliated colleges, could only stand with the approval of the Senate. A safety clause (no. 17), was written in to protect the religion of any non-Catholic who might attend the university: he was not to be required to attend any Catholic religious observance or instruction.[1]

Dr Leahy, after consulting Dr Derry, replied to Mayo's letter on the 19th, by listing eight points about the proposed Charter. (1) There was no provision except the authority of the Catholic prelates for securing soundness of faith and morals, and the bishops' authority could not be 'fully exercised in the present framing of the constitution'. (2) No effective provision was made for the appointment of professors sound in faith and morals, nor for removing those who were not. (3) Appointments were vested in the Senate, not in the Catholic bishops, 'which is objectionable'. (4) The bishops should at least have an absolute negative on appointments (although he was not sure that even that was enough). (5) 'In the Constitution of the Senate there is too much of the lay element, too little of the clerical.' (6) He supposed that Cardinal Cullen would be the first Chancellor, but after the first, that office ought to be filled by the election of the Senate, not the Convocation. The Chancellor ought always to be one of the four archbishops. (7) The numbers of the Senate ought to be variable, and not always fixed at twenty. And (8) 'A great objection to the proposed scheme is the want of a suitable endowment.'[2]

Leahy and Derry agreed to go to London at last, however, and an interview was arranged with Government representatives for 24 March. Cullen wanted to secure to the bishops the right of excluding morally harmful books and professors from the university, and apparently persuaded the two bishops to make this their major demand.[3] This was an important emphasis, for the objections listed by Leahy in his letter to Mayo amounted to just about the same exclusive Catholic claims which had caused the stalemate in the negotiations of February 1866.[4] Had Leahy not been prevailed upon, he would have stressed them all, and the compromise settlement for which Cullen was working would have been lost at once. Cullen was advised by Cardinal Reisach that if the professors were independent of episcopal control they would

[1] Mayo Papers, MS. 11217, 'Draft Royal Letter for Charter', 23 March 1868.
[2] *Parliamentary Papers*, 1867-8, LIII, 779.
[3] Woodlock Papers, Cullen to Woodlock, 23 March 1868.
[4] Cullen considered Leahy's letter to Mayo 'a little too decided to serve as a basis for negotiations'. Manning Papers, Cullen to Manning, 20 March 1868.

'become infected with Rationalism and Jansenism'.[1] As all the members of the Senate would be Catholics, he could see no difficulty in the way of granting the power of determining bad books and professors to the bishops: there was a good precedent in the Charter of the Laval University of Quebec, by which the Catholic archbishop, as Visitor, had this power given to him expressly.[2]

Cullen further prepared for the London meeting by addressing a letter to the committee of the National Association – which had just recommenced meetings after a long winter recess.[3] In it he remarked on the progress they had made on the education question, and adverted favourably to the proposed Catholic university. But all would be in vain, he warned, unless the enemies of this concession were shown to be in error, and that was something the Association could do. They must deny the 'deluded notion' that the Catholic laity desired to be protected from the ultramontanism of their bishops, and get the people to defend 'liberty of education' at 'this alarming crisis'.[4] He had reason to be alarmed. His worst fear that 'nationalist' priests would upset his diplomacy had just received partial realization in a speech (reported in the *Freeman*), by Father Conway,[5] in whom he recognized a notorious clerical *agent provocateur*, in which that priest 'has a rap at those pretended friends of Ireland who are trying to sell the country for a Charter to the Catholic University'.[6] Manning used his influence at the last minute to persuade Gladstone that he had done all he could 'to separate the Charter and the Endowment questions'.[7] But it has been seen that the draft 'Royal Letter' for the Charter, which formed the basis of the London meeting, had continued to leave the question of endowment an open question. In terms of the Church question also, many Tories were coming to the point where they would make their stand on 'levelling-up'.

The meeting in London took place on Tuesday 24 March. Leahy and Derry met Mayo and Malmesbury at the Irish Office and stated their

[1] Woodlock Papers, Cullen to Woodlock, 23 March 1868; and Manning Papers, Cullen to Manning, 20 March 1868.
[2] Woodlock Papers, Cullen to Woodlock, 23 March 1868.
[3] He may well have helped to end this recess (see chap. 4). The present crisis would be sufficient explanation of his motive for doing so.
[4] *The Times*, 23 March 1868, report of the National Association's committee of 22 March.
[5] Vol. 35 of the Propaganda *Scritture* has many references to the extreme conduct of Fr Conway, who was the parish priest of Headford.
[6] *Freeman*, 23 March 1868. Reported in a letter of Cullen's to Woodlock – Woodlock Papers, 23 March 1868.
[7] Gladstone Papers, B.M.Add.MS. 44249, f. 28. Manning to Gladstone, 24 March 1868.

views in a long interview.[1] The nature of the discussion was not recorded, but the result clearly left room for hope. Manning still felt the Government could satisfy the Irish bishops,[2] and the letter which the two deputed bishops addressed to Mayo subsequently reflected the position they had taken at the interview, especially as it was in fulfilment of the promise they made there, to put their views in writing.[3] Most significantly – and following Cullen's opinion – they dropped the demand for an endowment, 'appreciating the difficulty Government might experience' if they should continue to urge it. But they left on record their protest against the wealth of Trinity College and the State grant of £26,000 a year to the Queen's Colleges. Though there would not be an endowment, they still insisted that provision be made for the salaries of professors, for scholarships, and for 'other expenses'. On the proposal in general terms, they said that the plan most acceptable to the Irish bishops would consist in a modification of the existing Catholic University.[4] Accepting the Mayo plan, however, it ought also to be modified before it could receive the bishops' sanction. The Senate should not be able to veto appointments in the affiliated colleges, for, without the endowment of those colleges by the State, there was no justification for the State, acting through the university, to interfere in their internal arrangements. They also insisted on the naming of Cullen as first Chancellor, yet agreed to a provision in the constitution exempting any Protestants who might be enrolled as students from attendance at Catholic observances.[5]

The London meeting still left the plan as a serious proposition – at least as far as the Irish bishops were concerned, even if the public had been 'amused at the royal game of "goose" that has been going on between Lords Mayo and Malmesbury on the one side, and two prelates of the Roman Catholic Church on the other'.[6] Cullen still looked for a settlement before 'Mill and Fawcett get any influence' by a change of

[1] See Mayo's reference to the meeting, which he said lasted an hour and a half, in *Hansard*, cxcii, p. 1473 (12 June 1868).

[2] Gladstone Papers, B.M.Add.MS. 44249, f. 33, Manning to Gladstone, 28 March 1868.

[3] *Parliamentary Papers*, 1867-8, LIII, 779, Leahy and Derry to Mayo, 31 March 1868.

[4] The plea for a Charter for the existing Catholic University rather than for a new Catholic university was also made in a letter to the committee of the National Association by Dr O'Hea the Bishop of Ross, and read at a meeting of 7 April. *The Times*, 10 April 1868.

[5] *Parliamentary Papers*, 1867-8, LIII, 779, Leahy and Derry to Mayo, 31 March 1868.

[6] *The Ireland of To-day* ... by F.T.C.D., London, 1868, p. 13. The writer continued: 'Lord Mayo ought to be a keener statesman than to believe he could catch old birds with chaff.'

Administration. If only Mayo would concede the point about episcopal control of books and professors, it would certainly allow the bishops, for their part, to yield on other points 'where no principle is involved'.[1] And in Rome the Pope himself spoke warmly of Disraeli's attempt to improve the condition of the Irish Catholics.[2] The bishops waited for Mayo's reply to their written statement of the ground they had held at the meeting. They had to wait nearly six weeks.

Meanwhile in Parliament, Gladstone had given notice of his resolutions on the Church on 23 March,[3] and the Government had been defeated by fifty-six votes on 3 April at the end of the debate on Gladstone's motion for a committee to consider the Acts relating to the Established Church in Ireland.[4] Cullen, who had expressed himself anxious to get a university settlement before the Conservatives were displaced by the Liberals, had also hoped from the moment of their inception that Gladstone's resolutions would pass.[5] He hailed their passage with enthusiasm, enjoining their promoter to give them practical effect at once. Manning relayed this advice to Gladstone.[6] But Cullen was far from changing course on the university plan, which he still hoped to see pass. Could he not see that Gladstone's resolutions were intended to bury that plan? It is true that Cullen made no public declaration in favour of Gladstone's new policy at this time. Anyway, he had recently written of his suspicion of Gladstone. And it must not be forgotten that Mayo's reply to the bishops had not yet been received, and the chances for a university settlement seemed good. Could not Cullen see that even if something were to be worked out, it could not now get through the House of Commons? Perhaps he gambled on the course which in fact came to be taken by Gladstone: that of keeping the Conservatives in office. The Reform Bill had been passed in the spring, and Gladstone desired the elections to be held under the new register – and so did Cullen, who lent his support to the society set up in Dublin

---

[1] Woodlock Papers, Cullen to Woodlock, 25 March 1868.

[2] F.O. 43, vol. 101, Dispatch no. 32 from Odo Russell, 26 March 1868. Russell did not disclose any detail of the Government's plan to His Holiness.

[3] *Hansard*, CXCI, p. 32. See also Morley, *Life of Gladstone*, vol. I, p. 880; and Justin McCarthy, *The Story of Gladstone's Life*, London, 1898, p. 245.

[4] *Hansard*, CXCI, pp. 469 ff., 578 ff., 710 ff., 841 ff. See additionally chap. 7 for further results of this crisis.

[5] Woodlock Papers, Cullen to Woodlock, 25 March 1868.

[6] Gladstone Papers, B.M.Add.MS. 44249, f. 39, Manning to Gladstone, 8 April 1868. Manning was himself surprised by the rapidity of events, and the readiness with which English opinion took up the Church question. See his letter to Mgr Talbot of the 2 April 1868, quoted in Purcell, *Life of Cardinal Manning*, vol. II, p. 394.

for the registration of new voters. Rapid passage of the Charter before the elections seems still to have been in Cullen's mind; certainly Woodlock believed that Disraeli and Mayo would try to continue with the plan notwithstanding their defeat on the Church question.[1] For that he was glad. It still seemed better to him than anything they would get from any other Administration.[2] It is, therefore, hard to believe that however much Cullen may have approved the resolutions,[3] as a declaration of the principle for which the Irish Catholics had worked, that he switched policy in the middle of April from the university to the Church question.[4] Acton believed that he did. In his unpublished notes on 'Vaticana' he wrote, 'Manning a Liberal – only, however, for his own good. His negotiations with Disraeli – upset by Cullen.'[5] But this is clearly wrong: it was Manning who switched policy, not Cullen. It was not until the end of June, when Mayo finally refused to re-open the negotiations, that Cullen gave up hope. The emptiness of expecting anything suitable from the Liberals on the education question – which he always regarded as the most important – was brought home to him at this critical moment by Fawcett's tabling of a motion to open Trinity College.[6] Cullen supposed that when introduced, it would be carried against the Government as the resolutions had been, and he was sure it

[1] Kirby Papers, Woodlock to Kirby, no. 75, 15 April 1868. Mayo's letter to Abercorn of 3 May adds weight to this view – 'the situation is beset with every difficulty, but Disraeli is very confident and we may pull through'. He believed the Liberals were far more disorganized than were the supporters of the Government. Mayo Papers, MSS. 11161-11175 (Letter-books, 1868). Disraeli's confidence doubtless increased as it became apparent that the election would be fought on the Church question, for on that, he supposed, he could rely on the strength of Protestant feeling to secure a majority for the Conservatives.

[2] Kirby Papers. Woodlock to Kirby, no. 75, 15 April 1868; and Monsell Papers, Box 8319, Woodlock to Monsell, 14 April 1868.

[3] The contrast was emphasized by Horsman in the Commons' Committee on the Irish Establishment. 'The policy of the Government', he said, 'is to charter and endow a Roman Catholic University as a preliminary to endowing the Roman Catholic Church'; and the policy of Gladstone's resolutions was 'to divorce the State from all ecclesiastical styles and dignities in Ireland.' *Hansard*, cxci, p. 1405 (27 April 1868).

[4] As Buckle argued when he claimed, truly, that Gladstone's resolutions were an attempt to win over the Irish Catholics from supporting the Conservatives on the Charter question. Buckle, however, based his chronology on the letters of Manning to Disraeli, which ceased on 16 March, the very day on which Gladstone first declared against the continuance of the Establishment in Ireland. This was certainly no coincidence, but Manning's conclusion of the matter in no way bound the Irish bishops, who remained hopeful of a settlement of the Charter question. See Monypenny and Buckle, *op. cit.*, vol. II, p. 349.

[5] Cambridge University Library, (Acton) Add.MS. 5542, p. 17.

[6] *Hansard*, cxcii, p. 1041.

would 'do great mischief'.[1] Woodlock was, as always, of a like mind,[2] and asked how it was possible to meet the danger which, in the present circumstances of the House, was a most serious one. His answer was 'by urging on the Charter – the endowment does not seem to me for the moment necessary perhaps not expedient – of the Catholic University as proposed by Lord Mayo'.[3]

On 11 May, however, Mayo replied to the letter in which Leahy and Derry had put down the position they had held at the London meeting. He did not break off the negotiations, but rejected the conditions upon which the bishops had insisted. The Government, he explained, maintained that *all* appointments should be subject to the approval of the governing body of the university in order to preserve unity of action. They rejected the notion that the Chancellor should be a bishop, and intended, in their first nomination, to have a layman 'of rank, influence, and position'. A prelate would be 'inconsistent with one of the fundamental principles of such an institution, namely, that the future head of the governing Body should be elected by the University at large'. In fact the Government had rejected the bishops' proposals for the same reasons (although Mayo did not say so) which had caused Grey to reject those of 14 January 1866 – that the episcopal and Governmental views of the university were incompatible. Mayo put it thus:

> The object of the Government was to create an institution which, although denominational in character, would be thoroughly independent, self-governed, and free from any external influence, either political or religious. The proposals made in your letter would strike at the very root of these principles, and I am, therefore, with extreme regret, obliged to inform you that the recommendations contained in that letter cannot be entertained.[4]

Mayo must have realized that, although not referring in any way to future moves by either party, his letter would probably mean the end of the university plan, unless the bishops climbed down. He could not allow a settlement bought at too high a price. With the prospect of an election before the Government, their ability to lean on the 'no-Popery' cry which they imagined Gladstone's policy would stir up in the country would be weakened if their last act as an Administration had been one which gave in to the bishops' demands. Horsman had said in

---

[1] Kirby Papers, Cullen to Kirby, no. 154, 10 May 1868.

[2] *Ibid.*, Woodlock to Kirby, no. 75, 15 April 1868. Fawcett's plan, he wrote, would 'saddle upon our Catholic country the mixed system of Education in a way we never had it before, *viz.*, with all the influence of the wealth, the antiquity, and the learning of Trinity College'.

[3] Monsell Papers, Box 8319, Woodlock to Monsell, 14 April 1868.

[4] *Parliamentary Papers*, 1867-8, LIII, 779. Also quoted by James Macaulay, *Ireland in 1872*, p. 395.

the Committee on the Irish Church that the election would be fought on the question of Establishment and endowment, and this was generally accepted as the case.[1]

The bishops made no move on receiving Mayo's letter, but it became obvious to the press and the public that the negotiations were at an end when the official correspondence was published in the third week of May (1868).[2] The *Freeman* remarked that the 'Government would not accept the conditions proposed by the bishops, and the bishops, who had been led to believe the offer of the Government would have been more liberal, could not accept the scheme of the Government, which would appear to have been expressly fashioned in order to secure its rejection'. The Ministers had never really been in earnest, and the university they had proposed would not have worked even had it been endowed, and without endowment it would have been utterly ludicrous.[3] The *Express* welcomed the collapse of the negotiations: 'each party thoroughly mis- understood the views of the other'. The Mayo plan, it held, ought never to have been put forward, for not only did the parties at the negotiations at no point even approach agreement, but 'they have made a future agreement impossible, for we believe that no English Govern- ment will ever venture to propose that the Irish R.C. bishops should be indulged with the instrument of terrorism which they have demanded in the name of educational equality'.[4] There was much truth in that. At the weekly committee of the National Association of 26 May, Mac- Swiney, referring to the published correspondence, said 'the past week has taught the Irish people a lesson which will not be easily forgotten'. It was not to trust the disguise of toleration and hypocritical pro- fessions of the 'hereditary enemies of our creed and race'. As soon as the vote in Parliament on the Church Resolutions showed that the 'Irish vote was not to be caught in the Disraeli net', he observed, Mayo had dropped the Charter.[5] On the other hand, at least one Irish bishop thought that the Government's rejection of their proposals was related to the defeat in Parliament over Gladstone's resolutions. Dorrian felt that the Irish members should have supported the Government in the interests of the Charter and endowment 'instead of being so anxious for themselves'. Gladstone was further from the Catholic view than Disraeli,[6] and would 'never yield to the Bishops'

---

[1] *Hansard*, CXCI, p. 1406 (27 April 1868).   [2] *Parliamentary Papers*, 1867-8, LIII, 779.

[3] *Freeman*, 23 May 1868.   [4] *Express* (Dublin), 23 May 1868.   [5] *Freeman*, 27 May 1868.

[6] This is comparable with the opinion maintained by the *Dublin Review*. In April 1867 (p. 384), the *Dublin* held that Tory 'principles are a maimed and distorted version of principles originally Catholic; but Liberal principles are the absolute

views as Disraeli is inclined to do.' Had the anti-Catholic radicals and the Irish members not voted against Disraeli, Dorrian supposed that the Charter might well have continued to be practical politics.[1] It is difficult to see quite how, unless he can be taken to have assumed that Mayo's letter to the bishops reflected political tactic rather than genuine conviction on the part of the Government that they could never concede what the bishops asked. Manning also regarded the Parliamentary vote as decisive, taking it as his reason for ending communication with Disraeli. He began to turn his attention exclusively to the Church question.[2] But Cullen, Leahy and Derry still waited to see what Disraeli would do next, expecting, as later events were to show, that he would suggest some new approach in the Charter negotiations.

On 12 May, in reply to a request from Sir Colman O'Loghlen, member for Co. Clare, for a copy of the draft Charter to be placed before the House, Mayo had hinted that when the published correspondence between the Government and the two bishops was before them, steps might be taken regarding the Charter.[3] Perhaps he supposed the Irish bishops would write suggesting some compromise, but they in fact were waiting for him to do the same. And he had seen from the press reaction in Ireland that there was now no hope of winning Irish favour. So when, on the 28th of the month Murphy asked whether the Government intended any further action on the matter, Mayo declared that the question of the proposed university 'must be considered entirely at an end'. His reason was that the two prelates deputed to act by the hierarchy had declined the conditions set for its concession by the Government.[4]

If the Government were partly motivated by a desire not to condone ultramontane designs in view of the stand they would shortly have to take on the Church question at the elections, the appearance at this point of *Ireland in 1868, The Battlefield for English Party Strife* by Gerald FitzGibbon, one of the Masters in Chancery (Ireland), must have confirmed it.[5] He argued that should the new university be established, it would sharpen the distinction between the two religions in Ireland as never before, exposing the education of youth to 'the uncontrolled

opposite of Catholic principles, the principles against which the Church is now everywhere engaged in mortal struggle'. Dorrian was not, however, a Tory, and his belief that Disraeli should have been upheld turned on expediency not political principle.

[1] Kirby Papers, Dorrian to Kirby, no. 161, 15 May 1868.
[2] Shane Leslie, *Dublin Review*, October 1919, p. 170, Manning to Cullen, 15 May 1868.
[3] *Hansard*, CXCII, p. 112.
[4] *Ibid.*, pp. 955–6.
[5] Published in London, 1868. The preface is dated 25 May.

power and influence of the hierarchy'. Educated Catholics could see this, and dreaded an arrangement which would allow the propagation of religious prejudice and sectarian bigotry.[1] The Mayo plan was but an example of the usual exercise of influence by the Irish hierarchy. Statesmen competed for its support, and 'this has given that hierarchy a dogmatical control, and dictatorial power over every Ministry . . . by exciting and keeping up a never-ceasing agitation against the stability of the laws and institutions of the realm'.[2] Grant of a Charter would only place the Catholic gentry in final subjugation to the ultramontane hierarchy, and no safety measures such as an admixture of laymen in its constitution could prevent a denominational institution from becoming a sacerdotal preserve, imparting a discipline 'hardly tolerable in the dark ages in which it was invented', and over which the English Government would be able to exercise no more control that it did over the Propaganda in Rome.[3] It was by now evident, however, that FitzGibbon was preaching to the converted.

Mayo's announcement that the university question was closed had been coupled with his claim that it was the two bishops who had taken the initiative. But this was not entirely the case, for they had not replied to his letter of 11 May. Walsh argued that since the receipt of that letter, Leahy and Derry had been in consultation with their episcopal brethren in an attempt to draw up new safeguards for religion which would at the same time be within the limits of the Government's intentions.[4] This was very probably so. It has been seen that both parties awaited the first move of the other. But Walsh was surely unfair to Mayo when he emphasized the discrepancy between the six weeks which elapsed before he replied to Leahy's and Derry's letter of 31 March, and the mere two weeks allowed between his receipt of their note acknowledging his of 11 May – which came on the 16th – and his statement in the House on the 28th.[5] The former length of time occurred just at that point when the Government was facing attack in Parliament on the discussion of the

[1] Gerald FitzGibbon, *Ireland in 1868*, London, 1868, pp. 32-3.

[2] *Ibid.*, p. 51.

[3] *Ibid.*, p. 53.

[4] W. J. Walsh, *The Irish Question*, p. 39. But it was not true, as he alleged, that Mayo's ending of the proceedings by his announcement of the 28th, was 'to the amazement of everyone concerned'. It has been seen that the Irish press and the National Association had already written off the negotiations, and even Cullen, in a moment of despair, had supposed 'that all chance of getting a Charter for the Catholic University is now gone'. (Kirby Papers, Cullen to Kirby, no. 154, 10 May 1868.) But it must be noticed that this referred to a Charter for the existing Catholic University, and not to the 'Mayo Plan', about which he still sometimes entertained hope of successful issue.

[5] W. J. Walsh, *op. cit.*, p. 40. Walsh wrongly gives the last date as 29 May.

Gladstone resolutions. Mayo was not in a position to reply until he was certain that the Disraeli Administration was to be kept in office. This was not apparent until 7 May, on which day the Commons' Committee on the Established Church ended its sittings, all of Gladstone's resolutions having been agreed, but without any suggestion of a dissolution.[1] Mayo accordingly wrote to the bishops on the 11th, and on the 12th he even hinted in the House that action on the Charter was still a possibility. Presumably he was waiting for a reply from the bishops, and also testing public reaction on the publication of the official correspondence. But it had been established in that debate that the elections when they came would turn on the Irish Church question, and hence Mayo's anxiety to get the Charter question finalized one way or the other quickly. It is remarkable that he waited two weeks.

The question of which side terminated the negotiations was brought up in the House by Sir John Gray, and it may be safely assumed that he was acting as the mouthpiece of the bishops, determined to justify their part and sustain their claim that the negotiations ended as a result of misunderstanding, and so could be resumed. Sir George Bowyer intimated Gray's intention to Cullen, and asked his view of the case, 'whether the letter of the two prelates was an *ultimatum* to which no modification, compromise, or further negotiation was allowable'. Bowyer himself still hoped the negotiations could be renewed.[2] Gray had by no means written the negotiations off either. In a letter to Cullen written after his question in Parliament he could still feel that the Charter plan was 'not in as hopeful a condition as it was twelve months since.'[3] On 12 June, Gray asked bluntly for a copy of the communication by which Leahy and Derry had broken off the negotiations, and should it transpire that no such letter existed, he asked Mayo to point to that passage in any letter from the two bishops which was understood as intimating their wish to conclude the matter. He raised the important question, on which the whole difficulty turned, whether the Government had taken their letter of 31 March 'as suggestions and expression of opinions on matters then under consideration, or as a final and complete scheme from which they could not deviate?'[4] Mayo put the Government case. No such letter as had been asked for existed; but

---

[1] *Hansard*, CXCI, p. 1886 ff.

[2] Cullen Papers, Bowyer to Cullen, 12 June 1868.

[3] *Ibid.*, Gray to Cullen, 17 June 1868. He also showed once again the futility of hoping for a Charter from the Liberals.

[4] *Hansard*, CXCII, pp. 1472-3. It was this last point which Walsh meant (*op. cit.*, p. 40), when he wrote of Mayo taking the bishops' letter as an 'ultimatum'.

The principles professed by the right reverend prelates having been expressed in two letters, and also at a lengthened personal interview, we were naturally led to the conclusion that those were their settled opinions, and that from them they could not depart. Now, those were opinions upon matters of principle of the highest moment. They were, at the same time, entirely at variance with the opinions entertained by Her Majesty's Government . . . looking, therefore, at everything that has occurred, we consider the matter to be at an end, and it is not our intention to take any further steps with regard to it.[1]

Thus the Charter scheme of 1868 ended amid mutual confusion. In a letter to Leahy and Derry of 30 June, Mayo could only repeat the statement he had made in the House.[2] The Irish bishops turned away from the Charter and gave their attention to the Established Church, and to the Powis Commission which had just started its inquiry. Woodlock published a pamphlet in June advocating the establishment of a distinct Catholic university rather than of Catholic colleges attached to a mixed university. But it had no reference to the plan which had just collapsed, and looked to a new beginning.[3] Walsh compared the university proposals of 1866 and 1868, finding the absence of endowment as a common defect. The first had been a scheme for a Catholic college only, and the second a Catholic university.[4] But an advance had been made: it was not now suggested that the steps taken in 1866 should be retraced – the point that education in the Queen's Colleges was unsuited to Catholic requirements had been conceded by the Government.[5] There was no going back on that, and even Gladstone had to take up the Irish university question in this light, though he left it to the last of his reforming measures, and tackled it against the better judgment of a large slice of his own party.

One immediate result of the end of the Mayo plan was Manning's dropping of Disraeli. 'I felt that a ravine, I will not say a gulf, opened between us when the Resolutions on the Irish Church were laid upon the table of the House', he wrote to him on 2 December 1868.[6] It was not unnatural that Disraeli should feel disappointed with the man in

[1] *Hansard*, CXCII, p. 1474.

[2] W. J. Walsh, *op. cit.*, p. 40.

[3] Bartholomew Woodlock, *Catholic University Education in Ireland, A Letter to Mr Cogan, M.P.*, Dublin, 1868. See notice of it in the *Dublin Review*, July 1868, p. 235 ff., and in *The Times*, 9 June 1868.

[4] This distinction was apparently unclear to some, and Sir George Grey had to ask the Irish Secretary exactly what had been proposed in 1866 in order to clarify the members' minds. Was it a college or a university? Hansard, CXCII, p. 714 (22 May 1868).

[5] W. J. Walsh, *op. cit.*, p. 41.

[6] Monypenny and Buckle, *op. cit.*, vol. II, p. 349. Also quoted by Shane Leslie, *H. E. Manning*, p. 198.

whom he had reposed so much reliance during the preparatory stages of the plan, in the winter of 1867-8. He was indeed to speak of being stabbed in the back by Manning over this.[1] But the Catholics on their side were surprised by Disraeli's rapid abandonment of the plan; the *Freeman* later in the year contrasted his former willingness to concede 'sectarian education' with his subsequent change of mind.[2] It has been seen, however, that the causes and occasion of the breakdown of the scheme were complicated and confused. The bishops bid too high,[3] in the belief that their concessions would as a result be received with greater respect by the Government, although even so, their views were more extreme[4] than they were prepared to admit after the announcement that the negotiations were at an end. As everyone saw at the time, the bishops' and the Ministers' views of Catholic education were mutually exclusive, and it is most unlikely that a settlement could have been arrived at satisfactorily to both parties, even had events not 'swept the negotiation out of the negotiators' hands'.[5] But Cullen in his report to the Propaganda could not see the slight ground gained by the bishops since 1865 which Walsh noticed. He wrote,

My impression is that the Government was insincere. However, we have obtained some concrete result from the negotiations which were interrupted, and that is that the Goverment is determined not to give any guarantee to the Catholics against the teaching of heresy and rottenness [scostumatezze] in the Universities.[6]

Cullen's only gain was the wisdom of not dealing with the Government. And there the matter rested until first Fawcett, and then Gladstone took it up.

[1] Monypenny and Buckle, *op. cit.*, vol. II, p. 350: 'Whatever the degree of Manning's responsibility, the facts and dates suggest that the Roman Catholic authorities were diverted from adhesion to Disraeli's programme by Gladstone's superior bid.' Disraeli's accusation against Manning caused the latter to abandon all dealings with him. See Shane Leslie, *op. cit.*, p. 210; and also McClelland, *op. cit.*, p. 169, for an interesting assessment of Disraeli's charge.

[2] *Freeman*, 3 November 1868.

[3] Monypenny and Buckle, *op. cit.*, vol. II, p. 349. 'Dr Leahy and Dr Derry were not men of affairs, and . . . they asked for twice as much as they were prepared to take.' Though illustrating the point, this rather undervalues the bishops' stand on principle.

[4] Grey Papers, Aubrey de Vere to Grey, 1 June 1868.

[5] *Dublin Review*, April 1873, 'The Irish University Bill', p. 469. This article starts with a brief summary of the relations of the bishops and the Government over the university question since 1845.

[6] Propaganda, *Scritture* 36, Cullen to Barnabo, 24 June 1868.

CHAPTER SEVEN

Moves Towards Disestablishment
1866-8

THE position which the Irish Catholics adopted towards the existence among themselves of a Protestant Established Church was not one at which any Catholic could ordinarily have been expected to arrive. The unusual circumstances of Ireland induced them to accept and employ arguments which were far removed from the tradition of their Church. If any adjustment in the religious situation were to be considered, by the Catholic principle of Establishment, maintained in the Syllabus of Errors, they ought to have invoked Paley's majority principle and prepared themselves to displace the Protestant as the State religion. But they did not do so. Instead they took their stand on Voluntaryism and disestablishment, declaring a doctrine quite contrary to Catholic morality – that the State had no conscience and so was unable to compel Establishment. This was an advanced position, even for the 1860s, and in holding it they were siding, both theoretically and in practice, with the English Radicals and Dissenters who had been arguing along these lines with reference to England ever since the beginning of the century. It is in the working agreement between the National Association and the Liberation Society that this can be seen most clearly. Ireland represents an instance of Liberal Catholicism, but it was tempered with ultra-montanism, and just as in France, where the appearance of this combination, especially in the person of Lamennais, had posed such a dilemma for the Papacy, so in Ireland the question of education was the weak joint between them. The Irish Catholics may have argued for the voluntary system over the matter of religious endowment, but they did not scruple to ask for State endowment for their university and schools whilst at the same time denouncing the right of the State to interfere in them. This can be seen most clearly in 1869, when Dr Russell, the President of Maynooth, urged Gladstone to treat his college as an educational estab-lishment, and so entitled to continue to receive its (rather anomalous) State assistance, rather than as an ecclesiastical one, in which case, by the principle embodied in the Church Act, of non-recognition by the State of religious opinion, it should have – as it had eventually – to give up State endowment. Or again; in England Parliament had given aid to schools in denominational grants, but in Ireland the problem of 'endowing error' was avoided, except in the case of Maynooth, by the creation of a system of mixed secular education. This was, of course, one of the bishops major grievances, and their suggested solution was the adoption of the English method, which meant State denominational endowment.

The abolition of the Test and Corporation Acts in England in 1828, and the passage of Catholic Emancipation the following year had inaugurated a statutory modification of the State's position regarding religious belief which was to survive the century. The Marriage Act (1836), the abolition of religious tests in Scottish universities (1853), the admission of Jews to Parliament (1858), the abolition of Compulsory Church Rate (in England, 1868), and the University Test Act (1871), were signposts on the way. In the course of the century Parliamentary legislation weakened the canon law and the ecclesiastical courts still more, by removing many hitherto ecclesiastical causes to civil jurisdiction, so accelerating the withering away of the ecclesiastical parts of the Constitution. Safeguards to protect the religious Establishment were written into the Catholic Emancipation Act, but Establishments themselves were to fall. Precedents were created in the Colonies. The Canadian clergy reserves were abolished in 1854, and State aid for religion was withdrawn elsewhere – in New South Wales (1863), in Queensland and Tasmania (1866), in the West Indies (1868) and in Victoria (1870). Ireland was itself the scene of this sort of constitutional breakthrough in 1869. To the changing notion of the State which all this reflected, Ireland had contributed the Act of 1833, which was a supreme vindication of the power of the State to interfere in the Temporalities of Churches, and which ended the compulsory payment of Church cess. In 1857 Ministers' Money was abolished, and so, in 1867, was the Declaration against Transubstantiation – one of the safeguards of the Establishment.

These statutory changes touching religious belief did not indeed culminate in the collapse of the English Establishment. It was partly saved by timely reform,[1] carried mostly by laymen in the face of ecclesiastical opposition. Also, in Church debates in Parliament, moderates expressed a reluctance to legislate according to 'abstract principles' for fear of opening up precedents which could have a wider application than they were prepared to countenance; and by thus dealing with religious questions on the ground of expediency, they allowed the

[1] As Olive Brose argues in *Church and Parliament, The Reshaping of the Church of England, 1828–60*, Oxford, 1959.

Establishment to slip by to the present day. And unlike the position in Ireland, in England too many other parts of the constitutional fabric depended still on the legal existence of the Royal Supremacy to make its termination an easy matter. But the statutory changes removed the weight from much of the theoretical justification of the Establishment. 'It can hardly escape even cursory observation,' Gladstone was to write in this sense, in 1868, 'that the present century has seen a great increase in the instances of what is called political inconsistency.'[1] The multiplication of different religious opinions in society had made it very difficult still to hold to Hooker's notion of Parliament as the assembled laity of the Church. For statute was coming to recognize the legal existence of religious belief outside the Establishment, and to some men it seemed, therefore, that the continued exercise of State power over the Church of England was at first unjustifiable and then plainly monstrous. The appointment by *congé d'élire* of a bishop with unsound views, or the construction of doctrine in the judicial committee of the Privy Council, wherein sat men not of the Church upon whose doctrinal difficulties they were deliberating, came to seem more than merely anomalous. In one sense, it was a realization that Parliament had recognized society as frankly pluralist in its religious beliefs, which occasioned the lapse from the Establishment of first Newman and then Manning. Hurrell Froude's *Remarks on State Interference in Matters Spiritual*[2] had pointed the way. It was a commentary on the implications of the repeal of the Test and Corporation Acts and Catholic Emancipation, and the impossibility of considering them compatible with Hooker's theory of the State Church. Gladstone's odyssey from his early belief that the State had a conscience and so was able to select a religion on the grounds of its truth and accord it recognition and protection, to that revealed in his dealings with the Irish Church in the 1860s, followed exactly his realization that society was pluralist and that the new function of the State was therefore to act as neutral arbiter. In his *Chapter of Autobiography* (1868), he set a chronology to his changed attitude. Scarcely, he wrote there, had his 1838 book issued from the press, when 'I found myself the last man on the sinking ship'.[3] For the rest of his lifetime men were left wandering how long it would be before he turned his new position to its logical application in England and Wales.

Most English Dissenters – the Methodists were exceptional until the

[1] W. E. Gladstone, *Chapter of Autobiography*, London, 1868, p. 10.
[2] 1833; included in Froude's *Remains*, London, 1839, Part Second, vol. 1, p. 184.
[3] *Chapter of Autobiography*, p. 25.

mid-century – had argued that all churches should be cut free from the State, for their own good as well as in furtherance of 'religious equality'. They were then to be reconstituted on the basis on which they had themselves flourished, and on which the Irish Catholics had also created a vast religious network out of nothing since the end of the penal laws, namely, the *Voluntary Principle* (that congregations should maintain their own churches, either by voluntary contributions or by the bequests of the faithful. This was called 'levelling down' in the 1860s). Great difficulty had been encountered in proposing Church reforms when trying to determine which of the property of the Church had come originally from private bequest, which from royal gift, and what quantity represented the 'nationalty' given by the State at its institution for the furtherance of religion. The last source was explained by Coleridge,[1] and in Ireland his ideas were to be expounded by Aubrey de Vere. The Irish bishops cut across the confusion by renouncing what they held was still their valid claim to the ecclesiastical property, for it had been given for Catholic use before the Irish Reformation. As in England, questions of Church property caused men to look rather closely at just what had happened in the Reformation, and for Ireland, it was Cullen's nephew, Moran, who put the Catholic case.[2] They realized also, however, that by the Canon law principle of prescription (evidence of a hundred years' possession and use of property could be taken as proof of ownership) they would lose the ecclesiastical property of Ireland to the Protestants anyway, and so make disestablishment an ineffective means of securing 'religious equality'. Thus they made an even more drastic departure from the principles of their Church, and joined the English Dissenters and Radicals in demanding disendowment. They were to do to the Irish Establishment what Pius IX had been so horrified to witness in the Piedmontese Siccardi Laws. Disendowment was to be followed by the application of Irish ecclesiastical property to such purposes as the State might direct. Thus the old Appropriation Clause, which had so bedevilled the politics of the 1830s was to come up again as a live Parliamentary issue in the 1860s, and to be debated anew. One compromise with disendowment was *Concurrent Endowment* (or the distribution of ecclesiastical property and State aid indifferently among competing religions, usually, and as in the suggested application to Ireland, according to their numerical proportions. This was called 'levelling up' in the 1860s). It was rejected by all the Irish bishops except

[1] S. T. Coleridge, *On the Constitution of Church and State*, London, 1829.
[2] P. F. Moran, *The Episcopal Succession in Ireland during the reign of Elizabeth*, Dublin, 1866. (Also printed in the *Irish Ecclesiastical Record*.)

Moriarty, and eventually by Parliament, though not until after the Lords had withdrawn an amendment from the Church Bill in 1869 embodying the principle.

The Maynooth Grant was an example of concurrent endowment, as well as a standing contradiction to the existence of an Establishment. When it was made a permanent charge on the Consolidated Fund by Peel in 1845, Protestants objected that it compromised the State's conscience. Gladstone, in mid-swing from one position to another, resigned rather than act against the principles of his *State in its Relations with the Church* (1838). It was in fact a compromise, a transitional point in the mid-century around which men drew the opinions which were later to be brought out in the Irish Church debates. When that Church was abolished as an Establishment in 1871, the Maynooth Grant went with it. And so did the Irish *Regium Donum*, a comparable State endowment of Presbyterianism. The English recipients, to clear the way for their advancing notions of the State and religion, had given it up in 1852.

Ireland was perfectly suited for an attack on the bulwarks of the Establishment, for with its religious minority the Irish Church represented in an extreme form all the qualities which English Radicals and Dissenters were anxious to prove anomalous and unprincipled. The Religious census of England in 1851 had shown that the Established Church only just tipped the balance there, but in Ireland, the 1861 census provided statistical evidence of an overwhelmingly Catholic population in three of the four provinces. The disestablishment of the Irish Church could therefore proceed without delay, and its English promoters were determined to see it as a prelude for the future:

> It is immaterial that it was not so intended at the time. The Irish Church Act . . . not only marks a turning point in our national policy, but, in its object and leading features, it lays down the lines along which the ecclesiastical legislation for the future must necessarily travel. Nobody dreams that the Protestant Episcopal Church of Ireland can ever be re-established, or that any other Church can be established in its place. And with the legal equality of all churches formally recognized by law in one part of the three Kingdoms, it is inevitable that, sooner or later, the same even-handed justice must be done in the other parts also.[1]

There was a real sense in which the area and outline of debate on Church and State questions had been laid down in reference to England in the period from 1830 to 1850, and then passed to Ireland. There, the Catholic case against the Establishment both fulfilled that outline and

[1] *The Case for Disestablishment*, by members of the Liberation Society, rev. ed., London, 1894, p. 256.

provided a precedent for England. It had long been realized that Ireland would be the scene of the breakthrough, for the 1833 Irish Church Temporalities Act had in fact been an experiment in the sort of Church reform hoped for at home – a limited experiment.[1] But by the 1860s the limits were disregarded, and the demand was not for mere internal reform of the Irish Church, however radical, but its complete abolition as an Establishment, or, as the Irish Catholics put it, as 'a badge of conquest'. The Catholic bishops helped the enlargement of the design by adopting as their own the arguments framed with reference to the English stituation, and applying them successfully in Ireland. Voluntaryism and 'religious equality' were certainly not Catholic principles, but they became Irish ones in the hands of a national hierarchy working in articulated accord with the English Radicals and Dissenters. One significant difference appeared in this Irish application at the time. English Church reform was essentially lay-directed. The lay element was absent in Ireland – partly due to the nature of Roman Catholicism itself, which is in essence sacerdotally-directed, both in concept and in actuality, and partly to the almost entire absence of an educated Irish middle class. The two were linked by those who pointed out that it was the Church which kept the laity from the education which was available, either as a point of principle (that there was something inherently Catholic in 'enslaving the intellect'), or practically by forbidding Catholic attendance at mixed universities. But the absence of a lay element did not prevent the bishops from allying themselves with advanced principles.

Now the idea of a secular State, neutral between conflicting religious opinion, was a key element in nineteenth-century Liberalism. In grounding their arguments and making their stand in that concept, the Irish hierarchy endorsed the changing idea of the State in the most effective way they could. And so there occurred the paradox which had been apparent in the programme of the National Association: a Catholic hierarchy acting contrarily to the struggle of the Head of their Church with Liberalism. The sort of State which the Irish bishops appealed for, and which by their part in the disestablishment of a Church they helped to usher into existence, was just that type of State against which the Papal strictures were directed in the Syllabus of Errors and which they themselves regarded as an unsuitable educator. The Irish bishops worked diligently for the realization of that which the Pope most dreaded – *Libera chiesa in libero stato*.

[1] O. J. Brose, 'The Irish Precedent for English Church Reform', in *Journal of Ecclesiastical History*, VII, no. 2, 1956, p. 204.

In August 1859 it seemed to the *Daily News* that the question of the Irish Church Establishment 'sleeps so profoundly that there is, it appears, no likelihood of its awakening for some time to come'.[1] But the matter was not dead – it was only moribund in the area of political agitation. It had not ceased to be a grievance. O'Neill Daunt was stirring opinion about it in West Cork; and in 1857 Mr Justice Shee had written a pamphlet favouring religious equality.[2] The Catholic bishops were not so concerned with the Establishment as they were with education, although, as if to stake a claim for more active concern in the future, in their 1862 Resolutions they had framed one on the Protestant Establishment, 'from which they receive nothing in return but insult and dishonour'. Yet even then, they did not demand disestablishment; their petition was for exemption for Catholics from all taxation for the benefit of a Protestant ascendancy.[3] But events were turning towards a renewal of feeling against the Church. The *Kilkenny Journal* noticed as early as 1861 – evidently somewhat prematurely, however, and with a confusion of aspiration and fact – that the Church question was being taken up with warmth, 'and that one word from the saintly hierarchy' would inaugurate a movement for its settlement.[4] In 1863 MacHale described the Church as a 'hideous evil' in a public letter to the Chancellor of the Exchequer (Gladstone),[5] so recalling the reputation he had made for himself, when a young Maynooth professor, in his 'Hierophilus' Letters. And in that year also, Dillwyn moved in the Commons for a Select Committee of inquiry into 'the present distribution of endowments for religious purposes throughout Ireland', seeking an amendment of the arrangements which would be agreeable to persons of all religious professions there. The *Annual Register* took this as a sign that the Church question, which had slumbered since the abandonment of the Appropriation Clause, was again to become a political issue.[6] It was not alone. Woodlock saw Dillwyn's motion as an indication of renewed Parliamentary activity on the question.[7] But it was not until 1865 that Dillwyn moved in the House that the present position of the Irish Church was unsatisfactory, and so called for the early attention

[1] *Daily News*, 18 August 1859.

[2] William Shee, *A Proposal for Religious Equality in Ireland*, Dublin, 1857.

[3] *Resolutions adopted by the Archbishops and Bishops of Ireland at a meeting held in Dublin on the 6th, 7th, 8th, and 9th of May, 1862*. There is a copy in the Larcom Papers, MS. 7651.

[4] *Guardian*, 25 November 1863.

[5] Reported in the *Nonconformist*, 20 November 1861.

[6] *Annual Register*, 1863 (History).

[7] Kirby Papers, Woodlock to Kirby, no. 157, June 1863.

of the Government[1] – a famous motion, which inaugurated the Church question as a front-ranking political issue.

The delay in raising the matter again is partly a reflection of the continuing absence of agitation. Sir John Gray, denied that agitation was a necessary element in securing justice for Ireland: would they have to engender a great movement like that for emancipation before the Church question could receive serious attention? he asked Parliament in 1867.[2] This is a curious illustration of Gray's apparent failure to regard the potential of the National Association over-highly – for it was producing petitions as evidence of Irish agitation on the question, and it was intended to be – not indeed like the movement for emancipation – but a cultivator of public opinion. Henry Wilberforce had advised Moriarty in 1861 that petitions from every parish in Ireland would soon force the Government to do something about the Establishment.[3] That was before the National Association had come into being. But in 1865, with the Association in its first flood of enthusiasm, it was still necessary for Dillwyn to ask Monsell if he could get some Irishmen to support his motion against the Church. There were enough English Dissenters behind him, he explained, but there was little evidence of Irish feeling on the question. Monsell asked Cullen if it was possible for petitions to be got up to support him.[4] The National Association supplied them. Cullen was no doubt shaken at discovering how little was known of the Association and its objectives even among its friends in England. Once started however, it was the Church grievance which gave content to the working agreement between the Association and the Liberation Society. Yet the National Association, in selecting three heads for agitation had made each of them less powerful than they would have been had they stood singly, and together with the internal difficulty of the members in determining which of the three at any particular moment should receive priority, this gave a handle to their opponents. Thus in 1867 the venerable Protestant Bishop O'Brien of Ossory wrote that all Irish agitation seemed to be directed to questions other than that of the Establishment.[5]

1 *Hansard*, third series, vol. CLXXVIII, p. 383 (28 March 1865).

2 *Ibid.*, CLXXXVII, p. 100 (7 May 1867).

3 Monsell Papers, Box 8319, H. W. Wilberforce to Moriarty, 4 January 1861.

4 Cullen Papers, Monsell to Cullen, Easter Saturday, 1865. In May, Monsell made a similar request for Irish agitation, as the Irish M.P.s were embarrassed by allegations that their country was apathetic on the Church question. Cobden (who died in this year) had remarked to him that 'if forty Quakers had a religious grievance, they would make the government of the country impossible until it was redressed'. *Ibid.*, Monsell to Cullen, 30 May 1865.

5 James T. O'Brien, *The Case of the Established Church in Ireland*, second ed., London and Dublin, 1867, p. 40. O'Brien was a veteran of the Parliamentary debates on the Irish Church of the 1830s.

The Irish Religious census was a further cause of the delay. It had been held in 1861, but it was not until Hume, a Liverpool clergyman and a fellow of the Statistical Society of London, published a commentary on its findings in 1864 that the facts of the case could be laid before the public.[1] Hume dedicated his book to Dillwyn – but only to set that opponent of the Church on the right lines, for he used the statistical evidence of the proportions of Catholics and Protestants in Ireland to show that the anti-Church case was not so obvious as it might seem. Others were not to agree. Hume provided a table giving religious professions in the counties and provinces. This showed that out of the gross Irish population of 5,798,967, the number of Roman Catholics was 4,505,265. Members of the Established Church numbered only 693,357. There were also 45,399 Methodists, 523,291 Presbyterians, and 31,655 others. But he was not dismayed. He warned against 'generalizing from selected examples', especially when dealing with figures; 'for there is much which an inexperienced person cannot comprehend, and he grasps eagerly at such isolated facts as serve to confirm his previous crude deductions'.[2] Those who used the statistics which Hume had printed in so convenient a form were not to heed this, nor to believe his other conclusions. The drift of most of his argument was that Roman Catholics, though so overwhelming in numbers, especially in the three southern provinces, were not the intelligence of the country, and so did not count for as much, qualitatively, as did the Protestants.[3]

The 1861 census figures became the basis of the Catholic and English Dissenting case against the Irish Church. Speaking on Dillwyn's motion in 1865, Gathorne Hardy followed Hume in claiming that a 'close examination' of the figures did not leave them as conclusive as they had seemed. The 1851 English census, he said, had led to attacks on the position of the English Establishment, and now the same was happening with reference to Ireland.[4] Dillwyn had himself used the census figures

---

[1] A. Hume, *Results of the Irish Census of 1861.*   [2] A. Hume, *op. cit.*, p. 13.

[3] See, for example, his 'Social Pyramid' on page 57, which shows that at the top there were no Catholic Scripture-readers, needle-makers, artists in pearl, thimble-makers, plaster-of-Paris manufacturers, linen-thread manufacturers, or damask-designers; and at the bottom, that there were no Protestant flock-makers, carriage-brokers, pipers, sausage-makers, trotter-cleaners, fowl-skewer-makers, cordial-dealers, leather-breeches-makers, or brogue-makers. This sort of argument, that the Church made up for its lack of numbers by the intelligence and industry found in its ranks, was put most persuasively by James Byrne in the fifth essay of the well-known compendium, *Essays on the Irish Church*, Oxford and London, 1866, pp. 267 ff.

[4] *Hansard*, CLXXVIII, pp. 402–3. He argued that the figures showed a relative increase in the Protestant population of Ireland since 1834. The figures for that year had included Methodists and Wesleyans as members of the Establishment, but they were enunciated separately in the 1861 census. This relative increase was true, but Catholic

in the debate.[1] They were referred to with some frequency during Parliamentary discussion of the Church question up to 1869.[2]

The question of Catholic oaths had also to be aired before disestablishment could become practical politics for Roman Catholics, both in Parliament and among office-holders generally in Ireland. The oath prescribed in the Catholic Emancipation Act had been framed as a safeguard to the Protestant Constitution. As well as disclaiming the right of the Pope to absolve subjects from their allegiance, the oath also bound Catholics to 'abjure any Intention to subvert the present Church Establishment as settled by Law within this Realm . . . or weaken the Protestant Religion or Protestant Government in the United Kingdom'.[3] During the Commons' debate of the Irish Church Temporalities Act, in 1833, O'Connell had established the right of Catholic members to discuss Church temporalities despite the oath, on the ground that 'there was no inspiration in a certain number of pounds, shillings, and pence'.[4] A large gulf existed between that and discussion of disestablishment. In 1857, when considering the prospects for religious equality, Justice Shee had written of his 'clear conviction that Catholic members, however strong may be their impression of its expediency, ought not to vote' on questions touching the Establishment, so long as the oath continued to be 'among the conditions on which they were admitted to seats in Parliament'.[5] The difficulty recurred during debate on the Irish Church in the 1860s. Colonel Greville, speaking in 1866 on Gray's motion, referred to the oath, which, he said, must bar some from joining in that discussion.[6] And in 1867, Synan gave four reasons why the oath should not have that effect. He denied that the arguments of half a century past could bind Parliament, and that these arguments had any reference to constitutional changes. Also, the alteration in the oaths prescribed by

emigration must be set against it (a point made by Gladstone in his *Chapter of Autobiography*, p. 34). Gathorne Hardy also cited Hume's work as showing the beneficial effects of the Protestant West Connaught Mission (*Hansard, ibid.*, p. 418).

[1] *Hansard*, CLXXVIII, p. 387. In the same debate, Whiteside (p. 452) spoke of the 'petty juggling tricks with figures of which figures are always susceptible'.

[2] Speaking in the debate on Gladstone's motion for a Committee on the Acts relating to the Irish Establishment, on 2 April 1868, Lowe cited the census figures which, he said, illustrated the lines

> If, in England, for three million souls 'tis conceded,
> Two proper-sized bishops are all that is needed;
> 'Tis plain, for the Irish half-million who want 'em,
> One-third of a bishop is just the right quantum.
> *Hansard*, CXCI, p. 729.

[3] 10 Geo. IV, cap. 7, clause 2. [4] *Hansard*, XVIII (8 July 1833).
[5] William Shee, *op. cit.*, p. 5. [6] *Hansard*, CLXXXII, p. 1008.

the Emancipation Act he considered a conclusive declaration by Parliament that the Act was not final. Additionally, he asserted that it was a constitutional principle that Acts of the Legislature were founded on expediency and utility, to be altered according to the circumstances of the times'.[1] Yet it is clear that although Catholics were prominent in the debates on Dillwyn's and Gray's motions on the Church, which dealt with the questions of Church property and revenue, when it came, as it did in 1868, to Parliamentary debate on the existence or non-existence of the Irish Establishment altogether, the thirty-two Catholic members took no part, although, as Sir Frederick Heygate noticed, they voted.[2]

When the oath had been formulated, it had been assumed by Protestants that Catholics *would* endeavour to go beyond the limited terms upon which they were admitted to the Constitution. This suspicion had continued. Kingsley accused Newman of allowing equivocation and mental reservation in 1864, and Newman's famous reply became the *Apologia Pro Vita Sua*. Newman had there been forced to discuss the degree of equivocation allowed in the taking of oaths by St Alphonso de Liguori.[3] Protestants had come to suppose that Catholics always employed de Liguori when they wished to make an oath meaningless. The Harrowby Commission of inquiry into Maynooth, of 1855, had questioned several of the professors closely concerning the introduction of de Liguori's texts into the college curriculum.[4] O'Neill Daunt approved of all the cases where de Liguori deemed equivocation permissible,[5] but did not agree that Irish Catholics practised it in relation to their constitutional oaths. The Penal Days were a proof that Catholics would rather not take an oath abjuring their beliefs in order to receive the protection of the Constitution. It was paradoxical, he felt, that Catholics were attacked for alleged unreliability in swearing, when so

[1] *Hansard*, CLXXXVII, p. 147.

[2] *Ibid.*, CXCI, p. 1348 (27 April 1868). The debate on the resolutions was prior to the passing of the Promissory Oaths Bill but after the 1867 Oaths Act. It was the latter which allowed conscientious participation by Catholics in debates on Church principles, and it must therefore be concluded that their hesitation to speak stemmed from their desire not to prejudice the issue by giving it the appearance of being a Catholic-inspired move. Additionally, they were still rather cautious of Gladstone. But many had not been very happy about the Mayo Charter plan, and readily swung over to the Church question.

[3] See especially the *Apologia*, Fontana ed., 1959, Appendix 7, 'Lying and Equivocation', p. 349.

[4] *Parliamentary Papers*, 1855, XXII. See also the appendix of Patrick Murphy, *Popery in Ireland*, London, 1865, p. 289 ff., which quotes evidence from the 1855 Commission, and especially highlights Bishop Furlong's admission that de Liguori's *Moral Theology* 'is what I principally refer to'.

[5] Daunt, Journal, 26 March 1863.

many Anglican parsons declared their subscription to the Thirty-nine Articles without really believing them.[1] But the continuance of Protestant suspicion made the oath question a difficulty in the 1860s.

The oath probably explains why a few prominent Catholic politicians like Monsell, and Catholic peers, felt themselves precluded from attending the Aggregate Meeting of December 1864, or from joining the National Association, as A.M. Sullivan has suggested.[2] One of the three points of the Association was a frank declaration that the Establishment must be subverted. It has been seen that at the time of the Aggregate Meeting, some Protestants pointed to the oath and its apparent breach by those Catholics who had taken it. Prominent among these were Sir John Gray and Alderman MacSwiney. The opposition given to the customary vote of thanks to MacSwiney at the end of his year of office as Lord Mayor has also been mentioned. It was inspired by the same Protestant feeling. When Sullivan himself refused to take the oath on becoming a Dublin Councillor in 1862, he was fined £500 and disqualified.[3] The National Association saw the dangers, and through Gray it inaugurated a movement against 'obnoxious oaths' as one of its first acts. It was fought out in the Dublin Corporation, in a deputation to the Lord-Lieutenant, and in a Bill before Parliament.[4] There was a good colonial precedent available. In Melbourne, the Irish exile Gavan Duffy had secured the passage of an Act abolishing the Catholic oath and replacing it by an oath of allegiance common to all legislators and office-holders, in 1857.[5]

Monsell's Bill, of March 1865, followed the campaign against the oath got up by the National Association, and was supported by the Liberation Society.[6] But Monsell was not a member of the Association, which did not directly sponsor his action. The Bill was to substitute the existing oath of the 1829 Act for one which, while still declaring that the Pope had no civil jurisdiction in Britain, dropped the phrases about the Papal power of deposition. Those parts relating to subversion of the Establishment were also to be removed, and a simple oath of allegiance was to be taken instead. This followed the course taken in Melbourne by Duffy. In committee, on 21 March, Monsell spoke

---

[1] *Ibid.*, 15 February 1864. He published a letter in the *Cork Examiner* at this time, putting this argument.

[2] A. M. Sullivan, *New Ireland*, p. 311.　　　[3] *Ibid.*　　[4] See chap. 4.

[5] The Act was passed, as Duffy said, 'in deference to the scruples of Catholics', and 'in return for consenting to abolish state aid to religion'. Monsell Papers, Box 8319, Gavan Duffy to Moriarty, September 1857.

[6] Liberation Society Minute Books, vol. III (1862–7), p. 255. The Bill was debated and approved at the Council of 24 March 1865.

of the immorality of 'unnecessary oaths', and pointed out that the existing one was equivocal anyway.[1] It was imposed not only on the members of Parliament, but on Maynooth students, Catholic mayors, magistrates and councillors also.[2] Newdegate spoke of the Syllabus of Errors, and the urgent need to keep a protective oath against 'Papal Aggression'.[3] Yet Sir George Grey, for the Government, approved the Bill. It received a second reading on 17 May, when Grey said that it was not Catholics only who advocated the destruction of the Establishment, but Protestant Dissenters too,[4] so why should an oath afflict one class and not another, both sharing a common design? But Lefroy and Whiteside, moving the postponement of the Bill, spoke of the continuing need to protect the Church and the Constitution from Catholic subversion.[5] The Bill was passed by the Commons, but lost in the Lords by 21 votes, Earl Grey warning that the oath would not stop the struggle for the removal of the Irish Establishment, which would come 'sooner or later' anyway.[6] A comparable Bill was introduced for the Government by Sir George Grey in March 1866, enforcing a simple oath of allegiance,[7] which passed the Commons with only five dissentient votes. It also passed the Lords and received the royal assent on 30 April 1866.[8] Manning had urged Gladstone to see that the Bill had a favourable hearing in the Cabinet, and ensure that its excellence, which consisted in its purely civil references, would not be spoiled by the introduction of religious matters.[9] He also sent Gladstone the oaths of civil allegiance sanctioned by Rome for the Catholics of Ireland.[10] Cullen sent the Act to Cardinal Barnabo, explaining that the new simple oath of allegiance was 'such that one can oblige by it without any difficulty'. He was not so sure about the second clause of the Act, which dealt with succession questions. It seemed to him that the oath bound

---

[1] *Hansard*, CLXXVIII, pp. 26–7.   [2] *Ibid.*, p. 29.   [3] *Ibid.*, p. 31.

[4] *Ibid.*, CLXXIX, p. 463.

[5] *Ibid.*, pp. 432 ff., and pp. 450 ff.

[6] See *Annual Register*, 1865 (History), pp. 81 ff., for a summary of the arguments used in the debates on the Bill.

[7] The oath now read 'I, A.B., do faithfully swear that I will bear true allegiance to Her Majesty Queen Victoria, and defend her to the best of my power against all conspiracies whatever, which may be made against her power, crown, or dignity. SO HELP ME GOD.'

[8] See *Annual Register*, 1866 (History), p. 23; and John Brady, 'The oath of allegiance at Maynooth', in *Irish Ecclesiastical Record*, XCIV, 1960, p. 134. Also A. M. Sullivan's somewhat confused recollections in *New Ireland*, p. 313.

[9] Gladstone Papers, B.M.Add.MS. 44248, f. 286, Manning to Gladstone, 9 March 1866.

[10] *Ibid.*, f. 295, 'Copy of a Letter from Cardinal Litta, Prefect of the Propaganda, to Bishop Poynter, 26 April 1815'. Manning had copied this from Charles Butler, *Historical Memoirs of English Catholics*, London, 1821, vol. IV, p. 531.

them to be faithful to the Queen while she was a Protestant, and for that reason could be constructed to oblige them to be unfaithful should she become a Catholic. But if that should occur, Cullen said, 'we shall be more devoted to her than before'. He added, 'This is not the sense prescribed by the oath, but the words with which it is made up do not exclude a meaning in this sense'.[1]

On 30 April 1866, the Chief Secretary, Fortescue, announced the Government's intention of issuing a Commission to inquire into oaths taken by office-holders in Ireland, and by the Maynooth students.[2] This was constituted on 16 July. It was therefore somewhat prematurely that the member for Kildare, William Cogan introduced a Bill on 8 May for the abolition of the Declaration against Transubstantiation, the celebration of Masses, and the invocation of saints, etc. This was the other 'obnoxious oath' with which the Catholics were dissatisfied, and to which Monsell had also referred in 1865, when he spoke of the degrading scenes at Dublin Castle when Catholic Law-officers and Privy Councillors had to take an oath 'declaring the Roman Catholic religion to be damnable and idolatrous'.[3] Cogan took the view in 1866 that 'no one could pretend the interests of Protestantism were served' by the oath.[4] In his Bill a comparable oath would only be needed for two Irish officers, the Lord-Lieutenantcy and the Lord Chancellorship.

The allied oath taken at Maynooth was causing great irritation there. The suspicion entertained by Catholics in the Irish provinces of the integrity of Maynooth priests was probably because of the oath, and because they were educated at public expense. They were often 'suspected of being more or less in the English interest'.[5] When the Oaths Commission seemed certain to report in favour of some changes favourable to Catholics, the President of Maynooth, on the advice of Monsell, and after informing the Duke of Leinster, as Chairman of the Visitors, and the Chief Secretary, did not put forward the college freshmen to take their oaths at the January sessions (1867). He had assumed that a new oath would be approved during the Parliamentary session, and, anxious to report on this to the college Board, asked Monsell what the prospects were for a change.[6] Cullen also imagined that a settlement

---

[1] Propaganda, *Scritture 35*, Cullen to Barnabo, 9 May 1866. A printed copy of *An Act to Amend the Law relating to Parliamentary Oaths* is also bound in this volume of the *Scritture*.

[2] *Hansard*, CLXXXIII, p. 160.   [3] *Ibid.*, CLXXVIII, p. 25 (21 March 1865).

[4] *Ibid.*, CLXXXIII, p. 636 (8 May 1866).

[5] Daunt, Journal, 12 September 1865. This should be contrasted with Patrick Murphy's account of wholesale equivocation at the taking of their oaths by the Maynooth students; see *Popery in Ireland*, p. 161.

[6] Monsell Papers, Box 8319, Dr Russell to Monsell, 29 May 1867.

of the oath question 'quite favourably for the Catholics' was about to be made. He told the Propaganda that the Commission was almost certain to suggest acceptable formulae.[1]

He was not disappointed. The Oaths Commission found that,

although recent legislation has abolished certain oaths and converted others into declarations, the number of oaths still required to be taken is exceedingly large. Of these, many appear to us unnecessary, some even mischievous. We believe that every requirement of an unnecessary oath tends to detract from the solemnity of necessary oaths.[2]

The oath of allegiance was to be discontinued for students, officers and servants at Maynooth, and a simple declaration substituted.[3] The Declaration against Transubstantiation was to be abolished.[4] On 25 July 1867, the Home Secretary (Gathorne Hardy) promised a Bill to implement the main lines of the *Report*.[5] There was some unavoidable delay, however, for the Bill was most difficult to draft, almost a hundred Acts requiring to be repealed.[6] But the Bill was introduced and passed in 1868, its main provisions and its principle having already been conceded. It received the royal assent on 31 July in that year. By its terms, the number of persons required to take an oath was greatly reduced, and in the case of Ireland it was restricted to the few officers named in the Act, the most significant of whom were the Lord-Lieutenant, the Lord Chancellor, and the Commander of the Forces.[7] As a pamphleteer wrote at the time of the Act, 'now we are face to face with a coalition of Papists and Dissenters . . . to disestablish and disendow the only lawful successor of the ancient primitive Church'.[8] Catholic members of Parliament, and members of Irish corporations, were free to assail the Establishment as they would.

This is not the place to examine the history of the Church question in Parliament during the 1860s, except in so far as it was influenced by Catholic opinion. That influence was most felt in 1869, when actual propositions embodied in a Bill were held out to the Irish; in the few years preceding, the Catholic case was largely represented to Parliament by Sir John Gray of the National Association. But the stages of the debates were a curious re-enacting of those of the 1830s.[9] The Irish

---

[1] Propaganda, *Scritture*, 35, Cullen to Moriarty, 6 January 1867.
[2] 'Report of the Oaths Commission', in *Parliamentary Papers*, 1867, XXXI, 9.
[3] *Ibid.*, p. 40.   [4] *Ibid.*, pp. 11-12.   [5] *Hansard*, CLXXXIX, p. 78.
[6] John Brady, *op. cit.*, in *Irish Ecclesiastical Record*, XCIV, 1960, p. 134.
[7] 31 & 32 Vict. cap. 72. Promissory Oaths Act.
[8] James Briggs (an Anglican parson), *A Historical Survey of the relations that have subsisted between the Church and State of England and Ireland and the See and Court of Rome, from the Norman Conquest*, London, 1868, p. 44.
[9] Dillwyn's motion, 28 March 1865 (*Hansard*, CLXXVIII, pp. 383 ff.); Gray's motions,

bishops, in acting upon principles worked out by English Radicals and Dissenters in the first half of the century, were not basing their case upon outmoded grounds. All the questions raised in Parliament in the thirties were ploughed through a second time, and the whole matter of Church and State was raised. Even the men were often the same: Stanley (now Derby), Russell, Gladstone. Sir Robert Inglis, who in the thirties had gasped with unbelief as the entire fabric of the Tory Church seemed to be pulled down around him, was dead; but his mantle had fallen upon Newdegate in the Sixties.[1] The argument in debate was the same in quality as that over the Church Temporalities Act in 1833. The differences between the English and Irish branches of the United Church were emphasized by those anxious not to have Irish Disestablishment frustrated by fears of creating too obvious a precedent for England.[2] Supporters of the Establishment endeavoured to show the falsity of such distinction. Lord Cairns said in the Lords debate on Russell's motion for a Royal Commission (June 1867), that the attack was essentially perpetrated by those opposed to all religious establishments, who 'select the branch of the Established Church in Ireland because they think it is the weakest branch'.[3] In the committee on Gladstone's resolutions (1868) Disraeli cited Miall as just such a person.[4]

10 April 1866 (*ibid.*, CLXXXII, pp. 973 ff.), and 7 May 1867 (*ibid.*, CLXXXVII, pp. 96 ff.); Russell's motion, 24 June 1867 (*ibid.*, CLXXXVIII, pp. 354 ff. (Lords)); Maguire's motion, 10 March 1868 (*ibid.*, CXC, pp. 1288 ff.; Gladstone's resolutions, 23 March 1868 (*ibid.*, CXCI, pp. 32 ff.); Gladstone's motion, 30 March 1868 (*ibid.*, pp. 469 ff.); Commons' Committee on the Church, 27 April 1868 (*ibid.*, pp. 1338 ff.); Derby's question on the resolutions, 28 April 1868 (*ibid.*, pp. 1425 ff. (Lords)); Church Bill (Suspensory), Commons' first reading, 14 May 1868 (*ibid.*, CXCII, pp. 314 ff.; second reading, 22 May 1868 (*ibid.*, pp. 720 ff.); Committee, 5 June 1868 (*ibid.*, pp. 1185 ff.); third reading, 17 June 1868 (*ibid.*, pp. 1697 ff.); Lords debate on the Bill, second reading, 25 June 1868 (*ibid.*, pp. 2023 ff., and CXCIII, pp. 2 ff.).

[1] For accounts of the progress of the Church question in Parliament see R. B. O'Brien, *Fifty Years of Concessions to Ireland*, vol. II, Book VIII, esp. p. 233; Justin McCarthy, *Ireland Since the Union*, p. 194; Morley, *Life of Gladstone*, vol. I, Book V, p. 871, and Book VI, p. 891; A. M. Sullivan, *New Ireland*, eighth ed., p. 313; Justin McCarthy, *The Story of Gladstone's Life*, p. 243; J. T. Ball, *The Reformed Church of Ireland*, London, 1886, p. 259; H. Seddall, *The Church of Ireland*, Dublin, 1886, pp. 164 and 196; H. E. Patton, *Fifty Years of Disestablishment*, Dublin, 1922, Part I, p. 3; J. C. MacDonnell, *Life and Correspondence of William Magee*, London, 1896, vol. I, p. 208; R. G. Wilberforce, *Life of Samuel Wilberforce*, London, 1882, vol. III, p. 274; F. Warre Cornish, *The English Church in the Nineteenth Century*, London, 1910, vol. II, p. 288; F. D. How, *William Plunkett, A Memoir*, London, 1900, p. 64; The Liberation Society, *The Case for Disestablishment*, pp. 29, 88, 165 ff., 199, 241 ff., 255, 256; Earl of Selborne, *A Defence of the Church of England against Disestablishment*, new ed., London, 1887, pp. 215-17, 232-41, 244.

[2] See argument to this effect by Dillwyn in 1865, *Hansard*, CLXXVIII, p. 383; and by Gladstone, *ibid.*, p. 424.

[3] 24 June 1867. *Ibid.*, CLXXXVIII, p. 381.   [4] 30 April 1868. *Ibid.*, CXCI, p. 1671.

It is interesting that in December 1868, Cullen, reflecting upon the majorities in Parliament against the Establishment, should echo Cairns's and Disraeli's fears when he wrote 'the downfall of the Church in Ireland will be a great blow to Protestantism in England and elsewhere'.[1] Church property was asserted to be national property, and so freely at the disposal of Parliament,[2] and its defenders argued the rights of the Church as an aggregate of corporations.[3] Catholics were careful to separate the Church from its revenues when discussing reform, so avoiding the charge that they were infringing the oath they had taken under the Catholic Emancipation Act, but at the same time winning the confidence of waverers who would never consent to anything that could look like an attack on Protestantism *per se*.[4] Supporters of the religious *status quo* made out that any subversion of the Irish Church would lead into a general attack on property.[5] This was answered by citing the Act of 1833 as a precedent.[6] And other precedents were to hand – the abolition of the Canadian clergy reserves,[7] and in 1868 itself the ending of State support for the Church in the West Indies.[8] Both sides saw the difficulty there would again be over the question of what to do with the property, and there was talk of the Appropriation Clause[9] – much to the disgust of Chichester Fortescue who summarized the whole discussion of the Church by stating that 'at this time of the day, in the year 1868, Her Majesty's Government were painfully working up to the level of the Appropriation Clause of the year 1834. But it seemed that not even that point had been attained.'[10] Finally, as in the 1830s, the defenders of

[1] Spalding Letters, Cullen to Spalding, 12 December 1868.

[2] For example, The O'Donoghue in 1866, *Hansard*, CLXXXII, p. 1039; J. S. Mill in 1868, *ibid.*, CXC, p. 1517; and Roebuck in 1868, *ibid.*, CXCI, p. 712.

[3] For example, Whiteside in 1865, *ibid.*, CLXXVIII, p. 446; and Vance in 1867, *ibid.*, CLXXXVII, p. 119.

[4] See The O'Donoghue in 1865, *ibid.*, CLXXVIII, p. 393; Gray in 1866, *ibid.*, CLXXXII, p. 979. This was also the line taken by A. T. Lee in his influential pamphlet *Facts respecting the Present State of the Church in Ireland*, London and Dublin, 1865. Like Hume's, this pamphlet provided much of the material used by non-Irish members in Parliamentary debate.

[5] Gathorne Hardy in 1865, *Hansard*, CLXXVIII, p. 400; Lord Redesdale in 1868, *ibid.*, CXCIII, p. 17. This was a charge made by Master FitzGibbon against the Catholic clergy in his *Ireland in 1868*, p. 292.

[6] The O'Donoghue in 1866, *Hansard*, CLXXXII, p. 1038; Gray in 1867, *ibid.*, CLXXXVII, p. 101.

[7] Bernal Osborne in 1868, *ibid.*, CXCI, p. 781.

[8] Gladstone in 1868, *ibid.*, CXCI, p. 930.

[9] Grey in 1865, *ibid.*, CLXXVIII, p. 399. Bishop O'Brien of Ossory in 1867, *ibid.*, CLXXXVIII, p. 392; and Gladstone in 1868, *ibid.*, CXCI, p. 494.

[10] 10 March 1868, Maguire's motion for a Committee on the State of Ireland, *ibid.*, CXC, p. 1606.

the Church fell back on its legal safeguards – the Act of Union in which clause 5 had inseparably united the Churches of England and Ireland;[1] the terms of the Coronation Oath, which bound the sovereign to preserve the United Church inviolate;[2] and lastly that ground which had by now slipped from beneath Gladstone's feet, the maintenance of the Establishment by the State on the criterion of the truth of the doctrine it diffused.[3] Rather absurdly, this last position was accompanied by the suggestion that St Patrick was a Protestant.[4] The defenders further urged the case of the Irish Establishment as an integral part of the ties holding the empire together, and were met by the counter-argument that it was a local as well as an imperial question, and one calling for exceptional legislation.[5]

Although there was a reluctance in Parliament to enter into argument on 'abstract principle' when discussing the Establishment,[6] theories on the relations of Church and State were enunciated there. Gladstone wrote of his position over Dillwyn's motion (1865), 'For, agreeing with Mr Dillwyn as to the merits of the case, I held, as I have ever held, that it is not the duty of a minister to be forward in inscribing on the Journals of Parliament his own abstract views . . . until he conceives the time to be come when he can probably give effect to his opinion.'[7] The frequent references to Gladstone's *State in its Relations with the Church* (1838), and to the subsequent change in his opinions,[8] prompted him to

[1] For example, by Whiteside in 1865, *ibid.*, CLXXVIII, p. 443; Naas in 1867, *ibid.*, CLXXXVII, p. 159; Gathorne Hardy in 1868, *ibid.*, CXCII, p. 734, who said bluntly of the Suspensory Bill, 'This Act repeals the Union'. Gladstone argued that the endowments of the Church were not included in the terms of the Act of Union, see *Chapter of Autobiography*, p. 44.

[2] Gathorne Hardy in 1868, *Hansard*, CXCII, p. 734; Redesdale, in 1868, *ibid.*, CXCIII, p. 20. On 19 April 1869, Lord Redesdale asked a question in the Lords on the Coronation Oath. Since he 'believed the terms of the Oath condemned many proposals of the [Church] Bill', he asked if the Government intended any alteration in the text of the oath. *Ibid.*, CXCV, p. 1059.

[3] Gathorne Hardy in 1865, *ibid.*, CLXXVIII, p. 403; and Sir Michael Hicks-Beach in 1868, *ibid.*, CXCI, p. 1588.

[4] Catholics were quick to deny this: The O'Donoghue in 1866, *ibid.*, CLXXXII, p. 1035; Maguire in 1868, *ibid.*, CXC, p. 1303; and Gregory in 1868, *ibid.*, CXC, p. 1716.

[5] Gray in 1866, *ibid.*, CLXXXII, p. 1007; Fortescue in 1867, *ibid.*, CLXXXVII, pp. 169–70; and Lord Chelmsford in 1868, *ibid.*, CXCIII, p. 166.

[6] Fortescue, for example, in 1866, *ibid.*, CLXXXII, pp. 1016–17; and in 1867, the Duke of Argyll said in the Lords 'It is the misfortune of every discussion on the Church of Ireland . . . that we are plunged at once into a discussion of first principles'. *Ibid.*, CLXXXVIII, p. 402 (24 June 1867).

[7] *Chapter of Autobiography*, p. 44.

[8] By Whiteside, for example, in 1865, *Hansard*, CLXXVIII, p. 443; and by Lefroy in 1867, *ibid.*, CLXXXVII, p. 145. In that year also, Maguire justified Gladstone's changed views, since he was 'wisely following the example of Peel and adapting . . . to the altered circumstances of the time'; *ibid.*, CLXXXVII, p. 176 (7 May 1867).

lay out a theoretical case on his new position, first in the House, and then before the country at the polls – in the *Chapter of Autobiography* (1868).[1] In May 1867, speaking on Gray's motion, he outlined three situations in which Establishment was proper – but none of them applied to Ireland.[2] He had not yet committed himself to Disestablishment, and until March 1868 was merely censuring the Irish Church in such a way as left no doubt that action was needed. But it could have implied internal reform much more logically than actual disruption. Others speculated on the theory of Establishment. In June 1867 Earl Russell, introducing his motion in the Lords for a Royal Commission on the Church, quoted Paley and Warburton, as the prelude to a proposal of concurrent endowment.[3] When closing the debate on Maguire's motion in March 1868, Disraeli stressed the need for a connexion between religion and the State, without which the State became 'a mere affair of police'. That connexion was cemented by endowment.[4] But the theory of religious Establishment did not concern the Irish Catholics – although it deeply concerned the Papacy. The *Dublin Review*, had said in 1862 that it was 'not necessary for us to enter at large into the theory of the connection between the Church and the State'. This was because, citing Paley, Coleridge, and Chalmers, it could find no theory which would support the Irish example.[5] When the Irish bishops decided in 1867 upon their position in relation to the debate on the Irish Church, they also were unconcerned with the theory of the connexion of Church and State; for they totally eschewed any connexion and placed their whole support in the Voluntary system. They should have made it clear that they were acting, like Dupanloup, with reference to their own country only, and were not rejecting the great Catholic principle of the union of Church and State. It was the *Dublin Review* also, with an article by Gainsford in 1865, which, after contemplating the strictures of the Syllabus of Errors against those who believed not in that union, found itself able to absolve the Irish Catholics. 'Those who concur in desiring the abolition of the Church Establishment in Ireland,' wrote Gainsford, 'may still consistently maintain what opinions they please as to Church Establishments in general. The Irish Establishment is not . . . capable of

---

[1] In which he also wrote that it was 'by a practical rather than a theoretic test that our Establishments of religion should be tried', p. 62.

[2] 7 May 1867, *Hansard*, CLXXXVII, p. 129.

[3] 24 June 1867, *ibid.*, CLXXXVIII, pp. 355 ff.

[4] 16 March 1868, *ibid.*, CXC, p. 1781.

[5] *Dublin Review*, May 1862, 'The Established Church in Ireland' (by R. J. Gainsford), esp. pp. 318-9.

being supported by any theory or scheme of Church Establishments which has ever been propounded.'[1]

Disestablishment was one thing; disendowment quite another. The expedient of concurrent endowment, or 'levelling up', was suggested quite widely, both in the Catholic Church and in English opinion. The latter may be treated briefly. It is interesting to find Matthew Arnold among its promoters. He was disgusted by the *way* in which the Liberals intended to pull down the Irish Establishment; seeing, correctly, Dissent behind the principles on which it was to be done:

> It contended for the establishment of its own church-discipline as the only true one; and beaten in this contention, and seeing its rival established, it came down to the more plausible proposal 'to place all good men alike in a condition of religious equality'; and this plan of proceeding, originally taken as a mere second-best, became, by long sticking to it and preaching it up, first fair, then righteous, then the only righteous, then at last necessary to salvation. This is the plan for remedying the Nonconformists' divorce from contact with the national life by divorcing churchmen too from contact with it; that is, as we have familiarly before put it, the tailless foxes are for cutting off tails all round.[2]

Concurrent endowment was a way of preserving that contact with national life, but without the attendant evils of exclusive State interest. It had long been considered applicable to Ireland. Since the 'veto question' early in the century, and even beyond that, there had been plans to grant stipends, glebes and pensions to the Roman Catholic clergy. Pitt had strongly favoured something on these lines, and there had been actual proposals in 1825. Many could be found in the 1860s who still advocated such grants,[3] and they might well have been conceded had the Irish hierarchy intimated its willingness under the Derby–Disraeli Ministry.[4] But the hierarchy was almost united in opposing any State aids for reasons which will be seen later. In February 1866, Lord Lifford had outlined a whole plan of State support for the

---

[1] *Ibid.*, January 1865, 'The Irish Church Establishment' (also by Gainsford), p. 122.

[2] Matthew Arnold, *Culture and Anarchy*, Cambridge, 1960 ed., p. 32.

[3] For example: James Aytoun, *The Irish Difficulty*, pp. 9 and 21-4, and *The Irish Question*, London, 1686, pp. 33-8; *The Government Proceedings Against Fenianism* (anon), London, 1865, p. 13; Colonel Adair, *Ireland and her Servile War*, London and Dublin, 1866, pp. 31-2; J. G. V. Porter, *The State of Ireland in 1866: Its Chief Evils and their best possible Remedies*, Dublin, 1866, p. 18; G. R. Gleig, *Letters on the Irish Question*, London, 1868, p. 8; *Some Thoughts on the Irish Difficulty by an Irish Catholic M.P.*, London, 1868, pp. 17-18; *Ireland Regenerated*, Social Progress Pamphlet no. 1, London, 1868, p. 26; W. Maziere Brady, *Remarks on the Irish Church Temporalities*, Dublin, 1865, p. 23; James Godkin, *Ireland and her Churches*, p. 558.

[4] Cullen wrote to Manning in August 1867: 'The Government appear disposed to give some part of the property to the Catholic bishops and priests.' Quoted by Shane Leslie in *Dublin Review*, October 1919, p. 168.

priests in Ireland to the House of Lords.[1] Mayo favoured endowment, but saw the impossibility of carrying any proposal through a House in which the Government was in a minority. He felt that Ireland was especially suited to endowments.[2] The Voluntary system, he thought, worked unhappily among the Irish Catholics, as it had, so far, precluded men of birth or fortune from becoming engaged in the parochial system. Worse – that system had made the priests reflect the prejudices of the most violent of their congregations. As a system it could exist only by stressing 'points of difference, not of agreement with other churches . . . the country would soon be filled with controversy'. And most unfortunate of all, the Voluntary system 'wants permanence and Universality'.[3] Endowment was therefore essential, and as he was anxious to make concurrent endowment a reality in the university question, so he may well have favoured it for the Church.

Concurrent endowment was often suggested in Parliament as a solution to the Irish difficulty.[4] But it must be noted that it was essentially a compromise arrangement, favoured by those who saw the need for a connexion between Church and State, but uncertain as to the criterion upon which the State should select beliefs for protection and endowment. It was not quite saying that the State had no conscience: it was saying that its conscience was religious, but not discriminating over details. Those who supported concurrent endowment against Voluntaryism usually did it as a last prop for the revenues of the Church. But it would not have worked entirely to that end. As James Byrne showed, the system of general endowment was subject to similar defects as the Voluntary system, for it was necessary to make the endowment of each minister dependent on his having a sufficient congregation, and that made him dependent in some degree on his flock, and it still required that a demand must exist before the State could make it good by endowment of ministry.[5] Thus all the alarms of Chalmers against a free-trade

[1] *Hansard*, CLXXXI, pp. 1063 ff.: Roman Catholic Church (Ireland): Observations; Motion for a Paper (26 February 1866).
[2] Mayo Papers, MS. 11216, 'Notes on Maguire's Motion', 1868.
[3] *Ibid.*, 'Notes on Voluntary System' (no date).
[4] For example, by Pollard Urquhart in 1866, *Hansard*, CLXXXII, p. 1029; Earl Russell in 1867, *ibid.*, CLXXXVII, p. 116 and pp. 354, 362-7; Lord Clanricarde in 1867, *ibid.*, CLXXXVIII, p. 411; Peel Dawson in 1868, *ibid.*, CXCI, p. 607; Peel in 1868, *ibid.*, CLXXXVIII, p. 724; Earl Grey in 1868, *ibid.*, CXCII, p. 2060. It will be seen, in Chap. 8, that the Lords actually carried an amendment to the Church Bill in 1869 which embodied the principle of concurrent endowment. In December 1865, *The Times* came out in favour of giving the priests stipends.
[5] *Essays on the Irish Church*, Essay I, by J. Byrne, 'Establishment and Endowment of Religious Bodies by the State', p. 36. The essays favoured concurrent endowment, however.

in religion were relevant. Earl Grey wrote a pamphlet favouring con-current endowment,[1] and so did Earl Russell[2] – but Russell gave up the notion on the grounds that it was not practical politics after the vote in Parliament on Gladstone's resolutions.[3] Both were widely read, but the latter's, coming from the author of the Durham Letter, served only to increase Irish suspicion that concurrent endowment was a way of under-mining the independence of their Church.[4]

The Maynooth Grant, and the Irish *Regium Donum* to the Presbyter-ians, were examples of concurrent endowment which, because they were such, were to be swept away in the clauses of the Church Act of 1869. Yet both were held on to with tenacity by their recipients up to the last minute. They were always linked in Parliamentary debate,[5] and defen-ders of the Establishment tended to justify their continuance on the ground of expediency.[6] The Maynooth Grant had been a watershed in Gladstone's life. In the *Chapter of Autobiography*, he described it as 'a testing question for the foundations of the Irish Established Church'.[7] But although he had resigned in order to reject the theory of his 1838 book, this did not imply action on the Irish Church at that point. 'It is one thing to lift the anchor,' he wrote, 'it is another to spread the sails.'[8] The Irish Catholics, however, while keen to join the English Dissenters in imposing the Voluntary system of religious endowment in Ireland, were loathe to see it go. Cullen himself felt the end of the Grant would not hurt too much: the faithful might even contribute for Catholic education more readily when it became known that the education of priests was no longer to be supported by the Government.[9] The President of Maynooth was less sure, and aspired in 1868 to persuade Gladstone that the college

[1] Henry, Earl Grey, *Letter to John Bright respecting the Irish Church*, London, 1868 (26 March). See also his remarks favouring general endowment in his *Ireland, the causes of its present condition*, London, 1888, esp. pp. 34, 51-3, 62-73.

[2] John, Earl Russell, *Letter to the Rt. Hon. Chichester Fortescue on the State of Ireland*, London, 1868; and also his *Second Letter to Fortescue*, London, 1868.

[3] As he explained in his *Second Letter*, and in Parliament, *Hansard*, CXCIII, p. 240 (29 June 1868). Russell also gave his reasons for supporting endowment of the priests in his *Recollections and Suggestions, 1813–1873*, London, 1875, pp. 319-21.

[4] Daunt thought that Russell's attack on the existing arrangements of the Church was an empty bid for Irish support – Journal, 29 May 1867. Bishop MacEvilly of Galway said he would never trust any Government which contained the author of the Durham Letter – reported in a letter of W. K. Sullivan to Monsell, 13 April 1866; Monsell Papers, Box 8319.

[5] See, for example, the remarks of Pollard-Urquhart in 1866, *Hansard*, CLXXXII, p. 1029; of Derby in 1867, *ibid.*, CLXXXVIII, p. 417; and of Bright in 1868, *ibid.*, CXC, p. 1657.

[6] As by Hicks-Beach in 1868, *ibid.*, CXCI, p. 1588.

[7] *Chapter of Autobiography*, London, 1868, p. 26.

[8] *Ibid.*, p. 31.   [9] Kirby Papers, Cullen to Kirby, no. 154, 10 May 1868.

was educational, and not ecclesiastical, and so had a claim to be considered separately from the Church Act.[1] He did not succeed. Gladstone heard his arguments readily, but the principle of denominational endowment for educational purposes was as anathema to him as it was for ecclesiastical.

Regium Donum had been refused by its English recipients since 1852, but it continued in Ireland. It built a wall between the Ulster Presbyterians and their co-religionists in England and Scotland. The Ulster support for the principle of endowment, strongly upheld by Dr Henry Cooke, the Moderator,[2] ran strongly counter to English and Scotch Voluntaryism. The latter could not appreciate the difference made to Protestant Dissent by being encompassed about, as in Ireland, by an overwhelming and strong Catholic majority. But they correctly saw in the *Regium Donom* a great stumbling block to the attainment of Voluntaryism in Ireland. In 1860, Baxter, in moving in Parliament for the end of the grant, had spoken of its bad effects on the ministers who received it.[3] The Catholic Daunt described it as 'a bribe to the Presbyterian parsons to inoculate their flocks with a politico-religious fanatical hatred of Ireland'.[4] This was the theme generally taken by the *Nonconformist* and the Liberation Society in their opposition to it. The grant was held to have made the Ulster Presbyterians insensible to their independence and forgetful of their mission. English Dissent – hardly the body to cast the first stone – described the Irish Presbyterians as 'fast sinking into a mere political engine'.[5] Throughout the sixties the Ulstermen were in fact working to secure an increase of the grant – to the disgust of the Liberation Society,[6] who, as a result, when looking

[1] Gladstone Papers, B.M.Add.Ms. 44416, f. 78, Russell to Gladstone, 20 October 1868.

[2] See Dr Cooke's speech at the Hillsborough Protestant Demonstration of 30 October 1867 in J. L. Porter, *Life and Times of Henry Cooke*, London, 1871, p. 488. He said: 'I will tell you why I stand by the Church Establishment of this country, although I do not belong to it. . . . It is because I recognize in her a noble branch of the great Protestant tree planted in Europe by the hands of the Reformers' (p. 489). Dr Porter wrote that the demonstration was 'a Protestant coalition, on a broad and liberal basis, to resist the overthrow of national endowments' (p. 488). Cooke had a great following among Churchmen as well as Presbyterians. His life, wrote Cairns in 1871, 'was a large portion of the religious and public history of Ireland for the last half-century'. (Quoted in Porter's preface, p.v.)

[3] *Hansard*, CLVIII, p. 1618 (22 May 1860).

[4] Daunt, Journal, 23 November 1866.

[5] *Nonconformist*, 8 October 1862, 'A Regium Donum Eruption' – which linked the Orange rioting in Belfast with the low ethical qualities associated with those in receipt of State endowment.

[6] See the remarks made at their annual meeting in London on the 5 May 1864 in *Nonconformist*, 11 May 1864.

for an Irish ally to support them over Irish Disestablishment, were forced to unite with the Catholics instead. They were annoyed also because the receipt of the *Regium Donum* made it impossible for the Ulster Presbyterians to join the general movement of Dissent against the Maynooth Grant. They showed themselves extraordinarily flexible when they themselves dropped agitation against Maynooth in order to cement the alliance with the Irish Catholics.[1] In 1864, and again in 1865 the Irish Presbyterians asked for more.[2] By 1868, they had found a sympathetic Minister in Mayo.[3] In February of that year Dr Robert Montgomery, Moderator of the Irish General Assembly, had written to him about an increase of *Regium Donum*, especially as Derby had promised to look into the matter.[4] Mayo, whilst replying sympathetically, added that it was 'not a very fortunate moment to bring the question of any increase of religious endowment before the House of Commons'.[5] But they got up a deputation on 15 May.[6] The Government could not act because of the renewed difficulty of the endowment problem in Parliament with Gladstone's resolutions; but the question having exploded anyway, Mayo felt it right to defend the Presbyterians' request publicly, although he was careful to point out that it could not in fact be increased, 'because of the feeling of the country'.[7] This was the last official defence of the grant: it was abolished in 1869.

Two prominent Irish Catholics came forward with proposals for concurrent endowment, and their arguments and the refutations of them largely coloured the Irish Catholic discussion of the Church question up to 1868. They were Aubrey de Vere, and Bishop Moriarty of Kerry.

De Vere belonged to that group of Limerick converts which also included Dunraven and Monsell and who were all personally acquainted with Newman. Educated at Trinity College, and nurtured in Anglican notions of Church property, his terms of reference were almost wholly English. His views, even when – it might be said especially when – a

---

[1] See chap. 4. It could also be pointed out that by accepting the Maynooth Grant the Catholics were excluded from agitating against the *Regium Donum* – this point was made by R. H. Heron, *The Irish Difficulty*, p. 23.

[2] *The Times*, 6 February 1865. They sought to raise it to £100 p.a. for every congregation in excess of twelve families who could raise £35 p.a. on their own.

[3] W. W. Hunter, *A Life of the Earl of Mayo*, vol. I, p. 93.

[4] Mayo Papers, MS. 11216, Montgomery to Mayo, 25 February 1868. He wrote in London, where he was staying with a deputation.

[5] *Ibid.*, MS. 11216, Mayo to Montgomery, 25 February 1868.

[6] Bright rebuked 'their miserable subservience to the Tory and Church Party', *The Diaries of John Bright*, ed. R. A. J. Walling, London, 1930, p. 325.

[7] *Hansard*, CXCII, p. 807 (22 May 1868).

Catholic, after 1851, were strangely Tory and 'High Church'. He was strongly influenced by Sir Henry Taylor, F. D. Maurice; and especially by S. T. Coleridge – all of whom were family friends,[1] Wilfrid Ward wrote of him:

> From Coleridge he learnt to view religion, and especially Christianity, as the expression of the Universal mind of regenerate man – as something resting on wider and deeper experiences than belong to the life of one individual – and as in some inadequate manner the partial reflection of the infinite mind of God. Sectarianism, the outcome of self-confident private judgement, the attempt of the average individual man to construct a religion by means of his own defective dialectic, appeared to him in the highest degree unphilosophical.[2]

It was hardly surprising, therefore, that he should apply his Coleridgianism to his own Irish Catholic Church in the 1860s, and come up with a solution depending on endowment and opposed to any union between Catholics and sectarians. De Vere is now remembered – where he is remembered at all – for his poetry, but criticism of his pamphlets on endowment, like that of O'Neill Daunt who said he 'unluckily imports poetry into his politics',[3] was unfair in the sense in which it was meant. It is true that his thought and poetry were a reflection of that High Church–Lakeland atmosphere captured also in Faber, but his discussion of the Irish endowment problem was hardly 'poetical'. In his *Recollections*, de Vere referred to the dependence of his endowment theories on those of Coleridge: 'I quoted largely from what Coleridge says in his noble book "Church and State", on that sacred reserve or "nationalty" which the higher races never allowed to be wholly merged in individual properties.'[4] This was as easily applicable to Ireland as it was to England, except that the Catholic majority in Ireland made it imperative for the 'nationalty' of land set aside for the maintenance of the ministers of religion to be divided between the competing heirs of the early Church there. Coleridge had himself allowed his passion for 'nationalism' in religion, as de Vere explained to Earl Grey, and his aversion to the doctrine of 'double-allegiance', 'to make him refuse Catholic Emancipation to the Irish Catholics – a measure which of course conferred upon them great power in the State'.[5]

The High Church bent of his opinions is seen in his belief that the Church of England had somehow retained, suspended within its formularies, large deposits of Catholic doctrine which the Reformers

---

[1] Wilfrid Ward, *Aubrey de Vere, A Memoir*, London, 1904, chap. 2.
[2] *Ibid.*, p. 22.   [3] Daunt, Journal, 14 February 1867.
[4] *Recollections of Aubrey de Vere*, second ed., London, 1897, p. 336.
[5] Grey Papers, de Vere to Grey, 6 April 1868. He made the same point in his *Church Property and Secularisation*; reprinted in his *Essays*, London, 1889, p. 205.

had sought to eschew. This brought him close in intellectual sympathy to the early Tractarians, and this it was which led him to suppose that the idea he found in Hooker, that the State was not the originator, but the protector of Church property, was such a Catholic preservation.[1] His Tory–Coleridgianism expressed itself most cogently in his view of the purpose of ecclesiastical property:

> It is to provide for a nation's soul. It assumes that the persons composing a nation have souls, and that the training of souls costs money. Coleridge in his *Church and State* illustrates this subject with great felicity. . . . What is it that Ireland has lost by the alienation of the National Reserve? Citizenship and the sense of Citizenship. That Reserve, by some called 'the nationalty', becomes the primary test of what is, or is not, included in the nation. . . . The 'Voluntary System', when imposed upon a people by force, informs that people that that nation has no part in it, nor it in the nation. . . . But the National Reserve was created for the people, and especially for the poor: and it belongs to the clergy, accidentally and mediately, as they are the spiritual representatives of the people no less than their pastors. Constitutionally, they hold that Reserve, neither as a thing intrinsically their own, nor yet as the gift of the State which protects their rights, but as spiritual trustees for that nation which exists indivisibly in the twofold relations of Church and State. . . . Let us apply this to Ireland.[2]

De Vere gave his theories to the Catholic world in several pamphlets. The first was written in 1863 and republished in 1867, *The Church Establishment in Ireland illustrated exclusively by Protestant Authorities*. In 1866 came his *Church Settlement of Ireland, or Hibernia Pacanda*, followed in the next year by *Ireland's Church Property, and the Right Use of it*. And at the same time he published his *Church Property and Secularisation*. But it was in a letter to *The Times* in January 1866, on the subject of Fenianism, that de Vere first caught public attention for his concurrent endowment proposals. He agreed that religious equality was an essential part of the solution to the sort of Irish problems symptomized by Fenianism, but added that 'there is such a thing as levelling *up* as well as levelling *down*'. He quoted the solution suggested by Burke in 1795 to offset Jacobinism in Ireland – endowment of the Roman

[1] 'Church Property and Secularisation', in *Essays, Literary and Ethical*, p. 226.

[2] De Vere, *Hibernia Pacanda*, London, 1866, pp. 39–41. He also explained Coleridge's theory in *Church Property and Secularisation, Essays*, pp. 203 ff. Coleridge is there described as 'one of the greatest modern philosophers'. It is interesting that the other writer on the Irish question in the 1860s who was also influenced by Coleridge, came to the opposite conclusion – John Stuart Mill. The difference between the two men on this point illustrates a great nineteenth-century ideological conflict in microcosm. De Vere considered *Church Property and Secularisation* his most important tract, since it dealt with actual suggestions being made along the lines of secularization. When he re-published it in his *Essays* in 1889, it was with the added note 'still applicable to England' (p. 197). In the *Recollections*, he said that English endowments were endangered by the unhappy settlement in Ireland (p. 336).

Catholic priests. The modern Jacobins, he argued, were the Fenians.[1] It was only a hint, but it was received with alarm by the English Dissenters[2] and by Archbishop Leahy.[3] The *Dublin Review* also came out against the suggestion: English public opinion would never allow Irish Church property to be handed over to the Papists, and the Irish clergy themselves had shown no signs of wanting it.[4] De Vere was evidently surprised by the cold reception, and wrote to his friend Moriarty stressing that 'we must have the subject at our fingers' ends' to argue it effectively, and requesting statistics from Kerry on the adverse working of the Voluntary system there. He also expressed himself hurt that many had taken his hint about levelling up to mean State pensions for the clergy. This was not his plan. Pensions could never be anything but 'humiliation and a snare'. What he sought was the endowment of the Catholic Church with 'a fair and equal proportion of the Church property', and the rejection of any schemes which might secularize that property, 'especially through Catholic efforts'.[5] He was in too deeply to turn back, so he set about explaining his premises. Thus he wrote his *Hibernia Pacanda* in 1866.[6]

In March he opened communications with Earl Grey, whom he believed to be sympathetic to the idea of concurrent endowment,[7] and who in the previous month had spoken encouragingly during the Parliamentary debate on Lifford's observations on endowment of the Catholic clergy.[8] But the Church question had still not become crucial, and de Vere spent much of the rest of the year preparing his other pamphlets. In December 1866 Sir John Gray became alarmed at the prospect of de Vere's plans being introduced into the National Association, so ruining its working agreement with the English Voluntaries.[9] No doubt Gray expressed his apprehensions to Cullen, who,

---

[1] *The Times*, 19 January 1866. Its own comment on the letter was that 'the occasion is peculiarly favourable for making provision at the expense of the State for the Roman Catholic priesthood of Ireland'.

[2] *Nonconformist*, 24 January 1866, 'Proposed payment of the Irish Priesthood'.

[3] See his letter to the National Association condemning de Vere's theories, *The Times*, 25 January 1866.

[4] *Dublin Review*, April 1866, p. 493. But de Vere's letter in *The Times* is described as 'remarkably able', and is admitted to have 'attracted much attention'.

[5] Monsell Papers, Box 8319, de Vere to Moriarty, 28 January 1866.

[6] *Hibernia Pacanda*, London, 1866.

[7] Grey Papers, de Vere to Grey, 4 and 18 March 1868.

[8] 28 February 1866; *Hansard*, CLXXXI, p. 1082. But he had warned also that nothing approximating to the old Appropriation Clause could have his approval. Ward said that Grey prepared a plan of concurrent endowment on the lines suggested by de Vere, but did not follow it up as Russell rejected it. *Memoir*, p. 285.

[9] Daunt, Journal, 28 December 1866.

early in the new year, condemned de Vere's pamphlet in a letter to Kirby in Rome. He saw clearly that a fight over the application of the Church revenues was just what the Protestants were hoping would frustrate the attempts to disendow the Church, and depicted de Vere's plan as inaugurating such a conflict. He saw also that de Vere's two special claims for the Protestants – that they had a right to the ecclesiastical property by prescription and that their married clergy entitled them to special financial consideration – would leave little for the Catholics anyway.[1] In January, the National Association declared against concurrent endowment.[2] Gray continued to see the inherent threat to Catholic unity on the Church question in de Vere's ideas, however, and in July urged Cullen with the dangers which by then were reinforced with the appearance of a comparable plan by Moriarty.[3]

De Vere's *Church Property and Secularisation* also appeared in 1867. It was a complete statement of his plan. He now applied his Coleridgian theory so that,

> In dealing with it in Ireland it means that the Religious Equality should be reached, not by the secularization of her Church property, but by a just division of it, so far as it still remains, between the Catholics and Protestants; the Catholic portion being administered for religious purposes by a Catholic Board, and the Protestant portion by a Protestant Board.[4]

In a letter to Moriarty of March 1868, he elaborated the objects of the two Boards. They were to be left free to choose among the several purposes to which their respective shares of Church property should be applied: 'If the Bishops chose at a future time to include support of the clergy among such purposes, they would only have to apply for a new Act of Parliament extending the power of the Boards'.[5] He gave a warning about the implications of another course: 'The secularization of Ireland's Church property may sentence all property in both countries.'[6] He was also able to claim that his plan was 'the Catholic Course' – with justice – and Moriarty was to say the same. It was the Irish bishops who were departing from Catholic teaching by insisting on secularization. In his pamphlet, de Vere further argued against the alliance with English Dissent, for 'these allies will give no aid to Irish Catholics unless they adopt the principles of the English Sectaries'.[7] As

---

1 Kirby Papers, Cullen to Kirby, no. 3, 2 January 1867.
2 Daunt, Journal, 8 January 1867.
3 Cullen Papers, Gray to Cullen, 22 July 1867.   4 *Op. cit., Essays*, p. 197.
5 Monsell Papers, Box 8319, de Vere to Moriarty, 15 March 1868.
6 *Op. cit., Essays*, p. 199.
7 *Ibid.*, p. 229. In a letter to Earl Grey he developed his opposition to such an alliance, 'the most unnatural and mischievous of alliances', and pointed out that a

if in anticipation of Gladstone's *Chapter of Autobiography*, he turned also to deal with the problem of State conscience and division of endowments:

It is because it preserves a conscience, even when it has lost unity of faith, that it may and must do this. A State knows just as much about Revealed Truth as the Nation which it impersonates knows, and no more. If it confesses a unity of Faith which is desirable, but non-existent, it confesses a falsehood. If it confesses that a particular Nation, even though it has lost unity of Faith, still retains Christianity, and honours Religion according to its lights, it confesses the truth. If it confesses that to restore, as far as is possible, what was unjustly taken away is a Christian act, this is not to be branded as State Indifferentism. It is State Piety.[1]

The *Dublin Review* approved of the pamphlet, and hoped that the Irish bishops would give the suggested course regarding Church property 'their definite sanction'. The plan, it pointed out, was capable of being considered a restitution rather than an endowment, and this had never received their formal consideration. The time had not yet arrived when such a plan could be given practical effect, but it was rapidly coming.[2] Naas referred to de Vere's plan in his speech on Sir John Gray's motion in the Commons in May, but felt it involved great difficulties.[3] Russell, however, spoke favourably of it in the Lords in June.[4] De Vere was hopeful, and at the beginning of the very week in which the Irish bishops met and declared in favour of the Voluntary system, he wrote to Earl Grey expressing his belief that if a favourable opportunity should present itself for a 'Just Distribution', a much greater number of Catholics both clerical and lay would pronounce for it than anyone would at that moment be inclined to expect. Therefore Parliament should be induced to make such a settlement 'whether Ireland seeks it or denounces it'. In time the Catholics would avail themselves of the benefits opened up in that way.[5] He was not daunted by the Episcopal Declaration of 8 October 1867 condemning endowment. As he explained to Moriarty, with almost the quibble of a Tract Ninety, the bishops' resolution left the question of 'Distribution' untouched. They had affirmed that no endowment was to be given *to the*

voluntaryists' win in Ireland would provide a ready precedent for England. Grey Papers, de Vere to Grey, 6 February 1867.
[1] De Vere, *op. cit., Essays*, p. 207.
[2] *Dublin Review*, October 1867, 'An Irish Session', p. 516.
[3] *Hansard*, CLXXXVII, p. 163.
[4] *Ibid.*, CLXXXVIII, p. 365. This contrasts with Ward's statement that in 1866 Grey's plan of concurrent endowment had been quashed by Russell's opposition. *Memoir*, p. 285.
[5] Grey Papers, de Vere to Grey, 2 October 1867.

clergy in pensions, property or stipends, and that Church property should be given to benefit the poor. But clerical endowment had no necessary connexion with 'Distribution', and it was demonstrable that the poor would benefit immensely by the application of Church property to purposes both religious *and* charitable (such as denominational charity institutions, and the building of Churches); and equally clear that in a long view, the poor could not benefit from a secular application of the property.[1] It is evident that he had mistaken the whole spirit of the resolutions.[2]

As the Church question moved into its first critical phase, in Parliament in March 1868, de Vere was active in representing his case. He tried to get up petitions in each parish, demanding religious equality, but leaving the method of attaining it an open question, just – as he explained to Moriarty – as the Lay Declaration in favour of Disestablishment got up by the Earl of Fingall and other Catholic noblemen left it an open question.[3] Moriarty circulated such a petition in Kerry, and the Bishop of Limerick (Butler) did the same for one actually drafted by de Vere. Monsell advised in this.[4] He had decided against pressing the 'Distribution' case by public meetings, as they would become battle-grounds for the secularizing opposition, as well as being neutralized by Fenian speeches. He even sent one of his pamphlets to Mgr Moran, one of Cullen's secretaries, 'rather under the impression that he would regret my having renewed the controversy'. Moriarty he urged to use his political influence with Liberal Statesmen.[5] But Gladstone was not to follow his 'Distribution' plan, and in the full horror of realization that Gladstone intended to secularize Church property, de Vere was even driven at this time to consult with his opponent O'Neill Daunt.[6]

Aubrey de Vere had been able to claim that his plan was 'the Catholic course',[7] and that it was the Catholic bishops who departed from the teaching of their Church by insisting on disendowment and secularization. Only one of their number dissented – Moriarty.[8] Before the

[1] Monsell Papers, de Vere to Moriarty, 4 March 1868.

[2] In a letter to Moriarty immediately after their appearance (Monsell Papers, Box 8319, 12 October 1867), he had described them as 'warlike', but held them to be 'sufficiently *general*' to allow of such an interpretation as that put on them in his letter of 4 March 1868.

[3] Monsell Papers, Box 8319, de Vere to Moriarty, 4 March 1868. The Declaration is in *Parliamentary Papers*, 1867–8, LIII, 75.

[4] Monsell Papers, Box 8319, de Vere to Moriarty, 4 March 1868.   [5] *Ibid.*

[6] Daunt said of this, 'we correspond in as friendly terms now as if we had never been opposed to each other'. Journal, 30 March 1868.

[7] De Vere, *op. cit., Essays*, p. 200.

[8] Butler, Bishop of Limerick, also sympathized with the position held by de Vere and Moriarty, but he does not seem to have articulated his feelings.

Maynooth Commission in 1855 when questioned on the canons of the Council of Trent, he had upheld the proper and Catholic position of Churches endowed by the State, and a harmony of civil and canon law, although admitting that it 'does not exist with us'.[1] Over education, he had shown himself out of step in the sixties, and he had gone further than Cullen would allow in condemning the Fenians: now he was to support concurrent endowment on the Church question. For the feast of St Patrick (17 March) 1867, he wrote his *Letter on the Disendowment of the Established Church*, which was addressed to the clergy of the diocese of Kerry. It is a full account of the difficulties inherent in the Church question for Catholics, and for that, and because it received such wide publicity, it deserves close examination.[2]

Moriarty began by assuring the clergy that, although he was convinced of the soundness of the views he was to propose, he could not claim to speak with authority; 'we throw them out more for the purpose of discussion and eliciting your opinions, whether of adhesion or dissent'.[3] He then at once considered difficulties and objections which might be raised against Irish disendowment. First of these was whether Parliament had the moral right to deprive an individual or a corporate body of property long possessed. He upheld the sacredness of both forms of property; but all Catholics and many Protestants could answer that the Irish Establishment was not a rightful owner, that no prescription or statute could 'heal a title notoriously invalid from the first, and maintained only by the fraud and violence which marked its origin'.[4] The State, however, would not act on that principle. The measure would in fact be carried 'by the aid of those who hold that all endowment is wrong', that the State has an inherent right to control the Church, to appropriate her possessions, and that the Church has 'no rights but what the state chooses to allow'. These principles were false, and contrary to Catholic teaching. They were those used recently in Italy to despoil the Church.[5] He then took another line. If Catholics urged the disendowment of the State Church, may they not 'at no very distant time' become themselves the objects of a spoliation based on the precedent? Catholic charity was creating Catholic endowment in Ireland. Why should not the State take it away, as European governments had done to Church property there?[6] But they should really ask, what would be the effect on them spiritually of the disendowment of the Protestant Church? If the clergy of that Church were thrown on to the

---

[1] Harrowby Commission, *Parliamentary Papers*, 1855, XXII, 124 (13 October 1853).
[2] David Moriarty, *A Letter on the Disendowment of the Established Church*. As this is now rather difficult to find (there is a copy in the Mayo Papers), it is here summarized.
[3] *Ibid.*, p. 7.   [4] *Ibid.*, p. 8.   [5] *Ibid.*   [6] *Ibid.*, p. 9.

Voluntary system they would begin to make incursions into the Catholic fold; 'so long as the Protestant ascendancy is maintained, so long will Ireland remain steadfast in her allegiance to the true Church'. Where proselytism of Catholics had occurred, it had always been by missioners sent out by some voluntary society; but if disendowed, the Protestant clergy, dependent on their flocks for their incomes, would strive to enlarge them, and convert as many as possible.[1] It had also been said that the Establishment had preserved the Protestants from utter infidelity, and this helped Catholics indirectly, since it prevented the State attacking religion generally in the Voltairian manner.[2] Were these advantages to be thrown aside 'at the very time danger seemed imminent again?'[3]

Religious equality, he emphasized, must be conceded, whatever the difficulties, and he referred to Aubrey de Vere's *Church Establishment in Ireland* to prove the point. For the Establishment was 'an injustice unparalleled in the annals of tyranny'.[4] Some thought they could palliate the wrong by saying that the vast majority of landlords who paid tithe-rent-charge were Protestants anyway, and so that was no Catholic grievance. Yet it was again de Vere, in his *Hibernia Pacanda*, who exposed this sophism. Tithe-rent-charge was a tax on land, and the tenant paid it indirectly as part of his rent. Most of the Irish tenants were Catholic, and so *did* bear the burden of supporting the Establishment. They would have, indeed, to continue paying even if the Church should be disendowed, but the purpose to which the money would be applied would be different.[5] The existence of the Establishment also explained Irish disaffection, for it appeared as a clear proof of the unjust ascendancy of a conquering nation to those who would wish (foolishly) to sever ties with the British Constitution.[6] If disaffection were only a political evil, the clergy could have nothing to say about it, but 'it is a great moral evil'. It created a most dangerous state of conscience, for 'the law of God, enjoining obedience and allegiance to our civil rulers, is one of the clearest mandates of the Gospel'.[7] Only the removal of the Church ascendancy could cure disaffection and so allow men to obey the ordained powers without difficulty: 'we demand only the common rights of British subjects, of which the first is, that all shall be equal before the law'.[8] It should also be noticed that the Catholic Church was the rightful owner of all ecclesiastical property in Ireland,

---

[1] *Ibid.*, p. 12.   [2] *Ibid.*, p. 15.
[3] *Ibid.*, p. 16 – a reference to the forces gathering to overthrow the Papacy in Italy, and to Italian Liberalism, Mazzinianism and anti-Catholicism.
[4] *Ibid.*, p. 17.   [5] *Ibid.*, p. 19.   [6] *Ibid.*, p. 22.   [7] *Ibid.*, p. 23.
[8] *Ibid.*, p. 25.

with the exception only of that which the Protestants may have acquired since the Reformation. No concordat had ceded the Church property to the Crown, and Catholics acknowledged no prescription in this case. Further, the Catholic bishops had no right to alienate it, unless with the sanction of the Pope, for they were only possessors of it for the time being, with the right of usufruct. If they were to consult only political expediency they might well recommend an alienation of the property, and allow the State to withdraw all the religious endowments which the nation originally bestowed.[1]

Such a course, Moriarty continued, was one sure way of securing religious equality, but it seemed to him still that it would 'furnish a precedent and a sanction for unjust and sacrilegious spoliation'. Another course was open, 'more conformable to justice'. As the ecclesiastical revenues were originally set apart to supply the wants of the nation, and as it was unjust for them to be handed over to only a small section of it, the State should 'apply the ecclesiastical revenues to the service of all the churches that minister to the Irish people, and in the proportion in which the Irish people accept their ministration'.[2] This would not be too difficult to effect:

> The most obvious application of this principle would be realized if the whole Church income were paid to the imperial treasury, and thence disbursed to the different bodies requiring church ministers or ministrations, and in proportion to their numerical strength, as ascertained by the decennial census.[3]

But difficulty would be encountered in persuading the Catholic body to accept a share of the Church revenue. The clergy must continue to receive their personal support by the voluntary offerings of their flocks:

> We dare not condemn endowments. If we did the Church would condemn us. But we believe that where the voluntary system can be established, the Church will be more flourishing.[4]

Personal support of the clergy was not the whole cost of a national Church, however, and other expenses weighed heavily upon the poor people of Ireland. Why should not they use these other funds to alleviate the burden? The laity would welcome grants to help the building of churches or the maintenance of diocesan schools 'from the funds which our fore-fathers set apart for these purposes'.[5] They would then be exempted from a double taxation: one to maintain the Protestants and

---

[1] David Moriarty, *A Letter on the Disendowment of the Established Church*, p. 26. It is interesting to notice how some of de Vere's Coleridgianism has rubbed off on Moriarty.

[2] *Ibid.*, p. 27.   [3] *Ibid.*, p. 28.   [4] *Ibid.*   [5] *Ibid.*, p. 31.

one for their own Church. At this point he again referred to the pamphlets of Aubrey de Vere, identifying himself with their arguments,[1] and recommending them to the attention of statesmen. He drew to a close by reminding his readers of the objections which were his starting-point – objections no longer valid when not disendowment, but concurrent endowment, was suggested. The Protestant Church would continue to save the generality from infidelity: further, it might even lead men to Catholicity, for, in a pointed reference to the Oxford Movement, he adverted to those in that Church who, having no intercourse with Catholics, had yet by study and prayer attained the full measure of Catholic truth.[2] And although it was true that Ireland had little share in this movement, there were signs that it might follow the current renewal of spirituality in the Irish Protestants.[3]

The *Letter* was quite moderately received by Sir John Gray, which was surprising in view of his fears about de Vere's pamphlets and his later doctrinaire line on the Voluntary System in its fullness. Writing to Cullen, he neither approved nor disapproved it, but pointed to the difficulty of giving it practical effect – for political reasons. The Radicals in Parliament would never accept its principle, and he doubted if the Tories would consent to a plan which gave only a fractional part of the ecclesiastical revenues to their friends. Only the Whigs would be likely to entertain it, and they were Ireland's worst enemies.[4] *The Times* rather ignored the property proposals in the *Letter*, and confined its comment to Moriarty's exposure of the Establishment as the major cause of popular discontent. Its Irish correspondent regarded this as a correct view, and applauded the bishop, who, as he remarked, was already the favourite of the Irish conservatives on account of his frequent denouncing of the Fenians.[5] Moriarty himself sent a copy of the *Letter* to Earl Grey, evidently following de Vere's discovery that he

[1] *Ibid.*, p. 33.

[2] *Ibid.*, p. 37. He referred (p. 38) explicitly to 'Newman, Wilberforce, Faber, Ward, Manning and the host of learned ecclesiastics and laymen who followed these great leaders'.

[3] *Ibid.*, pp. 38-9. But in 1852 Archbishop Whately, who described 'Puseyism' as 'religion by proxy' had told Nassau Senior that it was not so prevalent in Ireland as in England: 'I was told that we should escape it; that, as we have the real thing, we should not adopt the copy; but I was sure that it would come. Ireland catches every disease after it has passed over England. Cholera came to us after you had had it – so did the potato-rot – so did Puseyism.' Nassau Senior, *Journals, Conversations and Essays relating to Ireland*, London, 1868, vol. II, p. 57.

[4] Cullen Papers, Gray to Cullen, 21 March 1867.

[5] *The Times*, 23 March 1867. Moriarty's *Letter* was also quoted in Parliament to show both that the Church was a real grievance in Ireland, and that endowment should go to Catholics. See, for example, this put by Attorney-General Warren in 1868, *Hansard*, CXCII, p. 776 (22 May).

was a man open to the sort of course they were both intent upon.[1] Like Sir John Gray, O'Neill Daunt was uncertain: he described Moriarty's work as 'a production of which it is hard to say whether it will do more harm or good'.[2] Henry Wilberforce wrote to express his delight. The *Letter* would make the English press give up its stock observation on the Irish Establishment – that 'it is felt to be a grievance by the English liberals but not by the Irish Catholics'. He believed that it would prove to be the 'beginning of the end' for the Irish Church. He expressed some doubt as to whether it had really done so much against infidelity as Moriarty had claimed, but he supposed that as Newman thought the same, he must be wrong himself.[3] Cullen did not denounce the *Letter*, but he ignored the principles and could see no point in it; sending a copy to Kirby, he added

> His plan, he says, has won for him the approbation of several great Statesmen. I am persuaded that the Parliament will never give back the old property of the Church to Catholics – nor will it give us a fair share. The only chance is to take away all from the parsons, and apply it to the public purposes. Protestants may do that, but they will never give anything worth taking to Catholics.[4]

Moriarty himself explained to Kirby that his *Letter* was in a way a reply to the bishops who had communicated to the National Association recommending secularization without any reference to the Holy See.[5]

He also expressed to Kirby his anxiety that his opinions might be misrepresented, and to safeguard his position he wrote an open letter to his clergy, published in the press, removing misconceptions which may have occurred over his pamphlet. He had been criticized for passing too lightly over the land question, and so devoted his space to showing the difficulties of legislating on that topic.[6] By July, Gray's attitude had hardened more. 'Dr Moriarty's Pastoral has given a force to de Vere's policy that it will be difficult to overcome', he wrote to Cullen from Westminster, and he was sure that it had left on Gladstone's mind an impression that the opponents of disendowment were now stronger, consisting in '1. Church of Ireland; 2. Presbyterians; 3. a respectable minority of Irish Catholics; and 4. the Anglicans of England.'[7] Cullen also came to see the danger to Catholic unity from Moriarty, who had

---

[1] Grey Papers, Moriarty to Grey, 23 March 1867.
[2] Daunt, Journal, 27 March 1867.
[3] Monsell Papers, Box 8319, H. W. Wilberforce to Moriarty, 1 April 1867.
[4] Kirby Papers, Cullen to Kirby, no. 128, 5 April 1867.
[5] *Ibid.*, Moriarty to Kirby, no. 131, 8 April 1867.
[6] *The Times*, 6 April 1867 – prints Moriarty's explanatory letter. In his *Letter on Disendowment*, he had said of the land question, 'we must confess ourselves incapable of offering any sure advice' (p. 6).
[7] Cullen Papers, Gray to Cullen, 22 July 1867.

now shown himself diverging from the other prelates on education as well as the Church, and he feared that Moriarty would be 'put forward by the High Catholics' to represent their views to the Government. He felt a bishops' meeting was needed to enable them to declare their views:[1] thus was planned the declaration against endowment of October 1867.

Moriarty himself saw the difficulty of his position, and intimated to de Vere, after the October resolutions, that it would be 'better not to raise questions now, but to watch the course things take'.[2] And this is what he seems to have done. Yet when the Church question was blown into life over Gladstone's resolutions in 1868, he could not resist representing his case to leading men of affairs. His views had already been canvassed in Parliament, and were widely respected.[3] To Monsell he wrote a long letter on the Church and the condition of Ireland, which, it has been suggested, may well have influenced Gladstone's decision to end the Mayo Charter scheme by the introduction of his resolutions.[4] In it he pleaded the case of religious equality as a necessary element in eradicating Irish disaffection, and ranged over the causes of it. Although the bishops wished the ecclesiastical property to be 'devoted to its secondary purpose of charity', he would himself 'include religion but not the support of the clergy'. He advised Monsell,

You must settle this question with the liberals. If you cannot agree upon the application of the Funds, then content yourself for the present with *disestablishing* the Protestant Church. Repeal that part of the Act of Union. Let the tithe-rent-charge be collected by the government which has a machinery ready made in the Income tax officials, and let the parsons be paid as they are now out of the Treasury until you settle the further question, What will you do with it?[5]

To Earl Grey he was encouraged to write during the crisis over the resolutions in Parliament, because of the publication of Grey's *Letter to*

[1] Kirby Papers, Cullen to Kirby, no. 294, 18 August 1867.

[2] Monsell Papers, Box 8319, Moriarty to de Vere, 12 October 1867.

[3] He was quoted, for example, by Naas in 1867, *Hansard*, CLXXXVII, p. 160; by Fortescue, *ibid.*, p. 169; by Russell, *ibid.*, CLXXXVIII, p. 359; by Cairns, *ibid.*, p. 372; and by Argyll, *ibid.*, p. 403.

[4] See chap. 6, p. 259.

[5] Gladstone Papers, B.M.Add.MS. 44152, f. 98, Moriarty to Monsell, 2 March 1868. This letter is reprinted in *Irish Historical Studies*, 1956-7, Select Document XVIII, p. 193, with notes by J. H. Whyte. Where, on p. 199, Whyte has square-bracketed a word as illegible in the last paragraph of the letter, it is in fact a Greek word – παιϛησια – somewhat corrupt Greek it is true, and Moriarty probably meant παιδεία (education). His meaning was that Parliament might well indulge itself in the education question (the Charter plan), but that a more pressing case should be urged upon them – the Church question. 'Prudence imposes on us a severe *reticentia*', he added.

John Bright (26 March 1868), which had supported the idea of concurrent endowment.[1]

The plan your Lordship proposes for the redistribution of the Ecclesiastical Revenues of this country, [he wrote], is substantially the same as what I suggested in a letter to my clergy last year, and what Mr Aubrey de Vere has been advocating with such power of argument and eloquence. I think that in the division he and I would be more liberal to the Protestant clergy than your Lordship or Earl Russell. The census may be the basis of redistribution, but it could not be the exact rule. No minority must get more than its numbers entitle it to. The person who has to minister to a hundred requires as large a stipend as the priest who ministers to ten thousand. He requires a larger stipend, for voluntary offerings will increase the stipend of him who ministers to a large congregation. We must also take into account that the parson is a married man.

He admitted that the bishops' resolutions of October 1867 were a difficulty, but since the respect for vested interests would prevent the redistribution of the funds of the Establishment for many years, 'we may leave the question to our successors', who would not, perhaps, be liable to political alliances like that between the bishops and the English Dissenters which would cause them to endorse secularization. Disestablishment was essential at once, to secure the legal equality of all Churches, but the revenues could be left in the custody of Parliament.[2]

Moriarty wrote to Gladstone himself on 22 April 1868, explaining that his opinions were shared by many in Ireland.[3] He asked Gladstone to look at the two proposals for dealing with the vested interests of the Protestant Church. It is evident that he had come, at that late hour, to see the right mode of handling them as the only hope for the success of any part of his own or de Vere's 'Distribution' plans. The two proposals were these. First Grey's, which would pay off vested interests from the imperial treasury or consolidated fund 'and leaving the Church property free and unencumbered for present application to the uses he proposes'. Second was Gladstone's own plan, which seemed to Moriarty to be one for selling out the property and giving compensation to the existing incumbents in ready cash. He feared that Grey's proposal was too generous for Parliamentary acceptance, and 'has also the inconvenience of prematurely settling another question which is better deferred to another time'. But Gladstone's supposed an unnecessary waste: far better to allow commissioners to take up the Church property and accumulate a fund to pay out vested interests, and to use the balance for distribution among the denominations for 'works of religion'; for

---

[1] Grey Papers, Moriarty to Grey, 2 April 1868.   [2] *Ibid.*

[3] Gladstone Papers, B.M.Add.MS. 44414, f. 280, Moriarty to Gladstone, 22 April 1868.

Churches, parochial-houses, and glebes. This would not be an endowment, but 'a relief to the laity who are heavily taxed for religious purposes'.[1]

The support of de Vere and Moriarty for concurrent endowment had most important effects upon opinion in Parliament, where those sympathetic to that course of action could quote Catholic authority for it. But they also provoked the National Association, aided by the Liberation Society, into declaration in favour of the Voluntary system. The Irish bishops, largely influenced by the proceedings in the Association, also came out decisively in favour of that system. It is important that the steps leading to the position of the majority party among the Irish Catholics on the Church question should be clarified.

The formation of the National Association at the end of 1864 had been among the most decisive causes of the reopening of the Church question. One of its three points – its chief one, as *The Irish People* and those favouring greater priority for the land question at the time of the rules dispute maintained – was the disestablishment of the Irish Church. In his speech at the Aggregate Meeting O'Neill Daunt had been careful to stress disendowment too, and so from the beginning the Association had had that plan inherently in its programme.[2] It had presented petitions in favour of Dillwyn's motion,[3] and in 1865 it had ended its long and crucial meeting on the rules, in June, by passing a resolution demanding the withdrawal of tithe-rent-charge.[4] In 1867 it had organized a petition against tithes, to be circulated in every parish in Ireland, but it was never so widely canvassed due to lack of funds.[5] The Association felt the opinion of the Catholic members of Parliament on the Church question at the meeting called by Dillon in December 1865. Daunt advised Dillon on the sort of proposals which might be made to them, and was, of course, enthusiastic that nothing short of complete disendowment would do. The members were not to be trapped into so advanced a position prematurely, however, and at the meeting Monsell told Dillon that the Catholics 'lost instead of gained' by placing the demands for the State Church on the grounds of Voluntaryism.[6]

It was in January 1866, after the publication of Aubrey de Vere's letter in *The Times*, that the National Association first reconsidered the question of disendowment. At a meeting on the 23rd of the month, a

---

[1] *Ibid.*   [2] See chap. 4.   [3] *Freeman*, 20 June 1865.

[4] *Ibid.*, Resolution proposed by Rev. R. Bellaney.

[5] Daunt, Journal, 20 June 1867.

[6] *Ibid.*, 30 November and 5 December 1865. Daunt observed 'Monsell is a whig, and gives whiggish counsel'. See also chap. 4.

letter from Archbishop Leahy of Cashel, a close friend of O'Neill Daunt, was read. It was, as *The Times* commented, de Vere's suggestions which were 'pointedly alluded to' by the Archbishop:

The question of a State provision for the Catholic clergy is, I perceive, again introduced. I take this opportunity to say that I, for one, am for the Voluntary principle, and for it alone, and that I am opposed to any measure that would make the Catholic Bishops or priests of Ireland the stipendiaries of the State in any shape or form. Although I do not by any means assume to speak for others, I believe I but express the sentiments and feelings of the Bishops and priests of Ireland.[1]

Daunt had written to Leahy on 27 December urging him to support the Voluntary principle.[2] The archbishop's letter to the Association was evidently the result. The two motions against the Church introduced to Parliament by Sir John Gray in 1866 and 1867 must also have represented the feeling of the committee of the Association, and in them he suggested complete disendowment. It is true that Gray did not represent himself in the House as spokesman of the Association, but this was no doubt because he was anxious not to give the opposition the handle of a 'popish confederacy' to grasp at and so defeat his intentions.[3] Even so, the Association was mentioned in the debates.[4] The Protestant Dublin *Mail*, noticing in February 1866 that the motion had been tabled, had described Gray as 'the agent of the R.C. bishops in Parliament' – which was not altogether an unfair description, but it is easy to see why Gray would not desire to see himself so prejudiced in a Protestant legislature.[5] Gray was also working with the Dublin Corporation, as he had on the oaths question in 1865, and a petition for disendowment emanating from Dublin was copied by the Corporations of Kilkenny and Waterford in support of his 1866 motion.[6]

[1] *The Times*, 25 January 1866; *Guardian*, 31 January 1866.

[2] Daunt, Journal, 27 December 1865. Daunt was convinced that the Government would suggest endowment of the priests following *The Times*'s declaration favouring such a course in its comment on the Dublin meeting of Irish members got up by Dillon (Journal, 15 December 1865). He also wrote to Dillon in the same manner as he did to Leahy, on 25 December 1865.

[3] In the 1866 debate, Whiteside said that the very wording of Gray's motion was identical with that made by the Papal Legate at the Aggregate Meeting of 1864. He went on to describe the National Association as an elaborate ultramontane plot, *Hansard*, CLXXXII, pp. 1045-66.

[4] By Peel Dawson, for example, in 1866, *ibid.*, CLXXXII, p. 1025; and by Lefroy in 1867, *ibid.*, CLXXXVII, p. 144.

[5] Dublin *Mail*, 15 February 1866. The same article, 'The Government and the Roman Bishops', went on to hint that, as with the university question, there might also be an 'arrangement' between the Government and the bishops over the Church. This was not so, but it illustrates the depth of Protestant distrust.

[6] As *The Times* noticed (9 April 1866), on the eve of Gray's motion. The Dublin petition was taken to London personally by MacSwiney (*The Times*, 10 April 1866).

Gray's motion was debated in Parliament on 10 April 1866, and from this point the National Association was central in the movement for the abolition of the Establishment. At a meeting in May a letter from Gainsford was read at a special meeting of the committee, urging them to action as the question was now 'ripe to be dealt with'. Only the debate on Parliamentary Reform was holding back the Legislature.[1] Kavanagh prepared 'county papers' to help the Association's propaganda on the Church. One on Wexford was submitted to the same meeting in May. The papers gave religious statistics of population, magistrates, educational institutions, the proportions of wealth in Protestant and in Catholic hands. In Wexford he pointed out that there were four to five Protestant High Sheriffs appointed for every one Catholic, and that four-fifths of the whole magisterial bench was Protestant.[2] The county papers all concluded with one remedy: 'religious equality'. It was probably the form of the county papers which suggested Gray's famous *Freeman's Journal Commission on the Church* (1868), which closely followed the material supplied by Kavanagh in his papers. In January 1867 the National Association received letters from several bishops 'recommending secularization', as Moriarty wrote to Kirby, 'without any reference to the Holy See'.[3] At the meeting on 8 January, one from the Bishop of Ross (O'Hea) demanded complete secularization. Cullen himself sent an important letter, praising the Association for its effective work on the Church question, especially in the form of petitions to Parliament. He was pleased that their chances of success were so greatly enhanced by the adhesion to the principle of disendowment of the 'large and powerful party in England' who were prepared to assist their own efforts. The Association, he repeated, was engaging successfully in the decisive task of informing public opinion on the right way of disposing of 'the fruitful source of all our evils' – disendowment.[4] A motion presented by O'Neill Daunt was passed unanimously. It demanded disendowment of the Church, and 'uncompromising Voluntaryism'.[5] This was decisive indeed. It was significant that this meeting had as its immediate background Sir John Gray's fears that the ideas of de Vere were about to be introduced into the Association by 'some persons'.[6] Gainsford's influence also was apparent in the form of the resolutions passed at the meeting. They declared the need for petitions on the Church question, and announced the gratitude of the Association to the English and Scots reformers (actually naming Bright) for helping their

[1] *Freeman*, 16 May 1866 (meeting of 15 May).   [2] *Ibid.*
[3] Kirby Papers, Moriarty to Kirby, no. 131, 8 April 1867.
[4] *The Times*, 10 January 1867.   [5] Daunt, Journal, 8 January 1867.
[6] *Ibid.*, 28 December 1866.

cause. The first two resolutions showed that, like some in the difficult moments of the Anti-Corn-Law League before them, the Association saw that only a reformed Parliament might secure the redress of their grievances, and no doubt the resolutions were also intended to reciprocate for help received:

> Resolved: That a Reformed Parliament being the readiest means by which the people of this country can obtain a satisfactory settlement of the Church, the Land, and the Education questions, it is therefore the duty of the executive committee of this Association to aid the movement for a more just and equitable representation of the people in parliament.
>
> That, as the House of Commons, as at present constituted, inadequately represents the people of the United Kingdom, and persistently refuses to legislate beneficially for Ireland, we hereby pledge ourselves to co-operate, by every means in our power, with the reformers in the three Kingdoms in their efforts to obtain an extension of the franchise, with vote by ballot.[1]

This was declaratory: the Association, beyond encouraging the Irish Catholic members to vote with the reformers in Parliament, did little else to fulfil the resolution. A meeting in Dublin on the 15th, chaired by MacSwiney, to give support to the English Reform League, was the only apparent concrete result of the resolutions. But even this meeting was not directly sponsored by the Association, though some of its members took part.[2] It is interesting to find a declaration favouring the ballot, for among the reasons proposed for its adoption early in the seventies was the belief that it would terminate the influence of the Irish priests over the voting habits of their flocks at elections.

In April the Association adopted a petition for disendowment, addressed to Parliament, which was circulated to each parish. It condemned the Establishment, declared Catholic determination not to seek the restoration of the Church property of Ireland, called for disendowment 'having due regard to existing vested interests', and, most importantly, asking Parliament 'to appropriate the revenues . . . to such secular purposes of public utility to the Irish people as to your wisdom shall seem desirable'.[3] In May came Gray's second motion on the Church also calling for disendowment, and in the following month the Association again resolved for the Voluntary principle, 'as best and safest for the Irish Catholic Church under the especial circumstances of her position', and to oppose any project of investing her with a portion of the Ecclesiastical State property at present in the possession of the

---

[1] *The Times*, 11 January 1867.   [2] *Ibid.*, 17 January 1867.
[3] Meeting of 27 April 1867, *Freeman*, 29 April 1867; motion of the Very Rev. B. Verdon.

Established Church.[1] One such project was Moriarty's. His *Letter* had been published in March. It was clearly in the minds of those at the meeting, for the secretary said at the beginning that it had been right to call the members together, although the bishops were nearly all in Rome, as the committee felt the Association should 'reiterate its declarations on the subject of the proposed scheme for endowing the Roman Catholic clergy out of the funds of the State Church Establishment – the more so as the Liberation Society and others seem to have been misled by a few writers, who only claim to speak for themselves, and who do not represent any considerable section of public opinion in Ireland'.[2] This was a dangerous state of affairs, and they could not afford to lose the support of that Society, especially as 'neither prelate, priest, nor layman belonging to the Association has ever expressed a dissent to our oft-repeated resolutions in favour of pure Voluntaryism in Church matters'. A letter was read from O'Neill Daunt urging total disendowment, and then the resolution was passed, the secretary adding again that it was 'merely a reiteration' of their previous ones.[3]

So it was that by the time the Church question became practical politics in Parliament with Gladstone's resolutions in 1868, the National Association had already opted for complete disendowment and secularization. Daunt was satisfied that the resolutions would have the support of the Association. He had been able to keep 'the committee of the National Association quite straight in this matter' of endowments. Even de Vere's pamphlets could not do much; 'I think the question is now beyond the reach of mischief from his misapplied talents,' he wrote in his Journal.[4] On 10 April a report on the Church question was presented by the committee to the Association. It demanded disendowment, but made one interesting point which was to be considered during the passage of the Church Bill in 1869 when it suggested that 'one act of restitution' could be welcomed – 'the restoration of the ruined abbeys, churches, and burial grounds of our forefathers, and their enclosure and maintenance undertaken by Catholics'. The report also suggested that Church revenues should be made into an Irish fund for secular purposes, and denied any claim on the grounds of prescription.[5] But the Church question did not occupy all the time of the Association, and in May a draft report before the committee stated that it was the land question

---

[1] *The Times*, 29 June 1867 (meeting of 27 June).
[2] *Freeman*, 29 June 1867.
[3] *Ibid.*   [4] Daunt. Journal, 6 April 1868.
[5] *The Times*, 10 April 1868. Carvell Williams wrote to the National Association in gratitude for the part they were taking on the Church question. His letter was read at the meeting on 26 May. *Freeman*, 27 May 1868.

which was the root of Irish evils.[1] That and similar assertions of the priority of the land question by members of the Association could be used as proof in Parliament that the Church was a 'sentimental grievance' only and that disendowment would not help the Irish peasantry.[2]

The National Association laid early plans for the inevitable general election, stressing the Church question. In this they were following the trend everywhere else in Britain. Their part will be glanced at later; but it should be noticed here that they did not, as in 1865, attempt to pledge candidates wholly to their programme. Instead they worked in the Liberal interest, and tried to get the local clergy to support Gladstone. Gray and MacSwiney introduced the Church question to the debates of the Dublin Corporation in September against the repeated protests of the Conservative opposition that it was no fit place for discussion of national political questions. Gray carried a motion in the Corporation for a petition to the Queen praying for disendowment.[3] It was also in September that the Meath clergy, who had seceded from the National Association at the end of 1865 after their failure to secure amended rules which emphasized the supremacy of the land question, found it necessary to declare that they still supported agitation on the Church question. They published a Declaration on disendowment, disclaiming alleged apathy on their part on that point. It was accompanied by a letter from Bishop Nulty to Sir John Gray, explaining that Conservatives had even misrepresented them as having rejected disestablishment and disendowment in the interests of tenant legislation. That was untrue. He showed it by citing the resolutions on the Church passed by the Meath clergy at their meeting in Navan on 29 August 1868, the first of which, on the Church, declared that they would 'earnestly and vigorously cooperate in every effort for its disendowment and disestablishment'.[4]

---

[1] *The Times*, 2 May 1868. The report was presented at the meeting of 26 May. *Freeman*, 27 May 1868.

[2] As, for example, by the Duke of Richmond in the Lords debate on 29 June on the Suspensory Bill. He cited the motion of Fr John Boylan (P.P., Crosserlaugh, Co. Cavan) at the National Association on 23 April, which had declared the urgency of a Land Bill, *Hansard*, CXCIII, p. 217. For Boylan's motion, see the *Freeman* report, 24 April 1867.

[3] *The Times*, 9 September 1868.

[4] *Ibid.*, 7 September 1868, which gives the texts both of the Declaration and of Nulty's Letter. In 1865 the Meath clergy had resolved that 'other agitations – such as that against the Established Church – are got up for party purposes . . .' and could not help the condition of the tenants. Their resolution of August 1868 explained: 'these words do not apply to the agitation now on foot against the Established Church, as they were spoken before this agitation came into existence . . . these words, in the context in which they stand, merely conveyed that the land question had the first

In establishing Catholic support for disendowment and secularization, the National Association was giving substance to the working agreement which it had evolved with the Liberation Society. Indeed, the agreement depended for its effect entirely on the Association swinging round to that position, for the English Dissenters could never agree to support Catholic educational claims, and their own counsels were not so much divided on land questions as ignorant of things seeming to be outside their terms of reference. The Liberation Society, especially through O'Neill Daunt,[1] heavily influenced the direction which the Association came to take on the endowments question, and through the Association, the bishops too. Looking back in July 1869 on his part in the Church question, Daunt traced the successful issue to united action for disendowment. After the incorporation of Voluntaryism into his speech at the Aggregate Meeting, all seemed set for a straightforward campaign

until Mr de Vere and some less able men got up a little agitation for a division of the spoils between the Catholic and the Protestant Churches. This project I successfully opposed in and out of the National Association. In the political position of Ireland our great and paramount need was the impartial disendowment of *all*; not the endowment of any. My admirable friend the Archbishop of Cashel (Dr Leahy) saw this very clearly: 'what we want', he wrote, 'is disendowment, not endowment'. Meanwhile the English Voluntaries agitated far and wide. They brought our question into every corner of England and Wales. Without their alliance the Irish Catholics could not rive the chain. On the other hand the English Voluntaries could have done nothing without us; for if we had been silent their efforts would have been plausibly met with the assurance that they were meddling with a question that did not concern them; and that the silence of the Irish Catholics demonstrated that we deemed the State-Church no grievance. In fact our joint-action was indispensable to success; and it was I who originally created, or promoted, our alliance. The English Voluntaries made the question so strong that Mr Gladstone found it worth his while to take it in hand.[2]

It will be remembered[3] that the Association and the Liberation Society had allied on the supposition that when the Irish Church had been pulled down, the Catholics would help, by their influence, the attack on other Establishments in Britain. But they were not to do so.

claim on the attention of the Legislature – that it was entitled to priority over all other questions for an immediate solution and settlement'; (Resolution IV). See also the *Guardian*, 9 September 1868, which, in reporting the proceedings, observed that no laymen had taken part.

[1] A. M. Sullivan selected Daunt and Gray as the two Irishmen 'who most largely contributed to the great purpose of Disestablishment'. *New Ireland*, p. 304.

[2] Daunt, Journal, 26 July 1869. It is important to realize that this is not the recollection of a man seeking to overdraw the object for which he had aspired, from the distance of many years. The note was written just after the passing of the Church Act.

[3] See chap. 4.

This may have been simply because Daunt had never impressed sufficiently upon the Association that co-operation was intended to be reciprocal, even though they had shown themselves conscious of reciprocation to the extent of supporting Bright's plea for aid in Parliamentary Reform, at least by resolving in its favour. More probably, however, it was because Irish Catholic Voluntaryism was a reflection of the peculiar circumstances of their country, and did not contain the element of positive anti-State-Church feeling so strong among English Dissenters.[1] And when the bishops came to consider Gladstone's university proposals in 1873, they found they were opposed by the English Dissenters: English Protestant feeling was roused by the Vatican Decrees, and the Irish bishops were treated to a demonstration of the inherent anti-popery of English Dissent. Finally, the Italian occupation of the Patrimony of St Peter in 1870 enabled them to see that in a general sense the advocates of disendowment were the 'Irreligious party'.[2] The *Dublin Review* had seen the difficulties in 1868, observing that the unfortunate aspect of the Church question was the connexion it was fostering between the Irish Catholics and English Liberals.[3]

In December 1862, O'Neill Daunt had hoped to secure episcopal adhesion to a movement for disestablishment, 'if the English Voluntaries consent to satisfactory terms of union'.[4] These had been arrived at[5] and after the National Association and the Liberation Society had both petititioned in support of Dillwyn's motion (1865), and it was made clear that they were capable of working in accord, it needed only the adhesion of the Irish bishops to the Voluntary principle for a united front to be created. But that was no small thing, and Daunt and the Society knew they would have to work diligently to obtain it. In the autumn of 1865 the Society put Daunt up to destroying a plan for the internal reform of the Irish Church proposed in *The Times* by Edward Hincks, a Co. Down parson. Daunt made his reply the occasion of a tremendous justification of the Voluntary principle.[6] Gray's motion in

[1] A. M. Sullivan, *op. cit.*, p. 300 n., who suggests this as the primary reason.

[2] E. S. Purcell noted that 'Archbishop Manning, perhaps, did not sufficiently consider that a large number of those who supported the Disestablishment of the Protestant Church in Ireland belonged to the irreligious party which is everywhere opposed to the Catholic principle of the union of Church and State'. *Life of Cardinal Manning*, vol. II, p. 394.

[3] *Dublin Review*, July 1868, 'The Irish Disestablishment', p. 80.

[4] Daunt, Journal, 8 December 1862.

[5] See chap. 4.

[6] *The Times*, 9 November 1865; Hinck's letter, 'How to Save the Irish Church'. Daunt's reply was anonymous, he signed himself 'An Irish Catholic'. *The Times*, 20 November 1865. The letter from Carvell Williams urging him to reply to Hincks was received by Daunt on 13 November.

1866 was a joint effort between Catholics and Dissenters, in the sense that a deputation from the Parliamentary committee of the Liberation Society met Gray and other Irish members in London and 'agreed on the terms of the proposed motion on the Irish Church Establishment',[1] although the initiation of a motion had been Gray's alone. In the debate in the Commons, Whiteside noticed the alliance at work, and asked if 'the Roman Catholic gentlemen ever reflected that they are now about to be made use of by the political children of the old Puritans?'[2] At the beginning of 1867, the Liberation Society were anxious that the Irish Church should again come before the notice of Parliament, and promised support for any motion Gray liked to propose.[3] It was becoming clear to the opponents of disendowment that the alliance was going to be formidable. In February of that year, de Vere wrote to Earl Grey that 'the alliance between Irish Catholics and English Radicals and Dissenters, through which it has been proposed to carry that plan into effect, appears to me the most unnatural and mischievous of alliances'.[4] And, as planned, Gray's motion in May 1867, was a manifestation of it, as Sir Frederick Heygate noticed during the debate, when he said that the movement in favour of the Voluntary system was 'one of purely English manufacture'.[5] In the Lords Debate on Earl Russell's motion for a Royal Commission on the Irish Church, in June, Lord Cairns was more explicit. It was mistaken, he said, to suppose that the growing agitation against the Church came from Ireland:

> The fact is, that it originated about two years ago with a body in this country . . . I refer to the Liberation Society. That body is conscientiously opposed to all Ecclesiastical Establishments. But they select the branch of the Established Church in Ireland because they think it is the weakest branch . . . and they accordingly proposed, about a couple of years ago, co-operation with the persons whom they regarded as the leaders of popular opinion in Ireland. . . .[6]

At the annual Council meeting of the Liberation Society held in London on May Day 1867, the secretary, Carvell Williams, referring to proposals for concurrent endowment, concluded that it would not be unlikely if in the beginning, 'measures relating to the Irish Church may call for the resistance instead of the support of the Committee'.[7] They did not have long to wait. An example of the type of measure apprehended by Williams was Sir Colman O'Loghlen's 'Roman Catholic

[1] Liberation Society Minute Books, vol. III (1862–7), p. 351. Reported to a Council on 2 March 1866.
[2] *Hansard*, CLXXXII, p. 1062 (10 April 1866).
[3] Liberation Society Minute Books, vol. III, p. 421. Council of 25 January 1867.
[4] Grey Papers, de Vere to Grey, 6 February 1867.
[5] *Hansard*, CLXXXVII, p. 117 (7 May 1867).
[6] *Ibid.*, CLXXXVIII, p. 381 (24 June 1867).   [7] *Nonconformist*, 2 May 1867.

Churches, Schools and Glebes (Ireland) Bill', which was discussed by the Council on the 24th of the month. By clause IV of the Bill, advances were authorized, in the form of loans, by the Commissioners of Public Works in Ireland, for the purchase of glebes and the erection of Catholic parochial-houses. This was a proposal which was to reappear in 1869. The Council objected to clause IV, and it seemed to them that the provisions of the Bill were of 'a doubtful character, in regard either to their practical operation, or to the principle on which they are based'.[1] The Bill was lost on its second reading in July, even after O'Loghlen had expunged the offensive clause IV as a result of representations from the Society.[2] Carvell Williams was becoming convinced that Fenianism would hasten a settlement of the Church question[3] – with justice, in view of the fact that it was Fenianism which convinced Gladstone of the urgency of doing something for Ireland. This, and the difficulty over endowments underlying O'Loghlen's Bill, persuaded him that he should go to Ireland to see things for himself, and, as the Committee said, 'for the purpose of conferring with the Society's friends, and of obtaining information for the future guidance of the Committee'.[4] In July the Government, following Russell's motion in the Lords for a Royal Commission on the Irish Establishment,[5] had constituted one, and Williams was doubtless anxious to see for himself the raw material on which it was to work,[6] although he agreed with Gray, who had written in his *Freeman* that 'the scope of the inquiry forbids any useful results'.[7] It was merely to look into rearrangements of the temporalities. But opposition to 'internal reform' of the Church was another element binding the Catholics and the English Dissenters. In June, the Society had also been worried by proposals in England and Ireland for con-current endowment – their anxiety, it will be remembered had trans-mitted itself to the National Association who had, as a result, reiterated their condemnation of endowment to quieten fears[8], and in this sense Carvell Williams's visit to Ireland was a probe to discover how much support de Vere, Moriarty and Monsell had there.

O'Neill Daunt prepared for his visit. The bishops were due to meet in October, and he must have realized that Carvell Williams's tour of the

---

[1] Liberation Society Minute Books, vol. III, p. 445. Council of 24 May 1867.

[2] *Ibid.*, p. 473. Council of 30 August 1867.

[3] Daunt, Journal, 16 March 1867.

[4] Liberation Society Minute Books, vol. III, p. 463. Committee of 2 August 1867.

[5] *Hansard*, CLXXXVIII, pp. 354 ff. (24 June 1867). On the work of the Commission, see J. T. Ball, *The Reformed Church of Ireland*, London and Dublin, 1886, pp. 266-7.

[6] But he did not meet any representative of the Established Church.

[7] *Freeman*, 12 August 1867.

[8] *Ibid.*, 29 June 1867. Special meeting of the National Association, 27 June.

country and the assurances he would offer of English support would be crucial in securing from them the desired resolution against endowment. He wrote off to several bishops pressing them to give Williams a good reception.[1] On arrival, the visitor went straight to Kilcascan (Co. Cork) to see Daunt, staying there the night of 6 September, and on the following day, after breakfasting at Skibbereen with Bishop O'Hea of Ross, he set out on his tour.[2] It lasted three weeks, and he visited Limerick, Cork, Queenstown, Fermoy, Thurles, Londonderry, Belfast and Rostrevor. He was three times in Dublin. He had interviews with six Catholic bishops, several Catholic M.P.s, agents of the press, Presbyterian and other Dissenting ministers, and also with the committee of the National Association.[3]

In his report to the Society's Council on his return to London early in October, he said that he had found great satisfaction everywhere in Ireland that they had sent over a representative. During the interviews he had set out four objects in each case. (1) To give an assurance of the close interest shown by the English liberal party in the Church question, and the determination of the Society to make it a prominent one at the next general election (it must be remembered that this was said before Gladstone had made it certain that the Church would be almost the sole issue at that election). (2) To urge the Irish into action which would impress English opinion with the need to deal with the question promptly. (3) To insist on 'the impartial disendowment of all sects in Ireland – as opposed to a policy of general endowment'; this he gave as the *only* condition on which the Society's influence could be expected. (4) To obtain and to offer practical suggestions for the adoption of measures by the Voluntaries of both countries.[4] In these conversations, he had received the impression that belief was spreading in all quarters that the Establishment was shortly destined to fall. He was convinced that most Catholics regarded it with feelings of decided hostility. The Presbyterians, while they were unlikely to unite against the Establishment, were at least opposed to the endowment of the Catholics; but they would probably only abandon the *Regium Donum* as part of a new policy of general endowment. Other dissenting bodies he found divided in their opinions on endowment, but noted, correctly, that they had no political influence anyway. But, most important, he reported that –

[1] Daunt, Journal, 23 August 1867.   [2] *Ibid.*, 6 and 7 September 1867.
[3] Liberation Society Minute Books, vol. III, p. 479. Council of 4 October 1867. It is unfortunate that there is no record of what passed at these meetings other than Williams's own general summary.
[4] *Ibid.*, p. 479. 'Report by Mr Carvell Williams on his visit to Ireland', 4 October 1867.

with scarcely an exception, the Roman Catholics whom he had met, had assured him that their body – on practical rather than theological grounds – would refuse to accept any of the endowments now possessed by the Protestant Establishment, and would insist on a policy of impartial disendowment, and that it was confidently expected that, at a meeting of the Roman Catholic bishops, to be held in Dublin on the 1st October, resolutions in that sense would be adopted.[1]

Nevertheless, because of the wide prevalence of a feeling that appeals to Parliament were useless, and because of the related strength of the Fenian movement, Williams did not report that an agitation on 'any great scale' would start in Ireland about the Church question. While the Society would get 'valuable co-operation' from Ireland, it must calculate most of its power and influence to lie in the English Liberal party.[2] The committee referred Carvell Williams's report to the Society's committee on the Irish Church 'to consider practical suggestions'.[3] Before that committee could report back, the resolutions of the Irish bishops supporting Voluntaryism were laid before the Council.[4] Williams's prediction had proved correct. It was on 25 October that the Irish committee recommended 'That it be suggested to the Committee of the National Association in Ireland that they should issue an address to English Liberals, urging them to action for the abolition of the Irish Establishment'.[5] Daunt was suggested as the best person to draft it. The other six points in their recommendations concerned press and lecture campaigns, and a proposal for a meeting of liberal politicians in London. They reflect Williams's advice that the Society's efforts would be best if largely confined to England.[6]

Now it is clear, therefore, that the combined actions of the National Association and the Liberation Society, goaded by Catholic proposals for concurrent endowment like those of de Vere and Moriarty, largely influenced the decision which the body of Irish bishops would make on the question of disendowment. That decision was issued to the Irish nation in the October resolutions of 1867, and it is interesting to trace the steps leading to it, and show the pressures brought to bear upon the bishops. They had to face the small but weighty opposition of Irish Catholics who sought general endowment. They were also cautioned by the *Dublin Review* against alliances with Liberals and Dissenters. Rome itself was, at least in its teaching, hostile to the sort of cause for which they opted, and the Syllabus of Errors remained as a condemnation of their actions which the bishops ignored. In 1868, the *Tablet*

---

[1] Liberation Society Minute Books, p. 480.   [2] *Ibid.*   [3] *Ibid.*, p. 481.
[4] *Ibid.*, p. 483. Council of 18 October 1867.
[5] In response to this, the National Association seems to have done nothing.
[6] *Ibid.*, p. 486. Report of Committee, 25 October 1867.

attacked them for ending the union between Church and State, and for supporting voluntaryism and secularization merely to applaud a party move of Gladstone's.[1]

In November 1864, when the informal preparations for the Aggregate Meeting were becoming known and speculated about, *The Irish People* had declared its recognition of a movement against the Church as honest and deserving of support if it was based purely upon the voluntary principle. 'Will Dr Cullen accept our principle?' the paper had asked. 'If not, we tell him, with profound respect, that we cannot recognize in him a practical enemy of the Church Establishment.'[2] They were to be surprised, for Cullen said of the Church at the Aggregate Meeting: 'I fully concur in the proposal to disendow it.'[3] The problem for the Voluntaryists, and especially for O'Neill Daunt, was to keep the Association, once formed, up to scratch on disendowment. Here he had the constant support of the Archbishop of Cashel. Leahy it was who wrote to the National Association in January 1866 urging them against any plan for Church property like that of de Vere; and who, in July of that year, advised Daunt to send out a circular note to all the bishops in his Province seeking their assistance in agitation for disendowment.[4]

Cullen was evidently sympathetic to disendowment throughout the period following the Aggregate Meeting, and for once he was not to be dogged in this by the opposition of MacHale. For as early as 1859 MacHale had assured Daunt of his adhesion to the principle of disendowment.[5] But Cullen wavered at times. In January 1867, writing to Kirby about de Vere's pamphlets, he actually outlined a solution on the lines suggested there:

> The only plan that can ever be carried out is to sell all the [Church] property, and put the amount in the hands of a Commission, to be applied as a sort of loan-fund for public useful purposes, such as building schools, Churches, colleges, etc. – in this way the clergy would not encounter the odium of receiving the tythes or a pension from government. As to giving the land to Catholics, the Protestants will never consent to it. The whole question is very intricate, and it will be difficult to get any good done.[6]

This was in fact very similar to de Vere's plan, which envisaged Commissions of Protestant and Catholic bodies to distribute Church

---

[1] *Tablet*, 4 April 1868. The *Tablet*'s conservatism came to an end in November, when the journal was bought for Manning. The new editor, Mgr Vaughan, supported disendowment, and the *Tablet* underwent a *volte face*.
[2] *Irish People*, 26 November 1864 – 'A New Association'.
[3] *Freeman*, 30 December 1864.   [4] Daunt, Journal, 3 July 1866.
[5] *Ibid.*, 8 November 1859.
[6] Kirby Papers, Cullen to Kirby, no. 3, 2 January 1867.

property, 'each body applying and distributing its portion through some instrumentality in which its clergy and laity should act conjointly'. The State should ensure that the funds were properly applied 'to moral and religious ends'.[1] But it is evident that Cullen's speculations were intended to be taken entirely hypothetically, for at the same time that he made them, Leahy was assuring Daunt that the cardinal was wedded to the Voluntary principle,[2] and at the National Association on 8 January, Cullen's letter endorsing it was read out.[3] In April, he suggested to Manning that the 'total disendowment' of the Church was the only solution to the Fenian troubles.[4]

It was just after this point that he seems to have asked Sir John Gray to ascertain Gladstone's position on the Church question. Gray had seen Gladstone in March about the Church, and the idea of an interview to discuss actual proposals had been mooted then.[5] Gray saw Gladstone for two hours on 22 July 1867 and came away with favourable impressions, letting Cullen know that *'personally* he is free to support any adjustment approved by Ireland, either the levelling *up* or the levelling *down'*. Gladstone was convinced, however, that de Vere's and Moriarty's pamphlets had increased the opposition to the latter course, but had expressed himself anxious to consider it as an *Irish* question, and deal with it accordingly, not prejudiced by the position of the English Establishment. Yet he felt great difficulty in taking up the question at once in Parliament, because of the divided opinions about endowment, and thought it dangerous to pledge to any plan until opinion became 'more developed and publicly expressed'. If this were done he would introduce a Bill to deal with the Church for the 'approved plan, be it *up* or *down'*. Gray asked Cullen to approve the course of securing a Bill from the Liberal party: they would be able to make sure that it was one for levelling down as the majority of the Irish members would support such a plan – only Monsell favoured levelling up.[6] It is surprising to find Gladstone at this relatively late point[7] in the Church question, apparently willing to countenance concurrent endowment should the Irish request it. He would have been awkwardly placed with his own

[1] Grey Papers, de Vere to Grey, 2 October 1867.
[2] Daunt, Journal, 4 January 1867.   [3] *The Times*, 10 January 1867.
[4] Cullen to Manning, 8 April 1867; quoted by Shane Leslie, *Dublin Review*, October 1919, p. 168.
[5] Cullen Papers, Gray to Cullen, 21 March 1867.
[6] *Ibid.*, Gray to Cullen, 22 July 1867.
[7] Yet in April of the previous year, at the time of Gray's motion, Gladstone had told Fortescue that he was by no means prepared to undertake to deal with the Church question – Carlingford Papers, CP. 1/7, Gladstone to Fortescue, 7 April 1866. Also quoted in Morley's *Life of Gladstone*, vol. 1, p. 873.

Liberal and Dissenting supporters had they done so. No doubt he counted on Gray's assurance that it was levelling down which would receive their support, and the bishops' resolutions in October therefore had the importance of making it clear to Gladstone personally that the way was now open for secularization.

With the knowledge that Gladstone waited on an Irish declaration Cullen proposed a meeting of the bishops for October, to deal with the university and education as well as the Church. 'The question of the endowments of the Protestant Church will soon be proposed in Parliament' he wrote to the Propaganda, pointing to the need to secure episcopal unanimity in order to avoid the scandal and frustration of a division.[1] Before it occurred, Carvell Williams's Irish tour took place, and the six bishops he met were doubtless impressed by his assurance of English support if their meeting should consecrate the Voluntary system.[2] Cullen was certain that Rome would not obstruct their path: when in Rome during the previous summer he had been advised by Antonelli that it would be fatal for the Irish Catholics to accept any endowment from the English Government. As Cullen later explained to Kirby, 'it was in accordance with that advice that I induced the other bishops to adopt the Resolutions'.[3] At the meeting, held during the first three days of October 1867, the bishops drew up the famous resolutions which declared that the Establishment -- maintained by property alienated from its rightful owners – should cease; that it should be disendowed; that the Catholics would not accept 'state pensions and government gifts' (quoting as authority for this the *Letter of Propaganda* issued by order of Pius VII in 1801, and the subsequent Papal Letter of 1805); and that the revenues of the Church should be used to alleviate the condition of the Irish poor. The text was emphatic in declaring that nothing new was done: the resolutions were merely a repetition of statements made by the Irish bishops in 1837, 1841 and 1843 – all refusing endowment. Cullen was pleased. 'I think we followed out exactly the recommendations of Cardinal Antonelli', he wrote.[4] This, in fact, was unlikely, for Antonelli probably confused the questions when speaking with Cullen in Rome. Probably it was only State endowment of the Irish Catholics against which he advised. In November 1868, he was to tell Odo Russell that he could never consent to Irish

1 Propaganda, *Scritture* 35, Cullen to Barnabo, 30 July 1867.
2 From the nature of his itinerary it is reasonable to assume that the six bishops he met were Butler, Keane, Delany, Dorrian, Archbishop Leahy and O'Hea (whom he is known to have met).
3 Kirby Papers, Cullen to Kirby, no. 126, 15 April 1868.
4 *Ibid.*, Cullen to Kirby, no. 368, 10 October 1867.

disendowment.[1] In the light of the Irish situation, Cullen apparently regarded the two questions as inseparable.

The resolutions,[2] Cullen believed, 'produced an excellent effect'.[3] O'Neill Daunt, on receiving them in a letter from Archbishop Leahy, said 'there is nothing now to interrupt our alliance with the English Voluntaries . . . Mr de Vere must, I think, feel himself rebuked by this unanimous resolution of the bishops'.[4] The resolutions got the widest publicity. They were warmly applauded by the *Nonconformist*, which compared the Catholic testimony in favour of Voluntaryism with the intransigence of the Protestant defenders of Church property, 'wishing that the comparison were less disadvantageous to Protestantism'.[5] Speaking in Parliament on his own motion on 10 March 1868 – a debate which turned out to be crucial for the Church question – Maguire quoted the resolutions to show that the problem of endowments was virtually settled.[6] Gladstone evidently acted on the assurance he had given to Gray in 1867, and at the end of that debate declared that the Establishment must cease. His own resolutions indicated that the Irish Catholic opinion, for which he had declared himself ready to wait, had been given. But while most men saw that the question of endowment had hardened as a result of the October resolutions of the bishops, de Vere and Moriarty still tried to save the day for their cause. The latter, who had been present at the bishops' meeting, explained to Earl Grey in the following year the reasons which had swayed the bishops. First, they had agreed that the Establishment and its revenues was hated by the Irish people 'with an intensity which surpasses every other national sentiment'. Secondly, they believed that 'the age of endowments is passed'. When a nation lost its unity of faith the support of religion ceased to be a national and become an individual duty. Thirdly, they thought that the Radical parties in England and Scotland would never consent to the endowment of the Catholic Church, and that without their aid the Irish Establishment could not be destroyed. 'To get rid of this Establishment', Moriarty emphasized, 'is the

[1] F.O. 43, vol. 101, Dispatch no. 48, 24 November 1868.
[2] For the text see Moran, *Writings of Cardinal Cullen*, vol. III, p. 71 (VII), 'Letter to the Clergy and Laity of the Diocese, transmitting the Resolutions adopted by the Irish Episcopate, 9 October 1867'. The resolutions are also referred to in the *Freeman's Journal Church Commission*, Dublin, 1868 (Seventeenth Report: on Voluntaryism). There is a copy of the resolutions in the Gladstone Papers, B.M.Add.MS. 44249, f. 92 – sent by Cullen to Manning in July 1869 at the time of the Lords' concurrent endowment amendment to the Church Bill.
[3] Kirby Papers, Cullen to Kirby, no. 126, 15 April 1868.
[4] Daunt, Journal, 8 October 1867.   [5] *Nonconformist*, 23 October 1867.
[6] *Hansard*, cxc, pp. 305-6.

most immediate and pressing necessity, and the bishops think that no self-seeking should delay for a moment this consummation.'[1] Moriarty still hoped, in 1868, to secure some form of general endowment. De Vere claimed that the October resolutions were amenable to an interpretation favourable to his plans too, since the bishops had not *explicitly* condemned the 'Distribution' scheme.[2] Both men were apparently unable to see that the bishops were right when they had said that the age of endowment was over, for that was just what the rise of Gladstone implied.[3]

The situation had now settled. The dialectic between the National Association, the Liberation Society, and the Irish prelates on one side, and the proposers of concurrent endowment on the other, had resulted in a coherent front on voluntaryism and secularization, with only a minority Catholic dissent. The Irish Catholic Church had come down in favour of what Mowbray was to describe in Parliament – in words the Papacy dreaded – as 'a free Church in a free State'.[4] The question was ripe for Gladstone's attention. It has been seen that in March 1868 he attempted to swing Catholic support away from the Mayo university plan and concentrate it on the Church.[5] His move was dictated by the need to prevent the concession of the denominational principle for university education in Ireland,[6] especially as the suspicion had continued to linger that State endowment might be included. Gladstone's occasion was determined by the fulfilment of the condition he had posed to Gray in 1867 – Irish Catholic commitment to a view on ecclesiastical endowment. This had come. And to confirm all, the Church question was one on which he would be able to turn Disraeli out, and put the Liberals into power. Manning caught the decisive swing, and while Parliament debated Maguire's motion, he turned his attention exclusively from the Charter to the Church and Land questions. It was in March that he published his *Ireland, A Letter to Earl Grey*, in which he

[1] Grey Papers, Moriarty to Grey, 2 April 1868.

[2] Monsell Papers, Box 8319, de Vere to Moriarty, 4 March 1868.

[3] Conservative defenders of the Church, who had wavered on the edge of general endowment, were more realistic and saw, as the Duke of Marlborough put it to Mayo, that 'the spirit of the Resolutions of the Irish bishops sufficiently shows that they will do nothing and take nothing'. Mayo Papers, MS. 11156, Marlborough to Mayo, 17 October 1867.

[4] *Hansard*, CXCI, p. 1515 (28 April 1868).   [5] See chap. 6.

[6] In his *Address* to the electors of south-west Lancashire in October 1868, Gladstone wrote of the Government plan: 'We refused to open a new source of discord through the establishment by the State of any denominational University. We repudiated the policy of universal endowment'. *Speeches of the Rt. Hon. W. E. Gladstone in South-west Lancashire*, Liverpool, 1868, p. iv.

gave assent to the Irish bishops' October resolutions,[1] and declared that the evils were so plain that 'the thirty Catholic members of the Commons are against the Church Establishment to the man'.[2]

Frequently when Parliament contemplated palliative measures for Irish Catholics, Protestant opposition attempted to block them by showing that there was no demand among the laity for any change. This was not to be possible with the Church question. In 1866 Kavanagh had announced to the National Association that the Establishment was a degradation felt keenly by the laity.[3] And this was shown to be true when, in February 1868, a *Declaration* of Irish Catholic laymen was signed by those who felt it proper 'to contradict publicly the assertion that we do not feel aggrieved by the present ecclesiastical settlement of Ireland'.[4] Organized by the Earl of Fingall, it was signed with thirteen columns of names, nearly a thousand in all.[5] *The Times* agreed that they were weighty names too,[6] and that the *Declaration* 'presents a formidable muster-roll against the hosts of the Protestant Defence Association'.[7] Also, in the provinces, Defence Association meetings began to be followed by meetings of lay Catholics to put the opposite case. This happened at Limerick in March, when the Earl of Dunraven, the Lord-Lieutenant of the County, convened such a counter-demonstration.[8]

Although it was foreign to the custom of the Catholic Church, there was a sense in which voluntaryism had come to be seen in Ireland as peculiarly suited to Catholicism there. After the penal days the Church had been rebuilt in Ireland entirely by voluntary contribution.[9] Archbishop Leahy felt it was possible also to prove 'that the early Irish Catholic Church was supported purely on the principle of

---

[1] H. E. Manning, *op. cit.*, p. 25. The *Letter* is also reprinted in Manning's *Miscellanies*, London, 1877, vol. I, p. 211.

[2] *Ibid.*, p. 6. He maintained the primacy of the land question, however, for 'in comparison with this question the others are light'. *Ibid.*, p. 28.

[3] *Freeman*, 19 April 1866 (meeting of 18 April).

[4] *Parliamentary Papers*, 1867–8, LIII, 75.

[5] Lord Castlerosse used it to show the Commons the extent of lay feeling, *Hansard*, CXC, p. 1734 (16 March 1868).

[6] It was signed by 12 peers, 4 Privy-Councillors, 86 Deputy-Lieutenants and M.P.s, 320 J.P.s, and nearly all the Catholic members of the Irish Bar, as well as numerous municipal officers.

[7] *The Times*, 20 February 1868. The Defence Association had just been established in Dublin, to act as a counterblast to Catholic agitation on the Church question.

[8] *Ibid.*, 17 March 1868.

[9] As Godkin demonstrated, using Dublin as an example, in *Ireland and her Churches*, p. 94. He noticed also, as others did, that the success of the West Connaught Mission of the Established Church was an essay in the Voluntary System. *Ibid.*, p. 393.

voluntaryism'.[1] In 1868 the *Freeman's Journal Church Commission*, in its Seventeenth Report, painted a glowing picture of the glories of the system, stressing the great sums the faithful gave to maintain religion in Ireland.[2] It had drawbacks, however. The poor contributed more than the rich – as Moriarty pointed out as an argument in favour of general endowment.[3] The unsatisfactory side of voluntaryism was presented to Rome in an anonymous memorandum written in the first three months of 1869, now preserved in the archives of Propaganda:

> The Catholic Church in Ireland has depended for three hundred years on the contributions of the faithful. This system, which is called Voluntary, has no doubt some great advantages for Ireland. However, it is not possible to deny that it is subject to a certain number of pitfalls, and amongst these, perhaps the greatest would be the avaricious spirit which naturally is inclined to develop in the clergy. Since the income of each individual is neither fixed nor predetermined, each tries to procure for himself as much as he can, with the result that in many parts of Ireland the people, however much attached to religion, and deeply Catholic, complain, and with full justification, of the excessive and continuous asking and squeezing to which they are subjected by the clergy.[4]

On the other hand, what the Irish bishops valued most, and as they had shown at the beginning of the century during the Veto controversy, was their independence. Endowment seemed to them to be a way of allowing the State to take it away. When the Government decided to appoint salaried Catholic military chaplains in 1865, Cullen was filled with alarm. 'It appears', he wrote, 'to be one of the usual attempts of England to interfere in Irish ecclesiastical affairs'; and when once they had enslaved the chap'ains, 'everything else follows.'[5] Those who would see general endowment in Ireland, had first to assure the hierarchy that this would not happen. Earl Russell said this when speaking on Lifford's motion for endowment in 1866.[6] Aubrey de Vere suggested a similar assurance in his *Hibernia Pacanda*,[7] and warned Earl Grey that it was a great difficulty to be overcome, especially as the Ecclesiastical Titles Act had shown that the anti-Catholicism of a Protestant State could still frame penal enactments.[8] Moriarty also saw the problem, and in his Maynooth Synod address in 1875 he was to give 'subserviency to the

---

1 Daunt, Journal, 29 December 1863 (notes on a letter from Leahy).
2 *Freeman's Journal Church Commission*, Dublin, 1868, pp. 373 ff.
3 And as Byrne wrote in his contribution to *Essays on the Irish Church*, pp. 32-3.
4 Propaganda, *Scritture*, 36. The place of this memorandum in the volume indicates that it belongs to January–March, 1869.
5 Kirby Papers, Cullen to Kirby, no. 157, 16 July 1865.
6 *Hansard*, CLXXI, p. 1073 (26 February 1866).
7 De Vere, *Hibernia Pacanda*, pp. 33-5.
8 Grey Papers, de Vere to Grey, 2 October 1867.

State' as one of the greatest perils into which a Church could fall.[1] In his *Letter to Earl Grey*, Manning referred to any proposal to grant State pensions to the Irish clergy as 'a plot against their independence'.[2] And it was to Manning that Cullen wrote echoing this sentiment in 1869, and stating that if the Lords' proposed concurrent endowment were carried into effect, its result would be to annoy and subject the clergy.[3] These fears were not entirely groundless. Clarendon exemplified the position the Catholics dreaded, and in 1868 Mgr Talbot was urged to make sure that he did not press for the endowment of the priests through Rome, as he would do it, Manning assured him, 'with the avowed intention of gaining a hold over them'.[4]

On 23 March 1868 Gladstone proposed his celebrated motion in the Commons, in the form of three resolutions. They called for the end of the Irish Establishment, with due regard to vested interests, for the confinement of the work of the Ecclesiastical Commission pending the final decision of Parliament on the Church, and for an address to the Crown praying that the Queen's interests in Irish temporalities be placed at the disposal of Parliament.[5] During the debate on 30 March on his motion to go into a committee on the question, Gladstone said that the occasion was not suitable to detail a plan.[6] But he was emphatic that it would be based, when presented, on disendowment[7] and secularization:

that which I renounce for the future is the attempt to maintain, in association with the State, under the authority of the State, or supported by the income of the State, or by public or national property in any form, a salaried or stipendiary clergy . . . when, after satisfying every just and equitable claim, we shall have to contemplate at some future time the application of a residue [of Church revenue], that residue will have, in my judgment, to be treated strictly and simply as an Irish fund for the benefit of Ireland.[8]

In a saving expression, which must have been intended to reassure the English Church that the Irish fate was not to be theirs too, he admitted a valid basis of Church property in Coleridgian terms:

[1] David Moriarty, *Sermons*, second ed., Dublin, 1906, p. 114.

[2] H. E. Manning, *Ireland, A Letter to Earl Grey*, p. 11.

[3] Manning Papers, Cullen to Manning, 13 July 1869.

[4] Purcell, *Life of Cardinal Manning*, vol. II, p. 399.

[5] *Hansard*, CXCI, p. 32. The resolutions are quoted in R. B. O'Brien's *Fifty Years of Concessions to Ireland*, vol. II, Book VIII, pp. 239-40.

[6] *Hansard*, CXCI, p. 471.

[7] On 17 March, Disraeli advised the Queen that Gladstone's actions would 'involve the whole question of Ecclesiastical endowment'. *Letters of Queen Victoria, 1862–78*, vol. I, p. 516.

[8] *Hansard*, CXCI, p. 472.

There is something in the idea of a national Establishment of religion, of a solemn appropriation of a part of the Commonwealth for conferring upon all who are ready to receive it what we know to be an inestimable benefit; of saving that portion of the inheritance from private selfishness, in order to extract from it, if we can, pure and unmixed advantages of the highest order for the population at large.[1]

But this, he said, was to view an Establishment on its 'etherial side', yet it had also 'a side of earth'. It was an appropriation of the fruits of labour, and unless the purposes for the appropriation were fulfilled, it could not be justified. Such was the case with Ireland.[2]

The resolutions must be seen for Gladstone, as they were by W. E. Williams, as the 'final expression of his policy in the most critical ten years of his life', and as the point at which, in his rise to the leadership of the Liberal Party, the 'last stage of a development and the first stage of a maturity' was reached.[3] But it was Fenianism which persuaded Gladstone of the *urgency* to act for the amelioration of Irish grievances – although he was careful to point out that it had not determined in any particulars the actual provisions which he was to propose.[4] Regarding the Church question, it has been suggested that the measure received its sanction from the Catholic adhesion to disendowment, which reassured him that the desire of his own Radical and Dissenting supporters was echoed in Ireland too. McClelland thinks it not unlikely that it was Manning's *Letter to Earl Grey* which finally convinced Gladstone that the time was now ripe for Disestablishment.[5] It is certainly true that – as Newdegate pointed out[6] – many of the arguments used in the Parliamentary debate were drawn from Manning's pamphlet. But it was written too late to influence Gladstone's timing of his attack on the Church, which had been arranged some months before Maguire's motion. In December 1867 Gladstone had written that 'the Irish Church, which has long been grave, is growing *awful*', and that the motion of which Maguire had given notice, while only with intent to 'occupy the ground', must cause them to consider the question.[7] In February Mayo had told J. T. Ball that 'a serious attack' on the Church was likely.[8] Gladstone gave his first notice of action on 16 March,[9] but it

---

[1] *Ibid.*, p. 493.   [2] *Ibid.*, p. 494.

[3] Williams, *The Rise of Gladstone to the Leadership of the Liberal Party, 1859–68*, p. 158.

[4] See Morley, *Life of Gladstone*, vol. I, p. 875; his observations are based on Gladstone's speech in *Hansard*, CXCVI.

[5] V. A. McClelland, *Cardinal Manning . . .*' p. 171.

[6] *Hansard*, CXCI, p. 1524 (28 April 1868).

[7] Carlingford Papers, CP. 1/10, Gladstone to Fortescue, 11 December 1867.

[8] Mayo Papers, MS. 11216, Mayo to Ball, 29 February 1868.

[9] *Hansard*, CXC, p. 1764.

had clearly been some months in preparation, as the events of the second half of 1867 had shown. The Manchester Fenian outrage in the autumn was probably the decisive factor for Gladstone. Manning's pamphlet, which appeared on 12 March, added justification,[1] but it cannot be seen in any way as determining events. In the *Chapter of Autobiography*, Gladstone himself did not explain the reasons which proved to his satisfaction that the time had come to deal with the Church. They must be 'treated elsewhere than in these pages', he wrote.[2]

Reflecting in 1888 on the resolutions, Earl Grey regretted the form in which they were made. Gladstone's speech of explanation, he noticed, had pledged the House to secularization without assigning plausible reasons for doing so. It left no real opportunity for the consideration of alternative schemes for endowment.[3] This was not actually true, for Gladstone had said that the occasion was not suitable for outlining actual plans; but it was certainly the case that, as Grey perceived, it was his intention to prejudice the House in favour of secularization from the outset. Grey was not alone. Matthew Arnold, appealing for members' abstention on the Church Bill, wrote that reasonable opinion would have liked an arrangement for 'the fair apportionment of the Church property of Ireland among the principal religious bodies there,' and that this had been ruled out of court by Liberal tactics:

> But we see that, instead of this, Liberal statesmen waited to trip up their rivals, if they proposed the arrangement which both knew to be reasonable, by means of the prejudice of their own Nonconformist extreme; and then, themselves proposing an arrangement to flatter this prejudice, made the other arrangement, which they themselves knew to be reasonable, out of the question.[4]

O'Neill Daunt was delighted with the resolutions and with Gladstone. 'The question has arrived at a great stage of importance', he wrote, 'when *he* thinks it worth his while to turn it into a test of party, and to propose resolutions of Disendowment and Religious Equality.' For that, they should thank their 'good allies' the English Voluntaries.[5] When the resolutions had been carried into Committee, he was convinced of

---

[1] Cullen thought it was 'excellent' and would 'do great good' (Woodlock Papers, Cullen to Woodlock, 16 March 1868). Cullen had in fact taken a large part in supplying Manning with material for the *Letter*, and also got Kavanagh to send statistical data. (See *ibid.*, Cullen to Woodlock, 2, 4 and 6 March 1868.) It was Cullen who supplied the information about Irish trade figures and drew Manning's attention to O'Reilly's *Return* of education statistics (1864) – see the *Letter* in Manning's *Miscellanies*, London, 1877, vol. I, pp. 223 and 231.

[2] *Chapter of Autobiography*, London, 1868, p. 46.

[3] Earl Grey, *Ireland, The causes of its present condition*, pp. 51-3.

[4] Matthew Arnold, *Culture and Anarchy*, 1960 ed., p. 201.

[5] Daunt, Journal, 25 March 1868.

success. All would go well, he wrote, if the Irish Catholics remained faithful to the English Voluntary alliance. He would see that the National Association committee did all it could for that end.[1] Dr Russell, the President of Maynooth, wrote to express the gratitude of Catholics to Gladstone for his resolutions.[2] Moriarty considered them wise and timely, since abolition of the Establishment was just what was needed to quieten the terrible disaffection in Ireland. The resolutions would produce 'an immense improvement in the popular feeling in Ireland'. Explaining this to Earl Grey, who had written to express disgust at Gladstone's action, the bishop speculated on the hope that concurrent endowment might still be possible at some future point when the ecclesiastical fund had finished paying out on vested interests.[3] Sir George Bowyer, the member for Dundalk, wrote to ask Cullen what he felt about Gladstone's proposals, adding that the least Catholics had a right to expect was the return of old Churches where the Catholic population was in a majority.[4] Cullen himself approved of the resolutions, giving the Propaganda information on the subject just after the House had voted to go into Committee on them:

> For several weeks throughout this Country we have been full of anxiety about the outcome of a question which was discussed in Parliament regarding the Established Church of Ireland. Mr Gladstone proposed to the House that the incomes which that Church had robbed from the Catholics at the time of the Reformation, and that all the privileges which that Church had enjoyed as the only one recognized by law, should cease. The debate was long and full of excitement. Disraeli and the other Ministers defended the Church with their swords unsheathed, and stated that they wanted to fight to the utmost to preserve it. However, the Protestant Church of Ireland has within it so many anomalies, and so many proofs of the injustice of its origin, that no art could sustain her; and when the time came to vote, 330 members of Parliament declared themselves for the abolition of the Protestant Church. . . . The Irish Protestants will resist in every conceivable manner the proposed deprivation, not so much for love of their Church, but because they have no other hope of surviving, without the possession of the riches of this world.[5]

It was characteristic of Cullen to think the worst of his opponents. But his news was well received in Rome as Kirby testified. Cullen told him that the vote had 'shaken Protestantism to its very foundations', not only

---

[1] *Ibid.*, 6 April 1868.
[2] Gladstone Papers, B.M.Add.MS. 44414, f. 208, Russell to Gladstone, 25 March 1868: 'The Resolutions of which you have given notice are by far the most important in regard to Ireland that have been laid on the table of the House since 1829.'
[3] Grey Papers, Moriarty to Grey, 2 April 1868.
[4] Cullen Papers, Bowyer to Cullen, 31 March 1868.
[5] Propaganda, *Scritture* 36, Cullen to Barnabo, 5 April 1868.

in Ireland, but in England too.[1] Cullen's approval of Gladstone's course was curious; on 17 March he had told Woodlock that he distrusted Gladstone, who was 'not a lover of justice', and feared that his opposition would prevent the Ministry from going on with the plan for chartering a Catholic university.[2] But at the same time he could not help applauding any attempt to deal with the Establishment based on the course outlined in the bishops' resolutions of October 1867. Yet he made no public declaration of support for Gladstone, presumably awaiting the fate of the Charter question. His silence was prejudiced by the action of the Dublin clergy, however, who, on the day of the Parliamentary vote on the motion for a Committee to consider the resolutions,[3] had offered prayers to the Queen of Sorrows for success. It was the Feast of the Seven Dolours. Cullen told Manning that he was sure this had contributed to the Parliamentary victory.[4] Manning communicated to Gladstone Cullen's approval of the resolutions and his belief that unless they were followed up there would be great dissatisfaction in Ireland. As Sir Shane Leslie wrote, 'during the battle for Disestablishment, Gladstone, through Manning, kept in touch with Cullen'.[5] Cullen was moderate: he felt the first resolution (which had declared that the Establishment should cease), was the most important, and he was convinced that 'if the Irish Church were disestablished, even though it retain all its endowments, the vastest step to mitigating and extinguishing the religious animosities of Ireland would be made'.[6] Manning had sent him a copy of Earl Grey's pamphlet,[7] and it was evidently with it in mind that Cullen told him that the Irish bishops would never consent to a share in the spoils of the Establishment – for the strange reason that 'our doing so would contribute to prevent any legislation'.[8] They would adhere instead to their resolutions. Manning tended to be rather indifferent over the endowments question, regarding disestablishment as

[1] Kirby Papers, Cullen to Kirby, 15 April 1868.

[2] Woodlock Papers, Cullen to Woodlock. 17 March 1868. Cullen felt Gladstone's lack of justice was shown by his pamphlet on Naples. The conflict in Catholic thinking is seen by de Vere's claim of the same year that Gladstone's hatred of injustice was witnessed in 'his fierce invectives against the old government of Naples'. De Vere to Spring Rice, 18 May 1868, quoted in Ward's *Memoir*, London, 1904, p. 287.

[3] 30 March 1868.

[4] Gladstone Papers, B.M.Add.MS. 44249, f. 39 – reported in a letter of Manning's to Gladstone, 8 April 1868.

[5] Leslie, *H. E. Manning*, p. 197.

[6] Gladstone Papers, B.M.Add.MS. 44249, f. 39, Manning to Gladstone, 8 April 1868.

[7] Leslie, *op. cit.*, p. 199 (quotation of Manning to Cullen, 2 April 1868).

[8] Gladstone Papers, B.M.Add.MS. 44249, f. 39, Manning to Gladstone, 8 April 1868 (a report of Cullen's letter).

the great thing.[1] It was probably Cullen's awareness of this that prompted his own hesitancy in explaining to Manning the real reasons why the bishops would not accept endowment – in the fear, no doubt, that Manning would recognize them as those which motivated English 'political' Dissent.

As the summer came on and Gladstone's ideas for the Church were given to Parliament there was some disquiet among the Irish Catholics. Bright, on whom the National Association had pinned so many hopes, and who had, as Trevelyan said, aspired to unite 'the English and Irish democracies',[2] produced suggestions so moderate as to cause them to lose faith in him. Bright tried to arrive at a solution for the Church difficulty which would avoid shocks; 'it is a great thing, I say,' he told the Commons during the debate on Maguire's motion, 'if you can make the past slide into the future without any great jar'.[3] This was not at all the sort of thing he had proposed at the Dublin banquet in his honour in 1866. Hinting now at mistaken views among members of the Liberation Society, he proposed to allow congregations of the Church of Ireland to have possession of their Churches and parochial-houses, with the abolition of State connexion and Crown appointments. The *Regium Donum* and the Maynooth Grant would cease. He had said that he imagined all Catholics would 'regard this as just',[4] but they were not to do so, and when he stuck to this position during the subsequent developments of the question in Parliament, even de Vere came to regard it as not even religious equality 'because it makes no equivalent to the Catholics for "fixed property" worth £2,500,000 which it would leave the Protestants'. Gladstone also intended to leave amounts of property to the disestablished Church, and de Vere argued the same lack of equality against his plan.[5]

When O'Neill Daunt realized the caution of Gladstone's proposals he called them 'a sham'.[6] Gladstone had spoken of giving a large slice of the Irish ecclesiastical revenues (three-fifths and perhaps even two-thirds) to the disestablished Church in perpetuity.[7] 'His purpose, as at

---

[1] Writing to Gladstone on 8 May, he remarked: 'Let the endowments be put overboard half-way between Galway and New York rather than mix them up with the question of your Resolutions.' Gladstone Papers, B.M.Add.MS. 44249, f. 51. Also printed in Leslie, *op. cit.*, p. 200.

[2] G. M. Trevelyan, *The Life of John Bright*, p. 388.

[3] *Hansard*, cxc, p. 1658 (13 March 1868).   [4] *Ibid.*

[5] Grey Papers, de Vere to Grey, 12 April 1868. Disappointment at Bright's action on the Church at this time prepared for the Irish revulsion against him for his later opposition to Home Rule, and led into the subsequent bitterness with which he was remembered in Ireland – see Justin McCarthy, *Ireland Since the Union*, p. 167.

[6] Daunt, Journal, 18 April 1868.

[7] *Hansard*, cxci, pp. 471 ff. (30 March); and pp. 930 ff. (3 April 1868).

present stated,' Daunt felt, 'seems to be investing one-eighth of the people with two-thirds of the Church property, in a mode well devised to protect the endowment from future attacks.'[1] This was, of course, just what Moriarty hoped would happen and he wrote to Gladstone with approval. But at the same time he made suggestions to avoid what he called the wastage in the plan. He recommended a fund, to be vested in a Commission, to administer the ecclesiastical revenues – paying out life-interests and compensation, and investing the residue. In this way, in a few years, a large sum would accumulate in the hands of the Commissioners which could then be employed as directed at that time. He meant – but did not say – directed to some sort of general endowment according to his own proposals. What he did hint to Gladstone was that the present plan had 'the inconvenience of prematurely settling another question [endowment] which is better deferred to another time'.[2]

O'Neill Daunt evidently communicated his disquiet to Carvell Williams in London, who consulted Manning,[3] and then made representations to Gladstone. The 'influential Irish Roman Catholic' who had approached him, he wrote, was concerned by 'your desire to permanently endow the Anglican Church in Ireland with a large portion of the property which it now holds as an Establishment'. He would like to know if the 'two-thirds' of the property merely represented an estimate of the compensations and life-interests, or if it was a *permanent* endowment.[4] Gladstone seems to have replied that it was his intention to give the Protestant clergy nothing beyond compensation for life interest.[5] The debates of 1869 were to show that even compensation could mean a huge sum. And Cullen's sanguine letter to the Propaganda on 24 June, explaining that 'the great question of the abolition of the Established Church of Ireland was successfully dealt with' – referring to the passage of the Suspensory Bill through the Commons[6] – was to prove hollow. The Bill was rejected by the Lords on the 29th of the same month.[7] The country, and the question, waited for the general election.

[1] Daunt, Journal, 18 April 1868.
[2] Gladstone Papers, B.M.Add.MS. 44414, f. 280, Moriarty to Gladstone, 22 April 1868.
[3] *Ibid.*, Add.MS. 44249, f. 51, Manning to Gladstone, 8 May 1868, where Manning relates his meeting with a 'leading nonconformist' on the church proposals. It was almost certainly Carvell Williams.
[4] *Ibid.*, Add.MS. 44415, f. 40. Williams to Gladstone, 12 May 1868.
[5] Daunt, Journal, 18 May 1868 (note on a letter received from Carvell Williams which had reference to communication with Gladstone).
[6] Propaganda, *Scritture* 36, Cullen to Barnabo, 24 June 1868.
[7] *Hansard*, CXCIII, p. 295.

At the same time the Church question was growing in urgency for the Irish hierarchy. The processions in support of the Manchester 'Martyrs' had allowed a degree of Fenian sympathy to overspill into areas of Irish society which had been hitherto wholly antipathetic. This feeling was tending to give a new priority to the land question, and those who emphasized that question could not always be relied upon to keep to the line sanctioned by the majority of the bishops. In January 1868, a meeting of Limerick priests headed by Dean O'Brien issued a *Declaration* in favour of repeal of the Union.[1] They had met to celebrate a requiem for the souls of the men executed at Manchester. It received wide notice,[2] although Mr Serjeant Barry exaggerated somewhat when he said in Parliament that it 'was daily receiving adherence from those who avowed their belief that the Imperial Parliament was either unable or unwilling to cope with the difficulties of Ireland'.[3] Yet sympathy there must have been, for large groups of clergy adhered to Home Rule early in the seventies, and Egan is surely right when he says that 'it can, therefore, be justly claimed that the Dean [O'Brien] was a pioneer of the Home Rule Movement which was formally launched in 1870 by Isaac Butt'.[4] Explaining his action at a subsequent meeting of Limerick priests on 20 January, O'Brien declared that those who had signed their Declaration now numbered 198, and he expressed some hope that the statesmanship of England would not overlook their grievances. Theirs was a movement, he said, 'which is simply the expression of opinion'. They passed resolutions calling for a national legislature for Ireland.[5] Aubrey de Vere certainly considered that their action inaugurated a new Repeal movement. O'Brien, he wrote to Earl Grey, 'doubtless looks to the aid he will receive from any long delay in the settlement of the Church Question'.[6] In Parliament, the Irish Attorney-General (Warren) quoted O'Brien's opinion that 'the Church established by the law is a premium to anti-national sentiment', and that the bishops would show themselves to be on the national side.[7]

It was also clear that a Church settlement alone would not give satisfaction to the seekers of Irish religious equality. The *Dublin Review* took the view that repeal of the Ecclesiastical Titles Act would be a good prelude to other Irish measures.[8] In fact it was not to be settled until

[1] *The Times*, 2 January 1868 (gives the full text of the Declaration). *Guardian*, 8 January 1868. Daunt, Journal, 18 January 1868.
[2] M. J. Egan, *Life of Dean O'Brien*, Dublin, 1949, p. 111.
[3] *Hansard*, cxcii, p. 773 (22 May 1868).   [4] M. J. Egan, *op. cit.*, p. 111.
[5] *The Times*, 23 January 1868.   [6] Grey Papers, de Vere to Grey, 28 June 1868.
[7] *Hansard*, cxci, p. 644 (31 March 1868).
[8] *Dublin Review*, July 1867, 'Irish Questions', p. 201.

after the Church question. But after the reports of the Select Committees of both Houses on the Act, in 1867 and 1868, it was obvious that Ecclesiastical Titles could not be considered separately from a general religious settlement.[1] The Party Processions Act was similarly placed. It had always been considered a grievance by Catholics and it was used against the demonstrations in support of the Manchester 'Martyrs'. Yet it was impartial in its operation, and the Orange leader, Johnston of Ballykilbeg, was imprisoned in March 1868 for violating its terms.[2] This stirred Orange bitterness, and Johnston was elected to a Belfast seat in the elections later that year. One smaller badge of religious inequality was settled before the elections, however, and this was by Monsell's Burials Act,[3] which enabled dissenters to have their own rites in the graveyards of the Established Church in Ireland. As Monsell pointed out,[4] this would benefit Presbyterians and Wesleyans as well as Roman Catholics.

The Irish bishops were also dismayed by the reappearance of the old 'no-Popery' cry as the elections came on. Cullen hoped that Disraeli's initial failure to get up the cry would continue, as he wrote to Kirby in April.[5] By the beginning of October he was less sure, and wrote again that 'Disraeli in his addresses shows the cloven foot; he says that the Catholics are endeavouring to give over the government of England to the Pope'.[6] In his speech on 3 April, during the debate on Gladstone's motion for a Committee to consider the Acts relating to the Irish Church, Disraeli had said that 'High Church Ritualists and the Irish followers of the Pope had been long in secret combination and are now in open confederacy'.[7] The House had greeted this with laughter; but the suspicions it symptomized were still latent in English society. The remark was much discussed.[8] The *Dublin Review* observed that if Disraeli was sincere 'he is as hopeless an anti-Catholic fanatic as Mr Whalley'.[9] The cause of Disraeli's repetition of the language of the

---

[1] *Parliamentary Papers*, 1867, VIII, 15; 1867–8, VIII, 185. (See chap. 8.)

[2] *The Times*, 7 March 1868.

[3] 31 & 32 Vict. cap. 103.

[4] *Hansard*, CXCI, p. 1069 (22 April 1868). Newdegate said in the same place – on the second reading of the Bill in the Commons – that Monsell was acting for the hierarchy (p. 1075). But this is unlikely. He acted on his own initiative.

[5] Kirby Papers, Cullen to Kirby, no. 126, 15 April 1868.

[6] *Ibid.*, Cullen to Kirby, no. 303, 8 October 1868.

[7] *Hansard*, CXCI, p. 924.

[8] See, for example, comment by the *Irish Times*, 15 April 1868; *Freeman*, 15 April 1868; Dublin *Mail*, 22 April 1868.

[9] *Dublin Review*, July 1868, 'The Irish Disestablishment', p. 81. And that was saying something. Whalley was the author of 'Patrick Murphy's' *Popery in Ireland* (1865).

Durham Letter was his conviction that Gladstone, in urging the Church question before the nation, had – as he told the Queen – 'mistaken the spirit of the times and the temper of the country'. He himself saw an accumulated passion ready to be let loose by the nation at the elections; he predicted a violent recurrence of 'no-Popery'. 'The abhorrence of Popery,' he continued, 'the dread of Ritualism, and the hatred of the Irish, have long been smouldering in the minds of the nation.'[1] Perhaps he mistook the signs he had read in the 'Murphyism' which had disrupted the English localities from time to time. The lectures of William Murphy on the evils of Popery had caused rioting and damage to property almost everywhere they had been given during 1867,[2] and again in 1868.[3] In May 1868 Murphy had to cancel meetings in Belfast due to fear of serious disturbances.[4] The *Nonconformist* accused Disraeli of abetting Murphy's excesses.[5] In July, it had even to warn its readers not to heed claims that Gladstone's policies would favour the growth of Popery: they should not mistake the providence of God, and above all, 'don't fancy that He has chosen Mr Disraeli to save the Reformation'.[6] But it was Disraeli who had mistaken the times, as the election results were to show – but only just, for after the Vatican Decrees Gladstone was faced with the ruin of his Irish policy by the strongest blast of 'no-Popery' to have shaken the country since 1850.

Cullen threw himself into the election struggle, expressing to Monsell his conviction that 'if there be any fair play, I hope the Liberal party will be greatly increased in Ireland'.[7] He interested himself in the selection of suitable candidates. In an open letter about the contested Wicklow election he asked for the choice of Liberals,[8] and he wrote to the Bishop of Galway (MacEvilly) about the need to select good men.

---

[1] *The Letters of Queen Victoria, 1862–78*, vol. 1, p. 517: Disraeli to the Queen, 23 March 1868.

[2] See *Annual Register*, 1867 (Chronicle), p. 79, June: reports of Murphy riots at Birmingham. On 17 June, Murphy said that 'The impudent demands of the Roman Catholics in the House of Commons in the present session had not been equalled since the days of William and Mary. They were reaping the fruits of the Catholic Emancipation Act.'

[3] *Ibid.*, 1868 (Chronicle), May and September – riots in Lancashire and Manchester. The hatred, brought out by Murphy's preaching, helps to explain Gladstone's defeat in south-west Lancashire in the 1868 election.

[4] *Freeman*, 27 May 1868, 'Attempted Murphyism in Belfast'.

[5] *Nonconformist*, 27 May 1868, 'Murphyism and Disraelism'.

[6] *Ibid.*, 29 July 1868, 'The No-Popery Cry'.

[7] Monsell Papers, Box 8319, Cullen to Monsell (no date), 1868.

[8] *Freeman*, 16 November 1868. Cullen's Letter to the Wicklow Clergy, 14 November 1868.

He was anxious that Wexford, where formerly he had been disturbed by the intervention of Young Ireland priests at elections,[1] should name a good Catholic.[2] O'Neill Daunt declined Bishop Furlong's invitation to stand for the constituency[3] Cullen's advice to MacEvilly in Galway produced interesting results in the election there. 'It could not be called with truth a *political* contest,' the bishop wrote afterwards, 'it was essentially religious.'[4] Cullen also gave his support to the Central Franchise Association, which aimed to register all the new voters enfranchised in Dublin City by the terms of the Reform Act.[5] The Irish Act, from which the redistribution clauses had been dropped, and which left Ireland with a £4 rating franchise in the boroughs, extended the suffrage in only a few places, however.[6] In Kerry, Moriarty worked in the Liberal interest. He and his clergy believed that 'no candidate aspiring to represent an Irish constituency in Parliament ought to be accepted unless on a distinct pledge to support the policy enunciated by Mr Gladstone with reference to the Established Church'.[7] The Bishop of Limerick (Butler) met the Bishop of Cloyne (Keane) in Cork during August, and agreed to accept no candidate 'except on a distinct pledge of opposing Disraeli and supporting Gladstone, at least until the Established Church is Disestablished and Disendowed'.[8] The Bishop of Dromore (Pius Leahy) addressed a circular to the electors, calling on them to vote for the candidate who supported Gladstone,[9] and the Catholic Primate, Dr Kieran, told the Louth clergy to return two Liberals for the county.[10] The Bishop of Galway rejected the Tory candidate in a published letter,[11] and at a meeting of the clergy at Athlone in October, Bishops McCabe and Gillooly directed the borough to adopt a Liberal.[12] It is quite clear that the Catholic bishops were emphatically on the side of Gladstone.

MacHale's published *Letter* on the election attacked landlords who coerced tenants into voting against conscience;[13] but when the elections were actually fought, it was the bishops and clergy who tended to

[1] The Wexford election in 1866 he felt had been unduly tampered with by Young Ireland priests, who had defied the bishop (Furlong) by interfering. Kirby Papers, Cullen to Kirby, no. 3, 2 January 1867.

[2] Monsell Papers, Box 8319, Cullen to Monsell (no date), 1868.

[3] Daunt, Journal, 22 June 1868.

[4] Kirby Papers, MacEvilly to Kirby, no. 11, 8 January 1869.   [5] See chap. 4.

[6] Sir Spencer Walpole, *The History of Twenty-Five Years*, London, 1904, vol. II, p. 201.

[7] Monsell Papers, Box 8319, Moriarty to Monsell (no date), 1868.

[8] *Ibid.*, Butler to Monsell, 16 August 1868.

[9] *The Times*, 9 November 1868.   [10] *Ibid.*, 10 November 1868.

[11] *Ibid.*, 9 October 1868.   [12] *Ibid.*, 31 October 1868.

[13] *Freeman*, 16 November 1868.

intimidation and irregularity, as the trials of the election petitions showed. At Cashel, Archbishop Leahy was examined about his alleged receipt of a £400 cheque during the election in November. He said he 'did not remember anything about' a cheque for the Christian Brothers given by the candidate's agent, and certainly did not use it. He did not call it bribery when on the eve of an election a candidate gave large sums for charity in his constituency. A £5 cheque given to a Father McNamara, he supposed, must have been 'for masses or for charity'. He had himself remained neutral in the contest,[1] and the commissioners hearing the petition apparently accepted this. But at the Sligo election, also in November, the commissioners reported that 'some of the acts of the Right Reverend Dr Gillooly, the R.C. Bishop, and of certain of his clergy . . . amounted to undue influence'.[2] On the Sunday preceding polling day, the bishop had addressed his flock in the Catholic parish church, saying that if any one of them voted for the Tory candidate (Knox), 'they would be considered rotten branches, and should be lopped off'. He had declared further, that those so voting would have to 'make reparation before they could be reconciled to God' – a phrase which the commissioners construed as ecclesiastical censure. At Drogheda an election petition trial revealed wholesale physical intimidation by the priests of those Catholics voting for McClintock. A Catholic mob led by a priest, patrolled the streets stoning those who would not vote their way. Giving evidence, a James Cahill declared that Father Matthews had instructed him to vote according to his conscience, and had then taken him to the polls and commanded him to vote for the candidate he named.[3] The election was voided. Clerical intimidation did not reach its high-water mark in 1868, however – that happened at the 1872 Galway election, after which a Catholic bishop (Duggan) was actually put on trial.[4]

As early as May, the National Association prepared for the elections. The committee resolved to prepare an Address, which would show up the misrepresentation of those who held that Ireland was apathetic on

[1] *Parliamentary Papers*, 1870, XXXII, 1, Report of the Commissioners appointed to inquire into corrupt practices at the last election for Cashel. Evidence of Dr Patrick Leahy, pp. 319 ff. The Commissioners found evidence of corruption, but Leahy was not implicated. They were satisfied that the cheque for £400, 'which was intended to influence the electors' in Munster's favour, and which was given to Edmund Leahy, the archbishop's brother in Sheffield, was not cashed. See their Report, pp. 5 ff.

[2] *Ibid.*, 1870, XXXII, 621, Report of Commissioners on Corrupt practices at the last Sligo election. Report, p. 627.

[3] *Ibid.*, 1868–9, XLIX, p. 47 (Evidence). Report of the Commissioners appointed to inquire into corrupt practices at the last election for Drogheda.

[4] See chap. 9.

the Church question.[1] In June MacSwiney told the Association that the electors must counteract 'the unprincipled cry of the Prime Minister who appeals to the fanaticism of English mobs'. Candidates must 'support the three questions now before the Country'.[2] It is important to notice that he did not ask for candidates pledged to the programme of the Association *as such*, for the policy of the 1865 election was abandoned, and the bishops and the Association gave their open support to the Liberals, refusing to seek out candidates of their own. Independent Opposition, checked in 1865, was now completely disregarded by the Association. The *Nonconformist* noticed the distinctive character of the Irish elections in

the hearty adherence of the Catholic clergy to what is described as 'the Gladstone policy on Irish questions,' and the pointed reference made by Liberal candidates to the necessity of thorough co-operation with 'the great Liberal Party in the sister Kingdom' . . . no one has a word to say about 'Nationalism', 'Fenianism', or any other vague crochet, but nearly all the Catholics who seek a Parliamentary seat are as unanimous in favour of tenant-right and denominational education as for the abolition of the Irish Church.[3]

It is apparent that in a sense the Association had done its job in diffusing its programme, and so could afford to leave the election to be fought on the same grounds as in England – for or against Gladstone.[4] Yet there was less religious rancour manifested in the Irish elections than was expected; even at the Belfast contested election there was no rioting.[5] The addresses of the Irish candidates in the Catholic interest reflected this; they did not mention the Association's programme by name, but nearly all of them included its three points as MacSwiney had hoped and as the *Nonconformist* observed.[6] Meanwhile, in October, Gladstone's speeches in south-west Lancashire made it certain that the election was a one-question affair – Ireland – and that the Church was the first part of Liberal policy. Speaking at Wigan on 23 October, Gladstone gave his adherence once more to secularization.[7] The country had his personal testimony before it: he had published his *Chapter of Autobiography*[8] on 22 September.

[1] *Freeman*, 27 May 1868. Committee of 26 May.
[2] *The Times*, 19 June 1868 (meeting of 16 June).
[3] *Nonconformist*, 9 September 1868.
[4] H. J. Hanham, *Elections and Party Management*, p. 201.
[5] *Dublin Review*, January 1869, p. 208.
[6] *Freeman*, 16 November 1868 (prints a large number of election Addresses).
[7] *Speeches of the Rt. Hon. W. E. Gladstone in South-west Lancashire*, Liverpool, 1868, p. 71.
[8] It is interesting that Newman wrote to tell Gladstone that his *Chapter* was 'most noble'. Perhaps he saw in it a similarity to his own *Apologia* – Gladstone Papers,

Only in Lancashire,[1] and in Ireland itself, did candidates in the election take up a distinctively Protestant line of the type imagined by Disraeli. The results showed that in Ireland the Liberals increased their lead. There were 56 Liberals, compared with 49 Conservatives returned for Irish seats in the 1865 election; in 1868, the proportions had become 65 to 40.[2] In the north Irish borough results, the Liberals won seats at Belfast, Londonderry, Carrickfergus, Newry and Dundalk, and as *The Times* remarked, 'the armour of Ulster conservatism, hitherto deemed impenetrable, has been shattered'.[3] It was clear that in Ulster large groups of Protestant Dissenters had combined with the Catholic electors.[4] 'The political attachment', *The Times* continued, 'between the Episcopalian and Presbyterian laity, which was rooted chiefly in the Orange system, and carefully cherished by the Conservative leaders, has been cleft by the Church Question and shorn of its strength.'[5] It is the more remarkable that this had happened in the face of an appeal to the Presbyterian electors by the dying Moderator Cooke to stand by the Establishment.[6] Yet it is here, in the surprising Liberal successes in Ulster, that the ground plan of Butt's Home Rule was laid out. Many Ulster Protestants could see the inevitability of disendowment, and were determined to join the Home Rule Movement after 1870 out of sheer political disillusionment with England. At a Grand Orange meeting at Lisburn on 1 July 1868, there had been those who had said that disendowment, if carried, would be met with a Protestant demand for repeal of the Union.[7] And in December the Grand Orange Lodge of Ireland, meeting in Dublin, resolved that disestablishment and disendowment would void the Act of Union, which would, in consequence, be maintained 'by superior physical force solely'.[8] In Dublin county Alderman MacSwiney lost to the Conservative. But in the city Pim and Corrigan were elected. Cullen himself went along to vote.

B.M.Add.MS. 44416, f. 244, Newman to Gladstone, 25 November 1868. Also referred to in Morley, *op. cit.*, vol. I, p. 884. The *Chapter* was reviewed in the *Dublin Review* of January, 1868, pp. 231 ff.

[1] H. J. Hanham, *op. cit.*, p. 215. He also discusses the support given to Disraeli by the Evangelical clergy in England.

[2] *Ibid.*, pp. 216-17.

[3] *The Times*, 23 November 1868. See also remarks by the *Annual Register*, 1868 (History), p. 171.

[4] Daunt was exultant at the Londonderry result – 'only conceive – Orange Derry!' he wrote in his Journal, 26 November 1868.

[5] *The Times*, 23 November 1868.

[6] J. L. Porter, *op. cit.*, p. 492; Cooke's 'Address to the Protestant Electors of Ireland', 24 October 1868.

[7] Daunt, Journal, 4 July 1868.

[8] *Dublin Review*, January 1883, 'Ireland under the Legislative Union', by W. J. O'Neill Daunt, p. 98.

Referring to Pim, he wrote to tell Kirby that 'I suppose no Cardinal ever voted for a Quaker before'.[1] No cardinal ever voted for a Liberal before either; but then one had never required their help. At the beginning of December Gladstone became Prime Minister.[2] His mission was to pacify Ireland.

[1] Kirby Papers, Cullen to Kirby, no. 355, 18 November 1868.
[2] Morley, *Life of Gladstone*, vol. 1, p. 886.

CHAPTER EIGHT

Government Legislation on Church and Land, 1869-70

HAVING taken so active a part in securing the return to the new Parliament of Liberals committed to Gladstone's policy, the Irish Catholics were anxious that legislation should be framed in accordance with their own views on the questions at issue. This meant 'exceptional legislation' – a demand for measures which, whilst inapplicable to the conditions of the other parts of the United Kingdom, should be passed for Ireland, having regard to Ireland's peculiar circumstances. But although the Irish demanded 'exceptional legislation' on the Church and land questions, they were not consistent, and on educational matters their demand was always that they had been unfairly – and exceptionally – treated, and that they were entitled to the denominational system obtaining in England. Gladstone himself could agree that the case of the Irish Church was clearly exceptional, but when in 1870 he came to realize the full difficulties of the questions involving the land, he modified his expressions about Ireland being governed according to Irish notions. 'What he meant to say', he explained to an Irish deputation in March of that year, 'was not that legislation for Ireland should proceed according to the behests of Irish opinion taken by itself, but in conformity with that opinion, as modified and qualified by public opinion in England and by public opinion in Scotland.'[1] Still, in the hopeful days at the start of the new Ministry, the Irish Catholics prepared for great things. The *Dublin Review* which had supported the principle of Independent Opposition throughout the closing decade, now remarked that Gladstone had fulfilled the conditions for which that policy had been formed: he had made their questions Cabinet questions of the first importance, and so must be supported fully.[2] This was also the condition upon which the revised rules of the National Association pledged its support to a Ministry, in accordance with the 1865 memorandum of Cullen.[3] The President of Maynooth, writing to Gladstone at the time of preparations for the Ministry in November 1868, had urged the need

[1] *The Times*, 7 March 1870.
[2] *Dublin Review*, January 1869, 'Ireland and the New Ministry', p. 203.
[3] See chap. 4.

for 'a thoroughly cordial understanding . . . between the Roman Catholic body in this country, and the new Government of which you will be the head'. Gladstone must show by his sympathy with their demands that lingering Irish suspicions of the Whigs were unfounded when applied to the new situation.[1] To some extent, Gladstone's policy rested on views of the Irish question which he had come to hold as a result of successful Irish presentation of their grievances. But on the Church question especially, though also on land, his position once arrived at reflected as much the prejudices of his English and Scottish supporters as it did his Irish – he himself spoke of the modification of Irish measures by home public opinion. In June 1869, *The Times* noticed that 'London is at present the chief source of Irish news',[2] and this sums up the lifting of Irish questions out of the hands of the bishops and the National Association, and into Parliament. Yet his measures were his own. Neither with the Church nor with the land Bills did Gladstone follow up amendments suggested by Irish Catholics. Perhaps this was because with both, the bishops announced their support for the Bills regardless of whether the modifications they put to him were accepted or not. They realized that the obstacles to overcome were great, and they were more anxious for imperfect legislation than for legislation which could never get through Parliament.

Dr Russell suggested that the first way of winning Irish confidence would be good Irish appointments. This was a test of sincerity. Catholics in office would assure those who still doubted, that the new Ministry intended to reverse the former policy of England towards Ireland. Monsell should be in the Cabinet, and O'Hagan should become the Irish Chancellor.[3] Moriarty told Gladstone the same thing, even naming the same men for office, and adding Fortescue to the Cabinet for good measure. Not since the days of O'Connell, he wrote, 'has the people's faith been so trustingly given as it now is to you'. A mistake was made in 1829 when the Emancipation Act was not followed up by Catholic appointments – the present new start should not go the same way. Appointments in which the Catholic people could have confidence would heal the division in Ireland: 'to effect this is the mission God has given to you'.[4] Maguire assured Gladstone in the same vein, and also suggested O'Hagan for Chancellor.[5] And so it was that O'Hagan

[1] Gladstone Papers, B.M.Add.MS. 44416, f. 246. Dr Russell to Gladstone, 25 November 1868.
[2] *The Times*, 7 June 1869.
[3] Gladstone Papers, B.M.Add.MS. 44416, f. 246.
[4] *Ibid.*, B.M.Add.MS. 44416, f. 273, Moriarty to Gladstone, 28 November 1868.
[5] *Ibid.*, B.M.Add.MS. 44416, f. 298, Maguire to Gladstone, 4 December 1868.

became the first Catholic Chancellor of Ireland, in December 1868.[1] Thomas Pope, a Dublin priest, expressed Irish feeling accurately if somewhat floridly: 'British Constitution! Whilst you elevate such dignitaries, and whilst your jurisprudence is presided over by such Lord High Chancellors – esto perpetua!'[2] But for a Catholic Cabinet appointment the Irish waited in vain. In May 1869, Cullen heard that Fortescue was to be made a peer, and told Monsell to get the office of Chief Secretary which would become vacant as a result. If it did not go to Monsell, Cullen asked him to use his influence to secure it for The O'Conor Don or Myles O'Reilly instead. 'As Mr Gladstone is so anxious to do justice to Ireland,' he wrote, 'I hope he will take this matter into consideration.'[3] But Fortescue was not elevated to the peerage yet, and when in the reshuffle of December 1870 caused by Bright's resignation from the Cabinet, Fortescue succeeded him at the Board of Trade, Lord Hartington became Irish Secretary, and Monsell the new Postmaster-General – without a Cabinet seat. Monsell expressed his disappointment to Gladstone; his presence in the Cabinet, he said, 'would have tended to promote objects you have very much to heart'.[4] Cullen had also tried to persuade Fortescue to give James Kavanagh a post, by presenting on his behalf a memorial to that end signed by several Catholic M.P.s and bishops.[5]

It was not until 1 March 1869 that the Church Bill received a first reading, and in the first two months of the year the Catholics waited anxiously. But their anxiety was not that the Bill would partially fail to satisfy their demands – this was to be an unpleasant shock still laid up for them – it was that Protestant opposition would arise in both England and Ireland. It was widely held that the election had given the pledge of the country to the secularization plan, and Gladstone always believed this, arguing it effectively against Disraeli in the Commons, who claimed that at the election the country had not pledged itself to any particular measure – 'no particular measure was then before it'[6] – but only to deal with the Irish Church. The report of the Royal Commission on the Church which had come out just before the election was set aside by Gladstone as irrelevant, and he correctly pointed out that no one in the debates had outlined a plan based on it, using this as evidence that

---

[1] *Guardian*, 16 December 1868. The first Catholic, that is, since 1690.
[2] Thomas Pope, *The Council of the Vatican and the Events of the Time*, p. 227.
[3] Monsell Papers, Box 8319, Cullen to Monsell, 21 May 1869.
[4] Gladstone Papers, B.M.Add.MS. 44152, f. 116, Monsell to Gladstone, 31 December 1870.
[5] Carlingford Papers, CP. 3/90, Cullen to Fortescue, 26 July 1869.
[6] *Hansard*, third series, cxciv, p. 466 (1 March 1869).

the Commissioners had undertaken only to reform 'that which is irreformable'.[1]

Catholic suspicion was not aroused by the attempts of Lord Cairns, the Ulster champion of Protestantism, to get sympathizers in Rome to elicit from the Papacy an expression of opinion adverse to Disestablishment, for the Catholics in Ireland knew nothing about it. But the Government took action when Lord Clarendon instructed Odo Russell to report on the matter.[2] Russell's reply showed that Cairns had been himself in Rome, and had spoken to Mgr Mardi about the Irish Church, but he had not seen Antonelli or Manning there, and was about to return to England in time for the meeting of Parliament. Russell was sure that no harm had been done. It was his belief that only the persuasions of Cullen or Manning could induce the Papal Administration to declare on the Irish Church question.[3] Meanwhile Rome – or at least Kirby the agent of the Irish episcopacy there – was receiving encouraging news from Ireland. MacEvilly wrote from Galway to say that it seemed certain after the election success that the Church Establishment was 'soon to be numbered among the things that were'.[4]

The National Association did not remain inactive in this period before the Bill was presented to Parliament. At its General Meeting on 12 January letters were read from the bishops which were to have the widest repercussions, even in Rome. Before the meeting there was a private conference of fifteen persons at the Association's rooms, to discuss the direction which the committee should give. O'Neill Daunt, hoping to secure secularization by the fulfilment of the suggested use of the Church funds made by the bishops in their resolutions of October 1867, describes in his Journal what passed:

> I was anxious to move a resolution advocating the payment of poor-rates from the ecclesiastical revenues; but I found most of our associates strongly opposed to a measure which they thought would confer a benefit on a body of men whom they hated as much as the landlords. I think this is a weak and short-sighted objection. The landlords would doubtless gain, but so would the tenants. . . . And it would deprive the bigots among them of all pretext of evicting Catholic tenants in order, as they say, to get Protestants who would contribute to defray their ecclesiastical expenses. I urged my views, but a prevalent notion of the Committee was 'to leave it all to Bright and Gladstone'.[5]

It is likely that the Bishop of Ross (O'Hea) gave Daunt some support over this. He was not at the private meeting nor at the following general

---

[1] *Hansard*, third series, CXCIV, p. 2114 (23 March 1869).
[2] Clarendon Papers, c. 475 (4), f. 206, Clarendon to Russell, 11 January 1869.
[3] *Ibid.*, c. 487, f. 17, Russell to Clarendon, 27 January 1869.
[4] Kirby Papers, MacEvilly to Kirby, no. 11, 8 January 1869.
[5] Daunt, Journal, 12 January 1869.

one, but in his letter which was read out at the latter, he warned the Association against unqualified support for Gladstone.[1] MacSwiney chaired the General Meeting, and the letters from the bishops were read out.[2] Cullen's referred to all three of the Association's points. One of them, the Church, was near to settlement, but it must be effected in the way they had always demanded. 'No measure', he wrote, 'save the total disestablishment of the State Church can be acceptable to us, as no other measure will introduce that religious equality which we desire.' If the glebes were given back to the Protestant clergy the Irish Catholics could not be satisfied, he continued. But the Association should take care not to relax its efforts on the land and education questions, though it would do well to repose its confidence in the justice of Bright and Gladstone. Archbishop Leahy congratulated the Association on its success: it had created a public opinion which was convinced of the urgency of the Irish measures they had suggested. 'No unworthy compromise will be accepted', he warned. Bishop Keane of Cloyne wrote suggesting that the Irish M.P.s should meet in Dublin or London and 'put forward as the condition of their support to Mr Gladstone's Ministry the concession of measures which they believe to be indispensable for the welfare of Ireland'. This was a propitious moment, for the people of Ireland were for the first time confident that at last English statesmen had realized the necessity of consulting Irish desires when attempting to legislate for Ireland. Bishop O'Hea of Ross expressed similar opinions, but additionally warned that the Irish members, who were in a 'serried phalanx to sustain Mr Gladstone', that in their 'devotedness to the man' they should not lose sight of the aspirations of Ireland – which would only be satisfied by complete religious equality, tenant-right, and free Catholic education. Disendowment of the Protestant Church would have, therefore, to be total.

MacSwiney read out letters from other prelates also, and, addressing himself to the meeting imparted his own conviction that they must resist what some had attributed to Gladstone, a policy of substantial re-endowment of the Irish Church after Disestablishment. O'Neill Daunt used his information about Gladstone's intentions on re-endowment (which he had procured through Carvell Williams),[3] to show that MacSwiney's fear was less well-founded than he imagined. He repeated

[1] *The Times*, 15 January 1869.

[2] *Ibid.* This report shows some confusion between the private meeting and that which followed it. See also: *Guardian*, 20 January 1869; *Nonconformist*, 20 January 1869; *Freeman*, 13 January 1869. (All of these print the texts of the bishops' letters.)

[3] *Ibid.* (Daunt's name is incorrectly given here as 'Dermott'.) On the reference to Carvell Williams, see chap. 7.

his suggestion that the revenues should be used to pay the poor rates, a measure which would 'unite all classes of Irishmen in one national brotherhood'.

The expressions of this meeting were evidently intended to remind the new Government that the Irish Catholics were watching every move whilst awaiting the provisions of the Church Bill. They produced one effect. Clarendon asked Odo Russell in Rome to find out what the Papal Government thought about the letters of the bishops at the meeting.[1] Russell was not able to discover anyone in Rome who had yet heard about them, and on 5 February he inquired of Antonelli. The cardinal replied that he had neither seen nor heard of them, but seemed annoyed and referred him to Manning with whose views on the Irish Church question he wished to be identified, and whom Lord Clarendon should consult if he would know anything about the position of Rome on that matter. On instructions from Clarendon, Russell pressed the Government's disapproval, both to Antonelli and to Manning, of 'the tone assumed by the Irish priesthood, who created difficulties when it was their manifest interest to remove them from the conciliatory course Mr Gladstone was endeavouring to follow'. Manning took Cullen's part, and argued that it was the duty of the Irish bishops 'to proclaim the truth until justice was done'. Russell conveyed, in gentle language, to both men, Clarendon's wish that the Irish bishops should not upset the boat. But as he sadly reported back 'of course the clergy must struggle to get as much as they can, after which they will, as usual, be ungrateful'.[2] *The Times* took a similar line to Clarendon's, by questioning seriously the prudence of the Association's 'recent demonstration' in Dublin. Had the episcopal letters been sent before the elections they would be intelligible; but the battle had been fought and won. 'What, then, is the meaning of the war-cry which the National Association has sounded?' All they were doing was putting weapons into the hands of their foes. The 'tone of mingled defiance and mistrust' which characterized the bishops' published letters did just that. Even if Cullen and the bishops had some misgivings about Gladstone's sincerity, *The Times* continued, 'it would have been wise to conceal them till some symptom appeared in justification of them'. As it was, their action had been fortunate not to have provoked a reaction in England unfavourable to any concessions.[3] This was prophetic, but English reaction waited upon the 'excesses' of the Vatican Council.

---

[1] F.O. 43, vol. 103B, Dispatch no. 8, 5 February 1869; and Clarendon Papers, c. 487, f. 21, Russell to Clarendon, 10 February 1869.
[2] Clarendon Papers, c. 487, f. 21.   [3] *The Times*, 19 January 1869.

The embarrassment offered to Gladstone by the bishops' letters was an indication to Clarendon that something would have to be done about Cullen. 'It is really too bad', he wrote, 'that this viper Cullen should be permitted to create difficulties in addition to those which already exist.' He greatly weakened the support on which Gladstone depended.[1] Clarendon, who was nothing if not an anti-Catholic, rather wrongly interpreted Cullen's intentions, which were not to stave off support from Gladstone, but to stimulate Gladstone's awareness that the Irish Catholics' demands were pointed. Cullen indeed was to announce his support for the Gladstone Church Bill at a later time; now he was merely goading him to action. Action came: on 8 February the Cabinet held their first discussion on the Church question, and Gladstone unfolded his plan. Its actual provisions had not been known before to at least Clarendon, who had written on 25 January that he had 'not the least idea' what they were;[2] and who, on the day of the Cabinet meeting, but before attending it, could confess himself confused by the question, which seemed 'a heap of complications'. The situation was made worse by Cairns's continued presence in Rome, and the fact that he had been joined by Gathorne Hardy. And he still smarted at the thought of the Irish bishops' additions to the difficulties, by which they assisted 'their heretical brethren in creating embarrassment to Gladstone'.[3] Even the Queen was difficult, expressing to Gladstone her regret that he should 'raise this question as he has', committing himself to 'so sweeping a measure'. She feared that disestablishment would only cause more trouble in Ireland, and perhaps even prove fatal to the Establishment in England.[4] But despite all this – or perhaps because of it – the Cabinet discussion on 8th February went well. 'No dissension or violent difference of opinion arose', Lord Kimberley wrote of the meeting.[5]

Clarendon did not have to do anything about Cullen, for Cullen acted on his own. On 8 February, at the Lord Mayor's dinner in Dublin, he spoke warmly of the Government's policy for Ireland and on 11 February he called on the new Lord-Lieutenant, Spencer, at the Viceregal Lodge in Dublin. It was the first time he had ever gone there, excepting only his intercession in 1867 for the life of the Fenian Burke. He had not attended Lord Spencer's first levée, but that was because, as *The Times* said, another archbishop attended who was entitled by law to

[1] Clarendon Papers, c. 475 (4), f. 210, Clarendon to Russell, 25 January 1869.
[2] *Ibid.*
[3] *Ibid.*, c. 475 (4), f. 214, Clarendon to Russell, 8 February 1869.
[4] *The Letters of Queen Victoria, 1862–78*, vol. I, p. 578, the Queen to Gladstone, 31 January 1869.
[5] *Journal of Events . . . 1868–74*, p. 2.

precedence, and a Catholic cardinal could hardly be expected to compromise himself by accepting it.[1] It is possible, as Clarendon suggested,[2] that Cullen's courtesy visit was on instruction from Rome, following Antonelli's irritation at the National Association letters. During his call, Cullen spoke to Spencer of the Church measure, education, and charities; 'his only bugbear', Clarendon reported to Odo Russell, 'appearing to be proselytism, with which I need not tell you the Government has nothing whatever to do, and which they never directly or indirectly assist'. Spencer was delighted by the visit, and by the cardinal's conciliatory tone on the Church question. Clarendon hoped that Antonelli and Manning would encourage him further in his 'improved course of conduct'.[3] Odo Russell believed that his 'gentle language' to Antonelli and Manning about the Irish bishops had been the cause of Cullen's visit.[4] He told Antonelli of it, and the Cardinal replied that he had heard all about it, and was charmed to hear 'qu'ils s'entendent si bien'.[5] And when in May, Clarendon again told Odo Russell to ask Antonelli to instruct the Irish bishops to use their influence sympathetically to the Government's policy, and the result was a Pastoral from Archbishop Leahy praising Gladstone's plans for Ireland, he was convinced that it was Clarendon's messages which had done it all. 'After eleven years of Roman experiences', he wrote, 'I confess myself *agreeably surprised*'.[6] At all events, Cullen's action softened the effect of the National Association meeting in January, and led to what *The Times* described as an 'entente cordiale' between the bishops and the Government, which was founded 'not merely upon the refinements of courtly amenity, but upon the solid basis of political sympathy'.[7]

There was one point about which the bishops made direct approach to Gladstone before he introduced his Bill. This concerned the old and historic Catholic sites in Ireland, and the suggestion was made that some should be returned to Catholic custody. This may have been sentiment, but it was powerful. Godkin noted this, attributing it to the strong hold exercised over Irishmen by the dead hand of the past – a past reminding them of the pillage of Catholic heritage:

[1] *The Times*, 13 February 1869.
[2] Clarendon Papers, c. 475 (4), f. 220, Clarendon to Russell, 22 February 1869.
[3] *Ibid.*
[4] *Ibid.*, c. 487, f. 27, Russell to Clarendon, 24 February 1869.
[5] *Ibid.*, c. 487, f. 31, Russell to Clarendon, 10 March 1869.
[6] *Ibid.*, c. 487, f. 61, Russell to Clarendon, 2 June 1869. He added: 'Facts certainly now prove that your messages are attended to at the Vatican with a promptitude that would rouse the envy of the four Catholic Powers.'
[7] *The Times*, 13 February 1869.

If meditation among the tombs of Ireland awaken such painful reminiscences in the minds of the laity – for they are an imaginative people, prone to brood over the past – how much more powerful must be the impression produced on the minds of the Roman Catholic priests. Some of the more aged of these have been educated upon the continent, and can tell their hearers of the grandeur and beauty of the cathedrals, abbeys, and colleges enjoyed by their church in Italy, France, and Germany. . . . Even the home-bred priests, who have never left their own country . . . constantly expatiate upon this theme. . . . They quote from such books as Cobbett's *History of the Reformation* descriptions of the spoliation of ecclesiastical property, and the demolition of famous religious houses.[1]

At the end of January 1869 Archbishop Leahy sent Gladstone a memorial from the Catholics of Cashel seeking possession of the old church on the Rock of the Kings (which belonged to the Establishment). It asked Gladstone to make provision in his forthcoming Church Bill for them to obtain it 'by purchase or somehow otherwise'. The memorialists did not ask this because they were Catholics, they affirmed, but because unless they took possession of the church it would decay completely – already it was a ruin, since in 1749 the Protestant Archbishop Price had unroofed it.[2] In an accompanying letter, Leahy saw a difficulty. The memorial suggested a course for embodiment in the Disendowment Bill which 'would be for so much an endowment of the Catholic Church, and so at variance with the principle of the measure'. This difficulty could be met if the Catholics were enabled to purchase the site from the State after disendowment. It was a site, he admitted, 'dear to all Ireland for its historical recollections'.[3] Cullen went further than that. Writing to tell Gladstone what he thought of the Church Bill in March 1869, he expressed his feeling that it was 'undesirable' that the twelve cathedrals should be restored to Protestant use by its provisions. This would appear in Ireland as a 'symbol of religious inequality', and the correct course would be to hand some of the old cathedrals over to the Catholics. In Dublin, the Catholics should have one of the two old cathedrals. He did not make the proviso about purchase that Leahy had; they would pay for maintenance and repair of the buildings, but not, apparently, for their acquisition in the first instance.[4] Cullen's suggestion can therefore be considered as an infraction of the

---

[1] James Godkin, *Ireland and her Churches*, pp. 5-6. Cobbett's *History of the Protestant 'Reformation' in England and Ireland* (Dublin, 1826), attempted to show, as its subtitle declared, 'how that event has impoverished and degraded the main body of the people in those countries'.

[2] Gladstone Papers, B.M.Add.MS. 44609, f. 20. 'R.C. Memorial seeking possession of the Old Church at Cashel', 25 January 1869.

[3] *Ibid.*, B.M.Add.MS. 44418, f. 232, Leahy to Gladstone, 30 January 1869.

[4] *Ibid.*, B.M.Add.MS. 44419, f. 198, Cullen to Gladstone, 11 March 1869.

principle of the Bill. Replying, Gladstone said that the Church Bill's provisions for the vesting of ecclesiastical sites was 'the most easy and satisfactory settlement', intended to include the interests of all communions. He had explained the course taken on this subject to several of the Irish members.[1]

Moriarty, writing to Fortescue in the same month, followed Leahy's caution and outlined a plan for Catholic acquisition of old Catholic sites by purchase. Thus they could get back St Patrick's Cathedral in Dublin, and the ruins of Cashel; the latter could then be restored just as Guinness had restored the former.[2] Gladstone saw these plans as threatening the principle of the Bill, but was able to use them, in turn, to persuade the Queen of the danger of over-generosity to the Protestant Church. He wrote to her in February:

> . . . to give to the disestablished Church the small portion of property conferred by the State since the Reformation, might give colour to a dangerous claim on the part of the R.C. Church to be reinstated in possession of the property presented to it by the State before the Reformation, and from this claim it might be difficult, on principle of equal dealing, to escape.[3]

The Cashel memorialists had affirmed that they asked not as Catholics, but simply to prevent the complete ruin of the site, and although this was not quite the case, Gladstone took them at their face value. By Clause 25 of the Church Act, disused places of worship of historic importance were vested in the Commissioners of Public Works (Ireland), to be preserved as national monuments.[4] The ruins of Cashel were so vested in 1871, and Dunraven wrote to Monsell, 'how sad this is . . . there ends the Archbishop's scheme'.[5]

The Commons went into Committee on 1 March and Gladstone moved leave to bring in his Bill 'to put an end to the Establishment of the Church in Ireland, and to make provision in respect of the temporalities thereof, and in respect of the Royal College of Maynooth'.[6] He explained

---

[1] Gladstone Papers, B.M.Add.MS. 44419, f. 209, Gladstone to Cullen, 13 March 1869.

[2] Carlingford Papers, CP. 3/85, Moriarty to Fortescue, 31 March 1869.

[3] *The Letters of Queen Victoria*, 1862–78, vol. i, p. 580, Gladstone to the Queen, 1 February 1869.

[4] 32 & 33 Vict. cap. 42. cl. 25 (1).

[5] Monsell Papers, Box 8319, Dunraven to Monsell, 4 September 1871.

[6] *Hansard*, cxciv, p. 412. Again, this is not the place to examine the Church Bill in Parliament except in so far as it touched Catholic interests. See: Commons' Committee on the Irish Church, 1 March 1869 (*ibid.*, pp. 412 ff.); Debates on the Bill (32 & 33 Vict. cap. 42); *Commons*, first reading (*ibid.*, pp. 466 ff.); second reading, 16 March 1869, (*ibid.*, pp. 1662 ff.); Committee, 15 April 1869 (*ibid.* cxcv, pp. 847 ff.); third reading, 31 May 1869 (*ibid.*, cxcvi, pp. 971 ff.). Lords' Debates, second reading, 14 June 1869 (*ibid.*, cxcvi, pp. 1637 ff.); Committee, 19 June 1869 (*ibid.*, cxcvii, pp. 686 ff.);

its details, ending with the heavy remark that 'the working of our constitutional government itself is upon its trial'.[1] The Bill's preamble made it clear that the whole was founded on the principle of total disestablishment and disendowment. The clauses made it clear that the intention was the secularization of the revenues, and the withdrawal of all assistance from the State to other Churches. The union of the Church of England and Ireland was to cease on 1 January 1871, on which day also the Irish Establishment would end. Protestant life interests were reserved or compensated; a Temporalities Commission appointed to deal with the revenues, the disestablished Church to be incorporated with a Representative Church Body; its doctrine and discipline to remain the same unless altered according to the constitution of the Church; ecclesiastical courts to cease; the Church to be empowered to hold Synods; the College of Maynooth was cut free from the State, its grant to cease, with compensation, and the *Regium Donum* also to cease. The churches in use at the time of the passing of the Act were to be conveyed to the new Body, subject to the life interests of the incumbents; the same was to take place with burial grounds; and the Temporalities Commissioners were to sell to the Church Body clerical residences and glebes. Special provision was also made for the Commissioners to dispose of any residue of Church estates by sales to the tenants, and as their purchase was to be assisted by State Loans, the Act was therefore the first to facilitate land purchase with the important precedent of State aid. Six thousand peasant proprietors were in fact created by the operation of the Act. Finally, of the £15 million of Church property which the State would take into its possession, £10 million was to be given back to the disestablished Church, and the balance was to be appropriated,[2] as the original preamble read, 'not for the maintenance of any Church or clergy, nor for the teaching of religion, but mainly for the relief of unavoidable calamity and suffering not touched by the poor law'.[3]

The Liberation Society worked to secure the passage of this Bill.[4] Since the visit of Carvell Williams in 1867, it had decided against active

---

third reading, 12 July 1869 (*ibid.*, pp. 1595 ff.), *Commons Debate on the Lords' amendments*, 15 July 1869 (*ibid.*, pp. 1891 ff.). *Lords' consideration of the Commons' amendments to their amendments*, 20 July 1869 (*ibid.*, CXCVIII, pp. 235 ff.). *Bill returned to the Commons*, 23 July 1869 (*ibid.*, p. 521); *Commons, Consideration of amendments*, 23 July 1869 (*ibid.*, pp. 564 ff.).

[1] *Hansard*, CXCIV, p. 465. [2] This is Gladstone's estimate. *Ibid.*, CXCVII, p. 1966.

[3] See Morley, *Life of Gladstone*, vol. I, p. 897; J. T. Ball, *The Reformed Church of Ireland*, pp. 271 ff.

[4] See Liberation Society Minute Books, vol. IV (1868–72), pp. 128, 131, 135, 137, 143, 145, 147, 151, on the Bill in the Commons; pp. 151, 153, on the Bill in the Lords; pp. 156, 157, 159, 160, on the Lords' amendments; p. 161, on the passing of the Bill.

work in Ireland, its only action there being the distribution of publications.[1] It had been satisfied by the bishops' resolutions of October 1867 that Catholics could be counted upon to support and agitate for total secularization, and this *principle* the Bill now incorporated. The Church question was the only common ground that the society had with the National Association and they were to fall away from each other after its settlement. Not only was this because they became actively divided over the Irish university question early in the seventies, but also because the Irish refused to fulfil the terms of their working agreement of the sixties. In May 1869 Monsell said in the Commons that the Irish had no wish to upset the Established Church in England.[2] This did not matter so much, for he had never belonged to the National Association. But in 1871 Miall introduced a Bill for English Disestablishment into the Commons, based on the Irish precedent,[3] and the Liberation Society appealed in vain for help from Ireland and the Association.[4] The Catholic union with the Dissenters was then at an end.

The first reading of the Bill on 1 March was quickly followed by varying Catholic reactions. Gladstone sent a copy to Cullen, who, in his reply on 11 March, said he felt that

the measures proposed in that Bill appear very well adapted to promote the interests of Ireland. Since it has appeared, I have seen several of my colleagues in the episcopacy, and many persons of every class among Catholics, and they all agree in expecting that the new legislation will inaugurate an era of peace and prosperity for this country.[5]

To prove his point, he quoted from a letter he had received from Bishop Furlong of Ferns – a name later to be notorious in England – which said that the Bill was 'at the same time the most practical that could be devised, and very indulgent to all interests concerned'. Cullen went on to suggest a few objections which, if attended to, would make the Bill even more acceptable. Some of the old cathedrals might well be given over to Catholic use. In order to help the introduction of small proprietors, all the see lands of the disendowed Church could be sold to the farmers in actual possession, though if this was not practical, it ought not to be allowed to interrupt the progress of the Bill. The surplus of ecclesiastical property was most properly to be used for charitable

[1] See Liberation Society Minute Books, vol. IV, p. 76, decision at the Council of 24 July 1868.

[2] *Hansard*, CXCVI, p. 1023 (31 May 1869).

[3] See *Annual Register*, 1871 (History), p. 92.

[4] Daunt, Journal, 19 April 1871. The appeal was made in the usual way, by a letter to Daunt from Carvell Williams.

[5] Gladstone Papers, B.M.Add.MS. 44419, f. 198, Cullen to Gladstone, 11 March 1869.

purposes, but this should not aid those institutions under the control of the Grand Juries in the provinces, since such places were 'nests of proselytism'. He had nothing to say about Maynooth. The sum allotted to it (£380,000), was small compared with Protestant compensation, but it would get on well enough with it. He ended by an expression of his gratitude for the measure.[1] In his reply, Gladstone explained that regarding the surplus the Bill was as yet incomplete, and a measure would be introduced later providing loans for the purchase of glebe-houses by all religious bodies.[2] Cullen went further in his support of the Bill. In a letter to the Dublin clergy he stated that if the measures proposed by the Prime Minister were accepted by Parliament, they would 'largely contribute to spread contentment and produce harmony among all classes'.[3]

Bishop Nulty, who had, in 1868, to reassure the country that he was still opposed to the Establishment despite the secession of his clergy from the National Association in 1865 over the land question, gave his support to the Bill too. 'With some trifling exceptions,' he wrote, 'it is grand.'[4] But other leading Catholics were less pleased. Aubrey de Vere tried to induce Moriarty to publish something which would show up the evils in the Bill. First among these was the fact that half of the Church property 'would be lost *forever*', not only to religion but to Irish purposes generally. Second was the 'elaborate arrangement' by which Catholics were to be prevented from recovering any of their cathedrals. This was galling, especially as in 1868 Bright had admitted that if the Protestant clergy retained the churches and glebe-houses, the Catholics were entitled to a corresponding 'fixed property'. Surely, he asked, the clergy and laity will not say that they regard this as a satisfactory settlement?[5] O'Neill Daunt was one of the laity who would not, and on reading the Bill in the newspapers, he prepared a criticism of it to send to the National Association.[6] He could see that to some extent it was 'a dis-endowing scheme, but objectionable in not going as far in that direction as Gladstone might have done with propriety and with full consideration for the vested-interests of existing incumbents'. The capitalization plan was in reality one of re-endowment of Protestantism. 'This is anything

1 *Ibid.* Cullen's point about the sale of see lands to the tenants – the principle of which was incorporated into the Church Act – has interesting affinities with the 'Bright clauses' in the 1870 Land Act.

2 *Ibid.*, Add.MS. 44419, f. 209, Gladstone to Cullen, 13 March 1869.

3 *The Times*, 15 March 1869.

4 Kirby Papers, Nulty to Kirby, no. 72, 5 March 1869.

5 Monsell Papers, Box 8319, de Vere to Moriarty, 2 March 1869. De Vere was in London to see the first stages of the Bill for himself.

6 Daunt, Journal, 8 March 1869.

The Catholic Church and Ireland in the Age of Rebellion

but "religious equality".[1] Thus was fulfilled his suspicion, for in the previous December he had written, 'I cannot unreservedly trust Gladstone.'[2]

Clarendon, who always thought the worst of Cullen, was surprised by his thankful acceptance of the Bill, supposing it must have been inspired by instruction from Rome.[3] The position of Rome had in fact changed somewhat. In November 1868 Cardinal Antonelli had asked Odo Russell about the course the new Government intended on the Irish Church question. Russell was not able to tell him – he did not then know anything beyond general principle. But a long conversation followed in which the cardinal 'distinctly said that the Church of Rome could never approve or sanction the principle of disendowment of any Church – or the principle of the separation of Church and State in any country'. Neither could they allow the clergy to be salaried by a non-Catholic Government.[4] Remarking on this conversation, Clarendon noticed its apparent incompatibility with Cullen's known opinion on the Irish Church. On hearing of Antonelli's words, Gladstone suggested some points to Clarendon which Odo Russell could make to the cardinal in Rome.[5] Antonelli apparently reacted favourably, and this will not seem strange if it was the case that his conversation with Russell on 24 November had reflected Cullen's fears that general endowment would follow disestablishment in Ireland. He now told Russell that he could not state Papal policy on the Church question until the reports at the Propaganda had been digested, but that in general the opinions publicly expressed by Cullen and Manning could be taken as being those of the Papacy.[6] In January, Russell pressed him to be rather more explicit by saying 'that it would be difficult for Her Majesty's Government to give the weight they might wish to the opinions of the Papal Government if they were precluded from quoting His Eminence's authority'. Antonelli replied that the English Government could consider the views of the Irish and English bishops, and 'more especially the opinions of Cardinal Cullen and Archbishop Manning on the Irish Church question, as the correct interpretation of the views and opinions of the Papal

[1] Daunt, Journal, 8 March 1869, He added: 'Gladstone proposes to employ a considerable share of the Church money in establishing lunatic asylums; possibly thinking that enlarged accommodation for demented patients will be rendered necessary when his measure shall have driven half the parsons and Orangemen mad.'

[2] Ibid., 26 December 1868.

[3] Clarendon Papers, c. 475 (4), f. 222, Clarendon to Russell, 8 March 1869.

[4] F.O. 43, vol. 101, Dispatch no. 48, 24 November 1868.

[5] Clarendon Papers, c. 475 (4), f. 196, Clarendon to Russell, 14 December 1868.

[6] F.O. 43, vol. 101, Dispatch no. 57, 22 December 1868.

Government'.[1] This was at least a little more definite. It was surprising that the strongly Gladstonian predilections vented in Rome by Manning found favour at the Vatican, especially as Gladstone was a known enemy of the Temporal Power, but it was so. The Pope had, as Odo Russell said, 'implicit faith and confidence in him'.[2] Clarendon saw Manning several times on his return to England, and no doubt learned directly from him, as Antonelli had indicated, what the policy of Rome was.[3] Antonelli approved the Church Bill when it had been presented. Russell reported:

> Cardinal Antonelli told me this morning [9 March] that he had read Mr Gladstone's speech of the 1st instant, on the Irish Church, with great interest, and that the plan proposed for solving that difficult question appeared to him both prudent and wise [aussi prudent que sage] because it gave full time for an equitable *rectification* of Church interests without bearing the character of a *confiscation* of Church property, like the odious measures adopted in Italy two years ago.[4]

Thus at the critical moment when the Church Bill lay before the country, but before the Commons' second reading, Cullen and Rome were in accord, despite the fact that, as Odo Russell pointed out, most of Antonelli's information on the Irish Church came from Manning, who was more Gladstonian than Cullen, and far more disposed to compromise on questions touching endowment. For Manning's influence was supreme in Rome now that Mgr Talbot had been carried off insane to Passy; and ordinarily he confided directly in the Cardinal Secretary of State, whereas Cullen dealt more with Barnabo, the Cardinal Prefect of the Propaganda.[5] Yet Antonelli was evidently satisfied that he had grasped Gladstone's policy, for he does not seem to have followed the subsequent debates on the Church Bill, and relied instead on 'impressions derived from Manning's and Cullen's correspondence'.[6] From his early disapproval, Antonelli had moved to warm approval of the Bill – but from that position he did not change. At a meeting with Clarendon in London on 5 April, Manning said that 'the course pursued by Gladstone was highly approved at the Vatican, and that although the disendowment of any church is not generally looked on with favour yet the mode in which it was proposed to distribute the revenue was quite in

[1] *Ibid.*, vol. 103B, Dispatch no. 4, 12 January 1869.
[2] Gladstone Papers, B.M.Add.MS. 44418, f. 144, Odo Russell to Clarendon, 13 January 1869. See also, Clarendon Papers, c. 487, f. 13.
[3] Clarendon Papers, c. 475 (4), f. 214, Clarendon to Russell, 8 February 1869, arranging the first meeting in London.
[4] F.O. 43, vol. 103B, Dispatch no. 11, 9 March 1869.
[5] Clarendon Papers, c. 487, f. 77, Russell to Clarendon, 14 July 1869.
[6] *Ibid.*

accordance with Catholic principles'.[1] And on the 21st Odo Russell was able to report that the Pope had himself told Count d'Arco how highly he approved of the Gladstone Church measure.[2]

On 16 March the Commons' debate on the second reading of the Bill began, with Disraeli opening with the cry that disestablishment and disendowment were quite separate matters, but that they had been confused at the elections and were confused now.[3] It was too late, however, to save the endowments on that tack, and after four days of debate the Bill passed its second reading with a majority of 118, on 23 March. Cullen remained quiet, but others in Ireland continued to be less happy. The Catholic parish priest of Kingscourt, a Father O'Reilly, wrote to the *Dublin Post* to say that the clause in the Bill which provided for the maintenance of the Protestant churches as national monuments, at public expense, had created feelings of surprise and dissatisfaction in his locality, and, he believed, in others also.[4] In reply to de Vere's appeal, Moriarty wrote a public letter to Fortescue on the Church Bill which, although welcoming its main provisions, put the criticisms made by de Vere.[5] The Dublin Protestants were more than critical. They published a solemn *Protest* in the form of a broadsheet, which declared that the papist organization of Ireland was now complete, led by a Cardinal-Legate, and that the only obstacle to the establishment of the Pope as supreme ruler in Ireland was the Royal Supremacy. It was 'with a view to remove this obstacle that the Roman Catholic clergy seek for the disestablishment of the Irish Church'.[6] In the same month a meeting addressed by Murphy at North Shields was attacked by four hundred armed Irishmen, and serious rioting resulted.[7] But opposition was not without its uses to supporters of the Bill, and as at this time the movement in favour of the release of the Fenian prisoners was spreading, McCabe, the Catholic Bishop of Ardagh, made virtue of necessity and published a letter against Fenianism and agrarian criminals, in which he hinted that the opponents of Gladstone's measure were the authors of agrarian outrage.[8]

The Commons went into Committee to consider the clauses of the Bill on 15 April, and on 5 May they came to Clause 39: the Repeal of the Maynooth Acts. A long discussion took place – the longest on any of the clauses. The sections of the Acts relating to the college which did

---

[1] Clarendon Papers, c. 475 (4), f. 228, Clarendon to Russell, 5 April 1869.
[2] *Ibid.*, c. 487, f. 41, Russell to Clarendon, 21 April 1869; d'Arco was Sir John Acton's father-in-law.
[3] *Hansard*, CXCIV, p. 1662.   [4] Quoted in the *Guardian*, 17 March 1869.
[5] *Ibid.*   [6] Quoted *ibid.*, 24 March 1869.
[7] *Annual Register*, 1869 (Chronicle), p. 22.   [8] *Guardian*, 24 March 1869.

not touch its legal existence were to be repealed, it was no longer to receive a State grant, although as in the case of the Church, life interests were to be attended to, and compensation was calculated at fourteen times the amount of the annual grant, to be given to the college as a capital sum. Debts owed by the trustees to the Board of Works which had accrued as a result of building expenses were released, and visitation was to cease. During the discussion, The O'Conor Don spoke for the Catholics in the House.[1] His claim that the Maynooth question related 'to educational, and not to religious endowments',[2] was the last statement of a long debate between Irish Catholics and Gladstone. It will be well to examine it in some detail, for over the Maynooth clause the Catholics felt their interests most closely touched, and it was over it also that the influence they tried to exert was to fail with the Government they had done so much to lift into power. It illustrates the extent to which Gladstone's measure rested on the English Radicals and Dissenters rather than upon the Irish Catholics. It was the former group who opposed continued endowment of Maynooth, and Gladstone sided with them to overrule Irish claims, some of which, like one put by Thomas Andrews, regretted the admixture of the Maynooth Grant with the Church question. Yet Andrews could see that disendowment of Maynooth was indispensable to the Church Bill in the sense that it 'floated into popularity a measure otherwise of doubtful acceptance with any large sections of the Protestants in the United Kingdom'.[3]

Even before the general election the President of Maynooth had approached Gladstone about the treatment the college should receive at the hands of a Liberal Government. In October 1868 Dr Russell had hoped that the election might pass off without it becoming necessary for the leading statesmen to enter much in detail regarding Maynooth, since it was a subject 'not likely to be very calmly discussed at the hustings'.[4] But it had proved not to be so. He therefore wished to let Gladstone know that Catholics had reconciled themselves to the cessation of the college's grant as a charge on the Consolidated Fund 'but beyond this they have maintained the most cautious reserve'.[5] Discussion of Maynooth in 1869 was to reveal the causes of that reserve, but Russell went in deep with his first probe. He told Gladstone that all Catholics felt it unfair to consider or deal with the Maynooth endowment '*simply in contrast with the Irish Church Endowment*'. He continued:

[1] *Hansard*, CXCVI, p. 142.   [2] *Ibid.*, p. 143.
[3] Thomas Andrews, *The Church in Ireland*, p. 40.
[4] Gladstone Papers, B.M.Add.MS. 44416, f. 78, Russell to Gladstone, 20 October 1868.
[5] *Ibid.*

There is no doubt that Maynooth is an *ecclesiastical*, but it is also an *educational* institution; and the true term of comparison for Maynooth as a State (or more properly, a public) establishment, would rather be Trinity College, Dublin, considered *as an Educational Establishment for the teaching of the Protestant clergy*. We consider that Maynooth is to be dealt with in contrast with Trinity College, and not with the Irish Church; and I may add that Mr Goldwin Smith volunteered to me the same view, and I have heard that this is also the view of Mr J. S. Mill, and of several others of the advanced Liberal Party.[1]

And even if, he continued, the case of Maynooth should be contrasted with the Church Establishment, it could then be pointed out that they would be unfairly treated, for it seemed likely from discussion of the Church question during the year that all the college could get in compensation would not compare to the scale of compensation the Church would receive. There could be no justice, and no religious equality, unless Maynooth was more handsomely provided for, and all Catholics were agreed on that.[2] Replying to this, Gladstone assured the President that nothing was yet settled, but thinking evidently of Fawcett's designs on Trinity College, he suggested one objection to Russell's proposed mode of dealing with Maynooth. If it were to be considered as an educational and not an ecclesiastical institution, Parliament could be held to interfere with it, to open it to laymen, regulate it 'as to tests in the manner which we have applied in the past and mean to apply further to Trinity College'. Alternatively, it might be said that because the college was entirely clerical, it must be treated as ecclesiastical by definition.[3]

Dr Russell admitted the difficulties Gladstone had raised, agreeing that if Maynooth should come to be dealt with as 'part of the *general scheme* of public education, I do not see how the alternative which you make could be evaded'. Yet he did not seek to have the college settled in general educational terms, but peculiarly treated with Trinity. Unlike Trinity, it was true, Maynooth was not a place of lay education, but like Trinity, it was especially endowed for clerical learning. It was uncertain how Trinity would be dealt with when the time came, but unless its specially Protestant character was abolished, Catholics would feel themselves entitled to claim for Maynooth 'consideration for an *analogous educational establishment*' on the lines of the Trinity settlement. And this would be complicated; for the bishops would never accept a mixed, lay and clerical, Maynooth. He gave ground a little – if the

[1] Gladstone Papers, B.M.Add.MS. 44416, f. 78, Russell to Gladstone, 20 October 1868.

[2] *Ibid.*

[3] *Ibid.*, B.M.Add.MS. 44417, f. 270, Gladstone to Russell, 28 December 1868. This letter is also in Dr Russell's Papers at Maynooth.

college could only with danger to its purposes be dealt with educationally, then he supposed that it must form part of a general settlement, but
if so, it must be on the principle of 'equal dealing with all the religious
communities'.[1] To establish their position, the President and Maynooth
professors decided to present a memorial to Gladstone. While this was in
preparation, during January, Gladstone and Russell continued to
communicate, Gladstone requesting, and receiving, information on the
running and nature of the college.[2] Russell also had time to consult
others about his original proposal to treat Maynooth educationally, and
they had apparently seen the dangers and advised against it. In its place
he therefore recommended to the Government an alternative course of
action, 'to find room for the permanent maintenance of the education
of our clergy under the general provisions which your avowed principle
of equal dealing towards all the communions will necessitate, as a set-off
against what it is proposed to have permanently in the hands of the
Protestants'. Further than this, and considering the temper of the
English and Scottish Liberal Party, he felt it would be injudicious to
make the maintenance of Maynooth, *as such*, any part of the Church
Settlement. The State should cease to provide for it, and then the religious difficulties which it created in the public mind would cease. But
material provisions would leave the college able to carry on without
State aid.[3]

This plan received curious support from Bruce when he spoke at
Lochwinnoch in Renfrewshire on 19 January. Replying to a questioner
who had asked if he would vote for the abolition of the Maynooth grant,
Bruce said that it must be part of a general settlement. The subject had
not yet been discussed by the Cabinet, but if the clergy of the disendowed Church were to be left with their houses and glebes, then the
Presbyterians and Catholics must not be left in a position of inequality.
The Government would thus have to decide whether to leave the
Protestant clergy without houses or glebes, or whether to give some form
of compensation to the other two denominational bodies, so securing
their equality. 'That subject', he added, 'is one which has to be considered.'[4] Russell read this speech in *The Times*, and was delighted,
writing to tell Gladstone that Bruce had put the matter on its 'true

[1] *Ibid.*, B.M.Add.MS. 44417, f. 290, Russell to Gladstone, 31 December 1868.

[2] C. W. Russell's Papers, Gladstone to Russell, 15 January 1869; Gladstone Papers,
B.M.Add.MS. 44418, f. 189, Russell to Gladstone, 20 January 1869.

[3] Gladstone Papers, B.M.Add.MS. 44418, f. 165, Russell to Gladstone, 18 January
1869.

[4] *The Times*, 20 January 1869.

footing'.[1] At the end of January, the Maynooth memorial arrived in London. It quoted the speech which Sir Robert Peel made in Parliament on 3 May 1845,[2] and showed that as the professors were 'in possession of offices fixed and permanent in law, we earnestly request that under any provision for us which may be substituted for the present, we may enjoy equal legal security, and that it may be conferred on us by an express enactment in the Bill by which the College may be disendowed'.[3] As Peel had received a deputation in 1845, the professors suggested one at this time should Gladstone wish it. The memorial was signed by the President and nineteen professors. Gladstone described it as 'most moderate'.[4]

Gladstone took the point, and his letter to Fortescue about the clauses to go into the Bill, written in February, shows that Maynooth compensation was considered in association with Protestant glebes.[5] But to some other Catholics, the objections suggested by Gladstone to Dr Russell's original proposal were not yet apparent. Aubrey de Vere told Moriarty early in March that Maynooth was 'a part obviously of the *University* not the *Church* Question!'[6] Meanwhile on 4 March the Bill's appearance had been approved by Russell, who thought it a 'skilful contrivance to provide for the numberless interests and varieties of interests which are involved in this prodigious social and political revolution'.[7] Gladstone was delighted, and hastened to explain that 'the case of Maynooth was the subject of much consideration, and I think that at last the right mode of proceeding was hit upon'. But the question was still not closed, and he anticipated that 'new points may emerge' in the debate.[8] More points were to emerge in the debates than he imagined, but it was the attempt to carry old points rather than new ones which characterized the proceedings.

Dr Russell did not let the matter rest there, however. He was anxious to make sure that the Maynooth clauses of the Bill, which were silent on the question, should give legal security to the life interests of individuals in the college.[9] Gladstone assured him that the drafting of the clause

[1] Gladstone Papers, B.M.Add.MS. 44418, f. 189, Russell to Gladstone, 20 January 1869.

[2] *Hansard*, LXXX, p. 143.

[3] B.M.Add.MS. 44798, f. 110, 'Maynooth Memorial', January 1869.

[4] Carlingford Papers, CP. 1/26, Gladstone to Fortescue, 30 January 1869.

[5] *Ibid.*, CP. 1/30, and CP. 1/36, Gladstone to Fortescue, 14 and 22 February 1869.

[6] Monsell Papers, Box 8319, de Vere to Moriarty, 2 March 1869.

[7] Gladstone Papers, B.M.Add.MS. 44419, f. 161, Russell to Gladstone, 4 March 1869.

[8] C. W. Russell's Papers, Gladstone to Russell, 5 March 1869.

[9] Gladstone Papers, B.M.Add.MS. 44419, f. 172, Russell to Gladstone, 7 March 1869.

was a legal matter and that all would be well – it was simply the case that when legislating, Parliament took no note of individual interests, but only of Trusts, and the Trustees would have legal security.[1] On 11 March, Cullen expressed himself satisfied with the arrangements in the Bill for Maynooth. 'Though the sum allotted to it appears small when compared with what is granted to Protestants and Presbyterians,' he wrote to Gladstone, 'in my opinion it will get on very well with its new endowment; but it appears reasonable that it should be exempted from visitations and other acts of State control to which it is now subjected.'[2] Bishop Furlong believed that if the sum granted as compensation could be invested, the college would be able to get along well.[3] But Gladstone was beginning to realize that the Maynooth clauses would receive a stormy treatment in Committee, especially from Aytoun, who opposed anything that could be construed as an endowment of the college. On 29 March, Gladstone wrote to Fortescue,

> It occurs to me that the question most awkward *for us* in the Committee on the Irish Church Bill may after all prove to be the 14 years [compensation adjustment] for Maynooth. And this seems so far likely, that I should be glad to know whether we could now take in hand the framing of a measure with regard to Trinity College, as a definite movement. I am not well enough acquainted with the subject to know whether this is practicable: but I think it deserves consideration. The defensive effect of the introduction of such a Bill I apprehend would be that it might prevent the Opposition from falling in *en masse* with the Aytoun faction. I conclude we should neutralize the University and seize on its behalf a large part of the endowments, leaving to the College as a denominational institution a portion of them for its own purposes.[4]

This plan was not followed up, although it is interesting to notice that the separation of Trinity College from the University of Dublin, which Gladstone suggested here, was to be the principle of his ill-fated university proposals of 1873. But in 1869 it was evidently considered inadvisable to attempt a quasi-settlement of the university question at the same time as the Church Bill: no doubt the endowments problem would have proved too embarrassing. It was to make an appearance on 4 May, when the House in Committee came to consider Clause 39 of the Bill. Whalley for the Opposition described the clause as 'levelling-up', and moved an amendment to have the visitation of the college continued, for should it be discontinued, 'the foreign power of the Papacy would be

---

[1] C. W. Russell's Papers, Gladstone to Russell, 9 March 1869.
[2] Gladstone Papers, B.M.Add.MS. 44419, f. 198, Cullen to Gladstone, 11 March 1869.
[3] *Ibid.*, Furlong's letter to Cullen quoted.
[4] Carlingford Papers, CP. 1/41, Gladstone to Fortescue, 29 March 1869.

left entirely without control'.[1] He went on to say that 'ordinary Protestants like himself [laughter] were opposed to it'.[2] Gladstone hastened to add that the position of Maynooth required special legal treatment: it was an existing corporation, and if the Maynooth Acts were wholly repealed that corporation would be destroyed.[3] Newdegate countered by saying that Maynooth property ought to be vested in the Commission appointed by the Bequests Act. He made an acute point when he said that incorporation of Maynooth was objectionable 'for the same category of reasons' which had induced Gladstone to find the incorporation of a Catholic university objectionable.[4] This was fair comment, but it went unanswered. Fielden remarked on the Pope's hatred of the principle of religious equality. Had the proposal to endow Maynooth – for that, he said, was what Clause 39 implied – been made at the elections the Liberals would not have got in.[5]

It was at this point that The O'Conor Don intervened. He had consulted with Dr Russell as to the course he should take, and Russell had advised him to make an additional claim on the part of the College Trustees 'for the repayment of the money expended by the Trustees, *from private funds* on repairs and buildings'.[6] But in the Commons' discussion, The O'Conor Don made his chief point the one which Russell had finally come to reject. He said that Catholics only asked for equal dealing, but the present question related 'to educational and not to religious endowments', and reminded the House that 'though Trinity College was not in the Bill . . . its consideration was postponed, not decided'.[7] When the Committee resumed on 6 May, Sir Hervey Bruce took up the question The O'Conor Don had thrown down. The University of Dublin and Maynooth were quite different, he said, 'since at the former, education was open for all, and at Maynooth it was only for Roman Catholics'.[8] Disraeli was shocked that compensation was apparently to be provided from the funds of the Establishment – it should come out of the Consolidated Fund.[9] But it was, as predicted, Aytoun who pressed home the objections. On 15 April he had introduced Maynooth into the debate, by protesting against the generosity of its proposed permanent endowment which the scale of compensation suggested. The effects would be evil; already the Maynooth Grant 'had enabled the hierarchy to educate boys into a priesthood the most powerful in Europe'.[10] Worse even than that was the principle at stake,

---

[1] *Hansard*, cxcvi, p. 108.   [2] *Ibid.*, cxcvi, p. 109.   [3] *Ibid.*, p. 112.
[4] *Ibid.*, p. 114.   [5] *Ibid.*, p. 121.
[6] Gladstone Papers, B.M.Add.MS. 44420, f. 81, Russell to Gladstone, 13 April 1869.
[7] *Hansard*, cxcvi, p. 146.   [8] *Ibid.*, p. 268.   [9] *Ibid.*, p. 292.
[10] *Ibid.*, cxcv, p. 874.

which savoured of broken pledges. 'The Government had gone to the polls and the question of "levelling-down" had been sanctioned', he said, '– the provision for Maynooth in the Bill goes against that principle.'[1] In the discussion of Clause 39 on 6 May, he repeated his charge of a broken pledge,[2] but it was too late, and the clause was agreed to. When it came to the Lords, on 6 July, it slid through without much opposition,[3] the House looking favourably upon a clause which went some of the way towards the grand design of concurrent endowment which they were attempting to graft into the Bill by their amendments.

Dr Russell was satisfied by the passage of the Maynooth clause,[4] hoping that some clause might be inserted at a later stage with provision for old age and sickness among those who were to enjoy life interests, as in the case of the Protestant clergy.[5]

This is a fit point to look briefly at the subsequent fate of Maynooth. When the Church Act came into effect in 1871, the *ex officio* trustees lapsed, and a sum of compensation fixed at £309,040 was granted. The debt of £12,704 owing to the Board of Works for building charges was remitted.[6] And as Healy wrote of the Act: 'There could be no more Government Commissions, no more lay visitations, no more vexatious and calumnious debates in Parliament about the College; and that in itself was something of a gain.'[7] In August 1869 the bishops had met at Maynooth to deliberate on the future of the college,[8] but it was not until 20 June 1871 that the first meeting of the Trustees took place under the new system. Cullen took the Chair, and the three archbishops and eight other prelates were present. The lay Catholics who were trustees resigned. The new Board invested £91,592. 7s. 2d. in a loan to Lord Granard, and the college's finances were generally reconstituted.[9] It was unfortunate that the 1869 Act made no reference to the 1795 Act of the Irish Parliament which established Maynooth, and which therefore remained unrepealed.[10] For by it, all the by-laws, rules, regulations and statutes agreed upon by the college Trustees had to be laid before the Lord-Lieutenant for his positive or negative approval if they were to have legal effect. This still bound the college after 1871.[11] A Bill to repeal the relevant Clause 4 of the 1795 Act, introduced to the Commons by

[1] *Ibid.*, p. 876.   [2] *Ibid.*, cxcvi, p. 302.   [3] *Ibid.*, cxcvii, p. 1108. (Clause 40 of the Act).
[4] Gladstone Papers, B.M.Add.MS. 44420, f. 236, Russell to Gladstone, 8 May 1869.
[5] *Ibid.*, Add.MS. 44420, f. 277, Russell to Gladstone, 17 May 1869. For Gladstone's cautious and unrevealing reply, see Dr Russell's Papers, Gladstone to Russell, 18 May 1869.
[6] James MacCaffrey, *History of the Catholic Church in the Nineteenth Century*, vol. II, p. 263.
[7] John Healy, *Maynooth College*, p. 480.   [8] *Freeman*, 2 September 1869.
[9] Healy, *op. cit.*, p. 485.   [10] 35 Geo. III, cap. 12.   [11] Healy, *op. cit.*, p. 481.

Hartington, the new Chief Secretary in July 1871, only received a first reading.[1] In June 1872, the college was provided with a 'visiting-committee', elected by ballot. At the Board in September, the President of the college was directed by the Trustees to ask for a Bill to repeal Clause 4 of the 1795 Act, in order to give legal effect to the new statutes made that year.[2] Nothing happened. But Gladstone had intended to do something – he had hoped to insert a clause to clear up the trouble into the University Bill in 1873. 'That, however, is at an end,' he wrote sadly to Dr Russell in March of that year, 'and all I can do will be to leave the Bill which has been drafted and is quite ready, to my successor, with a memorandum as to the necessity for it.'[3] Clause 4 of the 1795 Act remained on the statute book.

As, in May 1869, the Bill sifted through the House to the passage of its third reading on the last day of the month,[4] reaction in Ireland among those who had agitated the Church question continued to be varied. Cullen could not resist an invidious comparison between the amounts granted to Maynooth, and to the Protestants and Presbyterians. Yet he hoped the Bill would pass, expressing a fear that the Lords might reject it.[5] Daunt's earlier gloom at the Bill had been confirmed by the discussion in the Commons. At the beginning of June he described it as 'a dexterous fiscal swindle under the guise of religious equality'.[6] But Cullen's prediction was not to fall so very far from the mark: the Lords did not indeed reject the Bill – they rejected only its principle of general disendowment, and returned it to the Commons amended to allow concurrent endowment. The struggle over the Lords' amendments came to be a further occasion of the conflict between the principles of secularization and general endowment. Cullen and Manning were to spring to the defence of the voluntary system once again. On 29 June the Lords, having passed the second reading of the Bill with a majority of thirty-three, went into Committee to consider its clauses.[7] It was on 2 July that the Duke of Cleveland unsuccessfully moved an amendment to Clause 28, to provide glebe-houses for Roman Catholics and Presbyterians as well as for the disendowed clergy.[8] But on 12 July, Stanhope's amendment to the same clause was passed by seven votes: it provided glebes for the three denominations, and was a triumphal assertion of the

---

[1] *Hansard*, ccvii, p. 1543, Maynooth College Bill (12 July 1871).
[2] Healy, *op. cit.*, p. 492.
[3] C. W. Russell's Papers, Gladstone to Russell, 13 March 1873.
[4] By a majority of 114 – *Hansard*, cxcvi, pp. 971 ff.
[5] Spalding Letters, Cullen to Spalding, 22 May 1869.
[6] Daunt, Journal, 2 June 1869.   [7] *Hansard*, cxcvii, p. 686.
[8] *Ibid.*, pp. 1032-81.

principle of concurrent endowment.[1] The question of the glebes had complicated the measure from the start.

It will be remembered that Cullen's letter to the National Association on 12 January – the letter which had such wide repercussions – had condemned any proposal to re-endow the Protestant clergy with glebes. On the day preceding that meeting, Sir John Gray, then in London, had written to give Gladstone the views of Cullen and 'those whom I may term his ecclesiastical councillors' on the glebe question. He and Gladstone had recently met to discuss the matter; and Gray had held that if the Protestants should be left with the glebes after disestablishment, it could only be regarded among the Irish Catholics as 'the substitution of an unassailable for an assailable inequality'. He then gave the opinion of Cullen 'and his Council'. It was that the glebes and glebe-houses should remain in the possession of the existing incumbents for life, and as each life interest failed, a value should be put on them and they should be sold. The Protestants should have the first option of purchase, and the Commissioners who would be appointed to deal with the revenues of the disendowed church should grant loans with interest to enable the clergy to buy. Cullen believed that 'similar loans, out of the same fund, would prove a great boon to the Catholic population, who would gladly secure the repayment of loans for the purchase of glebes and the building of parochial-houses for their clergy'. He also hoped for 'the extension of this principle to all religious denominations'. It would have the further good effect of allowing the Catholics to rent old cathedrals for their worship.[2] Gladstone flatly turned down the idea: 'I think the Presbyterians and Nonconformists in Scotland and England especially might take fire if any permanent system of loans from a public fund for glebe-houses and Church repairs were proposed.'[3] His attitude helps to explain the Government's annoyance with Cullen's letter of 12 January.

Monsell saw Cullen on the 23rd, and they talked over the glebe question. Cullen said that to leave the glebes to the Established Church, and to give no equivalent to other demoninations, 'would be no settlement at all'. Monsell suggested a plan of his own, to value all the glebes and give the Protestants the right of pre-emption, allowing them to borrow money on the principle of the Land Improvement Act for the purpose. Catholics and Presbyterians were to be lent money at the same time to *build* glebe-houses, the sites to be provided by compulsory

[1] *Ibid.*, p. 1657.

[2] Gladstone Papers, B.M.Add.MS. 44418, f. 116, Gray to Gladstone, 11 January 1869.

[3] *Ibid.*, B.M.Add.MS. 44418, f. 150, Gladstone to Gray, 15 January 1869.

purchase powers as in the case of coastguard stations. Cullen agreed to this, and to the suggestion that the Protestants should have their glebes at the rate of the poor-law valuation, which would be much below their real value.[1] Cullen's willingness to accept the sort of arrangement implied by plans for glebe loans is surprising – it was contrary to secularization and State neutrality – but Gladstone went some of the way with him. Writing to him on 13 March, Gladstone promised that after the Church measure, 'Mr Fortescue will introduce a bill relating to loans for glebe-houses, and to the acquisition of sites and glebes, which may be regarded as a supplement to the Irish Church measure'.[2] In May, after the Government had given notice of its intention to do this, a fissure in the united front of the Irish Catholics and the Liberation Society became apparent. The Society resolved to oppose any such measure, and deputed Miall to make adverse representations to Gladstone.[3]

On 14 June the Church Bill had its second reading in the Lords. Cullen dreaded the possibility of their rejecting it, for, as he told Manning, this could lead to serious disturbances in Ireland. He also asked Manning to prevail upon Lord Gormanston, one of the few Irish Catholic peers, not to vote against the Bill. He had gone over to London with that expressed intention.[4] The Bill passed on the 18th, but, as Bishop Butler of Limerick wrote to Monsell, 'it were better, I think, that they had kicked it out', for now they would 'mutilate it in Committee'.[5] Clarendon informed Odo Russell that no one could say what the Lords would do in Committee, but it was certain that they were 'not unwilling to assist Catholics and Presbyterians in the shape of glebe-houses and lands'. The Government, he continued, would willingly allow this, but they were not in a position to do so, for the Scotch and Nonconformist members of the Liberal party would never consent, and 'we cannot break up the majority'.[6]

In the Committee the principle of disendowment was, as Morley wrote, 'reduced to a shadow'.[7] On the first day (29 June) Earl Grey

[1] Carlingford Papers, CP. 1/75, Monsell to Fortescue, 23 January 1869.

[2] Gladstone Papers, B.M.Add.MS. 44419, f. 209, Gladstone to Cullen, 13 March 1869.

[3] Liberation Society Minute Books, vol. IV, Council of 14 May 1869, p. 147.

[4] Manning Papers, Cullen to Manning, 8 June 1869. The letter is referred to by Shane Leslie, *H. E. Manning*, p. 202. Despite Manning's intercessions, Gormanston continued to support the Irish Church.

[5] Monsell Papers, Box 8319, Butler to Monsell, 19 June 1869.

[6] Clarendon Papers, c. 475 (4), f. 253, Clarendon to Russell, 28 June 1869. But, as the Government discovered, the Scots and Dissenters were as much opposed to glebe loans as they were to the gift of glebes.

[7] Morley, *Life of Gladstone*, vol. I, p. 905.

moved the immediate consideration of the preamble.[1] Westbury declared that as it stood it meant secularization, but that they should alter it and provide for the Roman Catholic clergy out of State resources.[2] He suggested the award of a lump sum to allow the purchase of glebes. O'Neill Daunt described this as a bribe to secure the acquiescence of the Catholics in the retention by the Protestant clergy of most of the revenues.[3] This was probably true. The preamble was rephrased to allow for an interpretation whereby the residue could be applied for religious purposes.[4] On 2 July, the Duke of Cleveland's amendment to Clause 28 provided glebe-houses for both Catholics and Presbyterians, but this was lost by 33 votes.[5] Yet on the 6th Lord Cairns successfully moved an amendment to Clause 68, postponing the application of the surplus by keeping it under the control of Parliament[6] – thus fulfilling the condition which Moriarty had argued would leave a later and less prejudiced Parliament free to retain the remnant of the funds for religious purposes.[7] The bishop was not himself in a position to comment upon this: throughout June and July he was confined at Killarney with illness. The Lords finished with the Bill on the 12th, and it passed its third reading. But when it passed, Lord Stanhope moved an amendment to Clause 28 (enactments with respect to ecclesiastical residences),[8] which gave free glebes to the three denominations. The Irish Methodists, as Gladstone was to observe, were left out 'in the cold'.[9] Stanhope's amendment, supported by Westbury and Earl Russell, passed by a majority of seven.[10] 'There is an extraordinary infatuation in the House for this scheme of giving glebes to the Catholic priests', Kimberley wrote in his journal on that day. 'It is an utterly impracticable proposal.'[11]

O'Neill Daunt did not wait for the lower house to debate the amendments. When the Lords had finished, he wrote a manifesto against the attempt to 'bribe' the priests with glebes, and sent it to the National Association.[12] Archbishop Leahy of Cashel and Bishop O'Hea of Ross wrote in support.[13] On the day following 'the unexpected vote of the Lords'

---

[1] *Hansard*, cxcvii, p. 689.   [2] *Ibid.*, p. 732.   [3] Daunt, Journal, 5 July 1869.
[4] Morley, *op. cit.*, vol. I, p. 905.
[5] *Hansard*, cxcvii, p. 1032. See also Spencer Walpole, *The History of Twenty-Five Years*, vol. II, p. 371.
[6] *Hansard, ibid.*, pp. 1228-54.   [7] See chap. 7.
[8] *Hansard*, cxcvii, p. 1632.
[9] Gladstone Papers, B.M.Add.MS. 44249, f. 81, Gladstone to Manning, 13 July 1869; in D. C. Lathbury, *Gladstone's Correspondence on Church and Religion*, vol. I, p. 162.
[10] *Hansard*, cxcvii, p. 1657.   [11] Kimberley *Journal*, p. 6.
[12] Daunt, Journal, 12 July 1869.   [13] *Ibid.*, 15 and 20 July 1869.

Gladstone wrote to Manning showing that the amendments, by allowing the concession of glebes, constituted 'a flat violation of all our pledges'. Stanhope's clause, he pointed out, differed from Cleveland's – which could be seen as a *corresponding* concession to the favourable terms on which glebe-houses were to be surrendered to the Protestant Church.[1] He urged Manning to exert his influence with Moore, Blake, and Blenner-hassett, who were prepared to support the Lords' amendments. Cullen also objected to the Lords' vote. He sent Manning a copy of the episcopal resolutions of October 1867 in which the bishops had pledged themselves to accept nothing from the State. 'The concurrent endowment of the Lords appears to be only a device to get an argument to defend the renewed endowment of the Protestant Church, and to silence us by throwing us some crumbs', he wrote. If the Lords should give £15 million to the Protestants, then on the principle of equality, they would have to give the Catholics £120 million, according to their numerical superiority. But this was not intended. He continued:

> It is certainly very insulting to the Irish Catholics to be told that they are put on a footing of equality with Protestants, whilst each Protestant gets as much as 120 Catholics. I am sure if the project of concurrent endowment be carried out, it will be made a pretext for annoying the Catholics and subjecting them to laws such as have been enacted for the management of Protestant glebes, etc. If the concurrent endowment were adopted, it would be difficult for us to maintain the voluntary system, whilst the endowments given us would be quite trifling and not sufficient to maintain one-tenth of our clergy.[2]

Cullen was evidently still anxious to secure glebe loans from the Government, but would never receive glebes as a gift. Manning handed Cullen's letter to Gladstone, and wrote at the same time to report on his efforts with those Irish members who were prepared to support the grant of glebes. G. H. Moore had in August to explain to Archbishop MacHale why he voted for glebes. It was because by Gladstone's Bill the Protestants retained them 'on the payment of a sum of money so trifling as to make it a mere cover' for a gift; and if that was the case, then on the terms of religious equality, the Catholics should be placed in a similar position. He had therefore approved of the course taken in the Lords.[3] Moore told Manning on 12 July that with few exceptions 'all the Irish members wished for glebes'.[4] But in speaking with Cogan

---

[1] Gladstone to Manning, 13 July 1869, as above.

[2] Gladstone Papers, B.M.Add.MS. 44249, f. 90, Cullen to Manning, 13 July 1869.

[3] Moore Papers, no. 782, Moore to MacHale, (?) August, 1869.

[4] Gladstone Papers, B.M.Add.MS. 44249, f. 84, Manning to Gladstone, 13 July 1869.

and Maguire[1] he found that this was not the case, for they would not allow them.[2] Moore, Blake and Blennerhassett were in fact the only Irish members who would. To Blake he wrote, Blennerhassett he evidently restrained, and Moore continued his stand. Thus Manning, who had gone to the House in order to fulfil Gladstone's wish that he should speak with them, saved one at least from using his influence for concurrent endowment.[3] He was unable to do anything about the *Dublin Review*, which in the same month, observed that 'the grant of glebes and of houses will be nothing more than a very inadequate act of restitution', but should only be accepted if they were vested in the hierarchy.[4]

Manning also warned Gladstone that the Government would be attacked if it should grant glebes, in just the same way as it had been over the Maynooth compensation. The glebes would undoubtedly be a great benefit to the poor Irish Catholics, but they could not 'compensate for the great public evil of stirring up the prejudices of the English Dissenters and the Scotch Presbyterians, or of raising mistrust between the people and clergy in Ireland'. And this, he thought, was 'a really imminent danger'.[5] On the next day, Cullen wrote to the Prime Minister to express his belief that 'the Bill will do no good in Ireland as it has been amended by the Lords'. Only the Fenians would profit, as it would confirm their thesis that no good could be done to Ireland by British legislation. The way the Lords had granted glebes would be regarded as an insult rather than an instalment of religious equality. The Protestants got far too much. The bishops would stand by the October resolutions of 1867, and 'perhaps, in the final arrangement of the question, it may not be useless to know how they feel'.[6] Cullen had written to Manning in the same sense on the same day, and Manning sent this on to Gladstone too.[7]

Yet it was not really Catholic representation which caused Gladstone to work for the obliteration of the Lords' amendments, for he had already said that they were contrary to the principle of the Bill – a principle on which the Government had been returned by the country

[1] On 21 March, Maguire had written to tell Gladstone that he would support the Bill because he, 'as an Irish Catholic, repudiate all notion of being levelled-up'. – Gladstone Papers, B.M.Add.MS. 44419, f. 249, Maguire to Gladstone, 21 March 1869.
[2] Manning to Gladstone, 13 July 1869, as above.
[3] See Leslie, *H. E. Manning . . .*, p. 202, and V. A. McCelland, *Cardinal Manning . . .*, p. 173.
[4] *Dublin Review*, July 1869, 'A Glance at Catholic Home Politics', pp. 181-2.
[5] Manning to Gladstone, 13 July 1869, as above.
[6] Gladstone Papers, B.M.Add.MS. 44421, f. 150, Cullen to Gladstone, 14 July 1869.
[7] *Ibid.*, B.M.Add.MS. 44429, f. 88, Manning to Gladstone, 14 July 1869.

at the elections. The Bill had gone back to the Commons on 15 July.[1] The story of the agreement reached between the Government and Lord Cairns, Disraeli and Archbishop Tait, is well enough known.[2] The principle of concurrent endowment was removed and the preamble again altered, so that in the final draft of the Bill, whilst not explicitly sanctioning secularization, it now read that after the satisfaction of just claims 'the property of the said Church of Ireland, or the proceeds thereof, should be applied in such manner as Parliament shall hereinafter direct'.[3]

The royal assent was given to the Church Act on 26 July, and on the 31st, Cullen related the events to the Propaganda, suggesting the broad benefit of the Act.

In the future, the Protestants will find themselves as the Catholics, without any privileges. Let us hope that this act of justice will have a good effect in Ireland. The poor Protestants are all very irritated. They never did imagine that England would have abandoned their cause.[4]

There was a great sense of relief in Ireland, and those who had agitated the Church question were almost wholly united in lauding the author of the Act. O'Donnell has truly said that joy at Gladstone's action was 'exultation at his castigation of the bygone devilry which had produced such lasting wrong'.[5] Manning told Gladstone that the benefit of passing the Act was 'simply *immense*',[6] and added later that it was 'the greatest act of the Legislature towards Ireland in our history', it inaugurated a new period in the history of the empire.[7] Gladstone himself thanked Manning 'for the firm, constant, and discriminating support' which he had given to the Bill throughout the arduous conflicts of its passage. He included Cullen in his thanks.[8] On 26 July, Cullen sent an expression of his gratitude to Fortescue whose support, he wrote, had rendered an invaluable service to Ireland in the Church Act,[9] and on the 27th the National Association met in Dublin. MacSwiney started the meeting by congratulating the members 'on the successful termination of the

---

[1] *Hansard*, CXCVII, p. 1891.   [2] See Morley, *op. cit.*, pp. 906 ff.
[3] 32 & 33 Vict. cap. 42.
[4] Propaganda, *Scritture* 36, Cullen to Barnabo, 31 July 1869.
[5] F. H. O'Donnell, *A History of the Irish Parliamentary Party*, London, 1910, vol. I, p. 17.
[6] Gladstone Papers, B.M.Add.MS. 44249, f. 95, Manning to Gladstone, 22 July 1869.
[7] *Ibid.*, f. 97, Manning to Gladstone, 24 July 1869.
[8] Gladstone to Manning, 24 July 1869, printed in D.C. Lathbury, *op. cit.*, vol. I, p. 163.
[9] Carlingford Papers, CP. 3/90, Cullen to Fortescue, 26 July 1869.

great struggle in favour of religious equality in Ireland'.[1] The Church question, now so happily concluded, he described as the Association's 'leading grievance'. He paid a tribute of gratitude to the Prime Minister, and to the English and Scottish allies of the Association, to Sir John Gray, the Dublin Corporation, and the Liberal members and press of Ireland. MacSwiney continued:

> The Bill may not be all that we could have wished, far from it, but taken as a whole, and considering the difficulties attending the passing of such a measure through powerful and hostile camps, I believe it would be a great risk to throw it out and trust to the future for a more just and equitable measure (hear, hear). Disestablishment is complete. Well, that alone is an enormous gain, and although Disendowment is not so fully carried out as the Bill originally contemplated . . . if the speedy carriage of the Church Bill hastened a settlement of the Land Question, I maintain that that consideration alone was worth far more than the few hundred thousand pounds borne off as booty – as my friend Mr O'Neill Daunt calls it – by the Disestablished and Disendowed party. Not the least beneficent of the many advantages of the Church Bill will be the extinction of that anti-Christian feeling which has for so many generations set Irishmen against Irishmen.[2]

These words were heavy with prophecy. MacSwiney's reference to Daunt was drawn from a letter he had sent to the meeting. Daunt was probably less pleased than any other Catholic with the Bill, which he had called 'a wretched abortion'[3] because disendowment seemed so incomplete. But he could not suppress the relief of others. Gladstone continued throughout the summer to receive expressions of gratitude from Irish Catholics. In August Bishop Conaty wrote to praise the first statesman since the Norman invasion, as he put it, to do justice to Ireland.[4] In September Kirby wrote similarly from Rome though in rather less exaggerated terms, and sent a book of religious engravings as a token of gratitude.[5] Later in the same month, Maguire assured him from Cork that there now existed 'a feeling of confidence in your Government – but far more in yourself – created by the passing of the Church Bill'.[6] And there needed to be, for despite the 'Triduum', a three-day religious celebration held in Dublin by Cullen in the middle of the month, in thanks for disestablishment,[7] and in spite of Kirby's

---

[1] *Freeman*, 28 July 1869.   [2] *Ibid.*

[3] Daunt, Journal, 24 July 1869.

[4] Gladstone Papers, B.M.Add.MS. 44421, f. 230, Conaty to Gladstone, 3 August 1869.

[5] *Ibid.*, B.M.Add.MS. 44422, f. 3, Kirby to Gladstone, 1 September 1869.

[6] *Ibid.*, B.M.Add.MS. 44422, f. 40, Maguire to Gladstone, 17 September 1869.

[7] Daunt did not like it – he could not yet see that the Church Act would do them any real good – and he disapproved 'of crowing for three successive days over a fallen foe'. Journal, 21 September 1869.

further assurance to Gladstone in December that Cullen and the bishops assembled in Rome for the Council were still filled with gratitude,[1] the National Association was preparing to deal with the land question, and so was Gladstone, and that would require the maximum amount of sympathy from the Irish if a settlement was to be concluded. The cracks could easily appear. The movement for the release of the Fenian prisoners, Liberal support for Italian national designs, and the Vatican Council, were all potentially destructive of good feeling between Gladstone and the Irish Catholics. Daunt warned them not to rely solely on the Prime Minister as 'the political saviour of Ireland', and feared that the bishops would get ensnared, especially as many of them, he thought, were 'easily caught with soft words'.[2] In April of the new year, the *Dublin Review* was able to look back on the 'brief days' of peace which descended on the Irish mind after the Church Act, but it had not lasted.[3]

One of the first ripples on the surface was stirred by the plan for glebe loans. Gladstone had promised this as a supplement to the Church measure in March 1869, with Cullen's approval. In November, Miall, who had been deputed to act for the Liberation Society on the question of glebe loans, wrote to warn Gladstone that if the matter came up in the next session of Parliament, many of the Dissenters who had supported his Administration would be forced reluctantly to vote against it. It was, he wrote, no doubt a small matter in itself, 'but it looks, or it *seems to look*, in the direction of Parliamentary aid to religious bodies, which the Nonconformists of England and Scotland believed to have been finally abandoned, as far at least as Ireland is concerned' in the Church Act.[4] But Gladstone was to redeem his pledge to Cullen, and despite the objections of O'Neill Daunt, the Irish bishops' support for glebe loans threw the Liberation Society and the National Association apart, even before the Irish had ignored the appeal to support Miall's motion for English Disestablishment, and before the university question drove a wedge between the Liberals and the Catholics. Gladstone was no doubt encouraged to hear from Rome that Odo Russell, who was trying to meet the Irish bishops at the Council, had gained an impression that they would even have liked to have accepted *gifts* of glebe-houses if they had not been disallowed.[5]

---

[1] Gladstone Papers, B.M.Add.MS. 44423, f. 212, Kirby to Gladstone, 10 December 1869.

[2] Daunt, Journal, 9 February 1870.

[3] *Dublin Review*, April 1870, 'Is Ireland Irreconcilable?', pp. 452-3.

[4] Carlingford Papers, CP. 1/67, Miall to Gladstone, 4 November 1869.

[5] Clarendon Papers, c. 487, f. 120, Russell to Clarendon, 24 January 1870.

The Glebe Loans (Ireland) Bill was introduced by Fortescue on 18 July 1870;[1] and moving a second reading on the 26th, he said its object was 'to give facilities for the erection of glebe-houses to members of other communions than the Disestablished Church'.[2] By the terms of the Bill, the Commissioners of Public Works (Ireland) were to be authorized to grant loans of up to two-thirds of the cost for the purchase of glebes. This was to last until 1875. Candlish condemned the Bill on the grounds Miall had suggested to Gladstone: it was based on the *principle* of endowment.[3] Gladstone himself hastened to soften the attack, by pointing out that the northern Presbyterians would be the greatest beneficiaries from the Bill.[4] Maguire admitted the need for Catholic glebe-houses and could not agree that the Bill rested on the principle of endowment – if it did, it could not have the support of the Irish bishops, who, in the Disestablishment struggle had repudiated any share in the spoils, and had done so 'to keep faith with the English members who supported them' as well as because it was 'a matter of pride and principle'. The present Bill would bring about visible religious equality.[5] Miall opposed it as 'something like the establishment of relations between the State and the different religious communities', but since it was but the 'fag-end of a measure already passed' he would not press opposition too far.[6] The Bill passed its third reading in the Commons on 2 August, with a majority of twenty-two votes.[7] As some Nonconformists had voted for its second reading, the Liberation Society, following Miall's line in the debate, considered it inadvisable to continue opposition to the measure.[8] O'Neill Daunt did not give up, and sent letters to the press against what he renamed 'The Priests' Bribery (Ireland) Bill'.[9] Sadly he had to admit that many of the priests welcomed it.[10] The Bill passed the Lords and became law on 10 August.[11] In August of the following year, an amending statute allowed loans for some additional purposes.[12]

The glebe loan question had pushed ahead into the period when Gladstone was redeeming the second pledge in his Irish policy. The 1870 Land Act followed a decade which had revealed the inadequacies of the Land Improvement (Ireland) Act of 1860, a decade of agrarian unrest.

---

[1] *Hansard*, CCIII, p. 477.   [2] *Ibid.*, p. 956.   [3] *Ibid.*, p. 959.
[4] *Ibid.*, p. 963.   [5] *Ibid.*, pp. 969-71.   [6] *Ibid.*, p. 976.
[7] *Ibid.*, p. 1482.
[8] Liberation Society Minute Books, vol. IV, Council of 29 July 1870, p. 264.
[9] Daunt, Journal, 30 July 1870.   [10] *Ibid.*, 2 and 13 August 1870.
[11] 33 & 34 Vict. cap. 112.
[12] 34 & 35 Vict. cap. 100. For the construction of both statutes, see W. G. Brooke, *The Irish Church Act, 1869*, new ed., Dublin, 1871, pp. 131 and 139.

The land question had featured among the grievances put forward by the hierarchy: it was in the 1859 Pastoral, and it formed one of the three points of the National Association's programme. But the position of the Church on the question was never really coherent. Like O'Connell, most of the bishops preferred to concentrate agitation on questions involving political right; and, also like him, they tended to steer clear of land problems. The policy of the National Association, as its name had suggested, was soaked in O'Connellism. But there could be no return to the Ireland of O'Connell's day: Young Ireland and the rising of 1848 had enduringly identified Irish nationalism with the land question. Cullen was anxious to keep all agitations with which the clergy had to do on a strictly constitutional basis, and he was always afraid that the agitation on land might spill over into something more militant. He had managed almost entirely to suppress the Young Ireland and Tenant League priests, but the spirit of those sympathies remained, and the behaviour of priests at Tenant-Right meetings in the later sixties, and the secession of Bishop Nulty and the Meath priests from the National Association in 1865, had pointed a warning which Cullen evidently heeded. He did not indeed ignore the land question – that would have been impossible – and anyway he had deep feeling for the poor and oppressed. But he spoke on it with the utmost caution, fearing above all things that too radical demands for changes in the land arrangements of Ireland would upset the basis of property rights everywhere. And this he regarded with horror; not simply because the Church over which he presided was fast becoming a very large property-owner, and because attacks on Papal temporal possessions together with his own attacks on the property of the Irish Establishment had shown that the world was prepared to allow the pillage of such property, but also because he saw in private property one of the dispensations of the Divine Laws. Fenianism was above all an example to the bishops of what could happen when those who felt sorely about the economic condition of the peasants allowed their anger to get beyond safe constitutional limits. There was general agreement among the Irish Catholics that the misery of the peasants was the direct result of the landlord-tenant Acts; it was naturally enough only the Protestants who argued that there was something inherent in the Catholic religion, or in the Irish themselves, which prevented their material advance.

This is not the place to examine the Irish land problem, but it is important to trace the manner in which it contributed to determine the courses of action adopted by the bishops, and finally to see how they reacted to Gladstone's measure in 1870. Except in Meath, where, after 1865 the clergy carried on their own Tenant-Right agitation, and in Tuam, where MacHale continued with rock-like perseverance to stand by the tenant programme of the 1850s, the Catholic bishops expressed themselves on the land question in the deliberations of the National Association. At the Aggregate Meeting in December 1864, Cullen had admitted the 'inextricable difficulties' of the land question, pointing to its most serious effect – emigration. In the twenty years since the Famine, he said on that occasion, Ireland had lost nearly three million of her people. But he had cautioned them against violent attempts to redress the attendant evils, and instead made the positive suggestion that they should call upon the legislature to grant to the tenants 'compensation for all valuable improvements'. In any change, however, 'the rights of property' ought to be recognized.[1] Archbishop Leahy of Cashel had moved a resolution at that meeting which asked for the concession Cullen had mentioned. The problem with using the National Association as the vehicle for expression of opinion on the land question was that it involved the Association in the disturbing issue of priorities, as has been seen before. Cullen's practical insistence on education and the Church as the most pressing questions was not accepted by all, and the disruption over the new rules in 1865 had shown that the land question could split the members. Yet one of its earliest acts had been the compilation of *Suggestions* by Dillon in April 1865, with a view to amending the ineffectiveness of the 1860 Act.[2] Dillon and the committee drew up a Land Bill, giving content to the suggestions made originally by Cullen and Leahy at the Aggregate Meeting, and the meeting of Irish members in Dublin in December 1865 drew up a similar one, and this was sent to Gladstone in February 1866 when it was known that the Government were considering land legislation.[3] In March 1865, as part of the National Association's agitation, Maguire had managed to get a Commons' Committee appointed to look into the operation of Cartwell's 1860 Act. Bishop Keane of Cloyne had been examined before it, and the result was a report which showed, as everyone had thought, that the Act was a dead letter.[4] But the report was the background to Fortescue's Bill in 1866,[5] and to that of Lord Naas in 1867, both of which, as Morley

---

[1] *Freeman*, 30 December 1864. See chap. 4.   [2] See chap. 4.

[3] Gladstone Papers, B.M.Add.MS. 44409, f. 213, John Dillon and Tristram Kennedy to Gladstone, 22 February 1866.

[4] Spencer Walpole, *op. cit.*, vol. II, p. 312; and *Dublin Review*, October 1865, 'The Irish Land Question', p. 463. For the Report, see *Parliamentary Papers*, 1865, XI.

[5] An outline of Fortescue's Bill is given in Black, *Economic Thought and the Irish Question, 1817–70*, p. 50. The Bill was withdrawn after the change of Ministry in June 1866.

wrote, were the roots for the measure of 1870.[1] Even over Fortescue's Bill, the National Association can be said to have been fairly active. Kavanagh told the meeting on 18 April 1866 that they had played a large part in convincing the Government of the need to act. In the last session they had organized 514 petitions on Tenant-Right, and 565 in the present one. He congratulated the Association on its emergence from the divisions over land which had characterized the previous year, to the position of united agitation for Tenant-Right[2] which they now held. At a Committee on 15 May MacSwiney said that they should discuss the Fortescue Bill in order to let their representatives in Parliament know what their opinions upon it were. He thought himself that it required very heavy amendment before it could become effective.[3] Bishop Gillooly said that Clause 29 of the Bill, which left the landlords with full power over improvements and did not give the tenants any right to compensation, although it referred only to written contracts, 'will nullify completely all the advantageous provisions made in the rest of the Bill'. If it could not be amended to secure full compensation, it must be opposed.[4] The question was referred to a Special Committee, but the Bill had been dropped by the new Government before they could do anything.

After the Bill of 1866, it became apparent that no measure so limited and so moderate in tenant compensation could be accepted by Ireland again. The changed feeling in Ireland brought about by the Fenian rebellion heightened the demands to be made in land legislation. Collison Black has noticed how Sir John Gray saw this and how he used his *Freeman's Journal* to propagate more comprehensive plans.[5] But Gray was inspired by the activities of the National Association: it was the Association which piloted them. Again this involved a difficulty. The disrupting potential of the land question meant that the Association tended to prefer declarations of principle to actual proposals, and at the same time the debate on land was turning on consideration of two broad plans, both touching principle and so forcing the Association to choose between then. They were (1) land purchase, and (2) fixity of tenure with compensation for improvements. The Association came to endorse the latter, but those more radical among the clergy tended to favour land purchase, like Nulty and the Meath priests. It meant the creation of some sort of peasant propriety, and was especially recommended by Bright and Mill. Those among the clergy who supported such schemes eulogized Mill, whose *England and Ireland* became their text-book.[6]

---

[1] Morley, *op. cit.*, vol. I, p. 917.   [2] *Freeman*, 19 April 1866.
[3] *Ibid.*, 16 May 1866.   [4] *Ibid.*   [5] Black, *op. cit.*, p. 52.
[6] J. S. Mill, *England and Ireland*, London, 1868. See also the criticism of Mill's

The *Dublin Review* had always favoured Mill's land plan (which was surprising in a conservative journal), but had seen as early as 1865 that 'whenever it shall be advanced in a Parliament of landlords, we may be sure of an outcry about Communism'.[1] This was to prove correct. During Gray's motion in May 1867, the Attorney-General for Ireland (Chatterton) said that the plan to despoil *Church* private property was 'full of the socialist and communist element'.[2] In June 1868 Lord Malmesbury observed that Manning's writing on the Irish land question was 'nothing but pure communism';[3] and it was Lord Dufferin who, when writing a reply to Mill's pamphlet in 1868, claimed that 'a more logical' statement of his doctrine was 'M. Proudhon's "La propriété c'est le vol".'[4] Manning, in his *Letter to Earl Grey*, had declared the priority of the land question. He had employed the old natural law labour theories about the origin of property, and claimed for them the authority of the Divine laws – which, since positive enactments must reflect them in order to be just, should be the guide to Parliament in dealing with Ireland. 'There is a natural and divine law', he had written, 'anterior and superior to all human and civil law, by which every people has a right to live of the fruits of the soil on which they are born, and in which they are buried.'[5] Manning quoted Butt to show the evils of eviction,[6] and based much of the detail of his arguments on Butt's findings. Nulty regretted that Mill's ideas were not taken up, and in 1881 he was to describe him as 'the deepest thinker of his day, and the ablest economist that every lived'. He had demonstrated 'the rottenness and injustice of the Irish laws of land tenure'.[7] Father Lavelle, the 'patriot-priest' of Partry, who was always the most radical of clerical land reform agitators – Mgr D'Alton described him as 'frankly a vigorous opponent of Irish landlordism'[8] – cited Mill to show that 'the land of Ireland, and the land of any country, belongs to the people of that country'.[9]

Cullen had himself desired to see the gradual creation of something like a peasant proprietorship, but his caution about due respect for existing property rights kept him away from Bright's and Mill's designs.

---

land purchase scheme in *Mr Mill's Plan for the Pacification of Ireland Examined*, by Lord Dufferin, London, 1868.

[1] *Dublin Review*, October 1865, 'The Irish Land Question', pp. 472-3.
[2] *Hansard*, CLXXXVII, p. 131 (7 May 1867).
[3] *Ibid.*, CXCII, p. 2074 (25 June 1868).   [4] Dufferin, *op. cit.*, p. 5.
[5] Manning, *Ireland, A Letter to Earl Grey* in *Miscellanies*, vol. I, p. 239.
[6] *Ibid.*, p. 244-5. See Isaac Butt's *Land Tenure in Ireland*, Dublin, 1866, p. 34.
[7] Thomas Nulty, *The Land Agitation in Ireland*, Manchester and London, 1881, p. 5.
[8] D'Alton, *History of the Archdiocese of Tuam*, vol. II, p. 358.
[9] Patrick Lavelle, *The Irish Landlord since the Revolution*, Dublin, 1870, pp. 8-9.
His quotation was from Mill's *Principles of Political Economy*, Book II, chap. 10.

He favoured first tenant compensation, and then, as Irish demands heightened after 1865, fixity of tenure too. This amounted to the second manner of dealing with the land question, and this had more support in England than land purchase which, as a solution, as Collison Black has shown, had little backing among economists during this period.[1]

In February 1867 Naas introduced a Bill for Tenant Improvements,[2] which would have authorized special Commissioners of Public Works to advance loans to enable Tenants to make improvements; but it was to prove merely the twenty-sixth Irish Land Bill since the Devon Commission – it was dropped. The Government assured the Irish members that it was intended as only a partial reform and not a total settlement, but they pointed out that its provisions were meaningless without fixity of tenure. Manning was to remark that this sort of legislation fell far behind that suggested by Derby's Government in 1852.[3] Moriarty, anxious to reply to criticism that he had ignored the land question, wrote in a *Letter* to his clergy that the undoubted benefits of compensation would have no practical value without fixity, both of rent and of tenure. But, unlike the Irish members in Parliament, he supported Naas's Bill, since loans for improvements would, he argued, prevent the poor tenants from being depressed into the condition of day-labourers for the richer ones.[4] He made the same point in May when he wrote, in a letter to Butt, that 'it riles me to see men who assume the leadership in a question like this shouting for compensation for improvements while they leave both tenure and rent in the arbitrary power of the landlord'. His apparent indifference on the land question had only reflected his inability to see a remedy in former plans of action.[5]

At the committee of the National Association on 23 of April 1867, Fr Boylan moved a resolution rejecting the Naas Bill as it 'falls immensely short of what is justly due to the tenantry of Ireland' since it did not grant compensation. His speech was a full-blown testimony for Tenant-Right, but he was careful to let the committee know that only petitions and action in Parliament should be used to secure it.[6] The motion was passed, but the Association did nothing else. Yet it had made itself clear on one thing: it was going to support alternative plans to land purchase. O'Loghlen's Bill of 1867 in Parliament, for the diminution of tenancy-at-will, was withdrawn, and Clanricarde's for all

---

[1] Black, *op. cit.*, p. 58.   [2] *Hansard*, CLXXXV, p. 532 (18 February 1867).
[3] H. E. Manning, *op. cit.*, vol. I, p. 249.   [4] *The Times*, 6 April 1867.
[5] Black (*op. cit.*, p. 53) quotes this letter of 26 May. Since he wrote, the Butt Papers have been renumbered, and the reference he cites, B. 40, will no longer find the letter. It would seem to be temporarily lost.
[6] *Freeman*, 24 April 1867.

land dealing by voluntary contracts, was referred to a Select Committee of the Lords in 1867, and again in 1868, but got no further. For the other side, as it were, O'Beirne, the member for Cashel, had moved for a grant of a million pounds to carry out Bright's scheme of land purchase.[1] Meanwhile the National Association and the bishops were using their time to secure a united policy on the Church question, and the bishops were waiting to see what the Government would do about Irish university education now that the Supplemental Charter had proved to be useless.

Although the hierarchy and the Government expended their time on these matters in 1868, the outburst of Fenian sympathy following the Manchester 'Martyrs' episode at the end of 1867, which had convinced Gladstone of the need to deal with Ireland, revealed the chronic condition of the Irish peasantry at the same time. During the Church discussions of 1868 there were many who said that it was the land and not the Church which had caused Irish disaffection. In the debate on Maguire's motion of March, Mill had elaborated his land purchase scheme at great length.[2] But it was in reply that Gladstone made it certain that it would never be entertained by any Government of which he was head. He would allow no more than 'the frank recognition of the principle of perfect security to the tenant for the proceeds of his capital and industry expended on the soil'.[3] Fortescue had argued similarly the need for exceptional legislation on Irish land, and urged the principle of his own Bill of 1866 'which reversed the rule of English law that the improvements effected by the tenant became at once the property of his landlord',[4] At the National Association's committee in May, a report was read from the special Land Committee which it had set up under McCarthy Downing. They had received letters from several parts of Ireland complaining of the 'growing evil' symptomized by the introduction of 'oppressive covenants into agreements for the letting of farms'. These contracts limited or prohibited the tenants' use of game, methods of cultivation, and in some cases even marriage was only to be allowed with the agent's permission. The committee feared that such contracts would prevent the tenants from voting according to conscience at elections. They reported that the Cardwell Act of 1860 had not benefited a tenant in a single instance. The Association's remedy was 'the enactment of a landlord and tenant law based on the simple principle of securing to the occupier the fruits of his industry and capital by making him an independent tenant on a sixty-one-years' lease, from

---

[1] See Black, *op. cit.*, pp. 59-60.   [2] *Hansard*, CXC, pp. 1520 ff.
[3] For the whole speech, see *ibid.*, pp. 1741 ff.   [4] *Ibid.*, p. 1602.

which vexatious, oppressive and degrading covenants should be rigidly excluded as contrary to public morals and public policy'.[1] It will be seen that the principle of Clanricarde's Bill of 1867 was hereby firmly rejected by the Association.

Speaking of Maguire's motion, Mayo had declared the Government's readiness to appoint a Royal Commission to examine the Irish land laws, with a view to new legislation.[2] But the Governmental crisis led to the end of that suggestion just as it killed the university plan, and for the rest of the year, and until the summer of 1869, the Church question occupied Parliamentary time, and as Collison Black writes 'the question of land reform became secondary'.[3] In January 1869 Cullen told the National Association (in a letter) that they could leave it to Gladstone and Bright to provide a measure 'to secure the rights of the tenants'.[4] At the end of April, Gladstone, speaking on the state of Ireland announced that 'the occupiers of the soil in Ireland may look with confidence to Parliament to do something about their discreditable condition'.[5] After the passing of the Church Bill, the National Association therefore turned itself to providing the sort of information which could be used to induce Gladstone to legislate accordingly. At the meeting on 27 July MacSwiney announced that the chairman of their special Land Committee, McCarthy Downing, would return to Dublin in a few days to organize a conference on the question. By Murphy's resolution, the secretary was instructed to communicate with the members of the Association throughout the country to elicit their opinion on land legislation and arrange the time of the conference. As MacSwiney said, 'both parties in the State having admitted the necessity of immediate legislation on the subject of the land, it behoves the people themselves, the tenant farmers, and all others interested in the question, to convene local meetings and to nominate delegates to confer with the central body in Dublin'.[6] In their Maynooth resolutions of 18 August – the last statement before they left to attend the Vatican Council – the bishops expressed their delight to find that the Government had declared itself ready to 'legislate for Ireland in accordance with the wishes of its people', and had shown by the Church Bill that they had meant it.[7] The tenth resolution dealt with the land question, of which a settlement was 'essential to the peace and welfare of the United Kingdom'. The bishops declared that,

---

[1] *Freeman*, 27 May 1868.

[2] *Hansard*, cxc, pp. 1379 ff. See also, Spencer Walpole, *op. cit.*, vol. ii, p. 313.

[3] Black, *op. cit.*, p. 62.   [4] *The Times*, 15 January 1869.

[5] *Hansard*, cxcv, p. 2028 (30 April 1869).   [6] *Freeman*, 28 July 1869.

[7] *Ibid.*, 2 September 1869, Resolution iv.

They recognize the rights and the duties of landlords. They claim, in the same spirit, the rights as they recognize the duties of tenants. They believe that the comparative destitutions, the chronic discontent, and the depressing discouragement of the people of Ireland, are, at this period of her history, to be attributed more to the want of a settlement of this question on fair and equitable principles than to any other cause. Therefore, in the interests of all classes, they earnestly hope that the responsible advisers of the Crown will take this most important subject into immediate consideration, and propose to Parliament such measures as may restore confidence, stimulate industry, increase national wealth, and lead to general union, contentment, and happiness.[1]

It will be noticed that they did not elaborate at all. 'It is not the office of the bishops to propose any definite scheme', the *Freeman* observed.[2] But they had done so in the past, at the National Association, and before Gladstone's Bill was before the country they were to meet in Rome to suggest to him the detailed provisions which they thought essential for inclusion. They were also more concerned about the education question, to which nine of the ten resolutions referred, although the Dublin *Express* was surely overdrawing the emphasis in the 'Maynooth Decalogue' when it described it as having only 'touched with a feeble hand the one topic which engages the attention of the people'.[3] Yet it is true that the emphasis does reflect the difficulty the hierarchy felt about the land question. The injustice was always clear to them, but they were terribly conscious that opting for a definite plan would almost certainly provoke suspicion and division.

This could be detected from the varying declarations made during the early autumn by the clergy in the provinces. In October, the clergy of the Mill Street Deanery in the Kerry diocese adopted four resolutions which called for both fixity of tenure with fair rents, and for the purchase by the State of the lands of absentee landlords with their resale to the occupiers, thereby creating a 'yeoman proprietary'. Land banks on the Prussian model would provide the capital to enable the purchase of the estates by peasants. Parliamentary representatives were to be asked to pledge themselves to these resolutions.[4] The *Freeman* came out in their support, noticing that in Kerry 'a common spirit animates clergy and laity' on the land question.[5] During the same month, reports were made in the Dublin press of tenant meetings, and the lists of those attending them showed a significant prominence of clergy.[6] On the 15th the diocesan Synod at St John's Cathedral in Limerick, presided over by their bishop, the moderate Dr Butler, resolved for tenant security with

---

[1] *Ibid.*, Resolution x.   [2] *Ibid.* (editorial comment).
[3] *Express* (Dublin), 4 September 1869.   [4] *Freeman*, 9 October 1869.
[5] *Ibid.*, 11 October 1869.   [6] *Ibid.*, 14 October 1869.

fair rents. Their second resolution was careful to safeguard landlords' rights – if they were not misused.[1] The support of the *Freeman* for the Kerry resolutions showed just how widespread was the desire that had grown in Ireland for fixity of tenure, and how it had stretched up to the top of the Catholic scale. When Lord Bessborough was rebuked in London for encouraging Gladstone to communicate with Sir John Gray over the land question, the Irish Lord Chancellor, O'Hagan, told them that 'the success or failure of the Land Bill depends on the *Freeman's Journal*; if it says, we accept this as a fixity of tenure, every priest will say the same, and *vice versa*'.[2] Early in January, Odo Russell reported that all the Irish priests he had seen in Rome were 'unanimous in saying that a great and immediate charge for the better would follow a Land Bill that established *fixity of tenure* in Ireland – all other questions are secondary in their opinion'.[3]

The Government land plan matured during the early autumn. At the end of July, Gladstone had asked Fortescue to see that a précis of the attempts at Irish land legislation since the Devon Commission should be prepared for him.[4] During September, Gladstone, Fortescue and Sullivan (the Irish Attorney-General) compared notes in writing, and in relating his impressions, Gladstone showed that he was 'unwilling to force a peasant proprietary into existence', and although it was now widely admitted that compensation must be granted, it no longer 'suffices to settle the question'. When the Cabinet discussed the measures, a committee would be formed to prepare a Bill.[5] The Cabinet discussions on Irish land started on 31 October 1870. Kimberley, who confessed that he had been unable to imagine a satisfactory plan before, admitted that the scheme Sullivan outlined in the Cabinet was very acceptable. It amounted, he wrote, to an extension of Ulster Tenant-Right to the whole of Ireland, and it was clear that Sullivan was 'the real author of the plan'. Fortescue he considered to have much less knowledge of the subject,[6] and Gladstone himself understood it far less closely than the Church question.[7] Thus the Bill was drafted, without

---

[1] *Freeman*, 21 October 1869 (from the *Limerick Reporter*).

[2] Morley, *Life of Gladstone*, vol. I, p. 926. See also Black, *op. cit.*, p. 53.

[3] Clarendon Papers, c. 487, f. 112, Odo Russell to Clarendon, 7 January 1870.

[4] Carlingford Papers, CP. 1/55, Gladstone to Fortescue, 30 July 1869.

[5] *Ibid.*, CP. 1/60, Gladstone to Fortescue, 15 September 1869. Extracts from the letter are quoted in Morley, *op. cit.*, vol. I, p. 922.

[6] Kimberley, *op. cit.*, p. 9.

[7] *Ibid.*, p. 11. In his unpublished Ph.D. thesis (Cambridge University Library 1963), 'Irish Land Reform and English Liberal Politics, 1865–70', E. D. Steele corrects this estimate of Gladstone's part. The Act was very largely the work of Gladstone', he wrote (Preface), and his thesis examines the place of the Act in Gladstone's view of Irish problems.

any reference to the Irish bishops or the opinions of the National Association. 'It was', Morley wrote of the drafting, 'almost a point of honour in those days for British Cabinets to make Irish laws out of their own heads.'[1]

Gladstone had reason to feel confident that his measure would win approval from the Irish prelates, however. Manning had written from Rome to let him know that they all spoke of him with 'genuine trust and regard'.[2] And Maguire heard the Pope, when he was presented by Bishop Keane, declare his pleasure that the English Government seemed willing to act justly towards Ireland. He published a report of the audience in the *Cork Examiner*, his own paper, and emphasized the Pope's best wishes for the forthcoming land legislation.[3] O'Neill Daunt was angry. It was wrong that the Pope should be exhibted to the public by Maguire 'as graciously expressing his hopes of a happy future for Ireland from the good dispositions of the English Government'.[4] But the Council in Rome was to cause Gladstone no little difficulty. He feared greatly, as he wrote to Lord Acton, that the high tide of ultramontanism which it was beginning to express would poison English opinion and adversely affect his attempts at a land settlement for the Irish Catholics.[5]

Meanwhile Odo Russell got to work in Rome. 'I am getting on much better with the Irish bishops than I expected', he wrote on 24 January 1870 to Clarendon, '– at first they were shy of me, but now they come and talk and ask me to communicate their ideas to you and Mr Gladstone.'[6] They were concerned as much with the effect to be produced by the condemnation of Fenianism as with the proposed Land Bill, but most wished Gladstone to know that 'fixity of tenure' would be the strongest blow Parliament could strike at Fenianism. Cullen, he related further, was 'not very accessible', but Manning was always ready to be useful.[7] On 5 February, Manning received three of the Irish bishops who had come to express the views of the other bishops on the land question, and they asked him to convey them to Gladstone in the strictest confidence. They were afraid that some of the points they considered vital would not find a place in the Bill. Especially, they looked for some protection against *capricious* evictions, and suggested local tribunals

[1] Morley, *op. cit.*, vol. I, p. 926.
[2] Gladstone Papers, B.M.Add.MS. 44249, f. 131, Manning to Gladstone, 17 January 1870.
[3] Reprinted in *The Times*, 21 January 1870, under the title, 'The Pope and the Irish Land Question'.
[4] Daunt, Journal, 1 March 1870.
[5] Gladstone to Acton, 8 January 1870: in D. C. Lathbury, *op. cit.*, vol. II, p. 51.
[6] Clarendon Papers, c. 487, f. 120, Russell to Clarendon, 24 January 1870.
[7] *Ibid.*

which could decide if the landlord was evicting for a proper reason or not; but *reasons* should exist, and they should be impartially adjudicated. Secondly, they hoped for security against high rents by some form of arbitration machinery. Thirdly, an outgoing tenant should receive what Ulster custom secured in the north – compensation for improvements and for 'good-will'. 'On all these points they are very decided and unanimous', Manning related. 'They urged also that they have so openly staked their influence over the people in the confidence of a satisfactory Land Bill, that if in this they seemed to have failed, their power for good will be gone.'[1] Their points were indeed discussed in London, and without revealing the issue, Clarendon let Russell know on the 7th of the month that he could 'assure the bishops that we have gone the fullest length of our tether in behalf of the Tenants, and that if we had made more inroads on the rights of property the Bill would have no chance of passing'.[2]

The Bill was introduced to Parliament by Gladstone and given its first reading on 15 February;[3] and he declared his doubt whether, at that moment, the legal position of the Irish peasant was 'materially better, or even better at all, than it was before the mitigation of the Penal Laws'.[4] The Bill allowed the tenant to claim damages for eviction according to a scale based on the rent, though a landlord would not be bound to give compensation if he had granted a lease for thirty-one years. It was therefore based on an extension of the principle of Ulster custom. It did also contain a small measure of land purchase, despite Gladstone's reservations. The 'Bright Clauses' enabled the Board of Works to advance up to two-thirds of purchase money, and provided for land sales where the owners and occupiers were able to reach mutually satisfactory terms. Yet only 877 tenants purchased their holdings under the provisions of the Act – most were unable to raise the initial one-third of the purchase price.[5] In an open letter to Manning in *The Times*, Gladstone explained the merit of the measure as that 'the man evicted without any fault . . . will receive whatever the custom of the country gives, and where there is no custom, according to a scale, besides whatever he can claim for permanent buildings or reclamation of land'.[6] But there was no fixity of tenure, and it was this which caused the *Freeman* to observe that the measure would 'leave the old sore unhealed, the Land

---

[1] Gladstone Papers, B.M.Add.MS. 44249, f. 135, Manning to Gladstone, 5 February 1870.

[2] Clarendon Papers, c. 475 (4), f. 280, Clarendon to Russell, 7 February 1870.

[3] *Hansard*, CXCIX, p. 333.   [4] *Ibid.*, p. 346.

[5] J. E. Pomfret, *The Struggle for Land in Ireland, 1800-1923*, Princeton, 1930, p. 90.

[6] Morley, *op. cit.*, vol. I, p. 928.

Question unsettled'.[1] It was quite well received elsewhere, however. The President of Maynooth regarded it as 'a greater success even than the Church Bill'.[2] Surprising support came from Father Lavelle, who had replied to Moore's sending him a draft of the Bill by confessing 'it is something better than even I expected'. There were defects in it (it is curious that he did not mention the absence of comprehensive fixity of tenure as one of these), but he hoped that it would pass 'even in its present shape'.[3] In Rome, Cullen told Manning that the bishops were unanimous in commendation of it. He had written off to Ireland giving it full support. Manning had not seen MacHale, and was told on inquiry that he too spoke favourably of the Bill. 'The other bishops spoke most warmly of it; which was not affected by one or two expressions of doubt whether in the scale for computing compensations the outgoing tenant is sufficiently protected.'[4] Odo Russell telegraphed the Foreign Office to let Clarendon know of the favour of the bishops.[5]

The expressions of doubt were to grow somewhat in significance as the bishops reconsidered the provisions of the Bill between sessions of the Council. At the end of February they drew up a memorandum detailing six major faults in it, and four lesser ones.[6] In sending it on to Gladstone, Manning explained in a note of his own that

The enclosed paper was drawn up by the Irish bishops, and brought to me by two of them with a request that I would forward it to you. They prefer for reasons of their own to communicate through a channel which cannot be regarded as official: and they desire me to say that though they feel strongly and unanimously on the subjects mentioned in their note, they regard your measure as a great boon to Ireland, and the beginning of a new and happier state. They say that as the measure now stands they fear it cannot be regarded as a settlement of the question.[7]

The accompanying memorandum, headed 'Amendments required in the Proposed Land Bill', outlined the principles of perpetuity of tenure and the adjustment of rent by a 'Land Court'. These principles, as J. L. Hammond has recognized, included the provision which became law in

[1] *Freeman,* 19 February 1870.
[2] Gladstone Papers, B.M.Add.MS. 44425, f. 9, Russell to Gladstone, 18 February 1870.
[3] Moore Papers, no. 810, Lavelle to Moore, 20 February 1870.
[4] Gladstone Papers, B.M.Add.MS. 44249, f. 139, Manning to Gladstone, 24 February 1870.
[5] F.O. 43, vol. 106, no. 50, Russell to Clarendon (telegram), 27 February 1870.
[6] See Gladstone Papers, B.M.Add.MS. 44249, f. 143 ('Amendments required in the Proposed Land Bill' – a full text); Morley, *op. cit.,* vol. I, p. 930; and J. L. Hammond, *Gladstone and the Irish Nation,* p. 101.
[7] Gladstone Papers, B.M.Add.MS. 44249, f. 141, Manning to Gladstone, 1 March 1870.

the 1881 Land Act.[1] But the bishops kept their word, and did not cease to support the Bill, even when it became apparent that their amendments were to be given no effect. On 6 March Gladstone wrote to thank Cullen for his favourable reception of the Bill, and mentioned amendments suggested by Cullen which Monsell had forwarded to him. He did not discuss these beyond a bare acknowledgement, however, but instead urged the Cardinal to use all his weight to put an end to the agrarian outrage that was sweeping through Ireland. 'Ireland has been strong in her controversy with Great Britain because she has had Justice on her side', he wrote; but if outrages continued, Justice 'will have changed sides in the controversy, conforming to the change in the balance of right and wrong'.[2] He was doubtless worried that the outrages, which were notoriously frequent in Westmeath and Mayo, would lead to a demand for more coercive measures in Ireland.[3] The outrages continued, and in 1871 Bishop Nulty was to argue that a really effective measure of relief for the rural poor was the only thing that could put an end to them.[4] On the 12th Cullen replied from Rome to Gladstone's letter. He said that there were defects in the Bill, but claimed that he was 'not sufficiently conversant with the Bill to point out these defects'. This was curious, for he had done just that in a letter to Monsell. Probably he did not wish to put anything in writing directly to the Prime Minister, preferring to make his views on detail known through intermediaries. He expressed regret at opposition to the Bill, and explained the Irish outrages by the presence in the country of Fenian *agents provocateurs* and a seditious press. The Government should deal heavily with both. But he wished to let Gladstone have an intimation of Irish gratitude. 'Whether your Land Bill will become law or not,' he finished his letter, 'Ireland is bound to be eternally grateful to you for the glorious efforts you have made to remove the effects of past grievances.'[5] If Cullen was amenable – more than amenable – the same could not be said for the National Association. Conjointly with the Tenant League, which had been established in 1869 by Butt and Dean O'Brien of Limerick, it got

[1] Hammond, *op. cit.*, p. 103.

[2] Gladstone Papers, B.M.Add.MS. 44425, f. 192, Gladstone to Cullen, 6 March 1870.

[3] Kimberley, *op. cit.*, p. 12, comments on the likelihood of demands for strong Government action to suppress crime in Ireland, and on the growing dissatisfaction with the Government for doing nothing.

[4] Thomas Nulty, *Letter of the Most Revd. Dr Nulty to Lord Hartington*, 26 April 1871 (a printed paper), p. 10. There is a copy in the Gladstone Papers: B.M.Add.MS, 44616, f. 139.

[5] Gladstone Papers, B.M.Add.MS. 44425, f. 243, Cullen to Gladstone, 12 March 1870. See reference to this exchange of letters in a letter by Clarendon in F.O. 361/1, Clarendon to Odo Russell, 7 March 1870 (in the Public Record Office).

up a deputation to Gladstone to assure him of their dissatisfaction with the incompleteness of the Land Bill. The deputation, which included MacSwiney, McCarthy Downing, Maguire, Synan, McEvoy, Gregory and Moore, saw the Prime Minister on 5 March, and were told that the Government could never 'carry exceptional legislation in the case of Ireland to a point which was calculated to produce a rupture of our social relations'.[1] It is evident that MacSwiney must have been uneasy about the deputation: he supported the Bill against opposition to it in the Dublin Corporation. Gray also attacked it in the Commons. The National Association wavered between its two leaders: and hence, probably, its unsure voice at this critical time. Its division over the Land Bill was a turning-point: the sharp disagreements which had characterized the introduction of land questions by the Association in 1865 were reappearing. It was from this point, in effect, that the Association was marked down for dissolution, even if the education question was still able, for a time, to lend it a sense of unity. The polarization of Gray and MacSwiney – of two wings of O'Connellism – indicated imminent trouble for the Liberal alliance.

The Bill started its second reading in the Commons on 7 March.[2] Neither here, nor later in the Lords, was it ever really hotly opposed,[3] but the attitude of the Irish members demonstrated the divided counsels in Dublin. They had met in Dublin in mid-February to determine their attitude to the Bill.[4] On the 10th, Sir John Gray said he would vote against the second reading 'because he knew that the Bill would be unsatisfactory to the people of Ireland'.[5] For this he was attacked by Monsell, who warned him of the 'tremendous responsibility' he had incurred by undervaluing the Bill and so endangering its chances.[6] Sir Colman O'Loghlen spoke in favour on the 11th; it was an honest compromise, and it was Ireland's misfortune that her people 'did not understand what a compromise was'.[7] McCarthy Downing, the chairman of the National Association's Land Committee, opposed the second reading on the same ground as Gray – that it did not secure fixity of tenure.[8] Nevertheless the Bill passed with a majority of 431, there being only eleven dissentients, eight of whom were Irish following Gray. In Committee, Gray and his Irish supporters tried to insert a new clause to establish 'permissive parliamentary tenant-right', which would have

[1] *The Times*, 7 March 1870.   [2] *Hansard*, CXCIX, p. 1373.
[3] Morley, *op. cit.*, vol. I, p. 928.
[4] Gladstone Papers, B.M.Add.MS. 44249, f. 139, Manning to Gladstone, 24 February 1870. Manning had thought the meeting a good sign: he was proved wrong.
[5] *Hansard*, CXCIX, p. 1681.   [6] *Ibid.*, p. 1703.   [7] *Ibid.*, p. 1777.
[8] *Ibid.*, p. 1803.

amounted virtually to fixity of tenure. Gladstone was firmly against it: 'I am irreconcilably opposed to granting fixity of tenure', he told the Committee.[1]

In Ireland divided counsel continued. As the Bill was undergoing its second reading in the Commons, a Galway priest denounced it from the altar of his chapel, and asked his congregation if those who rejected the Bill would say so. Instantly every man, woman and child present raised their hands, and on being asked further, if they would vote for a candidate who supported it, they all shouted 'never!'[2] This was not an isolated incident. In the Dublin Corporation, A. M. Sullivan moved a resolution condemning the Bill. Alderman Plunkett, a member of the National Association committee, supported him, holding that it could never satisfy the tenants. MacSwiney, however, voted against the resolution and declared that the Bill, though it had defects, 'contained a fair, rational, and just settlement of the question'.[3] The resolution was adopted. A. M. Sullivan was later to write that the Bill was a half-measure, 'and like all half-measures dealing with gigantic issues, did not receive even half-justice in popular estimation, but was wholly condemned and sweepingly denounced'.[4] But the Bill passed a third reading in the Commons without a division, and it also passed its second reading in the Lords in the same way.[5]

The bishops in Rome did what they could to throw their influence on to the side of the Bill. Clarendon had written to Odo Russell at the end of March to say that it was up to them 'to do their utmost to support the Land Bill' in their Lenten Pastorals.[6] Some did, and Cullen's, which appeared at the beginning of May, went a long way in favouring the Government and their Bill. 'In my opinion', he wrote in the Pastoral, 'it would be fatal policy to do anything to weaken their hands or assist in driving them from power'.[7] But the Vatican Council was itself having such an effect, as Gladstone wrote to Manning on 16 April.[8] 'From the commencement of the Council I have feared the consequences of (what we consider) extreme proceedings upon the progress of just legislation here', he wrote, adding, 'my anticipations have been, I regret to say, much more than realized.' The movement in Rome towards the

---

[1] *Hansard*, CXCIX, p. 1025 (19 May 1870). [2] *Guardian*, 9 March 1870.
[3] *The Times*, 17 March 1870. [4] A. M. Sullivan, *New Ireland*, p. 371.
[5] Morley, *op. cit.*, vol. I, p. 930.
[6] F.O. 361/1, Clarendon to Odo Russell, 28 March 1870 (in the Public Record Office).
[7] *Guardian*, 4 May 1870.
[8] Gladstone Papers, B.M.Add.MS. 44249, f. 152, Gladstone to Manning, 16 April 1870; printed also in D. C. Lathbury, *op. cit.*, vol. II, p. 52.

definition of Infallibility had produced an unfavourable reaction against concessions to Catholics among English Protestants. Gladstone saw this behind Newdegate's successful motion for a Select Committee for the inspection of Conventual and Monastic Institutions, on 29 March.[1] Gray presented a petition from the Dublin Corporation against the proposed inquiry. They had met to discuss it on 7 April.[2] Catholic feeling ran strongly against it, although Manning said that Rome welcomed it 'because they think that anything like persecution only strengthens the Faith'.[3] This had strange confirmation from Odo Russell. 'The bishops do not in reality mind the Parliamentary Inquiry into their Conventual establishments', he wrote, 'because they love a grievance, and will make the most of it to turn the sympathies persecution awakens to their account.'[4] Manning had told Odo Russell that 'nothing could touch the Irish race to the quick more surely than to meddle with convents'.[5] The President of Maynooth received a note from Gladstone which explained that the Government did not have the power to prevent the inquiry,[6] although it had been carried unexpectedly and against their wishes. The *Nonconformist* opposed Newdegate's inquiry too, on grounds of expediency. It would cause an explosion of sectarian animosity which could hardly benefit the country at that moment.[7] The *Dublin Review* attributed the whole thing to the spirit stirred by the preaching of Murphy, although the Catholics, accustomed to feigned attacks, had been taken by surprise when a real one was made.[8] When the Select Committee of Inquiry was appointed, on 10 May, it contained four Irish members[9] – a sop to the roused Irish feeling, for, as Newdegate explained (on the 23rd), 'the inquiry had no relation to that country'.[10] The inquiry troubled Parliamentary life for a couple of years,[11] and in the committee's report of 1871 it found that the penalties of the Emancipation Act[12] had not been enforced in any case, but that the consequences of its penal clauses, and the doctrine of

---

[1] *Ibid.* See *Hansard*, CC, pp. 872 and 1588.   [2] *Hansard*, CCI, p. 55.

[3] Gladstone Papers, B.M.Add.MS. 44426, f. 222, Russell to Gladstone, 15 May 1870.

[4] Clarendon Papers, c. 487, f. 166, Russell to Clarendon, 10 April 1870.

[5] Gladstone Papers, B.M.Add.MS. 44426, f. 224, Manning to Russell, 15 May 1870.

[6] C. W. Russell's Papers, Gladstone to Russell, 19 April 1870.

[7] *Nonconformist*, 4 May 1870.

[8] *Dublin Review*, October 1870, 'The Convent Committee', esp. pp. 271 and 291.

[9] The O'Conor Don, Burke, Gregory and Cogan. *Hansard*, CCI, p. 529.

[10] *Ibid.*, p. 1262.

[11] See *ibid.*, CCXIV, p. 526, 14 February 1873 (Monastic and Conventual Institutions Bill); CCXVI, p. 1650 (2 July 1873, ditto); and *Parliamentary Papers*, 1870, VII, 1, Report of the Committee of Inquiry, and 1871, VII, 181, Second Report.

[12] By clause 28 of 10 Geo. IV, cap. 7, religious orders were to be dissolved.

superstitious uses upon the dispositions of property, had occasionally been enforced in English and Irish courts.[1]

When Gladstone announced the success of Newdegate's motion in a telegram to Odo Russell, sent on 30 March, he had observed that 'Bishop Furlong's extraordinary letter is said to have contributed to the result'.[2] This letter had hardly followed Cullen's lead in supporting the Government; indeed, it became apparent to Russell that the Irish prelates were playing a double game, and this annoyed him:

> The Irish bishops are a hopeless set of humbugs – talking one way, writing another, and acting a third – ignorant, cunning, and deceitful like Neopolitans. To me their language is most satisfactory, full of praise and gratitude to Her Majesty's Government, but they do not act as they speak, and since Bishop Furlong has published his extraordinary letter, not one of them, or even of the English bishops, will in conversation with me blame, criticize, or venture to disagree with a Brother Bishop's published opinion![3]

Furlong's letter,[4] in Gladstone's opinion, had the effect of associating the Irish Land Bill with the ultramontane claims of the Roman Council.[5] It is clear that it must have dealt with the agrarian outrage in Ireland, and the possible ineffectiveness of the Bill, or the Peace Preservation Act, to deal with it. This would seem to be implied by Russell's letter of 10 April.[6] The association of ideas which Gladstone suggested was caused by Furlong's 'mode of discriminating between things secular and things spiritual'.[7] It is evident that he had put up higher claims for the clergy than Cullen had. And it therefore seems as though some of the bishops – those who did not keep the assurance that had been given to the Government through Manning at the beginning of March, that the Land Bill was still acceptable even if their amendments were not made – reflected the divided counsels on the Bill which obtained in Dublin and among the Irish at Westminster. Cullen did not attempt to elucidate the situation; no doubt he was anxious not to foster division on a question which he regarded secondarily to the Council itself, and to Irish education.

[1] *Parliamentary Papers*, 1871, VII, Report, p. vii. No Irishman gave evidence before the Committee.

[2] F.O. 43, vol. 105, 30 March 1870; and Gladstone Papers, B.M.Add.MS. 44426, f. 51.

[3] Clarendon Papers, c. 487, f. 166, Russell to Clarendon, 10 April 1870.

[4] There seems unfortunately to be no text available: yet it must have been very public for it to have influenced the Parliamentary vote as Gladstone said. *The Times* does not seem to have printed it.

[5] Gladstone Papers, B.M.Add.MS. 44249, f. 152, Gladstone to Manning, 16 April 1870.

[6] Clarendon Papers, c. 487, f. 166, Russell to Clarendon, 10 April 1870.

[7] Gladstone Papers, B.M.Add.MS. 44249, f. 152.

The Land Bill passed into law,[1] Gladstone prevailing over the changed atmosphere in Parliament and in the country.[2] As the Irish supporters of fixity of tenure had predicted, it proved to be ineffective and no true settlement, and opinion generally came to agree,[3] as did Gladstone himself in 1881. In that year also, Bishop Nulty laid the 1870 Act to rest when he remarked that it had 'positively aggravated and infused fresh vitality and vigour into many of the most galling characteristic injustices'.[4] But in one sense the Act was an important precedent: it was the first measure to recognize that the occupier as well as the owner had a right in the land.[5] In the long term, however, it was also a landmark in the growth of the feeling that Ireland could never expect anything good from English legislation. Dean O'Brien of Limerick felt that his Declaration of 1868 was never more relevant. 'We stand on the brink of the future which the "Limerick Declaration" two years ago shadowed forth', he now wrote to Butt. 'Landlords and Statesmen have only one remaining chance of saving us from coming confusion, and that is to permit us to make our own laws.'[6] The Home Rule movement had begun.

Gladstone, however, was concerned with one other attempt to pacify Ireland, and this also he saw endangered[7] by that increase of anti-Catholic feeling early in 1870 which he so much regretted as an impediment to ameliorating legislation, but to which he was to succumb himself in the later controversy over the Vatican Decrees. This was the repeal of the Ecclesiastical Titles Act, which, although it was not to occur until 1871, occupied Parliamentary time concurrently with the Land Bill. The Irish bishops had regarded the Act as a 'penal law' ever since it had passed in 1851, and it was the major cause of their bitterness with the Whigs. They resented the fact that their territorial titles were illegal, and although this was because of Clause 24 of the Emancipation Act, that Act had been a dead letter on this point, and it was the 1851 measure, passed amidst Protestant excitement over the 'Papal Aggression' allegedly attendant on the reconstitution of the English Hierarchy,

---

[1] 33 & 34 Vict. cap. 46.

[2] Gladstone Papers, B.M.Add.MS. 44249, f. 152, Gladstone to Manning, 16 April 1870.

[3] See, for example, A. M. Sullivan, *op. cit.*, p. 372; James Macaulay, *Ireland in 1872*, p. 271; and even the moderate Aubrey de Vere – *Recollections*, second ed., London, 1897, p. 338.

[4] Nulty, *The Land Agitation in Ireland*, p. 3.   [5] Black, *op. cit.*, p. 69.

[6] Butt Papers, O'Brien to Butt, 17 February 1870, quoted in Black, p. 70, with the old National Library of Ireland catalogue number, B. 34.

[7] Gladstone to Acton, 8 January 1870; printed in D. C. Lathbury, *op. cit.*, vol. II, p. 51.

which had underlined the inequality of their legal position. In 1867 a Commons' Select Committee which had examined both the Ecclesiastical Titles and the Catholic Relief Acts, reported that the former had 'proceeded upon a misapprehension of what the Brief of 1850 was intended to effect', and that Catholic territorial titles did not imply civil jurisdiction.[1] The greatest evil of the Act was stated correctly by Judge O'Hagan in his evidence: it was its tendency 'to separate the R.C. hierarchy from the civil government'.[2] A cordial intercourse between the bishops and the Government, which was prepared by the co-operation of the bishops in putting down Fenianism, could never be established whilst the Act remained on the Statute Book.[3] The evidence of Moriarty to the committee was important – he was highly regarded in Parliament for his moderation, and it is interesting that he was addressed in the committee by his illegal title as 'Bishop *of* Kerry'.[4] The Act, he said, had been totally ineffective; and the Catholics held it to be void:

> We never derived our jurisdiction from Parliament or from the Crown, and we believe that no power in the State can render the exercise of it either invalid or unlawful. As we know that episcopacy is of Divine institution, and that the authority by which we are appointed is of Divine institution, we consider that the law of the land might as well undertake the repeal of one of the Ten Commandments.[5]

The bishops' titles, he continued, were necessary to authenticate Catholic documents, and although several bishops in Ireland did not use theirs, this was only to preserve their independence by not placing themselves at the mercy of the law officers. He then made a long statement in which he upheld the Constitution and deplored the doctrine 'that all distinct nationalities have a right to choose their own form of Government'.[6] The withdrawal of the bishops from the National Board of Education, he said, had been caused by the Ecclesiastical Titles Act and the separation between the hierarchy and the government had followed that withdrawal.[7] Cullen was unhappy about Moriarty's evidence. He told Kirby that it contained 'many good things and many

---

[1] *Parliamentary Papers*, 1867, VIII, 15, Report of the Select Committee of the Commons on Ecclesiastical Titles and R.C. Relief Acts; Report, dated 2 August 1867, p. iii.

[2] *Ibid.*, Evidence, p. 1.   [3] *Ibid.*, p. 3.   [4] *Ibid.*, p. 43.   [5] *Ibid.*

[6] *Ibid.*, p. 45.

[7] *Ibid.*, p. 51. This point was denied by Sir Colman O'Loghlen in his evidence to the Lords' Committee in 1868. He claimed that the withdrawal of the bishops was caused by the policy of the Board itself. See *Parliamentary Papers*, 1867–8, VIII, Evidence, pp. 72 ff.

foolish things',[1] and probably the last point was one he considered foolish.

Earl Stanhope moved for the appointment of a Select Committee of the House of Lords to consider the Act, on 26 March 1868, saying that the question had caused 'a great amount of irritation'.[2] He reviewed the evidence of Moriarty and O'Hagan before the Commons' Committee and declared that the Act should end: there had been no single prosecution under it.[3] Earl Grey underestimated the situation, however, when he said that 'prejudice and passion on both sides had raised this question to undue importance'.[4] The Committee was constituted, and their Report of 16 June 1868, showed that the keen sense of injustice the Irish bishops had experienced in 1851 had not passed away with time, but the Act, the Committee felt, had *not* been ineffectual – it was a timely statement of the supremacy of the Sovereign, 'and there has not, since 1851, been any general or ostentatious infraction of the enactment of that year by those against whom it was directed'.[5] It had been claimed that the Act hindered Catholic bequests, and William Gernon, the Catholic secretary of the Irish Board of Charitable Donations and Bequests, was examined by the Committee on this point. He cited the 'George Hildebrand's Charity' case of 1865. The Archbishop of Tuam, holding the mensal parish of Westport (Co. Mayo) had been left a bequest of £70, and had signed the certificate with his episcopal title. When Gernon had showed MacHale that this was a contravention of the Titles Act, he had held out against signing himself simply by name – but had finally done so. This case, Gernon said, showed the humiliation and legal difficulties involved for the Catholic people of Ireland.[6] But when pressed he admitted that this was the only case he could think of in which the 1851 Act hindered a donor's or testator's intentions.[7] When questioned about Cullen, he was sure that the title of 'Cardinal' was not 'a contravention of the Ecclesiastical Titles Act, for that Act says nothing of Cardinals'.[8] The Committee, though it dealt mostly with Ireland (as had the Commons' Committee), did examine Bishop Grant of Southwark on the effects of the Act in England.[9] But on the basis of the

---

[1] Kirby Papers, Cullen to Kirby, no. 270, 29 July 1867.

[2] *Hansard*, CXCI, p. 239.   [3] *Ibid.*, p. 240.   [4] *Ibid.*, p. 252.

[5] *Parliamentary Papers*, 1867–8, VIII, 185, Report of the Select Committee of the House of Lords on Ecclesiastical Titles in Great Britain and Ireland; Report, p. iv.

[6] *Ibid.*, Evidence, p. 5.

[7] *Ibid.*, pp. 6–7.

[8] *Ibid.*, p. 7. He cited the recent case of 'Roger Palmer's Charity' in Dublin – the Bequests Board had accepted Cullen's title of Cardinal on the certificate without question.

[9] *Ibid.*, p. 57.

evidence, they were able to report that the Act had not 'as has sometimes been supposed, caused the Roman Catholics any real injury in the matter of charitable donations and bequests'.[1]

Correctly anticipating that the Lord's Report would retain the penalties of the Act, Manning got McEvoy to postpone a motion he was to make in the Commons for its repeal, on the grounds that it was better to wait until the Lords had afforded 'an open flank'.[2] McEvoy, M.P. for Meath and a member of the National Association, was the Catholic leader of the repeal agitation. In February 1869, he moved his third Bill for the repeal of the Act.[3] It only got a first reading, and at that time Newdegate said that the Church Bill made it inopportune.[4] When the Lords were amending the Church Bill in July, in fact, their discussion of Clause 13 made it apparent that after disestablishment, the Irish Protestant bishops would be rendered liable to the penalties of the Act. So Lord Colchester moved an amendment to except them from its operation, just as the Scottish Episcopalians had been excluded from it in 1851.[5] Lord Granard promptly said that the Catholic bishops, on the principle of religious equality, had a right to be exempted too.[6] And this caused Granville, for the Government, to admit that the present Bill would make it necessary to deal with the Titles Act afterwards.[7] So it was that in January 1870, Gladstone described the repeal of the Act as one of 'the wings of the Church Bill'.[8] Also in January, Manning, who was in Rome, received a subpoena under the Act, and this added urgency to the need for repeal. 'If you don't make haste I shall have the glory of martyrdom', he wrote to Gladstone.[9]

Kimberley was entrusted with the repeal Bill, which he accordingly introduced to the Lords on 19 May 1870.[10] The second reading, on the 27th of the month,[11] showed the difficulties for repeal Gladstone had anticipated from the backwash of the Vatican Council.[12] Even Kimberley admitted that he could have no part in the repeal of the Bill if it could prove to be – which it could not – a power against 'the extravagant pretensions put forward by the Court of Rome'.[13] In the Committee the

[1] *Parliamentary Papers*, 1867–8, VIII, Report, p. iii.
[2] Gladstone Papers, B.M.Add.MS. 44249, f. 55, Manning to Gladstone, 19 May 1868.
[3] *Hansard*, CXCIV, p. 186 (22 February 1869).   [4] *Ibid.*, p. 188.
[5] *Ibid.*, CXCVII, p. 884.   [6] *Ibid.*   [7] *Ibid.*, p. 885.
[8] Gladstone to Acton, 8 January 1870, in D. C. Lathbury, *op. cit.*, vol. II, p. 51.
[9] Gladstone Papers, B.M.Add.MS. 44249, f. 131, Manning to Gladstone, 17 January 1870.
[10] *Hansard*, CCI, p. 965.   [11] *Ibid.*, p. 1469.
[12] Gladstone Papers, B.M.Add.MS. 44249, f. 152, Gladstone to Manning, 16 April 1870.
[13] *Hansard*, CCI, p. 1475.

repeal Bill had a smooth passage – as a result of a private compromise agreement between Kimberley and Cairns on the latter's amendments,[1] but the Bill was withdrawn on 8 August when the Commons' amendments cut too deeply at its principle.[2] The Bill, reintroduced by the Attorney-General in the Commons in February 1871,[3] with the expression of his belief that the Church Act had rendered it 'a matter of absolute necessity'[4], was finally successful.[5] But if Moriarty was right, and it was the Ecclesiastical Titles Act which had driven the hierarchy and the Irish Executive apart, its repeal was not to bring them together. It had come too late. The country was just on the edge of the worst anti-Catholic feeling since 1851 itself.

There was still one more piece of legislation which was regarded in Ireland as a grievance, the Party Processions Act of 1850. This had the distinction of being an annoyance to both Green and Orange, and it was Johnston of Ballykilbeg, elected to Parliament for Belfast after his imprisonment for infringing the Act in 1868, who moved for its repeal. The Government were forced to take it up. The Act had operated fairly indiscriminately in the past, being enforced against Orangemen and Fenians alike. The processions and demonstrations attendant on the Fenian Amnesty movement were an obstacle to the repeal of the Act in 1869. Monsell, when urging Granville in January 1869 to deal with both matters together, pointed out that the Act was virtually made a dead letter by the recent growth in the scale of the processions organized by the Amnesty movement.[6] In March that year Johnston introduced a repeal Bill.[7] Seconding it for the Catholics, The O'Donoghue emphasized the uselessness of the Act; instead, 'he had faith in the impartiality of the Executive, in the resources of the common law, but above all, in the disposition of his Catholic brethren to make every sacrifice for the sake of union'.[8] But the Bill was withdrawn. It became evident when it was reintroduced the following year, that several Irish bishops were unhappy about the repeal of the Act. Speaking in the debate on the second reading of Johnston's Bill in March 1870, McCarthy Downing cited letters he had received from McGettigan, the Catholic Bishop of Raphoe, and Bishop Dorrian (both northern prelates), advising that it would be unwise to disturb the existing law.[9] For the Government,

[1] Kimberley, *Journal of Events*, p. 16.   [2] *Hansard*, CCIII, pp. 1683-4.
[3] *Ibid.*, CCIV, p. 273, first reading; *ibid.*, p. 780, second reading.
[4] *Ibid.*, p. 782.   [5] 34 & 35 Vict. cap. 53.
[6] Carlingford Papers, CP. 3/74, Monsell to Granville, 7 January 1869.
[7] *Hansard*, CXCIV, p. 1547, second reading, 16 March 1869.   [8] *Ibid.*, p. 1553.
[9] *Ibid.*, CC, p. 952. This is interesting, for the northern bishops' letters show that their fears were more that Orange outrages would harm them than that Fenian or Nationalist ones would.

Fortescue admitted that something would have to be done, but although they did not oppose the present Bill, they felt that some special legal regulation was still required. He promised action.[1] Accordingly Johnston withdrew his Bill, and in July Fortescue moved one 'directed against processions of all kinds in Ireland which were calculated to endanger public peace'.[2] Both Johnston and McCarthy Downing objected to this as a half measure, and to Clause 5, as a piece of 'exceptional legislation', by which the Lord-Lieutenant was empowered to ban processions by proclamation. On 12 March the Bill was put off for three months.[3] The principle of Johnston's original motion – complete repeal – was embodied in the Bill which Hartington introduced in April 1872.[4] It slid quietly through Parliament to receive the royal assent on 27 June.[5] James Macaulay suggested the reason when he wrote that 'as in the case of the Ecclesiastical Titles Act, discredit is brought on law if it remains unenforced and can be defied or evaded with impunity'.[6] By the time the Act passed, the Irish bishops were again involved in the university question.

---

[1] *Hansard*, cc, p. 945.   [2] *Ibid.*, ccii, p. 1677 (7 July 1870).
[3] *Ibid.*, cciii, p. 164.
[4] *Ibid.*, ccx, p. 1128 (11 April 1872). The Lords passed the second reading on 7 May – ccxi, p. 363.
[5] 35 & 36 Vict. cap. 22.   [6] James Macaulay, *op. cit.*, p. 312.

CHAPTER NINE

Episcopal Agitation: A Last Phase
1870-3

CLERICAL agitation in the sixties had resulted in Irish support for Gladstone. In their alliance with the English and Scottish Dissenters the Irish Catholics had formed one of the sectional alliances whose fusion, though temporary, constituted the Gladstonian Liberal Party in 1868. But the pressure for disestablishment and disendowment – for a free Church in a free State – which proved so effective up to 1869 in uniting the unlikely elements of Irish Catholicism and English Dissent, was removed by the Church Act. Inside Ireland itself, support for the Liberals collapsed by stages up to 1873, when the bishops used their influence upon the Irish members of Parliament to secure the rejection of Gladstone's University Bill, and therefore the fall of his ministry. Although the hierarchy had expressed temperate satisfaction with the 1870 Land Act, the National Association had divided over it. The rise of the Home Rulers with Isaac Butt's 'new departure' in 1870 was itself a sign that constitutional agitation within the existing structure of the Union, as embodied in the National Association, had passed the point where it could hope to win 'nationalist' support by showing that good could still be expected from the imperial Parliament. It was not only the lack of sympathy shown by the Government for the Pope's position which caused the Irish Catholics to draw away from the Liberals. The final occasion of that withdrawal was the University Bill in 1873; but a series of events in the early seventies had poisoned the relationship anyway and prepared for the severance when it came. It has been seen how the Vatican Council, Newdegate's Convents Inquiry, and continuing agrarian outrage, were obstacles thrown into the way which made legislation for Ireland more difficult for Gladstone. But before he came to deal with that question which the bishops had always regarded as the most important – education – English sympathy had vanished. The Westmeath and Mayo agrarian outrages, the Home Rule movement, the furore over Keogh's judgment in the Galway Election Trial, and the extraordinary O'Keeffe case were all strains on the English preparedness to deal dispassionately with Ireland. The Cullen era passed away with his death in 1878, but support for the Liberals had already gone. As early as 1873 it was clear that the future could only lie with the principle of Independent Opposition. The ground had been prepared for Parnell.

While the Land Bill was issuing through Parliament the Irish bishops were in Rome for the Vatican Council. Twenty-one bishops from Ireland were present of the Irish total of twenty-eight.[1] The Council was in many ways to show the fruits of Cullen's work – only two Irishmen were fervent Inopportunists up to the very end, but these two were Moriarty and MacHale, united now against the ultramontanism of the prelates supporting Cullen, but to be disunited again when back in Ireland on the Home Rule issue. Cullen himself took a most central part in the debates of the Council (Bishop Power of Killaloe wrote that 'Ireland is at the head of the Council')[2], and the Irish prelates generally showed very favourably by their organization. In 1871 Mgr Capel reported that 'during the Council the Pope had observed that the Irish bishops were much better disciplined and more united than the members of the English hierarchy'.[3] But Manning saw what the assembly in Rome had done to their chances at home. 'The Vatican Council seems to have laid a Circean spell upon the Liberal Party', he wrote in 1877. 'They have put off their former nature and have changed places with persecutors.'[4]

Pius IX had planned a general council ever since the promulgation of the Syllabus of Errors, but definite arrangements had been delayed, especially by the war between Austria and Prussia. It was in June 1867, when the bishops of the world were assembled in Rome for the eighteenth centenary of the martyrdom of SS Peter and Paul that the Pope made public announcement of the Council.[5] The bishops began to arrive in Rome in December 1869. 'It reminds one of the first Pentecostal Sunday', Kirby wrote to Gladstone.[6] The Irish bishops resided at the Irish College, where their discussions of the Fenian Condemna-

[1] Peadar MacSuibhne, 'Ireland at the Vatican Council', in *Irish Ecclesiastical Record*, April 1960, p. 211. Two Irish bishops died during the Council – Derry of Clonfert and McCabe of Ardagh.

[2] MacSuibhne, *op. cit.*, p. 298.

[3] F.O. 43, vol. 115, Dispatch no. 97, 29 June 1871, Jervoise to the F.O. This observation led the Pope to plan a new method of communication. A 'centre' was to be set up in Rome through which all the affairs of the English *and Irish* Church would be directed. An English prelate, with the rank of cardinal, should direct it. The plan came to nothing.

[4] H. E. Manning, *The True Story of the Vatican Council*, London, 1877, p. 198.

[5] Cuthbert Butler, *The Vatican Council, 1869–70*, pp. 63 and 65.

[6] Gladstone Papers, B.M.Add.MS. 44423, f. 212, Kirby to Gladstone, 10 December 1869.

tion Decree, the Peace Preservation Act and the Land Bill kept them in touch with matters at home, and where their host, Kirby, was also their Roman agent. The English Government, like others in Europe,[1] was apprehensive from the start that the Council would interfere with the existing relations of Church and State. Clarendon went so far as to describe the apprehension in terms of alarm, and this was 'augmented by the secrecy observed at the Vatican'.[2] Odo Russell was instructed by Clarendon and Gladstone to let Antonelli know that they hoped the Council would prove to be for 'the good of Humanity', but that they were conscious also 'that great danger to the peaceful relations of Church and State might ensue if the exaggerated views of extreme parties prevailed'. Antonelli agreed.[3] From the first intimation of the Council he had been opposed, fearing the reaction of the governments.[4] The English Government had become nervous in January 1868, when it became known that the Papacy was preparing to establish a hierarchy in Scotland. Antonelli had been warned then of the consequences that could follow a second 'Papal Aggression',[5] and Clarendon reminded Odo Russell in December that after the 'stout manifestations of Protestantism' elicited by the general election in Britain, a new hierarchy would 'really look like defiance'.[6] Happily for peace, the Papacy dropped the plan in January 1869 evidently after Manning had advised against it. 'The present friendly relations existing between Her Majesty's Government and the R.C. clergy in England precluded the adoption of a measure of so much importance . . . without previous notice or understanding', he explained.[7]

In fact the question of the relations of Church and State was not discussed by the Council, which ended amid a European war, although it was always present to haunt the proceedings.[8] And the Bavarian Government, which had hoped for intervention by the Powers (who were not represented, as they had been at Trent), approached the English Government with a view to their joint intervention.[9] Gladstone received the suggestion favourably, led on by Acton.[10] Manning was

---

[1] Butler, *op. cit.*, p. 11.
[2] Clarendon Papers, c. 475 (4), f. 253, Clarendon to Russell, 28 June 1869.
[3] F.O. 43, vol. 103 (8), Dispatch no. 58, 8 December 1869.
[4] Butler, *op. cit.*, p. 66.
[5] F.O. 43, vol. 101, Dispatch no. 14, 21 January 1868.
[6] Clarendon Papers, c. 475 (4), f. 196, Clarendon to Russell, 14 December 1868.
[7] To Odo Russell. F.O. 43, vol. 103B, Dispatch no. 1, 1 January 1869.
[8] Butler, *op. cit.*, p. 264.   [9] *Ibid.*, p. 270.
[10] Purcell, *Life of Cardinal Manning*, vol. II, p. 436; H. A. MacDougall, *The Acton-Newman Relations, The Dilemma of Christian Liberalism*, New York, 1962, p. 116; Butler, *op. cit.*, pp. 270-1.

released by the Pope from the oath of secrecy that hedged the members of the Council and prevented them from disclosing its proceedings. He was thus able to influence Odo Russell, and through him Clarendon, against Gladstone's disposition to intervene.[1] The Prime Minister could not carry the Cabinet with him and the intervention plan was abandoned. Manning was largely responsible, through the 'web of delicate and clinging diplomacy' which he had been able to spin round Odo Russell.[2] But Russell was no cypher, and he was persuaded by his own urbanity of outlook that Infallibility itself would never harm the civil allegiance of the subjects.[3] Gladstone was later to vindicate himself with Manning over the matter of the Vatican Decrees.

Cullen had no part in all this, though he was himself subject to Government pressure on the question of securing a condemnation of Fenianism by the Papacy.[4] He was a leader of the 'ultramontane' group at the Council pressing for the Definition of Infallibility ('Opportunists').[5] Four Irish bishops opposed: MacHale, Moriarty, Furlong and Pius Leahy.[6] For MacHale the question of Infallibility provided yet another occasion for him to air his opposition to Cullen, and although he was hardly as Gallican as Campana thought,[7] he did represent the old climate of Catholic opinion which Cullen had been sent to Ireland to sweep away. So in his way did Moriarty, although for him the older tradition was that of Archbishop Murray and of the 'Old Catholics' of England. The other two prelates, who were otherwise sound supporters of Cullen, were probably troubled by conscience, but they submitted quite early in the debates. It was not for the Definition of Infallibility that the Council was convened – it came up at a later point, and though Cullen had not himself articulated his support for the dogma in Ireland before 1870, it had been implicit in his view of the Papacy. Ward, however, had used the *Dublin Review* to propagate a far-reaching doctrine of Infallibility from 1863 onwards. He had not scrupled to call every Papal Bull the Word of God.[8] To Cullen belongs the distinction of having presented the formula which, with some slight modification, was

---

[1] Purcell, *op. cit.*, vol. II, p. 433; Butler, *op. cit.*, pp. 207 and 285.

[2] Lytton Strachey, *Eminent Victorians*, London, 1960, ed., p. 103.

[3] Blakiston, *The Roman Question*, p. xxxv.   [4] See chap. 3.

[5] In the archives of the diocese of Ardagh at Longford are preserved a collection of letters sent by Cullen to his secretary, Mgr Conroy, during the Council. They are not available for examination. Probably they will prove to be the source of the fullest and most intimate picture of the Irish at the Council when they are opened for study. It is known that they also deal with the unsuccessful attempt of Cullen to get Conroy elected to the see of Armagh.

[6] Butler, *op. cit.*, p. 176. The Australian bishops, all Irish, were Opportunists.

[7] Campana, *Il Concilio Vaticano*, vol. I, Part II, p. 772.   [8] Butler, *op. cit.*, pp. 57-8.

adopted for the Infallibility Decree; although it was not actually composed by him but by Cardinal Bilio.[1] This was in June 1870, but in May, during the crucial debate which determined whether the Definition would be put up or not, the clash of Cullen and MacHale had been clear. After Cullen's lengthy speech in favour, on the 19th, MacHale followed the next day by declaring that 'The simple Catholics of Ireland . . . did not think about or want these definitions; they held the doctrine practically, having sucked it with their mother's milk.' It could only raise 'controversies and troubles'.[2] The Archbishop of Cashel denied this on the following day.[3] An interesting question arose over Catholic Emancipation. On 17 March, Russell had telegraphed Gladstone to say that some of the English bishops would found their protest against Infallibility 'on the repudiation of that doctrine by their predecessors at the time of the Emancipation Act'.[4] The suggestion, which came from Acton, was probably taken up by Clifford and Errington, the two English bishops most staunchly in the minority. In the May debate, MacEvilly of Galway dealt with the point in his speech:

> The declaration made in 1826, before Emancipation, by the Irish and English bishops had been referred to – that the doctrine of Papal infallibility was one which Catholics were not bound to hold, and one which was not likely ever to be defined as an article of Catholic Faith. He said: Those bishops made that declaration; and I also from this ambo make the same declaration, namely, that it is not of Catholic Faith which all are obliged to believe under pain of heresy, that the Pope teaching *ex cathedra* is infallible; but by the Providence of God, in a short time it will not be possible to say so from this or any other pulpit.[5]

Again, in the debate on the text of the Decree on 18 of June, Cullen was met with MacHale's plea for the place of the bishops in the teaching of the Church.[6] To the end, MacHale and Moriarty were against the Definition though they declined their *non placet* in the final vote. They do not seem to have been present when the Irish prelates assembled at the Irish College on the evening of the day of the final vote on the dogma (18 July), to present an Address to Cullen in recognition of his great part in favour of the new dogma.[7]

---

[1] *Ibid.*, p. 355.   [2] Butler, *op. cit.*, p. 307.   [3] *Ibid.*, p. 308.

[4] Gladstone Papers, B.M.Add.MS. 44425, f. 269 (telegram), 17 March 1870.

[5] Quoted in Butler, *op. cit.*, p. 310, and taken from Mansi, *Collectio Conciliorum*, iv; speech of 25 May 1870.

[6] Butler, *op. cit.*, p. 357.

[7] Thomas Pope, *The Council of the Vatican and the Events of the Time*, p. 234. The text of the bishops' Address and Cullen's reply is in *Irish Ecclesiastical Record*, new series, vi, August 1870, pp. 638-40. Neither Moriarty nor MacHale were signatories of the Address.

The Council continued to hold sessions throughout the summer, but the Franco-Prussian war had led to the withdrawal of the French garrison from Rome, and on 20 September the Italians laid siege to the city. On 20 October the Pope issued an Apostolic Letter suspending the Council *sine die*.[1]

In Ireland the Infallibility Decree was accepted by the clergy, and, as Cullen wrote to Manning, there was no sign of dissension, though he feared that 'some few lawyers and government officials are following the guidance of Lord Acton'.[2] All the bishops had agreed to the Address sympathizing with the Pope's opposition to the Italian occupation of Rome, even though it described the Holy Father as '*infallibilis magister Ecclesiae*'. 'Dr MacHale and Dr Moriarty approved of everything', Cullen was relieved to report.[3] MacHale had been given a royal reception on his return to Tuam. His carriage was drawn by hand to the cathedral accompanied by a long procession of children. The entry of the city, as the *Civiltà Cattolica* observed,[4] was 'comparable to the hosannas given to Our Lord himself on his entry to Jerusalem'. At a feast in his honour in St Jarlath's College, MacHale declared that his opposition to Infallibility at the Council was explained by its inopportuneness, and did not concern the truth of the doctrine.[5] MacHale and Moriarty were never called on to make their formal assent to the Decree, nor were they asked to promulgate it, and it was not until the Synod of Maynooth in 1875 that they signed a joint Pastoral enforcing the Definition of Infallibility as an article of faith.[6]

Irish sympathy for the plight of the Pope was, in fact, a bond which helped to unite the bishops after their return from the Council. So was the increase in anti-Catholic feeling which the Council helped to foster in England. When he wrote to urge Gladstone to attend to Catholic feeling before acting on the Roman question, Bishop Gillooly warned him that 'whilst the anti-Catholic mania of the English people will keep alive national antipathies, the anti-Catholic action of the English Government would, in addition, foster disloyalty and rebellion, and counteract the effects of the best civil legislation'.[7] The city of Rome fell to the Italians on 20 September. On the 12th Cullen asked Manning to use all his influence to get two or three ships sent to Civita Vecchia. He hoped

---

[1] Butler, *op. cit.*, p. 416.
[2] Manning Papers, Cullen to Manning, 19 November 1870. Acton had some influence in Ireland too – he had been M.P. for Carlow.
[3] *Ibid.*   [4] Series VIII, p. 69.
[5] Campana, *op. cit.*, vol. I, Part II, pp. 772-3.   [6] Butler, *op. cit.*, p. 425.
[7] Gladstone Papers, B.M.Add.MS. 44428, f. 239, Gillooly to Gladstone, 30 November 1870.

the powers could be induced to declare the neutrality of Rome, on the same basis as Belgium, and pressed Manning to put this to Gladstone too.[1] On 19 October, after the fall of Rome, the Irish bishops sent a joint letter to their flocks, exhorting them to pray and to petition their members of Parliament to get the Government to do something to save the Pope.

> The words we address to you today, beloved brethren, come from hearts filled with sorrow and indignation. And how could it be otherwise, since we have to announce to you that our Holy Father, Pius IX, is a prisoner in the hands of his enemies.[2]

By mid-November Cullen was alarmed by affairs in Rome. He blamed Gladstone for the withdrawal of an English frigate from Civita Vecchia, and suggested that at their forthcoming meeting to support the Pope, some speakers should denounce the Prime Minister.[3] Meetings were held to express sympathy with the Pope, first at Wexford, Cork, Kilkenny and Belfast, and then, on 30 November, in Dublin. The bishops were unanimous about the text of their Address to the Pope.[4] Although it was true that Gladstone had no intention of saving the Pope's temporal sovereignty, he was doing more than Cullen evidently realized. Captain Salmon of H.M.S. *Defence* was ordered to stand by to receive the Pope should he decide to leave Rome, and the Government was prepared, as it had been in 1860, to give him asylum on British territory.[5] Sir George Bowyer and Lord Granard both approached the Government about the protection of Irish property in Rome – the Irish College and the monastery of San Clemente especially. Cullen remained despondent. 'Everything in Rome appears to go from bad to worse', he wrote in March of 1872. Still he feared for the safety of the Catholic colleges he knew so well.[6] And in the following December he asked Monsell if the British Government could not interfere at Rome, where, among the religious houses which he supposed were about to be suppressed, were the Irish and English Colleges.[7] His prayers were answered. The Government declared that they would stand by British ecclesiastical property if it should be attacked, and Monsell sent him a letter of Granville's to prove it.[8] Yet Cullen could see that the problem would be an enduring one. 'The Italian Government cannot be much

---

[1] Manning Papers, Cullen to Manning, 12 September 1870.
[2] *Irish Ecclesiastical Record*, new series, VII, p. 49.
[3] Manning Papers, Cullen to Manning, 19 November 1870.
[4] *Ibid.*
[5] See F.O. 43, vol. 114 for the many communications dealing with this.
[6] Manning Papers, Cullen to Manning, 10 March 1872.
[7] Monsell Papers, Box 8319, Cullen to Monsell, 26 December 1872.
[8] *Ibid.*, Cullen to Monsell, 26 February 1873.

depended on,' he wrote to Monsell, 'its financial difficulties will make it always look with a greedy eye upon every shred of ecclesiastical property.'[1]

If the Irish bishops found union in their sympathy for the greater sorrows of the Pope, they faced a division between themselves and the lower clergy over a movement which had started when they were away in Rome. The Home Rule movement of Isaac Butt had moderate aims – when compared with those of Parnell – but it was still an attempt to end the Union. O'Donnell wrote that the Home Rule movement had its immediate causes in two consequences of Fenianism, the revelation of the popularity attaching to the rejection of British law, and the feelings of sympathy and anger excited by the Fenian trials and punishments.[2] The importance of Butt's movement was that it united, if temporarily, all types of Irishmen, Protestant and Catholic, nationalist and con-servative: only the Liberals, supported by the Roman Catholic hierarchy, stood aloof as a body. The publicity which the nationalists gave to the conservative element in Home Rule had the useful result for the Gladstonian Liberals of providing them with a pretext for not joining.[3] Protestant support was lent as the fruit of wrath with the system which had allowed the Church of Ireland to be disestablished and disendowed. Daunt, an exceptional and prominent Liberal who joined the movement, wrote of this: 'In fact the ultimate effect of dis-endowment in promoting the repeal of the Union has been all along my leading reason for promoting disendowment.'[4] Butt's conversion to Home Rule was partly coloured by disestablishment but it was his efforts on behalf of the prisoners in the Fenian trials which gave him a nationalist character he had lacked before.[5] The Home Government Association of Ireland was founded as the result of a private meeting at the Bilton Hotel in Dublin on 19 May 1870.[6] Its programme was simply a domestic legislature, to deal only in Irish home affairs; the relationship of Ireland with England to become federal. The Association, like the National Association, was little more than a Dublin pressure group, not putting up candidates at by-elections, and without any local organization.[7] But unlike the National Association, it had the advantage of having only one point to its programme.

[1] *Ibid.*

[2] F. H. O'Donnell, *A History of the Irish Parliamentary Party*, London, 1910, vol. 1, p. 4.

[3] David Thornley, 'The Irish Conservatives and Home Rule, 1869–73', in *Irish Historical Studies*, XI, 1958–9, p. 208.

[4] Daunt, Journal, 20 May 1869.

[5] Terence de Vere White, *The Road of Excess*, pp. 186-7.

[6] A. M. Sullivan, *New Ireland*, pp. 339 and 344.   [7] D. Thornley, *op. cit.*, p. 208.

The Home Government Association was at first ignored by an authority who later adhered to it, Sir John Gray and his *Freeman's Journal*,[1] but the attitude of the Catholic lower clergy to it was also at first ambiguous. Only a few joined at the beginning of the movement – Daunt thought this was because they were suspicious of the Tory and Protestant names on the committee, names which also included Martin and Galbraith (a Fellow of Trinity College).[2] In 1873 the Bishop of Clonfert, Dr Duggan, told Daunt 'that if an Irishman were brayed in a mortar, two principles would be found indestructible – love of Catholicity, and hatred of England, which last was tolerably synonymous with attachment to Ireland'.[3] This was not unfair comment, and it would indeed have been surprising if some of the priests had not been attracted to Home Rule. A contributor to the *Dublin Review* wrote in 1872: 'the priests depend on the people as truly as the people depend on the priests'; and noticed how the priests acted 'to *organize* and *give effect* to a conviction which exists quite independently of themselves'.[4] In 1871 Dease observed to Monsell that his own parish priest, speaking of the Home Rule movement, had declared that the clergy were 'afraid not to go with the popular demand'.[5] The result of this sort of feeling was that many of the lower clergy were swept into the movement, though it is impossible to say quite how many. The Galway and Kerry elections in 1872 showed widespread support by the priests for Home Rule candidates – in fact it was they who put the Home Rulers in. But in Dublin there seems to be no evidence of the movement among the clergy. The support of the diocesan bishops would have been decisive in determining the allegiance of many of the priests to the new movement, but the position of the bishops often seemed uncertain. The Home Government Association would have welcomed their adhesion to the cause.[6] But Cullen, having supported and worked for the alliance between the hierarchy and the Gladstonian Liberals, would not see it undone now. In reply to an inquiry from Manning in 1871 regarding his position relative to Home Rule, Cullen replied,

I have determined to have nothing to do with the home rule movement for the present. The principal leaders in the movement here are professors of Trinity College who have never heretofore manifested any good feeling towards

[1] De Vere White, *op. cit.*, p. 241.   [2] Daunt, Journal, 15 July 1870.
[3] Daunt, *A Life Spent for Ireland*, p. 299.
[4] *Dublin Review*, October 1872, 'The Priesthood in Irish Politics', p. 276.
[5] Monsell Papers, Box 8319, J. A. Dease to Monsell, 9 June 1871.
[6] Daunt, Journal, 10 March 1871. In November 1873, the requisition for the Home Rule Conference (which inaugurated the League) was signed by only 420 priests. *The Times*, 17 November 1873.

the people of Ireland, and Orangemen who are still worse. Their object appears to be to put out the present ministry and get Disraeli into power, when they will all give up the present agitation and declare against home rule. The other leaders are editors of half-Fenian or anti-religious newspapers, and some few wrong-headed or disappointed Catholics who are ready to engage in any new project whatever it may be. Very few, perhaps ten or twelve priests, have taken a part in this agitation, but I think all the bishops and the great mass of the clergy seem determined to keep aloof.[1]

This made Cullen's position very clear, but it also showed him surprisingly out of touch. He went on to link the Home Rule leaders with the International – for which there was no basis in fact. He was accurate when he said that despite much noise in the press, the movement was not yet of any great power in Ireland. He continued:

The great mass of the people in Ireland are always ready to join any movement which is presented to them as something patriotic, but I think that the home rule is still looked on with suspicion by them on account of its leaders. Ere yesterday I was at a town called Moate in the Co. Westmeath, and I am sure ten thousand persons came to meet me on my arrival and all went on their knees to get my blessing. They all knew that I had always condemned Fenianism and that I had given no sanction to home rule. The line of action I am determined to follow is to look on until we shall know more about the tendencies of the system and its leaders.[2]

If Daunt was correct, however, in assuming that MacSwiney always acted for Cullen, the cardinal had not in fact merely waited on the turn of events. On 18 July 1871, Martin, Galbraith and Daunt had presented the Home Rule case at a meeting of the Dublin Corporation. MacSwiney, 'acting I suppose under Cardinal Cullen's inspiration', as Daunt remarked, moved the adjournment of consideration, but could find no seconder, and the body therefore resolved to pledge itself to the Home Rule movement.[3] Cullen's temporizing did not bring him any closer to sympathy with the new force in politics. In November 1873 he described it as 'the bubble of a movement'.[4] He dreaded that a revived Irish Parliament would 'at once pass laws to weaken and destroy the Church's action, and to restrain the bishops in the performance of their undoubted duty'.[5] There were occasional rumours that Cullen was

---

[1] Manning Papers, Cullen to Manning, 13 October 1871. Parts of this letter are referred to in V. A. McCelland, *Cardinal Manning*, pp. 177-8, and in Shane Leslie, *H. E. Manning*, p. 206.

[2] *Ibid.*

[3] Daunt, Journal, 22 July 1871.

[4] 4 November 1873, quoted in a letter of Gladstone to Granville. See J. L. Hammond, *Gladstone and the Irish Nation*, p. 114.

[5] Quoted in *Recollections of Aubrey de Vere*, p. 348.

swinging round,[1] but these were always false interpretations of his disappointment with the Liberals. In the autumn of 1873, *The Times*, noticing Cullen's disapproval of Home Rule correctly observed that 'he may still maintain an attitude of neutrality and reserve, while imposing no restrictions upon individual prelates who may think fit to cast in their lot' with Home Rule.[2] But it was in that year also that Manning expressed himself not unfavourably about Home Rule to Ullathorne. It had, he wrote, 'reclaimed many Fenians' and was 'like vaccination to smallpox', and whilst he had not committed himself, he was 'very tolerant about it'.[3] He might have added that he could hardly declare himself openly even had he wanted. The embarrassment to Cullen and Gladstone would have been too great, although to the latter he was frank enough in private, telling him in 1872 that if he would know the will of the Irish people, he would never get it 'with 30,000 English and Scots bayonets' holding the country down. He even suggested that British sovereignty was not rightful in Ireland.[4]

Cullen was wrong when he said that the Irish bishops would have nothing to do with Home Rule. In November 1870, Captain Dunne told Daunt that two bishops – whom he did not name – had spoken favourably of the Home Government Association.[5] But of those among the bishops who were supporters of the object of the Association in principle, all except one refused actual membership. Thus in the Westmeath election in June 1871, Bishop Nulty and the clergy worked for the Home Ruler, P. J. Smyth, so causing the two Liberal candidates to retire from the field.[6] J. A. Dease, one of the retiring Liberals, refused to declare for Home Rule although pressed hard to do so by clerical influence. But it is interesting that the bishop and many of the priests (as Dease wrote to Monsell), though they used all their weight for a Home Ruler, did so 'with bitter shame'; and Nulty told him privately that the priests 'were *afraid to oppose the popular feeling* that would be evoked' in

---

[1] Daunt, for example, wrote that 'A. M. Sullivan showed me a letter from the President of Maynooth, affirming that Cardinal Cullen has at last been converted to Home Rule'. Journal, 15 May 1873. Daunt, however, was unconvinced.

[2] *The Times*, 23 September 1873.

[3] Letter of 2 March 1873, quoted in Shane Leslie, *op. cit.*, p. 207. For comment on this, see V. A. McCelland, *op. cit.*, p. 178. Leslie wrote of Home Rule: 'Manning was perhaps the first prelate in the world to welcome it.' Daunt, usually so correct, had been quite wrong about Manning, whom he had considered 'a friend to the Legislative Union', Journal, 27 May 1870.

[4] Gladstone Papers, B.M.Add.MS. 44250, f. 55, Manning to Gladstone, 23 August 1872.

[5] Daunt, Journal, 15 November 1870.

[6] *Freeman's Journal*, 16 June 1871 (publishes Nulty's 'Letter' to the electors).

favour of Home Rule.[1] Nulty's reluctance continued, so that in March 1873 it was necessary for Daunt to write trying to persuade him to enlist in the cause. It is interesting that Duggan, the Bishop of Clonfert, who allegedly used intimidation at the Galway election, to favour Home Rule, was addressed by Daunt for the same reason at that time.[2] It is clear that the bishops, frightened of a rift between themselves, the people, and the lower clergy, were prepared to lend support to the Home Rule movement at conspicuous moments like election times, but were otherwise anxious not to become involved with it – perhaps because of Cullen's continued endorsement of Gladstonian Liberalism. But two bishops did lend their names to the movement at an early date: O'Hea of Ross, and MacHale. The former apparently gave informal support only,[3] and under the inspiration of Daunt.[4] MacHale was entirely for Butt's programme, and his name was among those on the governing body of the Home Government Association, but he attended none of its meetings and remained unmoved during the 1874 election.[5] This was probably as Mgr D'Alton suggested, because of his great age. Yet his age did not impair the political capabilities of his mind. When Daunt visited him in September 1873 he found the archbishop, over eighty years of age, in a fine state of mental agility – 'his intellect is still strong, and his shrewd sharp eye is as vigorous as ever'.[6] He had used this ability to favour the cause on paper, and it is interesting that he linked it with the education question. In May 1871 he published an open letter to Gladstone in which he declared:

English Statesmen feel, or affect to feel, much surprise at the growing and wide-spreading demand among the Irish people for the restoration of their native legislature. This demand is second only to their demand for perfect freedom and independence of Catholic education from all alien political influence – or rather distinct, as both objects are, they are associated in the minds of many, who look for home government as a necessary means to obtain the blessings of a Catholic education. . . . The longer educational justice is denied us, the louder and more pressing will be the demand for our own Parliament.[7]

It hardly needs to be said that Cullen did not envisage Home Rule as an expedient for securing Catholic education. Nor it may be

1 Monsell Papers, Box 8319, Dease to Monsell, 14 June 1871.
2 Daunt, Journal, 4 and 10 March 1873.
3 *Standard*, 10 November 1873.
4 Daunt, Journal, 15 November 1870.
5 D'Alton, *History of the Archdiocese of Tuam*, vol. II, p. 85.
6 Daunt, Journal, 7 September 1873.
7 *Freeman*, 11 May 1871.

supposed did Archbishop Leahy, upon whose deaf ears fell all Daunt's attempts at persuasion. He did at the end of 1870 agree to sound the other bishops on the question, but told Daunt of his 'distrust in the Dublin managers' of the movement.[1] On 2 April in the next year, Leahy explained his objections more extensively. The bishops, he wrote, lacked 'confidence in the motives of some of the Protestant leaders, who *look on the movement as identical with a movement against Rome Rule*'. To this Daunt replied that they were concerned with the acts and not with the motives of their Protestant allies, 'and that the very same objection would, if acted upon, have withheld us from taking part in the struggles for Catholic Emancipation and for Disestablishment'.[2] A. M. Sullivan thought the bishops held aloof from Home Rule and continued their alliance with Liberalism out of gratitude to Gladstone for the Church Act and in anticipation of his satisfaction on the education question. It was, he held, the mistrust of the Catholic Liberals which was the greatest impediment to the progress of Home Rule, despite successes for the new movement in the by-elections of 1871: Martin's election for Meath, Mitchell-Henry's for Galway, Smyth's for Westmeath and Butt's for Limerick.[3] Sullivan's opinion was probably the right one, and so was his belief that it was the hope of a good University Bill which kept the bishops loyal to an Administration which was otherwise revealing unpleasantly anti-Catholic tendencies.[4] Daunt felt it also explained why the priests in his locality, whilst supporting Home Rule, would not allow the publication of their names to that effect. 'I believe they are held in check by the bishops,' he wrote, 'who are in hopes of working an endowment for their University out of Gladstone.'[5] James Macaulay, that Protestant observer of the Irish scene, felt that the Catholic Church was likely to discountenance Home Rule as long as they could hope to get concessions from the Government.[6] Bishop Gillooly told Gladstone that 'in common with my brother bishops and our clergy', he was 'deeply anxious to promote peace and order through a just and cordial union between our countries'.[7] It is true that the failure of the University Bill in 1873 was the cause of an accession of strength

---

[1] Daunt, Journal, 29 December 1870.

[2] *Ibid.*, 3 April 1871. He repeated the argument that their Dissenting allies in Disestablishment had hoped to see a weakened Catholicism resulting from the new vigour of a Protestant Church released from State control.

[3] A. M. Sullivan, *op. cit.*, pp. 346–7.

[4] *Ibid.*, p. 349.

[5] Daunt, Journal, 12 November 1870.

[6] James Macaulay, *Ireland in 1872*, p. 78.

[7] Gladstone Papers, B.M.Add.MS. 44428, f. 239, Gillooly to Gladstone, 30 November 1870.

to the movement, but it only induced one bishop to join, Keane of Cloyne, even though, as reorganized by Butt during the same year into the Home Rule League, most of the Conservative element fell out.[1] The wounds of disestablishment by then seemed less raw to them, and with the sequence of events associated with the Galway election and the O'Keeffe case, new substance seemed to be given to the adage that Home Rule simply meant Rome Rule.[2]

The Galway and Kerry elections were demonstrations of the priests' loyalty to the cause of Home Rule. The former was to lead to an outburst of national feeling, and ended with the trial of a Catholic bishop for electoral intimidation. The Longford election in January 1870, which pointed the way, had been the occasion of unhappy division between the priests and a part of their flock, and the *Freeman* had described the election as 'perhaps one of the most lamentable in the history of this country'.[3] And that was saying something. The priests had been determined that their result should not be like that in Tipperary of November 1869, when the Fenian, O'Donovan Rossa, had swept the polls in the face of clerical opposition. The violent support they accorded to Greville-Nugent, and against Martin, at Longford, resulted only in a successful election petition.[4] But the elections at Tipperary and Longford inspired the Galway and Kerry priests to united action in 1872, and the result seemed to many observers to represent the highwater mark of clerical interference at Irish elections. The *Dublin Review* ran a series of articles revealing the excesses of the priests though upholding their right to participate in elections.[5] Their actions had raised again the entire question of the legitimacy of clerical intervention in political contests.

At Galway, the election on 6 February 1872 returned Captain Nolan,

---

[1] D. Thornley, *op. cit.*, p. 220. The Bishop of Cloyne and his clergy resolved in favour of Home Rule in September. *The Times*, 23 September 1873.

[2] Macaulay, *op. cit.*, p. 95.

[3] *Freeman*, 8 April 1870.

[4] For details of the election, see A. M. Sullivan, *op. cit.*, pp. 327 ff., and J. H. Whyte, 'The Influence of the Catholic Clergy on Elections in Nineteenth-century Ireland', in *English Historical Review*, LXXV, no. 295, 1960, pp. 253 ff.

[5] *Dublin Review*, July 1872, 'The Priesthood at Irish Elections', pp. 103-13; October 1872, 'The Priesthood in Irish Politics', pp. 257-91; January 1873, 'Irish Priests and Irish Landlords', pp. 120-37. In 1870, Lowry Whittle, the hammer of the Ultramontanes, had written on 'Irish Elections and the Influence of the Priests', in *Fraser's Magazine*, new series, I, 1870. His main purpose was to show that the priests organized and influenced the elections in order to pledge candidates to denominational education. 'As long as Ireland is without a middle-class, and the upper-class are regarded with such rooted distrust by the people,' he wrote (p. 58), 'some such organization is perhaps inevitable.'

the Home Rule candidate, and rejected Captain Trench. Nolan was subjected to a petition, and the evidence heard at its trial revealed that large-scale intimidation had been practised by the clergy, and a considerable violence of language had been used. Three bishops were implicated. It is interesting that Nolan (a Catholic) had prepared to contest the seat in December 1870, but had not done so because of allegations that fourteen families had been wrongly evicted from his property at Portacarron. In April 1871 he had submitted his innocence to the arbitration of A. M. Sullivan, Father Lavelle, and Sir John Gray, but had not proved it, and so agreed to compensate the evicted tenants. It was partly as a result of this chastening that he was able to stand as an anti-landlord candidate in 1872, and backed by the bishops and priests, he prevailed over the Trench family, whose proselytizing activities in West Connaught were frequently referred to by the clerical factions during the campaign.[1] After the election, the Lord-Lieutenant of Ireland (Spencer) reported to the Queen that 'the Catholic priesthood supported the Home Rule candidate with all the violence which they can use on occasions with great effect'.[2] The trial of the petition lasted six weeks,[3] and was heard before that man whom the Catholics most despised – the Catholic Judge Keogh. The evidence heard laid bare an incredible story, and even Bishop MacEvilly was plainly shocked, declaring that had he known of some of the alleged clerical excesses, he would have taken 'the most summary steps' to prevent outrages.[4] Two celebrated clerical agitators took an active part in Nolan's campaign – Peter Conway and Patrick Lavelle. MacHale, who himself voted for Nolan, was widely believed to have threatened the suspension of Father Walsh of Castlebar for not being active on that behalf, but MacHale denied this in evidence.[5]

It was the manner of Keogh's judgment, delivered at Galway on 27 May, as much as the shocking revelation of the evidence, which gave to the whole affair the qualities of sensationalism. If the evidence outraged English opinion, the judgment cut the Irish Catholics deeply. Keogh said in his judgment that the whole question was 'whether this election was free, or whether it was wholly controlled, from first to last, by the

[1] For accounts of the election, see P. J. Egan, *The Parish of Ballinasloe*, Dublin, 1960, pp. 268–9; *Annual Register* 1872 (History), p. 11; *Dublin Review*, July 1872, 'The Priesthood at Irish Elections', pp. 103 ff.; Whyte, *op. cit.*, p. 247; *Spectator*, 3 August 1872, 'The Irish Priesthood'.

[2] Spencer to the Queen, 11 February 1872, *The Letters of Queen Victoria, 1862–78*, vol. II, p. 191.

[3] From 1 April to 27 May.

[4] *Parliamentary Papers*, 1872, XLVIII, The Galway Election: Judgment, Report, and Evidence, Evidence, p. 552.

[5] *Ibid.*, p. 470.

hierarchy and clergy of the Roman Catholic Church'.[1] It would turn on the proof of 'undue influence' within the meaning of the Act.[2] He found an abundance of it, and his judgment, which lasted nine hours, was in effect a general and rather comprehensive execration of the operations of his Church. The campaign, he said, had started in July 1871 when the Archbishop of Tuam wrote a letter in the *Freeman's Journal* ('It is a Roman Catholic journal, Catholic among the Catholics'), in which he promised support for Nolan.[3] There followed a series of clerical meetings to back him.[4] Keogh then went on to speak of the violence of language employed against the Trench supporters. At a meeting in Gort, Father Lavelle had called Sir Thomas Burke, a Catholic landlord, but a supporter of Trench, a liar.[5] At the Newbridge meeting Father Murray had said of Nolan 'My reason for supporting him is that he is the nominee of Archbishop MacHale'.[6] All this so far was the customary manner of dealing with elections in Ireland, but the judge went further, to outline the evidence for believing that the priests had incited mobs to riot. 'What shall I say of the other outrages, too numerous to go through in detail?' he asked.[7] There was abounding evidence too, to illustrate the spiritual penalties held out to those who voted against the Catholic candidate. 'I have gone as far as I could through those horrid altar denunciations,' he said; 'now I am asked to believe that but for the exercise of this influence all religion would be lost.'[8] He could not do so; and the election was declared void. As if in summary of all, he had declared the whole matter 'the most astounding attempt at ecclesiastical tyranny which the whole history of priestly intolerance presents'.[9]

Keogh's report to the Speaker of the House of Commons was dated 11 June, and it was presented on the 13th.[10] There he found that the Archbishop of Tuam and the Bishop of Galway were guilty of undue

[1] *Parliamentary Papers*, 1872, XLVIII, Report, p. 5.

[2] 17 & 18 Vict. cap. 102: 'Every person who shall directly or indirectly, by himself or by any other person on his behalf, make use of, or threaten to make use of any force, violence, restraint, or inflict or threaten the infliction by himself, or by or through any other person, of any injury, damage, harm, or loss, *or in any other manner* practice intimidation upon or against any person, in order to induce or compel such person to vote or refrain from voting, or account of such person having voted at any election . . . or otherwise interfere with the free exercise of the franchise of any voter', shall be deemed guilty of 'undue influence', and the election voided.

[3] *Freeman*, 26 July 1871. See *Parliamentary Papers*, 1872, XLVIII, 8.

[4] *Parliamentary Papers*, 1872, XLVIII, 18.

[5] *Ibid.*, p. 19. Someone in the crowd had shouted, 'Ay, your rivirence, and a damned liar!'

[6] *Ibid.*   [7] *Ibid.*, p. 23.   [8] *Ibid.*, p. 44.   [9] *Ibid.*, p. 17.

[10] *Hansard*, third series, CCXI, p. 1669.

influence, but it was not proved that they had sanctioned or taken part in the denunciations of Trench. Although MacEvilly had stated in evidence that such altar denunciations were a direct violation of the Synodical decrees of the Church, Keogh could cite some proven instances where it had occurred.[1] He had also to report 'that a system of intimidation prevailed throughout the said county for many weeks preceding the said election', and that 'the voters throughout the county were, on the day of the polling, systematically conducted to the booths by the Roman Catholic clergy, who interfered actively in such polling'.[2] Keogh also submitted his findings to the Court of Common Pleas, and the Government was left with the problem of deciding how much action to take.

The Judgment provoked an immediate reaction in Ireland. The *Annual Register* noted the unbounded excitement: 'Never was a public man, not to say one of the judges of the land, an object of such unmeasured abuse as Mr Justice Keogh. It poured upon him in torrents from the Roman Catholic journals, whether professing Liberal, National, or Fenian politics. Their differences were for the time forgotten.'[3] No doubt was raised as to the legality – even to the justice – of the judgment,[4] though the *Dublin Review* pointed out that even had there been no intimidation at the polls, Nolan would still have been elected, for 'the effect of sacerdotal interference has been simply the election of that candidate whom the voters really preferred'.[5] And it was with great fairness that the *Annual Register* also observed that, 'The Judgment was conceived in a very one-sided spirit, and couched in very passionate and undignified language, and while it condemned with great force and just severity the high sacerdotal influence used in favour of Captain Nolan ... it justified the counter-combination of landlords for Captain Trench, and had nothing but panegyric for their conduct in the election.'[6] But in Ireland the condemnation of Keogh was much more fierce.

On 6 June, the *Freeman* printed a letter from MacHale on the extraordinary decision 'which took all Ireland by surprise'. His object was to caution the Catholic people of Ireland against taking any notice of Keogh's remarks on religion, and to show that the trial of the petition had itself been unusual, since matters 'totally irrelevant to the simple issue raised' had been called in evidence. Of Keogh himself, the archbishop considered it enough to condemn him because he was an advocate

---

[1] *Parliamentary Papers*, 1872, XLVIII, 74. [2] *Ibid.*
[3] *Annual Register*, 1872 (History), p. 79. [4] J. Macaulay, *Ireland in 1872*, p. 235.
[5] *Dublin Review*, July 1872, 'The Priesthood at Irish Elections', p. 103.
[6] *Annual Register*, 1872 (History), p. 79.

of mixed education. 'This I consider more important than to dwell on his chequered career', he wrote.[1] At the beginning of the month there had started a series of clerical meetings to condemn the judgment in the Galway case. The Cashel and Emly priests had passed resolutions censuring Keogh to which Archbishop Leahy appended his name.[2] On the 6th the Dublin clergy met under Cullen's chairmanship, and issued an Address to the people of Ireland. 'A great scandal has come upon us,' it began, 'rousing into almost unprecedented indignation the feelings of the whole nation.'[3] It might well have added that beneficial side-effects would result – as the *Freeman* had suggested the day before, when its leader declared that 'such a union of Irish prelates, priests, and people is sure to be manifested to all the world as has not been called for for many a previous generation'.[4] The Dublin Address continued:

> It is not our business to defend the political actions imputed to some of our clerical brethren, neither is it our right to sit in judgment on their conduct. Indiscreet zeal may have carried a few of them beyond the line of decorum. . . .

But of Keogh:

> Can he forget that the Nationality of Ireland meant simply the Catholic Church? Can he forget that it was in the sanctuary alone that the sacred fire of love of fatherland was preserved, awaiting better times, when it might be brought forth to burn more freely. . . . We must not conclude without putting on record our firm conviction that the courts of justice in Ireland will not retain the respect or command the confidence of our people, if men capable of thus insulting all they hold venerable and holy are allowed to preside on their benches.[5]

The censure of Keogh implied by the closing sequence of Cullen's Address did not fall on stony ground. The Kilkenny town council at once adopted a memorial calling on the Queen to remove Keogh from the bench. Bishop Furlong and the Wexford clergy passed resolutions with similar intent.[6] The judge was burned in effigy all over Ireland, but he was strongly supported by public feeling in England.[7] *The Times* reported that in Ireland 'he is branded as a perjurer, the colleague of a swindler and a felon'.[8] It was not only the 'betrayal' of the 1850s which was again fanned into political flame by the judgment. Keogh had also

[1] *Freeman*, 6 June 1872.   [2] *Ibid.*, 5 June 1872.   [3] *Ibid.*, 7 June 1872.
[4] *Ibid.*, 6 June 1872.
[5] For the text of the Address, see *Freeman*, 7 June 1872; *Express* (Dublin), 7 June 1872; *Annual Register*, 1872 (History), p. 82.
[6] *Freeman*, 8 June 1872.
[7] *Annual Register*, 1872 (History), p. 82. Some Catholic landlords assented to the principle of the judgment, however, and the Grand Jury of Leitrim resolved in its favour – see J. Macaulay, *op. cit.*, p. 240.
[8] *The Times*, 10 June 1872.

heard many of the Fenian trials, and if the public outrage of 1872 was comparable at all with anything, it was with the Irish excitement over the Manchester 'Martyrs' of 1867.

In a letter to the *Freeman* on 25 June, Lord Granard had referred to 'the scurrilous invective and the insulting accusations' of Keogh's judgment.[1] In the Commons on the 28th, Crichton called the attention of the Government to the letter and asked if its language was suitable in one who was Lord-Lieutenant of the County Leitrim.[2] And on 9 July, Midleton raised the matter in the Lords in the form of what he called 'a grave charge' against Granard. He should never have censured a judge anywhere but in the House.[3] For the Government, Spencer abstained from any opinion,[4] and it was left to Granard himself to declare that he had written in his private and not his public capacity.[5] The raising of the Granard letter in Parliament was the first skirmish in a considerable Parliamentary examination of the whole Galway case. Keogh had submitted two points of his judgment to the Common Pleas, and the court upheld him by 3 to 1, awarding the Galway seat to Captain Trench.[6] It was therefore up to the Government to announce its course of action, and this was done by the Irish Attorney-General (Dowse) on 23 July. Of the thirty-six persons named in the schedules of Keogh's report to the House, twenty-four were to be prosecuted for undue influence under the Corrupt Practices Act of 1854; and among them the Bishop of Clonfert, Dr Patrick Duggan, and nineteen Catholic clergymen. It was also announced that the Archbishop of Tuam and the Bishop of Galway would not be prosecuted as their part in the denunciations had not been proved.[7] On the 25th, the entire case was aired in the debate on Butt's motion for a Committee of the House to consider Keogh's report and the complaints that had been laid against it,[8] and as a result the case continued to receive Parliamentary attention throughout the year. On that day also, Bright advised Gladstone against the prosecutions.[9] The *Daily News* correspondent reported from Rome that the Pope had authorized the English and Irish bishops 'to protest, by means of Pastoral letters, against the determination of the British Government to prosecute the priests concerned in the Galway election proceedings'.[10]

As the time drew nearer for the trial of Dr Duggan, Jervoise, who had

---

[1] *Freeman*, 25 June 1872.   [2] *Hansard*, CCXII, p. 340.
[3] *Ibid.*, p. 859.   [4] *Ibid.*, p. 864.   [5] *Ibid.*, p. 865.
[6] *Annual Register*, 1872 (History), p. 82; *The Times*, 10 June 1872.
[7] *Hansard*, CCXII, pp. 1626-31.   [8] *Ibid.*, pp. 1763 ff.
[9] *The Diaries of John Bright*, ed. R. A. J. Walling, London, 1930, p. 349.
[10] *Daily News*, 26 July 1872.

succeeded Odo Russell in Rome, tried in November to discover whether Cullen had sought Papal influence in favour of those about to be prosecuted, as a rumour to that effect was receiving wide credence. Antonelli denied it: the Holy Father had never attempted 'to control the exercise of his vote by any citizen'. He expressed his disbelief that the Irish clergy could have been guilty of undue influence – but if that should be the case, they would surely be punished by their ecclesiastical superiors. It was true, he said, that Cullen had been in Rome during October, but everything he had said to the Pope and to himself had concerned the O'Keeffe case, and the Galway election had not been mentioned. But he would ask the Propaganda what they knew of it.[1] The question was not pursued by the Government; no doubt they were more alarmed to learn that Cullen had been interviewing the Pope about O'Keeffe than they were about the Vatican attitude to the Galway election.

The Duggan trial took place in February 1873. The Crown case rested on his utterance of the words 'Anathema, anathema, shall be hurled at any person who will not do as I recommend or as my clergy direct', and only one witness was produced to prove that he had spoken them, and he was a tradesman of Lord Clancarty's employ. The sole question was whether the words *were* spoken, and as this was not proved, the bishop was acquitted on 19 February. He retired to the south of France for three months to recover.[2] 'For the first time since the good grey head of Oliver Plunkett fell at Tyburn,' the *Freeman* noticed, 'a Prelate of the Irish Catholic Church stood as a criminal at the bar.'[3] No other convictions were obtained by the Crown either, for the rest of the cases were withdrawn.[4] But the entire affair had ruined the hopes of the Liberals in Ireland – unless Gladstone could save the situation and pull off a good University measure. Even the *Freeman* had seethed with anger at the Liberals, who had 'taken up the mantle of the priest-hunter'. The affair, it remarked, 'is enough to teach the Irish people to believe that "no good can come out of Nazareth"'.[5] It was no wonder that the Irish Catholics would not have the University Bill when it came.

One question which had been raised in the Galway case was to have great importance. It was Parnell who seized on the Ballot Act of 1872 as the perfect foundation for an Independent party.[6] The Act was in fact

[1] F.O. 43, vol. 119, Dispatches no. 65, 6 November and no. 66, 8 November 1872.

[2] For accounts of the trial, see *Freeman*, 27, 18, and 20 February 1873; Thomas Brett, *Life of Dr Duggan*, Dublin, 1921, p. 99; P. J. Egan, *The Parish of Ballinasloe*, Dublin, 1960, p. 269.

[3] *Freeman*, 20 February 1873.   [4] J. Macaulay, *op. cit.*, p. 241 n.

[5] *Freeman*, 25 July 1872.

[6] R. C. K. Ensor, *England, 1870–1914*, Oxford, 1936, p. 24; C. C. O'Brien, *Parnell and his Party, 1880–90*, Oxford, 1957, p. 34.

passed before the trial of the Galway election petition, but most speakers in the debate referred to the greater benefits it would bring to Ireland, and in opposing the second reading in the Commons in February, Liddell had referred to its recommendation 'on the strength of the Irish argument', and had also plainly alluded to the influence being prepared by the Home Rule priests at Galway and Kerry.[1] Captain Nolan, the still-seated victor of the Galway contest, replied to his remarks by accusing the landlords of dictating the votes of their tenants. With a dash of generosity which he later no doubt regretted, he admitted that the Ballot Act would prevent their influence but not that of the priests.[2] This was in fact true, and the Act[3] which so greatly emancipated the tenants from the electoral thrall of the landlords still left the priest the pulpit and – above all – the Confessional.[4] The Galway and Kerry elections were the last Irish county contests fought before the ballot was enforced, and in writing to the Queen on the disturbances at them, Spencer had looked to the Act as removing the occasion for abuses, as the 'mobs will not know which voters to attack or stop'.[5] In his appearance in the Galway petition trial, MacHale had been questioned on 'the attitude of the clergy to the ballot'. He had replied:

I have not the least doubt but that the clergy would hail it, on two accounts; first, because it would secure the complete freedom of the tenant-class and the immunity from landlord coercion; and secondly, it would screen the clergymen themselves from what is sometimes to them the very unenviable position of being obliged to come forward to defend the freedom and the rights of the tenantry.[6]

The Ballot Act had its most significant results in Ireland. But the fear that the priests would simply strengthen their influence by the assumption to themselves of that which the landlords could no longer wield, was not to prove so dire. In the mid-seventies the influence of the clergy at elections declined – partly because of episcopal alarm at the excesses of the Galway case, but more because of the rise of an Irish political party which had a Dublin caucus organizing the selection of candidates.[7] But the Ballot Act itself helped the decline: for by raising the average

[1] *Hansard*, CCIX, p. 474 (15 February 1872).

[2] *Ibid.*, p. 479.

[3] 35 & 36 Vict. cap. 32 (royal assent, 13 July 1872).

[4] In his judgment in the Galway case, Keogh reported a priest – whom he described as an 'insane disgrace to the Roman Catholic religion' – as having said 'they would use the Confessional under the ballot if they required it'. *Parliamentary Papers* 1872, XLVIII, 28; see *Dublin Review*, July 1872, p. 112.

[5] *The Letters of Queen Victoria, 1862–78*, vol. II, p. 191, 11 February 1872.

[6] *Parliamentary Papers*, 1872, XLVIII, Evidence, p. 470.

[7] Whyte, *op. cit.*, in *English Historical Review*, LXXV, no. 295, 1960, pp. 254-5.

number of polling stations in each county from four to twenty it made the customary sacerdotal arrangements for management of voting inapplicable.

The election in Kerry had been influenced by the Home Rule success in Galway just prior to it, and the victory of Blennerhassett over Dease came as a second blow to Liberalism.[1] But in Kerry the bishop used all his influence against Home Rule, unlike the bishops of the West. Unhappily for Moriarty, the Kerry priests were as faithful to the cause as had been their brethren at Galway. In January 1872 Cullen had urged Moriarty to support the Liberal Dease for the candidacy of Kerry. 'He is a good practical Catholic,' the cardinal had written, 'well acquainted with the wants of Ireland.'[2] This endorsement was not accepted by the Kerry priests. On 11 January, Moriarty addressed a *Letter* to the clergy and people of Kerry, in which he made it clear that he considered the Home Rule movement inopportune – when a Government was in power pledged to redress Irish grievances – and that its leadership, whilst containing some worthy men, also included 'dangerous revolutionaries'. He feared that something like the Parisian Commune might be established if Home Rule were to be given effect. He felt also that a general adoption in Ireland of that principle could only have the effect of throwing the Gladstone Government into the arms of the secularists, and thus a settlement of the education question favourable to Catholics would be postponed indefinitely.[3] But the priests waived caution, and they threw themselves into Blennerhassett's campaign. So the bishop issued a letter for the clergy alone on the 22nd of the month, in which he commanded them not to interfere in the contest in any parish but their own, 'in order to lessen, as far as possible, the appearance of disunion among the clergy at the coming election'. Violation of this instruction would be met with ecclesiastical censures.[4] Poor Moriarty, never popular because of his stand over Fenianism, and over the Church and education questions, was now attacked by the *Freeman* for sanctioning the 'unholy alliance' which had appeared at the election 'between the Liberal and Tory landlords'.[5] At least he had the support of Cullen this time, and, surprisingly, of The O'Donoghue.[6]

Concurrently with the two great Home Rule elections, there was occurring the first important round in a conflict which, touching on

[1] See A. M. Sullivan, *op. cit.*, pp. 349-63.
[2] Monsell Papers, Box 8319, Cullen to Moriarty, 5 January 1872.
[3] *Freeman*, 12 January 1872; *Annual Register*, 1872 (History), pp. 11 ff.
[4] *Freeman*, 25 January 1872.
[5] *Ibid.*, 10 February 1872.
[6] *Annual Register*, 1872 (History), pp. 11 ff.

matters central to the Irish agitation of the previous decade, seemed to summarize the hoplessness of achieving any real advance in the relations between English opinion and the Irish Catholic Church. The O'Keeffe case ran on until 1875, injecting poison into Parliamentary discussion of Irish questions and spreading discord in the Irish Church. It was debated at length both in Parliament and at the Vatican. James Macaulay could write, as early as the middle of 1872, that 'there are few who have not heard of Father O'Keeffe'.[1] His case, he wrote, 'will afford a most instructive view of the great questions now agitating the Roman Catholic Church – questions, the solution of which will influence the future history of Ireland'.[2]

It was in April 1871 that Cullen first intimated to Cardinal Barnabo at the Propaganda that all was not well in County Kilkenny:

> I am sorry to inform your Eminence of a grave scandal which at present causes distress in the Diocese of Ossory. . . .
> . . . It is caused by a certain O'Keeffe, Parish Priest of Callan. This person has undertaken legal proceedings against the Bishop and his curates, before civil courts. In addition to this, he is spreading the most serious slanders against the Bishop in pamphlets.[3]

Father Robert O'Keeffe had been trained at Maynooth, and had been for ten years Professor of Science and Languages at St Kyran's College in Kilkenny, before becoming parish priest of Callan in 1863. It is necessary to have a brief excursion into the famous collision which occurred between this priest and his bishop, and finally with Cullen.[4] O'Keeffe was manager of the Callan National Schools, and that these were well conducted under him was never called in question. But in September 1868, the Christian Brothers opened a school in Callan, and the children were all drawn away to it, so that when the National School inspectors visited in December, they found only seven boys there, whilst there were 220 at the Christian Brothers' establishment. O'Keeffe kept his own

---

[1] James Macaulay, *Ireland in 1872*, p. 183.

[2] *Ibid.*, p. 184.

[3] Propaganda, *Scritture* 36, Cullen to Barnabo, 30 April 1871. He sent some of O'Keeffe's work with the letter.

[4] This account is based principally on the very full details of the case given in numerous letters and papers in vol. 36 of the Propaganda *Scritture*; also on chap. XIII of James Macaulay's *Ireland in 1872*; and on the letters which O'Keeffe himself published as a pamphlet entitled *Cardinal Cullen and the P. P. Callan*, Dublin, 1872. Also used: *Parliamentary Papers*, 1872, LI, 649 (correspondence on O'Keeffe's dismissal by the National Board), 1873, LII, 305, 1874, LI, 617 (minutes of proceedings, and correspondence of the Board of National Education and the Callan Schools); 1876, LVIII, 675 (correspondence between the Local Government Board and O'Keeffe on his dismissal from the chaplaincy of the Callan Workhouse).

schools open, however, and a drift back took place. In June 1871 the average attendance there exceeded ninety. But to get the children back, he had told the parish that Bishop Walsh wished the National Schools of Callan to continue, and for this declaration the two curates of O'Keeffe, who ran the Friary Chapel, accused him from the altar of lying, and added that the bishop had authorized them to say so. He therefore brought an action for slander against his Diocesan and was non-suited, but an action against the curates, Neary and John Walsh, held, and both were convicted of slander. For taking action in a civil court he was then suspended, even though, as he explained to the Vicar-General, when he had written to Cullen about redress in an ecclesiastical tribunal, he had not been offered any assistance for such a course. Cullen did interfere in July 1871, suggesting that O'Keeffe should see him in Dublin so that the 'dissensions and disputes in Callan' might end.[1] This started a long correspondence with the cardinal, who cited the Bulls *In coena Domini* and *Apostolicae Sedis* to show that any priest who dragged ecclesiastics before civil courts would be liable to suspension. O'Keeffe countered this by quoting evidence given to the Committees of Parliament in 1825 and 1826 by Irish ecclesiastics, showing that Papal Bulls could not be received in Britain. This correspondence ended in November 1871 when O'Keeffe was suspended by Cullen.

In March 1872 Bishop Walsh wrote to the Commissioners of National Education in Dublin, informing them of O'Keeffe's suspension and his replacement as parish priest by a Father Martin. This last named also wrote to the Board requesting appointment as manager of the Callan National Schools. The Commissioners considered the case and on 23 April decided to receive and act on the bishop's certificate of suspension. O'Keeffe was thus dismissed by the Board, and subsequently the Poor Law Commissioners removed him from the chaplaincy of the Union Workhouse. When an action was brought before the Recorder of Dublin by the Callan National School teachers against the Education Commissioners for the amount of their salaries, it was decided that their contract was with the manager, O'Keeffe, who had been removed, so that the Board was not liable for payment. By this point in the case the main issue had become clear: two Government Boards and a Dublin court had accepted that an ecclesiastical censure could apparently be given what amounted to legal effect. In July 1872 the case came before Parliament. A small local Irish dispute, caused by two young curates calling their priest a liar, had become a major constitutional issue. Callan itself was bitterly split into two Catholic camps, and division was lapping

[1] *Cardinal Cullen and the P. P. Callan*, p. 10.

outwards to other Irish localities. To Protestants the case was plainly an example of ultramontanism receiving the support of administrative bodies. Cullen sadly informed the Propaganda that the Callan Protestants were subscribing to help defray O'Keeffe's legal expenses.[1]

In February 1872 O'Keeffe had written to tell Earl Russell that he had 'a real papal aggression to meet this time', and begged him to bring his case against the Poor Law Commissioners before the House of Lords. His only offence, he protested, was that he had sought redress in the courts of the land. 'Will your Lordship allow me to be punished as a criminal by a public board under control of Parliament for having done this?' he asked. 'I think you will not.'[2] To Gladstone he wrote that his treatment would raise 'a question of the utmost importance to the nation'.[3] In June he lost in the first of the proceedings he had instituted against Cullen before the Queen's Bench in Dublin. 'The case excites great interest', *The Times* remarked.[4] On 18 July, the Earl of Harrowby presented O'Keeffe's petition to the Lords, praying for redress against the action of his bishop, the Papal Legate, and the National Education Commissioners.[5] The Irish Lord Chancellor, O'Hagan, said[6] that with the question at issue between the bishop and the priest they had no concern; the question they must determine was 'under what circumstances the Commissioners of National Education in Ireland had found themselves coerced to deprive Mr O'Keeffe of the patronage and management of certain National Schools'.[7] He took the view that they had behaved quite properly[8] – if a man ceased to fill the position by right of which he had been appointed to the managership, it was natural for the Board to transfer the appointment to his successor.[9] The matter did not, however, end there. In August the member for Kilmarnock, Bouverie, raised it in the Commons by blaming the Commissioners for assisting Cullen in carrying out the claims of the hierarchy to be independent of lay tribunals,[10] but his protest gesture for a £100 reduction in the education vote was negatived. Meanwhile O'Keeffe himself was giving a wide interpretation to the evils which had encompassed him about. Following Bouverie's motion, he published a letter to Gladstone showing that 'certain theological opinions, which the State has always looked upon as inconsistent with true allegiance, and as subversive of civil and religious liberty, have been lately preached

---

[1] Propaganda, *Scritture* 36, Cullen to Barnabo, 15 February 1872.
[2] Gladstone Papers, B.M.Add.MS. 44433, f. 250, O'Keeffe to Earl Russell, 25 February 1872.
[3] *Ibid.*, B.M.Add.M.S. 444-33, f. 250, O'Keeffe to Gladstone, 26 February 1872.
[4] *The Times*, 10 June 1872.   [5] *Hansard*, CCXII, p. 1343.   [6] *Ibid.*, p. 1344.
[7] *Ibid.*   [8] *Ibid.*   [9] *Ibid.*, p. 1345.
[10] J. Macaulay, *op. cit.*, pp. 204–7; *The Times*, 6 August 1872.

from high places in this country'. These he defined, as would any Protestant, as ultramontanism. He accused Cullen of putting forward the claims of the Papacy to 'temporal sway' in Ireland. Even Catholic Emancipation, he postulated, would not have been conceded 'if the hierarchy of that time were imbued with the sentiments which Cardinal Cullen has imported from Rome'. The evils were quite manifest when 'public boards became the execution of Papal Bulls'. And action was imperative: 'I say the minister who thinks he can ignore such a state of things mistakes his duty.'[1]

Cullen himself went to Rome, and Antonelli said that he spoke of nothing but the O'Keeffe case whilst he was there, discussing it at length with the Pope.[2] Jervoise reported that it was on Papal instruction that O'Keeffe had been suspended.[3]

In April 1873, Bouverie (whom the *Freeman* styled 'an anti-Catholic bigot'), again broached the question in the Commons.[4] Manning wrote in May to warn Gladstone of the dangers of the case, which 'may involve the Government in a difficulty which they may not foresee,'[5] when dealing with the unpleasant situation caused by the collapse of the University Bill. Here Manning was right: for the end of the Bill and of of all hope of an educational settlement of any sort, meant that the Irish bishops were now released from any obligation to hold to the Gladstone Administration. They watched affairs in Parliament closely. On the 15th of the month, Hartington moved for the appointment of a Select Committee on the Callan Schools.[6] This was constituted on the 22nd,[7] and, like O'Keeffe himself, Vernon Harcourt showed the gravity of the question when he said 'it involved one of the largest questions which could possibly be conceived, and which was now agitating every part of Europe – namely, how far ecclesiastical authority was or was not to be

---

[1] Gladstone Papers, B.M.Add.MS. 44435, f. 35 (8 August 1872).

[2] F.O. 43, vol. 119, Dispatches nos. 65, 6 November and 66, 8 November, 1872.

[3] *Ibid.*, Dispatch no. 73, 19 November 1872. Barnabo had sent a Papal *Rescript* from the Propaganda on 31 May 1871, empowering Cullen to suspend O'Keeffe. (The text is in the *Dublin Review*, July 1873, p. 225.) Cullen told Moriarty in January 1872 that he had done everything in his power to avoid a suspension, but 'could not avoid doing so in the end'. He described O'Keeffe as proud and stubborn. Monsell Papers, Box 8319, Cullen to Moriarty, 5 January 1872.

[4] *Freeman*, 28 April 1873; *Hansard*, CCXV, p. 1140 (29 April).

[5] Gladstone Papers, B.M.Add.MS. 44250, f. 130, Manning to Gladstone, 8 May 1873.

[6] *Hansard*, CCXV, p. 2023.

[7] *Ibid.*, CCXVI, p. 319. The members of the Select Committee were Hartington, Cardwell, Gathorne Hardy, Whitbread, Burke and The O'Conor Don. The *Freeman* (24 May 1873), accepted the fairness of the selection.

supreme over the civil'.[1] In reply, Hartington assured the House that the scope of the inquiry was not so large; it was merely to ascertain the facts of a particular case.[2] At this juncture, on 27 May, the final verdict was declared in the case of *O'Keeffe* v. *Cullen*: O'Keeffe won, and was awarded $\frac{1}{4}d.$ nominal damages; the costs to be paid by the cardinal.[3] The *Freeman* commented on the favourable light in which the legal proceedings had left Cullen, so disappointing those who had hoped to see him exhibited as a proud and haughty prelate. 'The all-important fact, however, remains – that the first common law tribunal in the land has decided that every rescript, every document, every letter sent by His Holiness the Pope to his spiritual subjects in this country . . . is an illegal document.' Religious equality was 'destroyed at one blow'. The war waged by Bismarck against the freedom of the Church in Germany could not be worse.[4]

The Callan Schools Committee heard its evidence quickly, during the first half of June. The *Freeman* waited impatiently, transported by the potentialities of the case into a temporary supporter of the National Board. Surely, Gray asked through its columns, Parliament would not allow 'a deadly blow at Ireland's greatest temporal interest – the education of her youth?'[5] The Committee's report was issued on 18 June.[6] It referred the House entirely to the evidence, which showed that neither Cullen nor any of the other bishops had made any communication with the National Board on the Callan Schools question, with the exception only of Bishop Moran's formal notification that Martin had succeeded O'Keeffe.[7] Cullen, in fact, was shown never to have had dealings with the Board on any matter.[8] The case of Father Peter Daly was referred to several times, but it was no true precedent, for although he had remained manager of his National Schools, his suspension by his bishop (MacEvilly) had never been notified to the Board.[9]

On the basis of this, the Government decided to take no action, and let matters rest. But they could not prevent the continued upheaval of feeling in Ireland. The *Dublin Review* saw that the case could still 'upset the national system of education' and 'dislocate the relations between the Catholic Church in these countries and the State'.[10] And

---

[1] *Hansard*, CCXVI, p. 320.   [2] *Ibid.*, p. 322.   [3] *Freeman*, 28 May 1873.
[4] *Ibid.*   [5] *Ibid.*, 14 June 1873.
[6] *Parliamentary Papers*, 1873, IX, 1, Report on Circumstances of Dismissal by Commissioners of National Education in Ireland of Rev. R. O'Keeffe from the office of Manager of Callan Schools, etc.
[7] *Ibid.*, Evidence, p. 13 (by P. J. Keenan, Resident-Commissioner). Moran was Walsh's coadjutor.
[8] *Ibid.*, p. 141 (by Mr Justice Fitzgerald, a Commissioner since 1864).
[9] *Ibid.*, pp. 69, 87.   [10] *Dublin Review*, July 1873, 'The Case of Mr O'Keeffe', p. 211.

O'Keeffe himself did not stop agitating; nor did the peace return to the district of Callan, where 'rival altar denunciations were hurled, and the partisans of the two sides lived in constant strife'.[1] It was not until July 1875 that the last of the legal actions was heard – *O'Keeffe* v. *McDonald* (the Vicar-General).[2] The importance of the entire case was not really that O'Keeffe had made his point – he did not get his schools back – but that he had placed ammunition in the hands of those always ready to assail the Irish Catholic Church. 'If Mr O'Keeffe is successful in the conflict,' James Macaulay had written in 1872, 'it will be a national protest against the tyranny of the Ultramontane party.'[3] He had not been personally successful, but he had caused a major disruption in the Irish Church.

It was curious that the case should have presented the National Board in the character of a friend to the hierarchy, for the bishops had not ceased attacking the whole National System of education. During the autumn of 1869 they had prepared for the Powis Report on Primary Education in Ireland by the issue of the Maynooth resolutions. As early as July of that year, immediately following the settlement of the Church question, the National Association had declared that steps would have to be taken to settle education as well.[4] But it was the independent action of the bishops, in the Maynooth resolutions of August, which gave notice to the Government that Catholic educational demands must be dealt with. 'The Royal Assent was scarcely given to the Irish Church Act', the *Express* remarked on the resolutions, 'until Cardinal Cullen and his confréres raised a howl of religious discord.'[5] At Maynooth the bishops had again condemned mixed education, and called upon the clergy and laity 'to oppose by every constitutional means the extension or perpetuation of the mixed system'.[6] Since they had learned that the Government intended 'to legislate for Ireland in accordance with the wishes of its people', they wanted the Ministers to know that it was their wish to receive 'a complete system of education based upon religion'.[7] They demanded a share in the funds then given to the royal and endowed schools (Resolution VIII). As in the negotiations of 1865–8, in these resolutions the bishops again linked their demands on National education with higher education.[8] The resolutions were widely condemned by the English and

---

[1] J. Macaulay, *op. cit.*, p. 220.

[2] See P. J. Walsh, *Life of W. J. Walsh*, Dublin and Cork, 1928, p. 26.

[3] J. Macaulay, *op. cit.*, p. 228.   [4] *Freeman*, 28 July 1869; meeting of 27 July.

[5] *Express*, Dublin, 10 September 1869.   [6] *Freeman*, 2 September 1869: Resolution 1.

[7] *Ibid.*, Resolution IV.   [8] *Ibid.*, Resolutions V–IX.

Scottish press,[1] and to many it seemed that the opinion expressed by Bishop Magee to the House of Lords in June was true – that concerning education 'an alliance between the Ultramontanists and a Liberal Government on this question is quite impossible'.[2] This was also the sense implied when the *Nonconformist* warned the bishops that those in England who had supported them over religious equality would be found among their strongest opponents if they sought to implement the resolutions.[3] It was well known that the episcopal demands were not supported by the Irish laity, and it was up to the Government to deal equally for the whole Union – 'either to advance in the direction of secular education alike in England and Ireland, or in that of denominational educational endowment in both islands'.[4] The *Express* felt similarly: the real issue 'is not a struggle between the Irish people and the English Government, but a struggle between the Irish laity and the Irish priesthood'. The Government must not throw in their weight on the bishops' side.[5] Kavanagh wrote publicly to defend the resolutions, but he was too optimistic and too dependent on the power of statistics when he claimed that the differences of opinion among British Liberals on Irish education were only a result of their ignorance of the facts.[6] Cullen followed up the resolutions with a Pastoral on Catholic education at the beginning of September,[7] yet although he there instructed Catholic parents to remove their children from the Marlborough Street Model Schools in Dublin, by November a thousand Catholic children were still reported as in attendance.[8] But in reply to feelings like those expressed in the English press, a memorial of Irish lay Catholics was got up, which was signed by 888 who professed themselves in favour of the episcopal educational demands. It was presented in April 1870,[9] supported by a letter of Woodlock to *The Times*.[10] Everything now awaited the result of the Powis Commission.

Their report appeared in June 1870, and it is one of the most valuable documents in the history of Irish education.[11] It started with a *Historical Sketch of the System of National Education* which reviewed the entire

---

[1] *Express*, 10 September 1869.

[2] *Hansard*, CXCVI, p. 1869 (15 June 1869).

[3] *Nonconformist*, 8 September 1869, 'Mixed Education in Ireland'. At the National Association in July 1870, after the publication of the Powis Report, MacSwiney warned the members that the English Nonconformists would do all they could to resist it – he cited the *Nonconformist* as evidence. *Freeman*, 8 July 1870.

[4] *Ibid.*   [5] *Express*, 10 September 1869.   [6] *Freeman*, 18 September 1869.

[7] *Ibid.*, 2 September 1869.   [8] *Guardian*, 3 November 1869.

[9] *Express*, 7 April 1870.   [10] Printed in *Freeman*, 26 April 1870.

[11] *Parliamentary Papers*, 1870, XXVIII (8 vols.).

matter up to 1868, the year in which the Commission was constituted.[1] The actual recommendations were signed by Powis, Dunraven, the Protestant Bishop of Meath, Clonbrock, Morris, Brooke, Cowie, J. A. Dease, Stokes, W. K. Sullivan and Waldron. Three Commissioners did not sign – Kane, Wilson and Gibson, on the ground that 'it practically subverts the system of united education and favours the denominational system'.[2] The first recommendation was for the payment of teachers in proportion to the progress made by their pupils, and the Commissioners also believed that local management was necessary for the well-being of a school – the existing system in fact to continue – but the local contribution was to be raised by a rate of not more than threepence in the pound. The section of the report touching religion was the most important, however. First, in the case of a district with only one school: there, instead of excluding all religious teaching, the course should be adopted of placing all on an equality. Religious instruction should be confined to fixed hours. No child registered as a Protestant should be present when such instruction was given by a Roman Catholic, and vice versa. No child should be present at any religious observance to which the parents might object. School books were to be those allowed by the Commissioners of National Education for use in mixed schools. No religious emblems were to be exhibited in school hours.[3] In districts where there were two schools, with attendances of not less than twenty-five scholars, and which had been in existence for three years, they could relax these restrictions provided that the one prohibiting the presence of children of one religion at the instruction of those of another, continued to be enforced. Thus certain National Schools could become virtually denominational. It was also proposed that Christian Brothers' schools should receive grants. Among other recommendations was one for the compulsory acquisition of sites for schools, and another for the gradual extinction of the provincial Model Schools.[4] And it was suggested that, although all books in use must continue to have its authorization, the Board would cease publishing its own school books.

The *Freeman* welcomed the recommendations as 'a very decided step in the right direction, and as such will be received with satisfaction in Ireland'.[5] It considered the regulations proposed for religious instruction 'sufficiently ample to secure to all the benefits of the secular education of

[1] See James MacCaffrey, *History of the Catholic Church in the Nineteenth Century*, vol. II, p. 227.

[2] *Freeman*, 10 June 1870.

[3] *Parliamentary Papers*, 1870, XXVIII, vol. I, Recommendations, p. 526 (paragraph 42).

[4] See the special Report on Model Schools, District and Minor, by Cowie and Stokes; *ibid.*, vol. I, Part II, p. 739.

[5] *Freeman*, 6 June 1870.

the school without danger of interference with religion', although the Catholics still believed that religion could never be separated from secular instruction, and would continue to contend for a purely denominational system. The proposal that in districts with two schools, they should be regarded by the Board as denominational was given an unqualified approval as was the provision for the extinction of provincial Model Schools.[1]

It will be remembered that Cullen had been most careful in 1868 to keep Moriarty out of the Commission on the suspicion that he might declare himself for the mixed system. It is interesting that in his letter to the Commission of 10 June 1868, Moriarty avoided discussion of the principle of the National System, and wrote only on the manner of its operation.[2] This almost certainly reflected his desire not to upset the unanimity for which Cullen had worked so hard during that year. Cullen's own evidence to the Commission he made a manifesto of the Catholic case. He had collected data on the evils of secular education in America from Spalding in 1869, and similar matter from European countries, and, as he told Spalding, he used his three-days' appearance in examination to show 'how the mixed system is most dangerous'. He was hopeful that the National System would not last much longer; 'all the bishops are now united in condemning it' he added.[3] He was not the only episcopal witness (22 February 1869): Dr Dorrian of Down and Connor also gave evidence (9 June 1868),[4] so did Dr Keane of Cloyne (26 October 1868).[5] Dr Moriarty of Kerry, and the Archbishop of Armagh, Dr Kieran, sent letters to the Commission containing their views.[6] James Kavanagh was also examined.[7] Cullen was before the Commission for three days. He started by making a general statement[8] showing the necessity of having religion as the basis of all education. His replies to questions upheld the denominational system, and included a second statement on the evils for Catholics of the mixed system,[9] especially censuring the teaching of 'common Christianity'. In Dublin, he said, there was in practice very little mixed education, except in the Model and Workhouse Schools, though Belfast was torn by educational conflict.[10]

---

[1] *Freeman*, 6 June 1870.   [2] *Parliamentary Papers*, 1870, XXVIII, vol. VIII, p. 15.
[3] Spalding Letters, Cullen to Spalding, 22 May 1869.
[4] *Parliamentary Papers*, 1870, XXVIII, vol. III, p. 342.
[5] *Ibid.*, p. 675.   [6] *Ibid.*, vol. VIII, pp. 15 ff.   [7] *Ibid.*, vol. III, p. 395.
[8] *Ibid.*, pp. 1177 ff.   [9] *Ibid.*, pp. 1180 ff.
[10] *Ibid.*, p. 1179. In January of this year, he had told Monsell that this was true in many of the cities of the south; but in the west and north it was not so. Carlingford Papers, CP. 3/75, Monsell to Fortescue, 23 January 1869. In an open letter to Fortescue of 10 December 1869, Kavanagh said he had visited every National School in the Dublin district and found that there was 'not one school in Dublin attended by Catholic and Protestant children in any number'. *Freeman*, 13 December 1869.

The rational course would be to recognize *de facto* denominational education, and this was in effect what the Commissioners recommended. Cullen also reviewed the declarations of the bishops against the mixed system since the 1859 Pastoral,[1] and gave their claims over the education of the laity thus:

> Catholics admit the parental right over children; but not to the exclusion of the authority of the Church: when once Catholics have declared themselves subjects of the Church, as a matter of course they are bound as long as they remain Catholics, to be guided by the decisions and by the authority of the Church.[2]

Yet he did not demand the end of the National System. It was useless now, he realized, to revert to Lord Stanley's original principles, but 'the system as it stands could be reformed in such a way, without very much difficulty, as to render it satisfactory', and this was quite simply to be done by declaring all the schools denominational.[3] He was not aware of any more than a few Catholics who opposed their educational demands, and if the system became denominational it would not necessarily fall into the hands of the clergy.[4] When asked if he concurred in the Papal condemnation of the education of Catholics in purely secular knowledge, as given in the Syllabus of Errors, Cullen replied that it could be taken as the summary of all his evidence.[5]

When the evidence was published, Cullen was immediately attacked by the *Daily News* in London and the *Express* in Dublin for claiming that the Catholic laity went with his demands.[6] Kavanagh made a public reply, and at the same time welcomed the report as 'a highly important verdict, though unsatisfactory in many respects'.[7] In September a lay and clerical *Declaration* demanding denominational education was signed throughout the country.[8] The Government intended legislation based on the report, though Gladstone advised Fortescue, who was to deal with it, not to communicate with the Irish bishops about it because of the unfavourable state of public feeling.[9] In fact the legislation did not come – it was killed by the same difficulties which afflicted the Land Bill and the repeal of the Ecclesiastical Titles Act, a growth of anti-Catholic opinion in England. And coming as it did to supplement that feeling, the O'Keeffe case made it seem as if the 'Board of Commissioners is so irreclaimably under the power of the Romish hierarchy'[10] that any action

[1] *Parliamentary Papers*, 1870, XXVIII, vol. III, pp. 1182 ff. [2] *Ibid.*, p. 1219.
[3] *Ibid.*, p. 1233. [4] *Ibid.*, p. 1244. [5] *Ibid.*, p. 1259. [6] *Express*, 15 June 1870.
[7] *Freeman*, 24 June 1870. [8] *Ibid.*, 17 September 1870 (prints the text).
[9] Carlingford Papers, CP. 1/125(a), Gladstone to Fortescue, 19 August 1870.
[10] J. Macaulay, *op. cit.*, p. 382.

by the Government to reform the Irish National System could only strengthen the bishops' hands. Gladstone could not allow any such appearance, and the Powis recommendations remained unimplemented. This in turn caused the bishops to lose still more faith in his Government. In November 1870 Gillooly warned Gladstone that the Administration was on trial: legislation on education would prove the sincerity of their intentions.[1] It did not come.

The Catholics did not give up. On 20 April 1871 the National Association held a conference on the education question for the purpose of organizing petitions and bringing the matter before Parliament. When he wrote to wish it well, Cullen referred to the Paris Commune as 'a convincing proof of the evils of a godless system of education'.[2] Archbishop Leahy, in his letter to the conference said that as Gladstone had admitted the grievance and assured them of redress, 'the time has come for him to redeem his promise'.[3] The conference had before it the drafts of the papers which were later published under the name of a 'Committee of Irish Catholics', and which dealt with the need for a system of Irish intermediate education.[4] In 1870 the *Irish Ecclesiastical Record* had urged such a system.[5] Other action was taken to persuade the Government that legislation on educational questions was imperative. On 11 May, MacHale published an open letter to Gladstone, giving notice that 'no further toleration can be allowed to those delusive and insulting experiments by which it has been sought to win the confidence of the Irish people, and to persuade them to acquiesce in alien and antinational projects of instruction'. Nothing would satisfy them short of Catholic education.[6] In November, Monsell drew Gladstone's attention to a petition from Kerry and Limerick which had been got up by Bishops Moriarty and Butler. It made university demands, but also required educational equality at all levels, emphasizing the great sense of grievance the petitioners felt about it.[7] At a Catholic meeting at Maryborough in November, resolutions were passed favouring the episcopal policy.[8]

[1] Gladstone Papers, B.M.Add.MS. 44428, f. 239, Gillooly to Gladstone, 30 November 1870.

[2] *Freeman*, 22 April 1871.

[3] *Ibid.*

[4] *Intermediate and University Education in Ireland, by a Committee of Irish Catholics*, Part I, Intermediate Education, Dublin and London, 1872 (January).

[5] *Irish Ecclesiastical Record*, new series, VII, 1870–1, 'The Endowed Schools of Ireland', p. 97.

[6] *Freeman*, 11 May 1871.

[7] Gladstone Papers, B.M.Add.MS. 44152, f. 133. Fortescue has added to the copy (f. 139): 'This seems to me an excellent petition, most deserving of the attention of the Government.'

[8] *Express*, 21 November 1871.

But December brought the publication of *Roman Catholic Priests and National Schools*, a counterblast by Gerald FitzGibbon, the Master in Chancery. He repeated the claim that the laity did not wish the reforms demanded by their clergy, and held that every concession made by the Government only encouraged more demands. 'Nothing but the extirpation of what they call heresy will satisfy those who assert authority from heaven.'[1] The *Freeman's Journal* characterized the book as 'a scream of feminine shrillness and intensity, imploring the English Parliament not to grant to Ireland those education reforms which her people demand'.[2] In January of the new year, the Synod of the Church of Ireland upheld the National System and attacked the Catholic bishops, whose demands they resolved, were 'ultimately subversive of civil and religious liberty'.[3] Still the Catholics did not give up, and a reply was supplied at a meeting in Dublin on 17 January presided over by Cullen, which repeated all the arguments for Catholic education.[4] And at the same time, the papers by the 'Committee of Irish Catholics' were published. The National Association meeting on the 23rd was the occasion chosen by MacSwiney to declare that every Catholic in Ireland was for denominationalism, excepting only for 'a few impatient and ungovernable agitators'.[5]

The Irish received help from Manning, whose Pastoral in February supported the Irish claims on the ground that 'a Catholic nation has all right, human and divine, to Catholic Education'.[6] This encouraged Cullen to write to him on the situation: 'I fear we shall have great trouble with the education question. All our Catholics, rich and poor, are determined to have Catholic education. Some Government officials and adherents of State education, who are very few in number, are to be excepted.'[7] To Gladstone also he wrote stressing the unanimity of opinion among Catholics in Ireland:

It cannot be denied that the Catholics of Ireland have suffered for the past and are still suffering serious grievances in reference to education. They now expect that their wrongs will be redressed and that through your powerful influence some compensation will be made for past injustice, by establishing a

---

[1] Gerald FitzGibbon, *Roman Catholic Priests and National Schools*, Dublin, 1871, p. 42.

[2] *Freeman*, 29 December 1871: 'Master FitzGibbon Again.'

[3] *Ibid.*, 16 January 1872.

[4] *Ibid.*, 17 January 1872. Their published *Statement* is in the Gladstone Papers, B.M.Add.MS. 44433, f. 66.

[5] *Freeman*, 24 January 1872.

[6] *Ibid.*, 15 February 1872.

[7] Manning Papers, Cullen to Manning, 14 February 1872. See also *ibid.*, Cullen to Manning, 15 February, which thanks him for the Pastoral: 'Your defence of our religious educational claims is most conclusive.'

system of public instruction of which Catholics rich and poor may avail themselves for their children, without exposing their faith and morals to danger.[1]

Gladstone replied that the Government were still hoping to be able to deal with the question. The Endowed Schools Act of 1869, and the Forster Education Act of 1870 were the first steps for England; they hoped for a Scotch Act in 1872, and would then turn to Ireland. Each piece of legislation was 'intended to combine as far as circumstances permit, a certain consistency of general principle with a due regard to any peculiar features which each case may present'.[2] This should hardly have comforted the cardinal, for the legislation to which Gladstone referred had shown tendencies towards secularism, and a reference to the principle of the University Test Act in the letter seemed to confirm it. What Cullen wanted was the English system for Ireland: but when that cry was first made the English system was entirely denominational. It was now ceasing to be. But Cullen had not read the signs of the times, and in reporting Gladstone's views to Manning, while confessing that 'his answer is not very clear' he took it that 'he seems to say that in any Government measure on education the claims of the majority of the Irish nation will not be overlooked'.[3] To the Propaganda he sent a résumé of the educational questions raised in the Powis Report and in subsequent agitation.[4] The point which Gladstone had made with apparently insufficient emphasis to Cullen was put more clearly to Moriarty by Hartington, the Irish Secretary. 'The speeches which have lately been delivered at public meetings,' he wrote, 'and the requirements of the Roman Catholic Bishops (as I understood them), do appear to me to demand an amount of control on their part over the system of State Education which I do not think the Government or Parliament would be justified in conceding.'[5] In the same month, June, the *Dublin Review* wrote of the failure of the Government to do anything since the Powis Report. This 'disgraceful omission', it felt, was not due to the Prime Minister, but to the 'violent anti-Catholic prejudices' of his supporters.[6] This was probably true.

In December Cullen called on the bishops to meet in Dublin on 21 January 1873. It was to take stock of the state of affairs on the

[1] Gladstone Papers, B.M.Add.MS. 44433, f. 237, Cullen to Gladstone, 25 February 1872. There is a copy of the letter in the Cullen Papers.

[2] Cullen Papers, Gladstone to Cullen, 5 March 1872.

[3] Manning Papers, Cullen to Manning, 10 March 1872.

[4] Propaganda, *Scritture* 36, Cullen to Barnabo, 7 May 1872.

[5] Monsell Papers, Box 8319, Hartington to Moriarty, 11 June 1872. The recipient, he explained, could make this opinion public if he wished.

[6] *Dublin Review*, June 1872, 'Parliament and Catholic Education', p. 409.

education question; and to discuss the memorandum of the National Board which concerned agreements between managers and teachers, and which Cullen had made the subject of a *Letter* to his clergy in November.[1] When the bishops met they decided to approach Lord Chancellor O'Hagan about getting the text of the memorandum of agreement altered, and in this they were successful.[2] By this time the university question was again upon them, with a Bill maturing in London. As the bishops had kept the education question alive by constant agitation since the Church Act, so they had increasingly mixed their demands for university education with it. Early in 1873 Gladstone picked up the threads which Disraeli had been forced to let fall in 1868. But the National System he left as he found it. At the end of February 1873 he wrote to Fortescue to explain the position:

> As to the R.C. Bishops – it is too much to expect, perhaps to desire, that they should wholly quit their old ground. It would suffice the purpose in view that they should do what the Pope, I think Gregory XVI, did in the case of the Irish National Education, namely, leave each bishop free to take his own course on his own responsibility.[3]

The Cabinet took up the problem of higher education in November 1872. Morley wrote: 'Everybody knew that the state of University education in Ireland stood in the front rank of unsettled questions.'[4] The principle of the bishops' demands had not changed since the collapse of the Mayo plan in 1868 – although the conciliatory views of Disraeli had not survived. In November of 1868 the *Freeman* remarked on his new-found 'horror of sectarian education'.[5] In their Maynooth resolutions in August 1869, the bishops had declared that they 'clearly have a right to a Catholic University',[6] but should the Government consider it undesirable to increase the number of universities in the country, they would feel that religious equality had been

[1] *Freeman*, 12 November 1872 (text). On the Board's memorandum on agreements, see Cullen's letter to Monsell, 26 December 1872, in Monsell Papers, Box 8319; and his letter to Moriarty, 4 January 1873, *ibid*.

[2] Monsell Papers, Box 8319, Cullen to Moriarty, 20 February 1873.

[3] Carlingford Papers, CP. 1/179, Gladstone to Fortescue, 26 February 1873. Gladstone had prepared himself on the Papal view of education. In 1869 he had got Odo Russell to send him a copy of Leo XII's Bull *Quod Divina Sapientia* – 'on which is based', Russell had added 'the whole system of education of the Church of Rome'. F.O. 43, vol. 103B, Dispatch no. 13, 13 March 1869.

[4] Morley, *Life of Gladstone*, vol. II, p. 42: 'This time the problem was hardest of all, for it involved direct concession by nations inveterately Protestant, to a Catholic hierarchy having at its head an Ultramontane Cardinal of uncompromising opinions and inexorable will.'

[5] *Freeman*, 3 November 1868.

[6] *Ibid.*, 2 September 1869; Resolution v.

met if 'degrees, endowments, and other privileges enjoyed by their fellow-subjects of a different religion, be placed within the reach of Catholics'.[1] If the Government decided on one National University for Ireland 'for examining candidates and conferring degrees', then they should give the Catholics a distinct college of their own.[2] Finally, no settlement could be satisfactory unless the Queen's Colleges were rearranged on the denominational principle.[3] Indeed the difficulties of the bishops had increased. Their Catholic University was insufficiently well provided for. In July 1869 Woodlock, its Rector, had told Kirby that 'many of the dioceses are relaxing their support of the University – this year we are getting no collection from Waterford and Meath as well as from Tuam, and some of the dioceses in Connaught which have long since ceased to contribute'.[4] MacHale boasted to Daunt in 1873 that 'he had never given a farthing to the Catholic University, not deeming its spirit national'.[5] The Catholic laity signed a *Declaration* in 1870 to show that, as with the other points in the educational demands, the bishops had their support, contrary assertions notwithstanding.[6] Cullen feared that Fawcett's annual motions[7] to open up Trinity College would succeed: this, he argued, could only bring a new Queen's College into existence. He told Manning, on the occasion of Fawcett's motion in 1872, that if carried it would 'only add to the three Queen's Colleges already existing a fourth mixed college more wealthy and more mischievous than the rest'.[8] He urged Manning to persuade any members of Parliament he might meet to vote against the motion.[9] The *Freeman* had declared in 1869 that Fawcett's proposals, which amounted to making degrees accessible to Catholics through the very thing they could not accept, a mixed university, could not satisfy Irish demands. 'He is of the secularist class of educational reformers', it had explained.[10] The *Irish Ecclesiastical Record* pointed out that Catholics had everything to lose – their entire

[1] *Freeman*, Resolution VI.

[2] *Ibid.*, Resolution VII. In January, Cullen had told Monsell that he supported the idea of a National University with affiliated colleges. Carlingford Papers, CP. 3/75, Monsell to Fortescue, 23 January 1869.

[3] *Ibid.*, Resolution x.   [4] Kirby Papers, Woodlock to Kirby, no. 198, 7 July 1869.

[5] Daunt, Journal, 7 September 1873.

[6] *Parliamentary Papers*, 1870, LIV, 645; Copy of Declaration of the Catholic Laity of Ireland on the subject of University Education . . . lately laid before the Prime Minister. See also W. J. Walsh, *The Irish University Question, The Catholic Case*, Dublin, 1897, p. 49.

[7] For Fawcett's motions, see: 1869, *Hansard*, CXCVIII, p. 1197, 3 August; 1870, *ibid.*, CC, p. 1090, 1 April; 1871, *ibid.*, CCVIII, p. 694, 2 August; 1872, *ibid.*, CCX, p. 327, 20 March.

[8] Manning Papers, Cullen to Manning, 14 February 1872.

[9] *Ibid.*, Cullen to Manning, 10 March 1872.   [10] *Freeman*, 6 August 1869.

faith – by attendance at Trinity College, whereas Protestants had very little to fear, 'tolerating as they do the most varied forms of error'.[1] But it was going to be increasingly difficult to persuade the Liberals that they had a case to answer. When in January 1870 Bright said at Birmingham that there was now no Catholic grievance left in Ireland, Woodlock wrote to explain the university one.[2] The question had not changed. It remained where it had been in 1868,[3] but now the bishops were hanging on to the hope of Government legislation as never before – they were even holding back many of the priests from supporting Home Rule in anticipation of it – since it was the only chance left for the survival of the Catholic Liberalism which had been carefully built up during the previous decade.

It has been seen that Gladstone finally resigned from the settlement of Irish National education, leaving it to the bishops to treat with the existing system as they would. But he had always intended a university measure, and he also realized by the middle of 1872 that it was to be crucial. Fortescue was set to do the ground work on the proposed legislation as early as 1870 although Gladstone's advice to him in August of that year that there was no 'violent hurry' indicated that legislation would not be immediate.[4] By mid-1872 Fortescue had evidently had quite an extensive communication with Monsell on Irish university plans,[5] and it was through him that at an early date Fortescue learned of Cullen's 'unqualified adhesion' to the plan he had put – 'one neutral University, and denominational or other Colleges'[6] – the plan which was to form the core of Gladstone's proposals of 1873, the skeleton of which had been embodied in the bishops' Maynooth resolutions. Yet apart from this single, and most indirect, instance, Gladstone was careful to avoid the embarrassment of previous ministries on the question. There were no negotiations with the bishops, and no prior consultation.[7]

[1] *Irish Ecclesiastical Record*, new series, VI, 1869–70, p. 257.

[2] Kirby Papers, Woodlock to Kirby, no. 15, 13 January 1870.

[3] Almost the only new proposal made since then had been by Edward Howley, a Dublin barrister, in his *Universities and Secondary Schools of Ireland, with proposals for their Improvement*, Dublin and London, 1871. This had advocated capitation grants for both levels of education on the basis of the Trinidad scheme of 1869. For observations on this plan, see Alfred O'Rahilly, 'The Irish University Question', Part VII, in *Studies, An Irish Quarterly Review*, LI, 1962, especially pp. 149 ff.

[4] Carlingford Papers, CP. 1/124(a), Gladstone to Fortescue, 15 August 1870.

[5] *Ibid.*, CP. 1/176, Gladstone to Fortescue, 21 October 1872.

[6] *Ibid.*, CP. 3/75, Monsell to Fortescue, 23 January 1869. Cullen had also told him that Maynooth and Trinity College 'must be dealt with together'.

[7] 'No communications were opened with the bishops beforehand, probably from a surmise that they would be bound to ask more than they could obtain'. Morley, *op. cit.*, vol. II, p. 45.

In August 1870 Gladstone had written: 'It seems to me that in the main we *know* what we ought to give them whether they will take it or not.'[1] He had also to watch his own Nonconformist supporters. When the university plans were first discussed in the Cabinet, and when it had become clear that action was going to be taken, the Liberation Society had passed resolutions touching the proper course any legislation should take. Trinity College Tests were to be abolished, and the Society also resolved 'That it is desirable that the Government should be made aware of a private communication, forwarded at an early period, of the fact that any attempt to deal with the question in a contrary way will be seriously opposed by all classes of Nonconformists'.[2] This was to prove no idle threat.

Throughout November the Cabinet discussed the Irish university question almost exclusively. Kimberley reported no serious differences of opinion.[3] Manning wrote to let Cullen know that 'the Government are keeping their counsel so well that I have no knowledge of their intentions'. Remembering that in 1868 Cullen would have accepted a Charter without endowment, however, he advised him not to press for endowment now, as both sides of Parliament would refuse it.[4] Cullen accordingly prepared for action, writing to the Propaganda, 'it seems certain that within a short period Mr Gladstone will propose a law on . . . the Universities . . . and on this occasion it will be most necessary that the Bishops should unite together to obtain a University which will not be hostile to the Catholic Church'.[5] To the President of Maynooth Gladstone intimated in January (1873) that

We are approaching a third great and critical question, and the redemption of our last specific Irish *pledge*, though not the fulfilment of our last duty, for duty can never cease. If we fail, I think it will not be from an inadequate sense of the character of our engagement, nor from want of pains, nor from what is called the fear of man. From the nature of the case in part, but more from the temper of men's minds on this particular question, no plan can be proposed which will not attract much criticism; but I think, if upon the whole we are met in the same spirit as in 1869 and 1870, we may, please God, accomplish this step also towards the improvement of Ireland.[6]

[1] Carlingford Papers, CP. 1/125(a), Gladstone to Fortescue, 19 August 1870.

[2] Liberation Society Minute Books, vol. IV, Council of 25 November 1872, p. 486. A conference of the Society on the question in December resulted in a declaration in favour of a mixed system of Irish university education. *Ibid.*, p. 494.

[3] Kimberley, *op. cit.*, p. 35.

[4] Manning to Cullen, 8 December 1872; quoted by Shane Leslie, *Dublin Review*, October 1919, p. 184.

[5] Propaganda, *Scritture* 36, Cullen to Barnabo, 27 December 1872.

[6] C. W. Russell's Papers, Gladstone to Russell, 2 January 1873. Also in D. C. Lathbury, *Gladstone's Letters on Church and Religion*, vol. II, p. 144.

At the beginning of February Monsell forwarded a petition to him from 'the leading men of County Limerick' both Protestant and Catholic showing that a University Bill would be of little use if it did not also do something about intermediate education. It was signed by Bishop Butler and by Aubrey de Vere.[1] Gladstone ignored it, and the petitioners did not press their point, especially as on the 7th of the month Fawcett introduced another motion for the abolition of tests at Trinity College.[2] But Dr Russell did, and in writing to urge Gladstone not to confine the measure to universities, but to include intermediate education also, he pointed out that the absence of 'solid preparatory education' meant that Catholics would start unequally with Protestants, who had endowed secondary schools, in the competition of higher education.[3] Gladstone still took no notice; doubtless he was anxious that his plans should not be upset – as had been those of his predecessors – by allowing the Catholics to raise the entire education question simultaneously with that of its higher branches.

At the opening of the session, the Queen's Speech had referred to the university measure, which was to be for 'the advancement of learning' and framed 'with a careful regard to the rights of conscience'.[4] It was with the recitation of these words that the House went into Committee to consider Irish university education on 13 February. Gladstone spoke first on the question of intermediate education, though he said it was only 'for the sake of putting it aside'. He could not mix it with the present legislation, but hinted that it 'must arise as a consequence of any action we may take about Universities'.[5] This kept the ground clear, and would prevent the bishops from covering it with subsidiary demands as they had done in the 1860s. He next turned frankly to the difficulties which now beset them. 'I cannot wonder', he admitted, 'that apprehensions with respect to Ultramontane influence should enter into the minds of the British public whenever legislation affecting the position of the Roman Catholics in Ireland is projected.' But even so, it must not deter them from conceding claims of civil equality.[6] Then he presented the provisions of his Bill, which was later given a first-reading. It was, he said, 'a measure solely of the Government alone', as the governing body of Trinity College was associating itself with Fawcett's motion, and the Catholic bishops had not been approached.[7] The principle of the Bill was that which Monsell had put to Cullen in 1869. The University

[1] Gladstone Papers, B.M.Add.MS. 44152, f. 172, 4 February 1873.
[2] *Hansard*, CCXIV, p. 177.
[3] Gladstone Papers, B.M.Add.MS. 44437, f. 117, Russell to Gladstone, 8 February 1873.
[4] *Hansard*, CCXIV, p. 377.   [5] *Ibid.*, p. 379.   [6] *Ibid.*, p. 380.   [7] *Ibid.*, p. 381.

of Dublin was to be separated from Trinity College to become an Irish National University. It would have the exclusive privilege of granting degrees, and would be federal, with affiliated colleges. These were to be Trinity, the Queen's Colleges of Belfast and Cork, the Catholic College in Dublin, Magee College in Londonderry, and any others to be determined by Parliament in the first instance, and afterwards by the governing body. The Galway Queen's College was to be suppressed. The university was to be an examining body, but it was also to be nominally a teaching body with a staff of professors. The teaching of theology, modern history and ethics was not to be by the university, however, but by the constituent colleges, which were to be denominational although there were to be no religious tests for the university. The university was to be 'open'; anyone would be able to present themselves for examination and degree without attendance at the colleges. Trinity College was to retain its buildings. The governing body was to consist of a Chancellor, Vice-Chancellor, and twenty-eight members to be nominated in the first instance by Parliament. From 1875 to 1885 all vacancies would be filled alternately by the Crown and the University Council or governing body. The Senate would consist of all graduates, starting with those of Trinity College and the Queen's University, with special powers, which would last until 1878, to admit persons who had resided in other colleges (this would enable Catholics to join the Senate from the beginning). Every college with fifty members in *statu pupillari* could elect one member to the governing council, and those with 150 could elect two. The funds were to be provided by Trinity College and from the Consolidated Fund, and the remainder from the ecclesiastical funds of the disestablished Church.[1] Gladstone summarized all this as a move for 'abolition of Tests, open endowments, and emancipation of the University from the Colleges'. Parliament, he said, had recently dealt with Oxford and Cambridge, and would deal with Dublin University 'on the same principles'.[2] Thus it is clear that Irish experience engendered an interesting dialectic in British legislation: the university plans for Ireland of the mid-sixties had provided part of the background for the English Test Act – which Gladstone then tried to use to reform higher education back in Ireland.

From its first reading Cullen was against the Bill – as he explained when he called on Spencer at Dublin Castle on 25 February, for it

---

[1] *Hansard*, CCXIV, pp. 390 ff. See also, J. Macaulay, *op. cit.*, pp. 397-9; *Annual Register*, 1873 (History), pp. 7 ff.; Fergal McGrath, *Newman's University*, p. 492; Morley, *op. cit.*, vol. II, p. 46; W. J. Walsh, *op. cit.*, p. 42.

[2] *Hansard*, CCXIV, p. 404.

'perpetuated the mixed system of education to which he had always been opposed'.[1] The Lord-Lieutenant assured him that great care would be taken over the appointment of professors so that Catholics should be safe; to which Cullen replied that the similar assurances they had been given about Queen's College appointments had not been fulfilled. Spencer could not promise any amendment of the Bill, and expressed a wish that the Catholics should not embarrass the Government by their opposition. Cullen met that with the oblique remark that they would 'provide for the salvation of the souls committed to our care'.[2] As in 1868, so in 1873 Manning stepped in. He urged Cullen to accept the Bill, writing on 14 February to say that it would be best 'to make as much noise as will lead our enemies to believe that we do not like it, but to hold fast by the plan'. They would never get anything better, and opposition could only strengthen the Conservatives. 'All these are political reasons,' he ended, 'but I am here in sight of the storm signals.'[3] Manning reported his efforts with Cullen and the bishops to Gladstone, adding his awareness 'not only that I am more easily satisfied than they are, but am more easily satisfied than perhaps I should be if I were in Ireland'.[4] On the 25th Cullen gave more objections to Manning:

> I cannot see how we can in any way cooperate in carrying out the proposed measure, or remain silent whilst others undertake to promote. In the first place mixed education, or education without religion, is directly sanctioned by the establishment of a Queen's College in Dublin, to be called Trinity College. This institution will have the immense buildings of the present Trinity College, with its libraries and museums, all of which, or nearly all, are public property, and, besides, £50,000 per annum. Secondly, the new University will be a mixed teaching body endowed with immense revenues, which will serve to attract Catholic students. Mr Gladstone, in his speech, says that any of the present professors of Trinity College, who cannot be provided for in the new mixed College, may be appointed to chairs in the new University. In this way an ascendancy for Protestant teaching will be secured for the future.[5]

Manning let Gladstone have the gist of this, and also suggested that opposition in Ireland might be overcome if the Queen's University was continued as an examining body only, and by affiliating all Catholic

[1] Spencer to Gladstone, 25 February 1873; cited in J. L. Hammond, *op. cit.*, pp. 124-5.

[2] Manning Papers, Cullen to Manning, 2 March 1873 (in which Cullen reported the conversation of the previous month). See also Morley, *op. cit.*, vol. II, p. 48.

[3] Manning to Cullen, 14 February 1873, see Leslie, *Dublin Review*, October 1919, pp. 185-6.

[4] Gladstone Papers, B.M.Add.MS. 44250, f. 85, Manning to Gladstone, 15 February 1873.

[5] Manning Papers, Cullen to Manning, 25 February 1873. Also quoted by Leslie, *op. cit.*, p. 186.

colleges to it.[1] This amounted to the old Supplemental Charter, and Gladstone did not entertain it. Cullen wrote to Monsell in the same vein as in his letter to Manning. Whilst he admitted the advantage Catholics would have under the plan by being able to take degrees without going to the university, their benefits would be small, for as their college was poor few would have the means to prepare for the examinations. He regretted that Gladstone 'did not adopt a more liberal course'.[2]

The Irish bishops assembled in Dublin to discuss the Bill on 27 February. All expressed themselves greatly disappointed with it, and, as Cullen wrote to Manning, 'spoke against it much more strongly than I did in my letter to your Grace'. Only Dr Butler of Limerick attempted to defend it. They decided to send a petition to Parliament against 'everything in the bill that sanctions mixed education and against the way in which the endowments are distributed'. Cullen added, 'If we did less than we have done, the people here would be indignant with us, and our enemies would proclaim that we had changed our past decisions and approved of the mixed system'.[3] In view of subsequent events, it is important to notice that there was nothing directly in the resolutions of this meeting which prevented Irish members of Parliament from supporting the Bill in the House.[4] Manning wrote to Gladstone in this sense on 3 March, saying that Woodlock also believed that the bishops 'have not rejected the Bill'.[5]

The second reading also started on 3 March,[6] and it soon became clear that the Bill would be assailed by the Irish Catholic members as well as by the Conservatives and a Liberal group led by Fawcett. Osborne Morgan said on the first day that he certainly thought none the worse of the Bill because it was repudiated by the Catholic bishops; 'indeed, if it had received their unconditional approval he should believe there was some mischief lurking within it'.[7] Horsman, in opposing the reading, declared that any vote in its favour could only be regarded as one of confidence 'in Cardinal Cullen and his priests'. Miall's support

[1] Gladstone Papers, B.M.Add.MS. 44250, f. 97, Manning to Gladstone, 26 February 1873.
[2] Monsell Papers, Box 8319, Cullen to Monsell, 26 February 1873.
[3] Manning Papers, Cullen to Manning, 27 February 1873; see also Leslie, *H. E. Manning*, p. 211.
[4] Text of the resolutions in *Dublin Review*, April 1873, p. 451.
[5] Gladstone Papers, B.M.Add.MS. 44250, f. 107, Manning to Gladstone, 3 March 1873.
[6] *Hansard*, CCXIV, pp. 1223 ff. (3 March); *ibid.*, pp. 1398 ff. (6 March); *ibid.*, pp. 1617 ff. (10 March); *ibid.*, p. 1741 (11 March).
[7] *Ibid.*, p. 1227.

for the Bill, on the ground that it reflected the secular principle, must have made many of the Catholics stronger in adverse opinion than before.[1] Blennerhassett, the Home Rule victor of Kerry, observing that the cry of mixed education was taken up by the Liberals, sought to remind them 'that united education when it is free, when it is voluntary, when it is a liberation of the conscience, is one thing; but that united education when it is not free, when it is imposed on an unwilling people, when it is a coercion of the conscience, is quite another'.[2] The O'Conor Don found it necessary to deny again that the Catholic laity favoured mixed education,[3] and declared that the refusal to deal satisfactorily with higher education would increase the agitation for Home Rule.[4] The debate made it apparent that Gladstone was right when he hinted to Fortescue that the Irish members were being inspired by the hierarchy.[5] To the Queen he wrote that 'it is the opposition of the Roman Catholic bishops that brings about the present difficulty', for by 'working upon Liberal Irish members through their political interest in their seats' they had contrived a situation in which 'from twenty to twenty-five may go against the Bill'. He felt as a result that the Cabinet were now at liberty to throw it up.[6]

The condemnation of the measure in a Pastoral issued by Cullen on 9 March made matters worse.[7] On the 11th the second reading of the Bill, which Gladstone had declared a matter of confidence, was rejected by three votes; thirty-five of the forty-three Liberals who voted against were Irish. From the beginning Kimberley wrote, 'we have always foreseen that this question was the rock ahead on which we might make shipwreck'. Steer as they would, the danger seemed great, especially as 'it appears to be absolutely impossible to reconcile the pretensions of our Nonconformist and Roman Catholic supporters'.[8] Although the *Dublin Review* claimed emphatically that the bishops' resolutions had *not* bound the Irish members to vote against the Bill,[9] it was quite clear that it was the influence of the bishops which had secured the defeat of the Government. Gladstone was sure of it. For him, it was enough that they had declared the Bill should not pass in its present form, 'and the consequence is that I am saluted by their followers with an announcement that they must vote against a second reading', he explained

---

[1] *Hansard*, CCXIV, p. 1685.   [2] *Ibid.*, p. 1679.   [3] *Ibid.*, p. 1781.   [4] *Ibid.*, p. 1783.
[5] Carlingford Papers, CP. 1/180, Gladstone to Fortescue, 5 March 1873.
[6] Gladstone to the Queen, 8 March 1873; quoted by Morley, *op. cit.*, vol. II, pp. 49-50. His suggestion that the bishops used influence on members through constituencies is that made in Whittle's *Freedom of Education*, esp. p. 3.
[7] Morley, *op. cit.*, vol. II, p. 51.   [8] Kimberley, *op. cit.*, p. 35, 1 January 1873.
[9] *Dublin Review*, April 1873, 'The Irish University Bill', pp. 452-3.

desperately to Manning.[1] And even after the first shock, he held to this opinion. 'Your Irish brethren have received in the late vote of Parliament the most extravagant compliment ever paid them', he told Manning on the 13th of the month.[2] Gladstone resigned, but had to resume office after a week-long crisis caused by Disraeli's refusal to take over.[3] He was not allowed to lay down his burden until early in the next year, when, following a dissolution, the Conservatives secured a majority in an election in which a sizeable Irish Home Rule party was returned to Parliament. On 17 February 1874, Gladstone resigned.[4]

An immediate consequence of the defeat of the Government on its university measure was the passing of Fawcett's Bill to abolish tests at Trinity College, Dublin.[5] On 28 March the Bill he had introduced in February was withdrawn,[6] and he presented another measure on the same lines on the same day.[7] At the second reading in the Commons on 21 April it was in vain that The O'Donoghue objected to it as 'being an indirect and unworthy attempt to force upon the people of Ireland a University System against which they had solemnly protested'.[8] Sir John Gray said that he had always advocated the abolition of tests and so must support the Bill.[9] Ever since the passage of the Church Act, Gray had moved away from episcopal policy. He had led opposition to the Land Bill; his journal, the *Freeman*, had supported the Home Rulers at the Galway and Kerry elections; he had deserted the National Association in favour of Home Rule; and now he was found voting for a measure which Cullen had condemned as consecrating the mixed system of education. His withdrawal from orthodox Irish Catholic Liberalism was a barometer of changing opinion in Ireland. It was becoming clear that the union of the Irish Catholics with the Gladstonian party had not really survived the settlement of the Church question. Fawcett's Bill, passed in the Commons, had a successful passage through

---

[1] Gladstone Papers, B.M.Add.MS. 44250, f. 115, Gladstone to Manning, 8 March 1873. Kimberley was even more direct; 'The Irish Catholic members have received their orders from their masters, the Bishops, to vote against the Government', he wrote on the 8 March. *Journal of Events*, p. 36.

[2] Gladstone to Manning, 13 March 1873; quoted by Leslie, *Dublin Review*, October 1919, p. 190. Some Catholics attempted a defence. In 1874 the Bishop of Salford (Mgr Vaughan) wrote to Moriarty that 'Gladstone has to thank the Radicals for throwing him out. What could Catholics do when men like Bright pledged themselves to destroy denominational education but vote against them?' Monsell Papers, Box 8319, 17 February 1874.

[3] See Morley, *op. cit.*, vol. II, pp. 54 ff.

[4] R. C. K. Ensor, *England, 1870–1914*, Oxford, 1936, p. 26.

[5] See T. W. Moody, 'The Irish University Question of the Nineteenth Century', in *History*, XLIII, 1958, p. 101.

[6] *Hansard*, CCXV, p. 300.   [7] *Ibid.*, p. 304.   [8] *Ibid.*, p. 747.   [9] *Ibid.*, p. 760.

the Lords.[1] Cullen was forced back on the Catholic University, and in November he appealed to the Dublin clergy for their support, declaring that the events of the year had shown that nothing could be expected from the Government. 'Were the advocates of godless education and indifferentism to succeed in carrying out their projects,' he told the clergy, 'they would be reduced to a state of chaos and confusion.'[2]

In this last round with Gladstone on the education question the National Association had taken no decisive part. It was in fact fast moving towards its dissolution – which came at the end of the year. Some of its leading members, like O'Neill Daunt and Sir John Gray, had gone over to the Home Rulers, and although membership of other bodies was never taken to be incompatible with allegiance to the National Association, it greatly sapped its authority. Such local support as there had been for the Association was absorbed in the early seventies by the expanding farmers' and tenants' clubs. The bishops were disillusioned with the Liberal alliance. The swing away from political action is partially illustrated in the history of the Irish Catholic Union. This was fired by the example of the Catholic Union of Great Britain, founded in London in 1871 to promote general Catholic interests.[3] It was non-political. Lord Granard moved for a comparable Irish society, un-connected with the London Union. His Irish Catholic Union was launched at an inaugural meeting in Dublin on 26 November 1872. Two hundred persons attended on that occasion, many of them priests.[4] Granard became the President of the new society, which had the support of three members of Parliament – Davy, Cogan and Redmond. Its objects were general: to oppose the persecution of the religious orders throughout the world and interference with the authority of the Church in educational matters, and to promote the restoration of the Pope's temporalities.[5] The Catholic Union did not make much of an impression,

[1] It passed a second reading on 13 May. *Ibid.*, p. 1849. It was left to the Disraeli Ministry to carry on where Gladstone had been halted. In 1878 an Intermediate Education Board was set up in Dublin, and in 1879 a Royal University of Ireland was chartered. Maynooth had become a constituent college of the Catholic University in 1876, and in 1882 this became University College, given over to the control of the Jesuits in 1883. In 1909, a final settlement was tried by the creation of two new bodies to displace the Royal University. Thus the National University of Ireland and the Queen's University of Belfast came into being. The former was approved by the Catholic hierarchy and was soon virtually denominational.

[2] Letter of H. E. Cardinal Cullen to the Catholic Clergy, Secular and Regular of the Diocese of Dublin (6 November 1873), in *Irish Ecclesiastical Record*, new series, x, 1873–4, pp. 83–4.

[3] James MacCaffrey, *History of the Catholic Church in the Nineteenth Century*, vol. II, p. 76.

[4] *The Times*, 27 November 1872.   [5] *Ibid.*

however. On the day following its inception, at the opening of the new session of the Catholic University both Cullen and Granard made speeches, but neither of them mentioned the new venture.[1] And Aubrey de Vere, fearing 'any new movement which seemed to have a *party* character', had to write to Bishop Moriarty to find out what the Union was for.[2] *The Times* described it as 'a mysterious body'.[3] In January 1873 the Union did issue a *Declaration* outlining the Catholic requirements in any proposed legislation on the Irish university question, and these were clearly identified with those of the hierarchy.[4] The early reserve of the bishops therefore thawed, and Cullen, Leahy and nine other prelates were found at the Union's first annual conference on 3 December 1873, which was held, significantly, in St Kevin's Chapel at the Pro-Cathedral.[5] The *Freeman's Journal* had also come to give the Union a vague support, though Daunt regarded it as an attempt to uphold Gladstone against the Home Rulers.[6] He was mistaken, for the Catholic Union was entirely non-political. Even when Granard argued – as he did at the first annual meeting – for Parliamentary pressure to secure a settlement of Catholic education, he was careful to emphasize that the Union 'disclaimed all connexion with party politics'. Cullen did not speak.[7] In 1875 MacSwiney, who was a member, declared the need for a new political agitation since 'the Catholic Union cannot take up political subjects'.[8] Even so, it was inevitable that an Irish society would somehow involve itself with political questions, and members of the Union, which managed to have associates in every parish in the country,[9] took a small part in the 1874 elections in Connaught and Leinster.[10] They acted without the sanction of the officers of the Union.

The general election of February 1874 was in itself a clear indication of the breakdown of episcopal policy. Of the 103 new Irish members, fifty-nine were Home Rulers, thirty-two were Conservatives, and only twelve were Liberals, although there had been fifty-seven Liberals in

[1] *The Times*, 28 November 1872.

[2] Monsell Papers, Box 8319, de Vere to Moriarty, 1 December 1872.

[3] *The Times*, 30 January 1873.

[4] *Ibid.*

[5] *Ibid.*, 4 December 1873. But L. J. McCaffrey is exaggerating when he describes the Union as 'under the patronage of Cardinal Cullen'. 'Home Rule and the general election of 1874 in Ireland', in *Irish Historical Studies*, 1954, p. 191 n. Lord Granard was President. There had been no such office in the National Association.

[6] Daunt, Journal, 7 September 1873.

[7] *The Times*, 4 December 1873.

[8] *Freeman*, 4 October 1875.

[9] This is Granard's claim. *The Times*, 4 December 1873.

[10] L. J. McCaffrey, *op. cit.*, p. 201.

the old Parliament. Of the Home Rulers, forty-six were Catholics, and half of the total number of their party were landowners.[1] The dissolution of Parliament came as a surprise in Ireland,[2] and the Home Rule League, which had only been in existence for three weeks, had not yet prepared any sort of election machinery. A council, hurriedly called in Dublin by Butt, drew up an election Address, which invited the clergy to support them.[3] Many Liberals also declared for Home Rule during the campaign, and in some places Home Rule candidates appeared who were neither sponsored nor approved by the League in Dublin.[4] A large number of Home Rulers declared for denominational education and fixity of tenure, so securing the adhesion of the Catholic clergy and tenant farmers in their constituencies, although such local alliances not infrequently had the effect of scaring still more Conservatives away from Home Rule.[5]

The priests took a large part in the elections, especially in the selection of candidates – larger probably than the changed balance of interests resulting from the ballot and the Home Rule League might have suggested, but until the League's machinery was assembled they were still indispensable as local leaders of opinion even if their action tended to be unpredictable. They were to prove indispensable as local agents anyway, for when a strong directive political force existed, which was able to influence the lower clergy independently of the bishops, they were happy to work in its interest. Davitt's Land League and Parnell's Party were to show that. In the 1874 elections the priests were frequently able to ignore the influence of the bishops. In the Limerick County contest, occasioned by the elevation of Monsell to the peerage, but at once merged into the general election, both candidates supported Home Rule. Most of the clergy from the diocese of Limerick worked against W. H. O'Sullivan, whom Bishop Butler opposed on the grounds that he was a Fenian. The clergy of the Archbishop of Cashel's diocese, however, some of whom lived in the constituency, supported O'Sullivan although the archbishop himself remained neutral. A bitter contest resulted, not only between two factions of the clergy, but between the Limerick clergy and the 'nationalist' party.[6] O'Sullivan was successful. At Louth the priests supported A. M. Sullivan and Philip Callan, the Home Rule candidates, against Chichester Fortescue and O'Reilly Dease, the two Liberals. The Archbishop of Armagh, McGettigan, used his influence against the Home Rulers, published a letter in the press

---

[1] F. H. O'Donnell, *op. cit.*, vol. 1, p. 90.
[2] *The Times*, 26 January 1874.
[3] L. J. McCaffrey, *op. cit.*, p. 198.
[4] *The Times*, 2 February 1874.
[5] L. J. McCaffrey, *op. cit.*, p. 208.
[6] *The Times*, 23 January 1874.

which lauded Fortescue,[1] and called a clergy meeting to support him. His advice was flatly disregarded by the priests, and as a result of their activity, Sullivan and Callan were elected. Even in Mayo, where MacHale presided over a clergy meeting which selected a moderate Home Ruler, there was no accord; for although the priests were united in their decision, their failure to select Power, the more extreme popular choice, led to their execration at the hands of the trenchant among the constituents. As the clergy – Father Lavelle among them – left the meeting, they were groaned, and Bismarck, King William, and Judge Keogh, in an ironic reaction, were cheered.[2] Although most of the bishops were prepared to advise against extreme nationalists and Home Rulers, and to recommend Liberals, their influence was slight even over their clergy. During the actual contest, they tended to avoid intervention. In Dublin, a meeting of the Catholic clergy on 4 February, presided over by Cullen, advised the electors to vote for Pim and Brooks, the Liberals: 'the Home Rulers are dissatisfied with the clergy in consequence.'[3] Cullen took no further part in the election.

When the contests were over, the Home Rule members assembled in Dublin and resolved to constitute 'a separate and distinct party in the House of Commons'.[4] A new phase of Independent Opposition was opening up. The election was the most decisive indication of the decline of the Liberals in Ireland. 'The entire absence of any expression of gratitude or sympathy' for the Gladstone Ministry had, in the opinion of *The Times* correspondent, been the most remarkable characteristic of the Irish elections,[5] and this was true. The defeat of Chichester Fortescue at Louth ('he was the embodiment of the Irish policy of the Government')[6] symbolized 'the failure of the Liberals in their attempts since 1868 to merge the political elements of Irish disaffection in an English party of liberal reform principles'.[7]

The disastrous sequence of events in 1873–4 was followed by the pamphlet warfare between Gladstone and Manning over the Vatican Decrees, which revealed all the hidden anti-Catholicism which the Irish had suspected must lie in the English Liberals and ended all hope for the Irish bishops of salvaging anything from Gladstone's wrecked programme. Buckle believed that Manning misled Gladstone as he had Disraeli over the University Bill.[8] It is true that

1 *The Times*, 7 February 1874, and *Freeman*, 6 February 1874.
2 *Ibid.*, 5 and 6 February 1874. 3 *Ibid.*, 5 February.
4 A. M. Sullivan, *New Ireland*, p. 388. 5 *Ibid.*, 2 February 1874.
6 *Ibid.*, 10 February 1874. 7 L. J. McCaffrey, *op. cit.*, p. 210.
8 Monypenny and Buckle, *Life of Disraeli*, vol. II, p. 542.

after the collapse of the Bill Manning and Gladstone ceased to communicate, but probably this did not relate to the Bill – as Manning had frankly admitted to Gladstone all along that the Irish bishops were going to be difficult – but to the publication in 1874 of Gladstone's *The Vatican Decrees in their bearing on Civil Allegiance*.[1] Now that 'he had no longer the Irish vote to win or lose',[2] he was able to vent his feelings on the questions raised by the Council in 1870. Gladstone's thesis was that 'The Rome of the Middle Ages claimed universal monarchy. The modern Church of Rome has abandoned nothing, retracted nothing.'[3] He quoted Pius IX to show that the deposing power of the Papacy could still be exercised,[4] and asked 'in what way the obedience required by the Pope and the Council of the Vatican is to be reconciled with the integrity of civil allegiance?'[5] He did not regret the Irish reforms of his ministry, which had been effected in the interests of civil equality, and had no connexion with the doctrines held by those for whom they were passed.[6] But –

When Parliament had passed the Church Act of 1869 and the Land Act of 1870, there remained only, under the great head of Imperial equity, one serious question to be dealt with – that of higher Education. I consider that the Liberal majority in the House of Commons, and the Government . . . formally tendered payment in full of this portion of the debt by the Irish University Bill of February 1873. Some indeed think, that it was overpaid. . . . But the Roman Catholic prelacy of Ireland thought fit to produce the rejection of that measure, by the direct influence which they exercised over a certain number of Irish members of Parliament. . . . Their efforts were crowned with a complete success. From that time forward I have felt that the situation was changed, and that important matters would have to be cleared by suitable explanations.[7]

He could no longer believe, as he did before 1870, that there was nothing in the doctrines held by Roman Catholics which could impeach their 'full civil title'.[8]

The pamphlet created intense public excitement, and in its first two months (November and December 1874), it sold 145,000 copies.[9] Gladstone realized, as he wrote to Granville, that it would widen the breach between the Liberals and the Irish party.[10] Manning replied in 1875 after Gladstone had published a second tract (*Vaticanism*) in

---

[1] Purcell, *Life of Manning*, London, 1895, vol. II, p. 490.
[2] *Ibid.*, p. 471.
[3] W. E. Gladstone, *The Vatican Decrees in their bearing on Civil Allegiance, A Political Expostulation*, London, 1874, p. 11.
[4] *Ibid.*, p. 19.   [5] *Ibid.*, p. 43.   [6] *Ibid.*, pp. 59 and 61.   [7] *Ibid.*, pp. 59-60.
[8] *Ibid.*, p. 63.   [9] Morley, *op. cit.*, vol. II, pp. 126-7.
[10] Gladstone to Granville, 7 December 1874; quoted in J. L. Hammond, *op. cit.*, p. 138.

February 1875,[1] with his *Vatican Decrees in their bearing on Civil Allegiance*, in which he attempted to show that the Council had changed nothing touching civil obedience, which was 'as full, perfect, and complete since the Council as it was before'.[2] The controversy between the two men revealed some degree of bitterness. Its effects on Irish Catholic opinion were final. It coincided with the last critical phases of the O'Keeffe case, and seemed to come in support of that priest's contention that ultramontane doctrines, as taught in Ireland, were incompatible with loyalty. O'Keeffe himself even suggested to Gladstone some corrections he might make in his pamphlets.[3] For Cullen there could no longer be any question of having anything to do with a man so antagonistic to the Decrees he had worked hard at Rome to bring into being.

When he had closed the Commons debate on the University Bill in March 1873, Gladstone had testified to the high intentions of his Administration. 'To mete out justice to Ireland, according to the best view that with human infirmity we could form, has been the work, I will almost say the sacred work, of this Parliament', he had said.[4] But when he made his only visit to Ireland, in 1877, Cullen refused to dine with him at the Dublin Mansion House. 'Though Mr Gladstone rendered, or attempted to render services to Ireland for which she is most undoubtedly grateful,' he wrote to the Lord Mayor, 'yet it cannot be forgotten that for the last five years he has displayed a wonderful activity in injuring our religious interests.'[5] In Cullen is to be found a Liberal Catholic who lost his Liberalism when he came up against its antipathy to the old Catholic order. In the same place he said, 'no other statesman, however hostile, ever ventured to treat Pius IX as he has thought fit to do; besides, Mr Gladstone has been incessant in his attacks on the Vatican Council'. Cullen was evidently misled by the peculiar circumstances of Ireland's position relative to England, into supposing that the Liberalism he had found so loathsome when he saw its naked

[1] On the exchanges, see Morley, *op. cit.*, vol. II, pp. 123 ff., and Purcell, *op. cit.*, vol. II, p. 471 ff.

[2] H. E. Manning, *The Vatican Decrees in their bearing on Civil Allegiance*, London, 1875, p. 18.

[3] Gladstone Papers, B.M.Add.MS. 44446, f. 251, O'Keeffe to Gladstone, 27 February 1875.

[4] *Hansard*, CCXIV, p. 1863.

[5] Cullen Papers, Cullen to the Lord Mayor of Dublin, 5 November 1877. Yet Gladstone did chance to meet Cullen during the visit. Cullen told him that 'we could have given you a warmer reception if it had not been for certain pamphlets which we in Ireland did not like very well'. But he was otherwise cordial – Morley, *op. cit.*, vol. II, p. 179.

form at Rome in 1848 could be tamed for the service of the Irish Church. Now, after the shocks of 1873 and the ensuing public turmoil over the Vatican Decrees, he led a retreat from politics. The bishops and clergy returned to the quiescence from which they had emerged in 1859. At the Aggregate Meeting in December 1864, Archbishop Leahy had said that the prelates were 'come forth from the sanctuary to break a silence'. They had made their point; and Cullen had just managed to preserve a large measure of episcopal unity at the same time.

Early in August 1875 the collapse of any hope of renewed episcopal support for the Liberals, or any other political alliance or agitation, was underlined. Demonstrations to mark the O'Connell Centenary were organized by MacSwiney, who was again Lord Mayor of Dublin, and a committee which included Kavanagh, Smyth, Ignatius Kennedy, Canon Pope and Edmund Gray (now proprietor of the *Freeman* after the death of Sir John in April). With the exception of Gray, these men had all been members of the National Association committee. Home Rulers complained that the celebrations were being converted into a campaign to divert public sympathy from their cause: 'The imaginary greatness of the past was contrasted with the ineffectiveness and failure of to-day.'[1] The commemoration at the Pro-Cathedral on the 6th was attended by the four archbishops, twenty bishops and five hundred priests[2] – but it was Croke, the new Archbishop of Cashel, and not Cullen, who read the panegyric.[3] Cullen did not even walk in the outdoor procession with the visiting foreign bishops.[4] The outdoor demonstration was addressed by O'Hagan, the Catholic Lord Chancellor, but it was disrupted by the planned action of members of the Home Rule League, the Home Rule Confederation (of Great Britain), and the Amnesty Association, who called for Butt to speak. The celebration dinner in the evening was also broken up by the Home Rulers, MacSwiney leaving the chair in anger, and the lights flickering out on a scene of polarizing factions.[5]

MacSwiney, disgusted and humiliated, was also alarmed. He at once began probing opinion to discover reaction to a proposal for a new political agitation to provide an alternative to Home Rule. With a singular lack of tact, his probe took the form of a circular letter distributed throughout Ireland, calling for a National 'O'Connell Committee' in Dublin, and a new movement, to be called 'Faith and Fatherland'. Its objects were only vaguely defined: it would 'inform public opinion . . . by all legitimate means' on the settlement of 'temporal' and 'eternal'

[1] F. H. O'Donnell, *op. cit.*, vol. I, p. 133.   [2] *Ibid.*, vol. I, p. 136.
[3] T. de Vere White, *op. cit.*, p. 302.   [4] *Flag of Ireland*, 14 August 1875.
[5] See de Vere White, *op. cit.*, p. 304, and O'Donnell, *op. cit.*, vol. I, p. 136.

questions.[1] The occasion was strikingly similar to that which saw the formation of the National Association in 1864. Again an O'Connell celebration had brought together men who feared the potentialities of a rising national movement in Ireland; then the Fenians, now Home Rule. In his circular, MacSwiney had argued that 'a feeling largely prevails that the spirit of piety and patriotism, awakened by the Centenary celebrations, should be availed of to give practical effect to the principles of O'Connell'.[2] His proposal, which had the support of Smyth, was greeted by the Home Rulers with a contemptuous derision of 'Whig' politics, and by everyone else with indifference.[3] He was savagely attacked by the *Freeman*, which also had 'no hesitation in declaring that the heads of the Irish Church knew nothing of the matter until they received the circular of the Lord Mayor, which appears simply to have emanated from himself.'[4] The bishops remained silent while the Home Rulers' wrath spilled over 'Faith and Fatherland'. MacSwiney assured Gavan Duffy, who had returned to Ireland to visit friends and got caught up in the bitterness accompanying the demonstration, that Cullen supported his plan, and was prepared to guarantee the capital to establish a newspaper.[5] In their excitement many of the Home Rulers were prepared to associate Cullen with the new scheme.[6] But there is no evidence that he was involved: from the beginning of the O'Connell demonstration he had shown a marked caution of the turn of events, even though it was he who had solicited the Grand Cross of St Gregory for MacSwiney, from the Cardinal Prefect of Propaganda (Franchi), in recognition of his organization of the celebrations.[7] Like the other bishops, Cullen remained silent during the public outburst against MacSwiney. The latter, writing to the press to justify himself, accused the *Freeman* and the *Nation* of having conspired to kill the National Association by refusing to publish its proceedings. As the Catholic Union was non-political, he argued, there existed a good case for a new society to pick up the unfinished educational programme which the demise of the National Association had left behind.[8] The public did not agree, and 'Faith and Fatherland' was never established. The affair had shown that the rise of Home Rule, and the discrediting of the Liberal alliance, had made joint political action by the clergy and laity not only impossible but almost inconceivable.

[1] *The Times*, 16 September 1875, prints the text of the letter.
[2] *Ibid.*   [3] *Ibid.*, 24 September 1875.   [4] *Freeman*, 23 September 1875.
[5] Sir C. Gavan Duffy, *My Life in Two Hemispheres*, second ed., London, 1898, vol. II, p. 365.
[6] F. H. O'Donnell, *op. cit.*, vol. I, p. 137.
[7] *The Times*, 4 September 1875.   [8] *Freeman*, 4 October 1875.

In August 1875 the Synod of Maynooth was to show that with the curtailment of combined political activity the bishops had lost some of their unity. The university and education questions were there mulled over again,[1] but P. J. Walsh has noticed that of the divergences of opinion at the Synod little trace can be found in the published *Acta*, saving only MacHale's protest against the anti-national character of the Catholic University.[2] Also, Cardinal Barnabo's 'Letters of Instruction' to the Synod spoke unfavourably of abuses in the Church, 'attributed by people of experience in Irish affairs to the defective discipline of ecclesiastical seminaries in Ireland'.[3] The root question, education, was the one with which Cullen and the bishops were the least successful.

There is another sense in which the mid-seventies saw the end of a coherent sequence of events. A whole generation of the Catholic Church had passed away. It was true that MacHale lived on until 1881, and so into a new phase of the Irish question, but many of the more significant names were lost before that. Archbishop Leahy of Cashel died in 1875, followed by Bishop Furlong of Ferns and Sir John Gray in the same year, and by Moriarty of Kerry in 1877. Pius IX himself died in February 1878, confined and sadly, in the remnant of his former state which Antonelli, who had died in 1876, did so much to preserve. And in October, 1878, Cullen also followed the Head of his Church to the grave. A distinct era closed with the death of one more happy in his pastoral than in his political work. But the cardinal himself would admit of no such division of labour. 'Our business here then is to prepare ourselves for eternity,' he had advised his niece in 1846;[4] 'anything that is not directed to this object is lost.'

[1] R. Aubert, *Le Pontificat de Pie IX*, Paris, 1952, p. 398. See also the 'Pastoral Address of the Archbishops and Bishops of Ireland, assembled in National Synod at Maynooth, to their flocks', 20 September 1875, in *The Pastoral Letters . . . of Cardinal Cullen*, ed. P. F. Moran, vol. III, p. 656 (LXIX).

[2] P. J. Walsh, *Life of Archbishop Walsh*, Dublin and Cork, 1928, p. 27.

[3] John Healy, *Maynooth College, Its Centenary History*, Dublin, 1895, p. 520.

[4] Peadar MacSuibhne, *Paul Cullen and his Contemporaries, with their Letters*, Kildare, 1961, vol. I, p. 272.

Bibliography

of works referred to in the text

I. MANUSCRIPT SOURCES

A. ROME

ARCHIVES OF THE SACRA CONGREGATIO DE PROPAGANDA FIDE

Scritture riferite nei congressi, Irlanda. There are 45 volumes in the series, from 1625 to 1892. For the period covered by this book there are 4: volumes 33-6, (1857–73). The *Scritture* constitute one of the most valuable collections in the archives, and the most useful for the present purpose as they contain the letters sent in to the Propaganda from the Irish episcopate, as well as from any other persons in Ireland seeking to petition the Cardinal Prefect. The volumes for these years are not indexed, and only one (vol. 33) has folio numbering. Cullen's letters were usually in Italian, and passages quoted from them in this book are translations. The other prelates corresponded in Latin, and some petitions – that of the Galway laity against Father Daly in 1861, for example – are in English.

KIRBY PAPERS

At the Pontificio Collegio Irlandese, Via Santi Quattro, Rome. The correspondence of Mgr Kirby, now in the college archives, contains hundreds of letters from Irish bishops and priests. They are unbound, in folders, but an excellent calendar was made of them in 1954 by one of the students, Gerard McSorley. The letters are numbered, but it should be noticed that the series breaks in 1862, and from that date numbering starts afresh.

B. IRELAND

CULLEN PAPERS

In the archives of the Catholic Archdiocese of Dublin, Archbishop's House, Drumcondra. Like the archives of the Propaganda, these are not ordinarily open for inspection, and the Cullen Papers are unsorted and not numbered. The papers have had a disturbed history – they were taken to Australia by Cardinal Moran – and some appear not to have survived. Letters to Cullen from the Propaganda are lost, though often the copies of some of them are to be found in the *Acta* of the Sacred Congregation. It is clear that in time, when more sorting has taken place, the Dublin archives will be found to contain many more letters and papers of relevance to the subject of this book. Cullen himself did not keep a diary, and there are no autobiographical notes.

WOODLOCK PAPERS, AND LETTERS OF CULLEN TO SPALDING AND GILLOOLY

These have come from private collections in Ireland, and were kindly placed at my disposal by Father Peadar MacSuibhne of Kildare. The Woodlock letters (1866–8) deal almost exclusively with the university question, and Cullen's to Spalding (1864–9) and Gillooly (1858–65) with general affairs, especially Fenianism.

JOURNAL OF W. J. O'NEILL DAUNT

At the National Library of Ireland, Dublin. A full and sometimes rather rambling account of family as well as general political matters. But wherever it has been possible to check Daunt's report of an event, it has usually been found to be accurate to a surprising degree. Some extracts were edited and published by his daughter in 1896 as *A Life Spent for Ireland*. The Journal was maintained without a break throughout 1859–73. It is especially valuable for material on the Church question.

MONSELL PAPERS

National Library of Ireland; Box 8319. The papers include letters from Cullen and Bishop Moriarty, and are especially useful for illustrating the thought of lay Catholics on the questions agitated by the bishops. They are not numbered.

MAYO PAPERS

National Library of Ireland. The papers are now divided, those in Dublin referring to Mayo's years as Chief Secretary. They are in boxes, each of which contains several folders of letters or papers. His correspondence was wide, and among his papers are interesting items on Fenianism, and elections. A series on Church patronage and the Ecclesiastical Commission (MSS. 11212–11213, 11216), which fall outside the scope of this book – will be of great use to any student of Irish Protestantism in the period.

LARCOM PAPERS

National Library of Ireland. These relate to many activities of the Irish Executive as they came within the province of the permanent Under-Secretary. Sir Thomas Larcom kept a useful collection of press cuttings on political events, and where these are from provincial newspapers, they are sometimes the only surviving copies. The papers are bound and numbered.

G. H. MOORE PAPERS

National Library of Ireland. For the period 1859–73 there are around 200 items, but they are mostly peripheral at best to the present subject. Several letters, especially one by Dillon and one by Lavelle, have proved to be of the greatest importance, however.

C. W. RUSSELL'S PAPERS

At St Patrick's College, Maynooth, Co. Kildare. Rather a poor collection, but containing Gladstone's letters to Dr Russell over disestablishment.

C. ENGLAND

GLADSTONE PAPERS

British Museum. This vast collection requires no introduction. It is full of material of Irish interest, as well as containing Manning's letters to Gladstone.

DISPATCHES OF ODO RUSSELL (LORD AMPTHILL) FROM ROME

At the Public Record Office, Chancery Lane, London. The Dispatches form the series F.O. 43. They are bound. A most reliable source for Irish activities in Rome, and for the views of the Pontifical Government on Irish problems. They can be cross-referenced with –

CLARENDON PAPERS

Deposited at the Bodleian, Oxford. Especially useful Irish material from the earlier period of the fourth Earl Clarendon's Viceroyalty, but for this period his letters to Odo Russell, and Russell's replies are important. The papers are numbered and in folders.

CARLINGFORD PAPERS

In the possession of Lord Strachie at Sutton Court, Pensford, Bristol. They consist of letters to Chichester Fortescue, Irish Chief Secretary in 1865 and 1868; those from Gladstone having been partly used by Morley. A good collection on the Fenian Amnesty movement – hardly touched upon in this book. They are numbered and unbound.

GREY PAPERS

Deposited with the Durham Colleges, Prior's Kitchen, Durham. The papers of the third Earl Grey contain a valuable group of letters on the Church question from Aubrey de Vere. They are numbered and unbound.

MANNING PAPERS

With the Oblates of St Charles, St Mary-of-the-Angels, Bayswater. This important collection of Cardinal Manning's papers, which is well known, contains letters from Cullen, (1866–73), especially on the university question and disestablishment. They are not numbered: there is no catalogue.

MINUTE BOOKS OF THE LIBERATION SOCIETY

Together with other records of the Society, they are deposited at the London County Record Office, County Hall. The folios are numbered. The books illustrate the relationship between Irish Catholicism and English Dissent brought about by the Church question, but are thin for Irish material otherwise.

ACTON PAPERS

Cambridge University Library. A very little Irish material, but a great deal on the Liberal Catholics. Not much used in the present work, and that material which has, came from Acton's card indexes.

Note: The papers of David Moriarty, Bishop of Kerry, and John MacHale, Archbishop of Tuam, have been lost, presumed destroyed. This is unhappy: both were men of prominence in political affairs. The papers of Patrick Leahy, Archbishop of Cashel, are in the Diocesan archives at Thurles, but may not be consulted.

II. OFFICIAL PUBLICATIONS

HANSARD. Parliamentary Debates, Third Series (abb. *Hansard*).

PARLIAMENTARY PAPERS

Report on the Government and Management of Maynooth College, 1855, XXII, 1.

Report of the Commissioners appointed to inquire into Endowed Schools (Ireland), 1857–8, XXII (four parts).

Copy of Memorial of Roman Catholic Prelates relative to National Education in Ireland, 1860, LIII, 659.

Twenty-sixth Report of the Commissioners of National Education in Ireland, 1860, XXVI, 1. (*Note.* 'During the years subsequent to 1861, the history of the Board is to be found in the Parliamentary Papers, of which so much has been made, rather than in the Commissioners' Reports' – Powis Report, 1870. XXVIII, vol. 1, Part 1, p. 205.)

Report from the Select Committee (Commons) on Poor Relief (Ireland), 1861, X, 1.

Copy of a letter on the subject of National Education in Ireland, addressed to the Chief Secretary by certain members of Parliament, 1861, XLVIII, 683.

Return of Number of Children who regularly attend the National Schools in Ireland, between the 1st day of January, 1860, and the 1st day of January, 1861, classifying them according to their Religious Denomination, 1861, XLVIII, 715.

Copy of a Memorial lately presented to the Lord-Lieutenant of Ireland by the Lord Bishop of Down, Connor and Dromore, on the subject of National Education in Ireland, 1862, XLIII, 549.

Copies of Memorials to the Lord-Lieutenant of Ireland against recent changes in the Rules and Regulations of the Commissioners of National Education, 1864, XLVI, 371.

Report from the Select Committee (Commons) on the Tenure and Improvement of Land (Ireland) Act, 1865, XI, 402.

Correspondence between Her Majesty's Government and the Commissioners of National Education in Ireland, 1866, LV, 213.

Copies of Memorials addressed to the Secretary of State for the Home Department by Roman Catholic Prelates in Ireland, on the subject of University and National Education in Ireland, and of Correspondence relating thereto, 1866, LV, 243.

Report of the Select Committee of the House of Commons on Ecclesiastical Titles and R.C. Relief Acts, 1867, VIII, 15.

Report of the Commissioners appointed to inquire into corrupt practices at the last election for Tipperary, 1867, VIII, 147.

Copy of Answers prepared by the Board of National Education in Ireland, one by Judge O'Hagan, the other by the Resident-Commissioner, Rt. Hon. Alexander MacDonnell, on the subject of a letter by the Roman Catholic Bishops of January, 1866, to Sir George Grey, 1867, LV, 731.

Report of the Oaths Commission, 1867, XXXI, 1.

Report of the Select Committee of the House of Lords on Ecclesiastical Titles in Great Britain and Ireland, 1867-8, VIII, 185.

Correspondence relative to Proposed Charter to a Roman Catholic University (Ireland), 1867-8, LIII, 779, 791.

Declaration of the R.C. Laity of Ireland sent by the Earl of Fingall to the Chief Secretary, 1867-8, LIII, 75.

Return of the Number of Election Petitions, 1868-9, XLVIII, 410.

Report of the Commissioners appointed to inquire into corrupt practices at the last election for Drogheda, 1868-9, XLIX, 497.

Reports of the Select Committees of the House of Commons on Monastic and Conventual Institutions, 1870, VII, 1, 1871, VII, 181.

Report of the Commissioners on Primary Education in Ireland (Powis Commission), 1870, XXVIII (8 vols.).

Report of the Commissioners appointed to inquire into corrupt practices at the last election for Cashel, 1870, XXXII, 1.

Report, ditto, for Sligo, 1870, XXXII, 621.

Copy of Declaration of Heads of R.C. Colleges and Schools, and other Persons, lately laid before the Prime Minister, 1870, LIV, 601.

Copy of Declaration of the Catholic Laity of Ireland on the subject of University Education in Ireland, lately laid before the Prime Minister, 1870, LIV, 645.

Report of the Commissioners appointed to inquire into corrupt practices at the last election for Galway, with Judgments and Papers, 1872, XLVIII, 1.

Correspondence as to the Dismissal of the Rev. R. O'Keeffe, 1872, LI, 649.

Report of the Select Committee on the Circumstances of the Dismissal by the Commissioners of National Education in Ireland of the Rev. R. O'Keeffe from the Office of Manager of Callan Schools, etc., 1873, IX, 1.

Minutes of Proceedings and Correspondence of the Board of National Education, relating to Schools at Callan, 1873, LII, 305; 1874, LI, 617.

Memorial signed by Thirteen members of the National Education Board in Ireland for a full inquiry before a Parliamentary Committee into Case of the removal of Rev. R. O'Keeffe, 1873, LII, 429.

Correspondence between Local Government Board in Ireland and Rev. R. O'Keeffe, relating to his dismissal from the Chaplaincy of Callan Workhouse, 1876, LVIII, 675.

III. NEWSPAPERS AND PERIODICALS

The Times (London)
Guardian (London)
Freeman's Journal (Dublin)
   (abb. *Freeman*)
Nation (Dublin)
The Irish People (Dublin)
Cork Examiner (Cork)

Morning Mail (Dublin)
Morning Post (Dublin)
Express (Dublin)
Evening Packet (Dublin)
Irish Times (Dublin)
Northern Whig (Belfast)
Irishman (New York and Dublin)

Annual Register (London)
Dublin Review (Dublin, then London, 1863)
Rambler (London, ended 1862)
Irish Ecclesiastical Record (Dublin)
Tablet (London)
Battersby's (*Irish*) *Catholic Directory* (Dublin)

Any other newspapers cited in this work can be taken as extracted from the collection of cuttings in the Larcom Papers.

IV. WORKS BY CONTEMPORARIES

ADAIR, COL. F., *Ireland and her Servile War*, London and Dublin, 1866.

ANDREWS, THOMAS, *Studium Generale, A Chapter of Contemporary History*, London, 1867.

— *The Church in Ireland, A Second Chapter of Contemporary History*, London, 1869.

ARNOLD, MATTHEW, *Culture and Anarchy*, Cambridge, 1960 ed.

AYTOUN, JAMES *The Irish Difficulty, Five Letters to the Examiner*, London, 1866.

— *The Irish Question*, London, 1868.

BALL, J. T., *The Reformed Church of Ireland*, London and Dublin, 1886.

BRADY, W. MAZIERE, *Remarks on the Irish Church Temporalities*, Dublin, 1865.

— *The Episcopal Succession in England, Scotland, and Ireland, 1400 to 1875*, Rome, 1876. 3 vols.

BRIGGS, JAMES, *A Historical Survey of the relations that have subsisted between the Church and State of England and Ireland, and the See and Court of Rome, from the Norman Conquest*, London, 1868.

BRIGHT, JOHN, *The Diaries of John Bright*, ed. R. A. J. Walling, London, 1930.

BROOKE, W. G., *The Irish Church Act of 1869*, Dublin, 1871.

BUCKLE, G. E., ed., *The Letters of Queen Victoria*, second series, 1862–78, London, 1926. 2 vols.

BUTT, ISAAC, *Land Tenure in Ireland*, Dublin, 1866.

BYRNE, JAMES, and others, *Essays on the Irish Church*, Oxford and London, 1866.

CESARE, R. DE, *The Last Days of Papal Rome*, trans. Helen Zimmern, London, 1909.

CLANCARTY (WILLIAM LE POER TRENCH), *Ireland, Her Present Condition and What It ought to Be*, Dublin, 1864.

COBBETT, W., *History of the Protestant 'Reformation' in England and Ireland*, Dublin, 1826, 2 vols.

COLERIDGE, S. T., *On the Constitution of Church and State*, London, 1829.

CULLEN, PAUL, CARDINAL, *Letter to Lord St Leonards on the Management of the Patriotic Fund*, Dublin, 1857.

— *Letter . . . to the Rt. Hon. Thomas O'Hagan, M.P., and the Commissioners of National Education, on National Education*, Dublin, 1863.

— *The Pastoral Letters and Other Writings*, ed. P. F. Moran, Dublin, 1882. 3 vols.

DAUNT, W. J. O'NEILL, *Ireland and her Agitators*, Dublin, 1867 ed.

— *A Life Spent for Ireland*, ed. by his daughter, London, 1896.

DE VERE, AUBREY, *The Church Settlement of Ireland, or Hibernia Pacanda*, London, 1866.

— *Ireland's Church Property and the Right Use of It*, London, 1867.

— *Essays, Chiefly Literary and Ethical*, London, 1889.

— *Recollections*, second ed., London, 1897.

DOBBIN, O. T., *A Plea for Tolerance toward our fellow-subjects in Ireland who profess the Roman Catholic Religion*, London, 1866.

DUFFERIN, LORD, *Mr Mill's Plan for the Pacification of Ireland Examined*, London, 1868.

DUFFY, SIR CHARLES GAVAN, *My Life in Two Hemispheres*, London, second ed., 1898. 2 vols.

FITZGERALD, M., *Sermon on Fenianism*, Limerick, 1866.

FITZGIBBON, GERALD, *Ireland in 1868, The Battle-field for English Party Strife*, London, 1868.

— *Roman Catholic Priests and National Schools*, Dublin, 1871.

FITZPATRICK, W. J., *The Life, Times, and Correspondence of Dr Doyle*, Dublin, 1861. 2 vols.

Freeman's Journal Church Commission, Dublin, 1868.

F. T. C. D., *The Ireland of To-day, or The Inquisition and its Patrons*, London, 1868.

GLADSTONE, W. E., *Speeches in South-West Lancashire in October, 1868*, Liverpool, 1868.

— *A Chapter of Autobiography*, London, 1868.

— *Correspondence on Church and Religion*, ed. D. C. Lathbury, London, 1910.

— *The Vatican Decrees in their bearing on Civil Allegiance*, London, 1874.

See also Guedalla, Philip., ed. *Gladstone and Palmerston . . . correspondence*, 1928.

GLEIG, G. R., Letters on the Irish Question, London, 1868.

GODKIN, JAMES, *Ireland and her Churches*, London, 1867.

The Government Proceedings against Fenianism [anon], London, 1865.

GREGOROVIUS, F., *The Roman Journals of Ferdinand Gregorovius, 1852-74*, trans. G. W. Hamilton, London, 1911.

GREY, HENRY EARL, *Letter to John Bright respecting the Irish Church*, London, 1868.

— *Ireland and the Causes of its Present Condition*, London, 1888.

HARPER, S. B. A., *The Conspiracy against the Religion and Liberties of the States of the Church*, London, 1860.

HASLETT, WILLIAM, *The Queen's University in Ireland, The Supplemental Charter Considered*, Dublin, 1867.

HAUGHTON, SAMUEL, *University Education in Ireland*, London and Dublin, 1868.

HEALY, JOHN, *Maynooth College, Its Centenary History, 1795-1895*, Dublin, 1895.

HERON, R. M., *The Irish Difficulty and its solution by a System of Local Superintendence*, London, 1868.

HOWLEY, EDWARD, *The Universities and Secondary Schools of Ireland, with Proposals for their Improvement*, Dublin and London, 1871.

HUME, A., *Results of the Irish Census of 1861 with a special reference to the condition of the Church of Ireland*, London, 1864.

HUNTER, W. W., *A Life of the Earl of Mayo*, London, 1875.

HUTCH, WILLIAM, *Nano Nagle, Her Life, Her Labours, and their Fruits*, Dublin, 1875.

Ireland Regenerated, Social Progress Pamphlet no. 1, London, 1868.

The Irish Difficulty, being a review of the Debate in the House of Commons on Mr Maguire's Motion, by an Observer, London, 1868.

JOHNSTON, WILLIAM, *Ribbonism and Its Remedy, a Letter Addressed to the Earl of Derby*, Dublin, 1858.

KAVANAGH, J. W., *Mixed Education: The Catholic Case Stated*, Dublin, 1859.

KIMBERLEY, JOHN EARL, *A Journal of Events During the Gladstone Ministry, 1868-74*, ed. Ethel Drus. Camden Miscellany, XXI, 1859.

LASTEYRIE, JULES DE, *French Thoughts on Irish Evils*, trans. from *Revue de Deux Mondes* by Sir Justin Sheil, London, 1868.

LAVELLE, PATRICK, *The War in Partry, or Proselytism and Eviction*, Dublin, 1861.

— *The Irish Landlord since the Revolution*, Dublin, 1870.

LEE, A. T., *Facts respecting the present state of the Church in Ireland*, fourth ed., London and Dublin, 1865.

LIBERATION SOCIETY, *The Case for Disestablishment*, rev. ed., London, 1894.

LUCAS, EDWARD, *Life of Frederick Lucas*, London, 1886.

MACAULAY, JAMES, *Ireland in 1872, A Tour of Observation*, London, 1873.

MCCARTHY, JUSTIN H., *Ireland Since the Union*, London, 1887.

— *The Story of Gladstone's Life*, London, 1898.

MACDEVITT, JOHN, *University Education in Ireland and 'Ultramontanism'*, Dublin, 1886.

MACDONNELL, J. C., *The Life and Correspondence of Archbishop Magee*, London, 1896. 2 vols.

MAGUIRE, J. F., *Rome, Its Ruler and its Institutions*, second ed., London, 1859.

— *Pius the Ninth*, second ed., London, 1878.

MANNING, H. E., CARDINAL, *Rome and Revolution, A Sermon*, London, 1867.

— *Ireland, A Letter to Earl Grey*, London, 1868.

— *The Vatican Decrees in their bearing on Civil Allegiance*, London, 1875.

— *The True Story of the Vatican Council*, London, 1877.

— *Miscellanies*, London, 1877. 2 vols.

Members of the Liberation Society, *The Case for Disestablishment*, rev. ed., London, 1894.

MILL, J. S., *England and Ireland*, London, 1868.

MONSELL, WILLIAM, *A Lecture on the Roman Question*, London, 1860.

MORAN, P. F., *The Episcopal Succession in Ireland during the Reign of Elizabeth*, Dublin, 1866.

MORAN, P. F., ed., *The Pastoral Letters and Other Writings of Cardinal Cullen*, Dublin, 1882. 3 vols.

MORIARTY, DAVID, *A Letter on the Disendowment of the Established Church addressed to The Clergy of the Diocese of Kerry*, Dublin, 1867.

— *Sermons*, second ed., Dublin, 1906.

MORLEY, JOHN, *The Life of Gladstone*, second ed., London, 1905. 2 vols.

MURPHY, PATRICK, i.e. G. H. Whalley, M.P. , *Popery in Ireland*, London, 1865.

NEWMAN, J. H., CARDINAL, *Apologia Pro Vita Sua*, London, Fontana ed., 1959.

— *The Idea of a University*, London, 1907 ed.

NULTY, THOMAS, *The Land Agitation in Ireland, A Letter to the Clergy and Laity of Meath*, Manchester and London, 1881.

O'BRIEN, J. T., *The Case of the Established Church in Ireland*, second ed., London and Dublin, 1867.

O'BRIEN, R. B., *Irish Wrongs and English Remedies*, London, 1887.

— *Fifty Years of Concessions to Ireland, 1831-81*, London, 1883. 2 vols.

O'KEEFFE, ROBERT, *Cardinal Cullen and the P. P. Callan*, Dublin, 1872.

O'LEARY, JOHN, *Recollections of Fenians and Fenianism*, London, 1896. 2 vols.

O'REILLY, BERNARD, *John MacHale, His Life, Times, and Correspondence*, New York and Cincinnati, 1890. 2 vols.

O'REILLY, MYLES, W., *Two Articles on Education, reprinted from the Dublin Review*, London, 1863.

Pastoral Address of the Roman Catholic Archbishops and Bishops to the Catholic clergy and people of Ireland, Dublin, 1859.

PERCEVAL, JOHN, *Letter to the Rt. Hon. W. E. Gladstone on the separation of the Irish Church from the State, and in favour of a Dissolution of the Union*, London, 1868.

PERRAUD, ADOLPHE, *Ireland in 1862*, Dublin, 1863.

POPE, THOMAS, *The Council of the Vatican and the Events of the Time*, Dublin, 1871.

PORTER, J. G. V., *The State of Ireland in 1866, Its chief evils and their best possible remedies*, Dublin and London, 1866.

PORTER, J. L., *The Life and Times of Henry Cooke*, London, 1871.

RUSSELL, JOHN, 1ST EARL, *A Letter to the Rt. Hon. Chichester Fortescue on the State of Ireland*, second ed., London, 1868.

— *A Second Letter to Fortescue*, London, 1868.

— *Recollections and Suggestions, 1813-1873*, London, 1875.

SEDDALL, HENRY, *The Church of Ireland, A Historical Sketch*, Dublin and London, 1886.

SELBORNE, ROUNDELL PALMER, 1ST EARL OF, *A Defence of the Church of England against Disestablishment*, new ed., London, 1887.

SENIOR, NASSAU, *Journals, Conversations and Essays relating to Ireland*, London, 1868. 2 vols.

SHEE, WILLIAM, *A Proposal for Religious Equality in Ireland*, Dublin, 1857.

SMITH, GOLDWIN, *Irish History and Irish Character*, Oxford and London, second ed., 1862.

— *The Irish Question, Three Letters to the Editor of the Daily News*, London, 1868.

Some Thoughts on the Irish Difficulty, by an Irish Catholic M.P., London, 1868.

Statement adopted by the Graduates of the Queen's University in Ireland assembled in Public Meeting in Belfast, Wednesday, 6 December 1865, Dublin, 1865.

STOPFORD, E. A., *A Letter to the Rt. Hon. Alexander MacDonnell, Resident Commissioner of National Education, in Reply to 'The Catholic Case Stated'* etc., Dublin, 1859.

SULLIVAN, A. M., *New Ireland*, eighth ed., Glasgow, 1882.

SULLIVAN, W. K., *University Education in Ireland, A Letter to Sir John Acton*, Dublin, 1866.

WALLER, J. T., *Fenianism and Romanism*, Dublin, 1866.

WALPOLE, SIR SPENCER, *The History of Twenty-Five Years*, London, 1904. 2 vols.

WALSH, W. J., *The Irish University Question: The Catholic Case*, Dublin, 1897.

— *Trinity College and the University of Dublin*, Dublin, 1902.

WEBB, ALFRED, *Compendium of Irish Biography*, Dublin, 1878.

WHITTLE, J. L., *Freedom of Education: What it Means*, Dublin, 1866.

— 'Irish Elections and the Influence of the Priests', in *Fraser's Magazine*, new series, I, 1870.

WILBERFORCE, R. G., *Life of Samuel Wilberforce*, London, 1882 (3 vols.).

WISEMAN, NICHOLAS, CARDINAL, *The Sermons, Lectures, and Speeches delivered by H.E. Cardinal Wiseman during his Tour of Ireland in August and September, 1858; revised by His Eminence with a connecting narrative*, Dublin, 1859.

WOODLOCK, BARTHOLOMEW, *Catholic University Education in Ireland, a Letter to Mr Cogan, M.P.*, Dublin, 1868.

V. LATER WORKS

AUBERT, R., *Le Pontificat de Pie IX*, Paris, 1952.

AUCHMUTY, J. J., *Irish Education, A Historical Survey*, Dublin, 1937.

— 'Acton's election as an Irish Member of Parliament', in *English Historical Review*, LXI, 1946.

BARRY, P. C., 'The Holy See and the Irish National Schools', in *Irish Ecclesiastical Record*, fifth series, XCII, 1959.

BEALES, D. E. D., *England and Italy, 1859–60*, London, 1961.

BECK, G. A., ed., *The English Catholics, 1850–1950, Essays to commemorate the centenary of the restoration of the Hierarchy*, London, 1950.

BEGLEY, J., *The Diocese of Limerick*, Dublin, 1938.

BERKELEY, G. F-H., *The Irish Battalion in the Papal Army of 1860*, Dublin and Cork, 1948.

— *Italy in the Making*, Cambridge, 1932–40 (3 vols.).

BLACK, R. D. COLLISON, *Economic Thought and the Irish Question, 1817–70*, Cambridge, 1960.

BLAKISTON, N. A., ed., *The Roman Question, Extracts from the Despatches of Odo Russell from Rome, 1858–70*, London, 1962.

BRADY, JOHN, 'The Oath of Allegiance at Maynooth', in *Irish Ecclesiastical Record*, fifth series, XCIV, 1960.

BRETHERTON, C. H., *The Real Ireland*, London, 1925.

BRETT, THOMAS, *Life of Dr. Duggan*, Dublin, 1921.

BROSE, OLIVE, 'The Irish Precedent for English Church Reform, The Church Temporalities Act of 1833', in *Journal of Ecclesiastical History*, VII, no. 2, 1956.

— *Church and Parliament, The Reshaping of the Church of England, 1828–60*, Oxford, 1959.

BURTCHAELL, G. D., *Genealogical Memoirs of the Members of Parliament for Kilkenny*, Dublin and London, 1888.

BUTLER, CUTHBERT, *The Vatican Council, 1869–70*, London, 1962 ed.

CAHILL, E., *Freemasonry and the Anti-Christian Movement*, Dublin, 1929.

CAMPANA, EMILIO, *Il Concilio Vaticano*, Lugano, 1926. 2 vols.

Catholic Encyclopedia, English ed., New York, 1908.

CHADWICK, W. O., *Westcott and the University*, Cambridge, 1963.

'A Christian Brother', *Edmund Ignatius Rice and the Christian Brothers*, Dublin, 1926.

CORISH, P. J., 'Cardinal Cullen and Archbishop MacHale', in *Irish Ecclesiastical Record*, fifth series, XCI, 1959.

— 'Cardinal Cullen and the National Association of Ireland', in *Reportorium Novum*, vol. III, no. 1, 1962.

CORNISH, F. WARRE, *The English Church in the Nineteenth Century*, London, 1910. 2 vols.

COSTELLO, NUALA, *John MacHale*, Dublin, 1939.

CURRAN, M. J., 'Cardinal Cullen – Biographical Materials', in *Reportorium Novum*, vol. I, no. 1, 1955.

D'ALTON, E., *History of the Archdiocese of Tuam*, Dublin, 1928. 2 vols.

DARK, SYDNEY, *Newman*, London, 1934.

DEVOY, JOHN, *Recollections of an Irish Rebel*, London, 1929.

EDWARDS, R. DUDLEY, *Ireland and the Italian Risorgimento*, Dublin, 1960.

EGAN, M. J., *Life of Dean O'Brien*, Dublin, 1949.

EGAN, P. K., *The Parish of Ballinasloe*, Dublin, 1960.

ENSOR, R. C. K., *England, 1870–1914*, Oxford, 1936.

FITZPATRICK, J. D., *Edmund Rice*, Dublin, 1945.

FREEMANTLE, ANNE, ed., *The Papal Encyclicals*, New York, Mentor ed., 1956.

GILLESPIE, F. E., *Labour and Politics in England, 1850–67*, Duke University Press, 1927.

GUEDALLA, PHILIP, *Palmerston*, London, 1926.

— *Gladstone and Palmerston, being Their Correspondence, 1851–65*, London, 1928.

HALES, E. E. Y., *Pio Nono, A Study in European politics and religion in the Nineteenth Century*, London, 1956.

HAMMOND, J. L., *Gladstone and the Irish Nation*, London, 1938.

HANHAM, H. J., *Elections and Party Management in the Time of Disraeli and Gladstone*, London, 1959.

HOW, F. D., *William Conyngham Plunket, Fourth Baron Plunket and Sixty-first Archbishop of Dublin, A Memoir*, London, 1900.

LATHBURY, D. C., ed., *Correspondence on Church and Religion of W. E. Gladstone*, London, 1910. 2 vols.

LESLIE, SIR SHANE, 'Irish Pages from the Postbags of Manning, Cullen, and Gladstone', in *Dublin Review*, October, 1919.

— *H. E. Manning, His Life and Labours*, London, 1921.

MACCAFFREY, JAMES, *History of the Catholic Church in the Nineteenth-Century*, Dublin, Waterford, and St Louis (Mo.), 1909. 2 vols.

MCCAFFREY, L. J. 'Home Rule and the General Election of 1874 in Ireland', in *Irish Historical Studies*, 1954.

MCCLELLAND, V. A., *Cardinal Manning, His Public Life and Influence, 1865–92*, London, 1962.

MACDOUGALL, H. A., *The Acton-Newman Relations, The Dilemma of Christian Liberalism*, New York, 1962.

MCDOWELL, R. B., 'The Irish Executive in the Nineteenth Century', in *Irish Historical Studies*, IX, 1954–5.

MCGRATH, FERGAL, *Newman's University, Idea and Reality*, Dublin, 1951.

MACNAMEE, J. J., *History of the Diocese of Ardagh*, Dublin, 1954.

MACSUIBHNE, PEADAR, 'The Irish at the Vatican Council', in *Irish Ecclesiastical Record*, fifth series, April-May, 1960.

— *Paul Cullen and his Contemporaries, 1820–1902*, Kildare, vol. I, 1961, vol. II, 1962.

MANNING, B. L., *The Protestant Dissenting Deputies*, Cambridge, 1952.

MANSERGH, NICHOLAS, *Ireland in the Age of Reform and Revolution*, London, 1940.

MAXWELL, SIR HERBERT, *Life and Letters of George William Frederick, Fourth Earl of Clarendon*, London, 1913.

MONYPENNY, W. F., and BUCKLE, G. E., *Life of Disraeli*, rev. ed., London, 1929.

MOODY, T. W., 'The Irish University Question of the Nineteenth Century', in *History*, XLIII, 1958.

O'BRIEN, C. C., *Maria Cross, Imaginative Patterns in a Group of Catholic Writers*, London, 1963 ed.

— *Parnell and his Party, 1880–90*, Oxford, 1957.

O'BRIEN, W., and RYAN, D., ed., *Devoy's Post Bag, 1871–1928*, Dublin, 1948. 2 vols.

O'CONNELL, PHILIP, *The Diocese of Kilmore, Its History and Antiquities*, Dublin, 1937.

O'DONNELL, F. H., *A History of the Irish Parliamentary Party*, London, 1910. 2 vols.

O'RAHILLY, ALFRED, 'The Irish University Question', in *Studies, an Irish Quarterly Review*, LI, 1962.

PATTON, H. E., *Fifty Years of Disestablishment*, Dublin, 1922.

POMFRET, J. E., *The Struggle for Land in Ireland, 1800-1923*, Princeton, 1930

PURCELL, E. S., *Life of Cardinal Manning*, London, 1895.

RANDALL, SIR ALEC, 'A British Agent at the Vatican: The Mission of Odo Russell', in *Dublin Review*, 479, 1959.

SILLARD, P, A., *The Life and Letters of John Martin*, second ed., Dublin, 1901.

SMITH, D. MACK, *Cavour and Garibaldi, 1860*, Cambridge, 1954.

STOCKLEY, W. F., *Newman, Education, and Ireland*, London, 1933.

STRACHEY, LYTTON, *Eminent Victorians*, London, 1960 ed.

THORNLEY, DAVID, 'The Irish Conservatives and Home Rule, 1869–73,' in *Irish Historical Studies*, XI, 1958–9.

TREVELYAN, G. M., *The Life of John Bright*, London, 1913.

— *Garibaldi and The Making of Italy*, London, 1911.

TREVOR, MERIOL, *Newman, Light in Winter*, London, 1962.

WALSH, P. J., *William J. Walsh, Archbishop of Dublin*, Dublin and Cork, 1928.

WALSH T. J., *Nano Nagle and the Presentation Sisters*, Dublin, 1959.

WARD, WILFRID, *Aubrey de Vere, A Memoir*, London, 1904.

— *W. G. Ward and the Catholic Revival*, London, 1893.

WHITE, T. DE VERE, *The Road of Excess* [a life of Isaac Butt], Dublin, 1945.

WHYTE, A. J., *Political Life and Letters of Cavour*, Oxford, 1930.

WHYTE, J. H., *The Independent Irish Party, 1850-9*, Oxford 1958.

— 'The Appointment of Catholic Bishops in Nineteenth-century Ireland', in *Catholic Historical Review*, April 1962.

— 'The Influence of the Catholic clergy on elections in Nineteenth-century Ireland', in *English Historical Review*, LXXV, 295, 1960.

WILLIAMS, W. E., *The Rise of Gladstone to the Leadership of the Liberal Party, 1859–68*, Cambridge, 1934.

Index

Abercorn, Lord (Viceroy), 126
Acton, Sir John (Lord Acton), 17, 72, 130, 274, 395, 411, 414
Aggregate Meeting in Dublin (1864), 140, 141, 142-51, 155, 157, 160, 173, 180, 186, 188, 293, 319, 331, 387, 460
Agrarian crime, 86, 129, 133, 398, 409
All Hallows College, Dublin, 8, 78
America (United States), influence in Irish affairs, 15, 51, 86, 87, 91, 92, 97, 101, 102, 103, 104, 107, 124, 132, 133, 263, 265, 439
Amnesty movement, 125, 126, 368, 384, 407. Amnesty Association, 127, 128, 460
Ancient ecclesiastical buildings, suggested return to Catholics, 360-2
Andrews, Thomas, 240, 369
Anti-Catholic sentiment in Britain, 73, 193, 209, 210, 251, 326, 346-7, 355, 400, 401, 403, 409, 414, 457
Anti-Corn Law League, example of, 157, 322
Antonelli, Giacomo, Cardinal, 28, 31, 36, 42, 50, 51, 97, 114, 115, 122, 129, 130, 132, 133, 244, 333, 356, 358, 360, 366, 367, 411, 428, 434, 462
Appointments of Catholics to Irish offices, 37, 165, 354-5
Armagh Cathedral raid (1866), 125
Arnold, Matthew, on the Irish Church, 301, 340
Aytoun, James, 173n., 373, 374

Ball, J. T., 339
Ballot, vote by, 322, 456. Ballot Act (1872), 428, 429, 430
Barnabo, Alexander, Cardinal, 7, 28, 30, 62, 80, 103, 206, 215, 242, 294, 367, 431, 462
Barry, Serjeant, 123, 345
Belfast Catholic Institute, 210
riots (1864), 137-8
Bessborough, Lord, 394
Bible societies, work in Papal States, 44
Bills in Parliament
Charitable Bequests Amendment (1862), 80

Ecclesiastical Titles Act Repeal (1870), 406, 407
Fortescue's Land Bill (1866), 388, 391
Glebe-Loans, Ireland (1870), 385
Habeas Corpus Suspension, Ireland (1866), 222
Irish Church (1869), 158, 184, 323, 354, 355-83, 406
Land Bill (1870), 133, 172, 184, 354, 394-403, 410, 440, 453
Party Processions Act Repeal (1869, 1870, 1872), 407, 408
Promissory Oaths, 296
Roman Catholic Churches, Schools, and Glebes (1867), 328
Suspensory, Irish Church appointments (1868), 344
Tenant Improvement (1867), 390
Transubstantiation Declaration (1866), 107
University Bill (1873), 184, 421, 449-453, 457, 458, 459
Blennerhasset, R. P., 117, 430, 452
Board of Charitable Bequests, 201, 374, 405
of Public Works, 328, 369, 375, 385, 396
Bouverie, E. P., 433
Bowyer, Sir George, 58, 268, 279, 341, 415
Bright, John, 26, 142-3, 145, 153, 157, 173, 174, 176, 186, 223, 305n., 321, 326, 343, 355, 357, 365, 388, 389, 391, 392, 396, 427, 446, 453n.
Bruce, H. A., 203, 204, 205, 206, 207, 208, 209, 211, 212, 214, 232, 371
Bulls, Papal, reception in Britain, 434, 435
Burials Act (1868), 346
Burke, Thomas, 125, 126, 359
Butler, George, Bishop of Limerick, 14, 80, 84, 130, 136, 204, 206, 207, 222, 311, 348, 378, 393, 441, 448, 451, 456
Butt, Isaac, 72, 78, 127, 171, 345, 389, 390, 398, 409, 416, 420, 421, 422, 456, 460

Cairns, Sir Hugh (Lord Cairns), 77, 84, 199, 297, 298, 327, 356, 359, 379, 382, 407
Campden, Lord, 36
Canadian clergy reserves, 298
Cantwell, J., Bishop of Meath, 14
Capel, Mgr T. J., 410
Cardwell, Edward, 61, 67, 68, 69, 71, 72, 73, 74, 76, 78, 83, 209, 212
Carlisle, Lord (Viceroy), 63
Carlow College, 4, 235, 236
Cashel, Co. Tipp., Catholic memorial relating to, 361
Castlerosse, Lord, 47, 263
Catholic Case Stated, by James Kavanagh, 56-8
Catholic clergy, social and political influence of, 9, 14, 19, 28, 90, 99, 109, 111, 123, 254, 278, 287, 422n., 437, 456
   Defence Association, 20, 26, 185
   Union of Great Britain, 454
   Young Men's Society, 45, 104
Cavour, Count, 39, 42, 44, 46, 49
Census, of 1861, 3, 20, 146, 286, 290-1
Central Franchise Association, 181-2, 273, 348
Cess, Church, 21, 283
Chalmers, Thomas, influence of his thought in Ireland, 259n., 300, 302
Chaplains, Catholic military, 36, 58, 65, 337
Charter question, *see* University question
Christian Brothers, 24, 61, 79, 96, 97, 113, 349, 431, 438
Church building activities, 1, 15
Church question, *see* Protestant Establishment.
Civiltà Cattolica, 414
Clancarty, Lord, 4, 72, 77, 428
Clanricarde, Lord, 390, 392
Clarendon, 4th Earl, 5, 114, 116, 128, 129, 130, 133, 338, 356, 358, 359, 360, 366, 367, 378, 396, 397, 400, 411, 412
Cleveland, Duke of, 376, 379
Cobden, Richard, 38, 289n.
Cogan, W. H. F., 268, 295, 380, 454
Coleridge, S. T., influence of his thought in Ireland, 285, 300, 306, 307, 309, 338
Collins, P. P. Skibbereen, 90
Colonial precedents for legislation, 198, 283, 298
Commissions, Royal
   Irish Endowed Schools (1858), 52, 61
   Irish Establishment (1867-8), 245, 258, 300, 328, 355
   Oaths (1867), 295, 296

Primary Education, Ireland [Powis Commission] (1868-70), 18, 24, 69, 97, 245-7, 258, 264n., 280, 436, 437-441, 443
Conaty, Nicholas, Bishop of Kilmore, 166, 383
Concurrent Endowment, 96n., 108, 119, 192, 266, 285, 301, 302, 305-19, 338, 376, 377, 379-81
Conroy, George, Bishop of Ardagh, 7, 8, 412n.
Conservatives, Irish, 21, 174, 315, 324, 351, 456
Conway, Fr Peter, 271, 423
Cooke, Dr Henry, 304, 351
Corbally, M., 70
Cork Examiner, The, 66, 238, 395
Cork meeting on the education question (1859), 59-60
Corrigan, Sir Dominick, 202, 204, 235, 236
Crolly, William Archbishop of Armagh, 5
Cullen, Paul, Cardinal, 3, 4-12, 16, 17, 18, 26, 27, 28, 29, 30, 36, 47, 68, 74-5, 77, 79, 85, 100, 101, 233n., 294, 337, 346, 355, 375, 405, 410, 412, 413, 414, 415, 426, 428, 431, 432, 433, 434, 435, 455, 461, 462; – and Church question, 21, 146, 273, 274, 298, 301n., 303, 309, 316, 331-4, 338, 340n., 341-2, 344, 356, 364, 373, 376, 377, 378, 380, 381, 382, 383; – and Education, 23, 24, 25, 37, 53, 54, 57, 59, 60, 66, 67, 71, 72, 80, 82, 144, 155, 193, 195, 196, 197, 199, 200, 205, 206, 207, 208, 209, 211, 213, 214-5, 216, 218, 219, 220, 221, 222, 223, 224, 225, 227, 232, 241, 242, 244, 245, 246, 247, 248, 250, 256, 257, 258, 259, 260, 264, 265, 267, 268, 270, 271, 272, 281, 342, 437, 439, 440, 441, 442, 443, 444, 445, 447, 449, 450, 451, 452, 453, 462; – and Fenianism, 86, 88, 90, 92, 93, 94, 96, 97, 98, 101, 102, 113, 118, 119, 121, 122, 123, 125, 126, 127, 129, 132, 133, 134, 135, 145, 222, 398; – and Home Rule, 417, 418, 419; – and Italy, 39, 42, 43, 44, 45, 46, 48, 49, 78; – and Land question, 20, 37, 144-5, 365n., 386, 387, 389, 390, 392, 397, 398, 400, 402; – and the Liberals, 7, 8, 26, 27, 37, 70, 185, 186, 225, 347, 348, 352, 420, 430, 457, 459, 460; – and the National Association, 105, 135-89, Memorandum on the Rules of (1865), 163-6

Daly, Fr Peter, 16-17, 435
Daunt, W. J. O'Neill, 1, 7, 21, 31, 39, 99,
   138, 139, 147, 153, 154, 167, 174,
   177, 178, 179, 180, 181, 182, 185,
   288, 292, 303n., 304, 306, 311, 316,
   319, 320, 321, 323, 325, 326, 328,
   329, 331, 334, 340, 343-4, 348, 356,
   357, 365, 376, 379, 383, 384, 385,
   395, 416, 418, 419, 420, 421, 445,
   454, 455
De Vere, Aubrey, 123, 202, 204, 225, 285,
   305-11, 313, 315, 318, 319, 325, 327,
   328, 330, 331, 332, 334, 335, 337, 342n.,
   343, 345, 365, 368, 372, 448, 455
   Stephen, 47
Dease, J. A., 167, 170, 417, 419, 430, 439
Decree of Pius IX against Fenianism
   (1870), 131, 132, 133
Decrees of 1854 on the clergy and politics,
   27, 28-9, 35, 155
Delany, William, Bishop of Cork, 55, 59
Denominational schools, *see* Education
   question.
Denvir, Bishop of Down and Connor,
   141n.
Derby, 14th Earl of, 22, 34, 36, 37, 38,
   46, 55, 94, 122, 126, 147, 217, 228,
   234, 244, 245, 259, 297, 390, 440
Derry, John, Bishop of Clonfert, 14, 73,
   168, 214, 247, 256, 257, 258, 259,
   260, 263, 267, 268, 270, 271, 275,
   278, 279, 281n.
Devitt, Richard, 139, 142, 150, 156, 181
Devoy, John, 134
Dillon, John Blake, 137, 138, 139, 140,
   141, 142, 147, 153, 154, 155, 156,
   158, 159, 160, 161, 166, 167, 168,
   170, 171, 173, 174, 175, 176, 178,
   181, 182, 184, 186, 187, 188, 223,
   227, 319, 320n., 387
Dillwyn, Lewis, 159, 166, 180n., 288,
   289, 290, 292, 299, 319, 326
Disendowment, 20, 139, 147, 285, 301,
   314, 319, 321, 322, 324, 325, 327,
   329, 330, 331, 332, 338, 340, 348,
   357, 361, 378, 383
Disestablishment, *see* Protestant Establishment
Disraeli, Benjamin (Lord Beaconsfield),
   6, 7, 58, 228, 242, 244, 245, 252,
   256, 257, 258n., 259, 260, 264, 267,
   273, 274, 276, 277, 280, 281, 297,
   298, 300, 335, 341, 346, 347, 348,
   351, 355, 368, 374, 382, 444, 453,
   454n., 457
Dissenters, English and Scottish, 15, 82,
   153, 176, 177-81, 282, 284-5, 286,
   287, 289, 297, 301, 303, 304, 308,
   309, 318, 325-30, 333, 339, 343,
   369, 378n., 381, 384, 385, 409, 437,
   447, 452

Dixon, Joseph, Archbishop of Armagh,
   5, 12, 13, 38, 54, 55, 71, 136, 142,
   222
Dorrian, Patrick, Bishop of Down and
   Connor, 14, 29, 136, 138, 153, 161, 166,
   168, 172, 200, 210, 276, 277, 407,
   439
Doyle, James, Bishop of Kildare and
   Leighlin, 4, 16, 18
Dublin Cathedrals, Catholic claims to,
   361, 362
   Corporation, political activities of, 140,
   156, 157, 158, 167, 181, 293, 320,
   324, 383, 399, 400, 401, 418
Dublin Review, 1, 2, 26, 35, 40, 43, 45,
   48, 74, 82, 88, 96, 99, 123, 176, 185,
   186, 216, 225, 233, 248, 251, 300,
   308, 310, 326, 330, 345, 346, 353,
   381, 384, 401, 412, 417, 422, 425,
   435, 443, 452
Duffy, Sir C. Gavan, 27, 169, 293, 461
Duggan, James, Archbishop of Chicago,
   101, 102
   Patrick, Bishop of Clonfert, 349, 417,
   420, 427, 428
Dunkellin, Lord, 228, 232
Dunne, D. B., 199, 204, 221, 223
Dunraven, Lord, 47, 247, 305, 336

Eardley, Sir Culling, 9, 42, 44
Ecclesiastical Titles Act (1851), 26, 29,
   35, 37, 146, 337, 345, 346, 403-7,
   440
Economic condition of Ireland, 2, 80,
   144, 145, 393
Education Act, English (1870), 191, 229,
   443
Education question, 10-11, 22-4, 52-73,
   77, 82, 139, 140, 142, 144, 149, 175,
   191, 212, 226-9, 258, 260, 282, 420,
   436-44, 455, 462; – Catholic schools,
   23, 24, 144, 227; – Intermediate
   schools (and endowed), 23, 31, 52,
   53, 54, 448, 454n.; – National
   System of Education, 11, 21, 22, 55,
   60, 61-2, 63, 64, 67, 69, 71, 72, 80,
   82, 96, 119, 144, 155, 194, 198, 209,
   212, 217, 220, 226-9, 245, 246, 431,
   432, 435, 436, 438, 439, 440, 441,
   442, 444, 446; – National Board,
   22, 23, 24, 53, 57, 58, 69, 72, 73,
   77, 84, 191, 202, 221, 229, 260, 404,
   432, 433, 435, 436, 438, 439, 440,
   444
Edward, Prince of Wales, 29, 32, 94
Elections – General elections, *1859*, 34-7,
   45, 46; *1865*, 166, 167, 171-2;
   1868, 324, 346-52, 374; *1874*, 453,
   455-7

Emancipation, Catholic (Act of 1829), 137, 146, 283, 284, 291, 292, 293, 298, 306, 354, 401, 403, 413, 421
Emigration, 3, 71, 144, 148, 387
Encumbered Estates Act (1849), 15
Endowed Schools (England) Act (1869), 443
Episcopal meetings, 29, 60, 61, 62, 67, 76, 78, 102, 168, 204, 205, 206, 213-14, 246, 247, 333-4, 436, 437, 443-4, 451
Evictions, 43, 65, 423
Executive, Irish, 21, 29, 407

'Faith and Fatherland' movement, 460, 461
Famine, 11
Fawcett, Henry, 190, 240, 241, 249, 255n. 262, 272, 274, 281, 445, 448, 451, 453
Feeny, T., Bishop of Killala, 247
Fenianism, 3, 6, 40, 48, 51, 82, 85, 86-134, 135, 136, 141, 183, 188, 221, 243, 265, 307, 315, 328, 330, 332, 339, 345, 350, 386, 391, 416; Rome and –, 113-16, 129-33, 410; clergy and –, 90, 99, 105-13, 395, 404
Fermoy, Lord, 60
Fingall, Earl of, 311, 336
Fitzgerald, M., Administrator of Limerick Cathedral, 95
Fitzgibbon, Gerald, 277, 278, 442
Forde, Canon, of Dublin, 49, 151, 202
Fortescue, Chichester, 127, 171, 194, 212, 218, 219, 221, 223, 224, 228, 229, 230, 231, 232, 238, 262, 263, 295, 298, 354, 355, 378, 382, 387, 388, 391, 394, 408, 440, 446, 452, 456, 457
Freeman's Journal, The, 7, 8, 58, 65, 66, 70, 72, 80, 81, 84, 123, 125, 136, 138, 140, 149, 151, 157, 173, 183, 215, 228, 245, 247, 250, 251, 271, 276, 281, 328, 388, 393, 394, 396, 417, 422, 424, 425, 426, 427, 428, 430, 435, 438, 442, 444, 445, 453, 455, 461
Freeman's Journal Church Commission (1868), 11, 15, 321, 337
Freemasons, 93, 94, 133
Furlong, Thomas, Bishop of Ferns, 14, 36, 214, 292n., 348, 364, 373, 402, 412, 426, 462

Gainsford, R. J., 300, 321
Galbraith, J. A., 417, 418
Gallicanism in Ireland, 6, 13, 17, 22n.
Galway election (1872), 28, 349, 409, 417, 420, 422-30, 453; – Keogh's judgment on, 409, 423-7
Garibaldi, Giuseppe, 34, 39, 44, 49, 50, 79, 84-5, 116, 121, 177

Gavazzi, Fr, 44
Gillooly, Laurence, Bishop of Elphin, 14, 16, 61, 75, 103, 127, 136, 140, 142, 149, 153, 161, 166, 169, 182, 210, 214, 227, 348, 349, 388, 414, 421
Gladstone, W. E., 3, 26, 32, 37, 96, 127, 128, 133, 183, 184, 193, 243, 244, 276, 294, 297, 324, 328, 350, 352, 383, 403, 406, 409, 411, 412, 415, 419, 427, 457, 458, 459; – and Church question, 192, 259, 266, 273, 284, 299, 300, 303, 311, 316, 318, 325, 331, 332, 333, 334, 335, 338-47, 348, 350, 353-85; – and Education, 172, 190, 194, 195, 197, 212, 219, 223, 226, 227, 230, 245, 251, 255, 264, 265, 266, 268, 281, 317, 326, 335, 373, 376, 409, 421, 428, 440, 441, 443, 444, 446-53; – and Italian question, 38, 51, 461; – and Land question, 353, 385-403; – writings of, *State in its Relations with the Church* (1838), 286, 299, *Chapter of Autobiography* (1868), 284, 300, 303, 310, 340, 350, *Vatican Decrees in their Bearing on Civil Allegiance* (1874), 458, 459
Glebe-loans, 319, 357, 365, 372, 376, 377-81, 384-5
Godkin, James, 1, 15, 336n., 360-1
Gormanston, Lord, 378
Granard, Lord, 375, 406, 415, 427, 454, 455
Grant, Thomas, Bishop of Southwark, 405
Granville, Lord, 91n., 406, 407, 415, 458
Gray, Edmund, 460
Sir John, 7, 80, 137, 139, 156, 158, 171, 173, 175, 176, 181, 182, 212, 216, 223, 227, 245, 251n., 268, 279, 289, 292, 293, 296, 308, 309, 315, 316, 320, 324, 327, 328, 332, 334, 335, 377, 383, 388, 394, 399, 401, 417, 423, 435, 453, 454, 460, 462
Gregory XVI, 4, 444
Gregory, William, 263, 399
Grey, 3rd Earl, 178, 294, 303, 308, 310, 315, 317, 318, 334, 340, 341, 342, 378, 405
Grey, Sir George, 192, 195, 197, 198, 199, 200, 201, 202, 203, 205, 208, 209, 211, 212, 213, 216, 218, 226, 230, 236, 253, 280n., 294

Harcourt, Vernon, 434
Hardy, Gathorne, 190, 290, 296, 359
Harper, S. B., 39
Hartington, Lord, 355, 376, 405, 408, 434, 435, 443
Healy, Most Revd John, 6, 375
Hennessy, J. Pope, 48, 199

Heron, R. M., 4
Heygate, Sir Frederick, 91n., 292, 327
Home Government Association of Ireland, 416, 417, 419, 420
Home Rule Confederation, 460
  League, 422, 456, 460
  movement, 117, 134, 172, 345, 351, 409, 410, 416-22, 423, 429, 446, 452, 453, 454, 455, 456, 457, 460, 461
Horsman, E., 262, 274n., 275, 451
Howley, E., 446n.
Hume, A., 290
Hutch, William, 24

Independent Opposition, 6, 12, 26-7, 37, 70, 88, 135, 161, 162, 164, 167, 169, 170, 174, 176, 184, 188, 410, 457
Indifferentism, evils of, 11, 25
Infallibility, Definition of Papal (1870), 20, 401, 412-14
International Workingmen's Association, 134, 418
Irishman, The, 101, 133, 134
Irish Church Act (1869), 303, 304, 375, 382, 384, 392, 407, 409, 453, 458. *See also, Bill.* Irish Church
Irish College, Rome, 4, 30, 410, 413, 415
  Paris, 100
Irish Ecclesiastical Record, The, 8, 441, 445
Irish People, The, 5, 40, 87, 90, 95, 100, 124, 141, 145, 152, 171, 172, 188, 319, 331
Italian question, 11, 31, 33-4, 36, 37, 38-51, 65, 70, 177, 244, 384, 414, 415, 454, 459

Jervoise, H., 427, 434
Johnston, William (of Ballykilbeg), 346, 407, 408

Kane, Sir Robert, 197, 202, 219, 247
Kavanagh, J. W., 56-8, 65, 67, 68, 82, 84, 137, 139, 140, 156, 183n., 185, 215, 227, 229, 236, 321, 336, 340n., 355, 437, 439, 440, 460
Keane, William, Bishop of Cloyne, 14, 46, 62, 67, 70, 78, 80, 99, 127, 136, 142, 149, 159, 161, 164n., 168, 171, 348, 357, 387, 395, 422, 439
Kelly, T. J., 120, 121n.
Kennedy, Ignatius, 147, 460
  Tristram, 171
Kensington College, 197, 253n.
Keogh, Judge William, 6, 27, 104, 125, 141, 153, 195, 219, 423-7, 429n., 457
Kerry election (1872), 28, 117, 417, 422, 430, 453
Kickham, Charles, 87, 89, 91

Kieran, Michael, Archbishop of Armagh, 8, 171, 194, 348, 439
Kildare Place Society, 22, 227
Kilduff, John, Bishop of Ardagh, 142, 169, 214
Kimberley, Earl of, 359, 379, 394, 406, 407, 447, 452, 453n.
Kirby, Tobias, Archbishop of Ephesus, 7, 30, 101, 119, 341, 356, 383, 410, 411

Lamoricière, General, 49
Land Act (Cardwell's 1860), 159, 385, 387, 391
  (1870), 143, 385, 409. *See* also under *Bills.*
Landlord influence, 15, 28, 145, 356, 425
Land question, Irish, 20, 88, 110, 143, 144-5, 148, 149, 158, 159, 160, 161, 162, 170, 175, 181, 258, 316, 335, 345, 363, 383, 384, 385-403
Larcom, Sir Thomas, 113
Lawson, James, 202, 211
Laval University, Quebec, 80, 248, 271
Lavelle, Fr Patrick, 43, 71, 92, 93, 97, 99-105, 108, 111, 112, 118, 121, 125, 129, 130, 135, 136, 183, 389, 397, 423, 424, 457
Leahy, Patrick, Archbishop of Cashel, 2, 3, 13, 51, 54, 59, 61, 62, 73, 77, 87, 89, 91, 95, 136, 137, 139, 142, 148, 156, 166, 171n., 179, 180, 182, 186, 187, 220, 222, 247, 256, 257, 258, 259, 260, 263, 267, 268, 270, 271, 275, 278, 279, 281n., 308, 320, 325, 331, 332, 334, 336, 349, 357, 360, 361, 362, 379, 387, 421, 426, 441, 456, 460, 462
  Pius, Bishop of Dromore, 14, 54, 55, 127, 136, 214, 348, 412
Leo XII, 92
Liberal Catholicism, in Ireland, 10, 282, 459
Liberal Party and Ireland, 25-6, 136, 139, 140, 143, 153, 157, 161, 171, 172, 173, 174, 175-6, 177, 181, 184, 186, 193, 216, 225, 263, 266, 324, 326, 329, 330, 339, 350, 351, 353, 383, 409, 410, 416, 428, 437, 446, 452, 453, 456, 457, 459, 461
Liberation Society, 139, 147, 173, 174, 177-81, 182, 282, 289, 293, 304, 319, 323, 325-30, 335, 343, 363-4, 378, 384, 385, 447
Lifford, Lord, 301, 308
'Limerick Declaration' (1868), 121, 345, 403
London University, example of, 196, 197, 198, 199, 200, 202, 207, 214, 226, 251, 254
Longford election (1870), 422

Lowe, Robert, 121, 223, 230, 262n., 291n.
Luby, Thomas Clarke, 87, 89
Lucas, Frederick, 28

Macaulay, James, 408, 421, 431, 436
MacClosky, John, Cardinal, 132
MacDevitt, John, 190n.
MacEvilly, John, Bishop of Galway, 14, 16, 17, 43, 71, 79, 84, 102, 130, 153, 190, 303n., 347, 348, 356, 423, 424, 425, 427, 435
MacHale, John, Archbishop of Tuam, 3, 6, 12-13, 16, 17, 18, 20, 23, 25, 26, 29, 37-8, 39, 46, 53, 55, 59, 60, 63, 67-8, 71, 72, 73, 78, 99, 100, 101, 102, 103, 104, 105, 121, 125, 127, 138, 141, 142, 153, 154, 168, 169, 173, 180, 182, 188, 205, 206, 208, 212, 213, 215, 220, 222, 247, 260, 267, 268, 288, 331, 348, 380, 387, 397, 405, 410, 412, 413, 414, 420, 423, 424, 425, 427, 429, 441, 445, 457, 462
MacManus, T. B., 79, 94, 97-8, 122
MacNally, Charles, Bishop of Clogher, 30, 136
MacSwiney, Peter Paul, 127, 137, 139, 140, 141, 142, 153, 155-6, 157, 158, 166, 171, 172, 173, 178, 181, 183, 187, 226, 276, 293, 322, 324, 350, 351, 357, 382, 383, 388, 392, 399, 400, 418, 437n., 442, 455, 460, 461
Magee College, 210, 219, 449
Maguire, J. F., 2, 7, 30, 35, 40, 41, 42, 45, 47, 58, 59, 60, 69, 119, 123, 127, 137, 149, 153, 159, 160, 166, 173, 227, 248, 260, 262, 264, 268, 299n., 334, 339, 354, 381, 383, 385, 387, 395
Mail, The Dublin, 66, 78, 83, 152, 216, 225, 320
Malmesbury, Lord, 271, 272, 389
Manchester 'Martyrs', 116, 119, 120-4, 125, 126, 133, 183, 188, 340, 345, 346, 391, 427
Manning, H. E., Cardinal, 20, 40, 58, 89, 91, 111, 119, 126, 130, 132, 188, 191, 194, 195, 196, 219, 242-4, 245, 248, 251, 252, 256, 257, 264, 265, 267, 271, 272, 273, 274, 277, 280, 281, 284, 294, 326n., 331n., 335-6, 338, 339, 340, 342, 343, 344, 356, 358, 360, 366, 367, 378, 380, 381, 382, 389, 390, 395, 396, 397, 401, 402, 406, 410, 411, 412, 414, 417, 419, 434, 442, 443, 445, 447, 450, 451, 457, 458
Marriage Registration Act, Irish (1863), 77
Martin, John, 121, 122, 138, 157, 173, 181n., 417, 418, 421, 422

Maynooth, Royal College of St. Patrick, 6, 14, 53, 79, 98, 99, 203, 220, 240, 241, 248, 252, 269, 292, 294, 295-6, 312, 375, 376, 454n.; – and 1869 Church Act, 363, 365, 368-75
Grant question, 178, 179, 264, 283, 286, 303, 305, 343
Resolutions (1869), 392-3, 436, 437, 444, 446
Mayo, Earl of, 35, 55, 89n., 95, 96, 113, 117, 122, 228, 231, 234, 236, 238, 240, 245, 248, 250, 252, 253, 254, 256, 258, 260-1, 262, 264, 265, 267, 268, 271, 272, 273, 274, 275, 276, 277, 278, 279, 280, 302, 305, 310, 339, 387, 390, 392
Mazzinianism, 28, 46, 86, 98n., 126, 136
McCabe, Neil, Bishop of Ardagh, 348, 368
McCarthy Downing, 21, 128, 167, 168, 169, 391, 392, 399, 407, 408
McEvoy, Edward, 399, 406
McGettigan, Daniel, Archbishop of Armagh, 407, 456
Meath Tenant-Right Society, 170
Members of Parliament, Catholic, 54, 67, 69-70, 72, 175-6, 187, 243, 268, 380, 452
Mérode, Mgr de, 49
Miall, Edward, 177, 180n., 297, 364, 378, 384, 385, 451
Mill, John Stuart, influence in Ireland, 3, 272, 307n., 370, 388, 389
Ministers' Money, abolition (1857), 283
Mixed Education, *see* Education question
Monsell, William (Lord Emly), 47, 77, 79, 81, 127, 129, 166, 174, 180n., 193, 196, 199, 201, 202, 203, 204, 205, 206, 207, 208, 219, 222, 223, 224, 234, 235, 258, 259, 263, 289, 293, 295, 305, 311, 317, 328, 332, 346, 354, 355, 364, 377, 398, 399, 407, 415, 439n., 441, 446, 448, 456
Montalembert, Count, 32
Montefiore, Sir Moses, 42
Montgomery, Dr Robert, 305
Moore, G. H., 26, 27, 35, 138, 154, 168, 170, 173, 188, 380, 381, 397, 399
Moran, Patrick, Cardinal, 7, 8, 9, 233, 285, 311, 435
Morgan, Osborne, 451
Moriarty, David, Bishop of Kerry, 3, 7, 14, 19, 32, 46, 47, 49, 58, 69, 71, 79, 93, 111, 117, 118, 119, 121, 122, 125, 127, 128, 130, 132, 182, 202, 204, 206, 218, 222, 244, 246, 247, 258, 259, 286, 308, 309, 311, 312-18, 319, 321, 323, 328, 330, 332, 334, 335, 337, 341, 343, 348, 354, 362, 365, 368, 379, 390, 404, 405, 407, 410, 412, 414, 430, 439, 441, 462
Fr, of Philadelphia, 92

Montara, Edgar, 41-3, 72, 74
Mozley, Thomas, 132
Murphy Case (1859), 43
Murphy, John, Dean of Cork, 46
    William, 347, 368, 401
Murray, Daniel, Archbishop of Dublin,
    5, 18, 19, 22, 23, 25, 29, 412

Naas, Lord, *see* Mayo, Earl of
Napoleon III, 39, 42, 45
Nation, The, 24, 49, 57, 65, 66, 70, 122,
    140, 208, 222, 461
National Association of Ireland, 14, 26,
    29, 85, 101, 105, 108, 125, 127, 135-
    189, 193, 194, 195, 208n., 210, 216,
    226, 227, 271, 272n., 276, 278n.,
    282, 287, 289, 293, 308, 309, 316,
    319-25, 326, 330, 331, 335, 336, 341,
    343, 349, 350, 353, 354, 356-8, 360,
    364, 365, 377, 379, 382, 383, 384,
    385, 386, 387, 388, 390, 391, 392,
    395, 398-9, 400, 409, 416, 436, 441,
    442, 453, 454, 460, 461
National League, 138, 157, 181
National System of Education, *see* Educa-
    tion question.
Nationalism Irish, 117, 183, 350, 409,
    426
Newdegate, C. N., 106, 107, 126, 158,
    199, 263, 269n., 294, 401, 402, 406
Newman, J. H., Cardinal, 8, 25, 31, 32,
    58, 67, 78, 191, 193, 284, 292, 316,
    350n.
Newton, Charles, 50
Nolan, J. P., 422, 423, 424, 425, 429
Nonconformist, The, 47, 66, 153, 157,
    334, 347, 350, 401, 437
Nulty, Thomas, Bishop of Meath, 14,
    106, 142, 160, 161, 163, 168, 170,
    171, 182, 324, 365, 386, 388, 389,
    398, 403, 419, 420

Oath question, 146, 158, 167, 181, 283,
    291-6
O'Brien, Dominick, Bishop of Water-
    ford, 14, 28, 36, 113n., 214, 243, 247
O'Brien, James, Protestant Bishop of
    Ossory, 289
    Richard, Dean of Limerick, 156, 167,
    345, 398, 403
    William Smith, 80
O'Connell Centenary (1875), 460, 461
    Daniel, political heritage of, 9, 12, 26,
    136, 145, 147, 151, 156, 185, 254,
    291, 354, 386, 461
    Dean, of Dublin, 151, 251
    Monument meetings (1864), 108, 112,
    136-7, 157
O'Connor, Bishop of Saldes, 158
O'Conor Don, The, 80, 202, 228, 355,
    369, 374, 452

O'Donoghue, The, 48, 50, 69, 88n., 121,
    138, 166, 174, 194, 195, 197, 198,
    199, 205, 216, 221, 228, 407, 430,
    453
O'Donovan Rossa, Jeremiah, 128, 134,
    422
O'Ferrall, More, 46, 203
O'Hagan, Lord Thomas, 83, 201, 202,
    204, 207, 208, 354, 355, 394, 404,
    405, 433, 444, 460
O'Hea, Michael, Bishop of Ross, 14, 90,
    127, 136, 137, 142, 161, 166, 272n.,
    321, 329, 356, 357, 379, 420
O'Keeffe, Fr Robert, 100, 409, 422, 428,
    431-6, 440, 459
O'Leary, John, 6, 27, 87, 96
O'Loghlen, Sir Colman, 277, 327-8,
    390, 399, 404n.
O'Mahony, John, 86, 87, 101
Orange Society, 8, 21, 37, 81, 88, 136,
    137, 138, 141, 145, 151, 233, 304n.,
    346, 351, 407, 418
O'Reilly, Myles, 51, 58, 82, 150, 170,
    173, 195n., 201, 202, 208, 223,
    224, 227, 355
    Fr P. P., Kingscourt, 368
Oxford movement, influence in Ireland,
    306, 307, 315, 346

Packet, The, 13, 51, 58, 65, 66, 79
Palmerston, Lord, 35, 37, 38, 46, 48, 81
'Papal Aggression', 17, 26, 116, 294, 403,
    411
Papal Battalion of St Patrick (1860),
    50-1, 82, 89
    Army, Irish recruits, 113, 115, 122
    States, *see* Italian question
Parliamentary Committees
    Callan Schools (Commons) Committee
    (1873), 434, 435
    Conventual and Monastic Institutions
    (Commons) Committee (1870), 401,
    402, 409
    Ecclesiastical Titles and Catholic
    Relief Acts (Commons) Committee,
    (1867), 346, 404
    Ecclesiastical Titles (Lords) Com-
    mittee (1868), 346, 405-6
    Land Act (1860) (Commons) Com-
    mittee (1865), 159
    Poor Relief (Commons) Committee
    (1861), 74-6
    Religious Endowments in Ireland (Com-
    mons) Committee (1863), 288
Parliamentary Reform, 34-5, 228, 273,
    321, 322, 326
Parnell, C. S., 410, 416, 428, 456
Party Processions Act (1850), 81, 346,
    407-8
Pastoral of 1859, 1, 11, 18, 22, 56, 62,
    63-7, 70, 71, 125, 135, 144, 185, 386

Patriot, The Connaught, 93, 102
Peace Preservation Acts, 2, 133, 402, 411
Peel, Sir Robert (2nd Bart.), 25, 286, 372
(3rd Bart.), 25, 48, 76, 78, 79, 83, 199,
223, 230, 232, 234
Penal Laws, heritage of, 1, 9, 15, 285,
292, 396
Pim, J., 351, 352, 457
Pius VII, 333
IX, 5, 31, 34, 41n., 42, 46, 49, 94, 96,
114, 115, 116, 131, 207n., 215, 234,
273, 285, 367, 395, 410, 414, 415,
428, 458, 459, 462
Plunket, Lord, Protestant Bishop of
Tuam, 43, 187n.
Plunkett, Alderman, of Dublin, 151, 181,
400
Polish Rebellion, influence in Irish affairs,
40, 91, 107
Poor Law, Irish, 65, 73-7, 80, 83, 432, 433
Pope, Thomas, 7, 127, 355, 460
Powis Report, *see* Commissions, Royal
Presbyterians, Irish, 20, 54, 197, 210,
216, 304-5, 329, 351, 385
Promissory Oaths Act (1868), 292n., 296
Propaganda, Sacred Congregation of, 19,
29, 30, 60, 67, 87, 98, 101, 102, 116,
129, 185, 208, 215, 250, 337, 366,
428, 443
Proselytism, in Ireland, 9, 11, 21, 23, 43-4
65, 72, 73, 74, 140, 146, 228, 313
Protestant Establishment, 20, 21, 53, 80,
92, 110, 129, 140, 142, 143, 146, 162,
170, 174, 175, 176, 181, 183, 186,
188, 216, 252, 264, 266, 271, 273,
276, 280, 282, 391, 416
Protestantism, Irish, 65, 66, 82, 309
Protestant Defence Association, 336

Queen's Colleges and University, *see*
University question
Quo graviora (Encyclical, 1826), 92, 93

Rambler, The, 35, 36, 47, 52
Reform Act, Irish (1868), 348
League, 85, 181, 322
Regium Donum, 286, 303, 304-5, 329,
343, 363
Reisach, Cardinal, 270
Religious Orders, in Ireland, 14, 19
Reynolds, Alderman, of Dublin, 46, 106
Ribbonism, 86, 87, 95, 105, 106
Risorgimento, *see* Italian question
Royal Hibernian School, Dublin, 83
Russell, Dr C. W., 202, 247, 266, 268,
282, 303, 341, 353, 354, 369, 370,
371, 372, 374, 375, 397, 401 419n.
Lord John (Earl Russell), 17, 26, 31,
35, 37, 38, 39, 48, 111n., 117n.,
178, 211, 226, 228, 297, 300, 303,
308n., 310, 318, 337, 379, 433

Odo (Lord Ampthill), 6, 31, 36, 39,
42, 48, 51, 94, 114-15, 116, 122, 128,
129, 130, 131, 132, 133, 333, 356,
358, 359, 360, 366, 367, 368, 384,
394, 395, 397, 401, 402, 411, 412,
413, 428, 444n.
Ryan, P. P., Cahir, 130

Sadleir, John, 6, 27, 141, 153
St Jarlath's College, Tuam, 414
St Patrick's Brotherhood, 87, 93, 94-5,
98, 100, 101, 102, 103, 104
San Clemente, Rome, 415
Schools, *see* Education question
Scottish hierarchy proposals, 116, 411
Secularization, of ecclesiastical revenues,
309, 311, 314, 318, 321, 323, 325,
333, 335, 338, 350, 364
Severn, Joseph, 116
Shee, William, 288, 291
Spalding, Martin, Archbishop of Balti-
more, 9, 439
Spencer, Lord (Viceroy), 128, 130, 359,
360, 423, 427, 429, 449, 450
Stanhope, Lord, 379, 405
Stanley, Lord, *see* Derby, Earl of
Stephens, James, 86, 87, 88, 114, 120
Stoney, G. Johnstone, 18, 22, 61-2, 253-6,
257, 262
Stopford, E. A., 23, 56, 57, 58
*Suggestions for the Amendment of the
Landed Property (Ireland) Improve-
ment Act* (1865), 159, 160, 387
Sullivan, A. M., 34, 45, 49, 92n., 118n.,
121, 122, 123, 124, 139, 293, 400,
419n., 421, 423, 456
Sir Edward, 202, 394
Prof. W. K., 150, 193, 198, 199, 202,
204, 219, 221, 223, 224, 226, 230n.,
232, 234, 235, 236, 241, 438
Syllabus of Errors (1864), 10, 155, 158,
185-6, 221, 263, 282, 287, 294, 300,
330, 410, 440
Synan, E. J., 149, 167, 171, 291, 399
Synod of Maynooth (1875), 337, 414, 462
of Thurles (1850), 5, 17, 25, 52

Tablet, The, 28, 70, 112, 208, 330, 331n.
Tait, A. C., Archbishop of Canterbury,
382
Talbot, Mgr George, 243, 338, 367
Temporal Power, *see* Italian question
Temporalities Act (1833), 21, 283, 287,
291, 297, 298
Tenant Laws, 3, 38, 53, 65, 142, 143, 167,
171, 183n., 252, 387, 388, 389, 390,
396
League (of 1850s), 20, 26, 140, 185, 386
– (of 1869), 398
Tenant-Right, 73, 139, 188n., 386, 387,
388, 390, 394, 396, 399

Times, The, 42, 137, 152, 153, 156, 182, 186, 191, 209, 234, 236, 315, 320, 326, 336, 351, 354, 358, 359, 360, 371 396, 419, 426, 433, 437, 455, 457
Times, The Irish, 73, 112, 152, 162, 163, 168, 251
Tipperary election (1869), 128, 422
Tithe Rent-charge, 21, 184, 313
Trench, E. le P., 423, 424, 425, 427
Trinity College, Dublin, *see* University question
Tuam Synod (1858), 53, 60, 63

Ullathorne, Archbishop Bernard, 419
Ulster Protestantism, 4, 20, 53, 351
  Religious Revival (1859), 32
Ultramontanism, in Ireland, 10, 16, 17, 18, 19, 106, 209, 221, 251, 262, 278, 434, 436, 437, 448, 458, 459
Union, Act of (1800), 9, 29, 153, 157, 299, 345, 351, 409, 416
  Irish Catholic, 454, 455, 461
University question, 24-5, 58, 59, 68, 79-81, 82, 176, 185, 190-239, 240-81, 364, 391, 421, 444-54, 454n., 455, 462, – Catholic University, 15, 25, 32, 58, 59, 62, 65, 66, 67-8, 79-81, 82, 96, 192, 193, 194, 195, 197-239, 240-81, 445, 454, 455, 462; – English Universities, 79, 192, 196, 197, 252, 253, 254; – Queen's Colleges and University, 5, 25, 55, 59, 62, 64, 78, 79, 81, 96, 155, 192, 195, 197-239, 240-81, 445, 449, 450, 454n.; – Queen's University, Supplemental Charter, 190, 194, 226, 229-38, 240, 244, 245, 250, 252, 261, 269, 391, 451; – Trinity College, Dublin, 24, 79, 80, 96, 155, 192, 197, 198, 211, 213, 216, 238n, 245, 248, 249, 251, 255, 256, 260, 261, 263n., 264, 272, 370, 373, 374, 418, 446, 448, 449, 450, 453; – religious Tests at Trinity, 190, 240, 241, 242, 249, 274, 447, 448, 453
University Test Act (1871), 190, 191, 196, 242, 283, 443
Ursuline Order, in Ireland, 24

Vatican Council (1869-70), 5, 20, 117, 128, 129, 358, 384, 395, 400, 406, 409, 410-14, 458, 459

Decrees controversy, 244, 326, 347, 403, 412, 457-9, 460
Verot, Bishop of St Augustine's, Florida, 19
Veto question, 301, 337
Viale-Prelà, Archbishop of Bologna, 41
Victoria, H.M. Queen, 49, 78, 112, 127, 228, 259, 359, 362, 423
Voluntary System, 14, 15, 124, 147, 172, 175, 178, 282, 285, 287, 300, 302, 303, 304, 308, 315, 319, 321, 322, 323, 326, 329, 330, 331, 332, 333, 334, 335, 336-7, 340, 341

Waller, J. T., 98n, 108, 110, 118n.
Walsh, Edward, Bishop of Ossory, 14, 432
Walshe, James, Bishop of Kildare and Leighlin, 214
Walsh, W. J., Archbishop of Dublin, 193, 231, 255, 278, 280
Ward, Wilfrid, 306, 308n., 412
Warren, Attorney-General, 112, 248, 249, 268, 345
Westbury, Lord, 379
Whalley, G. H., 79, 107, 346, 373; – 'Patrick Murphy', 105, 106
Whately, Richard, Archbishop of Dublin, 11, 315n.
Whiteside, James, 92, 199, 294, 320n., 327
Whittle, J. L., 220-1, 422n., 452n.
Whyte, Nicholas, 160, 162n., 166
Wilberforce, Henry, 118n., 289, 316
Williams, J. Carvell, 177, 179, 180, 181, 327, 328-30, 333, 344, 357, 363
Wiseman, Nicholas, Cardinal, 1, 2, 32, 34, 35, 36, 196, 242, 243
Wodehouse, Lord (Viceroy), 158, 191, 195, 197, 198, 199, 200, 201, 202, 203, 207, 208, 209, 211, 222, 253
Woodlock, Barth., Bishop of Ardagh, 78, 79, 151, 156, 194, 199, 202, 203, 218, 219, 222, 223, 224, 225, 233, 236, 241, 244, 256, 257, 258, 259, 260, 267, 268, 269n., 274, 275, 280, 288, 437, 445, 446, 451

Young Ireland priests, 20, 27, 91n., 109, 118, 348, 386